WINEQUEST THE WINE DICTIONARY

BY

TED GRUDZINSKI

Published by WINEQUEST, Bay Shore, N.Y.

WINEQUEST

31 Belford Avenue · Bay Shore, NY 11706 · (516) 666-4216

Library of Congress Catalog Number 85-51370

ISBN 0-9615063-0-X

for Mary
with special thanks to Gordon and Kay

INTRODUCTION

Three years ago, after numerous frustrating efforts to quickly find the meaning of a few wine terms and wine estates only to find that it took too many books and too much time to find the answers, I decided that it was time to try to put together a reference dictionary that was complete, concise, easy to use and fast. This volume, then, is the fullfillment of that desire and I trust that it will provide in one book most of the answers to the questions most frequently asked: what is it? what does this mean? where is it from? what's it made of?

I have tried to include all of the kinds of items that are found in other books, on wine labels and wine lists, that might be of interest to the novice and to the professional; therefore, the entries include, all in strictly alphabetical order, and cross-referenced as much as possible, the following: wine terms, châteaux and estates, merchants and wineries, grape varieties, wine maladies, historical writings and important names, the principal hybridizers and scientists, wines, wine villages, districts, regions and countries, and the most often encountered abbreviations.

ENTRIES, IN GENERAL

Each entry is listed by its principal name, ignoring titles, first names, articles and prepositions, such as: *les, aux, bodega, clos, château,* etc. However, there are a few cases where an article or other word forms an intregal part of the name of a city or town, and is listed with the article or word first. In some cases two versions of the name-listing are given. For the purposes of alphabetization all interior short words are also ignored. The official designation of AOC, DOC, etc., if there is one, immediately follows the name or title.

The country of origin follows the main entry in parentheses (see below for the abbreviations used for the countries), and on the right, the founding date, re-founding date or other important dates. When available, the approximate acreage and annual production amounts are given at the end of the entry.

Abbreviations frequently encountered are found at the beginning of each letter of the alphabet, and include translations as well.

Ownership of wineries and estates as well as winemakers are not included, for the most part, since they change so often.

The exact blends of grape varieties also change frequently, and they are not included except for officially required grape varieties and percentages. However, a few examples of Bordeaux *château* blends are given.

There is no attempt to give a quality rating to a wine, except by universal or official status. If a wine or producer is listed it is because it is well-known, written about in books and articles or because it is widely available. No one-volume dictionary can be all-inclusive, so naturally many terms, estates and wineries have been omitted.

I have attempted to make the orthography of foreign words and the placement of accent marks as accurate as possible, allowing for local variations in spelling, many of which are given.

In the future, if there exists a demand for a more comprehensive treatment, we would like to hear from the readers of this book. At the same time, any corrections, new additions, updating information or ideas would be welcome, and will be reserved for a later edition.

Abbreviations Used

A.	Austria	Lat.	Latin
Alg.	Algeria	Leb.	Lebanon
Arg.	Argentina	Liech.	Liechtenstein
Aus.	Australia	Lux.	Luxemburg
Br.	Brazil	Mex.	Mexico
Bul.	Bulgaria	Mor.	Morrocco
C.	Canada	N.Z.	New Zealand
Ch.	Chile	P.	Portugal
Cyp.	Cyprus	R.	Romania
Cz.	Czechoslovakia	S. Af.	South Africa
E.	England	Sp.	Spain
F.	France	Sw.	Switzerland
G.	Germany	T.	Turkey
Gr.	Greece	Tun.	Tunisia
H.	Hungary	Ur.	Uraguay
I.	Italy	U.S.	United States
Is.	Israel	U.S.S.R.	Russia
J.	Japan	Y.	Yugoslavia

Not abbreviated - China, Egypt, Sweden

A

A.C. (F.)

The shorter form of A.O.C.

A.O.C. (F.)

The abbreviation for *Appellation d'Origine Contrôllée* (Controlled Name of Origin), the phrase which indicates that the wine has met certain minimum standards as set by law and guarantees that the wine is from the place stated on the label.

A.O.G. (Mor.)

The abbreviation for *Appellation d'Origine Garantie*, French for "Guaranteed Name of Origin," the highest rating for the best Moroccan wines.

A.P. (G.)

The abbreviation for *Amtliche Prüfungsnummer* (Official Test Number), indicating that the wine was tested on a date as indicated by the last three digits of the A.P. number.

a granel (Sp.)

In bulk, as opposed to in bottles.

a la castellana (Sp.)

A method of vine-training, in low bush-style, with no supports.

Abbaia (I.)

A red wine from Monti, in northeastern Sardinia; made from Malaga and Pascale grapes.

l'Abbaye, Clos de (F.)

An estate in the Bourgeuil district, Touraine region, Loire Valley. 18 acres.

l'Abbaye de Morgeot (F.)

A *Premier Cru* vineyard in Chassagne-Montrachet, Côte de Beaune district, Burgundy; produces red and white wines. 27 acres.

l'Abbaye de Santenay, Domaine de (F.)

An estate in Santenay, Côte de Beaune district, Burgundy. 30 acres, including Santenay les Clos de Tavannes – 5 acres, Les Gravières – 5 acres, La Comme – 2.5 acres and Chassagne-Montrachet Morgeot (red wine) – 1.2 acres.

abboccato (I.)

Slightly sweet.

Abbuoto (I.)

A red grape grown in the Latium region.

Abfüller (G.)

A bottler.

abocado (Sp.)

Slightly sweet.

Abouriou (F.)

A red grape grown in Cahors, southwestern France.

Abruzzi *also* **Abruzzo (I.)**

A region east of Rome, in central Italy; produces only two DOC wines: Montepulciano and Trebbiano d'Abruzzo.

Abruzzo Bianco (I.)

A white grape grown in central Italy; the same grape as the Trebbiano of Orvieto.

1

Abstich (G.)

Racking, the drawing off of wine from one vat to another in order to separate the clear wine from the lees; also called *soutirage* (French) and *travaso* (Italian).

Abtwingert (Liech.)

An estate attached to the *Rotes Haus* (a famous old mansion), in the Vaduz district.

Acacia (U.S.)   1979

A winery in Napa City, Napa Valley, northern California; produces Pinot Noir and Chardonnay wines, some from single vineyards. 15,000 cases. 50 acres.

acariose

A species of mite which feeds on the fruit and leaves of grape vines.

acescence

A wine malady caused by exposure to oxygen, resulting in the formation of a translucent grey film on the surface of the wine while in the vat. Acetic acid and ethyl acetate are produced, causing a vinegary taste; also called *piqûre* in France.

acerbe (F.)

Very sharp; harsh.

acetic acid

A volatile acid, a natural ingredient of wine in very small amounts; if excessive it spoils the wine. It is caused by oxidation of ethyl alcohol in the presence of the fungus *Mycoderma aceti*.

acetification

Another name for acescence.

Achaia Clauss (Gr.)   1861

An important producer in Patras; produces Demestica, Santa Helena, Mavrodaphne and other wines. 2 million cases.

Achkarren (G.)

A village in the Baden region, Bereich Kaiserstuhl-Tuniberg, Grosslage Vulkanfelsen. The vineyards are Schlossberg and Castellberg.

Achtel (G.)

A liquid measure equal to one-eighth of an *Eimer* (a keg); also, one-eigth of a liter.

acidification

The addition of tartaric acid to the must when the grapes are deficient in acidity; the same result may be obtained by adding immature grapes to the must, or by blending in wine with higher acidity.

Ackerman-Laurance (F.)   1811

A producer of sparkling wine in the Saumur district, Anjou region, Loire Valley. 300,000 cases.

acquit-à-caution *also* acquit (F.)

An official document accompanying all shipments of wines and spirits in France on which taxes have not been paid; also used for exports exempt from taxation and for shipments made in bond.

Aconcagua Valley (Ch.)

An important district north of Santiago, in central Chile; produces mostly red wines from Cabernet Sauvignon and Malbec grapes.

Adakarasi (T.)

A native red grape.

Adam, Les Caves (F.)   1770

An estate and merchant in Ammerschwihr, Haut-Rhin, Alsace region; 28 acres, including 7 acres of the Kaefferkopf vineyard.

Adams County Winery (U.S.)

A winery in Orrtanna, Pennsylvania, near Gettysberg; grows mostly *vinifera* grapes, especially Gewürztraminer. 3 acres.

Adanti, Fratelli (I.)

An estate in Arquata di Bevagna, Umbria region; produces Bianco, Montefalco Rosso, Rosato, Sagrantino and Vin Santo wines.

adega (P.)

A *bodega,* as in Spain, a wine shop or a wine-making and storing facility.

Adelaide (Aus.)

The capitol of South Australia, formerly, the center of the wine industry.

Adelmann, Weingut Graf (G.)

An estate in Steinheim-Kleinbottwar, Württemberg region. 37 acres, including vineyards in Kleinbottwar and Hoheneck.

Adelsheim Vineyard (U.S.)   1978

A winery in Newberg, Willamette Valley, northwestern Oregon; produces Pinot Noir, Chardonnay, Johannisberg Riesling and Sauvignon Blanc wines. 20 acres.

Adgestone (E.)   1970

A vineyard in Sandown, Isle of Wight; produces white wines made from Müller-Thurgau, Seyval Blanc and Reichensteiner grapes. 9 acres.

Adler Fels (U.S.)   1980

A small winery in Santa Rosa, Sonoma County, California; produces Cabernet Sauvignon, Chardonnay, Johannisberg Riesling and Gewürztraminer wines from purchased grapes. 5,000 cases.

Afames (Cyp.)

A red wine from the village of Platres; made from the Mavron grape.

Affenberg (F.)

A vineyard in Orschwihr, Haut-Rhin district, Alsace region.

Affenthaler (G.)

A red wine from Affental in the Baden region; made mostly from the Pinot Noir grape. The wine is referred to as "Monkey Wine" because it has a monkey molded on the side of the bottle.

afrothes (Gr.)

Sparkling wine.

d'Agassac, Château (F.)

An estate in Ludon, Haut-Médoc district, Bordeaux; classified in 1978 as a *Cru Grand Bourgeois Exceptionnel.* 8,000 cases. 85 acres.

Agawam (U.S., C.)

A red *labrusca* grape grown in Canada and the U.S.

AGE, Bodegas Unidas S.A. (Sp.)   1964

A large winery in Fuenmayor, Rioja Alta; produces several wines, including Siglo, made mostly from purchased grapes. 3 million cases.

Aghiloia (I.)

A strong, dry white wine (15% alcohol) from the Vermentino di Galluro DOC district, in northeastern Sardinia; made from the Vermentino grape.

Aghiorghitiko (Gr.)

A red grape grown in Greece.

Aglianichello (I.)

A red grape grown in the Campania region.

Aglianico (I.)

A red grape grown throughout southern Italy.

Aglianico dei Colli Lucani (I.)

A red wine from Irsina and Tricarico, in the northeastern Basilicata region; made from the Aglianico grape; can also be sparkling.

Aglianico del Vulture DOC (I.)

A red wine from the southeastern slopes of Mt. Vulture, in the northern Basilicata region; made from the Aglianico grape; can be made dry, sweet or *spumante;* often bottled out of the region.

d'Agostini (U.S.)   1856

A winery in Plymouth, Shenandoah Valley, Amador County, California; produces Zinfandel, Carignane, Moscato Canelli and Mission wines. 75,000 cases. 125 acres.

agrafe *also* **agraffe (F.)**

A clamp used to hold the cork during the final stages of making Champagne.

Agros (Cyp.)

A district in Cyprus which produces the most renowned, sweet muscat wine.

Aguascalientes (Mex.)

The region and state where the San Marcos vineyard and winery dominates the wine production.

Ahern Winery (U.S.)   1978

A winery in San Fernando, Los Angeles County, California; produces Pinot Noir, Zinfandel, Chardonnay and Sauvignon Blanc wines from purchased grapes. 4,000 cases.

Ahlgren Vineyard (U.S.)   1976

A winery in Boulder Creek, Santa Cruz County, California; produces Cabernet Sauvignon, Zinfandel, Chardonnay and Sémillon wines from purchased grapes. 1,200 cases.

Ahm *also* **Aum** *and* **Ohm (G.)**

An old term for a standard barrel equal to 30-36 gallons.

Ahmchen (G.)

A small barrel equal to 6.3 gallons.

Ahmeur bou Ahmeur (Alg.)

A red grape, the same as the Flame Tokay in the U.S.

Ahr (G.)

A region in northwestern Germany on the Ahr river; the Bereich is Walporzheim/ Ahrtal, the only Grosslage is Klosterberg; produces red and white wines from Riesling, Müller-Thurgau, Pinot noir and Portugieser grapes. 2,000 acres.

Ahrweiler (G.)

A red wine producing village in the Ahr region, Bereich Walporzheim/Ahrtal, Grosslage Klosterberg. The vineyards are: Daubhaus, Forstberg, Riegelfeld, Rosenthal, Silberberg and Ursulinengarten.

Ai Danil (U.S.S.R.)

A sweet, white wine from the southern Ukraine; made from the Pinot Gris grape.

Aigle (Sw.)

1. A town in the Chablais district, in the eastern Vaud region, which produces:
2. A white wine made from the Chasselas grape.

Aigrots, Les (F.)

A *Premier Cru* vineyard in Beaune, Côte de Beaune district, Burgundy. 55 acres.

aîné (F.)

Eldest, the elder; senior.

Airén (Sp.)

A white grape grown in several regions in Spain; also called Lairén.

Alabama (U.S.)

A state in the southeastern U.S.; it has one important winery: Perdido Vineyards, which makes wine from muscadine grapes.

alambrado (Sp.)

A bottle of wine which is wrapped in an open, light wire netting called an *alambre*.

alambre (Sp.)

A wire netting wrapped around the bottle of a good quality wine, which originally served to protect the label from alteration.

Alameda County (U.S.)

A region east of San Francisco Bay, California. Livermore Valley, which is well-known for its white wines, is in this region. 2,000 acres.

Alarije (Sp.)

A white grape grown in southwestern Spain.

Alavesa (Sp.)

A district in the Rioja region; produces wines which are similar to Rhône wines. 17,000 acres.

Alavesas S.A., Bodegas (Sp.)   1972

A winery in Laguardia, Rioja Alavesa district, Rioja region; produces several wines, including Solar de Samaniego from their own and purchased grapes. 1,000 acres.

Alba Flora (Sp.)

A white wine from Majorca.

Albalonga (G.)

A white grape – a cross of Rieslaner and Sylvaner grapes, developed at the State Viticultural Institute, in Würzburg-Veitshöchheim.

Alban (Lat.)

Ancient Roman wine of Alba, mentioned by Pliny.

Albán (Sp.)

One of many local names for the Palomino grape in the Jerez region.

Albana (I.)

A white grape grown in the Emilia-Romagna region.

Albana di Romagno, DOC (I.)

1. A district in the eastern Emilia-Romagna region, between Bologna and Rimini, which produces:

2. Dry, sweet and sparkling white wines made from the Albana grape.

Albanello (I.)

A white grape grown in Sicily; one of the grapes used in making Corvo wine.

Albariño (Sp.)

A white grape.

Albariño del Palacio (Sp.)

A very dry, white wine from Cambados, in the Galicia region of northwestern Spain; a *vino verde* (like *vinho verde* of Portugal); made from the Albariño grape.

Albariza (Sp.)

An area around Jerez; produces the best *Fino* and *Manzanilla* Sherries. The soil is chalky-white.

albariza (Sp.)

The type of soil best suited to grow grapes for making Sherry. It contains 40% chalk, the rest is clay and sand.

Albarolo *also* **Erbarola (I.)**

A white grape grown in the Liguria region.

Albarona (I.)

A white grape grown in the Tuscany region.

Alben (G.)

Another name for the Elbling or Kleinberger grape; also known as the Klemperich grape.

alberello (I.)

A method of vine-training in which the vines are trained as low bushes; also known as head-trained.

Albert Grivault, Cuvée (F.)

A white wine from the Hospices de Beaune, Côte de Beaune district, Burgundy. The *cuvée* is composed of the following vineyard: Meursault Les Charmes Dessus – 1.2 acres. 225 cases.

Albillo (Sp.)

A white grape grown in northwestern Spain.

Albrecht (F.)

An estate in Orschwihr, Haut-Rhin, Alsace region; 50 acres, including Clos Himmelreich (part of the Pfingstberg vineyard) – 4 acres.

Albury (Aus.)

An old district in New South Wales.

Alcamo DOC (I.)

1. A town and large district in northwestern Sicily, which produces:

2. A light, dry, white wine made from 80% Catarratto Bianco grapes with some Damaschino, Grecanico and Trebbiano grapes.

Alcañon *also* Alcañol (Sp.)

Another name for the white Viura grape grown in the Rioja region; it is also known as Macabeo in Catalonia.

alcohol

A principal and important component of wine. During fermentation, sugar is converted into alcohol by enzymes in the yeast. It is responsible for the preservation of wine. Alcoholic content is expressed as percentage of volume. Natural (unfortified) wines contain 7-16% alcohol.

aldehyde

A component of wine produced by oxidation of alcohol, which helps account for the bouquet.

Alderbrook Vineyards (U.S.)   1983

A winery in Healdsburg, Sonoma County, California; produces Chardonnay and Sauvignon Blanc wines. 8,000 cases. 60 acres.

Aleatico (I.)

1. A red grape of the Muscat family, similar to the Black Muscat grape, which produces sweet, aromatic red wines in various parts of Italy.

2. A sweet, red wine from the southwestern Tuscany region; made from the Aleatico grape. 15-16% alcohol.

Aleatico di Gradoli DOC (I.)

A sweet, red dessert wine from the hills west of Lake Bolsena, in the northern Latium region; made from the Aleatico grape.

Aleatico di Portoferraio (I.)

A sweet, red wine from Elba, in the Tuscany region; made from the Aleatico grape.

Aleatico di Puglia DOC (I.)

A sweet, red wine from the Apulia region; made from the Aleatico di Puglia grape with some Negroamaro, Malvasia Nera and Primitivo grapes. It is sometimes fortified.

Alella DO (Sp.)

1. A town and district just northeast of Barcelona, in the Catalonia region, which produces:

2. Red, white and rosé wines, the red and rosé made from Tempranillo and Garnacha grapes, and the white from Xarel-lo, Pansa Rosada and Garnacha Blanca grapes; most of the wines are white.

d'Alesme-Becker, Château Marquis (F.)

An estate in Margaux, Haut-Médoc district, Bordeaux; classified in 1855 as a *Troisième Cru*. It has existed since at least 1616; in the 19th century it was known as Becker. 5,000 cases. 30 acres.

Alexander Valley (U.S.)

A district in northeastern Sonoma County, California; it is a part of the Russian River Valley.

Alexander Valley Vineyards (U.S.)   1975

A winery in Healdsburg, Alexander Valley, northern Sonoma County, California; produces Cabernet Sauvignon, Merlot, Chardonnay, Johannisberg Riesling and Gewürztraminer wines. 20,000 cases. 250 acres.

Alexander's Crown (U.S.)

A vineyard in Alexander Valley, Sonoma County, California; produces Cabernet Sauvignon wines made by Sonoma Vineyards.

Alexant, Charles (F.)

An estate in Meursault, Côte de Beaune district, Burgundy. 12 acres, including: Puligny-Montrachet Les Folatières – 2.5 acres, Volnay-le Village – 1.2 acres, Beaune Les Bressandes – 1.7 acres, Corton – .8 acre, Meursault Clos des Bouches Chères – 2 acres and Meursault Côte de Beaune Clos de la Baronne – 2.5 acres.

Aleyor (Sp.)

A red wine from island of Majorca, in the Mediterranean Sea.

Alezio (I.)

A village in the southern tip of the Apulia region, which produces red and rosé wines made from Negroamaro and Malvasia Rossa grapes.

Alföld (H.)

The Great Plain: a large region in Hungary, east of the Danube River, which contains half of Hungary's vineyards.

Alfrocheiro Preto (P.)

A red grape grown in the Dão region.

Algarve (P.)

A region along the southern coast, which produces ordinary red and white regional wines.

Algeria

A country in northern Africa, a large producer of mostly red wine. It now has 525,000 acres and ranks as the 8th largest producer in the world. The wines are mostly coarse and high in alcohol. The best wines are made in the Coteaux de Mascara district.

Aliança-Vinicola de Sangalhos, Caves (P.)   1920

A large company in Anadia, Bairrada region; produces still and sparkling wines.

Alicante DO (Sp.)

1. A district around Alicante, in the Levante region, southeastern Spain, which produces:

2. Red and white wines. The red wines are made from the Monastrell grape and the white wines are made from Verdil, Fartó, Merzeguera, Pedro Ximénez and Airén grapes.

Alicante-Bouschet (F.)

1. A red hybrid grape – a cross of Teinturier du Cher, Aramon and Grenache; developed by L. and M. Bouschet in France during the 19th century. It is one of the few grapes containing red juice and is grown in the French Midi, Algeria and California.

2. A red wine made by Papagni Vineyards, California, made from the Alicante-Bouschet grape.

Alicante Negro (Sp.)

A red grape grown in the Galicia region.

Aligoté (F.)

1. A white grape grown in Burgundy, which produces:

2. A white wine designated as Bourgogne Aligoté AOC. It is frequently used in the making of a drink called Kir.

Alkoomi (Aus.)   1971

A small winery in Frankland, Western Australia; produces numerous varietals and Port wine. 30 acres.

All Saints (Aus.)   1864

An old winery in northeastern Victoria; produces sweet Muscats and Port-style wines as well as Cabernet Sauvignon, Shiraz, Chardonnay, Riesling, Marsanne and others. 260 acres.

Allandale (Aus.)   1977

A small winery in New South Wales; produces Cabernet Sauvignon, Chardonnay and Sémillon, some from purchased grapes. 12 acres.

Allegrini (I.)

An estate in Fumane di Valpolicella, Veneto region; produces Amarone, Pelara and Valpolicella wines. 18,000 cases. 75 acres.

Allegro Vineyards (U.S.)   1978
first wine 1980

A winery in Brogue, Pennsylvania; produces hybrid and *vinifera* wines. 15 acres.

Alleinbesitz (G.)

Exclusive ownership; sole proprietorship; a *monopole*.

Allesverloren EWO (S. Af.)   1974

An estate in Malmesbury, in the Swartland W.O. district; produces red wines and Port-style wines. 400 acres.

Allobrogian (Lat.)

An ancient grape from Gaul, grown in Italy; mentioned by Cato.

Almadén (U.S.)   1852

A large winery in San José, Santa Clara County, California, with wineries also in San Benito County and Fresno County. Almaden produces over 50 different wines and sparkling wines, some of which are under the Charles LeFranc label. From almost a thousand acres in Santa Cruz and Santa Clara Counties, only 20 are left in San José. 7,000 acres in San Benito, Monterey and Alexander Counties.

Almansa DO (Sp.)

A district west of Alicante, in the La Mancha region, southeastern Spain; produces robust red wines.

Almarla Vineyards (U.S.)   1979

A winery in Mathersville, eastern Mississippi. 35 acres.

Almendralejo (Sp.)

1. A town and district in the Extremadura region, in southwestern Spain; produces ordinary wines and wine for making brandy.

2. A red grape grown in the Extremadura region.

Almeria (U.S.)

A white *vinifera* grape, from which the Calmeria grape was developed in 1950.

Almissa (Y.)

A sweet, red wine from the Dalmatia region.

Almonte (I.)

A red wine from Frontignano, near Todi, in the Umbria region; made from Sangiovese, Barbera and other grapes.

almude (P.)

An old measure equal to 25 liters.

aloque (Sp.)

A type of red wine made from a blend of red and white grapes.

Aloxe-Corton AOC (F.)

1. A village in the Côte de Beaune district, Burgundy; produces red and white wines. The most important vineyards are the *Grands Crus* of Corton, Corton-Renardes, Corton-Bressandes, Corton-Charlemagne and Corton-Clos du Roi. 600 acres.

2. Red and white wine from Aloxe-Corton; it can be a blend from any vineyard in that village. Some vineyards in neighboring Ladoix-Serrigny and Pernand-Vergelesses may use the appellation Aloxe-Corton, and 3 vineyards may use the Corton or Corton-Charlemagne appellation.

Alpha (U.S.)

An American, red hybrid grape which is very high in acid and very hardy.

alqueira (P.)

A wine measure of 11.5 kilograms of grapes, or 16 liters of wine, equal to about 3 gallons.

Alsace (F.)

An important wine-producing region of northeastern France. The region is a 75-mile long narrow strip which runs along the Rhône river and is divided into two districts, the Bas-Rhin in the north and the Haut-Rhin in the south; produces mostly dry, white wines, some late-harvest sweet wines and some red wines. The wines are identified on the label according to the varietal grape: Riesling, Gewürztraminer, Sylvaner, Muscat etc., and use mostly German names. The best wines can be legally labeled *Grand Cru, Grand Vin* or *Grand*

Réserve. Sometimes the vineyard name will appear on the label. 30,000 acres.

Alsheim (G.)

A village in the Rheinhessen region, Bereich Nierstein, Grosslagen Krötenbrunnen and Rheinblick. The vineyards are: Fischerpfad, Frühmesse, Römerberg and Sonnenberg in Grosslage Rheinblick and Goldberg in Grosslage Krötenbrunnen. 1,500 acres.

Alta Vineyard Cellar (U.S.)   1979

A winery in Calistoga, Napa Valley, California; produces only Chardonnay wine. 2,000 cases. 10 acres.

altar wine

Any wine used for sacramental or religious ceremonies in church, synagogue or home.

Altenbaumberg (G.)

A village in the Nahe region, Bereich Schloss Böckelheim, Grosslage Burgweg. The vineyards are: Kehrenberg, Laurentiusberg, Rotenberg, Schlossberg and Treuenfels.

Altenberg (F.)

A vineyard in Bergheim, Haut-Rhin district, Alsace region; produces Gewürztraminer, Riesling and Pinot Blanc wines.

Altenberg (F.)

A vineyard in Wolxheim, Bas-Rhin district, Alsace region.

Altenbourg (F.)

A vineyard in Sigolsheim, Haut-Rhin district, Alsace region; produces Riesling wines. 135 acres.

Altesse (F., Sw.)

1. A white grape grown in the Savoie region of southeastern France and in Switzerland.

2. A white wine from Switzerland; made from the Altesse grape.

Altintaş (T.)

A white grape grown in Turkey.

altise (F.)

A beetle which feeds on grape leaves so that only the veins remain in a lacey pattern.

Alto Adige DOC (I.)

The northern half of the Trentino-Alto Adige region of northeastern Italy, also known as the South Tyrol, and Südtiroler in German. The DOC covers many different varietal wines which must contain 95% of the grape named on the label.

Alto Douro (P.)

The Upper Douro region, around the River Douro, in northeastern Portugal, where Port wines are made.

Alto Estate EWO (S. Af.)   1920

A hillside estate in the Stellenbosch district; produces Cabernet Sauvignon wine. 250 acres.

Alushta (U.S.S.R.)

A red wine from the city and district of Alushta, in the Crimea region of the Ukraine.

Alva (P.)

A white grape grown in northwestern Portugal.

Alvarelhão (P.)

A red grape grown in Portugal; it is one of the grapes used to make red Vinho Verde; also called Pilongo.

Alvarinho (P.)

1. A white grape grown in the Vinho Verde district.

2. A white wine from the Vinho Verde district; made from the Alvarinho grape.

Alvear S.A. (Sp.)   1729

An estate in Montilla, Córdoba; produces many styles of Montilla wine. 350 acres.

Alzey (G.)

A village in the Rheinhessen region, Bereich Wonnegau, Grosslage Sylbillenstein. The vineyards are: Kapellenberg, Pfaffenhalde, Römerberg, Rotenfels and Wartberg. It is the home of a famous viticultural school. 1,800 acres.

Am Wagwam (A.)

A district just northwest of Vienna, along the Danube River, in the Lower Austria region.

amabile (I.)

Semi-sweet.

Amadieu, Pierre (F.)   1920

An estate and merchant in Gigondas, Rhône region; owns 200 acres of Gigondas.

Amador County (U.S.)

An important region in the central Sierra foothills, California; produces mostly Zinfandel wine. The Shenandoah Valley is the most important district in the region. 1,000 acres.

Amador Foothill Winery (U.S.)   1980

A small winery in Plymouth, Shenendoah Valley, Amador County, California; produces Cabernet Sauvignon, Zinfandel, Chenin Blanc, Sauvignon Blanc and white Zinfandel wines. 3,000 cases. 8 acres.

Amanda, Vinicola (I.)

A winery in Sava, east of Taranto, in the southern Apulia region; produces Primitivo and other wines.

Amandiers, Les (F.)

A vineyard in Riquewihr, Haut-Rhin district, Alsace region; produces Muscat wine. It is a *monopole* owned by Dopff & Irion.

amarognolo (I.)

A slight bitter taste present in many Italian white wines.

Ambassador's Vineyard (U.S.)

A vineyard in Los Olivos, Santa Ynez Valley, Santa Barbara County, California; produces Riesling wine; owned by Firestone Vineyard.

Amber Drops (I.)

A sweet, white wine from the Isle of Ischia, in the Campania region; made from the Biancolella grape. This wine ages well.

Amber Dry (E.)

The commercial name in England for Clairette du Languedoc wine.

Ambonnay (F.)

A village in the Côte d'Ambonnay district, Champagne region; produces a *Grand Cru* Champagne from mostly red grapes.

d'Ambra Vini d'Ischia (I.)

A winery on the island of Ischia, Campania region; produces Amber Drops, Biancolella, Forastera and Per'e Palummo wines. 150,000 cases.

Ambrato di Comiso (I.)

A sweet, white wine from Comiso, southeastern Sicily; made from red grapes: Calabrese, Frappato di Vittoria, Nerello Mascalese and Damaschino, vinified without the skins. 13-17% alcohol.

amelioration

Any of several methods of treating grape juice in order to improve the quality of the wine, such as the addition of sulphur, sugar or new wine.

Americano *also* Americanas (Sw.)

The Swiss name for the Isabella grape, an American red grape grown in New York State and Brazil.

amertume (F.)

A disease of wine caused by bacteria, which reduces glycerine and increases acidity, making the wine bitter and acetic.

Amigne (Sw.)

One of several local white grapes grown in the Valais region.

Aminean (Lat.)

An ancient Roman grape and wine; mentioned in Virgil's *Georgics II.*

Aminteon *also* **Amynteon (Gr.)**

1. A town and district in Macedonia, northern Greece, which produces:

2. A red wine.

Amiot, Veuve (F.)   1844

A producer of sparkling wines in St.-Hilaire-St.-Florent, Saumur district, Anjou region, Loire Valley. 250,000 cases.

Amiot Père et Fils, Pierre et Guy (F.)

An estate in Chassagne-Montrachet, Côte de Beaune district, Burgundy; 20 acres, including Montrachet – .3 acre, Chassagne-Montrachet En Cailleret – 1.7 acres, Puligny-Montrachet Les Demoiselles – .8 acre and Chassagne-Montrachet Clos St.-Jean (red) – .8 acre.

Amity Vineyard (U.S.)   1976

A small winery in Amity, Willamette Valley, northwestern Oregon; produces Pinot Noir, Pinot Noir Nouveau, White Riesling, Sémillon and Chardonnay wines. 15 acres.

Ammerschwir (F.)

An important village in the Haut-Rhin district, Alsace region. The most well-known vineyard is Kaefferkopf.

Amontillado (Sp.)

A dry type of Sherry, not as pale and light as *Fino* and sometimes slightly sweet.

Amoroso (Sp.)

A type of sweetened Oloroso Sherry made for English markets.

Amoureuses, Les (F.)

A *Premier Cru* vineyard in Chambolle-Musigny, Côte de Nuits district, Burgundy. 13 acres.

Ampeau, Robert et Michel (F.)

An estate in Meursault, Côte de Beaune district, Burgundy. 25 acres, including Puligny-Montrachet Les Combettes – 1.7 acres, Meursault Les Perrières – 2.5 acres, Les Charmes – 1.2 acres, Blagny La Pièce-sous-le-Bois – 2 acres, Auxey-Duresses Les Écusseaux – 2.5 acres, Volnay Les Santenots – 4 acres, Pommard – 2.5 acres, Beaune Clos du Roi – 1.2 acres and Savigny Les Lavières – 1.6 acres.

Ampelidaceae

The botanical family to which grapevines belong; it is divided into ten *genera*, one of which is important for wine making: the *genus Vitis, sub-genus Euvites*, of which the most important species are *Vitis vinifera* and *Vitis labrusca*. The *Vitis vinifera* species of grapes accounts for the best wines in the world.

ampelography

The study of grapes.

amphora

A large, two-handled vessel used in ancient Rome and Greece for storing wine.

Ampurdán-Costa Brava DO (Sp.)

A district near Figueras, in the northeastern Catalonia region of northeastern Spain; produces mostly rosé wines and some red and white wines. The red and rosé wines are made from Garnacha Tinta and Cariñena grapes and the white wines are made from Macabeo and Xarel-lo grapes.

Amselfelder (Y.)

A German name for the wine made from the Pinot Noir grape when sold to Germany and Austria; produced in the Kosovo district, in southern Yugoslavia.

Amtliche Prüfungsnummer (G.)

"Official Test Number," a number printed on the wine label indicating that the wine was tested and approved for a designation of *Qba* or *QmP.*

Amynteon *also* **Aminteon (Gr.)**
See **Aminteon**.

Anapa (U.S.S.R.)

A town and district in southwestern Russia; produces wines from Cabernet Sauvignon, Pinot Noir, Pinot Gris, Aligoté, Sauvignon, Sémillon and Riesling grapes.

Anbaugebiet *also* **Gebiet (G.)**

A region. There are 11 regions in Germany: Ahr, Baden, Franken, Hessische Bergstrasse, Mittelrhein, Mosel-Saar-Ruwer, Nahe, Rheingau, Rheinhessen, Rheinpfalz and Württemberg. Each region contains one or more *Bereiche*.

Anderson Vineyard, S. (U.S.)   vines 1971
                                   winery 1979

A winery in Yountville, Napa Valley, California; produces Chardonnay wine and champagne, some from purchased grapes. 3,000 cases. 35 acres.

Anderson Wine Cellars (U.S.)   **1980**

A small winery in Exeter, Tulare County, California; produces Ruby Cabernet and Chenin Blanc wines. 2,000 cases. 20 acres.

André (U.S.)

A brand of inexpensive, bulk-produced sparkling wines made by Gallo.

André, Pierre (F.)

The owner of La Reine Pédauque, in Aloxe-Corton, a wine company which operates 4 estates in the Côte de Beaune district, Burgundy. See **Reine Pédauque, La.**

Andrés (C.)   **1967, 1961**
                                 in British Columbia

A large winery in Winona, eastern Ontario.

Andron-Blanquet, Château (F.)

An estate in St.-Estèphe, Haut-Médoc district, Bordeaux; classified in 1978 as a *Cru Grand Bourgeois Exceptionnel*. 7,500 cases. 37 acres.

añejado (Sp.)
Aged.

añejo *also* **viejo (Sp.)**
Old.

Aney, Château (F.)

An estate in Cussac, Haut-Médoc district, Bordeaux; classified in 1978 as a *Cru Bourgeois*. 50 acres. 10,000 cases.

Angelica (U.S.)

A sweet wine, sometimes fortified, made in California, usually from the Mission grape.

Angelliaume, Léonce (F.)

An estate in Cravant-lès-Coteaux, Chinon district, Touraine region, Loire Valley.

d'Angelo, Fratelli (I.)   **1944**

A winery in Rionero, Basilicata region; produces Aglianico del Vulture, Malvasia and Moscato wines. 10,000 cases.

l'Angélus, Château (F.)

An estate in St.-Émilion, Bordeaux; classified in 1955 as a *Grand Cru Classé*. 14,000 cases. 62 acres.

Angera (I.)

1. A village in the Lombardy region, which produces:
2. A red wine made from a blend of Bonarda, Barbera and Nebbiolo grapes.

d'Angerville, Marquis (F.)

An estate in Volnay, Côte de Beaune district, Burgundy. 35 acres, including Volnay Clos des Ducs Monopole – 5 acres, Caillerets – 1.2 acres, Fremiet – 4 acres, Champans – 10 acres, Taille-Pieds – 2.5 acres and Meursault Les Santenots – 2.5 acres.

Anges, Domaine des (F.)   **1973**

An estate in Mormoiron, Côtes du Ventoux district, in the southern Rhône region; produces red wine made from Grenache, Syrah, Carignan and Cinsault grapes. 20 acres.

Anghelu Ruju (I.)

A sweet, red wine from Alghero, in north-western Sardinia, made from semi-dried Cannonau grapes. 18% alcohol.

Angiolini, Mario (I.)

An estate in Rami di Ravarino, Emilia-Romagna region; produces Lambrusco wine. 12,000 cases.

Angles, Les (F.)

A *Premier Cru* vineyard in Volnay, Côte de Beaune district, Burgundy. 9 acres.

l'Angludet, Château (F.)

An estate in Cantenac-Margaux, Haut-Médoc district, Bordeaux; classified in 1932 as a *Cru Bourgeois Exceptionnel*. 10,000 cases. 70 acres.

Angoris (I.)   **1648**

A large estate in Cormons, Friuli-Venezia Giulia region; produces Colli Orientali, Isonzo and sparkling wines. 500,000 cases. 450 acres.

Angoves (Aus.)   **1910**

A large estate west of Renmark, in South Australia; produces Rhine Riesling, Sauvignon Blanc, Chenin Blanc and Gewürztraminer wines. 500 acres.

anguillules (F.)

See **Eelworms**.

Anheuser, Weingut Ökonomierat August E. (G.)   **1869**

An estate in Bad Kreuznach, Nahe region. 150 acres, including several parcels of vineyards in Kreuznach, Winzerheim, Norheim and Niederhausen-Schlossböckelheim.

Anheuser, Weingut Paul (G.)   **1888**

An estate in Bad Kreuznach, Nahe region. 135 acres, including vineyards in Kreuznach, Schlossböckelheim, Niederhausen, Altenbamberger, Norheim and others.

Añina (Sp.)

An important district west of Jerez, in the Sherry region.

Anjou AOC (F.)

1. An important large region west of Touraine, in the Loire Valley, northwestern France, which gets its name from Angers, the largest city in the region; produces principally white wines made from the Chenin Blanc grape and red and rosé wines primarily from the Cabernet Franc grape. It is divided into the districts of Coteaux de la Loire, Coteaux du Layon, Coteaux de l'Aubance, Coteaux de Loir, Saumur and Coteaux de Saumur. The most well-known smaller districts are Bonnezeaux, Quarts de Chaume, Saumur-Champigny and Savennières.

2. The AOC designation for red, white and rosé wines from the Anjou region; the red and rosé are made from Cabernet Franc, Cabernet Sauvignon, Gamay, Pineau d'Aunis, Cot and Groslot grapes, the white from Chenin Blanc, Chardonnay and Sauvignon grapes. A Mousseux AOC is also produced.

Anjou Coteaux de la Loire AOC (F.)

A district in the Anjou region of the Loire Valley; produces dry and sweet white wines made from the Chenin Blanc grape.

Annaberg Stumpf-Fitz'sches Weingut (G.)

A small estate in Bad Dürkheim-Leistadt, Rheinpfalz region; owns part of the Anneberg vineyard in Kallstadt. 12 acres.

Annarella (I.)

A local white grape grown in Nicastro, in the Calabria region.

ano (P.)

Year of a vintage.

anreichern (G.)

To enrich; to add sugar to must in order to raise its alcohol content; to sugar must or wine.

Anreicherung (G.)

Chaptalization, the process of adding sugar to the must; also called *Verbessernung*.

Anselmi (I.)

A winery in Monforte d'Alpone, Veneto region; produces Bardolino, Soave and Valpolicella wines.

Ansonica di Giglio (I.)

1. A white grape grown in the Tuscany region.

2. A white wine from the Isle of Giglio, off the coast of southern Tuscany; made from the Ansonica di Giglio grape.

anthracnose

A fungus disease of the vine which causes the formation of stains on the shoots, leaves and fruit.

Antide Midan, Cuvée (F.)

A wine from the Hospices de Nuits, Côte de Nuits district, Burgundy. The *cuvée* is composed of one vineyard in Nuits-St.-Georges: Les Porets – .5 acre.

Antinori, Marchesi L. and P. (I.)   1385

A winery in Florence, Tuscany region; produces Aleatico, Chianti Classico, Galestro, Orvieto Classico, San Giocondo, Tignarello, Vin Santo, rosé and sparkling wines. 550 acres.

Antoniolo (I.)

An estate in Gattinara, Piedmont region; produces Gattinara, Santa Chiara and Spanna wines.

Apalachee Vineyard (U.S.)   1983

A winery in North High Shoals, Georgia; produces Cabernet Franc, Carmine and Riesling wines. 13 acres.

apéritif (F.)

Any drink taken before a meal, usually a wine such as dry Sherry, Champagne or fortified and flavored wines such as Lillet, Dubonnet or vermouth.

Apetlon (A.)

A village in the Burgenland region of eastern Austria; produces white Seewinkel wines made near the Neusliedlersee.

Aphrodite (Cyp.)

A well-known, medium-dry, white wine from Cyprus.

apoplexy

A fungus disease of the vine and other plants, caused by a cryptogamic growth entering the wood and emitting an enzyme that kills the wood ahead of it. The vine dies in the hottest part of the summer.

Appellation Complète (Lux.)   1935

A wine control law in Luxembourg, similar to the AOC laws of France, regulated by the Commission of the Marque National.

Appellation d'Origine Contrôllée; AOC; AC (F.)

1. French for "Controlled Name of Origin," the laws in France designed to guarantee the origin and quality of French wines, regulating geographical limits of production, varieties of grapes grown, the alcoholic content, grape yields, viticultural practices and wine making. The laws established several categories of wine quality: AOC wines – the highest quality, VDQS wines – the second level wines, *Vin de Pays* (formerly *Appellation d'Origine Simple*) and *Vin de Table*, which has no regional designation. *Vin de Consommation Courante* (VCC) is another category of regional wine, used for wines of the Midi. The laws were begun in 1905 and solidified in 1935. The governing body is the *Institut National des Appellation d'Origine des Vins et Eaux-de-Vie* (INAO). Similar laws exist in Germany, Italy and other countries.

2. A designation on the label indicating the highest quality of French wine and that the wine adheres to the laws applicable to that district or region.

Appellation d'Origine Garantie, AOG (Mor.)

1. French for "Guaranteed Name of Origin," the laws designed to guarantee the

origin and quality of the wines of Morocco; similar to the AOC laws of France.

2. The AOG designation indicates the highest quality wines.

Appellation d'Origine Simple (F.)   1927

French for "Simple Name of Origin," a predecessor of the *Appellation Contrôllée* law. It was passed in 1927 and regulated which grapes could be grown in which area. It was replaced by the AOC laws of 1935.

•Aprilia DOC (I.)

1. A town and district south of Rome, in the southwestern Latium region, which produces:

2. Red and white varietal wines made from Merlot, Sangiovese and Trebbiano grapes, each made from 95% of the grape listed.

Apulia *also* Puglia (I.)

1. A region in southeastern Italy, in the "heel of the boot." It is the largest wine-producing region in Italy, producing 291 million gallons a year. There are 18 DOC districts in this region.

2. A red wine from Martina Franca, in the southern Apulia region; made from a blend of Primitivo, Negroamaro and Malvasia Nera grapes.

d'Aquéria, Château (F.)

A famous estate in the Tavel district, Rhône region; produces rosé wines principally from the Grenache grape; also makes red Lirac wine. 105 acres.

Aquilea DOC (I.)

A village and district in the southeastern Friuli-Venezia Giulia region. It was granted DOC status in 1976; produces the following varietal wines: Cabernet (Sauvignon, Franc or a blend of both), Merlot, Pinot Bianco, Pinot Grigio, Refosco, Riesling Renano and Tocai Friulano.

Arad (R.)

A city and district in the Banat region of western Romania; produces red and white wines. The red wine is made from Caber-net Sauvignon, Merlot and Cadarka grapes and the white wine is made from the Fe-tească grape.

Aragón (Sp.)

1. A region in northeastern Spain; produces red, rosé and white wines.

2. A red grape grown in the La Mancha region.

Aragosta (I.)

A white wine from Alghero, northwestern Sardinia; made from the Vermentino grape.

arame (P.)

A wire mesh covering sometimes used on some bottles of old *reserva* wines.

Aramon (F.)

A grape grown in southern France, California and Algeria. It is very productive and makes ordinary wines, low in alcohol and light in color.

Arbanne (F.)

A grape grown in the Champagne region in small amounts.

Arbois (F.)

A white grape grown in the Touraine region, Loire Valley; also called Pineau Menu.

Arbois AOC (F.)

The best known district in the Jura region of southeastern France; produces red and white wines and is especially known for rosé wines; the red wines are made from Trousseau, Poulsard and Pinot Noir grapes, the rosé from Poulsard grapes and the white from Savagnin, Chardonnay and Pinot Blanc.

Archanes (Gr.)

A district near Herklion, Crete; produces red wines.

archbishop (E.)

A mulled claret wine, similar to a bishop (mulled Port).

d'Arche, Château (F.)

An estate in Sauternes, Sauternes district, Bordeaux; classified in 1855 as a *Deuxième Cru*. The name is taken from the 18th century owner, Comte d'Arche (1733-1789). Château d'Arche-Lafaurie was once joined to this estate but is now a separate growth. 7,500 cases. 90 acres.

d'Arche-Lafaurie, Château (F.)

An estate in Sauternes, Sauternes district, Bordeaux; classified in 1855 as a *Deuxième Cru*. It was once part of Château d'Arche. 4,300 cases.

d'Arches, Château (F.)

An estate in Ludon, Haut-Médoc district, Bordeaux; classified in 1978 as a *Cru Bourgeois*. 1,700 cases. 10 acres.

d'Arcy Wine Cellars, Bernard (U.S.) 1982

The new name of the Gross Highland Winery, in Absecon, New Jersey; newly planted with *vinifera* and hybrid grapes.

Ardenghesca (I.)

A white wine from Montalcino, Monte Antico district, in the Tuscany region; made from a blend of Trebbiano and Malvasia grapes.

are (F.)

A European metric measure of land equal to 100 square meters. Ten *are* = 1 *hectare*.

d'Arenberg (A.)

See **Osborn d'Arenberg.**

aréomètre *also* mustimètre (F.)

A device for measuring specific gravity, similar to the *Oechsle* and *Baumé* methods. It measures the amount of sugar or alcohol in wine or must.

Argentina

The fifth leading wine producing country with 750,000 acres producing 800 million gallons per year. Vineyards have been in existence since the 16th century. The Malbec grape produces 2/3 of the red wines and the whites are made mostly from Torrontes Sanjuanir and Pedro Ximénez grapes with some European grapes (Sémillon, Sauvignon, etc.). The Mendoza province produces 75% of the wine. Moët et Chandon makes Champaña there.

Argeş (R.)

A town and district in central Romania, north of Piteşti and just south of the Carpathian Mountains; produces varietal white wines, especially Fetească Regala; also Sauvignon, Riesling and Tămîioasă.

Argillats, Aux (F.)

A *Premier Cru* vineyard (in part) in Nuits-St.-Georges, Côte de Nuits district, Burgundy. 6 acres.

Argillats, Les (F.)

A *Premier Cru* vineyard (in part) in Nuits-St.-Georges, Côte de Nuits district, Burgundy. 18 acres.

Argillières, Les (F.)

A *Premier Cru* vineyard in Pommard, Côte de Beaune district, Burgundy. 9 acres.

Argillières, Clos des (F.)

A *Premier Cru* vineyard in Prémeaux, Côte de Nuits district, Burgundy. 10.5 acres.

argol

Tartar deposits in wine casks; when scraped off these deposits are made into cream of tartar for use in making baking powder.

Argonaut Winery (U.S.)   grapes 1972
                                winery 1976

A small winery in Ione, Amador County, California; produces Zinfandel and Barbera wines. 2,000 cases.

Arinto (P.)

A white grape grown in the Dão, Bucelas, Bairrada and other regions.

Arinto do Dão (P.)

A white grape grown in the Dão region, related to the German Riesling; also called Assario Branco.

Aris

A white hybrid grape – a cross of *Riparia* and Gamay crossed with Riesling; developed at the Federal Research Institute, Geilweilerhof, Germany.

Arizona (U.S.)

A state in the southwestern U.S. where only experimental planting is done. There are no commercial vineyards or wineries.

arjoado (P.)

A system of training vines on wires stretched between trees.

Arkansas (U.S.)

A state in the U.S. which has two large wineries and about a dozen small wineries. 5,000 acres.

Arlots, Clos des (F.)

A *Premier Cru* vineyard in Prémeaux, Côte de Nuits district, Burgundy. 16 acres.

Armand, Comte (F.)

An estate in Pommard, Côte de Beaune district, Burgundy; owns Pommard Clos des Épeneaux Monopole – 13 acres.

armazen (P.)

A wine lodge; a storage facility or warehouse.

Armenia (U.S.S.R.)

A republic of the U.S.S.R. near Iran and Turkey; produces mostly sweet, red and white wines made from Verdelho, Sercial, Aligoté, Muscat and Voskheat (Voskevaz) grapes.

armillaria root-rot

A fungus disease of the vine which develops on the shoots, trunk and roots; also called *pourridié* in France.

Arnauld, Château (F.)

An estate in Arcins, Haut-Medoc district, Bordeaux; classified in 1932 as a *Cru Bourgeois*. 3,000 cases. 25 acres.

Arneis dei Roeri (I.)

1. A white grape grown in the Roeri hills around Alba, in the southern Piedmont region, which produces:

2. A dry, white wine made from the Arneis dei Roeri grape.

Arnoison (F.)

Another name for the Chardonnay grape.

Arnoux Père et Fils (F.)

An estate in Chorey-lès-Beaune, Côte de Beaune district, Burgundy. 37 acres, including Beaune *Premier Cru* – 5 acres, and some acreage in Aloxe-Corton, Savigny and Chorey.

arroba (Sp.)

A wine measure of 11.5 kilograms of grapes, or 16 liters of wine, equal to about 5 gallons.

l'Arrosée, Château (F.)

An estate in St.-Émilion, Bordeaux; classified in 1955 as a *Grand Cru*. 15,000 cases. 62 acres.

Arrowfield (Aus.)   1969

A large winery in Upper Hunter Valley, New South Wales; it has the largest vineyard in Australia; produces Cabernet Sauvignon, Shiraz, Rhine Riesling, Sémillon and Chardonnay wines. 1,200 acres.

Arroyo Seco Vineyards (U.S.)

A large vineyard in Greenfield, Salinas Valley, Monterey County, California; produces Chardonnay, Cabernet, Merlot and Petite Sirah wines for Monterey Peninsula Winery. 350 acres.

Arsinöe (Cyp.)

A dry, white wine.

Arthur Girard, Cuvée (F.)

A red wine from the Hospices de Beaune, Côte de Beaune district, Burgundy. The *cuvée* is composed of the following vineyards in Savigny: Les Peuillets – 2.5 acres and Les Marconnets – 2 acres.

Artimino (I.)

An estate in Artimino, near Florence, in the Tuscany region; produces Carmignano, Chianti, Vin Ruspo, Vin Santo and other wines. 300 acres.

Artique-Arnaud, Château (F.)

The former name, in 1855, of Château Grand-Puy-Ducasse, in Pauillac, Bordeaux.

Arvelets, Les (F.)

A *Premier Cru* vineyard in Pommard, Côte de Beaune district, Burgundy. 20 acres.

Arvelets, Les (F.)

A *Premier Cru* vineyard in Fixin, Côte de Nuits district, Burgundy. 8 acres.

Arvier (I.)

A village in the Valle d'Aosta region; produces Enfer d'Arvier DOC wine made from the Petit Rouge grape.

Arvine (Sw.)

One of several old, white grapes grown in the Valais region. The Petite Arvine is a related grape.

Arvino (I.)

A red grape grown in the Calabria region; also called Gaglioppo and Magliocco.

asciutto (I.)

Dry (referring to a wine).

ascorbic acid

An ingredient frequently added to wines as an anti-oxidant.

Ashtarak (U.S.S.R.)

A white, fortified wine from Armenia SSR.

Aspiran (F.)

A red grape grown in the Languedoc region of southern France.

Asprinio (I.)

A white grape grown in the Campania and Basilicata regions.

Asprino *also* **Asprinio (I.)**

1. A white, *frizzante* wine from Ruoti, in the northwestern Basilicata region; made from the Asprinio grape. It is popular in Naples.

2. A white, *frizzante* wine from Caserta and Aversa, in the Campania region; made from the Asprinio grape; also very popular in Naples.

Assario Branco (P.)

A white grape grown in the Dão region; also called Arinto do Dão.

assemblage (F.)

1. In Bordeaux and other regions, the blending or mixing of the wines made from different grape varieties to produce the finished wine.

2. In Champagne, Burgundy and other regions, a blending of wines from different vineyards within a single village.

Assmannshausen (G.)

1. A village in the Rheingau region, Bereich Johannisberg, Grosslagen Burweg and Steil. The vineyards are Berg Kaiserstein-fels in Assmannshausen-Aulhausen (Grosslage Burgweg), Frankenthal in Assmannshausen (Grosslage Steil), and Hinterkirch and Höllenberg in Assmanns-hausen-Aulhausen (also in Grosslage Steil). It produces:

2. Red and white wines. The red wine is made from the Spätburgunder (Pinot Noir) grape and the white wine is made from the Riesling grape.

Associated Vintners (U.S.)   1967

A small winery in Redmond, near Seattle, Washington; produces Cabernet Sauvignon, Pinot Noir, Gewürztraminer, Chardonnay, Sémillon and White Riesling wines. 30 acres.

Assumption Abbey (U.S.)

A label for varietal wines formerly used by Brookside Vineyard Co., in Guasti, Cucamonga district, San Bernardino County, southern California.

Assyrtiko (Gr.)

A white grape grown in the Greek islands.

Asti (I.)

A city and district in the central Piedmont region, in northwestern Italy; known for its sparkling white wine, Asti Spumante, made from Muscat grapes and Moscato d'Asti, a still wine made from Muscat grapes.

Asti Spumante DOC (I.)

A sweet, white, sparkling wine from the Asti district, in the Piedmont region; made from Moscato Bianco or Moscato di Canelli grapes. The *Charmat* method is usually used.

Aszar-Neszmely (H.)

A district north of Mór, in the northern Transdanubia region of northwestern Hungary; produces white wine from the Ezerjó grape. Officially rated White Wine of Excellent Quality. 4,500 acres.

aszú (H.)

Polish for "dried" or "raisined," referring to the grapes used in making Tokaji wine.

Athenaeus (c. 170-230 B.C.) (Gr.)

An ancient Greek author who wrote *Deipnosophistae*, which contains discussions on wine-making and different kinds of wines.

attemperators

Metal coils immersed in fermenting vats through which hot or cold water is pumped to control the temperature of the must.

Attems, Conti (I.)

An estate in Lucinico, Friuli-Venezia Giulia region; produces Collio and Isonzo wines. 17,000 cases. 80 acres.

Attica (Gr.)

A region of Greece around Athens, famous for Retsina and Hymettus wines.

Aubaine (F.)

Another name for the Chardonnay grape.

Aubin Blanc (F.)

A white grape grown in the Lorraine region.

Aucerot (Aus.)

In the New South Wales region, another name for the white Auxerrois grape.

l'Aumérade, Domaine de (F.)

An estate in Pierrefeu, northeast of Toulon, in the southern Provence region.

Aurora *also* Aurore (U.S.)

An American, white, hybrid grape grown in New York State. The grape is known as Seibel 5279.

Ausbau (G.)

The maturing of new wine in the vat or cask.

Ausbruch (A., G., H.)

German for the purest free-run juice, or the first pressing of dried grapes; similar to *Trockenbeerenauslese*. The term is used for sweet Austrian wines and Hungarian Tokaji Aszú wines.

Auslese (G.)

"Selection," or "choice," the term applied to high-quality German and Austrian wines, referring to the specially selected bunches of grapes; rather sweet and rich.

Ausone, Château (F.)

A famous estate in St.-Émilion, Bordeaux; classified in 1955 as a *Premier Grand Cru Classé;* placed at the top of the list of 12 *Premiers Grands Crus Classées* along with Château Cheval-Blanc; named after Ausonius, the fourth century Roman poet. Made from 50% Merlot, 50% Cabernet Franc grapes. 2,500-2,800 cases. 18 acres.

Aussey *also* Osey

See **Osey.**

Aussey, Les (F.)

A *Premier Cru* vineyard (in part) in Volnay, Côte de Beaune district, Burgundy. 7 acres.

Australia

An important wine producing country; produces over 83 million gallons annually. The main regions are New South Wales (especially Hunter River Valley), Victoria and South Australia; there are also some vineyards in Western Australia, Queensland and Tasmania. Most of the vines planted are European, the Cabernet Sauvignon, Shiraz (Syrah), Riesling and Chardonnay being the most important. 220,000 acres.

Austria

The German-speaking country that produces wines similar to German wines, primarily from the Riesling, Traminer (or Gewürztraminer) and Grüner Veltliner grapes. The principal regions are Lower Austria, Burgenland, Styria and Vienna. 80 million gallons. 170,000 acres.

Auvernier (Sw.)

A village in the Neuchâtel district, in the Vaud region; produces white and rosé wines.

Auxerrois (F.)

1. A white or pink grape (Auxerrois Blanc and Auxerrois Gris) grown in the Lorraine region.

2. In the Cahors district, the name for the Malbec or Côt grape.

3. A district around Auxerre, west of Chablis, in the Burgundy region; it includes Irancy, Saint-Bris, Chitry and several other communes. The AOC wines are various *Bourgogne* and *Crémant* designations.

Auxerrois (G.)

In Germany, the name for a clone of the Pinot Blanc grape.

Auxey-Duresses AOC (F.)

A village in the Côte de Beaune district, Burgundy; produces dry white and red wines. It has 9 *Premier Cru* vineyards.

Avaux, Les (F.)

A *Premier Cru* vineyard in Beaune, Côte de Beaune district, Burgundy. 33 acres.

Avaux, Cuvée Clos des (F.)

A red wine from the Hospices de Beaune, Côte de Beaune district, Burgundy. The *cuvée* is composed of the following vineyard in Beaune: Les Avaux – 5 acres. 675 cases.

Avdat (Is.)

Red and white table wines produced by the Carmel Winery. The red wine is made from the Carignan grape and the white wine is made from Sauvignon Blanc and Clairette grapes.

Aveleda Lda, Quinta da (P.)   1947

An estate in Porto; produces *vinho verde* wines: Casal Garcia (dry), Aveleda (semisweet) and Quinta da Aveleda (dry).

Avelsbach (G.)

A village in the Mosel-Saar-Ruwer region, Bereich Saar-Ruwer, Grosslage Römerlay. The vineyards are: Altenberg, Hammerstein, Herrenberg, Kupp and Rotlay; sometimes listed as Mosel, sometimes as Ruwer wine; considered as a part of the city of Trier. 120 acres.

Avesso (P.)

A white grape grown in the Vinho Verde region.

Avillo (Sp.)

The name in the Catalonia region for the Picpoule grape.

Avize (F.)

A village in the Champagne region; produces one of the most highly regarded wines of the Côte des Blancs, rated a *Grand Cru*; grows mostly red grapes.

Ay (F.)

A village in the Marne Valley near Épernay, in the Champagne region; known for its underground cellars. Produces a *Grand Cru* Champagne from red grapes.

Ayala (F.)   c. 1860

A Champagne producer in Ay. 60 acres. 900,000 bottles.

Ayl (G.)

A village on the Saar River, in the Mosel-Saar-Ruwer region, Bereich Saar-Ruwer, Grosslage Scharzberg. The vineyards are: Herrenberger, Kupp and Scheidterberger. 270 acres.

Aymaville (I.)

A village in the Valle d'Aosta region of northwestern Italy; produces red wine from the Petit Rouge grape.

Azal *also* Azal Tinto (P.)

A red grape grown in the Vinho Verde region.

Azal Branco (P.)

A white grape grown in the Vinho Verde and Dão regions.

azienda agraria *also* azienda agricola (I.)

A farm, or vineyard.

B

B.A. (G.)

The abbreviation for *Beerenauslese* (selected berries).

B.A.T.F. (U.S.)

Bureau of Alcohol, Tobacco and Firearms, a division of the U.S. Treasury Department.

B. & G. (F.)   1725

Barton and Guestier, a merchant in Blanquefort, Bordeaux region.

BV (U.S.)   1899

Beaulieu Vineyards, Napa Valley, California.

ba-xiangpin-chiu (China)

Sparkling wine.

Băbească Neagră (R.)

A red wine from Nicoreşti, Focşani district, province of Moldavia, in eastern Romania; made from a local grape of the same name.

Babic (Y.)

A red grape grown in the province of Dalmatia.

Babich Wines (N.Z.)   1916

A winery in Henderson, Aukland district, North Island; produces Cabernet, Pinot Noir, Pinotage, Riesling, Gewürztraminer, Müller-Thurgau and Chenin Blanc wines. 80 acres.

Baccala Winery, William (U.S.)   1981

A winery in Ukiah, Mendocino County, California; produces Chardonnay and Sauvignon Blanc wines from their own and purchased grapes. 140 acres. 30,000 cases.

Baccanale (I.)

A dry or semi-sweet red wine from the Baccanale district, northern Latium region, north of Rome, around Lake Bracciano; made from a blend of Cesanese, Cabernet Franc and Carignano grapes.

Bacchus *also* **Bacchos (Lat.)**

The ancient Roman God of wine.

Bacchus (G.)

A white hybrid grape – a cross of Sylvaner and Riesling crossed with Müller-Thurgau; developed at the Federal Research Institute, Geilweilerhof, Germany. Named after the ancient Roman God of wine.

Bacchus (U.S.)

A red hybrid grape.

Bacharach (G.)

1. A *Bereich*, one of two in the Mittelrhein region. The *Grosslagen* are Schloss Reichenstein and Schloss Stahleck.

2. The principal town in the Mittelrhein region, Bereich Bacharach, Grosslage Schloss Stahleck. The vineyards are Hahn, Insel Heylesern Wert, Kloster Fürstental, Mathias Weingarten, Posten and Wolfshöhle.

Bachelet-Ramonet Père et Fils (F.)

An estate in Chassagne-Montrachet, Côte de Beaune district, Burgundy. 28 acres, including Bâtard-Montrachet – 1.2 acres, Chassagne-Montrachet Premier Cru – 5 acres (Cailleret, La Romanée, Grandes Ruchottes, Grande Montagne, Morgeot), Clos St.-Jean – 2.5 acres and Morgeot (red) – 6 acres.

Bacheroy-Josselin (F.)   1973

A *négociant* in Chablis, Burgundy; controls Domaine Laroche – 55 acres and Domaine La Jouchère – 135 acres.

Bacigalupi (U.S.)   first wine 1979

The label used by Healdsburg Winegrowers for Chardonnay and Pinot Noir wines made at Belvedere Wine Co. in Healdsburg, Sonoma County, California.

back-blending (Aus.)

The process of adding small amounts of grape juice to the wine after fermentation to give it a fresh, fruity taste. *Süss-reserve* is the German equivalent.

Backsberg Estate EWO (S. Af.)   1969

An estate between Stellenbosch and Paarl, in the Paarl district; produces Cabernet, Chardonnay, Chenin Blanc, Sauvignon, Shiraz and Steen wines. 400 acres.

Backus (U.S.)

A vineyard in Oakville, Napa Valley, California; grows Cabernet grapes for Phelps Vineyards winery. 7 acres.

Baco, Francois (1865-1947) **(F.)**

A French teacher and hybridizer from Belus in Landes, in the Armagnac region, who developed 7,000 hybrid grapes, of which Baco 1 and Baco 22A are important, especially in New York.

Baco 1, *or* **Baco Noir**

A red hybrid grape – a cross of *V. riparia* and Folle Blanche grown in N.Y. State and France.

Baco 22A

A white hybrid grape – a cross of Folle Blanche and Noah used in making Armagnac; also called Baco Blanc.

Baco Noir (U.S.)

1. A red hybrid grape; also known as Baco 1.

2. A red wine from New York State; made from the Baco 1 grape.

Badajoz (Sp.)

A town and district in southwestern Spain; produces red wine from Almendralejo, Garnacho and Morisca grapes and white wine from Cayetana, Pedro Ximénez, Palomino, Lairén, Moscatel and Macabeo grapes.

Badascony (H.)

1. A district in the Transdanubia region, on the northwestern shore of Lake Balaton; produces white wines mostly from Szurkebarat and Kéknyelü grapes, and some from Furmint, Sárgamuskotály and Wälschriesling grapes. Officially rated White Wine of Outstanding Quality. 6,000 acres.

2. The mountain for which the Badascony district is named.

Badascony Kéknyelü (H.)

The best-known white wine of Badascony; made from the Kéknyelü grape.

Baden (G.)

A region in southwestern Germany; produces white wine, made mostly from the Müller-Thurgau grape and some red wine made from the Spätburgunder grape. The *Bereiche* are Badische Bergstrasse/Kraichgau, Badisches Frankenland, Bodensee, Markgräflerland, Kaiserstuhl-Tunibert, Breisgau and Ortenau. 35,000 acres.

Baden (A.)

A village south of Vienna, in the Lower Austria region; produces white wine made from Rotgipfler and Zierfändler grapes; also produces some red wine.

Badia a Coltibuono (I.)

An estate in Gaiole, Tuscany region; produces Chianti Classico, Vin Santo and other wines. 100 acres.

Badische Bergstrasse/Kraichgau (G.)

A *Bereich*, one of seven in the Baden region. The *Grosslagen* are Hohenberg, Mannaberg, Stiftsberg and Rittersberg. 4,300 acres.

Badisches Frankenland (G.)

A *Bereich*, one of seven in the Baden region. The *Grosslage* is Tauberklinge. 1,300 acres.

Badisches Weingut, Markgräflich (G.)

An estate in Durbach, Baden region; owns vineyards in Durbach, including the *monopole* Schloss Staufenberg. 70 acres.

Badoux, Henri (Sw.)   1908

An estate in Aigle, Vaud region; produces Aigle les Murailles, Pinot Noir and Pinot Gris wines. 125 acres.

Badstube (G.)

A *Grosslage*, one of ten in Bereich Bernkastel (Mittel-Mosel), in the Mosel-Saar-Ruwer region. The vineyards are Bratenhöfchen, Doctor, Graben, Lay and Matheisbildchen, all in the village of Bernkastel.

Baga (P.)

A red grape grown in the Bairrada region. It produces 90% of the wines in that area.

bagaço (P.)

Marc; pomace; the residue of skins, pips, and stalks after the pressing of the grapes.

Bagrina (Y.)

A white grape grown in Serbia.

Bahans-Haut-Brion (F.)

The second wine of Château Haut-Brion.

Bahèzre de Lanlay, Cuvée de (F.)

A white wine from the Hospices de Beaune, Côte de Beaune district, Burgundy. The *cuvée* is composed of the following vineyards: Meursault-Charmes Les Charmes Dessus – 1.2 acres, Meursault-Charmes Les Charmes Dessous – 1 acre. 450 cases.

Baileys (Aus.)   1870

A winery in Glenrowan, northeastern Victoria; known for sweet Muscat and Tokay wines and unusual rich reds made from Cabernet and Shiraz grapes. 100 acres.

Bailly, Père et Fils (F.)

An estate in Les Loges, Pouilly-Fumé district, Upper Loire region, Loire Valley. 30 acres.

Bailly-Reverdy et Fils, Bernard (F.)

An estate in Bué, Sancerre, Upper Loire region. 25 acres, including Clos du Chêne Marchard – 3 acres.

Bailly Vineyard, Alexis (U.S.)   1977

A winery in Hastings, Minnesota, near Minneapolis; grows mostly hybrid grapes. 10 acres.

Bairrada (P.)   1979

A recently demarcated region south of Oporto; produces red, some white and sparkling wines. 46,500 acres.

Baixo Corgo (P.)

One of 3 districts of the demarcated region of Oporto's vineyards, in the Upper Douro region. The other two districts are Cima Corgo and Douro Superior.

Baja California (Mex.)

An important region of northwestern Mexico.

Balac, Château (F.)

An estate in St.-Laurent, Haut-Médoc district, Bordeaux; classified in 1978 as a *Cru Bourgeois*. 27 acres. 5,000 cases.

Baladí (Sp.)

A white grape grown in the Montilla district, used in making sherry-like wines.

Balatonfüred-Csopak (H.)

A district in the Transdanubia region, on the northeastern shore of Lake Balaton, in western Hungary; produces white wine from Wälschriesling, Sylvaner, Furmint and other grapes. Officially rated White Wine of Outstanding Quality. 5,000 acres.

Balatonmellik (H.)

A district in the Transdanubia region on the northern shore of Lake Balaton, in western Hungary; produces white wine from Wälschriesling, Sylvaner, Ezerjó and Mézesfehér grapes. Officially rated White Wine of Excellent Quality. 7,000 acres.

Balbach Erbern, Bürgermeister Anton (G.)

An estate in Nierstein, Rheinhessen region. 45 acres, with vineyards in Nierstein, including Hipping, Pettenthal, Ölberg, Bildstock and others.

Balbaina (Sp.)

One of the principal districts in the Sherry region, west of Jerez.

Baldinelli Vineyards (U.S.)　　　　1972

A small winery in Plymouth, Shenandoah Valley, Amador County, California; produces Cabernet and Zinfandel wines. 6,000 cases. 70 acres.

Baleau, Château (F.)

An estate in St.-Émilion, Bordeaux; in 1969 was added to the 1955 classification as a *Grand Cru Classé*. 8,000 cases. 40 acres.

Balestard-La-Tonnelle, Château (F.)

An estate in St.-Émilion, Bordeaux; classified in 1955 as a *Grand Cru Classé*. 4,000 cases. 20 acres.

Balgownie (Aus.)　　　　1969

A winery near Bendigo, central Victoria; produces primarily Cabernet, Shiraz, Pinot Noir and Chardonnay wines. 5,000 cases. 30 acres.

Balland et Fils, Bernard (F.)

An estate in Bué, Sancerre district, Upper Loire region; produces red, rosé and white wines. 20 acres.

Ballard Canyon Winery (U.S.)　　　　1978

A winery in Solvang, Santa Ynez Valley, Santa Barbara County, California; produces Cabernet, Chardonnay and Johannisberg Riesling wines. 5,000 cases. 40 acres.

Balling

A hydrometer scaled to measure the sugar content of grape juice, indicating the percentage of sugar by weight. Similar to Brix.

Ballot-Millot (F.)

An estate in Meursault, Côte de Beaune district, Burgundy. 17 acres, including Meursault Les Genevrières 1.2 acres, Les Charmes – 1.2 acres, Beaune Les Épenottes – 2.5 acres, Volnay Les Santenots – 1.2 acres and Puligny-Montrachet Premier Cru – .8 acre.

balseiro (P.)

A large wooden vat that rests on legs.

balthazar *also* balthasar (F.)

A large bottle for Champagne, holding the equivalent of 16 normal bottles, or about 13 liters, or 432 ounces.

Balverne Winery and Vineyards (U.S.)　　　　1980, planted 1973

A winery in Windsor, Chalkhill district, Sonoma County, California; produces Cabernet, Zinfandel, Scheurebe, Sauvignon Blanc, Gewürztraminer, Johannisberg Riesling and Chardonnay wines. 22,000 cases. 250 acres.

Banat (Y.)

A district in the province of Vojvodina, Serbia; produces red and white varietal wines.

Banat (R.)

A region in western Romania. It consists of Tomnatec, Termia Mare (the Plain) and the hill vineyards of Buziaş, Recaş, Miniş, Ghiroc, Baratke, Pîncota and Şiria; produces red wines: Cabernet and Kadarka and white wines: Creaţa, Majărcă and Steinschiller.

Banat Riesling (H.)

The Italian Riesling grape, not the true Johannisberg Riesling.

Bandiera (U.S.)　　　　1937, 1975

A winery in Cloverdale, northern Sonoma County, California, formerly the California

Wine Company; produces Cabernet, Pinot Noir, Zinfandel, Chardonnay, Johannisberg Riesling and Sauvignon Blanc wines.

Bandol AOC (F.)

1. A village and district west of Toulon, in the southwestern Provence region, which produces:

2. Red, white and rosé wines, the red and rosé made from the Mourvèdre, Grenache and Cinsault grapes, and the white from Clairette, Ugni Blanc, Bourboulenc and Sauvignon grapes.

Banfi, Villa (I.)   1977

A large winery in Montalcino, Tuscany region; produces Asti Spumante, Brunello, Cabernet Sauvignon, Chianti, Chardonnay and other wines; the largest exporter of Italian wines to the U.S. 750 acres.

Banholzer Wine Cellars (U.S.)   1974

A vineyard and winery in Hesston, near Lake Michigan, in the northwestern corner of Indiana, the largest in the state; produces wines from hybrid grapes as well as Cabernet, Pinot Noir, Chardonnay and Gewürztraminer wines; also unusual blends of hybrid and *vinifera* grapes. 70 acres.

Banyuls AOC (F.)

1. A town and district in the Côtes du Roussillon district, Roussillon region, in southern France; produces VDN; best known wine is Banyuls Grand Cru, made from 75% Grenache grapes.

2. A sweet red wine (VDN) from the Côtes du Roussillon district, in southwestern France; made from Grenache, Muscat, Malvoisie and Maccabéo grapes.

Barale, Fratelli (I.)   1870

A winery in Barolo, Piedmont region; produces Barolo, Barbera and Dolcetto wines.

Barancourt (F.)   1969

A Champagne producer in Bouzy, shared by 3 growers using only 10% purchased grapes; also makes Bouzy Rouge (Coteaux Champenois). 600,000 bottles. 115 acres.

Barande, la (F.)

A vineyard in Givry, Côte Chalonnaise district, Burgundy.

Barbacarlo DOC (I.)

A red wine from Broni, Oltrepò Pavese district, in the Lombardy region; made from a blend of Barbera, Croatina, Uva Rara, and Ughetta grapes.

Barbadillo S.A., Antonio (Sp.)   1821

A large Sherry producer in Sanlúcar de Barrameda; produces mostly Manzanilla but also many other types as well, including some table wines. 2,000 acres.

Barbaresco DOCG (I.)

1. A town and district in the Piedmont region; includes the towns of Barbaresco, Neive and Treiso, which produces:

2. A red wine made from the Nebbiolo grape.

Barbarossa (I.)

A local red grape grown in the Emilia-Romagna and Liguria regions.

Barbarossa di Bertinoro (I.)

A red wine from Bertinoro, south of Ravenna, in the eastern Emilia-Romagna region; made from the Barbarossa grape.

Barbaroux (F.)

A red grape grown in Cassis, in the Provence region.

Barbe, Château de (F.)

An estate in Villeneuve, Côtes de Bourg district, Bordeaux. 130 acres.

Barbeito (P.)

A producer of Madeira wines.

Barbera (I.)

An important red grape grown in Italy, especially in the Piedmont region (Asti, Monferrato and Alba). It is also grown in California.

Barbera d'Alba DOC (I.)

A red wine from Alba, near Barolo and Barbaresco, in the south central Piedmont region; made from the Barbera grape.

Barbera d'Asti DOC (I.)

A red wine from Asti, in the central Piedmont region; made from the Barbera grape.

Barbera dei Colli Tortonesi DOC (I.)

A red wine from Tortona, east of Alessandria, in the southeastern Piedmont region; made from either 100% Barbera grapes or blended with up to 15% Freisa, Bonarda Piedmontese or Dolcetto grapes.

Barbera di Linero (I.)

A red wine from the Colli di Luni district, near La Spezia, in the eastern Liguria region; made from the Barbera grape.

Barbera del Monferrato DOC (I.)

A red wine from the Asti district, in the central Piedmont region; made from the Barbera grape blended with 10-15% Freisa, Grignolino or Dolcetto grapes.

Barberani (I.)

An estate in Orvieto, Umbria region; produces Lago di Corbara, Orvieto Classico and Rosato wines. 30,000 cases. 75 acres.

Barbi, Fattoria dei (I.)

An estate in Montalcino, Tuscany region; produces Brunello, Brusco, Moscatello and Vin Santo wines. 12,000 cases. 75 acres.

Barbier S.A., René (Sp.)

A winery in San Sadurní de Noya, Barcelona, Catalonia region; produces still and sparkling wines.

Barboursville Vineyard (U.S.)   1976

A winery in Barboursville, Virginia; produces Cabernet, Merlot, Chardonnay and Riesling wines. 250 acres.

Barca Velha (P.)

Portuguese for "Old Boat," a red wine from Meão, northern Douro Valley, in northern Portugal; made from a blend of Port grapes: Tinta Roriz (60%), Amarela (15%), Touriga Francesca (20%) and other grapes. The name may refer to the old sailboats that used to carry the wine down the Douro River.

Barcelo (P.)

A white grape grown in the Dão and Douro regions.

Barceló S.A., Hijos de Antonio (Sp.) 1876

A *bodega* in Málaga; produces a wide range of Málaga wines.

Bardenheier's Wine Cellars (U.S.)   1873
first planting 1970

A large winery in St. Louis, Missouri, which blends and bottles California wines as well as their own wines from hybrid grapes. It is the largest winery in the state. 70 acres.

bardo (P.)

A system of vine-training on wires stretched between wood or granite pillars.

Bardolino DOC (I.)

1. A village and district in the Veneto region, northwest of Verona, which produces:

2. Red and rosé wines made from a blend of Corvina, Rondinella, Molinara and Negrara grapes.

Bärenblut (U.S.)

German for "Bear's Blood," a red wine from Beringer Vineyards, Napa Valley, California; made from a blend of Grignolino and Pinot Noir grapes.

Barengo Winery (U.S.)   1934

A large winery in Acampo, north of Lodi, San Juaquin Valley, central California, once known as the Acampo Winery owned by C. Mondavi; produces a complete line of wines. 600,000 cases. 650 acres.

Baret, Château (F.)

An unclassified estate in Villenave-d'Or-non, Graves district, Bordeaux. 4,500 cases of red and white wine. 60 acres.

Bargetto Winery (U.S.)   1933

A winery in Soquel, Sanata Cruz County, California. Produces Cabernet, Zinfandel, Chardonnay, Pinot Blanc, Johannisberg Riesling, Moscato and dessert wines from purchased grapes. 40,000 cases. 2nd label is Santa Cruz Cellars.

barile (I.)

A barrel.

Barjac, Guy de (F.)

An estate in Cornas, northern Rhône region. 5 acres.

Barjumeau-Chauvin, Château (F.)

An unclassified estate in Sauternes, Sauternes district, Bordeaux. 900 cases. 8 acres.

Barker, Château (Aus.)   1973

A winery in Mount Barker, Western Australia; produces Cabernet, Shiraz, Pinot Noir, Rhine Riesling and other wines. 5,000 cases. 40 acres.

Barnes (C.)   1873

A winery in St. Catherines, near Niagara Falls, Ontario, the oldest winery in Canada; produces wines made mostly from *labrusca* grapes.

Barolo DOCG (I.)

1. A village and district in the southern Piedmont region; the district also includes the villages of Roddi, Verduno, Grinzane, Diano d'Alba, La Morra, Castiglione, Falletto, Serralunga d'Alba and Monforte d'Alba. 25,000 acres. It produces:

2. A red wine made from the Nebbiolo grape.

Baronnie, La (F.)

See **Bergerie, La.**

Baroque (F.)

A white grape grown in the Southwest region.

Barossa Valley (Aus.)

An important district north of Adelaide, in South Australia.

Barr (F.)

A village in the northern Bas-Rhin district, Alsace region.

Barre, Clos de la *also* La Barre (F.)

A *Premier Cru* vineyard in Volnay, Côte de Beaune district, Burgundy. 3 acres.

Barre, Clos de la (F.)

An unclassified vineyard in Meursault, Côte de Beaune district, Burgundy; a *monopole* of Comtes Lafon. 5 acres.

barrel

A container for aging, storing, transporting, and sometimes fermenting wine, usually made of oak. A U.S. barrel holds 31.5 gallons; a British barrel holds 36 imperial gallons.

barrica (Sp.)

Spanish for the French *barrique*, or barrel.

barrique (F.)

A French barrel or hogshead, especially the *barrique Bordelaise*, or Bordeaux hogshead; holds 225 liters, or 288 bottles, or 24 cases. In Bordeaux 4 *barriques* equals 1 *tonneau*.

barriquot (F.)

An old French word for a keg, or small barrel.

Barsac AOC (F.)

1. A town and district within the Sauternes district, Bordeaux region, near Sauternes; produces very sweet white wines made from Sémillon and Sauvignon Blanc grapes. Classified in 1855 along with Sauternes.

2. The sweet, white wine made in Barsac, in the Sauternes district, which by AOC law may be labeled either Barsac or Sauternes.

Bársonyos-Császár (H.)

A white wine district northwest of Mór, in the Transdanubia region, northwestern Hungary; produces white wines like Mór, made from the Ezerjó grape.

Bart, André (F.)

An estate in Marsannay-La-Côte, Côte de Nuits district, Burgundy. 25 acres, including Bonnes Mares – 1 acre, Chambertin-Clos de Bèze – 1 acre, and vineyards in Fixin and Santenay.

Barton & Guestier *also* B & G (F.)   1725

A merchant in Blanquefort, Bordeaux; blends and ships wine from several regions.

Bas-Beaujolais (F.)

The southern half of the Beaujolais region. It is considered to be of lower quality than the northern section. The soil is more chalky, with less granite.

Bas des Duresses, Les (F.)

A *Premier Cru* vineyard in Auxey-Duresses, Côte de Beaune district, Burgundy. 6 acres.

Bas-Médoc (F.)

The northernmost section of the Médoc district of Bordeaux. The terrain is flatter, with less gravel in the soil, resulting in lower quality wines than the Haut-Médoc further south. There are no classified growths in this part of the Médoc.

Bas-Rhin (F.)

The northern half of the Alsace region, generally held to be of somewhat lower quality than the Haut-Rhin in the south.

Bas des Teurons, Le (F.)

A *Premier Cru* vineyard in Beaune, Côte de Beaune district, Burgundy. 18 acres.

Basedow's (Aus.)   1895

A small winery in the Barossa Valley, north of Adelaide, in South Australia; produces red wines, including Shiraz, and Port wines. 3,000 cases.

Basilicata (I.)

A lesser-known region of southern Italy, between Apulia, Campania and Calabria; produces only one DOC wine: Aglianico del Vulture.

Bassenden Estate (Aus.)   1951

A small winery in Bassenden, near Perth, Swan Valley, in Western Australia; produces red wines made from the Grenache grape. 3,000 cases. 5 acres.

Basserman-Jordan, Weingut Dr. Von (G.)

An estate in Deidesheim, Rheinpfalz region; owns vineyards in Deidesheim, Forst, Ruppertsberg, Dürkheim and Ungstein. 115 acres.

Basses Mourettes (F.)

A *Premier Cru* vineyard in Ladoix-Serrigny, Côte de Beaune district, Burgundy. The wine may also be sold as Aloxe-Corton. 2.5 acres.

Basses-Vergelesses, Les (F.)

A *Premier Cru* vineyard partly in Pernand-Vergelesses (45 acres) and partly in Savigny-lès-Beaune (4.5 acres), Côte de Beaune district, Burgundy; may also be sold as Aloxe-Corton.

Bassot, Thomas (F.)   1850

A merchant in Gevrey-Chambertin, Côte de Nuits district, Burgundy.

bastard (E.)

A sweet wine, white or tawny, sold in England in the Elizabethan period; mentioned by Shakespeare.

Bastardo (P.)

An important red grape used in making Port, one of 16 "first quality grapes"; also grown in the Bairrado region, and is possibly the same grape as the Trousseau of France.

Bastide-Neuve, Domaine de la (F.)

An estate in Le Cannet-des-Maures, northeast of Toulon, in the Côtes de Provence district, Provence region.

Bataillière *also* **Bataillère (F.)**

A *Premier Cru* vineyard in Savigny-lès-Beaune, Burgundy; also known as Les Vergelesses. 42 acres.

Batailley, Château (F.)

An estate in Pauillac, Haut-Médoc district, in the Bordeaux region; classified in 1855 as a *Cinquième Cru;* made from equal amounts of Cabernet Sauvignon, Cabernet Franc and Merlot grapes. 130 acres.

Bâtard-Montrachet AOC (F.)

A *Grand Cru* vineyard, partly in Puligny-Montrachet (15 acres) and partly in Chassagne-Montrachet (14.5 acres), Côte de Beaune district, Burgundy; produces white wines made from Chardonnay grapes. There are about 35 owners. 3,800 cases. 29.5 acres.

Battistina (I.)

A winery in Novi Ligure, Piedmont region; produces Cortese di Gavi wines. 50 acres.

Baudes, Les (F.)

A *Premier Cru* vineyard in Chambolle-Musigny, Côte de Nuits district, Burgundy. 9 acres.

Baudoin, Clos (F.)

A vineyard in Vouvray, Touraine region, Loire Valley; owned by Prince Poniatowski. 44 acres.

Baudot, Cuvée (F.)

A white wine from the Hospices de Beaune, Côte de Beaune district, Burgundy. The *cuvée* is composed of the following vineyards: Meursault Les Genevrières Dessus – 1.5 acres, and Les Genevrières Dessous – 1.5 acres. 450 cases.

Baudrand et Fils (F.)

An estate in Chassagne-Montrachet, Côte de Beaune, Burgundy; owns Chassagne-Montrachet Clos St.-Marc Monopole, part of Clos St.-Jean, Mercurey Clos Marcilly Monopole and vineyards in Puligny-Montrachet, Santenay and Savigny-lès-Beaune.

Baulet, Clos (F.)

A *Premier Cru* vineyard in Morey-St.-Denis, Côte de Nuits district, Burgundy. 8 acres.

Baumard, Domaine des (F.)

An old estate in Logis de la Giraudière, Anjou region, Loire Valley; produces Quarts de Chaume (15 acres), Coteaux du Layon, Savennières (28 acres) and other wines. 65 acres.

Baumé (F.)

A hydrometer scaled to measure the density of musts and sweet wines; 1 degree *Baumé* is approximately equal to 1.8 degrees Brix.

Bayerische Bodensee (G.)

A very small *Bereich,* one of 4 in the Württemberg region, Grosslage Lindauer Seegarten, containing only one village, Nonnenhorn, with 2 vineyards: Seehalde and Sonnenbüchel.

Bayle, Château (F.)

An estate in Sauternes, Sauternes district, Bordeaux; classified in 1855 as a *Premier Cru.* The name was later changed to Château Guiraud.

Bazenet, Fernand (F.)

An estate in Saint-Romain, Côte de Beaune, Burgundy; owns vineyards in Saint-Romain (red and white). 11 acres.

Béarn AOC (F.)

1. An old province in southwestern France, known for Jurançon, a sweet white wine.

2. A district east of Bayonne, in southwestern France, producing red, rosé and white wines.

3. The wines from the Béarn district, the red and rosé made from the Tannet, Fer, Pinenc, Courbu Noir, Cabernet Franc and Sauvignon and Manseng Noir grapes, and the white made from Petit Manseng, Gros Manseng, Courbu, Lauzet, Baroque, Sauvignon and Sémillon grapes.

Beatty Ranch (U.S.)

A vineyard in Angwin, Napa Valley, California; produces Cabernet and Zinfandel grapes for Cakebread Cellars winery. 30 acres.

Beau-Site, Château (F.)

An estate in St.-Estèphe, Haut-Médoc district, Bordeaux; classified in 1978 as a *Cru Grand Bourgeois Exceptionnel*. 12,000 cases. 62 acres.

Beau Val Wines (U.S.)   1979

A small winery in Plymouth, Amador County, California; produces Zinfandel, Petite Sirah, Barbera, Sauvignon Blanc and other wines. 3,000 cases. 7.5 acres.

Beaucastel, Domaine de (F.)   1832

An estate in the Châteauneuf-du-Pape district, Rhône region; produces red and white wine. 200 acres.

Beaujeu, Clos (F.)

A winery in Chavignol, Sancerre district, Upper Loire region, Loire Valley.

Beaujolais AOC (F.)

A district in southern Burgundy, where red wine from the Gamay grape is produced as well as a small amount of white wine from the Chardonnay or Pinot Blanc grape. It was established in the 11th century and was called Bellijocum. In 1260 it was granted a charter by the Sire of Beaujeu. Most Beaujolais wine is fruity and is drunk young. The AOC classifications are: Beaujolais – 9% alcohol, at least 85% Gamay; Beaujolais Supérieur – 10% alcohol; and Beaujolais-Villages. The 9 *Crus* each have their own AOC: Brouilly, Chénas, Chiroubles, Côte de Brouilly, Fleurie, Juliénas, Morgon, Moulin-à-Vent and St.-Amour.

43,000 acres. 18.5 million gallons per year. 45 miles long, up to 10 miles wide.

Beaujolais Supérieur AOC (F.)

Beaujolais wine with an alcoholic content of at least 10%.

Beaujolais-Villages AOC (F.)

The AOC designation for wine from any or several of 40 *communes* in the northern part of the Beaujolais district, and usually of higher quality than plain Beaujolais or Beaujolais Supérieur.

Beaulieu, Château de (F.)

A large estate in Rognes, Coteaux d'Aix-en-Provence district, Provence. 700 acres.

Beaulieu Vineyards (U.S.)   1899

A famous old winery in Rutherford, Napa Valley, California; renowned for Georges de Latour Private Reserve Cabernet. Other vineyards are at Oakville and in the Carneros district. The famous wine maker was André Tchelistcheff from 1938-1973. Wines include Cabernet, Pinot Noir, Gamay Beaujolais, Sauvignon Blanc, Chardonnay, Johannisberg Riesling, Muscat Blanc, Muscat de Frontignan, and Grenache Rosé. Vintage sparkling wine has been made since 1955. 250,000 cases. 1,000 acres.

Beaumes (F.)

A vineyard section of Hermitage, northern Rhône region; grows white grapes.

Beaumes-de-Venise AOC *and* VDN (F.)

A town near Gigondas, in the Côtes du Rhône-Villages district, southern Rhône region; produces sweet white wine (VDN) made from the Muscat de Frontignan grape and dry red wine (AOC) from Grenache, Cinsault, Mourvèdre and Carignan grapes.

Beaumont, Château (F.)

An estate in Cussac, Haut-Médoc district, Bordeaux; classified in 1978 as a *Cru Grand Bourgeois*. 15,000 cases. 140 acres.

Beaumonts, Les also **Beaux-Monts (F.)**

A *Premier Cru* vineyard in Vosne-Romanée, Côte de Nuits district, Burgundy. 6 acres.

Beaune AOC (F.)

1. An important city in Burgundy, in the Côte de Beaune district. Many wine firms originate here as well as the Hospices de Beaune. It is the center of the Burgundian wine trade. There are 36 *Premier Cru* vineyards, but no *Grand Cru* vineyards. 120,000 cases of red, 5,000 cases of white. 1,300 acres.

2. The AOC red and white wine from Beaune.

Beaunois (F.)

The local name in Chablis for the Chardonnay grape.

Beauregard (F.)

A *Premier Cru* vineyard in Santenay, Côte de Beaune district, Burgundy. 82 acres.

Beauregard, Château (F.)

An estate in Pomerol, Bordeaux. 4500 cases. 32 acres.

Beauregard, Château de (F.)

An estate in Bizanet, Corbières district, Languedoc region. 28,000 cases. 105 acres.

Beaurenard, Domaine de (F.)

An estate in Châteauneuf-du-Pape, southern Rhône region; also owns La Ferme Pisan (Côtes du Rhône); produces red wine made from 70% Grenache, 10% Syrah, 10% Mourvèdre and 10% Cinsault grapes. 70 acres.

Beaurepaire (F.)

A *Premier Cru* vineyard in Santenay, Côte de Beaune district, Burgundy. 42 acres.

Beauroy (F.)

A *Premier Cru* vineyard in the *communes* of Poinchy and Beines, Chablis district, Burgundy; it also usually includes the Troêmes vineyard as part of Beauroy.

Beauséjour-Bécot, Château (F.)

An estate in in St.-Émilion, Bordeaux; classified in 1955 as a *Premier Grand Cru*. Until 1869 the two Beauséjour estates were one property (Beauséjour-Fagouet). 70% Merlot, the rest is Cabernet Franc and some Cabernet Sauvignon. 8,000 cases. 19 acres.

Beauséjour-Duffau-Lagarrosse, Château (F.)

An estate in St.-Émilion, Bordeaux; classified in 1955 as a *Premier Grand Cru*. 4,000 cases. 12 acres.

Beaux-Bruns, Aux (F.)

A *Premier Cru* vineyard in Chambolle-Musigny, Côte de Nuits district, Burgundy. 6 acres.

Beaux-Monts, Les also **Beaumonts (F.)**

A *Premier Cru* vineyard in Vosne-Romanée, Côte de Nuits district, Burgundy. 13 acres.

Bécade, Château La (F.)

An estate in Listrac, Haut-Médoc district, Bordeaux; classified in 1978 as a *Cru Bourgeois*. 14,000 cases. 70 acres.

Bechtheim (G.)

A village in the Rheinhessen region, Bereich Wonnegau, Grosslagen Gotteshilfe and Pilgerpfad. The vineyards are: Geyersberg, Rosengarten and Stein in Grosslage Gotteshilfe; Hasensprung and Heiligkreutz in Grosslage Pilgerpfad.

Becker, J. (F.)

An estate and merchant in Zellenberg, Haut-Rhin district, Alsace region. 25 acres.

Beckstein (G.)

A village in the Baden region, Bereich Badisches Frankenland, Grosslage Tauberklinge. The vineyards are Kirchberg and Nonnenberg.

Beerenauslese (G., A.)

A selection of individual grapes from the selected bunches, producing a superior wine, richer and sweeter than *Auslese* and *Spätlese* wines.

Beerenlay (G.)

A *Grosslage*, one of ten, in Bereich Bernkastel, Mosel-Saar-Ruwer region. Only part of Leiser is in this *Grosslage*. The vineyards are: Niederberg-Helden, Rosenlay and Sussenberg. The remaining vineyard of Leiser is Schlossberg, in Grosslage Kurfürstlay.

beeswing

A light, thin crust, resembling the wing of a bee; it is found in some old Port bottles.

Beiras (P.)

A region in northeastern Portugal; produces red wines and some whites.

Bel-Air (F.)

A *Premier Cru* vineyard in Gevrey-Chambertin, Côte de Nuits district, Burgundy. 8 acres.

Bel Air, Château (F.)

An estate in Lalande de Pomerol, Bordeaux. 4,000 cases. 25 acres.

Bel-Air, Château (F.)

An estate in St.-Estèphe, Haut-Médoc district, Bordeaux; classified in 1932 as a *Cru Bourgeois*. 1,400 cases. 10 acres.

Bel-Air Lagrave, Château (F.)

An estate in Moulis, Haut-Médoc district, Bordeaux; classified in 1932 as a *Cru Bourgeois*. 4,500 cases. 30 acres.

Bel-Air-Marquis d'Aligre, Château (F.)

An estate in Soussans-Margaux, Haut-Médoc district, Bordeaux; classified in 1932 as a *Cru Bourgeois Exceptionnel*, but was not classified in 1978. 4,000 cases. 40 acres.

Bel Arbres (U.S.)

The second wine of Fetzer Vineyards, Mendocino County, California.

Bel-Orme-Tronquoy-de-Lalande, Château (F.)

An estate in St.-Seurin-de-Cadourne, Haut-Médoc district, Bordeaux; classified in 1978 as a *Cru Grand Bourgeois*. 12,000 cases. 62 acres.

Belair, Château *also* Bel-Air (F.)

An estate in St.-Émilion, Bordeaux, next to Château Ausone; classified in 1955 as a *Premier Grand Cru*. The wine is composed of 60-65% Merlot, the remainder Cabernet Franc. 4,000 cases. 30 acres.

Beldi (Tun.)

A native white grape of Tunisia.

Belgrave, Château (F.)

An estate in St.-Laurent, Haut-Médoc district, Bordeaux; classified in 1855 as a *Cinquième Cru*. 22,000 cases. 100 acres.

Beli Pinot *also* Beli Burgundec (Y.)

The Yugoslavian name for the Pinot Blanc grape and the wine made from that grape.

Belin, Maison Jules (F.)   1817

An estate in Prémeaux, Côte de Nuits district, Burgundy. 32 acres, including Nuits-St.-Georges Clos des Forêts St.-Georges Monopole – 17.5 acres, Clos de l'Arlot (red and white) Monopole – 10 acres and Côte de Nuits-Villages Clos du Chapeau Monopole – 4 acres.

Bell'Agio (I.)

A semi-sweet, white wine from northwestern Sicily; made from the Moscato grape; produced by Rallo & Figlio.

Bell Canyon Cellars (U.S.)

The second wine of Burgess Cellars, St. Helena, Napa Valley, California.

Bella Napoli Winery (U.S.)   1934

A winery in Manteen, San Joaquin Valley, central California; produces Chenin Blanc, Chardonnay, Carignan and Grenache wines. 500 acres.

Bella Oaks Vineyard (U.S.)

A vineyard in Oakville, Napa Valley, California; produces Cabernet Sauvignon and White Riesling grapes for wines made by Heitz Cellars. 40 acres.

Belland, Domaine Joseph (F.)

An estate in Santenay, Côte de Beaune district, Burgundy. 33 acres, including Les Gravières – 4 acres, La Comme – 2.5 acres, Beauregard – 7.5 acres and Chassagne-Montrachet Clos Pitois Monopole (red and white) – 7.5 acres.

Bellandais (F.)

A red hybrid grape grown in the Rhône region; also called Siebel 14596.

Belle Rive, Château (F.)

An estate in Chaume, Rochefort-sur-Loire, Anjou region, Loire Valley; produces Quarts de Chaume wine. 40 acres.

Belle Terre Vineyards (U.S.)

A vineyard in Healdsburg, Alexander Valley, Sonoma County, California; produces Cabernet, Chardonnay, Gewürztraminer and Riesling grapes for Château St-Jean winery. 150 acres.

Bellerive, Château (F.)

An estate in Valeyrac, Médoc district, Bordeaux; classified in 1978 as a *Cru Bourgeois.* 4,500 cases. 25 acres.

Bellerose, Château (F.)

An estate in Pauillac, Haut-Médoc district, Bordeaux; classified in 1978 as a *Cru Bourgeois.*

Bellerose Vineyard (U.S.)   1979

A winery in Healdsburg, Dry Creek Valley, Sonoma County, California; produces Cabernet, blended with Cabernet Franc, Merlot, Malbec and Petit Verdot grapes. 10,000 cases. 50 acres.

Bellet AOC (F.)

A small district north of Nice, in the eastern Provence region; produces red and rosé wines from a blend of Grenache, Cinsault, Braquet and Folle Noire grapes, and white wines from a blend of Rolle, Roussanne, Clairette, Bourboulenc and Chardonnay grapes. 100 acres.

Bellet, Château de (F.)

An estate in St.-Romain de Bellet, Bellet district, in the eastern Provence region.

Bellevue, Château (F.)

An estate in St.-Émilion, Bordeaux; classified in 1955 as a *Grand Cru Classé.* 3,000 cases. 16 acres.

Bellevue, Château de (F.)

An estate in Villié-Morgon, Beaujolais district, Burgundy. 30 acres of Morgon AOC.

Bellone (I.)

A white grape grown in the Latium region.

Belvedere Wine Company (U.S.)

A winery in Healdsburg, Sonoma County, California; produces single-vineyard varietal wines from well-known vineyards: Bacigalupi Chardonnay, Robert Young Cabernet, Winery Lake Pinot Noir. 6,000 cases.

Ben Ean (Aus.)

A well-known vineyard in the Lower Hunter Valley district, New South Wales, owned by Lindeman's Winery.

bench grafting

A method of grafting in which the scion (top of the vine) and the root stock are joined in a nursery and placed in soil after the graft has healed.

Beni Carló (Sp.)

Another name for the Mourvèdre grape.

Benicarló (Sp.)

1. A town north of Valencia, in the Castellón de la Plana district, the Levante region.

2. The red wine from Benicarló which, because of its strength, was used in the 19th century to bolster Bordeaux wines.

Benmarl Vineyard (U.S.)   1971

A small winery in Marlboro, Hudson River Valley region, New York; produces Chardonnay, Seyval Blanc, Baco Noir, other hybrid wines and blends. 70 acres.

Benoit, Château (U.S.)   1980

A winery near Dundee, Willamette Valley, northwestern Oregon; produces Pinot Noir, Chardonnay and Johannisberg Riesling wines. 5,000 cases. 40 acres.

Bensheim (G.)

A village in the Hessische Bergstrasse region, Bereich Starkenberg, Grosslage Wolfsmagen. The vineyards are: Hemsberg, Kalkgasse, Kirchberg, Paulus and Streichling.

bentonite

A clay (hydrated silicate of aluminum) used as a clarifying or fining agent in white wine. It swells in liquid and forms a paste, after which it is stirred into the wine, usually 100 grams per hectoliter, diluted first into 2 liters or more of water. It prevents protein precipitation and discoloration from copper; its use is allowed by law.

Béquignol (F.)

A minor red grape grown in the Blayais district, Bordeaux.

Berberana, S.A. Bodegas (Sp.)   1877

A large winery in Cenicero, Rioja Alta region; produces wines from their own and purchased grapes, mostly from the Tempranillo grape. 2 million cases. 1,200 acres.

Bereich (G.)

A district, or sub-region, of which there are officially 31; a Bereich wine is from a well-defined area around a particular town producing a wine blended from the lesser quality vineyards of that town; hence, a somewhat inferior wine, e.g., Bereich Bernkastel.

Bergat, Château (F.)

An estate in St.-Émilion, Bordeaux; classified in 1955 as a Grand Cru Classé. 2,000 cases. 10 acres.

Bergerac AOC (F.)

A city and district in the Southwest region, east of Bordeaux; produces red wines from Cabernet Sauvignon, Cabernet Franc, Merlot, Malbec and Fer grapes; and white wines from Sémillon, Sauvignon, Muscadelle, Ondenc and Chenin Blanc grapes. Monbazillac, a sweet white wine, is the most well-known wine from the district.

Bergerie, La (F.)   1904

A merchant (now called La Baronnie) in Pauillac, Bordeaux region.

Bergkelder (S. Af.)

A large winery in the Stellenbosch district; makes and distributes many fine Estate (EWO) wines.

Bergstrasse/Kraichgau (G.)

A Bereich, one of seven, in the Baden region. The Grosslagen are Hohenberg, Mannaberg, Rittersberg and Stiftsberg.

Bergweiler-Prüm Erben, Weingut Zach. (G.)

An estate in Bernkastel-Kues, Mosel-Saar-Ruwer region. 24 acres, including parts of Bernkasteler Badstube, Bratenhöfchen, Doktor, Graben, Lay, Matheisbildchen, Schlossberg and Johannisbrünnchen; also, parts of important vineyards in Graach, Wehlen, Zeltingen, Erden and Brauneberg.

Beringer (U.S.)   1876, 1971

An old winery in St. Helena, Napa Valley, California; produces a wide range of varietal and blended wines from grapes grown in St. Helena, Yountville, Knight's Valley and Carneros Creek. The second wine is Los Hermanos. 200,000 cases. 1,800 acres.

Berkeley Wine Cellars (U.S.)   1970

The label used for some of the wines made by Wine and The People Winery in Berkeley, Alameda County, California.

Bermet (Y.)

A Yugoslavian vermouth from the Fruška Gora district of the Vojvodina Province, north of Serbia.

Bernarde, Domaine de la (F.)

An estate in Le Luc, north of St. Tropez, in the Provence region. Produces red, white and rosé wines. 16,000 cases. 200 acres.

Bernardine, La (F.)

An estate in Châteauneuf-du-Pape, southern Rhône region; owned by Chapoutier. 70 acres.

Bernardins, Domaine de Castaud Maurin (F.)

An estate in Beaumes-de-Venise, southern Rhône region. 3,000 cases of VDN and red wine. 40 acres.

Bernardo Winery (U.S.)   1889

A small winery in San Diego, San Diego County, southern California; produces table and dessert wines. 4,000 cases.

Bernkastel (G.)

A *Bereich*, one of four, in the Mosel-Saar-Ruwer region. The *Grosslagen* are Badstube, Beerenlay, Kurfüstlay, Michelsberg, Münzlay, Nacktarsch, Probstberg, Sankt Michael, Schwarzlay and Vom Heissen Stein. Most of the great wine villages and vineyards of the region are in Bereich Bernkastel.

Bernkastel-Kues (G.)

A famous village in the Mosel-Saar-Ruwer region, Bereich Bernkastel (Mittel Mosel), Grosslagen Badstube and Kurfürstlay. The vineyards are Bratenhöfchen, Doctor, Lay and Matheisbildchen in Grosslage Badstube; and Johannisbrünnchen, Kardinalsberg, Rosenberg, Schlossberg, Stephanus-Rosengärtchen and Weissenstein in Grosslage Kurfürstlay. 500 acres.

Beronia, Bodegas (Sp.)   1970

A winery in Ollauri, Rioja Alta region. 25 acres.

Berrière, Château la (F.)

An estate in La Chapelle Basse-Mer, Muscadet de Sèvre-et-Maine district, Muscadet region, Loire Valley. 75 acres.

Berrywine Plantation (U.S.)   1973

A winery in Mount Airy, Maryland; produces wines from hybrid grapes. 5 acres.

Bersano (I.)   1896

A winery in Nizza Monferrato, near Asti, in the Piedmont region; produces Barolo, Barbaresco, Barbera, Dolcetto, Moscato and sparkling wines; made from their own and purchased grapes. 100,000 cases. 300 acres.

Bertagna, Éts (F.)

An estate in Vougeot, Côte de Nuits district, Burgundy. 30 acres, including Vougeot Premier Cru – 7.5 acres, Vougeot Clos de la Perrière Monopole – 6 acres, Échézeaux – 3.7 acres, Clos de la Roche – 1.2 acres, Clos St.-Denis – 1.2 acres and Gevrey-Chambertin La Justice – 3.7 acres.

Bertani (I.)

A winery in Verona, Veneto region; produces Amarone, Bardolino, Valpolicella, Soave and rosé wines; made from their own and purchased grapes. 185,000 cases. 500 acres.

Bertheaut, Guy (F.)

An estate in Fixin, Côte de Nuits district, Burgundy. 17 acres, including Fixin Les Arvelets – 1.6 acres, Cras – 4 acres and Gevrey-Chambertin – 2.5 acres.

Berthets, Domaine des (F.)

An estate in Chénas (or Moulin-à-Vent), Beaujolais district, Burgundy.

Bertille-Seyve (F.)

The name used by Bertille Seyve Sr. for the hybrid grapes he developed beginning in 1895.

Bertins, Les (F.)

A *Premier Cru* vineyard in Pommard, Côte de Beaune district, Burgundy. 9 acres.

Bertins, Château Les (F.)

An estate in Valeyrac, Médoc district, Bordeaux; classified in 1978 as a *Cru Bourgeois Being Reconstituted*. 6,000 cases. 50 acres.

Bertolli (I.)

An estate in Castellina Scalo, Tuscany region; produces Chianti, Chianti Classico, Orvieto and other wines under the name of Alivar. 75,000 cases.

Bertram's Devonvale Estate EWO (S. Af.)

An estate in the Stellenbosch district; produces Cabernet, Shiraz and Pinotage wines.

Bertrands, Domaine des (F.)

An estate in Le Cannet-des-Maures, north of St. Tropez, in the Provence region.

Berzamino (I.)

A local name for the Marzemino grape in the Lombardy region.

Besancenot-Mathouillet, Domaine (F.)

An estate in Beaune, Côte de Beaune district, Burgundy. 25 acres, including Beaune Cent-Vignes – 7.5 acres, and parts of Beaune Bressandes, Clos du Roi and Toussaints.

Bessac, Caves Eugène (F.)

A merchant in Châteauneuf-du-Pape, southern Rhône region; produces wines from Châteauneuf-du-Pape, Tavel, Côte-Rôtie, Hermitage and Côtes du Rhône made from purchased grapes. 200,000 cases.

Béssards, Les *also* Bréssards (F.)

One of the best vineyards in Hermitage, northern Rhône region; produces red wines.

Besserat de Bellefon (F.)   1843

A Champagne producer in Reims, Formerly in Ay; the *cuvée de prestige* is Brut Intégral. 1.8 million bottles.

Best Exhibitor of Show (Aus.)

The highest honor awarded to a wine in Australia.

Best's Concongella (Aus.)   1866

An old winery in the Great Western district, central Victoria; produces Shiraz, Pinot Meunier, Chardonnay, Chasselas and Rhine Riesling wines. 7,000 cases. 50 acres.

Beta (U.S., C.)

An American and Canadian red hybrid grape – a cross of *Vitis labrusca* and *Vitis riparia*.

Bétault, Cuvée Hugues et Louis (F.)

A red wine from the Hospices de Beaune, Côte de Beaune district, Burgundy. The *cuvée* is composed of the following vineyards in Beaune: Les Grèves – 2.2 acres, La Mignotte – 1.2 acres, Les Aigrots – 1 acre, Les Sizies – 1 acre and Les Vignes Franches – .5 acre. 875 cases.

Beugnons (F.)

A *Premier Cru* vineyard in Chablis, Chablis district, Burgundy; usually included as part of the Vaillons vineyard.

Beurot *also* Burot (F.)

The Pinot Beurot or Pinot Gris grape, grown in Burgundy.

Beychevelle, Château (F.)

An estate in St.-Julien, Haut-Médoc district, Bordeaux; classified in 1855 as a *Quatrième Cru*. The name, acquired around 1587, is a corruption of *Basse-Voile* (or *baissez les voiles*), a command to lower the sails of a boat as it passed by the 14th century castle. This was the salute to the Admiral of France, the Duc d'Epernon, the new owner. The present building dates from 1757. 25,000 cases. 150 acres.

Beyer, Jean (F.)

An estate and merchant in Epfig, Bas-Rhin district, Alsace region. 15 acres.

Beyer, Léon (F.)   **1580**

An estate and merchant in Eguisheim, Haut-Rhin district, Alsace region. 40 acres.

Beyerman, Henri et Oscar (F.)   **1620**

Merchants in Bordeaux.

Beylerce (T.)

A native white grape.

Beylot (F.)   **1740**

A merchant in Libourne, Bordeaux region.

Bianca Tenera (I.)

A white grape grown in the Campania region.

Biancame *also* **Bianchello (I.)**

A white grape grown in the Marches region.

Bianchello *also* **Biancame (I.)**

A white grape grown in the Marches region.

Bianchello del Metauro DOC (I.)

1. A district in the Metauro River Valley, in the northeastern Marches region, which produces:

2. A white wine made from the Bianchello (Biancame) grape with 5% Malvasia Toscana.

Bianchetta Trevigiana (I.)

A white grape grown in the Valdadige district, Trentino-Alto Adige region.

bianco (I.)

White.

Bianco d'Alessano (I.)

A local white grape grown in the Apulia region.

Bianco di Campociesa (I.)

A sweet white wine from the Valpolicella district, in the Veneto region; a *recioto* wine produced by Masi.

Bianco di Castelfranco DOC (I.)

A white wine from Castelfranco, near Modena, in the central Emilia-Romagna region.

Bianco dei Colli Maceratesi DOC (I.)

1. A district near Macerata, in the southeastern Marches region, which produces:

2. A white wine made from 50% Trebbiano Toscano, 30-50% Maceratino and Malvasia and 15% Verdicchio grapes.

Bianco di Custoza DOC (I.)

A white wine from Custoza, southwest of Verona, in the Veneto region; made from Trebbiano Toscano, Garganega and Tocai grapes; similar to Soave.

Bianco della Lega (I.)   **since 1980**

A white wine from the Chianti Classico district, in Tuscany, made from Trebbiano and Malvasia grapes.

Bianco Pisano San Torpè DOC (I.)   **1980**

1. A district in Tuscany, covering the same area as the Chianti Colline Pisane district, which produces:

2. A white wine made from the Trebbiano grape with some Malvasia and Canaiolo Bianco added.

Bianco di Pitigliano DOC (I.)

1. A district in Pitigliano and Manciano, in southern Tuscany, which produces:

2. A white wine made from Trebbiano, Greco or Grechetto, Malvasia and Verdello grapes.

Bianco dei Roeri (I.)

A white wine from Reori, near Alba, in the southern Piedmont region; made from 50% Arneis and 50% Nebbiolo grapes.

Bianco di Scandiano DOC (I)

1. A district in Scandiano, west of Modena, in the Emilia-Romagna region, which produces:

2. White wines, sweet, dry or sparkling, made from Sauvignon, Malvasia di Candia and Trebbiano grapes.

Bianco Toara (I.)

A dry white wine from Toara, in the Colli Berici district, near Vicenza, in the Veneto region; made from the Garganega grape.

Bianco della Valdinievole DOC (I.)

1. A district around Pescia, in the northern Tuscany region, which produces:
2. A white wine made from Trebbiano grapes.

Bianco Vergine della Valdichiana DOC (I.)

1. A district south of Arezzo, in the eastern Tuscany region, which produces:
2. A white wine made from 70-85% Trebbiano, with Malvasia and other grapes.

Biancolella (I.)

A white grape grown in the Campania region, southern Italy, blended with Forastera grapes to make white Ischia wine.

Biancone (F.)

A white grape grown in Corsica.

Biblino (I.)

An ancient wine of Sicily praised by the Greek poet, Hesiod (8th century B.C.) and by Pliny.

bica-aberta (P.)

The Portuguese equivalent of *en blanc*, i.e. without skins, to make a white wine from red grapes.

Bical da Bairrada (P.)

A white grape grown in the Dão and Bairrada regions; also called Borrado das Moscas.

Bichot, Albert et Cie (F.)   1831

A large company in Beaune, Burgundy; controls Domaine du Clos Frantin, which owns Chambertin – .8 acre, Richebourg – .2 acre, Clos de Vougeot – 1.3 acres, Vosne-Romanée Aux Malconsorts – 4.4 acres, Grands Échézeaux – .6 acre, Échézeaux – 2.5 acres and parts of Corton-Languettes, Gevrey-Chambertin, Vosne-Romanée, and

Nuits-St.-Georges; also controls Long-Dépaquit, in Chablis.

Bidot-Bourgogne (F.)

An estate in Pommard, Côte de Beaune, Burgundy. 12 acres, including Pommard les Epenots – .6 acre and vineyards in Volnay and Beaune.

Bienvenues-Bâtard-Montrachet AOC (F.)

A famous vineyard in Puligny-Montrachet, Côte de Beaune district, Burgundy, officially classified as a *Grand Cru*; it was formerly sold as Bâtard-Montrachet or as Criots-Bâtard-Montrachet. Produces white wine. 6 acres.

Biffar, Weingut Joseph (G.)

An estate in Deidesheim, Rheinpfalz region; owns vineyards in Deidesheim and Ruppertsberg. 30 acres.

Bigi & Figlio, Luigi (I.)   1881

A winery in Ponte Giulio di Orvieto, Umbria region; produces Est! Est!! Est!!!, Orvieto, Rosso and Vino Nobile di Montepulciano wines. 200,000 cases.

Bijelo (Y.)

White.

Bilbainas S.A., Bodegas (Sp.)   1901

A winery in Haro, Rioja Alta; produces Brillante, Cepa de Oro, Viña Paceta, Viña Pomal, Viña Zaco and sparkling wines. 230,000 cases. 700 acres.

Billard-Gonnet (F.)

An estate in Pommard, Côte de Beaune district, Burgundy. 30 acres, including Pommard Premier Cru – 14 acres (Rugiens, Clos de Berger, Jarollières, Pézerolles, Charmots, Chaponnières, Poutures and Bertins).

Billardet, Cuvée (F.)

A red wine from the Hospices de Beaune, Côte de Beaune district, Burgundy. The *cuvée* is composed of the following vineyards in Pommard: Petits-Épenots – 1.5 acres,

Les Noizons – 1.2 acres, Les Arvelets – 1 acre and Les Rugiens – 1 acre. 680 cases.

Billards, Domaine de (F.)

An estate in Pontanevaux, Beaujolais district, Burgundy; produces Saint-Amour *(Cru Beaujolais)* wine.

Billaud-Simon, J. (F.)　　　　　1955

An estate in Chablis, Burgundy; owns Chablis Les Clos – 1.5 acres, Vaudésir – 1.5 acres and parts of Mont-de-Milieu, Montée de Tonnerre and Vaillons.

Billecart-Salmon (F.)　　　　　1818

A Champagne producer in Ay; the special *cuvées* are Cuvée N.F. Billecart Vintage Brut and vintage Blanc de Blancs. 500,000 bottles.

Biltmore, Château (U.S.)　　　　1977

A winery in Asheville, western North Carolina; produces wines made from *vinifera* and hybrid grapes. 75 acres.

Bingen (G.)

1. A village in the Rheinhessen region, Bereich Bingen, Grosslage Sankt Rochuskapelle. The vineyards are: Bubenstück, Kapellenberg, Kirchberg, Osterberg, Pfarrgarten, Rosengarten, Scharlachberg, Schelmenstück, Schlossberg-Schwätzerchen and Schwartzenberg. 1800 acres.

2. A *Bereich*, one of 3 in the Rheinhessen region. The *Grosslagen* are Abtei, Adelberg, Kaiserpfalz, Kurfürstenstück, Rheingrafenstein and Sankt Rochuskapelle.

Bingen Wine Cellars (U.S.)　　　1974

The former name of Mount Elise Vineyards, in Bingen, Washington.

Biondi-Santi (I.)　　　　　　　1840

An estate in Montalcino, Tuscany region; originator of Brunello di Montalcino wine; produces Brunello wine. 4,000 cases. 30 acres.

Birkmyer Vineyards (U.S.)

A vineyard in Napa, Napa Valley, California; produces Riesling grapes for Stag's Leap Wine Cellars. 17 acres.

Birkweil (G.)

A village in the Rheinpfalz region, Bereich Südliche Weinstrasse, Grosslage Königsgarten. The vineyards are: Kastanienbusch, Mandelberg, and part of Rosenberg.

Biscardo (I.)

A winery in Bussolengo, Veneto region; produces Amarone, Bardolino and Soave wines; also handles wines from several other regions. 270 acres.

Bischöflichen Weingüter Trier (G.)

An estate in Trier, Mosel-Saar-Ruwer region; a combination of the Bischöfliches Priesterseminar, Hohe Domkirche and Bischöfliches Konvikt estate holdings; owns vineyards in 15 Mosel, Saar and Ruwer villages. 260 acres.

Biser (Y.)

Semi-sparkling.

bishop (E.)

A mulled Port, a drink made with Port wine, sugar, orange and cloves, usually heated and flambéed before being poured.

Bitouzet, P. (F.)

An estate in Savigny-lès-Beaune, Côte de Beaune district, Burgundy. 5 acres, including Savigny Les Lavières – 1.2 acres and Aloxe-Corton Valozières – .8 acre.

Bize et Fils, Simon (F.)

An estate in Savigny-lès-Beaune, Côte de Beaune district, Burgundy. 25 acres, including Savigny Les Vergelesses – 7 acres, Les Marconnets – 1.6 acres and Les Guettes – 2 acres.

Bizolière, Domaine de la (F.)

An estate in Savennières, Anjou region, Loire Valley. 45 acres, including 9 acres of

La Roche aux Moines, 15 acres of Savennières and other vineyards as well.

Blaauwklippen Estate EWO (S. Af.) 1972

An estate in Stellenbosch, recently restored; produces red and white varietal wines, including Zinfandel, and blended wines. 18,000 cases. 300 acres.

Black Corinth (U.S.)

A red *vinifera* grape grown in California, also called Zante Currant.

Black Hamburg

A red grape, grown in the U.S. and England; in Germany and Austria it is called the Trollinger, Blauer Malvasia, Gross Vernatsch, and Frankenthaler; in Italy, Schiava Grossa.

Black July (Br.)

A red grape grown in Brazil.

Black Mountain (U.S.)

A vineyard in Healdsburg, Alexander Valley, in Sonoma County, California; produces Zinfandel, Chardonnay and Sauvignon Blanc grapes for Joseph Phelps and J.W. Morris Wineries. 100 acres.

Black Muscat (U.S.)

A red grape grown in California; also called Muscat Hamburg.

Black Pearl (U.S.)

A red *labrusca* grape.

black rot

A fungus disease of the vine characterized by the formation of stains speckled with black which appear on the leaves and cause the fruit to shrivel and turn brown.

Black Spanish

A red hybrid grape; also called Jacquez or Lenoir.

Black Velvet (E.)

A drink, originating in England, made from Champagne mixed with Stout.

Blagny AOC (F.)

A hamlet (*hameau*, in French) between and behind Meursault and Puligny-Montrachet, in the Côte de Beaune district, Burgundy; produces red and white wines, sometimes sold as Meursault or Puligny-Montrachet.

Blagny, Domaine de (F.)

An estate in Meursault, Côte de Beaune district, Burgundy. 28 acres, including Meursault Blagny La Genelotte Monopole (red and white) – 7.5 acres, La Pièce-sous-le-Bois – 5 acres, Sous le Dos d'Âne – 5 acres, Puligny-Montrachet les Chalimeaux – 1 acre and Hameau de Blagny – 5 acres.

blanc (F.)

White.

Blanc, Le Clos (F.)

A *Premier Cru* vineyard in Pommard, Côte de Beaune district, Burgundy. 10.5 acres.

Blanc, Domaine du Mas (F.)

An estate in Banyuls-sur-Mer, Roussillon region; produces Collioure and Banyul wines. 35 acres.

blanc de blancs (F.)

"White from whites," meaning a white wine made from white grapes, used especially with regard to Champagne made from Chardonnay grapes.

Blanc de Cossan (I.)

A white wine from Cossan, near Aosta, in the Valle d'Aosta region; made from the Grenache grape.

Blanc d'Euvézin (F.)

A white grape grown in the Lorraine region.

Blanc Fumé (F.)

In the Poilly-Fumé district, the local name for the Sauvignon Blanc grape.

Blanc Fumé de Pouilly AOC (F.)

1. A district in the Upper Loire region, Loire Valley, made up of Pouilly-sur-Loire

and six surrounding communes; identical to Pouilly-Fumé AOC district; it produces :

2. A dry white wine made from the Sauvignon Blanc grape.

Blanc de Morgex (I.)

A white wine from the Valle d'Aosta region grown in high altitudes; made from the Blanc de Valdigne grape.

blanc de noirs (F.)

"White from reds," meaning a white wine made from red grapes, a term used mostly for Champagnes made from Pinot Noir grapes.

Blanc Ramé (F.)

A white grape; also called Pineau de Charentes.

Blanc de La Salle (I.)

A white wine from the Valle d'Aosta region; made from the Blanc de Valdigne grape.

Blanc de Valdigne (I.)

A white grape grown in the Valle d'Aosta region.

Blanc de Vougeot, Clos, *also* **La Vigne Blanche (F.)**

1. A *Premier Cru* vineyard in Vougeot, Côte de Nuits district, Burgundy. 4.5 acres; it produces:

2. A white wine made from the Chardonnay grape.

Blanca-Roja *also* **Blanquirroja (Sp.)**

In the Rioja region, another name for the white Malvasía grape.

Blanchards, Les (F.)

A *Premier Cru* vineyard in Morey-St.-Denis, Côte de Nuits district, Burgundy. 4.5 acres.

Blanches Fleurs, Les (F.)

A *Premier Cru* vineyard in Beaune, Côte de Beaune district, Burgundy. 3 acres.

Blanchots (F.)

A *Grand Cru* vineyard in Fyé, Chablis district, Burgundy.

Blanck (F.)

An estate in Kientzheim, Haut-Rhin district, Alsace region. 52 acres, including Schlossberg – 8 acres (Riesling) and Furstentum – 15 acres (Gewürztraminer).

blanco (Sp.)

White.

Blandy's (P.)   1811

A producer of Madeira wines.

Blankenhorn KG, Weingut Fritz (G.)

An estate in Schliengen, Baden region; owns vineyards in Schliengen and Badenweil. 35 acres.

Blanquette de Limoux AOC (F.)

1. A district around Limoux, southwest of Carcassone, in the Languedoc region of the Midi, which produces:

2. A sparkling wine made from 90% Mauzac and 10% Clairette and Chardonnay grapes. See **Vin de Blanquette** (a still wine).

Blanquirroja *also* **Blanca-Roja (Sp.)**

In the Rioja region, the local name for the white Malvasía grape.

Blatina (Y.)

1. A red grape grown in Yugoslavia.

2. A red wine from the Bosnia-Herzegovina region; made from the Blatina grape.

Blauburgunder (G., A.)

In Germany and Austria, the name for the Pinot Noir grape.

Blauer Malvasier (G.)

In Germany, a local name for the Trollinger grape; also called Frankentaler, Gross Vernatsch and Meraner Kurtraube; in Italy called Schiava Grossa, in the U.S. called the Black Hamburg.

Blauer Portugieser (A.)

A red grape grown in Vöslau; in the U.S. called Early Burgundy, in parts of France called Portugais Bleu.

Blauer Wildbacher (A.)

A native red grape from the Styria region.

Blaufränkischer

A red grape (possibly the Gamay grape) grown in Austria, Hungary, Yugoslavia and other eastern European countries; in Germany also called the Lemberger.

Blauklevner (G.)

In Germany, another name for Pinot Noir grape.

Blaye AOC *also* Blayais AOC (F.)

1. A city in the Bordeaux region, across the Gironde River from the Haut-Médoc district, which produces:

2. Red and white wines, the red made from Cabernet Sauvignon, Cabernet Franc, Merlot, Malbec and Cot grapes, and the white from Sauvignon, Sémillon, Muscadelle, Folle Blanche and Frontignan grapes, which can be sweet or dry.

Blázquez S.A., Hijos de Agustin (Sp.)
1795

A Sherry producer in Jerez de la Frontera; produces a wide range of Sherries.

blending

A process of selective mixing of: a) different grapes to make wine, b) different wines to achieve a desired style, c) different vintages to obtain a consistent taste from year to year. Most Champagnes, all Sherry, Port, red Bordeaux and California generic wines are blended in one way or another.

Bleufrancs (F.)

The French name for the red Blaufränkischer grape, also known as Franconia and Limberger.

blind tasting

The tasting of wines without any identifying information, except the obvious one of color, in an attempt to ascertain the identity of the wine through taste, aroma and color.

Blomac, Château de (F.)

An estate in Blomac, near Capendu, Minervois district, Languedoc region; produces red wines. 260 acres.

Blondeau, Cuvée (F.)

A red wine from the Hospices de Beaune, Côte de Beaune district, Burgundy. The *cuvée* is composed of the following vineyards in Volnay: Champans – 1.5 acres, Taille Pieds – 1.5 acres, Ronceret – 1 acre and En l'Ormeau – .5 acre. 500 cases.

Blondeau-Danne (F.)

An estate in St.-Aubin, Côte de Beaune district, Burgundy. 30 acres, including vineyard parcels in Volnay, Meursault, Puligny-Montrachet, Chassagne-Montrachet, Saint-Aubin and some Criots-Bâtard-Montrachet

Bôa Vista, Quinta (P.)

One of the best known *quintas* of the Alto Douro region, northeast of Peso da Regua; owned by Offley Forrester Lda.

Boais (P.)

One of the four grapes used to make Carcavelos wines.

Boal *also* Bual (P.)

1. A white whine grape grown in southern Portugal and in Madeira.

2. A Madeira wine which is rich, full and sweet, but not as sweet as Malmsey.

Bobal (SP.)

A red grape grown in the La Mancha region.

Boberg WO (S. Af.)

An official designation for fortified wines made in the Paarl and Tulbagh districts.

Boca DOC (I.)

1. A village and district north of Gattinara, in the northern Piedmont region, which produces:
2. A red wine made from 45-70% Nebbiolo grapes blended with Vespolina and Bonarda grapes.

boccale (I.)

A decanter.

Böckelheim, Schloss (G.)

See **Schloss Böckelheim.**

Bocksbeutel (G.)

A squat, flat-sided bottle used for wines from the Franken and Baden regions.

Bockwingert (Liech.)

An estate in the Vaduz district, Liechtenstein; produces a light red wine made from the Blauburgunder grape.

bocoy (Sp.)

A butt or cask; a chestnut barrel used for shipping Spanish wines. 65-70 liters or 172-185 U.S. gallons.

bodega (Sp.)

1. A large place for storing wines, usually above ground.
2. A wine shop.
3. A winery or wine company.

bodeguero (Sp.)

A *bodega* owner.

Bodengeschmack (G.)

Earthy taste, a term used to describe a wine; also called *Bodenton.*

Bodenheim (G.)

A village in the Rheinhessen region, Bereich Nierstein, Grosslage Sankt Alban. The vineyards are: Burgweg, Ebersberg, Heitersbrünnchen, Hoch, Kapelle, Kreuzberg, Leidhecke, Mönchspfad, Reichsritterstift, Silberberg and Westrum. 1,300 acres.

Bodensee (G.)

A *Bereich*, one of 7, in the Baden region. The only *Grosslage* is Sonnenufer. 750 acres.

Bodenton (G.)

Earthy taste, a term used to describe a wine; also called *Bodengeschmack.*

Boeckel, E. (F.)   1853

An estate and merchant in Mittelbergheim, Bas-Rhin district, Alsace region; owns 50 acres in Mittelbergheim, Andlau, Barr and Heiligenstein, including 12 acres of Wibelsberg, in Andlau (Riesling), 4 acres in Brandluft, in Mittelbergheim (Riesling) and 1.2 acres of Chardonnay vines.

Boeger Winery (U.S.)   1973

A winery in Placerville, El Dorado County, California, rebuilt on the site of the old Fossati Vineyard; produces Cabernet, Zinfandel, Merlot, Chardonnay, Sauvignon Blanc, Sémillon and blended red and white wines. 10,000 cases. 20 acres.

Boğazkeasi (T.)

A red grape grown in southeastern Turkey.

Boğazkere (T.)

A red grape grown in Turkey.

Bogdanuša (Y.)

A white grape grown in the Dalmatia region of the Republic of Croatia.

Bogle Vineyards Winery (U.S.)   1979

A winery in Clarksburg, Yolo County, California; produces Petite Sirah and Chenin Blanc wines. 15,000 cases.

Bohemia (Cz.)

A province in western Czechoslovakia; the only important wine district is north of Prague and includes the towns of Litoměřice, Mělnik, Roudnice and Velké Zernoseky; produces mostly white wines from Riesling, Traminer, Sylvaner and Chardonnay grapes and red wines from Blauer Burgunder, Portugieser and St. Laurent grapes. 1,000 acres.

Boillet, Cuvée (F.)

A red wine from the Hospices de Beaune, Côte de Beaune district, Burgundy. The *cuvée* is composed of the following vineyard in Auxey-Duresses: Les Duresses – 2 acres. 225 cases.

Boillot, Domaine Henri (F.)

An estate in Volnay, Côte de Beaune district, Burgundy. 55 acres, including Puligny-Montrachet Clos de la Mouchère Monopole – 10 acres, Pucelles – 1.2 acres, Meursault Les Genevrières – 2.5 acres, Volnay En Chevret, Caillerets – 2 acres, Les Angles – 4 acres, Pommard Les Jarollières – 3.2 acres, Les Rugiens – 1.2 acres and Beaune Les Épenottes – 1.2 acres.

Bois, Clos du (U.S.)   vineyards 1960
                           winery 1980

A winery in Healdsburg, Dry Creek Valley, Sonoma County, California; produces Cabernet, Pinot Noir, Chardonnay, Gewürztraminer and Johannisberg Riesling wines. The secondary label is River Oaks. 50,000 cases. 1,200 acres.

boisé (F.)

Woody, in taste.

Boisseaux, Domaine Gaston (F.)

An estate in Beaune, Côte de Beaune district, Burgundy. 18 acres, including Beaune Montée Rouge – 11.5 acres, Savigny Les Peuillets – .6 acre and Chorey-lès-Beaune – 6.2 acres.

Boisseaux-Estivant (F.)   1878

A merchant in Beaune, Côte de Beaune district, Burgundy.

Boisset, Jean-Claude (F.)   1961

An estate and merchant in Nuits-St.-Georges, Côte de Nuits district, Burgundy. 25 acres, including vineyards in Gevrey-Chambertin.

Boisset Vineyard (U.S.)   1980

A vineyard and future winery in Rutherford, Napa Valley, California; owned by Jean-Claude Boisset of Burgundy; produces Cabernet, Chardonnay and Sauvignon Blanc wines. 55 acres. 10,000 cases.

Boix-Chevaux (F.)

A vineyard in Givry, Côte Chalonnaise district, Burgundy.

Bolivia

A minor wine-producing country in South America. 5,000 acres.

Bolla (I.)   1883

A large winery in Verona, Veneto region; produces Amarone, Bardolino, Soave and Valpolicella wines. 1.4 million cases.

Bolle & Cie (Sw.)   1842

An estate and merchant in Morges, Vaud region; owns several other estates; produces Dorin, Dézaley and other wines. 90,000 cases. 25 acres.

Bollenberg (F.)

A vineyard partly in Westhalten and partly in Orschwihr, Haut-Rhin district, Alsace region; grows Muscat, Riesling and Gewürztraminer grapes.

Bollinger (F.)   1829

A Champagne producer in Ay; the special *cuvées* are R.D. and Vielle Vignes Françaises (Blanc de Noirs). 1.2 million bottles. 350 acres.

Bombino *also* Bombino Bianco *also* Bonvino (I.)

A white grape grown in the Abruzzi, Apulia and Latium regions; related to the Trebbiano Nostrano or Trebbiano d'Abruzzo grape.

Bombino Nero (I.)

A red grape grown in the Apulia region.

bombona (Sp.)

A large, pear-shaped earthen vessel for storing wines; it has a 30-liter capacity.

Bomita (Sp.)

A white grape grown in southwestern Spain.

Bon Blanc (F.)

Another name for the Colombard grape; also called Chasselas in the Seyssel district, Savoie region; also called Pied-Tendre and Blanquette.

Bonacina, Gianni (I.)

The author of *"Lo Stivale in Bottiglia"* (*"The Boot in Bottle"*), a wine encyclopedia.

Bonarda *also* Bonarda di Gattinara (I.)

A red grape grown in the Emilia-Romagna, Lombardy and Piedmont regions; also grown in Argentina and Brazil.

bonbonne (F.)

A large jug usually with a wicker or straw covering used for storing and shipping inexpensive wine; also called *Dame-Jeanne* or Demijohn.

bonde (F.)

A barrel stopper, or bung.

Bondola (Sw.)

A red grape grown in the Ticino region and used in making Nostrano, a blended wine.

Bonfoi EWO (S. Af.)

An estate in the Stellenbosch district; produces white wines.

Bonneau, Château (F.)

An estate in St.-Seurin-de-Cadourne, Haut-Médoc district, Bordeaux; classified in 1978 as a *Cru Bourgeois*. 3,000 cases. 12 acres.

Bonneau de Martray, Domaine (F.)

An estate in Savigny-lès-Beaune, Côte de Beaune district, Burgundy. 28 acres, including Corton – 6.5 acres and Corton-Charlemagne – 21 acres.

Bonnes Mares AOC (F.)

A *Grand Cru* vineyard partly in Chambolle-Musigny and partly in Morey-St.-Denis (the greater part in Chambolle-Musigny), Côte de Nuits district, Burgundy. 38 acres.

Bonnet, Château (F.)

An estate in Chénas, Beaujolais district, Burgundy.

Bonnet, F. (F.)   1922

A Champagne producer in Oger, south of Épernay. 120,000 bottles. 22 acres.

Bonnezeaux AOC (F.)

1. A town in the Coteaux-du-Layon district, Anjou region, Loire Valley; classified in 1951 as a *Grand Cru*. 250 acres. It produces:
2. Sweet white wines made from the Pineau de la Loire (or Chenin Blanc) grape.

Bonny Doon Vineyard (U.S.)   1983

A winery in Santa Cruz, Santa Cruz County, California; produces Cabernet, Chardonnay, Pinot Noir and Sirah wines. 20 acres. 4,000 cases.

Bonvin Fils, Charles (Sw.)   1858

An estate in Sion, Valais region; produces Fendant wine (under the names of Sans Cullotte, La Gachette, Château Conthey and Brûlefer) and Dôle wine. 60 acres.

Bonvino *also* Bombino Bianco (I.)

See **Bombino**.

Boordy Vineyard (U.S.)   1945

A small winery in Riderwood, just north of Baltimore, Maryland, one of the first wineries to grow French hybrid grapes in the U.S.; produces white, red and rosé wines from hybrid grapes. 7 acres.

Boppard (G.)

An important village in the Mittelrhein region, Bereich Rheinburgengau, Grosslage Gedeonseck. The vineyards are: Elfenlay, Englestein, Fässerlay, Feuerlay, Mandelstein, Ohlenberg and Weingrube.

bor (H.)
Wine.

Bordeaux AOC *also with* Clairet, Mousseux or Rosé (F.)
1. A city and region in southwestern France, the most famous and largest wine region in France, department of the Gironde, itself the largest department of France. There are at least 40 AOC place-names designating different wines: Bordeaux Rouge, Bordeaux Blanc, Médoc, Blaye, Bourg, Graves, St.-Émilion, Pomerol, Sauternes, etc. Many of the oldest and most renowned château estates are located in this region.

2. A red or white wine from anywhere in the Bordeaux region, a generic wine usually blended from several growers from different communes.

Bordeaux mixture
A mixture of copper sulfate and slaked lime used as a fungicide in Europe and the U.S. It is sprayed on the vines in the summer to prevent mildew and oïdium.

Bordeaux Supérieur AOC (F.)
A designation for red, white and rosé wines from the Bordeaux region, with .5% more alcohol than Bordeaux AOC. Côtes de Castillon, Côtes de Francs and Haut-Bénauge carry the Bordeaux Supérieur designation.

Bordeleau (Is.)
A red *vinifera* grape grown in Israel.

Bordo (Br.)
A hybrid grape grown in Brazil.

Borgo Conventi (I.)   1876
An estate in Farra d'Isonzo, Friuli-Venezia Giulia region; produces Collio, Sauvignon Blanc and Tocai wines. 4,000 cases. 17 acres.

Borgogno & Figli, Giacomo (I.)
An estate in Barolo, Piedmont region; produces Barbera, Barolo and Dolcetto wines.

Borie-Lalande, Château (F.)
An estate in St.-Julien, Haut-Médoc district, Bordeaux; classified in 1932 as a *Cru Bourgeois*; now owned by Château Ducru-Beaucaillou. 45 acres. 4,500 cases.

Borie-Manoux (F.)
A merchant in Bordeaux; owns Châteaux Batailley, Beau-Site and Trottevielle.

Borniques, Les (F.)
A *Premier Cru* vineyard in Chambolle-Musigny, Côte de Nuits district, Burgundy. 3 acres.

Bornóva Misketi (T.)
A sweet white muscat wine from Bornóva, near Izmir, in the Aegean region of western Turkey.

Borraçal (P.)
A red grape grown in the Vinho Verde region.

Borrado das Moscas (P.)
A white grape grown in the Dão region; also called Bical da Bairrada.

Borra's Cellar (U.S.)   1975
A small winery in Lodi, San Joaquin Valley, California; produces Barbera and Carignane wines. 500 cases. 30 acres.

Bosca & Figli, Luigi (I.)   1831
A large estate in Canelli, Asti district, Piedmont region; produces Asti Spumante, Barbaresco, Barbera, Barolo, Dolcetto, Gavi, Gignolino, Canei and sparkling wines. 700 acres.

Boscarelli, Poderi (I.)   1963
An estate in Cervignano di Montepulciano, Tuscany region; produces Chianti, Colli Senesi and Vino Nobile di Montepulciano wines. 3,000 cases. 22 acres.

Bosché Vineyard (U.S.)
A vineyard in Rutherford, Napa Valley, California, owned by John Bosché; pro-

duces Cabernet grapes for Freemark Abbey winery. 15 acres.

Bosco (I.)

A white grape grown in the Cinqueterre district, Liguria region.

Bosco, Ca' del (I.)   1968

An estate in Erbusco, Lombardy region; produces Franciacorta, rosé and sparkling wines. 25,000 cases. 95 acres.

Bosco Eliceo (I.)

A red wine from the plains around the Comacchio Lagoon, near Ferrara, in the eastern Emilia-Romagna region; made from the Uva d'Oro grape.

Boscq, Château Le (F.)

An estate in St.-Estèphe, Haut-Médoc district, Bordeaux; classified in 1978 as a *Cru Bourgeois*. 4,000 cases. 32 acres.

Boskydel Vineyards (U.S.)   1976

A winery near the town of Lake Leelenau, in northern Michigan; produces red wine from De Chaunac grapes and white wine from Vignoles grapes. 20 acres.

Bosnia-Herzegovina (Y.)

A large state in west central Yugoslavia; produces Žilavka wine, the best-known white wine of the region.

Bosquet, Domaine du (F.)

An estate in the Vins de Sables district, Languedoc region (the Midi); produces red wines: Vins des Sables du Golfe du Lion; owned by Domaines Viticoles des Salins du Midi.

bota (Sp.)

1. A 1-liter wine bag.
2. A 500-liter (132-gallon) wine barrel used to store and age wines.
3. A 500-600-liter Sherry butt.

Botrytis cinerea

A fungus that attacks overripe grapes, especially white grapes, under certain cli-matic conditions, producing a rich, sweet, dessert wine of extraordinary quality and flavor; Sauternes and Riesling wines of Germany and California are frequently made in this way; also called "noble rot." See **Pourriture Noble.**

Bott Frères (F.)

A merchant in Ribeauvillé, Haut-Rhin district, Alsace region. 30 acres in Ribeauvillé, Hunawihr and Beblenheim.

Bott-Geyl (F.)   1910

An estate and merchant in Beblenheim, Haut-Rhin district, Alsace region; owns Sonnenglanz vineyard – 5 acres (Gewürztraminer).

Botticino DOC (I.)

1. A town and district near Brescia, in the Lombardy region, which produces:
2. A red wine made from the Barbera grape with some Marzemino, Schiava Gentile and Sangiovese grapes.

bottle-fermented

Fermented a second time in the bottle, referring to the process of making Champagne and other sparkling wines; the *méthode Champenoise.*

bottle sickness

A temporary malady of wine when first bottled or when transported overseas or long distances on land. The wine seems to be unbalanced and harsh until rested a few weeks or months.

Bouchaine Vineyards (U.S.)   1924, 1980

A winery in the Carneros district, southern Napa Valley, California; formerly, the Garetto Winery; produces Pinot Noir, Chardonnay and Sauvignon Blanc wines. 90,000 cases.

Bouchard Aîné et Fils (F.)   1750

An old estate, merchant and shipper in Beaune, Côte de Beaune district, Burgundy. 55 acres, including Mercurey Clos La Marche Monopole – 7.5 acres, Clos du Chapitre – 10 acres, Mercurey Blanc – 3.8

acres; also makes wine of the Domaine Dr. Henri Marion – 15 acres: Chambertin Clos de Bèze – 4.8 acres, Fixin La Mazière – 3.3 acres and Côte de Nuits-Villages – 7.5 acres.

Bouchard Père et Fils (F.)   **1731**

The largest estate in the Côte de Beaune district, in Beaune, Burgundy. 200 acres, including Le Corton – 9 acres, Corton-Charlemagne – 7.5 acres, Savigny Les Lavières – 10 acres, Beaune Les Teurons – 8.6 acres, Les Marconnets – 5.4 acres, Clos de la Mousse Monopole – 8 acres, Les Grèves Vigne de l'Enfant Jesus Monopole – 10 acres, Clos-Landry Monopole – 4.4 acres, Beaune du Château – 11.5 acres (a blend of parts of some 17 *Premier Cru* vineyards), Pommard Les Rugiens – 1 acre, Les Combes – 2 acres, Volnay Caillerets – 9 acres, En Chevret – .6 acre, Taille-Pieds – 2.5 acres, Chanlin – 1 acre, Fremiet Clos de la Rougette Monopole – 4 acres, Chambertin – .4 acre, Montrachet – 2.8 acres, Chevalier-Montrachet – 3.6 acres, Meursault Les Genevrières – 3.6 acres and Beaune du Château Blanc – 10 acres (a blend of vineyards); also distributes wine of Château de Vosne-Romanée and Château de Mandelot (Hautes-Côtes de Beaune).

bouché (F.)

Of a wine bottle, stoppered with a cork.

Boucher, Aimé (F.)   **1900**

A merchant in Huisseau-sur-Cosson, Touraine region; produces Chinon, Bourgueil and other Touraine wines, Vouvray, Pouilly Fumé, Sancerre and Crémant de Loire. 75,000 cases.

Bouchères, Les (F.)

A *Premier Cru* vineyard in Meursault, Côte de Beaune district, Burgundy. 10.5 acres.

Boucherottes, Les (F.)

A *Premier Cru* vineyard mostly (21 acres) in Beaune and partly (4 acres) in Pommard, Côte de Beaune district, Burgundy. 25 acres, total.

Bouchet *also* **Gros-Bouchet** *also* **Bouchy (F.)**

In St.-Émilion and Pomerol, the name for the Cabernet Franc grape.

boucheur (F.)

One who forces a cork into a bottle, especially a bottle of Champagne.

bouchon (F.)

A cork.

bouchonné (F.)

Corked, or corky, said of a wine spoiled by a bad cork.

Bouchots, Les (F.)

A *Premier Cru* vineyard in Morey-St.-Denis, Côte de Nuits district, Burgundy. 5 acres.

Bouchotte, Valentin (F.)

An estate in Savigny-lès-Beaune, Côte de Beaune district, Burgundy. 12 acres, including Savigny Haut Jarrons – 5 acres.

Bouchy (F.)

A red grape grown in the Madiran district, Southwest region; also the local name for the Cabernet Franc grape in St.-Émilion and Pomerol.

Boudin, Adhémar (F.)

An estate in the Chablis district, Burgundy. 22 acres, including 5 acres of Fourchaume.

Boudots, Aux *also* **Les Boudots (F.)**

A *Premier Cru* vineyard in Nuits-St.-Georges, Côte de Nuits district, Burgundy. 16 acres.

Boudriotte(s), La, Les (F.)

A *Premier Cru* vineyard in Chassagne-Montrachet, Côte de Beaune district, Burgundy; produces red and white wines. 45 acres.

Bouffants, Clos des (F.)

An estate in Verdigny, Sancerre district, Upper Loire region, Loire Valley. 25 acres.

Bougros (F.)

One of 7 *Grand Cru* vineyards in Chablis, Chablis district, Burgundy.

Bouis, Château le (F.)

An estate in Gruissan, Corbières district, Languedoc region; produces rosé and white wines. 17,000 cases. 90 acres.

Bourboulenc (F.)

A white grape grown in the Rhône region for making white wine, and one of the 13 grapes permitted to be used in making the red Châteauneuf-du-Pape wine; also grown in the Midi and in Israel.

Bourdieu, Château le (F.)

An estate in Vertheuil, Haut-Médoc district, Bordeaux; classified in 1932 as a *Cru Bourgeois*. 15,000 cases. 130 acres.

Bourée Fils, Pierre (F.)   1864

An estate in Gevrey-Chambertin, Côte de Nuits district, Burgundy. 8 acres, including Charmes-Chambertin – 2 acres and Gevrey-Chambertin Clos de la Justice Monopole – 5 acres.

Bourg *also* Bourgeais *also* Côtes de Bourg *all* AOC (F.)

1. A town (Bourg) and district across the Gironde River from Margaux, in the Bordeaux region, which produces:

2. Red wines made from Cabernet Sauvignon, Cabernet Franc, Merlot and Malbec grapes, and sweet or dry white wines from Sémillon, Sauvignon and Muscadelle grapes.

Bourgeot, Ernest (F.)

An estate in Fixin, Côte de Nuits district, Burgundy; owns vineyards in Gevrey-Chambertin, Chambolle-Musigny and Fixin. 10 acres.

Bourgneuf-Vayron, Château (F.)

An estate in Pomerol, Bordeaux. 4,000 cases. 22 acres.

Bourgogne AOC (F.)

1. Burgundy.

2. Red, white and rosé wines from various parts of Burgundy; the red and rosé wines are made from the Pinot Noir or the Gamay grape (the César and Tressot grapes, however, may be used in the Chablis and Auxerrois districts); the white wines are made from the Chardonnay grape, but may contain some Pinot Blanc and Pinot Beurot grapes.

Bourgogne Aligoté AOC (F.)

A white wine from the Burgundy region made from the Aligoté grape, with up to 15% Chardonnay grapes permitted.

Bourgogne Aligoté de Bouzeron AOC (F.)   1979

A new AOC designation for the white wine from Bouzeron, between Chagny and Rully, in the Côte Chalonnaise district, Burgundy; made from Aligoté grapes.

Bourgogne Clairet AOC (F.)

Rosé wines from the Burgundy region made from the Pinot Noir grape (or the César and Tressot grapes in the Chablis district); essentially the same as Bourgogne Rosé AOC.

Bourgogne Grand Ordinaire AOC (F.)

A designation for red, white and rosé wines of the region, made from the same grapes as Bougogne AOC except that for the white wine the Sacy and Melon de Bourgogne grapes may also be used. This is the lowest classification of Burgundy wines.

Bourgogne Hautes-Côtes-de-Beaune AOC (F.)

A designation for red, white and rosé wines from the hills behind the Côte de Beaune, Burgundy. Pinot Noir, Chardonnay and Pinot Blanc grapes must be used.

Bourgogne Hautes-Côtes-de-Nuits AOC (F.)

A designation for red, white and rosé wines from the hills behind the Côte de

Nuits, Burgundy. Pinot Noir, Chardonnay and Pinot Blanc grapes must be used.

Bourgogne Irancy AOC (F.)

Red and rosé wine from Irancy, southwest of Chablis, in the Auxerrois district, Burgundy. Pinot Noir, Tressot and César grapes may be used.

Bourgogne Passe-Tout-Grains *or* **Passe-toutgrains AOC (F.)**

Red and some rosé wine from anywhere in Burgundy made from a blend of Pinot Noir (at least a third) and Gamay grapes.

Bourgueil AOC (F.)

1. A village and district in the western Touraine region, Loire Valley, which produces:

2. A red or rosé wine made from Cabernet Franc and Cabernet Sauvignon grapes.

Bouscaut, Château (F.)

An estate in Cadaujac, in the Graves district, Bordeaux region; classified in 1959 as a *Cru Classé* for red and white wine. Red wine – 10,000 cases, 77 acres; white wine – 1,500 cases, 15 acres.

Bouschet, M. (F.)

A hybridizer who developed the Alicante-Bouschet grape in the 19th century, grown in southern France and Algeria.

Bousquet, Château de (F.)

An estate in Bourg, Côte de Bourg district, Bordeaux. 148 acres.

Bousse d'Or (F.)

A *Premier Cru* vineyard in Volnay, Côte de Beaune district, Burgundy; a *monopole* owned by the Domaine de la Pousse d'Or. 5 acres.

Bousselots, Aux (F.)

A *Premier Cru* vineyard in Nuits-St.-Georges, Côte de Nuits district, Burgundy. 11 acres.

Boussey (F.)

An estate in Monthélie, Côte de Beaune district, Burgundy. 25 acres, including Volnay Taille-Pieds – .6 acre, Monthélie Les Champs Fulliet – 2.5 acres, Pommard – 2 acres and some Meursault.

Boutari & Son S.A., J. (Gr.)　　　　　**1879**

An estate in Stenimachos, Naoussa, in Macedonia, northern Greece; produces Grande Reserve Boutari (red) and other wines. 30,000 cases.

bouteille (F.)

A bottle.

bouteille couleuse (F.)

A leaky bottle; a bottle of wine that has evaporated or leaked because of a faulty cork.

Boutières (F.)

A *Premier Cru* vineyard in Cheilly-les-Maranges, Côte de Beaune district, Burgundy. Red and white wines.

boutique

A small winery, usually in California or Australia, specializing in making small amounts of fine wines of individual character.

Bouvet-Ladubay (F.)　　　　　　　　　　**1851**

A producer of sparkling wines in St.-Hilaire-St.-Florent, Saumur district, Anjou region, Loire Valley.

Bouvier (A.)

A native white grape grown in the Burgenland region; also grown in Serbia, Yugoslavia.

Bouzeron (F.)

A commune just north of Rully, in the Côte Chalonnaise district, Burgundy; produces red and white wines designated as Bourgogne AOC. A new AOC designation was granted in 1979 for Bourgogne Aligoté de Bouzeron.

Bouzy (F.)

A village in the Côte d'Ambonnay district, Champagne region; rated *Grand Cru*; grows red grapes for Champagne and red still wine.

Bovale (I.)

A red grape grown in Sardinia.

Bowen Estate (Aus.)   1972

A vineyard and winery in the Coonawarra district of South Australia; produces Cabernet, Shiraz, Rhine Riesling, Chardonnay and blended red wines. 2,500 cases. 40 acres.

Boyd-Cantenac, Château (F.)

An estate in Margaux, Haut-Médoc district, Bordeaux; until 1860 was one property with Château Cantenac-Brown and was known as Château Boyd in the 1855 classification; classified in 1855 as a *Troisième Cru*. 5,500 cases. 45 acres.

Bracciola (I.)

A local grape grown in the Tuscany region.

Brachetto (I.)

A red grape grown in the Piedmont region; produces dry, semi-dry and sparkling wines.

Brachetto d'Acqui DOC (I.)

1. A district around Acqui Terme, south of Asti, in the Piedmont region, which produces:

2. A slightly sweet red, semi-sparkling wine, made from the Brachetto grape.

Brachetto d'Alba (I.)

1. A district around Alba, south of Asti, in the Piedmont region, which produces:

2. A red, semi-sweet, semi-sparkling wine made from the Brachetto grape.

Brachetto d'Asti (I.)

1. A district around Asti, in the Piedmont region, which produces:

2. A red, semi-sparkling, slightly sweet wine made from the Brachetto grape.

Bramaterra DOC (I.)

1. A village and district west of Gattinara, in the Piedmont region, which produces:

2. A red wine made from 50-70% Nebbiolo grapes blended with Croatina, Bonarda and Vespolina grapes.

Branaire-Ducru, Château (F.)

An estate in St.-Julien, Haut-Médoc district, Bordeaux region; during the 18th century known successively as Château Duluc and Château Branaire-du-Luc; classified in 1855 as a *Quatrième Cru*. 18,000 cases. 120 acres.

Brancelho (P.)

A red grape grown in the Monção district, Vinho Verde region.

Brancellao (Sp.)

A red grape grown in the Galicia region of northwestern Spain.

Brand (F.)

A *Grand cru* vineyard in Turckheim, Haut-Rhin district, Alsace region. 75 acres.

Brander Vineyard (U.S.)   1979

A small winery in Santa Ynez, Santa Barbara County, California; produces a Cabernet Sauvignon wine blended with Merlot and Cabernet Franc grapes, and a Sauvignon Blanc wine blended with Sémillon grapes. 5,000 cases. 40 acres.

Brandluft (F.)

A vineyard in Mittelbergheim, Bas-Rhin district, Alsace region.

brandy

A strong alcoholic drink made from distilled wine, and is produced in most regions of the world. Cognac and Armagnac are the finest examples of brandies.

Brane-Cantenac, Château (F.)

An estate in Cantenac-Margaux, Haut-Médoc district, Bordeaux; in the early 19th century known as Château de Gorce; classified in 1855 as a *Deuxième Cru*. 30,000 cases. 210 acres.

Braquet (F.)

A local red grape grown in Bellet, in the Provence region.

Braucol *also* Brocol (F.)

A local red grape grown in the Gaillac district, Southwest region.

Brauneberg (G.)

A village in the Mosel-Saar-Ruwer region, Bereich Bernkastel, Grosslage Kurfürstlay, formerly called Dusemond. The vineyards are Hasenläufer, Juffer, Juffer-Sonnenuhr, Kammer, Klostergarten, Mandelgraben, and Filzen, which was added later. 700 acres.

Brazil

A country in South America. Vines have been planted since the 17th century. It has 170,000 acres of vines; 20% are *Vitis vinifera*, the rest are hybrids of *Vitis labrusca*. It produces Barbera, Bonarda, Merlot, Syrah, Moscato, Riesling and Trebbiano grapes. Martini and Rossi, Cinzano and Moët & Chandon have operations there.

Brédif, Marc (F.)   1893

An estate and merchant in Rochecorbon, Touraine region, Loire Valley; produces Vouvray wine.

Breganze DOC (I.)

1. A village and district north of Vicenza, in the Veneto region, which produces:

2. Numerous varietal and blended wines; the Bianco is made from 85% Tocai, the Rosso from 85% Merlot; the varietals are stated on the labels.

Breisgau (G.)

A *Bereich*, one of seven, in the Baden region. The *Grosslagen* are Burg Lichteneck, Burg Zähringen and Schutterlindenberg. 3,500 acres.

Brenner (G.)

A fungus disease of the vine occuring mostly in Germany; it causes browning between the veins of basal leaves.

Brenot Père et Fils (F.)   1876

An estate in Santenay, Côte de Beaune, Burgundy; owns Bâtard-Montrachet – .8 acre, Santenay Les Gravières – 1.2 acres, some Montrachet, Puligny-Montrachet, Chassagne-Montrachet and Santenay (white).

Brentano'sche Gutsverwaltung Winkel, Baron von (G.)   1804

An estate in Oestrich-Winkel, Rheingau region; owns vineyards in Winkel: Hasensprung, Jesuitgarten, Gutenberg and Dachsberg. 25 acres.

Bresparolo (I.)

A white grape grown in the Breganze district, in the Veneto region; also called Vespaiolo.

Bressande, La (F.)

A *Premier Cru* vineyard in Rully, Côte Chalonnaise district, Burgundy.

Bressandes, Les (F.)

A *Premier Cru* vineyard in Beaune, Côte de Beaune district, Burgundy. 50 acres.

Bressandes, Les (F.)

A *Grand Cru* vineyard in Aloxe-Corton, Côte de Beaune district, Burgundy. 43 acres.

Bressardes, Les *also* Bessardes (F.)

One of the best vineyards in Hermitage, northern Rhône region; grows red grapes.

Breton (F.)

The local name for the Cabernet Franc grape in the Touraine and Anjou regions.

Bretterins, Les (F.)

A *Premier Cru* vineyard in Auxey-Duresses, Côte de Beaune district, Burgundy; also called La Chapelle. 5 acres.

Bretzenheim (G.)

A village in the Nahe region, Bereich Kreuznach, Grosslage Kronenberg. The vineyards are: Felsenköpfchen, Hofgut, Pastorei and Schlossgarten.

Breuil, Château du (F.)

An estate in Cissac, Haut-Médoc district, Bordeaux; classified in 1978 as a *Cru Bourgeois*. 12,000 cases. 50 acres.

Briante, Château de (F.)

An estate in Brouilly, Beaujolais district, Burgundy.

Briarcrest (U.S.)

The name of a 100% Cabernet wine made by the Clos du Bois winery, Sonoma County, California.

bricco (I.)

A steep incline or hill.

Bricco del Drago (I.)

A red wine from San Rocco Seno d'Elvio, near Alba, in the Piedmont region; made from a blend of Dolcetto and Nebbiolo grapes.

Bricco Manzoni (I.)

A red wine from Monforte d'Alba, south of Alba, in the south central Piedmont region; made from a blend of Dolcetto and Nebbiolo grapes.

Bridane, Château La (F.)

An estate in St.-Julien, Haut-Médoc district, Bordeaux; classified in 1978 as a *Cru Bourgeois*. 6,000 cases. 40 acres.

Bridgehampton Winery (U.S.) vines 1978, 1st wine 1982

A winery in Bridgehampton, South Fork, Long Island region, New York; only the first vintage was vinified at another winery; produces Chardonnay, Riesling, Pinot Noir, Gamay, Merlot and other wines. 2,500 cases. 26 acres.

Bright (C.)   1874

An old winery near Niagara Falls, Ontario, specializing in *vinifera* varietals, especially Pinot Noir and Chardonnay. 1.200 acres.

Brillette, Château (F.)

An estate in Moulis, Haut-Médoc district, Bordeaux; classified in 1978 as a *Cru Grand Bourgeois*. 8,000 cases. 70 acres.

Brindisi DOC (I.)   DOC since 1979

1. A famous seaport and district in the southern Apulia region, which produces:

2. Red and rosé wines made from the Negroamaro grape with some Malvasia Nera, Sussumariello, Montepulciano and Sangiovese grapes.

Bristol Cream (E.)

A sweetened old Oloroso Sherry bottled in Bristol, England by Harvey's.

Bristol Milk (E.)

An Oloroso Sherry, less sweet than Bristol Cream, bottled by Harvey's, of Bristol, England.

British Columbia (C.)

A province of Canada; the Okanagau Valley produces wines from hybrid, *vinifera* and *labrusca* grapes.

Brix (U.S.)

A hydrometer scaled to measure the percentage of sugar, by weight, in grape juice; similar to Balling; a number followed by the word "Brix" represents the percentage of sugar in the juice or the wine.

Brocard et Fils, E. (F.)   1890

A merchant in Beaune, Côte de Beaune district, Burgundy.

Brocard, Louis (F.)

An estate in Couchey, Côte de Nuits district, Burgundy. 10 acres, including 2.5 acres of vines in Fixin.

Brochon (F.)

A minor commune in the Côte de Nuits district, between Fixin and Gevrey-Chambertin, Burgundy. Some red wines are sold as Gevrey-Chambertin, the rest as Côte de Nuits-Villages or Bourgogne.

Brocol *also* Braucol (F.)

A local red grape grown in the Gaillac district, Southwest region.

Brokenwood (Aus.)   1973

A small winery in New South Wales, Lower Hunter Valley district; produces Cabernet, Hermitage, Pinot Noir and Chardonnay wines. 2,000 cases. 45 acres.

Brolio, Castello di (I.)

A well-known producer of Chianti Classico. See **Ricasoli, Barone.**

Bronte Winery (U.S.)   1933, winery 1943

A winery near Hartford, southeastern Michigan; French hybrids were planted there in 1953 and produced the first commercial wine in the U.S. labeled as a French hybrid grape (Baco); also produces sparkling wines. 50 acres.

Brookside Vineyard Company (U.S.) 1832

A large winery in Guasti, Cucamonga district, San Bernardino County, southern California; produces nearly 100 wines under various labels, including Assumption Abbey, Guasti and Vache. 800,000 cases. 3,000 acres.

Brotherhood Winery (U.S.)   1839

A winery in Washingtonville, Hudson River Valley region, New York State; produces wines from native *labrusca* grapes bought from various parts of New York.

Brouillards (F.)

A *Premier Cru* vineyard (in part) in Volnay, Côte de Beaune district, Burgundy. 15 acres.

Brouilly AOC (F.)

The most southerly of the *Crus Beaujolais*, made up of several communes, including

Cercié and Odénas, in the Beaujolais district, Burgundy. The center section, around Mont Brouilly, is called Côte de Brouilly and has its own AOC; produces red wine made from Gamay grapes. 2,500 acres.

Broustet, Château (F.)

An estate in Barsac, Sauternes district, Bordeaux; classified in 1855 (then called Broustet-Nérac, when Château Nairac was a part of Broustet) as a *Deuxième Cru*. 3,000 cases. 40 acres.

Brown Brothers (Aus.)   1889

An old winery in Milawa, northeastern Victoria; produces Cabernet, Shiraz, Rhine Riesling, Chardonnay, Chenin Blanc, Traminer, Sémillon, sweet Muscat and many other wines from their own and purchased grapes. 75,000 cases. 300 acres.

Brown Sherry (Sp.)

A dark, sweet, oloroso sherry.

broyage (F.)

Crushing or mashing (of grapes).

Bruce, David Winery (U.S.) planted 1961, winery 1964

A small winery in Los Gatos, in the Santa Cruz mountains, Santa Clara County, California; produces Cabernet, Pinot Noir, Zinfandel, Petite Sirah, Johannisberg Riesling, Chardonnay and Pinot Noir Blanc wines. 18,000 cases. 25 acres.

Bruck, Lionel J. (F.)   1807

An estate and merchant in Nuits-St.-Georges, Côte de Nuits district, Burgundy (now controlled by Cruse); owns Corton Clos du Roi – 9 acres and Nuits-St.-Georges Les St.-Georges – .7 acre.

Brugo, Agostino (I.)   1894

An estate in Romagnano Sesia, Piedmont region; produces Gattinara, Ghemme and Spanna wines.

Brûlées, Aux (F.)

A *Premier Cru* vineyard in Vosne-Romanée, Côte de Nuits district, Burgundy. 10 acres.

Bründlmayer, Weingut (A.)   1581

An estate in Langenlois, Lower Austria region; produces Grüner Veltliner, Müller-Thurgau, Rheinriesling and Ruländer wines. 11,000 cases. 85 acres.

Brunello (I.)

A red grape, related to the Sangiovese, grown in Montalcino, in the Tuscany region; also called Sangiovese Grosso.

Brunello di Montalcino DOCG (I.)

1. A district around Montalcino, south of Siena, in the Tuscany region, which produces:
2. A famous red wine made from the Sangiovese Grosso (Brunello) grape, capable of long aging, 50 years or more.

Brunesco (I.)

A red wine from the Colli Altotiberini district, in the northern Umbria region.

Brunet, André (F.)

An estate in Meursault, Côte de Beaune district, Burgundy. 20 acres, including Meursault Les Charmes – 4 acres, Les Genevrières – .3 acre, Volnay Les Santenots – .8 acre and Meursault *Premier Cru* (red) – 1.7 acres.

Brunet, Cuvée (F.)

A red wine from the Hospices de Beaune, Côte de Beaune district, Burgundy. The *cuvée* is composed of the following vineyards in Beaune: Les Teurons – 2 acres, Les Bressandes – 1.5 acres, La Mignotte – 2.2 acres and Les Cents Vignes – 1 acre. 550 cases.

brunissure (F.)

"Browning," an adverse condition of the vine in which leaf-browning occurs, caused by overproduction due to insufficient pruning; the leaves drop off and the quality of the fruit suffers.

Brünnerstrasse (A.)

A narrow district between Falkenstein, north of Vienna, and Brünn, south of Vienna, in the Weinviertel district, Lower Austria region.

Brunori & Figlio, M. (I.)   1972

An estate in Jesi, the Marches region; produces Verdicchio wine.

Brusco dei Barbi (I.)

A red wine from Montalcino, in the Tuscany region; made from Brunello grapes using the *governo* process; produced by Fattoria dei Barbi.

Brussels Convervatory Grape

Another name for the Trollinger grape.

Brussonnes, Les *also* Les Brussolles (F.)

A *Premier Cru* vineyard in Chassagne-Montrachet, Côte de Beaune district, Burgundy; produces red and white wines. 44 acres.

brut (F.)

Dry, applied to Champagne. It is normally the driest style, with 0-1.5% dosage added.

bruto (P.)

"Brut," applied to sparkling wines.

Bruzzone, V.B. (I.)   1860

A winery in Strevi, Piedmont region; produces Brachetto, Dolcetto, Asti Spumante, and Gavi wines and also several other sparkling wines. 100 acres. 20,000 cases.

Bryczek, Domaine Georges (F.)

An estate in Morey-St.-Denis, Côte de Nuits district, Burgundy. 12 acres, including Morey-St.-Denis Clos-Sorbés – 8 acres, Morey- St.-Denis – 2.5 acres; also a Cuvée du Pape Jean-Paul II.

Bual (P.)

See **Boal**.

Buçaco (P.)

Red and white wines from the Palace Hotel do Buçaco, near Luso, in the Bairrada region, south of Oporto. 35 acres.

Bucciarossa (I.)

A red wine from the Piedmont region; produced by Vallana.

Bucelas *also* **Bucellas (P.)**

1. A village and district north of Lisbon, which produces:

2. A dry white wine made from Arinto (65%) and Esgana Cão grapes.

Buckingham Valley Vineyards (U.S.) 1966

A small winery in Buckingham, Pennsylvania; produces wines from hybrid grapes. 10 acres.

Budai (H.)

A white grape.

Buehler Vineyards (U.S.)   1978

A small winery in St. Helena, Napa Valley, California; produces Cabernet, Zinfandel, Pinot Blanc and Muscat wines. 8,000 cases. 60 acres.

**Buena Vida Vineyard (U.S.)   1978,
                                                   vines 1974**

A winery in Springstown, in central Texas; produces wines made from French Hybrid grapes.

Buena Vista Winery (U.S.)   1857, 1943

A winery in Sonoma, Sonoma Valley, California; closed in the 1870's, reopened in 1943; originally built by Agoston Haraszthy; produces Cabernet, Zinfandel, Pinot Noir, Sylvaner, Green Hungarian, Riesling, Fumé Blanc and Chardonnay wines. 100,000 cases. 700 acres in Carneros Creek district.

Buergen (F.)

A vineyard in Zellenberg, Haut-Rhin district, Alsace region.

Buffalo (U.S.)

A red hybrid grape grown in the southeastern U.S.

Buffet, Mme. (F.)

An estate in Volnay, Côte de Beaune district, Burgundy. 15 acres, including Volnay Champans – 1.2 acres, Clos des Chênes – 2.5 acres and Pommard Les Rugiens – .3 acre.

Bugey (F.)

A district in the Savoie region of southeastern France; produces red, white, rosé and sparkling wines under various Vin du Bugey VDQS designations.

Buhl, Weingut Reichsrat von (G.)

An estate in Deidesheim, Rheinpfalz region; owns vineyards in Forst, Deidesheim and Ruppertsberg. 240 acres.

Buisson (F.)

An estate in Saint-Romain, Côte de Beaune district, Burgundy; produces red and white Saint-Romain wines. 12 acres.

Bukettraube (G.)

A white hybrid grape from Germany grown in South Africa.

Bükkalja (H.)

A district in northeastern Hungary; produces white wines made from Léanyka, Wälschriesling and Mézesfehér grapes. Rated officially as White Wine of Excellent Quality. 10.000 acres.

Bulgaria

A country in Eastern Europe; wines marketed here are varietals and brand names for blended wines. Local grapes such as Misket, Dimiat, Kadarka, Mavrud, Pamid and some western European grapes are grown. 130 million gallons.

bulk process

A process of making sparkling wines by fermenting the wine a second time in tanks, or large closed vats, instead of in individual bottles; similar to the *Charmat* process.

Bully Hill (U.S.)   1970

An estate in Hammondsport, Finger Lakes region, New York State; owned by Walter S. Taylor; produces varietals and blends from hybrid grapes, some *labrusca* varieties and bottle-fermented brut champagne. 25,000 cases.

Bundesweinprämierung (G.)

The national wine award, given each year to the best wines of Germany; awarded by the *Deutsche Landwirtschafts Gesellschaft* (DLG).

Bundner Herrschaft (Sw.)

A district in eastern Switzerland, near Liechtenstein; produces wines made from the Blauburgunder and Completer grapes.

bung

A stopper for a wine barrel or cask, made of wood or other material, sometimes wrapped with linen to acheive a tighter seal, and sometimes acting as an escape valve for CO_2 gas.

Buonamico, Fattoria del (I.)   1954

An estate in Montecarlo, Tuscany region; produces Montecarlo Bianco and Rosso di Cercatoia wines. 7,000 cases. 50 acres.

Bura (I.)

A local name for the Tocai Friulano grape in the Colli Bolognesi district, Emilia-Romagna region.

Burdin, Joanny (F.)

A grower who, with his son, Remy, developed Burdin 4503, a red hybrid grape, Burdin 5201, a white wine grape, and Burdin 7705 (Florental), a red grape.

Burg Hornberg, Weingut (G.)

An estate in Neckarzimmern, Baden region; owns vineyards in Neckarzimmern and Michelfeld. 50 acres.

Burgaw (U.S.)

A red muscadine grape, a *Vitis rotundifolia* variety.

Burgenland (A.)

One of 4 regions in Austria, south of Vienna, along the eastern border. It was part of Hungary until 1921. 75,000 acres.

Burger (G.)

A German white *vinifera* grape grown in California; also called Monbadon.

Bürgermeister (G.)

A mayor.

Bürgerspital zum Heiligen Geist (G.) 1319

A large estate in Würzburg, Franken region; owns vineyards in Würzburg (especially the Stein vineyard), Randersacker and other towns. 335 acres.

Burgess Cellars (U.S.)   1943, 1972

A winery northeast of St. Helena, Pope Valley district, Napa Valley, California; was originally Souverain Cellars; produces Cabernet, Zinfandel, Chardonnay and Johannisberg Riesling wines from their own and purchased grapes. Bell Canyon Cellars is the 2nd label. 30,000 cases. 75 acres.

Burghoffer Père et Fils (F.)

An estate in Mittelwihr, Haut-Rhin district, Alsace region. 15 acres, including Mandelberg vineyard – 1 acre.

Burgundy *also* Bourgogne (F.)

1. A famous historical wine region in eastern France, a narrow stretch of important vineyards 100 miles long, from Dijon south to Lyon, but also including the Chablis and Auxerrois districts near Auxerre, some 60 miles northwest of Dijon. The main districts are: Chablis, in the north, Côte d'Or, divided into Côte de Nuits and Côte de Beaune, the Côte Chalonnaise, or Chalonnais, Mâcon, or Mâconnais, and Beaujolais. The region produces great red wines from the Pinot Noir grape, equally great wines from the Chardonnay grape, Beaujolais wines from the Gamay grape and Chablis wines from the Chardonnay grape. Some rosé and sparkling wines are also produced. 100,000 acres. 20 million cases.

2. A generic red wine made in California, New York State and other regions of the world made from a blend of grapes and usually sold in jugs as an inexpensive table wine.

Bürklin-Wolf, Weingut Dr. (G.)

An estate in Wackenheim, Rheinpfalz region; owns extensive vineyards in Wackenheim, Forst, Deidesheim and Ruppertsberg. 250 acres.

Burle, Edmond (F.)

An estate in Gigondas, southern Rhône region; produces Gigondas and Vacqueyras wines.

Buschino (I.)

A white wine from the northeastern Veneto region, on the Piave River, made from Picolit and Verduzzo grapes.

Bussière, Clos (F.)

A *Premier Cru* vineyard in Morey-St.-Denis, Côte de Nuits district, Burgundy. 7.5 acres.

butt (E.)

A standard cask, variable in size, used in Britain, having the capacity of 491 liters (129.6 gallons) for ale, Sherry or Málaga and 573 liters (151.3 gallons) for any other wine.

Buttafuoco DOC (I.)

"Sparks of Fire," a red wine, sometimes semi-sparkling, from Castana, Oltrepò Pavese district, in the southwestern Lombardy region; made from Uva Rara, Croatina and Barbera grapes.

Butteaux (F.)

A *Premier Cru* vineyard in Chablis, Chablis district, Burgundy; it is usually considered part of the Montmains vineyard.

butyric acid

One of several volatile acids present in wine in small amounts.

Buxy (F.)

A commune included in the Monfagny AOC, in the Côte Chalonnaise district, Burgundy.

Buzbağ (T.)

A red wine from eastern Turkey, near Elâziğ, made from the Öküzgözü grape.

Buzzetto (I.)

A white grape grown in the Liguria region; also called the Lumassina grape.

Buzzetto di Quiliano (I.)

A white wine made in several villages around Quiliano, near Savona, in the Liguria region, made from the Buzzetto grape.

Buzzinelli, Fratelli (I.)

An estate in Cormons, Friuli-Venezia Giulia region; produces Collio wines.

By, Château de (F.)

An estate in Bégadan, Médoc district, Bordeaux; classified in 1978 as a *Cru Bourgeois*. 4,000 cases. 20 acres.

Bybline (Gr.)

An ancient Greek or Phoenician sweet wine, originally from Byblos, in northern Syria, and made in Thrace; mentioned by Hesiod.

Bynum, Davis Winery (U.S.)   1973

A small winery in Healdsburg, Russian River Valley, northern Sonoma County, California; produces Pinot Noir, Cabernet, Merlot, Petite Syrah, Zinfandel, Chardonnay, Fumé Blanc, Gewürztraminer wines and Sherries. 20 acres. 20,000 cases.

Byrd Vineyards (U.S.)   1972

A winery in Myersville, Maryland; produces wines made from *vinifera* grapes (Cabernet, Chardonnay, Sauvignon Blanc, Gewürztraminer) and hybrid grapes. 15 acres.

Byrrh (F.)

A well-known French brand of apéritif made from wine, with quinine and brandy added.

C

CK (U.S.)

A brand name for jug wines from the Charles Krug Winery (C.Mondavi) in Napa Valley, California.

CVNE (Sp.) 1879

Compañia Vinícola del Norte de España, a large winery in Haro, Rioja Alta; produces several wines: Cune, Imperial, Viña Real, etc. 330,000 cases. 700 acres.

ca' (I.)

Casa (house).

Caballero S.A., Luis (Sp.) 1795

A Sherry producer in Puerto de Santa Maria; produces Sherries under its own name and that of Burdon.

Cabanne, Château La (F.)

An estate in Pomerol, Bordeaux. 3,000 cases. 20 acres.

Cabardès VDQS *also* **Cotes du Cabardès et de l'Orbiel (F.)**

A designation for red and rosé wines from north of Carcassonne, in the Languedoc region; made from Carignan, Cinsault, Grenache, Mourvèdre and other grapes.

Caberat (Br.)

In Brazil, the name for the Cabernet grape.

Cabernet

The shorter name for the Cabernet Sauvignon grape (or wine), especially in Bordeaux and California. In some other regions of France, however, especially in the Loire Valley, it usually refers to the Cabernet Franc grape. In Italy it may mean either grape or both grapes blended together.

Cabernet d'Anjou AOC *also* **Cabernet d'Anjou-Val-de-Loire (F.)**

A designation for rosé wine from the Anjou region; made from Cabernet Franc, Cabernet Sauvignon, or both.

Cabernet Franc (F.)

An important red grape, grown in the Bordeaux region, especially in St.-Émilion; also grown in the Loire Valley for red and rosé wines; also called Bouchet or Gros-Bouchet in St.-Émilion and Pomerol, Bouchy in Madiran and Breton in the Saumur and the Touraine (Loire Valley).

Cabernet de Saumur AOC (F.)

A designation for rosé wine from the Saumur district, Anjou region; made from Cabernet Sauvignon, Cabernet Franc, or both.

Cabernet Sauvignon

A red grape grown principally in Bordeaux as well as California and Australia, and more recently, in Italy; it is frequently blended with Merlot and/or other grapes; in California also used to make rosé and even Port wines.

Cabet, Cuvée (F.)

A wine from the Hospices de Nuits, Côte de Nuits district, Burgundy. The *cuvée* is composed of Nuits-St.-Georges Didiers St.-Georges – 5 acres (combined with Cuvée Jacques Duret).

Cabrières VDQS (F.)

A district around Béziers, Coteaux du Languedoc district, Languedoc region (the

Midi); produces rosé wines made from Carignan, Cinsault and Grenache grapes.

Cacaboué (F.)

A rare, local white grape grown in the Savoie region.

Cacc'e Mmitte di Lucera DOC (I.)

Italian dialect for "Drink it down and fill it up again," a red wine from Lucera, in the northern Apulia region; made from Uva di Troia, Montepulciano, Sangiovese, Malvasia Nera, Trebbiano Toscano, Bombino Bianco and Malvasia Bianco grapes.

Cacchiano, Castello di (I.)   12th cent.

An old estate in Monti, Tuscany region; produces Chianti Classico wines.

Cáceres (Sp.)

A district and province in the Extremadura region of southwestern Spain; produces red and white wines.

Cáceres, Bodegas Marqués de (Sp.)   1970

A French-influenced winery in Cenicero, Rioja Alta; produces red and white wines under several brand names from grapes grown by local growers. 200,000 cases. 1,500 acres.

Cache cellars (U.S.)   1978

A small winery in Davis, Solano County, California; produces Cabernet, Zinfandel, Pinot Noir and Chardonnay wines.

Cadarka also **Cadarca, Kadarka (R.)**

A red grape grown in the Banat region, the same grape as the Hungarian and Bulgarian Kadarka.

cadastro (P.)

A register of vineyards.

**Cadenasso Winery (U.S.)   1906, new site
                                              1926**

A winery in Fairfield, Solano County, California; produces Cabernet, Pinot Noir, Zinfandel, Grignolino, Chenin Blanc and Grey Riesling wines. 260 acres.

Cadet-Bon, Château (F.)

An estate in St.-Émilion, Bordeaux; classified in 1955 as a *Grand Cru Classé*. 1,000 cases. 10 acres.

Cadet-Piola, Château (F.)

An estate in St.-Émilion, Bordeaux; classified in 1955 as a *Grand Cru Classé*. 4,500 cases. 20 acres.

Cadillac AOC (F.)

1. A town on the right bank of the Garonne River, opposite Sauternes, in the Bordeaux region, which produces:

2. Sweet, white wines, made from Sauvignon, Sémillon and Muscadelle grapes.

Cadlolo Winery (U.S.)   1913

A large winery in Lodi, San Joaquin Valley, California; produces bulk wines, from their own and purchased grapes. 5 acres.

Caecuban (Lat.)

An ancient Roman wine, mentioned by Horace and Athanaeus.

Cafaggio, Villa (I.)

An estate in Panzano, Tuscany; produces Chianti Classico wine. 11,000 cases. 85 acres.

Cagnasso Winery (U.S.)   1977

A winery in Marlboro, Hudson River Valley region, New York; produces wines from hybrid grapes. 10 acres.

Cagnina (I.)

1. A local name for the red Canaiolo Nero grape grown in the eastern Emilia-Romagna region, which produces:

2. A sweet red wine from Bertinoro, in the eastern Emilia-Romagna region, made from the Cagnina grape.

Cahors AOC (F.)   AOC since 1971

1. A town and district, north of Toulouse, in the Southwest region, which produces:

2. A red wine made from the Malbec, Merlot, Tannat and Jurançon grapes.

3. In the Bordeaux region, another name for the Malbec grape.

Cailleret, *also* Chassagne (F.)

A *Premier Cru* vineyard in Chassagne-Montrachet, Côte de Beaune district, Burgundy; produces white wine only. 15 acres (including En Cailleret).

Cailleret *also* Clos du Cailleret (F.)

A *Premier Cru* vineyard in Puligny-Montrachet, Côte de Beaune district, Burgundy. 13.5 acres.

Cailleret, En (F.)

A *Premier Cru* vineyard in Chassagne-Montrachet, Côte de Beaune district, Burgundy; produces red wine only. 15 acres, including Cailleret (Chassagne).

Cailleret(s), En (F.)

A *Premier Cru* vineyard in Volnay, Côte de Beaune district, Burgundy. 7 acres.

Cailleret Dessus (F.)

A *Premier Cru* vineyard in Volnay, Côte de Beaune district, Burgundy. 37 acres.

Caillerets, Les (F.)

A *Premier Cru* vineyard in Meursault, Côte de Beaune district, Burgundy. 3.5 acres.

Cailles, Les (F.)

A *Premier Cru* vineyard in Nuits-St.-Georges, Côte de Nuits district, Burgundy. 9.5 acres.

Caillet, Georges (F.)

An estate in Pommard, Côte de Beaune, Burgundy. 16 acres, including Pommard les Charmots – 1.2 acres and Beaune Premier Cru.

Caillou, Château (F.)

An estate in Barsac, Sauternes district, Bordeaux; classified in 1855 as a *Deuxième Cru*. 35 acres. 3,700 cases.

Caillou Blanc de Château Talbot (F.)

A white wine of Château Talbot, in St.-Julien, Haut-Médoc region, Bordeaux; made from Sauvignon Blanc grapes. 5 acres.

Cain Cellars (U.S.)　　　　　　1981

A winery in St. Helena, Napa Valley, California; produces Cabernet, Merlot and Sauvignon wines. 12,000 cases. 70 acres.

Cainhos (P.)

A red grape grown in the Vinho Verde region.

Caiño (Sp.)

A red grape grown in Galicia, in northwestern Spain.

Cairanne (F.)

One of the *communes* of the Côtes du Rhône-Villages district, in the southern Rhône region; produces red, white and rosé wines.

Cakebread Cellars (U.S.)　　　　1973

A small winery in Oakville, Napa Valley, California; produces Cabernet, Zinfandel, Sauvignon Blanc and Chardonnay wines. 15,000 cases. 22 acres.

Calabrese (I.)

A red grape grown in Sicily.

Calabria (I.)

A region in southern Italy, the "toe of the boot." Cirò is the most well-known of the DOC wines.

Calagraño (Sp.)

A white grape grown in the Rioja region; also called Cayetana in southwestern Spain.

calcic salt

See **casein.**

Calcinaia, Villa (I.)　　　　　　1523

An estate in Greve, Tuscany; produces Chianti Classico, Bianco Secco and Vin Santo wines. 23,000 cases. 75 acres.

Caldaro *also* **Lago di Caldaro,** *and* **Kalterersee DOC (I.)**

1. A lake and district south of Bolzano, in the Trentino-Alto Adige region, which produces:

2. A red wine made from the Schiava Grossa, Schiava Gentile and Schiava Grigia (Grossvernatsch, Kleinvernatsch and Grauvernatsch) grapes; some Pinot Nero (Blauburgunder) and Lagrein grapes may be included.

caldaro (I.)

An almond-flavored wine from the southern Trentino-Alto Adige region.

Cálem & Figlio Ltd., A.A. (P.)   **1859**

A Port producer in Porto. 50 acres, including Quinta da Foz and 3 other vineyards; the wine is made from their own and purchased grapes.

Calera Wine Company (U.S.)   **1975**

A winery in Hollister, San Benito County, California; produces Pinot Noir, Zinfandel and Zinfandel Essence (sweet) wines. 6,000 cases. 25 acres.

California (U.S.)

The most important wine-producing state in the U. S.; the most well-known regions are Napa and Sonoma counties. 750,000 acres.

California Growers Winery (U.S.)   **1936**

A winery in Tulare, Tulare County, San Joaquin Valley, California; produces many varietal wines as well as sherries and sparkling wines. 600,000 cases. 2,000 acres.

California Wine Company (U.S.)   **1937**

A former winery in Cloverdale, northern Sonoma County, California; now the owner of Bandiera, Arroyo Sonoma, Sage Creek and Potter Valley wineries.

Calissanne, Château de (F.)

An estate in Lançon-de-Provence, in the Provence region.

Calissano & Figli, Luigi (I.)   **1872**

A winery in Alba, Piedmont region; produces Barolo, Barbaresco, sparkling and other wines. 500,000 cases.

Callaway Vineyard and Winery (U.S.)   **planted 1969, winery 1974**

A winery in Temecula, Riverside County, southern California; produces Cabernet, Zinfandel, Petite Sirah, Johannisberg Riesling, Chenin Blanc, Santana (a late-harvest Riesling), Sauvignon Blanc and Sweet Nancy (a botryticized Chenin Blanc) wines. 80,000 cases. 140 acres.

Calmeria (U.S.)

A white *vinifera* grape developed in 1950 from the Almeria grape.

Calò, Giuseppe (I.)   **1938**

An estate in Alezio, Apulia region; produces several red and rosé wines. 12,000 cases.

Calon-Ségur, Château (F.)

An estate in St.-Estèphe, Haut-Médoc district, Bordeaux; classified in 1855 as a *Troisième Cru*. 25,000 cases. 145 acres.

Calouères (F.)

A *Premier Cru* vineyard in Morey-St.-Denis, Côte de Nuits district, Burgundy. 3.5 acres.

Calvet & Cie. (F.)   **1818**

A large company in Bordeaux, at one time a single company before a son created another Calvet company in Beaune, Burgundy; owns several châteaux in Bordeaux.

Calvet S.A. (F.)   **1870**

A large firm in Beaune, Burgundy, built by the son of the original Calvet as a branch of the Bordeaux firm, and later separated.

Camaralet (F.)

A local white grape grown in southwestern France, and used in making Jurançon wines.

Camarate (P.)

1. A red grape, also called Mortagua; grown in the Dão and Ribatejo regions.

2. A red wine made near Setúbal, in central Portugal; made from Periquita, Merlot and Cabernet Sauvignon grapes.

Camarèse (F.)

A local red grape grown in the Côtes du Rhône-Villages district, southern Rhône region.

Cambas, Andrew (Gr.)   1869

A merchant in Athens; produces a wide range of still and sparkling wines.

Cambiaso Winery (U.S.)   1934

A winery in Healdsburg, Russian River Valley, northern Sonoma County, California; produces Barbera, Cabernet, Petite Sirah and Sauvignon Blanc wines as well as jug blends from their own and purchased grapes. 60 acres. 175,000 cases.

Camensac, Château (F.)

An estate in St.-Laurent, Haut-Medoc district, Bordeaux; classified in 1855 as a *Cinquième Cru*. 22,000 cases. 150 acres.

Camigliano (I.)

An estate in Montalcino, Tuscany region; produces Bianco, Brunello and Rosso wines. 33,000 cases. 170 acres.

Camilleri, Giuseppe Steri (I.)   1966

An estate in Naro, Sicily; produces Steri Bianco and Rosso wines. 65 acres.

Camina (G.)

A red grape – a cross of Portugieser and Spätburgunder; developed at the Federal Research Institute, Geilweilerhof, Germany.

Campania (I.)

A region around Naples, in southwestern Italy; produces well-known wines, including Lacrima Christi, Falerno, Greco di Tufo and Taurasi.

Campaux, Domaine des (F.)

An estate in Bormes-lès-Mimosas, in the Provence region.

Campbell's (Aus.)   1870

A winery in Rutherglen, Murray River Valley, Victoria; produces Shiraz, sweet Muscat, Tokay and Port wines. 25,000 cases. 100 acres.

Campbell's Early (U.S.)

An American red grape of the *lambrusca* family used in making red wine in Washington; also called Island Bell.

Campidano di Terralba DOC (I.)

1. A district around Terralba, south of Oristano, in southwestern Sardinia, which produces:

2. A red wine made from 80% Bovale grapes blended with some Pascale, Greco Nero and Monica grapes.

Campiglione (I.)

A dry red wine made near Cavour, southwest of Torino, in the central Piedmont region; made from a blend of Nebbiolo and other grapes.

Campii Raudi (I.)

One of the vineyards and wines of A. Vallana, a producer of Spanna wines in the Piedmont region.

Campo Fiorin (I.)

A red wine from the Valpolicella district, Veneto region; a Valpolicella wine mixed with the lees of Amarone, re-fermented into a more full-bodied wine; made by Masi.

Campo Romano (I.)

A red wine made near Alba, in the south central Piedmont region; made from Freisa and Pinot Nero grapes.

Campo Viejo S.A., Bodegas (I.)   1963

A large winery in Logroño, Rioja Alta region; produces wines under several brand names from their own and purchased grapes and purchased wine. 700 acres.

Camus Père et Fils (F.)

An estate in Gevrey-Chambertin, Côte de Nuits district, Burgundy. 42 acres, including Chambertin – 4 acres, Latricières-Chambertin – 3.7 acres, Charmes-Chambertin – 7.5 acres, Mazoyères-Chambertin – 10 acres and Mazis-Chambertin – 1 acre.

Canada

A country in North America; since it is north of the U.S. it produces wines mostly from *labrusca* grapes, and very few from hybrid and *vinifera* grape varieties. 25,000 acres.

Canada Muscat (U.S.)   1961

A New York State white, hybrid grape – a cross of Hamburg Muscat and Hubbard.

Canaiolo *also* Canaiolo Nero (I.)

A red grape, one of many used in Chianti and other red wines from Tuscany, Rubesco wine from Umbria and other wines from Latium. Also called Cagnina.

Canaiolo Bianco (I.)

A white grape grown in Tuscany.

Canaiolo Nero (I.)

A red grape, the same as Canaiolo. Also called Cagnina in the Emilia-Romagna region.

Cañamero (Sp.)

1. A town southwest of Guadalupe, in the Cáceres district of the Extremadura region, which produces:

2. Red and white wines; the reds are made from Garnacha, Morisca, Palomino Negro and Tinto Fino grapes; the whites are made from Alarije, Bomita, Airén and Marfil grapes, frequently made into a Sherry-style wine, with up to 15% alcohol.

Canandaigua Wine Company (U.S.)

A large winery in Canandaigua, Finger Lakes region, New York State; produces branded, blended wines such as "Rich-

ard's Wild Irish Rose" and "Virginia Dare." 300 acres.

Canard-Duchêne (F.)   1868

A Champagne producer in Ludes, south of Reims; the *cuvée de prestige* is Charles VII Brut (since 1968). 2.3 million bottles. 125 acres.

Canary (Sp.)

A wine from the Canary Islands, off the coast of North Africa, well-known in the Elizabethan era, mentioned by Shakespeare and Ben Johnson. Known as Canary Sack and Palma Sack.

Candia dei Colli Apuani DOC (I.)

1. A new district near Carrara, in the northwestern corner of the Tuscany region, which produces:

2. White wine made from Vermentino and Albarola grapes.

cane

A mature shoot of the vine, which bears leaves and fruit.

Cane Ridge (U.S.)

A label used by the Colcord Winery, in Paris, Kentucky; produces wines from hybrid grapes. 37 acres.

Canepa, Viña José (Ch.)

A large winery in Camino lo Sierra, in the Maipo Valley, central Chile; produces Cabernet Sauvignon, Sémillon, Moscatel and other wines. 1,200 acres. 500,000 cases.

cannellino (I.)

Semi-sweet, referring to one of the styles of Frascati white wine; produced in the Latium region.

Canneto *also* Canneto Amaro (I.)

A red wine from Canneto Pavese, in the Oltrepò Pavese district, southern Lombardy region; made from Barbera, Croatina and other grapes.

Cannonau (I.)

1. A red grape grown in Sardinia.

2. Various red, white and rosé wines from Sardinia made from the Cannonau grape.

Cannonau di Sardegna DOC (I.)   1980

Red and rosé wines, (dry and sweet) from many areas on the island of Sardinia; made from 90% Connonau grapes and some Bovale, Carignano, Pascale, Monica and Vernaccia di San Gimignano grapes. 13 – 18% alcohol.

Canon, Château (F.)

An estate in St.-Émilion, Bordeaux; classified in 1955 as a *Premier Grand Cru*; made from 53% Merlot, 45% Cabernet Franc and some Cabernet Sauvignon grapes. 9,000 cases. 50 acres.

Canon Fronsac AOC (F.)

A designation for red wine from the Fronsac district, Bordeaux, but from the better vineyards; made from the two Cabernets, Merlot and Malbec grapes.

Canon-la-Gaffelière, Château (F.)

An estate in St.-Émilion, Bordeaux; classified in 1955 as a *Grand Cru Classé*. 12,500 cases. 50 acres.

cantara (P., Sp.)

A wine measure equal to an *arroba* in Spain and an *alqueira* in Portugal, or about 11.5 kilograms of grapes, or 16 liters of wine (about 3 gallons).

Canteiro *also* **Vinho Canteiro (P.)**

A special type of Madeira wine which is matured in the heat of the sun instead of being artificially heated in the *estufado*.

Cantemerle, Château (F.)

An estate in Macau, Haut-Medoc district, Bordeaux; classified in 1855 as a *Cinquième Cru*. 8,000 cases. 55 acres.

Cantenac (F.)

A village in the Haut-Médoc region, Bordeaux. The wines from this village are bottled under the Margaux AOC.

Cantenac-Brown, Château (F.)

An estate in Cantenac-Margaux, Haut-Médoc district, Bordeaux; classified in 1855 as a *Troisième Cru*, when it was part of Château Boyd-Cantenac; the present name was in use from 1860. 75 acres. 13,000 cases.

Cantenac-Prieuré, Château (F.)

An estate in Cantenac-Margaux, Haut-Médoc district, Bordeaux; classified in 1855 as a *Quatrième Cru*; in 1953 the name was changed to Prieuré-Lichine. 25,000 cases. 140 acres.

Canterrane, Domaine de (F.)

An estate in Trouillas, Roussillon region; produces Rivesaltes, Muscat de Rivesaltes and Côtes du Roussillon wines. 370 acres.

Cantharide, Domaine de la (F.)

An estate in Visan, southern Rhône region; produces mostly red wines from Grenache, Syrah and Mourvèdre grapes.

cantina (I.)

A winery or cellar.

Cantina del Camino (I.)

A vineyard in Maggiora, in the Piedmont region; produces a Spanna wine made by A. Vallana.

cantina sociale (I.)

A wine co-op. There are approximately 800 *cantine* in Italy, accounting for more than 40% of the wine production.

Cantrie, Château de (F.)

An estate in La Cantrie, Muscadet de Sèvre-et-Maine district, Muscadet region, Loire Valley. 25 acres.

cap

The mass of grape stems, pips and other solids which collect and rise to the top of the fermenting vat when red wine is being made.

Cap Bon (Tun.)

A district in northeastern Tunisia, known for its dry and sweet Muscat wines.

Cap Corse (F.)

1. A peninsula on the northeastern tip of Corsica, which produces:

2. Red, white and rosé wines, sweet and dry, under the Vin de Corse Coteaux du Cap Course AOC designation; made from Muscat and Vermentino grapes.

Cap-de-Mourlin, Château (F.)

An estate in St.-Émilion, Bordeaux; classified in 1955 as a *Grand Cru Classé*. 7,000 cases. 40 acres.

Capannelle (I.)

An estate in Gaiole, Tuscany region; produces Chianti Classico and Capannelle Bianco wines. 1,500 cases. 8 acres.

Caparone (U.S.)   1980

A small winery in Paso Robles, San Luis Obispo County, California; produces Cabernet, Merlot, Zinfandel and Nebbiolo wines. 4,000 cases. 10 acres.

Caparzo, Tenuta (I.)

An estate in Montalcino, Tuscany region; produces Brunello and Rosso dei Vigneti di Brunello wines. 35 acres.

capataz (Sp.)

A cellarmaster.

Cape Mentelle (Aus.)   1969

A winery in Margaret River, Western Australia; produces Cabernet, Shiraz, Zinfandel and Chenin Blanc wines. 42 acres.

Capena Bianco DOC (I.)

A white wine from Capena, in the northern Latium region, northeast of Rome; made from 55% Malvasia, 25% Trebbiano and some Bellone and Bonvino grapes.

Capezzana, Tenuta di (I.)   15th cent.

An estate in Carmignano, Tuscany region; produces Capezzana Bianco, Carmignano, Chianti Montalbano, Ghiaie, Vin Ruspo, Vin Santo and other wines. 60,000 cases. 200 acres.

Capbern, Château (F.)

An estate in St.-Estèphe, Haut-Médoc district, Bordeaux; classified in 1978 as a *Cru Grand Bourgeois Exceptionnel*. 7,500 cases. 80 acres.

Capitain-Gagnerot (F.)

An estate in Ladoix-Serrigny, Côte de Beaune, Burgundy. 20 acres, including Corton Renardes and La Maréchaude – 2 acres, Aloxe-Corton les Moutottes – 2.5 acres, Les Lolières – 4 acres, Corton-Charlemagne – .3 acre, Clos de Vougeot – .4 acre and Ladoix Côte de Beaune – 7.3 acres.

Capitans, Château des (F.)

An estate in Juliénas, Beaujolais district, Burgundy.

Capitel San Rocco (I.)

Red and white wines from San Rocco, in the Valpolicella district, Veneto region; the white wine is made from Garganega and Durello grapes, the red is a Valpolicella wine with the lees of Amarone added near the end of the fermentation.

Capitulare de Villis (Lat.)

A well-known writing of Charlemagne (742-814), containing regulations for growing grapes and making wine.

Capléon-Veyrin, Château (F.)

An estate in Listrac, Haut-Médoc district, Bordeaux; classified in 1932 as a *Cru Bourgeois*. 2,300 cases. 12 acres.

Caprettona (I.)

A local name in the Campania region for the Coda di Volpe grape.

Capri DOC (I.)

1. An island off the coast of central Campania, which produces:

2. Red and white wines, the red made mostly from Piedirosso grapes with some

Barbera and Tintore grapes, and the white made from Falanghina, Greco and Biancolella grapes.

Capriano del Colle DOC (I.)

1. A town and district south of Brescia, in the Lombardy region, which produces:

2. Red and white wines; the red is made from Sangiovese, Marzemino, Barbera and some Merlot grapes; the white is made from the Trebbiano grape.

Capuzzo, Mario (I.)

An estate in Castagnole Monferrato, southeastern Piedmont region; produces Barbera, Grignolino, Roché and Saraprino wines.

caque (F.)

A large basket used in Champagne to collect the grapes at harvest time; holds 150-175 lbs. of grapes; also called *mannequin*.

Caracchioli (I.)

An estate in San Prospero, Emilia-Romagna region; produces several types of Lambrusco wines including a Lambrusco Bianco.

Caradeux, En (F.)

A *Premier Cru* vineyard in Pernand-Vergelesses, Côte de Beaune district, Burgundy; the wine may also be sold as Aloxe-Corton. 50 acres.

carafe, carafon (F.)

A decanter or bottle for serving ordinary wines. A *carafon* is a small *carafe*.

Caramino (I.)

A red wine from Fara, near Ghemme, in the northeastern Piedmont region; made from the Nebbiolo grape.

caratello (I.)

A keg or small barrel.

carbon dioxide

A gas produced when sugar is fermented by the action of yeast, approximately equal in weight to the alcohol produced. Usually the carbon dioxide is allowed to escape except in sparkling wines, beer and cider.

carbonic maceration

To make red wine whole grapes are put into a closed vat in a carbonic gas atmosphere, although some grapes are crushed naturally by weight; fermentation takes place spontaneously within the grapes without the addition of yeasts, and carbon dioxide is produced. The process lasts 5-10 days and produces a somewhat fruity wine.

Carbonnieux, Château (F.)

An estate in Léognan, Graves district, Bordeaux; classified in 1959 as a *Cru Classé* for red and white wines. 170 acres. 20,000 cases.

carboy

A large bottle with a wicker or wooden frame; a demijohn.

Carcannieux, Château (F.)

An estate in Queyrac, Médoc district, Bordeaux; classified in 1978 as a *Cru Bourgeois*. 8,000 cases. 40 acres.

Carcavelos (P.)

1. A town and district west of Lisbon, which produces:

2. A sweet or medium-dry, fortified white wine made from Galego Dourado, Boais, Arinto and Espadeiro grapes.

Cardinal (U.S.)

A red *vinifera* grape – a cross of Flame Tokay and Ribier; bred in 1946 in California.

Cardonne, Château La (F.)

An estate in Blaignan, Médoc district, Bordeaux; classified in 1978 as a *Cru Grand Bourgeois*. Owned by Lafite-Rothschild since about 1973. 30,000 cases. 150 acres.

Carelle Dessous (F.)

A *Premier Cru* vineyard (in part) in Volnay, Côte de Beaune district, Burgundy. 5 acres.

Carelle sous la Chapelle (F.)

A *Premier Cru* vineyard in Volnay, Côte de Beaune district, Burgundy. 9 acres.

Carema DOC (I.)

1. A village and district in the northwestern Piedmont region, which produces:

2. A red wine made from the Nebbiolo grape.

Carey Cellars, J. (U.S.)   1977

A winery in Solvang, Santa Ynez Valley, Santa Barbara County, California; produces Cabernet, Merlot, Chardonnay and Sauvignon Blanc wines. 45 acres. 4,000 cases.

Carey Winery, Richard (U.S.)   1972

A winery in San Leandro, western Alameda County, California; produces Cabernet, Zinfandel, Blanc Fumé and Chenin Blanc wines from purchased grapes. The winery closed down in 1981.

Carignan *also* **Carignane (F.)**

A red grape, the most common in France, grown in the Midi, in the Provence and Rhône regions, and in California. A large-yielding grape, it produces a red wine with low acidity and tannin; used as a blending grape.

Carignano (I.)

In Sardinia, the name for the Carignan grape of France; also called Uva di Spagna.

Carignano del Sulcis DOC (I.)

1. A district encompassing the islands of San Pietro and Sant' Antioco, off the southwestern coast of Sardinia and including the southwestern corner of Sardinia known as Sulcis; it produces:

2. Red and rosé wines made from the Carignan grape blended with Monica, Alicante and Pascale grapes.

Carillon, Domaine Père et Fils (F.)

An estate in Puligny-Montrachet, Côte de Beaune district, Burgundy. 25 acres, including Mercurey En Champs Martin – 1.2

acres, Chassagne-Montrachet Les Macherelles (red) – 1.2 acres, Les Chenevottes – 1.2 acres, Puligny-Montrachet Les Combettes – 1.2 acres, Champ Canet – 1.2 acres, Les Referts – 2.5 acres, Puligny-Montrachet (red) – 1.2 acres and some Saint-Aubin.

Cariñena DO (Sp.)

1. A town and district in the Aragón region of northern Spain, which produces:

2. Red and rosé wines made from Bobal, Cariñena, Juan Ibañez and Garnacho Negro grapes and white wines from the Garnacho Blanco and Viura grapes. The reds may contain up to 18% alcohol.

3. The red grape which originated in this area and in France is called the Carignan grape.

Carlos (U.S.)

A white muscadine grape grown in the southeastern United States.

Carman (U.S.)

A red American grape grown in eastern Texas and in the southeastern U.S.

Carmel (Is.)

A brand name of wines produced by the following:

Carmel Wine Grower's Co-operative (Is.)

A large co-op in Richon-le-Zion and Zichron-Jacob, Israel; produces most of the wines in the country; produces Cabernet Sauvignon, Petite Sirah, Grenache Rosé, Sauvignon Blanc and other wines.

Carmel Wine Company (Is.)

A company set up in New York as the agent for handling the wines exported from Israel to the U.S. and Canada.

Carménère (F.)

A red grape grown in the Bordeaux region.

Carmes-Haut-Brion, Château Les (F.)

An unclassified estate in Pessac, Graves district, Bordeaux; produces red wines. 1,600 cases. 10 acres.

Carmignano DOC (I.)   1975

1. A district northwest of Florence, within the Chianti Montalbano district, Tuscany region, which produces:

2. A red wine similar to Chianti but with the addition of 6-10% Cabernet Sauvignon.

Carmine (U.S.)

A red grape developed in California by H. P. Olmo – a cross of Ruby Cabernet and Merlot; similar to Cabernet but with a greater yield.

Carnelian (U.S.)

A red grape developed in California by H.P. Olmo – a cross of Ruby Cabernet and Grenache; also known as B12.

Carneros (U.S.)

A district in southern Napa and Sonoma Counties, California; produces Pinot Noir and Chardonnay grapes.

Carneros Creek Winery (U.S.)   1973

A winery in Carneros Creek, south of Napa, Napa Valley, California; produces Cabernet, Pinot Noir, Zinfandel and Chardonnay wines from their own and purchased grapes. 15,000 cases. 10 acres.

Carnevale, Giorgio (I.)   1880

An estate in Rocchetta Tanaro-Cerro, near Asti, in the Piedmont region; produces Barbaresco, Barbera, Barolo, Brachetto, Dolcetto, Freisa, Grignolino, Nebbiolo, Cortese and Moscato wines. 30,000 cases.

Cároli Vineyard (U.S.)   1950's

A winery in New Windsor, Maryland; produces wines from hybrid grapes.

Carolina Blackrose (U.S.)

A red hybrid grape grown in Texas.

Caronne Ste.-Gemme, Château (F.)

An estate in St.-Laurent, Haut-Médoc district, Bordeaux; classified in 1978 as a *Cru Grand Bourgeois Exceptionnel*. 18,000 cases. 90 acres.

Carrascal (Sp.)

One of the best-known districts in the Sherry region, north of Jerez.

Carricante (I.)

A local white grape grown in Sicily.

Carrières, Les (Fr.)

A *Premier Cru* vineyard in Chambolle-Musigny, Côte de Nuits district, Burgundy. 2 acres.

Carrières, Les (F.)

A *Grand Cru* vineyard in Ladoix-Serrigny, but sold as Corton, Côte de Beaune district, Burgundy. 1 acre.

Carruades de Château Lafite (F.)

Formerly, the second wine of Château Lafite-Rothschild, in Pauillac, Haut-Médoc district, Bordeaux; made from vines under 12 years old; made as early as 1878, and discontinued after 1967. See **Moulin des Carruades.**

Carrubier, Domaine du (F.)

An estate at La Londe-lès-Maures, in the Provence region.

Cartaxo (P.)

1. A town and district in the Ribatejo region, northeast of Lisbon, which produces:

2. Red, white and rosé wines, the red made from Trincadeira, Mortagua and João de Santarem grapes and the white from Fernão Pires, Terrantez, Rabo de Ovelha, Boais and Jampal grapes.

Carte, Château La (F.)

An estate in St.-Émilion, Bordeaux; classified in 1955 as a *Grand Cru Classé*. 2,500 cases. 11 acres.

Cartizze *also* Superiore di Cartizze (I.)

1. A town in the Conegliano-Valdobbiadene DOC district, north of Treviso, in the Veneto region, which produces:

2. Dry and sweet, white wines and sparkling wines made from Prosecco grapes

with some Pinot Bianco and Pinot Grigio grapes.

carvalho (P.)

Oak.

Carvalho, Ribeiro & Ferreira (P.)   1898

A merchant in Lisbon; produces Garrafeira, Dão, Serradayres and Vinho Verde wines.

Cas Rougeot, Le (F.)

A *Premier Cru* vineyard in Monthélie, Côte de Beaune district, Burgundy.

Casa Concha, Marqués de (Ch.)

A red wine from the Maipo Valley, in central Chile; made from Cabernet grapes by Concha y Toro.

Casa do Douro (P.)

One of three regulating offices of the *Instituto do Vinho do Porto* controlling the production of Port wines, this one in charge of the viticulture and classification of the vineyards.

Casa Larga (U.S.)   1978, grapes 1974

A small winery in Fairport, northwest of Lake Canandaigua, Finger Lakes region, New York; produces Chardonnay, Riesling, Cabernet, Pinot Noir and hybrid wines. 2,000 cases. 12 acres.

Casa Nuestra (U.S.)   1980

A winery in St. Helena, Napa Valley, California; produces Chenin Blanc, Zinfandel and Gamay wines. 1,000 cases. 12 acres.

Casa de Sonoma (U.S.)

A red wine made and bottled in 1947 by El Gavilan Winery, Santa Rosa, California; made from Cabernet grapes; recorked and released in 1982 by Sebastiani Vineyards.

Casabello Winery (C.)   1966

A large winery in Penticton, at the southern end of Okanagan Lake, British Columbia; produces "estate" wines made from hybrid and *vinifera* grapes grown in the Osoyoos vineyard.

Casal de Azenha (P.)

A red wine from the Colares district, produced by da Silva.

Casal Thaulero (I.)

A large co-op winery in Roseto degli Abruzzi, Abruzzi region; produces Montepulciano and Trebbiano wines. 60,000 cases.

Casar de Valdaiga (Sp.)

A claret-style red wine from the El Bierzo district, in the León region, northwestern Spain.

Cascade (U.S.)

A red hybrid grape, Seibel 13053.

Cascade Mountain Vineyard (U.S.)

A winery in Amenia, Hudson River Valley region, New York; produces wines made from hybrid grapes. 25 acres.

Cascal (P.)

A white grape grown in the Vinho Verde region.

case

A wooden or cardboard box containing 12 fifths, 12 liters, 24 half-bottles, 48 splits, 6 magnums, or 4 three-liter or four-liter bottles.

casein

A protein substance used to clarify white wines. It is made from milk (present as calcic salt), washed, dried and ground. Doses of 5-20 grams per hectoliter are used for clearing wines and 25-30 grams per hectoliter for preventing oxidation or maderization.

Casillero del Diablo (Ch.)

A red wine from the Maipo Valley, in central Chile, produced by Concha y Toro; made from Cabernet grapes.

cask

A wine barrel of various sizes made of wood and bound with metal hoops.

Cassady (U.S.)

A grape which is crossed with the Concord to produce the Niagara grape.

Cassayre-Forni Cellars (U.S.)   1976

A winery in Rutherford, Napa Valley, California; produces Cabernet, Zinfandel, Chardonnay and Chenin Blanc wines from purchased grapes. 7,000 cases.

casse, cuprous (copper)

A wine malady caused by the wine coming in contact with copper, after which copper sulfide and protein may form a precipitate in the presence of light and the absence of air, thereby ruining the wine.

casse, ferric (iron)

A disease of wine caused by contact with iron, which contaminates the wine, causing cloudiness and the formation of a gray deposit when exposed to oxygen. White casse is due to ferric phosphate, blue casse is due to ferric tannate.

casse, oxidasic

A disease of wine produced by an enzyme which causes the wine to become cloudy and change color when exposed to oxygen. The enzyme is caused by the presence of over-ripe or moldy grapes. Red wines turn brown and white wines turn yellow.

casse, protein

A disease of wine caused by excessive protein matter in white wines.

Casse-Têtes (F.)

An unclassified vineyard in Meursault, Côte de Beaune district, Burgundy.

Cassemichère, Château de la (F.)

An estate in Vallet, Muscadet region, Loire Valley; produces Muscadet wines. 65 acres.

Cassis AOC (F.)

1. A village and small district southeast of Marseille, in the Provence region, which produces:
2. White wines made from Clairette, Ugni Blanc, Marsanne, Sauvignon and other grapes, and red and rosé wines made from Grenache, Cinsault, Carignan and Mourvèdre grapes.

Castel Chiuro (I.)

Red and white wines from Valtellina district, Lombardy region; produced by Negri. The white is made from Pinot and Riesling grapes and the red from Nebbiolo grapes.

Castel Frères (F.)

A merchant in Bordeaux; blends and bottles mostly branded VCC wines.

Castel Grifone (I.)

A rosé wine from the Torgiano DOC district, in the Umbria region; made from Sangiovese, Canaiolo, Montepulciano and Ciliegiolo grapes; produced by Lungarotti.

Castel Mitrano (I.)

A red wine from Mitrano, near Brindisi, in the southern Apulia region; made from Negro and Malvasia Nera grapes.

Castel del Monte DOC (I.)

1. A town and district in the central Apulia region, which produces:
2. Red, white and rosé wines, the red made from Uva di Troia, Bombino Nero, Montepulciano and Sangiovese grapes, the white from Pampanino, Trebbiano Toscano, Trebbiano Giallo, Bombino Bianco and Palumbo grapes, and the rosé from Bombino Nero, Montepulciano and Uva di Troia grapes in different proportions from the red wine.

Castel Oualou, Domaine de (F.)

An estate in Roquemaure, Lirac district, southern Rhône region; produces red wines made from Syrah and Mourvèdre grapes, rosé wines made from Cinsault, Grenache and Clairette grapes and white wines made from Ugni Blanc, Clairette and Picpoul grapes. 130 acres.

Castel-Roubine (F.)

An estate in Lorgues, in the Provence region.

Castel San Giorgio (I.)

Red and white wines from Fregene, north of Rome, in the Latium region; the red wines are made from Merlot, Montepulciano and Pinot Nero grapes; the white wines are made from Malvasia, Trebbiano, Sauvignon and Sémillon grapes.

Castel San Michele (I.)

A red wine from San Michele all'Adige, in the Trentino-Alto Adige region of northeastern Italy; made from Cabernet and Merlot grapes; produced by the Instituto Agrario Provinciale.

Castel di Serra Spumante (I.)

A dry, sparkling wine from the Gavi district, in the Piedmont region; made from Cortese and Pinot Blanc grapes.

Castelão (P.)

A red grape grown in the Bairrada region as well as other parts of southern Portugal.

Castelgiocondo (I.)   1975

A large estate in Montalcino, Tuscany region; produces Brunello and Rosso wines. 20,000 cases. 435 acres.

Castelgreve (I.)

A large co-op winery with almost 200 growers in Mercatale Val di Pesa, Tuscany region; also called Castelli del Grevepesa; produces Chianti Classico, Valgreve Bianco and Vin Santo wines. 150,000 cases. 2,000 acres.

Castelino (P.)

A red grape grown in the Torres Vedras region, north of Lisbon.

Castell (G.)

A village in the Franken region, Bereich Steigerwald, mostly in Grosslage Herren-

berg and partly in Grosslage Schild. The vineyards are: Bausch, Feuerbach, Hohnart, Kirchberg, Kugelspeil, Reitsteig, Schlossberg and Trautberg.

Castell del Remei (Sp.)

An estate in Penelles, Catalonia region; produces wines from Spanish and French grapes.

Castell'in Villa (I.)   1968

An estate in Castelnuovo Berardenga, Tuscany; produces Chianti Classico, Bianco della Val d'Arbia and Vin Santo wines. 50,000 cases. 150 acres.

Castell'sches Domänenamt, Fürstlich (G.)

An estate in Castell Unterfranken, Franken region; owns vineyards in Castell. 100 acres.

castellana, a la (Sp.)

A method of training vines in low-bush style, with no supports.

Castellare (I.)

An estate in Castellina in Chianti, Tuscany region; produces Chianti Classico wines. 5,000 cases.

Casteller DOC (I.)

1. A large district south of Trento, in the Trentino-Alto Adige region, which produces:

2. A light red or rosé wine made from Schiava, Merlot and Lambrusco grapes.

Castelli di Jesi (I.)

The shorter name for Verdicchio dei Castelli di Jesi DOC district, in the Marches region.

Castelli Romani (I.)

1. A district southeast of Rome, in the Latium region, also known as Colli Albani and Colli Romani. It consists of 6 DOC districts which produce mostly white wines. They are: Colli Albani, Colli Lanuvini, Frascati, Marino, Montecompatri Colonna and Velletri (red and white).

2. Any of the above wines, popular in Roman restaurants, made in the hills southeast of Rome.

Castello d'Illasi (I.)

A red wine from the Valpolicella district, in the Veneto region that has been allowed to re-ferment after having been added to the lees of Amarone wine; produced by Santi.

Castello di Montalbano (I.)

A vineyard of A. Vallana, near Gattinara, in the Piedmont region.

Castello di Montoro (I.)

A red wine from Montoro di Narni, in the southern Umbria region; made from Sangiovese, Merlot, Barbera and Montepulciano grapes.

Castello di Roncade (I.)

1. A red wine from Roncade, east of Treviso, in the Veneto region; made from a blend of Cabernet Sauvignon, Cabernet Franc, Merlot, Malbec and Petit Verdot grapes, produced by:
2. An estate of the same name.

Castello di Torre in Pietra (I.)

1. A red wine from Torre in Pietra, northwest of Rome, in the Latium region; made from Sangiovese and Montepulciano grapes; produced by:
2. An estate of the same name.

Castelsegonzano (I.)

A red wine from Segonzano, northeast of Trento, in the Trentino-Alto Adige region; made from the Pinot Nero grape.

Castéra, Château du (F.)

An estate in St. Germain d'Esteuil, Médoc district, Bordeaux; classified in 1978 as a *Cru Bourgeois*. 14,000 cases. 90 acres.

catador (Sp.)

A wine taster.

Catalonia (Sp.)

A region in northeastern Spain, with Barcelona and Tarragona as the principal cities; the most well-known district is Penedès and the town of San Sadurní de Noya is the center for Spanish sparkling wines.

Catarratto (I.)

A white grape grown in Sicily.

Catawba (U.S.)

1. An American red grape of the *Vitis labrusca* discovered about 1800 in North Carolina, near the Catawba River; it is thought to be a natural hybrid; grown in Ohio and New York to make red and white wines.
2. Red or white wine made from the Catawba grape.

Cato the Censor (234-149 B.C.) (Lat.)

The author of *De Agri Cultura*, the earliest Roman account of vine growing and wine making, also called *De Re Rustica*.

Cattin, Théo (F.)

An estate in Voegtlinshoffen, Haut-Rhin district, Alsace region. 45 acres.

caudle (E.)

A hot, sweetened, spiced wine or ale with beaten egg yolk added.

cava (Sp., P.)

1. A cellar where sparkling wines are made only by the Champagne method (*méthode Champenoise*).
2. A name given to sparkling wines made by the Champagne method.

Cavallotto, Fratelli (I.)

An estate in Castiglione Falletto, Piedmont region; produces Barbera, Barolo, Dolcetto, Grignolino, Nebbiolo and other wines. 40 acres.

cave (F.)

A cellar.

Cave Co-opérative des Grands Crus de Tavel (F.)   1937

A co-op winery in Tavel, Rhône region; 140 members; accounts for over 50% of all Tavel wine.

Cavendish Cape (S.Af.)

A Sherry-style wine made by the KWV.

Cavendish Manor (E.)   1974

A vineyard in Cavendish, Sudbury, Suffolk, England; produces a white wine from the Müller-Thurgau grape. 10 acres.

caviste (F.)

A cellerman.

Càvit (Cantina Viticoltori Trento) (I.) 1957

A large co-op of some 4,000 growers in Trento, Trentino-Alto Adige region; produces a variety of still and sparkling wines. 8 million cases. 17,000 acres.

Cayetana (Sp.)

A local white grape grown in southwestern Spain; the same as the Calagraño grape from the Rioja region.

Caymus Vineyard (U.S.)   1972

A winery in Rutherford, Napa Valley, California; produces Cabernet, Pinot Noir, Zinfandel, Johannisberg Riesling and Chardonnay wines. Second label is Liberty School. 70 acres. 20,000 cases.

Cayuga Vineyard (U.S.)   1981

A vineyard in Ovid, on the western shore of Lake Cayuga, Finger Lakes region, New York State; produces wines from Chardonnay, Riesling, Dutchess and hybrid grapes. 45 acres.

Cayuga White (U.S.)

A white hybrid grape, a cross of Seyval Blanc and Schuyler, bred in 1972 at Geneva Station, New York State; also called Geneva White, or GW3.

Cazatiers, Les (F.)

A *Premier Cru* vineyard in Gevrey-Chambertin, Côte de Nuits district, Burgundy. 22.5 acres.

Cazaux, Clos des (F.)

An estate in Vacqueyras, in the Côtes du Rhône-Villages district, Rhône region.

Cecchi & Figlia, Luigi (I.)   1893

A winery in Castellina in Chianti, Tuscany region; produces Bianco della Lega, Chianti, Chianti Classico and Galestro wines; also owns the Villa Cerna estate, a Chianti producer.

Cecubo (I.)

A red wine from Gaeta, on the southwestern coast of the Latium region; made from Abbuoto, Negroamaro and other grapes.

Cedar Hill Wine Company (U.S.)   1970

A winery in Cleveland Heights, Ohio; produces Pinot Noir, Chancellor and Chambourcin wines which are made and sold at the owner's restaurant.

Cèdres, Les (F.)

A brand name of Châteauneuf-du-Pape wine; produced by Paul Jaboulet.

Cellatica DOC (I.)

1. A village and district north of Brescia, in the Lombardy region, which produces:
2. A red wine made from Schiava Gentile, Barbera, and Marzemino (locally known as Berzamino) grapes.

cellier (F.)

A building where the wine is made or stored, also called *chai*, or *cuverie*.

Cellier aux Moines (F.)

A vineyard in Givry, Côte Chalonnaise district, Burgundy.

Cellier des Princes, Les (F.)   1924

A co-operative in Courthézon, Châteauneuf-du-Pape district, Rhône region; it produces wine for 180 vineyard owners.

Cencibel (Sp.)

A red grape grown in La Mancha, another name for the Tempranillo grape.

Cent Vignes, Les (F.)

A *Premier Cru* vineyard in Beaune, Côte de Beaune district, Burgundy. 59 acres.

Centurian (U.S.)

A red hybrid grape – a cross of Ruby Cabernet and Grenache; bred by Dr. Harold Olmo, at Davis, in 1973; makes a heavy red wine.

cep (F.)

A vine stock.

cepa (P. *and* Sp.)

A vine stock.

Cépa Velha (P.)

A white wine from Monção, in the Vinho Verde region; made from the Alvarinho grape.

cépage (F.)

A grape variety.

Cerasuolo DOC (I.)

A rosé wine from the Montepulciano d'Abruzzo district, in the Abruzzo region; made from Montepulciano grapes, with up to 15% Sangiovese grapes.

Cerasuolo di Vittoria DOC (I.)

1. A district around Vittoria, in southeastern Sicily, which produces:

2. A light red wine made from Calabrese and Frappato di Vittoria grapes with some Grosso Nero or Nero Mascalese grapes. The wine is also called Frappato.

Ceratti, Umberto (I.)

An estate in Caraffa del Bianco, Calabria region; produces Greco di Bianco and Mantonico di Bianco wines.

Cerceal (P.)

A white grape grown in Dão and Bairrada regions.

Ceretto (I.)   1935

An estate in Alba, Piedmont region; produces Barbaresco, Barbera, Barolo, Dolcetto and Nebbiolo wines. 100 acres, partly rented.

Cereza (Arg.)

A native red grape.

Cérons AOC (F.)

1. A town and district north of Barsac, Bordeaux region, which produces:

2. Sweet white wines made from Sémillon, Sauvignon Blanc and Muscadelle grapes; some dry wine is also made. 465,000 gallons.

Certan-Giraud, Château (F.)

An estate in Pomerol, Bordeaux. 1,200 cases. 7 acres.

Certan-Marzelle, Château (F.)

An estate in Pomerol, Bordeaux. 1,300 cases. 10 acres.

Certan-de-May, Château (F.)

An estate in Pomerol, Bordeaux. 1,500 cases. 10 acres.

Cerveteri DOC (I.)

1. A village and district northwest of Rome, in the Latium region, which produces:

2. Red wine from Sangiovese, Montepulciano and some Cesanese grapes, and white wine from 50% Trebbiano, 35% Malvasia and other grapes (Tocai, Verdicchio) at no more than 15%.

Cesanese DOC (I.)

1. A red grape grown in the Latium region, which produces:

2. A red wine, dry, sweet or *frizzante*, from 3 small DOC districts: Cesanese del Piglio, Cesanese di Affile and Cesanese di Olivano Romano; made from Cesanese di Affile and Cesanese Comune grapes.

Cesanese di Affile DOC (I.)

1. A grape grown in Affile, east of Rome, in the Latium region, which produces:

2. Red wines, sweet, dry or sparkling.

Cesanese Comune (I.)

A red grape, a sub-variety of the Cesanese, grown in the Latium region.

Cesanese di Olivano Romano DOC (I.)

1. A district around Olivano Romano, east of Rome, in the Latium region, which produces:

2. Red wines, similar to the above.

Cesanese del Piglio DOC (I.)

1. A district southeast of Rome and including Piglio, Anagni and Paliano, in the Latium region, which produces:

2. A red wine made from the Cesanese grape.

César (F.)

A local red grape grown in the Auxerrois district, near Chablis, Burgundy region; also called Romain.

Cesare, Pio (I.)   1881

An estate and winery in Alba, Piedmont region; produces Barbaresco, Barbera, Barolo, Dolcetto, Grignolino and Nebbiolo wines; made from their own and purchased grapes. 21,000 cases. 40 acres.

Cesari (I.)

An estate in Castel San Pietro, Emilia-Romagna region; produces Albana, Sangiovese and Trebbiano wines.

Chabiots, Les (F.)

A *Premier Cru* vineyard in Morey-St.-Denis, Côte de Nuits district, Burgundy. 5.5 acres.

Chablais (Sw.)

1. A district around Aigle, in the eastern part of the Vaud region, which produces:

2. White wines made from the Chasselas grape.

Chablis AOC (F.)

1. A city and district southeast of Paris, in the northern Burgundy region. The district includes 19 communes - none of which appear on the labels. The *Grand Cru* vineyards are: Vaudésir, Les Preuses, Blanchots, Les Clos, Valmur, Grenouilles, Bougros and (unofficially) La Montonne. The *Premier Cru* vineyards used to number around thirty, but now are grouped into 12 main vineyards, which are: Beauroy (Beauroy and Troesmes), Côte de Léchet, Fourchaume (Fourchaume, Côte de Frontenay and Vaupulent), Les Fourneaux (Les Fourneaux, Côte des Près-Girots, and Morein), Mélinots (Mélinots, Les Épinottes and Roncières), Montée de Tonnerre (Montée de Tonnerre, Châpelot and Pied d'Aloup), Montmains (Montmains, Butteaux and Forêts), Monts de Milieu, Vaillons (Vaillons, Beugnons, Châtains, Les Lys and Séché), Vaucoupin, Vaudevey and Vogros (Vogros and Vaugiraut). Originally, 1,000 acres, now over 3,000 acres and continually growing, of which 250 acres are *Grand Cru*, 1,000 acres are *Premier Cru*, 1,500 acres are Chablis, and 300 acres Petit Chablis.

2. White wines made from the Chardonnay grape, divided into four AOC designations: Chablis *Grand Cru* (with the name of the vineyard), Chablis *Premier Cru* (with the name of the vineyard), Chablis, and Petit Chablis.

Chablis (U.S. and others)

A dry or semi-dry white wine made from any number of grape varieties blended together, and bottled mostly in 1.5-, 3- and 4-liter jugs.

Chablisienne, La (F.)

A co-op winery in Chablis, Burgundy; produces mostly bulk wines.

Chaboeufs, Les (F.)

A *Premier Cru* vineyard in Nuits-St.-Georges, Côte de Nuits district, Burgundy. 7 acres.

Chabond, Jean-François (F.)

An estate in St.-Péray, Rhône region. 17 acres.

Chabriots, Les (F.)

A *Premier Cru* vineyard in Chambolle-Musigny, Côte de Nuits district, Burgundy. 3.5 acres.

Chacolí (Sp.)

A white wine from Guernica, Guetaria and Zarauz, in the Basque region (northern Navarra region) of northern Spain made in the *vino verde* style, low in alcohol (9-11%); made from Ondarrubi Zuria (white) or Ondarrubi Beltza (red) grapes.

Chaffots, Les (F.)

A *Premier Cru* vineyard in Morey-St.-Denis, Côte de Nuits district, Burgundy. 3 acres.

Chagny (F.)

A commune north of Rully, in the Côte Chalonnaise district of Burgundy; produces white wines and some red wines.

chai (F.)

A wine shed; a storage area above ground; a building where the wine is made; also called *cellier*, or *cuverie*.

Chaignots, Aux (F.)

A *Premier Cru* vineyard in Nuits-St.-Georges, Côte de Nuits district, Burgundy. 14 acres.

Chaillots, Les (F.)

A *Premier Cru* vineyard in Aloxe-Corton, Côte de Beaune district, Burgundy. 8 acres.

Chaine-Carteau, En la (F.)

A *Premier Cru* vineyard (in part) in Nuits-St.-Georges, Côte de Nuits district, Burgundy. 6.5 acres.

Chaintres, Château de (F.)

An estate in Dampierre-sur-Loire, Saumur-Champigny district, Anjou region, Loire Valley; produces red and white wines. 50 acres.

Chaize, Château de la (F.)

A large estate in Odénas (Brouilly), Beaujolais district, Burgundy. 250 acres.

Chalet Debonné (U.S.)   1971

A winery in Madison, Ohio; produces wines made from Concord and hybrid grapes. 8,000 cases. 40 acres.

Chalk Hill Vineyard (U.S.)

A vineyard in Windsor, Russian River Valley, Sonoma County, California, owned by Sonoma Vineyards; produces Chardonnay wine from grapes grown there.

Chalkidiki (Gr.)

1. A district in Macedonia, in northern Greece, which produces:
2. Red wines made from the Limnio grape.

Chalon-sur-Saône (F.)

A city in central Burgundy, in the Chalonnais district, south of the Côte de Beaune district; produces red and white wines from neighboring vineyards under the Bourgogne AOC designation.

Chalone Vineyard (U.S.)   1966,
1st wine 1960

A winery and vineyard in Soledad, Monterey County, California, situated on the Pinnacles Mountains 2,000 feet above the Salinas Valley; produces Cabernet, Pinot Noir, Chardonnay, Pinot Blanc and Chenin Blanc wines. Other labels are Galivan and Edna Valley Vineyard. 120 acres. 10,000 cases.

Chalonnais, *also* Côte Chalonnaise (F.)

A district in central Burgundy, the name derived from Chalon-sur-Saône; produces red wine from Pinot Noir, Pinot Liebault and Pinot Beurot grapes and white wine from Chardonnay and Pinot Blanc grapes grown in the vineyards around Givry, Mercurey, Montagny and Rully; sparkling wines are also made.

Chalybon

An ancient wine of Syria and Damascus; a favorite of Persian Kings, mentioned in the Bible.

Chambave Rouge (I.)

A red wine from Chambave, in the Valle d'Aosta region; made from Gros Vien, Dolcetto and Barbera grapes.

Chambers (Aus.)   1860

An old winery near Rutherglen, in northeastern Victoria; produces Muscat, Tokay, Amontillado and various red wines. 120 acres.

Chambert, Château (F.)

An estate in St.-Estèphe, Haut-Médoc district, Bordeaux; classified in 1978 as a *Cru Bourgeois*. 20 acres.

Chambertin AOC (F.)

A famous *Grand Cru* vineyard in Gevrey-Chambertin, Côte de Nuits district, Burgundy. 70 acres, half of which is the Clos de Bèze.

Chambertin-Clos de Bèze AOC (F.)

A famous *Grand Cru* vineyard in Gevrey-Chambertin, Côte de Nuits district, Burgundy. May also be labeled Chambertin. 38 acres.

Chambéry (F.)

A city in the Savoie region well-known for the production of vermouth.

Chambolle-Musigny AOC (F.)

A famous commune in the Côte de Nuits district, Burgundy; known as Cambolla in 1110, and as *Campus Ebulliens* in Latin, *Champ Boillant* in French, meaning "Boiling Field," named after a turbulent stream; later named Chambolle-Musigné; produces mostly red wine and a little white wine. The *Grand Cru* vineyards are Les Musigny and part of Les Bonnes-Mares. Of the twenty *Premiers Crus*, Les Amoureuses and Les Charmes are the most well-known.

Chambourcin (F.)

A red hybrid grape, also known as Joannes Seyve 26205.

Chamboureau, Château de (F.)

An estate in Epiré, Savennières district, Anjou region, Loire Valley; produces Savennières and other Anjou wines. 35 acres.

chambrer (F.)

To bring a red wine up from cellar temperature to room temperature. The best method is to bring it to the kitchen to be slowly warmed at least one hour ahead of serving.

Chamisal Vineyard (U.S.)   vines 1972, winery 1980

A winery in San Luis Obispo, San Luis Obispo County, California; produces Cabernet and Chardonnay wines. 55 acres.

Champ(s) Canet (F.)

A *Premier Cru* vineyard in Puligny-Montrachet. Côte de Beaune district, Burgundy. 10 acres.

Champ-Clou (F.)

A *Premier Cru* vineyard in Rully, Côte Chalonnaise district, Burgundy.

Champ-Ducour, Clos du (F.)

An estate in Moulin-à-Vent, Beaujolais district, Burgundy.

Champ(s) Pimont *also* Champimont (F.)

A *Premier Cru* vineyard in Beaune, Côte de Beaune district, Burgundy. 45 acres.

Champ Poureau (F.)

A vineyard in Givry, Côte Chalonnaise district, Burgundy.

Champagne (F.)

1. A famous region centered around Épernay and Reims, northeast of Paris; produces primarily white and rosé sparkling wines and some still wines made from Chardonnay and Pinot Noir grapes with some Pinot Meunier, Arbanne and Meslier grapes allowed. The region is divided into the following districts: Côte d'Ambonnay, Côte d'Épernay, Côte des Blancs, Côte de Vertus, Montagne de Reims and Vallé de la Marne. 55,000 acres.

2. The famous sparkling wines originally made in the Champagne region of France, but also made in the U.S. and in other countries; produced by causing a second fermentation in each bottle of wine and capturing the carbon dioxide gas while disposing of the sediment in a lengthy and delicate process. White Champagne may be made from Chardonnay, or Pinot Noir or a blend of the two grapes and rosé from Pinot Noir grapes. Still wine from the region is now called Coteaux Champenois (formerly called Champagne Nature).

Champagne method

The traditional way of making a sparkling wine, by causing a second fermentation in each bottle, as done in the Champagne region, rather than in tanks (bulk, or *Charmat* method); called *méthode Champenoise*, in French.

Champagnon, Louis (F.)

An estate in Chénas, Beaujolais district, Burgundy. 12 acres.

Champanel (U.S.)

An American red hybrid grape grown in Texas.

champanex (F.)

A hexagonal device that mechanically accomplishes the *remuage* (riddling) of Champagne; it can have a capacity of 500 bottles. Also called *gyropalette*, and in Spain, *girasol*.

Champans (F.)

A *Premier Cru* vineyard in Volnay, Côte de Beaune district, Burgundy. 28 acres.

Champeaux, (F.)

A *Premier Cru* vineyard in Gevrey-Chambertin, Côte de Nuits district, Burgundy. 17 acres.

Champet, Émile (F.)

An estate in Ampuis, Côte-Rôtie district, Rhône region; owns 4 acres of Côte-Rôtie.

Champimonts *also* Champ(s) Pimont (F.)

A *Premier Cru* vineyard in Beaune, Côte de Beaune district, Burgundy. 45 acres.

Champitennois *also* Petite Chapelle (F.)

A *Premier Cru* vineyard in Gevrey-Chambertin, Côte de Nuits district, Burgundy. 10 acres.

Champlot (F.)

A *Premier Cru* vineyard in St.-Aubin, Côte de Beaune district, Burgundy. 20 acres.

Champonnet (F.)

A *Premier Cru* vineyard in Gevrey-Chambertin, Côte de Nuits district, Burgundy. 8 acres.

Champs Canet (F.)
See **Champ Canet.**

Champs Fulliot, Les (F.)

A *Premier Cru* vineyard in Monthélie, Côte de Beaune district, Burgundy. 21 acres.

Champs Gain, Les (F.)

A *Premier Cru* vineyard in Chassagne-Montrachet, Côte de Beaune district, Burgundy. 30 acres.

Champs-Perdrix, Aux (F.)

A *Premier Cru* vineyard in Nuits-St.-Georges, Côte de Nuits district, Burgundy. 5.5 acres.

Champs Piments (F.)
See **Champimonts.**

Champy Père et Fils (F.)   1720

A merchant and estate in Beaune, Côte de Beaune, Burgundy. 18 acres, including Clos de Vougeot – 6 acres, Savigny La Dominode – 4.3 acres, Beaune Le Clos des Mouches – 4.3 acres and Les Avaux – 4.3 acres.

Chancellor

A red hybrid grape, also known as Siebel 7053 – a cross of S. 5163 and S. 800.

Chandon, Domaine (U.S.)   1973, winery 1977, first wine 1976

·Moët-Hennessy's large winery in Yountville, southern Napa Valley, California; produces sparkling wines: Brut, Blanc de Noirs, Blanc de Blancs and others made from Pinot Noir, Chardonnay, Pinot Blanc, Gamay, Ugni Blanc and Flora grapes. 250,000 cases. 1,300 acres.

Chandon de Briailles, Domaine (F.)

An estate in Savigny-lès-Beaune, Côte de Beaune district, Burgundy. 45 acres, including Savigny Les Lavières – 7.5 acres, Pernand-Vergelesses Île des Vergelesses – 10 acres, Corton Les Bressandes – 7.5 acres, Clos du Roi – 2.5 acres, Les Maréchaudes – 1.2 acres and Corton (Blanc) – .8 acre.

Chanière, La (F.)

A *Premier Cru* vineyard (in part) in Pommard, Côte de Beaune district, Burgundy. 25 acres.

Chanlin (F.)

A *Premier Cru* vineyard in Volnay, Côte de Beaune district, Burgundy. 10 acres.

Chanlins-Bas, Les (F.)

A *Premier Cru* vineyard in Pommard, Côte de Beaune district, Burgundy. 18 acres.

Chanson, Cuvée Paul (F.)

A white wine from the Hospices de Beaune, Côte de Beaune district, Burgundy. The *cuvée* is composed of one vineyard in Corton: Coton-Vergennes – .7 acre. 68 cases.

Chanson Père et Fils (F.)   1750

A shipper and grower in Beaune, Côte de Beaune district, Burgundy. 100 acres, including Beaune Clos des Fèves – 9 acres, Les Bressandes – 3.5 acres, Les Grèves – 5.7 acres, Le Clos des Mouches – 11 acres, Les Marconnets – 9 acres, Clos du Roi – 6.5 acres, Champs Pimont – 7.5 acres, Les Teurons – 10 acres, Les Blanches Fleurs – 3 acres, Savigny La Dominode – 4 acres, Les Marconnets – 5.5 acres and Pernand-Vergelesses Les Vergelesses – 16 acres.

Chante-Alouette (F.)

1. One of the important vineyard sections in Hermitage, Rhône region; grows white grapes.
2. A white Hermitage wine, produced by Chapoutier.

Chante-Cigale, Domaine (F.)

An estate in Châteauneuf-du-Pape, Rhône region; produces red wine made from 80% Grenache, 10% Syrah, 5% Mourvèdre and 5% Cinsault grapes. 100 acres.

chantepleure (F.)

1. In Anjou, a tube (*pipette*) used for removing wine for tasting or analysis from a large container or cask.
2. The wooden spigot of a wine barrel.

chapeau (F.)

A cap consisting of grape solids (skins, pips, etc.) which forms on the top of the vat during the fermentation process.

Chapelle, La (F.)

A *Premier Cru* vineyard in Auxey-Duresses, Côte de Beaune district, Burgundy, now split into two vineyards: Bretterins and Reugne.

Chapelle, La (F.)

1. A vineyard section in Hermitage, Rhône region; red and white grapes are grown.
2. A red Hermitage wine, produced by Paul Jaboulet; the grapes are from Le Méal and Les Bressards vineyards.

Chapelle, Domaine de la (F.)

An estate in Châteauneuf-de-Gadagne, Côtes du Rhône district, Rhône region.

Chapelle-Chambertin AOC (F.)

One of 9 *Grand Cru* vineyards in Gevrey-Chambertin, Côte de Nuits district, Burgundy. 15 acres.

Chapelle-Madeleine, Château (F.)

An estate in St.-Émilion, Bordeaux; classified in 1955 as a *Grand Cru Classé*. 100 cases. 2.5 acres.

Chapelot (F.)

A *Premier Cru* vineyard in Fyé, Chablis district, Burgundy; usually included as part of the Montée de Tonnerre vineyard.

Chapitre (F.)

A *Premier Cru* vineyard in Rully, Côte Chalonnaise district, Burgundy.

Chapitre, Clos du (F.)

A *Premier Cru* vineyard in Fixin, Côte de Nuits district, Burgundy. 11 acres.

Chapitre, Clos du (F.)

A *Premier Cru* vineyard in Gevrey-Chambertin, Côte de Nuits district, Burgundy. 2.5 acres.

Chaponnières, Les (F.)

A *Premier Cru* vineyard in Pommard, Côte de Beaune district, Burgundy. 8 acres.

Chapoutier, M. (F.)   1808

A large estate and merchant in Tain-L'Hermitage, Rhône region. 175 acres, including 7 acres of Côte-Rôtie, 76 acres of Hermitage, 15 acres of Crozes-Hermitage, 15 acres of St.-Joseph and 66 acres of Châteauneuf-du-Pape; Chante-Alouette and Sizeranne are brand names.

Chappellet (U.S.)   1967

A winery in St. Helena, on Pritchard Hill, Napa Valley, California; produces Cabernet, Merlot, Chardonnay, Johannisberg Riesling and Chenin Blanc wines; the second wine is Pritchard Hill. 25,000 cases. 100 acres.

Chaptal, Jean Antoine (1756-1832) (F.)

A chemist and Minister of the Interior, who, in 1801, developed the practice of chaptalization. See below.

chaptalization

The process of adding sugar to must during *remontage* in order to increase the potential alcohol level; this process also decreases excessive tartness of some wines by precipitating the production of cream of tartar; cane or beet sugar is added to red wines and cane sugar is added to white wines; developed by Dr. Chaptal in 1801, it is allowed by law in Burgundy and Bordeaux and in Germany (but not for *Qualitätswein*); not permitted in California.

Chapuis (F.)

An estate in Aloxe-Corton, Côte de Beaune district, Burgundy. 28 acres, including Corton – 12.5 acres (from several vineyards) and Corton-Charlemagne – 1.6 acres.

Charal (C.)   1968, 1975

A winery in Blenheim, Ontario; produces Chardonnay, Riesling and other wines. 60 acres.

Charbaut et Fils, A. (F.)

A Champagne producer in Épernay; Charbaut Certificate is the *cuvée de prestige*. 130 acres. 2.5 million bottles.

Charbono *also* Charbonneau (I.)

An Italian red grape, now grown in California, usually used as a blending wine, but occasionally produced as a varietal.

Chardonnay (F.)

A white grape grown principally in Burgundy, Champagne and California, believed to be a variant of the Pinot Blanc grape; also known as Arnoison, Aubaine, Beaunois, Melon Blanc and Melon d'Arbois.

Charente wines (F.)

Light, thin, tart white wines produced in the Charente region; used to make Cognac, but also sold locally as red or white table wines.

Charlemagne (F.)

A famous *Grand Cru* vineyard partly in Aloxe-Corton and partly in Pernand-Vergelesses, Côte de Beaune district, Burgundy; may be sold as Corton-Charlemagne (white wine) or Corton (red or white wine). The name Charlemagne has not been used for some years. 84 acres.

Charlemagne (742-814) (F.)

Charles I (Charles the Great), King of the Franks, Emperor of the West; author of *Capitulare de Villis*, which contains regulations governing vineyards and winemaking.

Charlotte Dumay, Cuvée (F.)

A red wine from the Hospices de Beaune, Côte de Beaune district, Burgundy. The *cuvée* is composed of the following vineyards: Corton-Renardes – 5 acres, Corton-Les Bressandes – 2.5 acres and Corton-Clos du Roi – 1 acre. 575 cases.

Charmat, Eugène (F.)

The French scientist who, in 1910, developed a process for making sparkling wines in tanks instead of in the bottle.

Charmat process (F.)

The process of making sparkling wines in bulk instead of in the bottle, invented by Eugène Charmat in 1910 in France. The wine is put into a tank and heated for 12-16 hours to artificially age it. It is then cooled and pumped into a second tank to which yeast and sugar is added; it ferments again for 10-15 days to obtain the necessary carbonation, after which it is pumped into a third tank to be clarified by refrigeration, filtered and finally bottled. This process is not permitted in the Champagne region.

Charmes, Aux (F.)

A *Premier Cru* vineyard in Morey-St.-Denis, Côte de Nuits district, Burgundy. 3 acres.

Charmes, Les (F.)

A large vineyard in Lugny, Mâconnais district, Burgundy. 198 acres.

Charmes, Les (F.)

A *Premier Cru* vineyard in Chambolle-Musigny, Côte de Nuits district, Burgundy. 12.5 acres.

Charmes, Les (F.)

A vineyard in Villié-Morgon, Beaujolais district, Burgundy. 250 acres.

Charmes-Chambertin AOC (F.)

A famous *Grand Cru* vineyard in Gevrey-Chambertin, Côte de Nuits district, Burgundy; it usually includes Mazoyères-Chambertin. 11,500 cases. 75 acres total.

Charmes Dessous, Les (F.)

A *Premier Cru* vineyard (in part) in Meursault, Côte de Beaune district, Burgundy; usually sold as Les Charmes. 31 acres.

Charmes Dessus, Les (F.)

A *Premier Cru* vineyard in Meursault, Côte de Beaune district, Burgundy; usually sold as Les Charmes. 38 acres.

Charmots, Les (F.)

A *Premier Cru* vineyard in Pommard, Côte de Beaune district, Burgundy. 8 acres.

Charneco (P.)

An ancient Port wine, c. 16th century, mentioned by Shakespeare; it was probably a Bucelas wine, since Charneco is near Bucelas.

Charnières, Les (F.)

A *Premier Cru* vineyard (in part) in Savigny-lès-Beaune, Côte de Beaune district, Burgundy. 5 acres.

Charnières, Les *also* Charrières (F.)

A *Premier Cru* vineyard in Morey-St.-Denis, Côte de Nuits district, Burgundy. 6 acres.

charnu (F.)

Fleshy; full-bodied.

charpenté (F.)

Well-built, well-structured, with generous amounts of alcohol and other elements.

Charrières, Les *also* Charnières (F.)

A *Premier Cru* vineyard in Morey-St.-Denis, Côte de Nuits district, Burgundy. 6 acres.

Chassagne *also* Cailleret (F.)

A *Premier Cru* vineyard in Chassagne-Montrachet, Côte de Beaune district, Burgundy; produces white wines only. 15 acres total, with En Cailleret (red wine only).

Chassagne-Montrachet AOC (F.)

A commune in the southern end of the Côte de Beaune district, Burgundy. It has 3 *Grand Cru* (Criots-Bâtard-Montrachet, part of Le Montrachet and part of Bâtard-Montrachet) and 14 *Premier Cru* vineyards. 165,000 gallons red, 99,000 gallons white wine. 860 acres.

Chasse-Spleen, Château (F.)

An estate in Moulis, Haut-Médoc district, Bordeaux; classified in 1978 as a *Cru Grand Bourgeois Exceptionnel*. 20,000 cases. 125 acres.

Chasselas (F.)

A white grape grown in the Pouilly-sur-Loire district, in the Savoie and in Alsace; also called the Gutedel in Germany, the Fendant in Switzerland, and the Chasselas Doré and Sweetwater in Australia.

Chasseloir, Château de (F.)

An estate in St.-Fiacre-sur-Maine, Muscadet Sèvre-et-Maine district, Loire Valley. 60 acres.

Chassy (F.)

A village in the Côtes du Rhône-Villages district, Rhône region.

Chatains (F.)

A *Premier Cru* vineyard in Chablis, Chablis district, Burgundy; usually included as part of the Vaillon vineyard.

château (F.)

French for a castle, palace, mansion or hall; a wine estate or winery where vines are grown and wine is usually made and bottled. Bordeaux wine is usually bottled under the *château* name (or *Clos*, or *Domaine*). In the U.S. and other countries a *château* name is frequently used as the name of a winery, for example: Château Montelena, Domaine Chandon and Clos Du Val, in California.

château-bottled

A designation on wine labels meaning that the wine was made and bottled at the estate or winery listed on the label and sometimes at a *chai* of the same owner on another property in the same district. In California, estate-bottled is similar in meaning.

Château-Châlon AOC (F.)

1. A village and district, also including Domblans, Minetru, and Nevy-sur-Seille, in the Jura region of eastern France, which produces:

2. A white, sherry-like wine known as *"vin jaune,"* made from the Savagnin grape and sold in flat, squat, flask-shaped bottles.

Château-Gai (C.)   1890

A winery near Niagara Falls, Ontario; produces a variety of different wines from purchased grapes.

Château-Grillet AOC (F.)   1830

1. An estate of 7.4 acres with its own AOC designation, near Vérin, in the Condrieu district, northern Rhône region, which produces:

2. A famous white wine made from the Viognier grape.

Châteaumeillant VDQS (F.)

A town and district south of Bourges, in the Upper Loire region, Loire Valley; produces red wine made from Gamay and Pinot Noir grapes, some white wine made from the Melon grape and *vin gris*. Other important villages are St.-Maur, Vesdun, Reigny and Urciers.

Châteauneuf-du-Pape AOC (F.)

1. French for "New Castle of the Pope," a famous town and district in the southern Rhône region; the district also includes Bédarrides, Courthézon, Orange and Sorgues, and produces:

2. A red or white wine usually made from different blends of Grenache, Mourvèdre, Syrah, Muscardin, Vaccarese, Counoise, Picpoule, Cinsault, Clairette, Bourboulenc, Terret Noir, Picardin and Roussanne grapes for the red, and blends of Clairette, Bourboulenc, Roussanne, Grenache Blanc and Picpoul for the white.

Chatelain, Jean-Claude (F.)

An estate in Les Berthiers, Pouilly-Fumé district, Upper Loire region. 25 acres.

Chatelet, Château Le (F.)

An estate in St.-Émilion, Bordeaux; classified in 1955 as a *Grand Cru Classé*. 700 cases. 7 acres.

Châtelots, Les (F.)

A *Premier Cru* vineyard in Chambolle-Musigny, Côte de Nuits district, Burgundy. 6 acres.

Châtenay, Samuel (Sw.)   1796

A well-known estate and merchant in Boudry, Neuchâtel region; produces many wines under several domaine names. 50 acres.

Chatenière, La (F.)

A *Premier Cru* vineyard in St.-Aubin, Côte de Beaune district, Burgundy; produces red and white wines. 25 acres.

Châtillon-en-Diois AOC (F.)   1974

1. A village and district around Die, in the southeastern Rhône region; the district also includes 11 other villages around Die, the most important of which are Menglon, St.-Romain and Laval d'Aix; 150 acres. It produces:

2. A red, white or rosé wine, the red and rosé made from Gamay Noir, Syrah and Pinot Noir grapes, and the white from Aligoté and Chardonnay grapes. All wine is made by Cave Co-op de Die.

Chatillonne, La (F.)

One of the best vineyards in the Côte-Rôtie district, in the Côte-Blonde section, in the northern Rhône region.

Chauché Gris (F.)

A white grape grown around Poitiers, in west central France, and in California, where it is known as the Grey Riesling grape.

Chaumes, Les (F.)

A *Grand Cru* vineyard (in part) in Aloxe-Corton, Côte de Beaune district, Burgundy. 2.5 acres.

Chaumes, Les (F.)

A *Premier Cru* vineyard in Vosne-Romanée, Côte de Nuits district, Burgundy. 18 acres.

Chaunac, De (F.)

A red hybrid grape grown in Canada; also known as Seibel 9549.

Chautauqua (U.S.)

A lake, town and region in the southwestern corner of New York State, on the southeastern shore of Lake Erie.

Chauvenet, F. (F.)   1853

A producer of still and sparkling Burgundy wine in Nuits-St.-Georges, Côte de Nuits district, Burgundy.

Chauvenet, Jean (F.)

An estate in Nuits-St.-Georges, Côte de Nuits district, Burgundy. 17.5 acres, including Nuits-St.-Georges Les Vaucrains – 1.2 acres, Nuits-St.-Georges *Premier Cru* - 4 acres and Vosne-Romanée.

Chauvin, Château (F.)

An estate in St.-Émilion, Bordeaux; classified in 1955 as a *Grand Cru Classé*. 4,000 cases. 25 acres.

Chave, Gérard (F.)   1481

An estate in Mauves, Hermitage district, northern Rhône region; owns Hermitage – 25 acres.

Chefoo (China)

1. A town on the Shantung peninsula, in eastern China, which produces:

2. Red wine similar to Port and white wine similar to Sherry.

Cheilly-les-Maranges AOC (F.)

A village in the southern end of the Côte de Beaune district, Burgundy; produces red and white wines usually sold as Côte de Beaune-Villages. The three *Premier Cru* vineyards, totalling 108 acres, are La Boutière, Les Maranges and Plantes-de-Maranges.

Chelois

A red hybrid grape, also known as Seibel 10878 – a cross of Seibel 5163 and Seibel 5593; grown in the eastern and mid-western U.S.

Chénas AOC (F.)

1. A village and a *Cru Beaujolais*, most of which is within the Moulin-à-vent AOC. 600 acres. It produces:

2. A red wine made from the Gamay grape.

Chêne Marchand, Clos du (F.)

A vineyard in Bué, Sancerre district, Upper Loire Region, Loire Valley; it has several owners. 75 acres.

Chênes, Clos des (F.)

A *Premier Cru* vineyard (in part) in Volnay, Côte de Beaune district, Burgundy. 40 acres.

Chénevery, Les (F.)

A *Premier Cru* vineyard (in part) in Morey-St.-Denis, Côte de Nuits district, Burgundy. 8 acres.

Chenevottes, Les (F.)

A *Premier Cru* vineyard in Chassagne-Montrachet, Côte de Beaune district, Burgundy; produces red and white wines. 28 acres.

Chenin Blanc

A white grape grown primarily in the Loire valley, especially in Vouvray, and in California and South Africa to make sweet or dry white wines. In the Loire Valley it is called the Pineau de la Loire and Blanc

d'Anjou, and in South Africa it is called Steen.

Chenin Noir (F.)

A red grape grown in the Loire Valley; also called Pineau d'Aunis.

Chenôve (F.)

A village in the northern Côte de Nuits district, Burgundy. Its wine only qualifies for Bourgogne AOC.

Cherbaudes (F.)

A *Premier Cru* vineyard in Gevrey-Chambertin, Côte de Nuits district, Burgundy. 5 acres.

Cheseaux, Aux (F.)

A *Premier Cru* vineyard in Morey-St.-Denis, Côte de Nuits district, Burgundy. 6 acres.

Cheusots, Aux (F.)

A *Premier Cru* vineyard in Fixin, Côte de Nuits district, Burgundy. 4.5 acres.

Cheval-Blanc, Château (F.)

A famous estate in St.-Émilion, Bordeaux; classified in 1955 as a *Premier Grand Cru*. With Ausone, it is placed at the top of the list of 12 *Premiers Grands Crus*. It was a part of Château Figeac until the 19th century. 14,000 cases. 87 acres.

Chevalier, Château (U.S.)   1891, 1969

A winery in St. Helena, Napa Valley, California; produces Cabernet, Pinot Noir, Chardonnay and Riesling wines. 10,000 cases. 60 acres.

Chevalier, Domaine de (F.)

An estate in Léognan, Graves district, Bordeaux; classified in 1959 as a *Cru Classé* for red and white wines. 4,500 cases of red, 1,000 cases of white. 35 acres.

Chevalier-Dubois (F.)

An estate in Ladoix-Serrigny, Côte de Beaune district, Burgundy. 20 acres, including Corton-Charlemagne – .4 acre,

Corton – 2.5 acres, Aloxe-Corton and La-doix Côte de Beaune.

Chevalier-Montrachet AOC (F.)

A famous *Grand Cru* vineyard, situated directly above the Montrachet vineyard, in Puligny-Montrachet, Côte de Beaune district, Burgundy. 16 acres.

Chevalier de Stérimberg, Le (F.)

A white wine from Hermitage, northern Rhône region, made from Marsanne and Roussanne grapes; produced by Jaboulet.

Chevalière, La (F.)

One of the best vineyards in the Côte-Rôtie district, Côte-Brune section, northern Rhône region.

Cheverny VDQS (F.)

1. A district around Cour-Cheverny, near Blois, in the eastern Touraine region, Loire Valley, which produces:

2. Red, rosé and white wines; the reds and rosés are made from Gamay Noir, Cabernet Franc, Cabernet Sauvignon, Pinot Noir and Malbec grapes; the whites from Chenin Blanc, Sauvignon, Arbois (or Pineau Menu) and Romorantin grapes.

Chevillon, Maurice (F.)

An estate in the Nuits-St.-Georges, Côte de Nuits district, Burgundy. 33 acres, including Nuits-St.-Georges Aux Chaignots – 7.5 acres, Les Cailles – 5 acres, Les St.-Georges – 1.8 acres, La Roncière – 5 acres and Les Pruliers – 4 acres.

Chevre, Château (U.S.)　　　　1973, first wine 1979

A winery in Yountville, Napa Valley, California; produces Merlot wine. 2,000 cases. 20 acres.

Chevret, En (F.)

A *Premier Cru* vineyard in Volnay, Côte de Beaune district, Burgundy. 15 acres.

Cheysson-lès-Fargues (F.)

An estate in Chiroubles, Beaujolais district, Burgundy. 55 acres.

Chian (Gr.)

A sweet wine from ancient Greece, praised by Horace.

Chianti DOCG (I.)

1. A district in the Tuscany region, the largest DOC district in Italy; divided into seven zones: Chianti Classico – between Florence and Siena, Chianti Colli Aretini – east of Chianti Classico, Chianti Colli Fiorentini – south and east of Florence, Chianti Colli Senesi – around Montalcino, Montepulciano and east of San Gimignano, Chianti Colline Pisane – southeast of Pisa, Chianti Montalbano – west of Florence and Chianti Rufina – east of Florence. 7,000 or more growers. 1 million acres.

2. The famous red wine from the Chianti district; made from 50-80% Sangiovese, 10-30% Canaiolo, 10-30% Malvasia and Trebbiano and up to 5% Colorino grapes. The blend was changed in 1984, raising the amount of Sangiovese (75-90%) and lowering the amount of Canaiolo (5-10%), Trebbiano and Malvasia (5-10%) grapes. The name is derived from the Latin word *Clangor*, which means trumpet call. Chianti was known in the 13th century when it was white wine; the red was then known as Vermiglio or Florence Red. Chianti is now sold mostly in Bordeaux bottles instead of *fiaschi*.

Chianti Melini (I.)

See **Melini.**

Chianti Putto (I.)

An organization of growers, all DOC, in the Chianti district, representing 1,900 properties in all the zones except Chianti Classico. Their emblem is a baby Bacchus with a vine.

Chiaretto (I.)

A rosé wine from the Riviera del Garda Bresciano DOC district, west of Lake Garda, in the Lombardy region; like the red, it is made from Groppello, Sangiovese, Barbera and Marzemino grapes.

Chiarli – 1860 (I.)   1860
An estate in Modena, Emilia-Romagna region; produces several Lambrusca wines. 130,000 cases. 250 acres.

Chiaro di Bruna (I.)
A white wine from the Colli Altotiberini district, in the northern Umbria region, made from Trebbiano grapes with some Malvasia Bianca and other grapes.

Chiavennasca (I.)
A local name in the Valtellina district, Lombardy region, for the Nebbiolo grape.

Chicama Vineyards (U.S.)   1971
A vineyard and winery on Martha's Vineyard island, Massachusetts; produces Cabernet, Pinot Noir, Gamay Beaujolais, Chardonnay and Riesling wines and two Russian varietals, Mzvani and Rkatsiteli. 35 acres.

Chichet, Mas (F.)
An estate in Chemin de Charlemagne, Roussillon region; produces red and rosé wines made from Cabernet Sauvignon, Merlot, Grenache and Syrah grapes. 60 acres.

Chicotot, Auguste (F.)
An estate in Nuits-St.-Georges, Côte de Nuits district, Burgundy. 10 acres, including Nuits-St.-Georges Les St.-Georges – 2.5 acres, Les Vaucrains – .7 acre and some Les Procès and Les Pruliers.

Chicotot, Lucien (F.)
An estate in Nuits-St.-Georges, Côte de Nuits district, Burgundy. 9 acres, including Nuits-St.-Georges Les St.-Georges – 2.5 acres and Les Vaucrains – .7 acre.

Chile
An important wine-producing country in South America, and one of the few that can grow ungrafted *vinifera* grapes, because of the absence of *phylloxera*, the destructive plant louse. The main production is of varietal wines from Cabernet Sauvignon, Merlot, Malbec, Chardonnay, Sauvignon Blanc, Sémillon and Riesling grapes. The Maipo Valley is the best region for wine. 160 million gallons. 280,000 acres.

Chiles Valley (U.S.)
A small district, east of Rutherford, in Napa Valley, California.

China
Small amounts of wines are produced in several regions of eastern China. Most are sweet and high in alcohol, like Port and Sherry. There are about 50,000 acres of vines. Tsingtao, Chefoo and Great Wall are the best-known wines.

Chinon AOC (F.)
1. A town and district in the Touraine region, Loire Valley, which produces:

2. Red, white and rosé wines, the red and rosé made from the Cabernet Franc grape, and the white from the Chenin Blanc grape.

Chiroubles AOC (F.)
1. A village and a *Cru* Beaujolais in the Beaujolais district, Burgundy. 800 acres. It produces:

2. A red wine made from the Gamay grape.

Chiusa, Tenuta La (I.)
A small estate in Magazzini di Portoferraio-Elba, on Elba Island, Tuscany region; produces Elba wines. 1,000 cases. 11 acres.

chlorosis
A disease of the vine during which the leaves and stems turn yellow from lack of chlorophyll, usually due to an iron deficiency.

Chopin-Gesseaume, D. (F.)
An estate in Nuits-St.-Georges, Côte de Nuits district, Burgundy. 12 acres, including Nuits-St.-Georges Les Pruliers – 1.2 acres, Les Cailles – .6 acre and Les Chaignots – .5 acre.

chopine (F.)
A pint, or half-liter.

Chorey, Château de (F.)

An estate in Chorey-lès-Beaune, Côte de Beaune district, Burgundy. 30 acres, including Chorey-lès-Beaune – 2.5 acres.

Chorey-lès-Beaune AOC (F.)

A village in the Côte de Beaune district, Burgundy; produces red and white wine sold as Chorey-lès-Beaune or as Côte de Beaune-Villages. There are no *Premier Cru* or *Grand Cru* vineyards.

Chorny Doktor (U.S.S.R.)

A sweet, red dessert wine from the Crimea region, in the Ukraine SSR.

Chouacheux, Les (F.)

A *Premier Cru* vineyard in Beaune, Côte de Beaune district, Burgundy. 12.5 acres.

Christian Brothers (U.S.)   1882, 1930

A large winery in Mont La Salle, northwest of Napa city, Napa Valley, California; produces a large variety of generic, varietal and fortified wines. 1,500 acres in Napa Valley, 1,200 acres in Fresno County. 4 million cases.

Chumai (U.S.S.R.)

A sweet, red wine from Moldavia SSR, made from the Cabernet grape.

Chusclan (F.)

A commune in the Côtes du Rhône-Villages district, southern Rhône region; produces red, white and rosé wines.

Cignano, Podere di (I.)

An estate in Bagnoro Montoncello, Tuscany region; produces Chianti Colli Aretini and other wines. 35,000 cases. 145 acres.

Cilento (I.)

Red and rosé wines from Cilento, south of Salerno, in the Campania region; made from Primitivo, Guarnaccia and other grapes.

Ciliegiolo (I.)

A red grape grown in the Tuscany region.

Cilurzo and Piconi (U.S.)   vines 1967, winery 1978

A small winery in Temecula, Riverside County, in southern California; produces Cabernet, Petite Syrah, Chenin Blanc and Fumé Blanc wines. 40 acres.

Cima Corgo (P.)

The middle of the three sections of the Oporto (Port) vineyards in the Upper Douro region, considered the best of the three. The other two are Baixo Corgo and Douro Superior.

Cinque Castelli (I.)

Italian for "five castles," one of the vineyards of A. Vallana, near Gattinara, in the Piedmont region.

Cinqueterre DOC (I.)

1. A district consisting of Corniglia, Manarola, Monterosso, Riomaggiore and Vernazza, in the eastern Liguria region, which produces:

2. A white wine made from Bosco grapes with some Albarola and Vermentino grapes.

Cinquième Cru (F.)

Fifth Growth, the lowest category of estates in the 1855 classification of red Médoc wines of the Bordeaux region.

Cinsault *also* Cinsaut (F.)

A red grape, one of many used in making Châteauneuf-du-Pape wine, as well as other Rhône wines, and also grown in Algeria, South Africa (where it is called Hermitage) and California.

Cinzano, Francesco (I.)   18th cent.

A winery in Torino, Piedmont region; produces Asti Spumante and other sparkling wines, vermouth and other still wines.

Cirial (Sp.)

A white grape grown in the La Mancha region.

Cirò DOC (I.)

1. A town and district in eastern Calabria region, which produces:

2. Red, white and rosé wines, the red and rosé made from 95% Gaglioppo grapes with some Greco and Trebbiano Toscano grapes and the white from the Greco Bianco grape.

Cisa Asinara dei Marchesi di Gresy, Tenuta (I.)

An estate in Barbaresco, Piedmont region; produces Barbaresco, Dolcetto and Nebbiolo wines. 120 acres.

Cissac, Château (F.)

An estate in Cissac, Haut-Médoc district, Bordeaux; classified in 1978 as a *Cru Grand Bourgeois Exceptionnel*. 10,000 cases. 65 acres.

Citran, Château (F.)

An estate in Avensan, Haut-Médoc district, Bordeaux; classified in 1978 as a *Cru Grand Bourgeois Exceptionnel*. 13,000 cases. 130 acres.

citric acid

An acid found in grapes and to a lesser extent in wine.

claie (F.)

A straw or cane mat for drying grapes used in making VDN.

Clair-Cautin (F.)

An estate in Santenay, Côte de Beaune district, Burgundy. 19 acres, including Santenay Les Clos de Tavannes – 1.2 acres, La Comme – 2.5 acres and Santenay (white) – .6 acre.

Clair-Daü (F.)   1818

An important estate in Marsannay-La-Côte, Côte de Nuits district, Burgundy. 88 acres, including Chambertin Clos de Bèze – 5 acres, Chappelle-Chambertin – 1 acre, Clos St.-Jacques – 5 acres, Étournelles St.-Jacques – 1 acre, Lavaux St.-Jacques – .5 acre, Cazetiers – 2.5 acres, Combe aux Moines – .4 acre, Musigny – .8 acre,

Bonnes Mares – 7.5 acres, Chambolle-Musigny Les Amoureuses – .5 acre, Clos de Vougeot – 2.2 acres, Savigny Dominode – 4.8 acres, Santenay – 5 acres.

clairet (F.)

A light red wine, at one time applied to the wines of Bordeaux, as well as to a red wine mixed with some white wine to lighten it; the origin of the English term "claret."

Clairette (F.)

A white grape grown in the Rhône region, the Midi, and in Algeria.

Clairette de Bellegarde AOC (F.)

A white wine from the commune of Bellegarde, Languedoc region, in southern France; made from the Clairette grape. 160,000 gallons.

Clairette de Die AOC (F.)

1. A district around Die, along the Drôme River, including two dozen other villages, in the east central Rhône region, which produces:

2. A sparkling white wine made from varying blends of Clairette and Muscat de Frontignan grapes; some still wine is also made. 500,000 cases.

Clairette du Languedoc AOC (F.)

1. A district composed of a dozen villages west of Montpellier, in the central Languedoc region, which produces:

2. A white wine made from the Clairette grape. Another version of the wine is made from overripe grapes and allowed to maderize with 3 years aging and is called *rancio* (Sherry-like).

Clape, La VDQS (F.)

1. A village and district east of Narbonne, in the Coteaux du Languedoc district, Languedoc region, southern France, which produces:

2. Red, rosé and some white wines, the red and rosé made from various blends of Carignan, Grenache, Cinsault and Terret Noir grapes, and the white from Clairette, Bourboulenc and Picpoul grapes.

Clape, Auguste (F.)

An estate in Cornas, northern Rhône region; owns Cornas – 13.5 acres.

Clare, Château La (F.)

An estate in Bégadan, Médoc district, Bordeaux; classified in 1978 as a *Cru Bourgeois*. 9,000 cases. 45 acres.

Clare Estate, Château (Aus.)

An estate in Auburn, Clare/Watervale district, in South Australia; produces Cabernet and Rhine Riesling wines.

Clare Riesling (Aus.)

Another name for the Sémillon grape and the wine made from it in South Australia; also known as Crouchen.

Clare/Watervale (Aus.)

A small district around Clare and Auburn, 80 miles north of Adelaide, in South Australia; produces high-quality red and white wines including Cabernet, Shiraz and Rhine Riesling.

Clarendon Estate (Aus.)   1970

A winery in Clarendon, in South Australia; produces Cabernet, Shiraz, Chardonnay, Rhine Riesling and Gewürztraminer wines. 100 acres.

claret (E.)

The British term for Bordeaux wines, derived from *clairet,* the French word for a light red or rosé wine.

clarete (Sp., P.)

Any light red wine, especially in the Rioja region.

Clarke, Château (F.)

An estate in Listrac, Haut-Médoc district, Bordeaux; classified in 1932 as a *Cru Bourgeois,* and in 1978 as Being Reconstituted; bought by Baron Edmond de Rothschild (Lafite), enlarged and replanted in 1973. 345 acres. 50,000 cases.

Clarke Vineyard (U.S.)   1983

A Winery in Stonington, northeastern Connecticut; produces wines made from Chardonnay, Pinot Noir, Riesling and hybrid grapes. 10 acres.

clarry (E.) *also* clarré (F.)

A Medieval wine drink, probably made with claret mixed with honey and spices.

Clary, Château de (F.)

An estate in Roquemaure, Lirac district, southern Rhône region. 135 acres.

classico (I.)

Classic, of better quality, finer; a traditional or original part of a district.

Clastidio (I.)

Red, white and rosé wines from Casteggio, in the Oltrepò Pavese district, Lombardy region; the red and rosé are made from Barbera, Uva Rara and Croatina grapes; the white from Riesling Italico and Pinot grapes.

Clastidium (I.)

A white wine from Broni, in the Oltrepò Pavese district, in the Lombardy region; made from Pinot Nero and Pinot Grigio grapes and aged in oak.

clavelin (F.)

A squat, flat-sided bottle used in the commune of Château–Châlon, Jura region, for *vin jaune.*

Clavoillons (F.)

A *Premier Cru* vineyard in Puligny-Montrachet, Côte de Beaune district, Burgundy. 14 acres.

Clefs d'Or, Les (F.)

An estate in Châteauneuf-du-Pape, Rhône region; also makes a white wine made from Grenache Blanc and Bourboulenc grapes. 62 acres. Also owns Domaine de Beaumefort in Beaumefort, Côtes du Rhône district – 30 acres.

Clémencey Frères (F.)

An estate in Couchey, Côte de Nuits district, Burgundy. 12 acres, including Fixin Les Hervelets – 5 acres.

Cléray, Château du (F.)

An estate in Vallet, Muscadet de Sèvre-et-Maine district, Muscadet region, Loire Valley; also makes some Gros Plant wine. 75 acres.

Clerc-Milon-Mondon, Château (F.)

An estate in Milon (Pauillac), Haut-Médoc district, Bordeaux; classified in 1855 as a *Cinquième Cru*; bought by Baron Philippe de Rothschild (Mouton) in 1970. 8,000 cases. 65 acres.

Clerget, Domaine (F.)

An estate in Volnay, Côte de Beaune district, Burgundy. 12 acres, including Volnay Caillerets – .8 acre, Clos du Verseuil Monopole – 1.6 acres, Les Santenots – 2 acres, Carelle sous la Chapelle – 1.6 acres and Pommard Les Rugiens – 1.6 acres.

Clerget, Félix (F.)   1270

An estate in Pommard, Côte de Beaune district, Burgundy. 45 acres, including Pommard Les Rugiens – 2 acres, Pommard *Premier Cru* - 12 acres (Arvelets, Charmots, Saucille, Chanières, Clos Blanc and Chanlins Bas), Volnay En Cailleret – .8 acre, Les Mitans – 2.5 acres, Puligny-Montrachet Champs Gain – .8 acre, Beaune Les Grèves – 1.7 acres, Les Aigrots – 6.2 acres, Saint-Désiré – 7.5 acres, Corton-Renardes – 1 acre, Corton-Vergennes – 2 acres and Clos de Vougeot – .8 acre.

Clerget, Raoul (F.)   13th cent.

An estate and merchant in St.-Aubin, Côte de Beaune district, Burgundy; produces St.-Aubin and other wines.

Clerget, Roger (F.)

An estate in Pommard, Côte de Beaune district, Burgundy. 35 acres, including Pommard Les Rugiens – 1.2 acres, Les Épenots – 1.2 acres, Les Pézerolles – 4 acres, Clos Blanc – 1.2 acres, Savigny Les Vergelesses – 4 acres and Aloxe-Corton – 2.5 acres.

Clerget, Veuve A. (F.)

An estate in Chambolle-Musigny, Côte de Nuits district, Burgundy. 15 acres, including Échézeaux – .5 acre, Chambolle-Musigny Les Charmes – 1.6 acres and some Vosne-Romanée, Morey-St.-Denis and Vougeot.

Cles, Barone de (I.)   16th cent.

An estate in Mezzolombardo, Trentino-Alto Adige region; produces Chardonnay, Lagrein, Pinot Grigio, Teroldego Rotaliano, Trentino and other wines. 23,000 cases. 75 acres.

Clevner *also* Klevner *or* Klebrot (G.)

1. In Alsace, the name for the Pinot Blanc grape.
2. In Switzerland, the name for the Blauburgunder, or Pinot Noir grape.

climat (F.)

In Burgundy, the name for a vineyard, or a designated parcel of vineyard; a *cru*, or growth.

Climat du Val *also* Clos du Val (F.)

A *Premier Cru* vineyard in Auxey-Duresses, Côte de Beaune district, Burgundy. 23 acres.

Climens, Château (F.)

An estate in Barsac, Sauternes district, Bordeaux; classified in 1855 as a *Premier Cru*; the wine is made entirely from Sémillon grapes; considered nearly equal in quality to Château d'Yquem. 6,000 cases. 75 acres.

Clinet, Château (F.)

An estate in Pomerol, Bordeaux. 3,300 cases. 15 acres.

Clinton (U.S.) *also* Clinto, Crinto, Grinto (I.)

An American red grape grown in the eastern and midwestern U.S. and in the eastern Veneto region of Italy, used to made red wine; also for blending and as root stocks for grafting.

Clinton Vineyard (U.S.)　　　　　1977

A small winery in Wetmore, Hudson River Valley region, New York; produces Seyval Blanc, White Riesling and Chardonnay wines. 4,000 cases. 12 acres.

clone

A group of individual plants which are propagated asexually from one single source and which retains the special characteristics of the source plant. Different clones of any one grape variety exist, having different characteristics.

clos (F.)

An enclosed vineyard; a vineyard that was formerly walled but still retains the name *clos*. The name is used in many regions of France and California.

Clos, Les (F.)

A *Grand Cru* vineyard in Chablis, Chablis district, Burgundy.

Closeau, Au (F.)

A *Premier Cru* vineyard in Gevrey-Chambertin, Côte de Nuits district, Burgundy. 1.5 acres.

Closel, Domaine du (F.)

An estate in St.-Georges-sur-Loire, Savennières district, Anjou region, Loire Valley; produces Savennières and other Anjou wines. 40 acres.

Closerie, Château La (F.)

An estate in Moulis, Haut-Médoc district, Bordeaux; classified in 1978 as a *Cru Bourgeois*. 2,300 cases. 17 acres.

Clotte, Château La (F.)

An estate in St.-Émilion, Bordeaux; classified in 1955 as a *Grand Cru Classé*. 2,500 cases. 12 acres.

Clous, Aux (F.)

A *Premier Cru* vineyard (in part) in Savigny-lès-Beaune, Côte de Beaune district, Burgundy. 38 acres.

Cloux (F.)

A *Premier Cru* vineyard in Rully, Côte Chalonnaise district, Burgundy.

Clusière, Château La (F.)

An estate in St.-Émilion, Bordeaux; classified in 1955 as a *Grand Cru Classé*. 1,200 cases. 8 acres.

Coan (Gr.)

An ancient Greek wine from the Island of Cos.

Cochineal *also* Cochnilles (F.)

A scale insect which attaches itself to the vines and feeds on the sap, thus weakening the vines.

cochylis

A species of moth, the larvae of which feed on the grapes.

Cockburn Smithes & Cia Lda (P.)　　1815

A Port producer in Vila Nova de Gaia; owns Quinta do Tua, Quinta da Santa Maria, Quinta do Val, Quinta do Coelho and Quinta do Atayde; produces several Ports: Director's Reserve, Special Reserve Tawny, etc. 600 acres.

Cococciola (I.)

A white grape grown in the Abruzzo region.

Coda di Volpe (I.)

A white grape grown in the Vesuvio district, Campania region. The local name is Caprettona.

Códega (P.)

A white grape grown in the Douro region for table wines.

Codo (P.)

A white grape grown in the Beiras district, east of the Dão region, in northern Portugal.

Codorníu S.A. (Sp.)

A winery in San Sadurní de Noya, west of Barcelona, in the Catalonia region; produces only sparkling wines from purchased grapes. 3 million cases.

Cogno, Elvio (I.)

An estate in La Morra, Piedmont region; produces Barbera, Barolo, Dolcetto and Freisa wines.

Col d'Orcia (I.)

A large estate in Montalcino, Tuscany region; produces Brunello, Novembrino and Rosso wines. 12,000 cases. 200 acres.

Col Sandago (I.)   1960

An estate in Pieve di Soligo, Veneto region; produces Cabernet Sauvignon, Coste delle Pergole, Merlot, Pinot Grigio, Val de Brun and Wildbacher wines. 50,000 cases. 200 acres.

Colacicchi, Bruno (I.)

An estate in Anagni, Latium region; produces Romagnano and Torre Ercolana wines.

Colares (P.)

1. A town and district West of Lisbon, which produces:

2. Red and white wine; the red made from the Ramisco grape, and the white made from Arinto, Malvasia and Dona Branca grapes grown in sandy soil. The red requires very long aging (10 years in wood) to show its true quality.

Colcord Winery (U.S.) vines 1970
                                    wine 1976

A winery near Paris, Kentucky; produces Villard Blanc, Chelois and other hybrid wines; bottled under the Cane Ridge label. 37 acres.

Cold Duck (U.S.)   1930

A sparkling wine from N.Y. State and Michigan, made by blending red and white sparkling wines.

Cole Ranch (U.S.)

A vineyard in Mendocino County, California; grows Riesling grapes for Château St. Jean and Fetzer wineries. 40 acres.

Colella, Santoro (I.)

An estate in Pratola Peligna, Abruzzi region; produces Montepulciano, Pinot Grigio, Riesling, Traminer, Trebbiano and Veltliner wines.

colheita (P.)

Vintage.

Colin, François (F.)

An estate in Chassagne-Montrachet, Côte de Beaune district, Burgundy, with vineyards in Chassagne-Montrachet (red and white). 15 acres.

collage (F.)

The process of fining and clarifying the wine by adding egg white, isinglass, gelatin, casein, blood or clay to bring suspended solids to the bottom of the vat.

collar

The narrow label on the neck of the bottle; *collerette*, in French.

Collard Brothers (N.Z.)   1946

A winery in Henderson, Aukland district, North Island; produces Rhine Riesling, Müller-Thurgau, Gewürztraminer, Sylvaner, Cabernet and Merlot wines. 60 acres.

Collavini, E. (I.)

An estate in Corno di Rosazzo, Friuli-Venezia Giulia region; produces Colli Orientali, Collio and Grave wines. 22,000 cases. 55 acres.

Colle del Calvario (I.)

Red and white wines from Grumello, east of Bergamo, in the Lombardy region; the red wine is made from Merlot, Cabernet and Marzemino grapes and the white wine is made from Pinot Bianco and Pinot Grigio grapes.

Colle Picchioni (I.)

A red wine from Marino, in the Castelli Romani district, south of Rome, in the Latium region; made from Merlot and Cesanese grapes with some Sangiovese and Montepulciano grapes.

collerette (F.)

The collar, or label on the neck of a wine bottle.

Collet et Fils, Domaine Jean (F.)

An estate in the Chablis district, Burgundy; owns Valmur – 1.3 acres, Vaillons – 9 acres, Montmains – 11 acres, Épinotte – 7.5 acres, Monts-de-Milieu – 1.3 acres, Montée de Tonnerre – 1 acre and Chablis – 12.5 acres.

colli (I.)

Hills.

Colli Albani DOC (I.)

1. A district from Albano and the area around Lake Albano, south of Rome, in the Castelli Romani district, Latium region, which produces:

2. White wines made from Malvasia and Trebbiano grapes.

Colli Altotiberini DOC (I.)   DOC in 1978

1. A district around Città di Costello, in the northern Umbria region, which produces:

2. Red, white and rosé wines, the red and rosé made from Sangoivese and Merlot grapes, and the white from Trebbiano and Malvasia grapes.

Colli Berici DOC (I.)

A district near Vicenza, in the Veneto region; the red and white wines are varietals and are named for the grape from which they are made: Cabernet, Garganega, Merlot, Pinot Bianco, Sauvignon, Tocai Italico and Tocai Rosso.

Colli Bolognesi DOC (I.)

A district southwest of Bologna, in the Emilia-Romagna region. Most of the red and white wines are varietals and are named after the grape from which they are made: Barbera, Merlot, Pinot Bianco, Riesling Italico (or Pignoletto), Sauvignon and Bianco (Albana and Trebbiano grapes).

Colli di Bolzano DOC (I.)

1. A district around Bolzano, in the Trentino-Alto Adige region, which produces:

2. Light, red wines made from the Schiava grape.

Colli Euganei DOC (I.)

A district around Padua, in the Veneto region, which produces red and white wines: Bianco, made from Garganega, Sauvignon, Serprina and Tocai grapes, Moscato, from Moscato Bianco grapes and Rosso, from Cabernet, Barbera, Merlot and Raboso grapes.

Colli Lanuvini DOC (I.)

1. A district around Lanuvio, south of Rome, in the Latium region, which produces:

2. A white wine made from Malvasia, Trebbiano, Bellone and Bonvino grapes.

Colli Morenici Mantovani del Garda DOC (I.)

1. A district north of Mantua, in the southeastern Lombardy region, which produces:

2. Red, white and rosé wines, the red and rosé made from Rondinella, Merlot and Rossanella grapes and the white from Garganega and Trebbiano grapes.

Colli Orientali del Friuli (I.)

A district around Cividale del Friuli, in the eastern Friuli-Venezia Giulia region, which produces a dozen varietal wines, each named after the grape from which it is made.

Colli Perugini DOC (I.)

1. A district covering the hills southwest of Perugina, in the Umbria region, which produces:

2. Red, white and rosé wines; the red and rosé wine is made from the Sangiovese grape with some Merlot, Barbera and Montepulciano grapes; the white wine is made from Grechetto, Malvasia and Trebbiano grapes.

Colli Piacentini DOC (I.)   1983

A new district around the Piacenza hills, in the western Emilia-Romagna region, producing several varietal wines.

Colli Tortonesi DOC (I.)

A district around Tortona, in the southeastern Piedmont region, which produces two varietal wines: Barbera and Cortese.

Colli del Trasimeno DOC (I.)

A district around Lake Trasimeno, west of Perugia, in the Umbria region; produces red and white wines, the red wine made from Sangiovese, Ciliegiolo, Montepulciano and Gamay grapes, the white wine made from Malvasia, Trebbiano, Verdello and Grechetto grapes.

Collignon, Cuvée Madeleine (F.)   1977

A red wine from the Hospices de Beaune, Côte de Beaune district, Burgundy. The *cuvée* is composed of one vineyard in Gevrey-Chambertin (the only *cuvée* from the Côte de Nuits): Mazis-Chambertin – 4 acres. 675 cases.

Colline, Le (I.)   c. 1950

An estate in Gattinara, Piedmont region; produces Barbaresco, Ghemme and Monsecco wines. 45 acres.

Colline de Sarre et Chesallet, La (I.)

A red wine from Sarre and Chesallet, west of Aosta, in the Valle d'Aosta region; made from Petit Rouge and Gamay grapes.

Collio *also* Collio Goriziano DOC (I.)

1. A district in the eastern part of the Friuli-Venezia Giulia region, in northeastern Italy, which produces:

2. A wide variety of red and white varietal wines and Collio wine, a white wine made from Ribolla, Malvasia and Tocai grapes.

Collioure AOC (F.)

1. A village in the northern tip of the Banyuls district, Roussillon region, in the Midi, which produces:

2. A red wine made from the Grenache, Mourvèdre, Cinsault and some Carignan grapes.

Colmar (F.)

The largest town in Alsace and the center of the region's wine trade.

Colobel

A red hybrid grape, also called Seibel 8357 – a cross of Seibel 6150 and 5455 grapes, and because of its red juice used as a *teinturier* (coloring grape) in blends.

Colombar (S. Af.)

A white grape, the Colombard of France, grown in the Stellenbosch district; mostly used in blending.

Colombard, French Colombard (F.)

A white grape grown mostly in the Cognac and Armagnac regions, but also in South Africa and in California, where it is used for generic wines and as a varietal.

Colombier Monpelou, Château (F.)

An estate in Pauillac, in the Haut-Médoc district, Bordeaux; classified in 1978 as a *Cru Grand Bourgeois*. 30 acres. 5,000 cases.

Colony (U.S.)   1887

The brand name for Italian Swiss Colony wines, originally in Asti, northern Sonoma County, California.

Colorado (U.S.)

A state in the southwestern United States, where some *vinifera* grapes have been planted since 1973, and one commercial winery has been built in 1978.

Colorado Mountain Vineyards (U.S.) 1974

The only winery in the state of Colorado, located in Golden; produces Johannisberg Riesling, Chardonnay and Gewürztraminer wines. 20 acres.

Colorino (I.)

A red grape grown in the Tuscany region.

Coltassala (I.)

A red wine from the Tuscany region; made from a blend of Sangiovese and Mammolo grapes; produced by Castello di Volpaia.

coltivatore (I.)

A cultivator, or grower.

Columella (1st century, A.D.) (Lat.)

An ancient Roman author who wrote *De Re Rustica* (c. 60 A.D.), in which he describes vineyards and wine-making.

Combe-aux-Moines (F.)

A *Premier Cru* vineyard in Gevrey-Chambertin, Côte de Nuits district, Burgundy. 12 acres.

Combe d'Orveau, La (F.)

A *Premier Cru* vineyard in Chambolle-Musigny, Côte de Nuits district, Burgundy; one of the 3 sections of Le Musigny vineyard. 12.5 acres.

Combes, Les (F.)

A *Premier Cru* vineyard in St.-Aubin, Côte de Beaune district, Burgundy; produces red and white wines. 37 acres.

Combes, Les (F.)

A *Grand Cru* vineyard (in part) in Aloxe-Corton, Côte de Beaune district, Burgundy.

Combes-Dessus, Les (F.)

A *Premier Cru* vineyard (in part) in Pommard, Côte de Beaune district, Burgundy. 7 acres.

Combettes, Les (F.)

A *Premier Cru* vineyard in Puligny-Montrachet, Côte de Beaune district, Burgundy. 16.5 acres.

Comblanchien (F.)

A commune south of Nuits-St.-Georges and Prémeaux, in the Côte de Nuits district, Burgundy; produces red and white wines sold as Côte de Nuits-Villages.

Combottes, Aux (F.)

A *Premier Cru* vineyard in Chambolle-Musigny, Côte de Nuits district, Burgundy. 5 acres. See also **Les Combottes.**

Combottes, Aux (F.)

A *Premier Cru* vineyard in Gevrey-Chambertin, Côte de Nuits district, Burgundy. 12.5 acres.

Combottes, Les (F.)

A *Premier Cru* vineyard in Chambolle-Musigny, Côte de Nuits district, Burgundy. 5 acres.

Cometta (I.)

A local red grape grown around Perugia, in the Umbria region.

Comissão de Viticultura da Região dos Vinhos Verdes (P.) 1929

A governmental commission formed in 1929 to regulate the wines from the Vinho Verde region.

Commandaria (Cyp.)

A legendary, sweet, red wine from Cyprus; made from dried Mavron and Xynisteri grapes. The most notable wines come from the villages of Kalokhorio, Zoopiyi and Yerassa, north of Limassol.

Commaraine, Clos de la (F.)

A *Premier Cru* vineyard in Pommard, Côte de Beaune district, Burgundy. 10 acres.

Comme, La (F.)

A *Premier Cru* vineyard in Santenay, Côte de Beaune district, Burgundy. 80 acres.

Commonwealth Winery (U.S.)   1977

A winery in Plymouth, Massachusetts; produces varietal wines made from hybrid and *vinifera* grapes.

communal wine (F.)

Wine grown and made from the area around one specific village or *commune* (township); a village wine, usually blended from several vineyards.

commune (F.)

A village, township or parish and its vineyards.

Compañía Vinícola del Norte de España (Sp.)

See **CVNE.**

Completer (Sw.)

A rare, local, white grape grown in the Bundner Herrschaft district, in eastern Switzerland; it is used to make sweet white wine.

Concannon Vineyard (U.S.)   1883

An old winery in Livermore, Livermore Valley, Alameda County, California; produces Cabernet, Pinot Noir, Petite Sirah, Sauvignon Blanc, Muscat Blanc and Rkatsiteli wines, and Château Concannon (a sweet Sauvignon Blanc). 75,000 cases. 250 acres.

Concha y Toro (Ch.)   1883

One of the largest wineries in Chile, in the Maipo Valley, central Chile; produces Cabernet, Sauvignon, Riesling, Casillero del Diablo, Marqués de Casa Concha and St. Emiliana Cabernet wines. 4,000 acres. 1 million cases.

Concord (U.S.)

An important American red grape of *Vitis labrusca* developed in Concord, Massachusetts by Ephraim Wales Bull during 1843-1849; grown extensively in the eastern and midwestern U.S. and in Canada where it produces sweet wines and sweet Kosher wines.

Conde de Caralt (Sp.)

A winery in San Sadurní de Noya, west of Barcelona, in the Catalonia region; produces still and sparkling wines.

Conde de Santar (P.)

An estate near Viseu in the Dão region, which produces red and white Dão wines, the red made from Mortagua, Baga de Louro and Tourigo grapes, and the white from Arinto, Fernão Pires and Azal Branco grapes, aged and bottled by Carvalho, Ribeiro & Ferreira of Lisbon. 150 acres. 60,000 cases.

Condemine, Domaine de la (F.)

An estate in Paulhan, Clairette du Languedoc district, Languedoc region. 15 acres.

Condrieu AOC (F.)

1. A village and small district of only 35 acres south of Vienne, in the northern Rhône region. The district also includes Vérin, Limony and St.-Michel-sur-Rhône as well as the famous Château-Grillet, and produces:

2. A white wine made from the Viognier grape.

Conestoga Vineyards (U.S.)   1963

A winery in Birchrunville, east of Valley Forge, Pennsylvania; produces wines made from hybrid and *labrusca* grapes.

confrérie (F.)

A wine society.

Confuron et ses Fils, Domaine Jean (F.)

An old estate in Prémeaux, Côte de Nuits district, Burgundy. 25 acres, including Clos de Vougeot – 1.2 acres, Bonnes Mares – .7 acre, Nuits-St.-Georges Les Chaboeufs – 1.2 acres and Les Vaucrains – .7 acre.

Confuron-Jayer, J. (F.)

An estate in Vosne-Romanée, Côte de Nuits district, Burgundy. 7.5 acres, including Clos de Vougeot – .7 acre and Vosne-Romanée Les Suchots – 4 acres.

congé (F.)

An official document accompanying shipments of wines and spirits stating that taxes have been paid.

congius (Lat.)

An old Roman wine measure equal to one-eigth of an *Amphora*, or about 3 liters.

Congress Springs Vineyards (U.S.)   1892, 1976

A small winery near Saratoga, in the Santa Cruz mountains, Santa Clara County, California; produces Cabernet, Pinot Noir, Zinfandel, Sémillon, Sauvignon Blanc and Pinot Blanc wines. 5,000 cases. 10 acres.

Conn Creek Winery (U.S.)   1974

A winery in Rutherford (originally in St. Helena), Napa Valley, California; produces Cabernet, Zinfandel and Chardonnay wines. Their second wine is Château Maja. 20,000 cases. 150 acres.

Connecticut (U.S.)

A state in the northeastern United States, which had very few wineries because of the high license fees until 1978, when they were reduced.

Conoy Winery (U.S.)   1972

A winery near Bainbridge, Pennsylvania; produces wines made from de Chaunac and Aurora grapes. 27 acres.

Conseillante, Château La (F.)

An estate in Pomerol, Bordeaux. 30 acres. 3,500 cases.

Consejo Regulador (Sp.)

The Regulatory Council, the official governmental organization which sets up requirements for and supervises the *Denominación de Origen* wines, first set up in 1926 (for Rioja wines) and still continues to designate regions and districts.

consorzio (I.)

A group of growers and shippers who have organized in order to affect some control of the use of place names and the quality of their wines; also, a local wine society.

Consorzio Romagnoto Vini Tipici (I.)

See **Corovin.**

Constantia WO (S.Af.)

1. A town and district south of Capetown, at one time famous for its Muscat wines, which now produces:

2. Red and white varietal wines made from Cabernet Sauvignon, Shiraz, Pinotage, Chenin Blanc, Riesling and Kerner grapes.

Conterno, Aldo (I.)

An estate in Monforte d'Alba, Piedmont region; produces Barbera, Barolo, Dolcetto, Freisa and Grignolino wines. 8,000 cases. 37 acres.

Conterno, Giacomo (I.)   1770

An estate in Monforte d'Alba, Piedmont region; produces Barbera, Barolo and Dolcetto wines.

Conteville (Aus.)   1966

A small winery in Wanneroo, north of Perth, in the Swan Valley district, Western Australia; produces Cabernet Sauvignon, Rhine Riesling and Gewürztraminer varietal wines and a dry Frontignan wine. 6,000 cases. 50 acres.

Contini, Attilio (I.)

An estate in Cabras, Sardinia; produces Vernaccia di Oristano wines.

Contra Costa County (U.S.)

A region east of San Francisco and just south of Alameda County, northwestern California. 4,000 acres.

Contratto, Giuseppe (I.)   1867

A winery in Canelli, Piedmont region; produces Barbaresco, Barbera, Barolo, Freisa, Cortese, Asti Spumante and Contratto Brut wines.

Contrie, Clos de la (F.)

An estate in St.-Nicolas-de-Bourgueil, Touraine region, Loire Valley. 20 acres.

Cook, R. and J. (U.S.)   1978

A winery in Clarksburg, in the Sacramento River Delta, Yolo County, California; produces Cabernet, Petite Sirah and Chenin Blanc wines. 400 acres. 40,000 cases.

Cook's New Zealand Wine Company (N.Z.)   1968

A winery in Te Kauwhata, North Island, also plantings in Gisborne and Riverhead; produces Cabernet, Pinot Gris, Riesling Silvaner, Gewürztraminer, Golden Chasselas, Pinotage, Pinot Meunier, Chardonnay and many other wines. 400 acres.

Coonawarra (Aus.)

A famous small district on the southern tip of South Australia; produces Cabernet, Shiraz and Rhine Riesling wines.

cooper

1. A craftsman who makes barrels and casks.

2. A merchant who samples wines at bottling time.

3. To make or repair casks or barrels.

4. To store in barrels.

cooperage

1. The assembly of barrels.

2. The manufacture and repair of barrels.

3. The fee charged for the work of the cooper.

co-operative

A jointly owned and operated winery or cellar.

copper sulfate

Cupric sulfate, also called blue stone and blue vitriol, a copper salt used as a fungicide.

Copertino DOC (I.)

1. A village and district around Copertino, in the southern Apulia region, which produces:

2. Red and rosé wines made from Negroamaro, Malvasia Nera, Montepulciano and Sangiovese grapes.

copita (Sp.)

A specially shaped glass which tapers toward the top, used for drinking Sherry.

Coquard-Loison (F.)

An estate in Flagey-Échézeaux, Côte de Nuits district, Burgundy. 12.5 acres, including Grands Échézeaux – .5 acre, Clos de Vougeot – 1 acre, Échézeaux – 2.5 acres, Clos de la Roche – .8 acre and some Gevrey-Chambertin and Vosne-Romanée.

Cora, G. & L. Fratelli (I.)

A merchant in Torino, Piedmont region; produces Asti Spumante and other sparkling wines.

Corbans Wines (N.Z.)   1902

An old winery in Henderson, West Aukland, North Island; also plantings in Whenuapai, Gisborne and Tolaga Bay; produces Cabernet, Claret from Cabernet and Pinotage, Chardonnay, Riesling Sylvaner, Chenin Blanc and fortified wines. 1,000 acres.

Corbara (I.)

1. A lake southeast of Orvieto, in the Umbria region.

2. A red wine from an area around Lake Corbara; made from the Sangiovese grape.

Corbeaux, Les (F.)

A *Premier Cru* vineyard in Gevrey-Chambertin, Côte de Nuits district, Burgundy. 8 acres.

Corbières VDQS (F.)

1. A large district (85,000 acres) southwest of Narbonne, in the Languedoc region, which produces:

2. Red, white and rosé wines, the red and rosé made from Carignan, Cinsault, Grenache, Mourvèdre, Terret noir, Picpoul and Syrah grapes, and the white from Clairette, Malvoisie and Bourboulenc grapes.

Corbin, Château (F.)

An estate in St.-Émilion, Bordeaux; classified in 1955 as a *Grand Cru Classé*. 8,500 cases. 30 acres.

Corbin-Michotte, Château (F.)

An estate in St.-Émilion, Bordeaux; classified in 1955 as a *Grand Cru Classé*. 4,000 cases. 18 acres.

Cordero di Montezemolo, Paolo (I.)

An estate in La Morra, Piedmont region; produces Barolo and Dolcetto wines. 2,500 cases. 32 acres.

Cordier (F.)   1877

A merchant in Bordeaux; owns Châteaux Gruaud-Larose, Talbot, Lafaurie-Peyraguey and Clos des Jacobins.

cordon (F.)

A method of vine-training in which the fruit-bearing canes emenating from a single, short trunk are trained horizontally on wires.

cordon de royat (F.)

A variation of cordon-training of vines.

Cordtz Brothers Cellars (U.S)   1906, 1980

A re-established winery in Cloverdale, Sonoma County, California; produces Cabernet, Zinfandel, Chardonnay, Gewürztraminer and Sauvignon Blanc wines. 15,000 cases. 50 acres.

Corgette, Domaine de la (F.)

An estate in St.-Romain, Côte de Beaune district, Burgundy; controlled by Roland Thévenin. See **Thévenin.**

Corgoloin (F.)

A commune in the southwestern Côte de Nuits district, Burgundy; the wines are blended and sold as Côte de Nuits-Villages AOC.

Cori DOC (I.)

1. A village and district south of Rome, in the Latium region, which produces:

2. Red and white wines; the red wines are made from 40-60% Montepulciano, 20-40% Nero Buoni di Cori and 10-30% Cesanese grapes, and the white wines from Malvasia and Trebbiano grapes.

Coria (I.)

An estate in Vittoria, Sicily; produces Cerasuolo, Moscato, Slicchiato, Villa Fontane and other wines. 1,200 cases. 7 acres.

Corinto Nero (I.)

A red grape grown in Sicily.

Coriole (Aus.)   1969

A small winery south of Adelaide, in the Southern Vales district, South Australia; produces mostly red wine: Cabernet and Shiraz, and some white wine: Rhine Riesling and Chenin Blanc. 7,000 cases. 160 acres.

cork

A stopper for wine bottles usually made of cork; some are now made of plastic or composition cork.

corkage

A fee charged in a restaurant for opening and serving wine brought in by the patron.

corkscrew

A device used to extract corks from bottles; basically, a strong metal spiral with a handle.

corky

A term used to describe wine that has been spoiled by a bad cork; *bouchonné*, in French.

Cornas AOC (F.)

1. A village and small district (180 acres) northwest of Valence, in the northern Rhône region, which produces:

2. A red wine made from the Syrah grape.

Coron Père et Fils (F.)   1879

An estate in Beaune, Côte de Beaune district, Burgundy. 8 acres, including Beaune Les Cent Vignes – 2 acres, Clos du Roi – 2 acres, Champs Pimont – 2.5 acres, Les Grèves – 1.2 acres and Le Clos des Mouches – .5 acre.

Corovin (Consorzio Romagnolo Vini Tipici) (I.)   1968

A large co-op group in Forli, Emilia-Romagna region; produces many wines including Albana, Lambrusco, Sangiovese and Trebbiano; made from grapes of 12,000 growers. 3 million cases.

Corowa (Aus.)

A town and district in southern New South Wales.

Corriola (P.)

A hybrid grape grown in the Vinho Verde region.

Corse (F.)

The French-owned island of Corsica.

corsé (F.)

Robust; full-bodied.

Corsica also Corse (F.)

An island in the Mediterranean Sea, south of France and west of Italy; it is owned by France but the language is an Italian dialect; produces red, white and rosé wines mostly from local Italian-related varieties. Eight wines carry the Vin de Corse AOC designation, of which the most well-known are Vin de Corse, Patrimonio and Coteaux d'Ajaccio. 8 million gallons. 20,000 acres.

Cortaillod (Sw.)

1. A village west of Neuchâtel, on the north shore of Lake Neuchâtel, in the Neuchâtel district, Vaud region, which produces:

2. A red wine made from the Pinot Noir grape.

Cortese (I.)

A white grape grown in the Piedmont region, especially in Gavi, and to a lesser extent in Lombardy.

Cortese dell'Alto Monferrato DOC (I.)

1. A district south of Alessandria, in the southeastern Piedmont region, which produces:

2. A white wine made from at least 85% Cortese grapes.

Cortese di Gavi DOC also Gavi DOC (I.)

1. A district around Gavi, in the southeastern Piedmont region, which produces:

2. A white wine made from the Cortese grape, made also in a *spumante* version.

Corton- (F.)

A peculiarity in Burgundy, that any vineyard name following the name of Corton- is considered a *Grand Cru*; they include: Bressandes, Charlemagne, Chaumes, Clos du Roi, Fiètres, Grèves, Languettes, Maréchaudes, Meix, Pauland, Perrières, Pougets, Renardes, Vigne-au-Saint and small parts of other vineyards in Aloxe-Corton; Carrières, Grands Lolières, Moutottes, Rognet, Toppe au Vert and Vergennes in Ladoix-Serrigny; and Charlemagne in Pernand-Vergelesses. If one of those vineyard names follows Aloxe-Corton then it is a *Premier Cru*, since several vineyards are designated partially *Grand Cru* and partially *Premier Cru*.

Corton, Le AOC (F.)

A *Grand Cru* vineyard mainly in Aloxe-Corton, with small parts in Pernand-Vergelesses and Ladoix-Serrigny, Côte de Beaune district, Burgundy; it is sub-divided into several vineyard plots; produces red and white wines. 30 acres.

Corton-Charlemagne AOC (F.)

A *Grand Cru* white-wine vineyard, partly in Aloxe-Corton and partly in Pernand-Vergelesses, Côte de Beaune district, Burgundy. 40 acres.

Corton-Grancey (F.)
See **Grancey, Château.**

Cortons, Clos des (F.)
A *Grand Cru* vineyard in Ladoix-Serrigny (when used with Corton), Côte de Beaune district, Burgundy; a *monopole* of Faiveley. 7.5 acres.

Corvées, Clos des (F.)
A *Premier Cru* vineyard in Prémeaux, Côte de Nuits district, Burgundy. 19 acres.

Corvées-Paget, Les (F.)
A *Premier Cru* vineyard in Prémeaux, Côte de Nuits district, Burgundy. 5 acres.

Corvetta (I.)
A local red grape grown in the Umbria region.

Corvina (I.)
A red grape grown in the Bardolino and Valpolicella districts, in the Veneto region.

Corvo. Duca di Salaparuta (I.)   1824
Italian for "crow," a brand of red, white and sparkling wines from Casteldeccia, just east of Palermo, in northwestern Sicily. The red wine is made from Calabrese, Nerello Mascalese and Perricone grapes and the white and sparkling wines from Catarratto, Inzolia and Trebbiano grapes. Produced by the Duca di Salaparuta from purchased grapes. 600,000 cases.

Cos d'Estournel, Château (F.)
An estate in St.-Estèphe, Haut-Médoc district, Bordeaux; classified in 1855 as a *Deuxième Cru;* named after the Isle of Cos (or Caux), near Rhodes. 25,000 cases. 150 acres.

Cos-Labory, Château (F.)
An estate in St.-Estèphe, Haut-Médoc district, Bordeaux; classified in 1855 as a *Cinquième Cru*. 40 acres. 5,000 cases.

cosecha (Sp.)
The harvest year; vintage year.

cosechero (Sp.)
A vineyard owner.

Cossart, Gordon & Co. (P.)   1745
A producer of Madeira wines.

Cosson, Héritiers (F.)
An estate in Morey-St.-Denis, Côte de Nuits, Burgundy. 24 acres, including Clos des Lambrays Monopole – 22 acres and Morey-St.-Denis Clos des Sorbés – 2 acres.

Costanti, Podere Emilio (I.)
A small estate in Montalcino, Tuscany region; produces Albatro, Brunello, Chianti Colli Senese and Vermiglio wines. 1,200 cases. 9 acres.

Coste, Château La (F.)
An estate in Le Puy-Ste.-Réparade, in the Provence region.

Costières du Gard VDQS (F.)
1. A large district of almost 10,000 acres west of Nîmes, in the eastern part of the Languedoc region of the Midi, which produces:
2. Red, white and rosé wines, the red and rosé made from Carignan, Cinsault, Mourvèdre, Grenache, Syrah and other grapes, and the white from Clairette, Bourboulenc and Ugni Blanc grapes.

Costozza (I.)
A village and estate in Costozza di Longare, south of Vicenza, in the Colli Berici district, Veneto region; produces special quality varietal wines made from Cabernet Franc, Picolit, Pinot Nero, Riesling and other grapes.

Cot *also* Côt (F.)
In the Loire Valley, the name for the Malbec grape; also called Cahors, Auxerrois, Pressac and Pied-Rouge.

Cotat, François & Paul (F.)
A small estate in Chavignol, Sancerre district, Upper Loire region, Loire Valley.

Côte, La (Sw.)

A district on the northern shore of Lake Geneva, in the Vaud region; produces Dorin and Salvagnin wines.

côte (F.)

A vineyard slope or hill.

Côte de Beaune AOC (F.)

1. The southern half of the Côte d'Or district, in Burgundy, almost 15 miles long; produces red and white wines (80% red). 7,500 acres. 19 communes. 7 *Grand Crus* (all but one, Corton, are white).

2. The AOC name for blended red wine from anywhere in the Côte de Beaune district.

Côte de Beaune-Villages AOC (F.)

A red wine made from a blend of several of 16 *communes* in the Côte de Beaune district, Burgundy; those *communes* are: Chassagne-Montrachet, Cheilly-lès-Maranges, Chorey-lès-Beaune, Dezize-lès-Maranges, Ladoix-Serrigny, Meursault, Monthélie, Pernand-Vergelesses, Puligny-Montrachet, Saint-Aubin, Saint-Romain, Sampigny-lès-Maranges, Santenay, and Savigny-lès-Beaune. Aloxe-Corton, Beaune, Pommard and Volnay are specifically excluded.

Côte des Blancs (F.)

1. A district in the Champagne region, south of Épernay, which includes Cramant and Avize, and is planted with Pinot Blanc and Chardonnay grapes.

2. The unofficial term for the southern half of the Côte de Beaune district in Burgundy, including Chassagne, Puligny, Blagny and Meursault, where mostly white wines of high quality are made; also called Côte de Meursault.

Côte Blonde (F.)

The southern half of the Côte-Rôtie vineyards, in the northern Rhône region; the soil is limestone, and for the most part white Viognier grapes and some red Syrah grapes are grown here and are frequently blended with grapes grown in the Côte Brune.

Côte-Boudin (F.)

One of the best vineyards in the Côte Brune section of the Côte-Rôtie vineyards, northern Rhône region.

Côte-de-Brouilly AOC (F.)

A *Cru* Beaujolais in the center of the Brouilly vineyards and higher up on Mont Brouilly, in the Beaujolais district, Burgundy; produces red wine from the Gamay grape. 600 acres.

Côte Brune (F.)

The northern half of the Côte-Rôtie vineyards, in the northern Rhône region; the soil is clayey and the Syrah grape is grown, frequently blended with grapes grown in the Côte Blonde.

Côte Chalonnaise (F.)

A district just to the west of Chalon-sur-Saône and south of the Côte de Beaune district, Burgundy; it consists of Bouzeron, Givry, Mercurey, Montagny and Rully, and produces red and white wines from Pinot Noir, Gamay, Chardonnay, Pinot Blanc and Aligoté grapes.

Côte de Dijon (F.)

A district south of Dijon, north of the Côte d'Or, which used to be an important wine-producing district of Burgundy, and included vineyards in Dijon, Larrey, Chenôve, Marsannay-la-Côte, Couchey, and even Fixin.

Côte de Fontenay (F.)

A *Premier Cru* vineyard in La Chapelle-Vaupelteigne, in the Chablis district, Burgundy; usually included as part of the Fourchaume vineyard.

Côte de Lèchet (F.)

A *Premier Cru* vineyard in Milly, Chablis district, Burgundy.

Côte de Meursault (F.)

See **Côte des Blancs #2.**

Côte de Nuits (F.)

The northern section of the Côte d'Or district, the most famous section of Burgundy, where the finest red Burgundies are produced from the Pinot Noir grape. It is named after the principal town, Nuits-St.-Georges. 12 miles long. 12 communes. 3,500 acres.

Côte de Nuits-Villages AOC (F.)

Red or white wine from any of the following *communes* in the Côte de Nuits district, in Burgundy: Brochon, Comblanchien, Corgoloin, Fixin and Prissey.

Côte d'Or (F.)

The most famous district of Burgundy, south of Dijon, from Fixin in the north to Santenay in the south, where the finest red and white wines are made from the Pinot Noir and the Chardonnay grape. It is divided into the Côte de Beaune and the Côte de Nuits.

Côte Roannaise VDQS (F.)

The designation for red and rosé wine from Roanne, in the Upper Loire region, Loire Valley; made from Gamay grapes.

Côte Rôtie (F.)

A *Premier Cru* vineyard in Morey-St.-Denis, Côte de Nuits district, Burgundy. 5 acres.

Côte-Rôtie AOC (F.)

1. A small district of 750 acres around Ampuis, in the northern Rhône region, which produces:

2. A red wine made from the Syrah grape sometimes blended with the Viognier grape.

coteau, plural: coteaux (F.)

A hillside; usually used to denote minor regions and districts, frequently of VDQS status.

Coteaux d'Aix-en-Provence VDQS (F.)

A district around Aix-en-Provence, in the Provence region; produces red, white and rosé wines, the red and rosé made from

Grenache, Carignan, Cinsault, Mourvèdre, Counoise and Cabernet Sauvignon grapes, and the white from the Clairette, Ugni Blanc, Sémillon and other grapes.

Coteaux d'Ajaccio AOC (F.)

A district around Ajaccio, in southwestern Corsica, producing red and rosé wines from Sciacarello grapes and white wine from Vermentino grapes.

Coteaux d'Ancenis VDQS (F.)

A district around Ancenis, in the Muscadet region, Loire Valley; produces red, white and rosé varietal wines from Chenin Blanc, Malvoisie, Gamay and Cabernet Franc grapes.

Coteaux de l'Aubance AOC (F.)

A district along the Aubance River, south of Angers, in the Anjou region, Loire Valley; produces sweet white wines made from the Chenin Blanc grape, and rosé wines from the Cabernet Franc grape.

Coteaux des Baux-en-Provence VDQS (F.)

A district around Baux-de-Provence, south of Avignon, in the western Provence region; produces red, white and rosé wines similar to the Coteaux d'Aix-en-Provence wines.

Coteaux du Cap Corse AOC (F.)

A district in northern Corsica; produces red, white, rosé and VDN wines.

Coteaux de Carthage (Tun.)

Red, white and rosé wines from Carthage, Tunisia.

Coteaux Champenois AOC (F.) 1974

The AOC since 1974 for white, red and rosé still wines from the Champagne region; made from Pinot Noir, Pinot Meunier and Chardonnay grapes; from 1955-1974 it was known as *Vin Nature de Champagne*.

Coteaux du Giennois VDQS (F.)

A district south of Gien, Upper Loire region, in the eastern Loire Valley; produces red and rosé wines made from Pinot Noir and Gamay grapes, and white wines from Sauvignon Blanc and Chenin Blanc grapes.

Coteaux de Khanguet (Tun.)

An important district in Tunisia, southeast of Tunis.

Coteaux du Languedoc VDQS (F.)

The general name for any of 15 VDQS wines from the central part of the Languedoc region.

Coteaux du Layon AOC (F.)

A district along the Layon River, south of Angers, in the Anjou region, Loire Valley; produces sweet white wines made from the Chenin Blanc grape. If the name "Chaumes" is added, then the wine can only be from Rochefort-sur-Loire.

Coteaux du Loir AOC (F.)

A small district north of the Loire River and north of Tours, along the Loir River (a tributary of the Loire River), in the Touraine region, Loire Valley; produces red, white and rosé wines, the red and rosé wines made from Gamay, Cot, Cabernet Franc, and Pineau d'Aunis grapes, and the white from the Chenin Blanc grape.

Coteaux de la Loire (F.)

See **Anjou Coteaux de la Loire.**

Coteaux du Lyonnais VDQS (F.)

A designation for red, white and rosé wines from Lyon, in southern Burgundy; the red and rosé wines are made from the Gamay grape, and the white made from Chardonnay, Aligoté and Melon de Bourgogne grapes.

Coteaux de Mascara (Alg.)

A district in the hills around Mascara, in the Oran region, producing red, white and rosé wines.

Coteaux de la Méjanelle VDQS (F.)

A designation for mostly red and rosé wines from northeast of Montpellier, in the Languedoc region; made from Carignan, Cinsault and Grenache grapes.

Coteaux de Pierrevert VDQS (F.)

A designation for red, white and rosé wines from Pierrevert, northeast of Aix-en-Provence, in the western Provence region; the red and rosé wines are made from Carignan, Cinsault and Grenache grapes, and the white is made from Clairette, Marsanne and Roussanne grapes.

Coteaux de Saint-Christol VDQS (F.)

A designation for red wine from Saint-Christol, west of Lunel, in the Languedoc region; made from Carignan, Cinsault and Grenache grapes.

Coteaux de Saumur AOC (F.)

A designation for semi-sweet, white wines from the Saumur district, Anjou region, Loire Valley; made from Chenin Blanc grapes, similar to Vouvray wine.

Coteaux de Tlemcen (Alg.)

A district around Tlemcen, west of Oran; produces red, white and rosé wines.

Coteaux de Touraine (F.)

Another, and unofficial, name for the Touraine region, Loire Valley.

Coteaux du Tricastin AOC (F.)   since 1974

An AOC district for the area east of the Rhône River, between Montélimar and Bollène, in the southern Rhône region; produces red, white and rosé wines, the red and rosé wines made from Grenache, Mourvèdre, Cinsault, Carignan and Syrah grapes, and the white from Grenache Blanc, Clairette, Picpoul, Bourboulenc and Ugni Blanc grapes.

Coteaux du Vendômois VDQS (F.)

A designation for red, white and rosé wines from Vendôme, northeast of Tours, in the Touraine region, Loire Valley; the red and rosé are made from Cabernet, Gamay, Pinot Noir and Pineau d'Aunis grapes, and the white is made from Chenin Blanc and Chardonnay grapes.

Coteaux de Vérargues VDQS (F.)

A designation for red and rosé wines from Vérargues, northwest of Lunel, in the Languedoc region; made from Carignan, Cinsault, Grenache and Aramon grapes.

Côtes d'Agly VDN (F.)

A district in the Roussillon region, northwest of Perpignan; produces sweet fortified wines (red, and white and rosé) made from Grenache, Malvoisie and Muscat grapes.

Côtes d'Auvergne VDQS (F.)

A district between Limoges and Lyons, in central France; produces red, white and rosé wines, the red and rosé from Gamay and Pinot Noir grapes, and the white from Chardonnay grapes.

Côtes de Bergerac AOC (F.)

The designation for red wines from the Bergerac district, east of Bordeaux, in the Southwest region; made from the two Cabernet grapes, Merlot, Malbec and Fer grapes.

When the word "Moelleux" is added to the above designation, then it applies to a sweet white wine made from Sémillon, Sauvignon and Muscadelle grapes grown in the same district.

Côtes de Blaye AOC (F.)

The designation for dry or sweet white wines from the Blayais district, in the Bordeaux region, made from Sauvignon and Sémillon grapes.

Côtes de Bordeaux Saint-Macaire AOC (F.)

A district north of Langon and just south of the Entre-Deux-Mers district, in the Bordeaux region; produces sweet white wines made from Sauvignon, Sémillon and Muscadelle grapes.

Côtes de Bourg AOC (F.)

A designation for red and dry white wines of the Bourgeais district, in the Bordeaux region. See **Bourg.**

Côtes du Buzet AOC (F.)

A district around Buzet, southeast of Bordeaux, in the Southwest region; produces red, white and rosé wines, the red and rosé made from the two Cabernets, Merlot and Malbec grapes, and the white from Sauvignon, Sémillon and Muscadelle grapes.

Côtes du Cabardès et de l'Orbiel VDQS (F.)

See **Cabardès.**

Côtes Canon Fronsac (F.)

See **Canon Fronsac AOC.**

Côtes de Castillon AOC (F.)

A district around Castillon-la-Bataille, just east of St.-Émilion, in the Bordeaux region; produces red wines made from the two Cabernet grapes, Merlot and Malbec grapes.

Côtes de Colombe (U.S.)   1969

A small winery in Banks, Willamette Valley, northwestern Oregon; produces Cabernet, Pinot Noir and Chardonnay wines. 10 acres.

Côtes de Duras AOC (F.)

A district around Duras, 70 miles southeast of the city of Bordeaux, near Bergerac, in the Southwest region; produces red wines from Cabernet, Merlot and Malbec grapes, and white wines from Sémillon, Sauvignon, Muscadelle, Ondenc, Ugni Blanc and Mauzac grapes.

Côtes de Forez VDQS (F.)

A designation for red and rosé wines from west of Lyon, in the Upper Loire region, Loire Valley; made from the Gamay grape.

Côtes de Francs AOC (F.)

A designation for red and white wines from an area east of Pomerol, Bordeaux region, under the Bordeaux Supérieur AOC.

Côtes de Fronsac (F.)

See **Fronsac AOC.**

Côtes du Fronton *also* Côtes du Frontonnais AOC (F.)

A district north of Toulouse, in the Southwest region; produces red and rosé wines made from the local Negrette grape with some Cabernet, Syrah, Cinsault, Malbec, Gamay, and Mauzac grapes.

Côtes du Jura *also* Côtes du Jura Mousseux AOC (F.)

The designation for red, white and rosé wines from the Jura region of eastern France; the red and rosé (also *vin gris)* made from Pinot Noir, Poulsard and Trousseau grapes, and the white from Savagnin, Chardonnay and Pinot Blanc grapes.

The *mousseux* wines are made by the *méthode Champenoise.*

Côtes du Lubéron VDQS (F.)

A district north of Aix-en-Provence, in the southeastern Rhône region; produces red, white and rosé wines, the red and rosé wines are made from Grenache, Carignan and Cinsault grapes and the white wines are made from Bourboulenc and Grenache Blanc grapes.

Côtes de la Malepère VDQS (F.) VDQS in 1982

A designation for red and rosé wine from an area around Carcassonne, in the Languedoc region; made from Cinsault, Cot, Cabernets Franc and Sauvignon, Merlot, Grenache and Syrah grapes.

Côtes du Marmandais VDQS (F.)

A designation for red and white wines from around Marmande, southeast of the Bordeaux region, in the Southwest region; the red wine is made from Abouriou, Gamay, Malbec, Merlot and the two Cabernet grapes, the white from Sauvignon Blanc, Sémillon and Ugni Blanc grapes.

Côtes de Montravel AOC *also* Haut-Montravel (F.)

A designation for sweet, white wine from certain select *communes* in the Montravel district, east of St.-Émilion, in the Southwest region; made from Sémillon, Sauvignon and Muscadelle grapes.

Côtes des Près Girots (F.)

A *Premier Cru* vineyard in Fleys, Chablis district, Burgundy; usually included as part of the Les Fourneaux vineyard.

Côtes de Provence AOC (F.)   1977

A district covering most of the southeastern Provence region; produces red, white and rosé wines, the red and rosé from Grenache, Cinsault, Mourvèdre, Carignan, Cabernet and Syrah grapes, and the white from Clairette, Ugni Blanc, Sauvignon, Sémillon and Vermentino grapes.

Côtes du Rhône AOC (F.)

1. The official name for the entire Rhône region of vineyards along the Rhône River from Vienne south to Avignon.

2. The designation for red, white and rosé wines from the entire Rhône region that do not warrant a higher classification.

Côtes du Rhône-Villages AOC (F.) since 1967

Wines from at least 17 *communes* in the southern Côtes du Rhône; the *communes* are: Beaumes-de-Venise (red wine only), Cairanne, Chusclan, Laudun, Rasteau (not VDN), Roaix, Rochegude, Rousset-les-Vignes, Sablet, St. Gervais, St. Maurice-sur-Eygues, St. Pantaléon-les-Vignes, Séguret, Vacqueyras, Valréas, Vinsobres and Visan; produces mostly red wines and some white and rosé wines. The label reads: the village name, and underneath, in smaller letters, Côtes du Rhône Appellation Contrôlée.

Wines labeled as Côtes du Rhône-Villages are blends of wine from several of the 17 villages.

Côtes du Roussillon AOC (F.)   1977

A district mostly south of Perpignan, in the Roussillon region, that was formerly called Grands Roussillons; produces red, white and rosé wines, the red and rosé made from Carignan, Cinsault, Grenache,

Mourvèdre and other grapes, and the white from Maccabéo grapes.

Côtes du Roussillon-Villages AOC (F.)

The designation for superior red wines from certain villages northwest of Perpignan, in the Roussillon region.

Côtes de Saint-Mont VDQS (F.)

A designation for red, white and rosé wines from an area north of Tarbes, in the Southwest region; the red and rosé wines are made from Tannet, Merlot and the two Cabernet grapes; the white is made from Meslier, Jurançon, Picpoul and Sauvignon grapes.

Côtes de Saussignac AOC (F.)

A district around Saussignac, southwest of Bergerac, in the Southwest region; produces white wines made from Sauvignon, Semillon, and Muscadelle grapes.

Côtes de Toul VDQS (F.)

A district in the Lorraine region; produces mostly light rosé wines (*vin gris*) made from Gamay, Pinot Noir and Pinot Meunier grapes.

Côtes du Ventoux AOC (F.)

A district around Mount Ventoux, in the southeastern Rhône region; produces red, white and rosé wines similar to Côtes du Rhône wines.

Côtes du Vivarais VDQS (F.)

A district in the southern Rhône region, on the west bank of the Rhône River, between Viviers and Pont St.-Esprit; produces red, white and rosé wines similar to Côtes du Rhône wines; made from Grenache, Cinsault, Carignan, Syrah and Gamay grapes.

Côtes du Zaacar (Alg.)

A district around Algiers; produces red and white wines.

Coteşti (R.)

A town in the Focşani district, province of Moldavia, in eastern Romania; produces red and white varietal wines from a variety of grapes.

Cotnari (R.)

A sweet white wine from the Province of Moldavia, in northeastern Romania, known since at least 1646; made from the Grasă grape.

Coturri and Sons, H. (U.S.)　　1979

A winery in Glen Ellen, Sonoma County, California; produces several varietal wines made from purchased grapes.

Coucherias, Aux (F.)

A *Premier Cru* vineyard (in part) in Beaune, Côte de Beaune district, Burgundy. 55 acres.

Couderc, Georges (1850-1928) (F.)

A French hybridizer from the Ardèche; known for developing the Couderc Noir grape.

Couderc Noir (F.)

A red hybrid grape grown in France and Brazil; also called Couderc 7120.

Coufran, Château (F.)

An estate in St. Seurin de Cadourne, Haut-Médoc district, Bordeaux; classified in 1978 as a *Cru Grand Bourgeois*. 30,000 cases. 150 acres.

Couhabort (F.)

A local grape grown in Madiran; also called Pinenc.

Couhins, Château (F.)

An estate in Villenave-d'Ornon, Graves district, Bordeaux; classified as a *Cru Classé* (white only) in 1959. 1,800 cases. 25 acres.

coulant (F.)

French for "running," light, fresh, easy to drink, low in alcohol.

Coulée de Serrant, Clos de la (F.)

A vineyard and estate in Savennières, Anjou region, Loire Valley; has its own AOC

– Savennières Coulée de Serrant, which is rated a *Grand Cru*; produces dry white wine (formerly sweet) made from the Chenin Blanc grape. 17 acres.

couleuse (F.)

Leaky; having evaporated in the bottle from a bad cork.

coulure (F.)

Blossom fall, a condition caused by bad weather at flowering time; blossoms or embryonic berries fall from the vines.

Couly-Dutheil (F.)   1910

A merchant in Chinon, Touraine region; owns several estates: Clos de l'Écho, Clos de l'Olive and Domaine René Couly. 45,000 cases. 80 acres.

Counoise (F.)

A red grape grown in the Rhône (including Châteauneuf-du-Pape wines), Provence and Languedoc regions.

coupage (F.)

The blending of wines from different *communes* in the making of Champagne.

coupé (F.)

Cut; blended or watered down.

Courbu (F.)

An old, local white grape grown in the Jurançon district, in the Southwest region; also called Sarrat.

Courcel, Domaine de Mme Bernard de (F.)

An estate in Pommard, Côte de Beaune district, Burgundy. 32 acres, including Pommard Les Épenots – 20 acres and Pommard Les Rugiens – 2.5 acres.

Courcelles, Château de (F.)

An estate in the Beaujolais-Villages district, Burgundy.

Couronne, Château La (F.)   1874

An estate in Pauillac, Haut-Médoc district, Bordeaux; classified in 1932 as a *Cru Bour-*

geois Exceptionnel; begun in 1874. 700 cases. 7 acres.

Coursodon, Gustave et Pierre (F.)

An estate in Mauves, St.-Joseph district, northern Rhône region; owns St.-Joseph – 17 acres.

court noué (F.)

A viral disease of the vine caused by a virus which lives in the soil (usually associated with *phylloxera*) and affects the vine leaves, turning them yellow in patches along the veins and causing them to become misshapen; called "fan leaf" in English.

courtier (F.)

1. A wine-broker.

2. In Alsace, a gourmet.

Courtis, Domaine Pierre des (F.)
1st vintage 1977

An estate in the Chablis district, created from Bois de Milly, formerly classified as Petit Chablis. 25 acres.

Coury Vineyards, Charles (U.S.)   1966
1st wine 1972

A winery in Forest Grove, Tualatin Valley, northwestern Oregon; a part of Reuter's Hill Vineyards since 1978; produces Cabernet, Riesling, Gewürztraminer, Chardonnay, Sylvaner and Muscat Ottonel wines. 60 acres.

Cousiño Macul (Ch.)   1882

An estate in Santiago; produces Chardonnay, Riesling, Sémillon, Cabernet and other wines. 300,000 cases. 900 acres.

Couspaude, Château La (F.)

An estate in St.-Émilion, Bordeaux; classified in 1955 as a *Grand Cru Classé*. 2,000 cases. 11 acres.

Coutelin-Merville, Château (F.)

An estate in St.-Estèphe, Haut-Médoc district, Bordeaux; classified in 1978 as a *Cru Grand Bourgeois*. 4,000 cases. 27 acres.

Coutet, Château (F.)

An estate in Barsac, Sauternes district, Bordeaux; classified in 1855 as a Premier Cru. 80% Sémillon, 20% Sauvignon grapes. 90 acres. 7,500 cases.

Coutet, Château (F.)

An estate in St.-Émilion, Bordeaux; classified in 1955 as a *Grand Cru Classé*. 3,500 cases. 30 acres.

Coutière, La (F.)

A *Premier Cru* vineyard in Ladoix-Serrigny, Côte de Beaune district, Burgundy; may be sold as Aloxe-Corton. 3.5 acres.

Couvent, Château Le (F.)

An estate in St.-Émilion, Bordeaux; classified in 1955 as a *Grand Cru Classé*, the smallest classified growth in Bordeaux. 200 cases. 1 acre.

Couvent-des-Jacobins, Château (F.)

An estate in St.-Émilion, Bordeaux; classified in 1969 as a *Grand Cru Classé*. 4,000 cases. 20 acres.

Cowra (Aus.)

A district, west of Sidney, in central New South Wales.

crackling

Semi-sparkling; *frizzante, pétillant, crémant,* or *perlé.*

Craigmoor (Aus.)   1858

An old winery in the Mudgee district of New South Wales, northwest of Hunter Valley; produces red, white, Port-style and Muscat wines made from Cabernet, Shiraz, Pinot Noir, Chardonnay, Sémillon, Traminer, Sauvignon Blanc and Trebbiano grapes. 22,000 cases. 130 acres.

Cramant (F.)

A village south of Épernay, in the Côte des Blancs district, Champagne region; produces one of the highest rated wines of the Côte des Blancs, a *Grand Cru*, rated at 100%.

Cras, Aux *also* Les Cras (F.)

A *Premier Cru* vineyard in Beaune, Côte de Beaune district, Burgundy. 12 acres.

Cras, Aux (F.)

A *Premier Cru* vineyard in Nuits-St.-Georges, Côte de Nuits district, Burgundy. 8 acres.

Cras, Les (F.)

A *Premier Cru* vineyard in Meursault, Côte de Beaune district, Burgundy. 10 aces.

Cras, Les (F.)

A *Premier Cru* vineyard in Vougeot, Côte de Nuits district, Burgundy. 10.5 acres.

Cras, Les (F.)

A *Premier Cru* vineyard in Chambolle-Musigny, Côte de Nuits district, Burgundy. 10.5 acres.

Crato Branco (P.)

A white grape grown in southern Portugal.

Crato Preto (P.)

A red grape grown in southern Portugal.

Cream Sherry (P.)

Sweetened Oloroso Sherry made for British and U.S. markets.

Creața (R.)

A white grape grown in the Banat region, in southwestern Romania; also called Riesling de Banat.

crema (Sp.)

In Málaga, a term denoting sweet or semi-sweet wines.

Crema Viñera, La (U.S.)   1979

A winery in Petaluma, Sonoma County, California; produces Pinot Noir and Chardonnay wines from grapes purchased from Ventana Vineyards (Monterey). Other labels are Petaluma Cellars and Sonoma Mountain Cellars. 7,500 cases.

Crémade, Domaine de la (F.)

An estate in Mouries, in the Provence region.

Crémant AOC (F.)   1975

White, semi-sparkling wine from the Champagne, Alsace, Burgundy and Loire Valley regions; made from red and white grapes; allowed since 1975.

crémant (F.)

Creaming; lightly sparkling.

Crémat, Château de (F.)

An estate and merchant in Bellet, Provence region. 6,500 cases. 30 acres.

crème de tête (F.)

In Sauternes, Bordeaux, a wine from the first crushing, considered the best; also called *"vin de tête."*

Crème du Vien de Nus (I.)

A red wine from Nus, near Aosta, in the Valle d'Aosta region; made from Vien de Nus, Petit Rouge and Merlot grapes.

crémeux (F.)

Creamy.

Crépy AOC (F.)

A small district of 150 acres in Douvaine, Ballaison and Loisin, near Lake Geneva, in the Savoie region, southeastern France; produces a light white wine, some of it sparkling, made from the Chasselas grape.

Crescini Wines (U.S.)   1980

A small winery in Soquel, Santa Cruz County, California; produces Cabernet, Petite Sirah and Chenin Blanc wines from purchased grapes.

Cresta Blanca Wine Company (U.S.)   1880, 1946

A large winery in Ukiah, Mendocino County, California, and part of the Guild Winery; started originally at Livermore, Alameda County; produces Zinfandel, Petite Sirah, and Sémillon wines, and many generic and dessert wines from purchased grapes from several regions of the state. 100,000 cases.

Crete (Gr.)

An island south of Greece; the best-known districts are Archanes and Peza, which produce red wines made from the Romeiko, Mandilari, Kotsifali and Liatico grapes.

Creuseford, Gérard (F.)

An estate in Auxey-Duresses, Côte de Beaune district, Burgundy. 20 acres, including Auxey-Duresses Le Val – 5 acres, Meursault Le Poruzot – 1.2 acres and some Volnay.

Creux de la Net (F.)

A *Premier Cru* vineyard in Pernand-Vergelesses, Côte de Beaune district, Burgundy; may be sold as Aloxe-Corton. 7.5 acres.

criadera (Sp.)

Spanish for "nursery"; the "nursery" casks used to age wines that use the *solera* system.

criado (Sp.)

Aged, matured.

crianza (Sp.)

Spanish for "nursed," i.e., aged, blended.

Cribari and Sons, B. (U.S.)

A large winery in Fresno, San Joaquin Valley, California; formerly Roma Wines, now part of Guild Wineries, a large co-operative; produces generic and varietal jug wines.

Criolla (Sp.)

A red grape of Spanish origin grown in Argentina, Mexico and California (known in the latter as the Mission grape).

Criolla Grande (Arg.)

A native red grape.

Criots-Bâtard-Montrachet AOC (F.)

A *Grand Cru* vineyard in Chassagne-Montrachet, Côte de Beaune district, Burgundy. 7 owners. 3.5 acres.

Crno (Y.)

Red.

Croatia (Y.)

One of the 6 states in Yugoslavia, in the northwest; includes the provinces of Slavonia, Istria and Dalmatia; produces about a third of all Yugoslavian wine.

Croattina (I.)

A red grape grown in the Lombardy region.

Crochet, Lucien (F.)

An estate in Bué, Sancerre district, Upper Loire region; owns 35 acres of the Clos du Chêne Marchand vineyard.

Crock, Château Le (F.)

An estate in St.-Estèphe, Haut-Médoc district, Bordeaux; classified in 1978 as a *Cru Grand Bourgeois Exceptionnel.* 10,000 cases. 70 acres.

Croft & Cía Lda (P.)   1678

A Port producer in Vila Nova de Gaia; owns Quinta da Roêda, and the Delaforce and Morgan brands. 250 acres.

Croft Jerez S.A. (Sp.)   1970

A Sherry producer in Jerez de la Frontera, an expanded operation of the well-known Port shipper. 1,200 acres.

Croix, La (F.)

A vineyard section of Hermitage, in the northern Rhône region; produces red wine.

Croix, Château La (F.)

An estate in Pomerol, Bordeaux. 2,000 cases. 20 acres.

Croix, Domaine de la (F.)

An estate in Croix-Valmer, in the Provence region.

Croix-de-Gay, Château La (F.)

An estate in Pomerol, Bordeaux. 3,000 cases. 15 acres.

Croix de Jamanot, La (F.)

A vineyard section of Hermitage, in the northern Rhône region.

Croix-Noires, Les (F.)

A *Premier Cru* vineyard in Pommard, Côte de Beaune district, Burgundy. 10.5 acres.

Croizet-Bages, Château (F.)

An estate in Pauillac, Haut-Médoc district, Bordeaux; classified in 1855 as a *Cinquième Cru;* part of what was an old estate of Bages in the 18th century; also called Calvé-Croizet-Bages, owned by Julien Calvé from 1853-1930. 60 acres. 8,000 cases.

Cromin, Clos du (F.)

An unclassified vineyard in Meursault, Côte de Beaune district, Burgundy; very old vines. 3.8 acres.

Cronin Vineyards (U.S.)   1980

A small winery in Woodside, San Mateo County, California; produces Cabernet, Zinfandel, Pinot Noir and Chardonnay wines from purchased grapes.

Croque-Michotte, Château (F.)

An estate in St.-Émilion, Bordeaux; classified in 1955 as a *Grand Cru Classé.* 5,000 cases. 25 acres.

crossing *also* cross-bred

A grape produced by the cross-pollinization of two varieties within the same species (e.g., of two varieties of *vinifera* grapes), and therefore not a hybrid, but a *métis.* Some experts, however, consider any cross a hybrid.

Crosswood Vineyard (U.S.)   1983
vines 1981

A winery in North Stonington, northeastern Connecticut; produces *vinifera* wines. 20 acres.

Crots, Aux (F.)

A *Premier Cru* vineyard (in part) in Nuits-St.-Georges, Côte de Nuits district, Burgundy. 21 acres.

Crouchen (Aus.)

In South Australia, the name for the Sémillon grape, grown in the Barossa Valley; also called Clare Riesling and Hunter Riesling.

Crozes-Hermitage AOC (F.)   since 1952

A village and district, including ten other villages, around Tain-l'Hermitage, in the northern Rhône region; the other villages are: Serves, Erôme, Gervans, Larnage, Mercurol, Chanos-Curson, Beaumont-Monteux, Pont-de-l'Isère and Roche-de-Glun; produces red wine from the Syrah grape and some white wine from Roussanne and Marsanne grapes. 1,500 acres.

cru (F.)

A growth; a vineyard; a *château* estate.

Cru Artisan (F.)

A former classification of Bordeaux wines, ranking just below *Cru Bourgeois* and above *Cru Paysan.*

Cru Beaujolais (F.)

A superior *commune* or vineyard area in the northern Beaujolais district, Burgundy. The 9 *Crus* produce the best wines in the district and each has its own AOC; they are: Brouilly, Côte de Brouilly, Chénas, Chiroubles, Fleurie, Juliénas, Morgon, Moulin-à-Vent and St.-Amour. 10,000 acres.

Cru Bourgeois (F.)

A classification of Bordeaux wines of the Médoc district that rank below the *Grands Crus Classés* of 1855; the first official list was published in 1932; a new classification was made in 1966 and revised in 1978.

The unclassified growths of the Sauternes and Graves districts are also referred to as *Crus Bourgeois.*

Cru Classé (F.)

A classified growth, an official designation of a superior growth or vineyard.

Cru Exceptionnel (F.)

A classification (more correctly, *Crus Bourgeois Supérieurs Exceptionnels*) of six Bordeaux (Médoc) growths in 1932, ranking one step below 5th Growth and above the *Cru Bourgeois.* In the 1966 classification (revised in 1978) 18 growths were classified as *Crus Grands Bourgeois Exceptionnels.*

Cru Paysan (F.)

French for Peasant Growth, a ranking of Bordeaux wines below the quality and size of the *Cru Bourgeois* (Bourgeois Growth); it is no longer used.

Cruse & Fils Frères (F.)   1819

A merchant in Bordeaux; owns several *châteaux*, including Pontet-Canet and Giscours.

Crusius, Weingut Hans and Peter (G.)

An estate in Traisen, Nahe region; owns vineyards in Traisen, Norheim, Niederhausen and Schlossböckelheim. 30 acres.

Crusserey, Camille (F.)

A grower in Fixin, Côte de Nuits, Burgundy. 10 acres, including Fixin Les Hervelets – 2.5 acres and Clos du Meix Trouhans Monopole – 5 acres.

crust

The sediment in an old Port wine, which collects and hardens on the sides of the bottle.

Crusted Port (P.)

A blended port wine which throws a crust or sediment, as does Vintage Port; it is aged longer in wood, then bottled; therefore, it is not as long-lived as Vintage Port nor is it considered as good; usually a blend of several vintages.

cruzetas (P.)
T-shaped uprights of wood or concrete used to string wires on which vines are trained; used in the Vinho Verde region.

Cryptogam
A genus of fungus, some of which cause vine diseases.

cuba de fermetação (P.)
A fermenting vat.

Çubuk (T.)
A red grape grown in central Turkey.

Cucamonga Valley (U.S.)
A small district east of Los Angeles, between Ontario and Fontana, San Bernardino County, California.

Cucamonga Vineyard Company (U.S.)
                              1870, 1961, 1976
A large winery in Cucamonga, San Bernardino County, California; the first bonded winery in California; produces bulk wines, bulk champagne, and some varietal wines. 1 million cases.

culaccino *also* **culaton (I.)**
In the Piedmont region, the dregs from the bottom of the bottle, which are saved till the next day and given to friends.

Cullen's (Aus.)   1971
A winery in Willyabrup, Margaret River district, Western Australia; produces Cabernet, Rhine Riesling, Sauvignon Blanc, Sémillon and Chardonnay wines. 6,000 cases. 50 acres.

cultivar (S. Af.)
A grape variety.

cunacho (Sp.)
A wicker basket used to hold the harvested grapes.

Cune (Sp.)
See **CVNE.**

cup (E.)
A punch, usually wine- or champagne-based.

cupa (Lat.)
An ancient Roman vat or barrel.

Curé-Bon-la-Madeleine, Château (F.)
An estate in St.-Émilion, Bordeaux; classified in 1955 as a *Grand Cru Classé*. 2,000 cases. 13 acres.

Cusona, Fattoria di Guicciardini Strozzi (I.)   16th cent.
An estate in San Gimignano, Tuscany region; produces Chianti, Vernaccia and Vin Santo wines. 45,000 cases. 125 acres.

cuvaison *also* **cuvage (F.)**
The vatting time, or fermentation time.

Cuvaison Vineyard (U.S.)   1970
A winery in Calistoga, Napa Valley, California; produces Cabernet, Zinfandel and Chardonnay wines from purchased grapes until newly acquired vineyards are ready. Second label is Calistoga Vineyards. 10,000 cases. 400 acres.

cuve (F.)
A large vat used for fermentation.

cuve close (F.)
A special, hermetically-sealed vat for making *mousseux* or sparkling wines by the *Charmat* process.

cuve fermée (F.)
A closed vat used to ferment red wine, frequently with a layer of carbon dioxide above the must.

cuvée (F.)
1. The contents of a wine vat; a vatting.
2. A vineyard parcel or special plot or section.

3. In Champagne and California, a particular blend of champagne or a special lot or batch of wine.

cuvée de prestige (F.)

A special, expensive, deluxe Champagne, e.g. Dom Pérignon, Comtes de Champagne, Cristal, Fleur de Champagne, etc.

cuvier *also* **cuverie (F.)**

A winery building where the wine is made or stored; also called *chai* and *cellier.*

Cuvillo y Cía S.A. (Sp.)   **1783**

A Sherry producer in Puerto de Santa Maria; produces several types of Sherry.

Cviček (Y.)

A rosé wine from southern Slovenia.

Cyrot-Chaudron, Cuvée (F.)   **1981**

A new red wine from the Hospices de Beaune, Burgundy; the *cuvée* is made up of several vineyard parcels in Beaune.

Cynthiana (U.S.)

A red hybrid grape; also called Norton in Virginia, U.S.

Cyprus

An island in the eastern Mediterranean Sea; grows mostly red grapes, especially the local Mavron grape, and some white grapes, the Xynisteri and the Muscat. The most well-known wines are Commandaria, a sweet wine made from Mavron and Xynisteri grapes, Othello, a red, Kokkineli, a rosé, and Aphrodite and Arsinoë, white wines.

Cyprus Sherry (Cyp.)

A whole range of quality Sherry-style wines from the Island of Cyprus; made from local grapes using the *solera* system.

Czechoslovakia

A country in eastern Europe which produces wines made in a region north of Prague, and also from a large region southeast of Brno; made from German grapes: Rhine Riesling, Traminer, Sylvaner, Müller-Thurgau, Blauburgunder and others. 100,000 acres.

D

D.L.G. (G.)   1885

Deutsche Landwirtschafts Gesellschaft (German Agriculture Society), the organization which awards the *Bundesweinprämierung*, the national wine award.

D.O. (Sp.)   1926, 1972

Denominacion de Origen (Designation of Origin), the wine laws designed to control the quality and labeling of Spanish wines, begun in 1926 and centralized in 1972.

D.O.C. (I.)   1963

Denominazione di Origine Controllata (Controlled Denomination of Origin), a designation of wines requiring certain minimum standards of quality.

D.O.C.G. (I.)   1983

Denominazione di Origine Controllata e Garantita (Controlled and Guaranteed Denomination of Origin), an upgrading of the DOC designation of wines, requiring more rigid standards of quality.

D.O.S. (I.)   1963

Denominazione di Origine Semplice (Denomination of Simple Origin), a designation for local wines of ordinary character made from grapes traditionally grown in the area.

D.R.C. (F.)

The abbreviation for *Domaine de la Romanée-Conti*, a famous estate in Vosne-Romanée, Côte de Nuits district, Burgundy. See **Romanée-Conti, Domaine de la.**

da pronta beva (I.)

Italian for "to be drunk young."

Dabuki *also* **Dabouki (Is.)**

A native grape.

Dagueneau, Serge (F.)

An estate in Les Berthiers, Pouilly district, Upper Loire region, Loire Valley. 25 acres.

Dahlem Erben KG, Dr. (G.)   1702

An estate in Oppenheim, Rheinhessen region. 65 acres, including vineyards in Oppenheimer Sackträger, Herrenberg, Schloss, Kreuz, Herrengarten and Daubhaus; also owns vineyards in Dienheim.

Daldini, Figli di Alberto (Sw.)   1883

An estate in Lugano-Crocefisso, Ticino district; produces Merlot wine. 20 acres.

Dalmatia (Y.)

A province of the state of Croatia, from Zadar to Dubrovnik, on the southern coast; produces red wines: Plavina, Babic and Plavac, and white wines: Maraština, Pošip, Grk, Vugava and Bogdanuša.

Dama delle Rose (I.)

A rosé wine from Mezzolombardo, in the Trentino-Alto Adige region; made from the Merlot grape.

Damaschino (I.)

A white grape grown in Sicily.

Dame, Mas de la (F.)

An estate in Les Baux-de-Provence, in the Provence region.

Dame Blanche, Château La (F.)

An estate in Le Taillan, Haut-Médoc district, Bordeaux; it is actually the white wine of Château du Taillan.

Dame-Jeanne *also* bonbonne (F.)

French for "Lady Jane":

1. A demijohn, a large glass bottle with a 1-10 gallon capacity, used to store and transport wines and spirits.

2. In Bordeaux, a 2.5 liter bottle, more than a magnum, less than a double magnum.

Dames de la Charité, Cuvée (F.)

A red wine from the Hospices de Beaune, Côte de Beaune district, Burgundy. The *cuvée* is composed of the following vineyards in Pommard: Les Épenots – 1 acre, Les Rugiens – 1 acre, Les Noizons – 1 acre, La Refène – 1 acre and Les Combes Dessus – .5 acre. 400 cases.

Dames Hospitalières, Cuvée (F.)

A red wine from the Hospices de Beaune, Côte de Beaune district, Burgundy. The *cuvée* is composed of the following vineyards in Beaune; Les Bressandes – 2.5 acres, La Mignotte – 1.5 acres, Les Teurons – 1.25 acres and Les Grèves – 1 acre. 625 cases.

Damodes, Aux (F.)

A *Premier Cru* vineyard (in part) in Nuits-St.-Georges, Côte de Nuits district, Burgundy. 33 acres.

Damoy, Domaine Pierre (F.)

An estate in Gevrey-Chambertin, Côte de Nuits district, Burgundy. 22 acres, including Chambertin Clos de Bèze – 12.5 acres, Chambertin – 1.2 acres, Chapelle-Chambertin – 5.5 acres and Gevrey-Chambertin Tamisot – 3.7 acres; some wine is domaine-bottled, some sold in bulk.

Dão (P.)

1. A river and region southeast of Porto, centered around Viseu, in northern Portugal, which produces:

2. Red and white wines; the red made from Touriga Nacional, Alvarelhao, Jaen, Alfrocheiro Preto, Tinta Amarela, and Tinta Pinheira grapes, and the white from Arinto do Dão, Borrado das Moscas, Cerceal, Barcelo, Encruzado and Verdelho grapes, all approved varieties; other varieties are also used.

Dar bel Amri (Mor.)

A district east of Rabat; produces red wines.

Daringa (Aus.)

A small winery south of Adelaide, in the Southern Vales district, South Australia; produces Cabernet and Shiraz wines.

Darnat, Héritiers (F.)

An estate in Meursault, Côte de Beaune district, Burgundy. 3 acres, including Meursault Les Cras Clos Richemont Monopole – 1.7 acres.

Darona, Pierre (F.)

An estate in St.-Péray, Rhône region. 22 acres, some owned and some rented.

Darviot, Henri Jean (F.)

Domaine Darviot, an estate in Beaune, Burgundy. 40 acres, including Beaune Les Grèves – 2 acres, Le Clos des Mouches – 2.5 acres, Les Aigrots – 2 acres, Montagne St.-Désiré – 5 acres, Meursault La Goutte d'Or – 1.2 acres, Meursault Clos de la Velle Monopole – 2.5 acres, Monthélie Clos Gauthey Monopole – 2.5 acres, Monthélie Les Duresses – 2 acres and some Savigny.

Dassault, Château (F.)

An estate in St.-Émilion, Bordeaux; classified in 1969 as a *Grand Cru Classé*. 8,000 cases. 45 acres.

Daubhaus (G.)

A *Grosslage* in Bereich Johannisberg, in the Rheingau region; includes the village of Hochheim and 3 other villages.

Dauvissat, René (F.)

An estate in Chablis, Burgundy. 18 acres, including Les Clos – 3.7 acres, Les Preuses – 2.5 acres, Forêts – 9 acres and some Séchet.

Dauzac, Château (F.)

An estate (formerly Dauzats) in Labarde-Margaux, Haut-Médoc district, Bordeaux; classified in 1855 as a *Cinquième Cru*; it was unknown until the mid-19th century. It was here that the Bordeaux mixture was first used for vine protection. 14,000 cases. 100 acres.

de-acidification

The process of blending overly acid wines with low-acid wines, thereby reducing the total acidity in the finished wine.

De Leu Winery, Château (U.S.)

See **Leu Winery, Château de.**

De Loach Vineyards (U.S.)   1975
winery 1979

A winery in Santa Rosa, in the Russian River Valley district, Sonoma County, California; produces Zinfandel, Pinot Noir, Chardonnay, Gewürztraminer, Fumé Blanc and White Zinfandel wines. 15,000 cases. 130 acres.

De Re Rustica (Lat.)

1. A book by the ancient Roman author, Marcus Varro, in which he describes vine-growing and wines; it is also known as *Rerum Rusticarum Libri.*

2. A book by the ancient Roman author, Columella, in which he describes vineyards and wine-making.

3. A book written by Cato the Censor, in which he describes vine-growing and wine-making; also called *De Agri Cultura.*

De Vite (I.)

1. A white grape – a cross of Riesling and Trollinger grapes, which produces:

2. A white wine from Egna, in the northern Trentino-Alto Adige region.

De Zoete Inval Estate EWO (S. Af.)

A classified estate just south of Paarl, in the Paarl district.

Dealul Mare (R.)

A district southeast of the Carpathian Mountains, in southeastern Romania; includes the state-owned experimental vineyard of Valea Călugărească; produces red wines made from Pinot Noir, Merlot and Cabernet grapes, and white wines from Wälschriesling, Ruländer, Fetească Regala, Graša and Tămîioasă grâpes.

Débaudière, Domaine de (F.)

An estate in Vallet, Muscadet de Sèvre-et-Maine district, Loire Valley; produces Muscadet sur Lie wine. 22 acres.

Debina (Gr.)

A white grape grown in Epirus, in northwestern Greece.

débourbage (F.)

1. The process of racking the wine, a cleansing process in which grape juice is run off into a vat after pressing and allowed to rest 24 hours to allow solids to fall to the bottom. In white wines it refers to the process of separating the solids from the must before fermentation.

2. The practice of delaying the fermentation for a day.

Debröi Hárslevelü (H.)

1. A district in the Matraalja region of northeastern Hungary, which produces:

2. A dry white wine made from the Hárslevelü grape.

decant

To carefully pour wine from a bottle into another serving vessel; the sediment should remain in the original bottle, thus preventing it from being stirred up in the wine when pouring. Decanting also aerates the wine.

decanter

A serving vessel for wine, usually of clear crystal.

Deckrot (G.)

A red grape – a cross of Ruländer and Fäbertraube; developed at the State Viticultural Institute, Freiburg im Breisgau, Germany.

Decugnano dei Barbi (I.)

An estate in Corbara di Orvieto, Umbria region; produces Orvieto Classico, Brut Spumante and Rosso wines.

Deer Park Winery (U.S.)   1979

A winery in Deer Park, Napa Valley, California; produces Zinfandel, Chardonnay and Sauvignon Blanc wines. 5,000 cases. 7 acres.

**Deerfield Vineyards Wine Cellars (U.S.)
1974**

A winery in Edenton, North Carolina; produces red and white wines from native grapes, including a dry blend of Scuppernong and Delaware grapes.

Defrance, René (F.)

A grower in Fixin, Côte de Nuits, Burgundy; owns vineyards in Fixin. 10 acres.

dégorgement (F.)

The process of releasing the sediment in a bottle of champagne after the 2nd fermentation by uncorking the bottle briefly, after having worked the sediment close to the cork and freezing the neck.

dégustation (F.)

A tasting.

Dehlinger (U.S.)   1976

A winery in Forestville, west of Santa Rosa, Sonoma County, California; produces Cabernet, Pinot Noir, Zinfandel and Chardonnay wines. 8,000 cases. 15 acres.

Deidesheim (G.)

An important village the Rheinpfalz region, Bereich Mittelhaardt-Deutsche Weinstrasse, partly in each of the Grosslagen Mariengarten, Schnepfenflug an der Weinstrasse, and Hofstück. The vineyards are: Nonnenstück, in Grosslage Hofstück; Letten in Grosslage Schnepfenflug; and Grainhübel, Herrgottsacker, Hohenmorgen, Kalkofen, Kieselberg, Langenmorgen, Leinhöhle, Maushöhle and Paradiesgarten in Grosslage Mariengarten.

Deinhard, Gutsverwaltung (G.)

An estate in Deidesheim, Rheinpfalz region; owns vineyards in Deidesheim, Forst and Ruppertsberg. 46 acres.

Deinhard, Gutsverwaltung (G.)   1900

A large estate in Bernkastel-Kues, Mosel-Saar-Ruwer region; owns vineyards in Bernkastel (including 4 acres of the Doktor vineyard), Graach, Wehlen and other Mosel towns. 70 acres.

Deinhard, Weingut Dr. (G.)

Another estate in Deidesheim, Rheinpfalz region; owns other vineyards in Deidesheim, Ruppertsberg and Forst. 100 acres.

Deinhard, Weingut des Hauses (G.)

A large estate in Oestrich-Winkel, Rheingau region; owns vineyards in Oestrich, Hallgarten, Mittelheim, Winkel, Johannisberg, Geisenheim and Rüdesheim. 140 acres.

Deinhard & Company (G.)

A large merchant company in Koblenz am Rhein; owns several estates in the Mosel, Rheingau and Rheinpfalz regions.

Deipnosophistae (c. 228 B.C.) **(Gr.)**

A book by the ancient Greek author, Athenaeus, in which he describes a banquet, wines and wine-making.

Deiss, Marcel (F.)

An estate in Bergheim, northern Haut-Rhin district, Alsace region.

Delaforce Sons & Co. (P.)   1868

A Port producer in Vila Nova de Gaia; uses grapes from Quinta da Corte.

Delagrange, Bernard et Fils (F.)

An estate in Volnay, Côte de Beaune, Burgundy. 50 acres, including Volnay Caillerets – .8 acre, Champans – .8 acre, Pommard Les Chanlins Bas – .8 acre and Beaune Les Boucherottes – .8 acre.

Delaporte, Vincent (F.)

An estate in Chavignol, Sancerre district, Upper Loire region. 25 acres.

Delas Frères (F.)   1835

An estate and merchant in Tournon, northern Rhône region. 50 acres, including Clos Bouché in Vérin (Condrieu) – 5 acres, Cornas – 12 acres, Côte-Rôtie – 6 acres, Hermitage – 24 acres and some St.-Joseph and Crozes-Hermitage.

Delaware (U.S.)

A native American hybid red grape, spicy and aromatic; considered one of the best U.S. grapes; grown principally in Ohio and New York State.

Delegat's Vineyard (N.Z.)   1947

A winery in Henderson, Aukland district, North Island; produces Cabernet, Riesling, Chardonnay and Müller-Thurgau wines. 50 acres.

Delegrange-Bachelet (F.)

An estate in Chassagne-Montrachet, Côte de Beaune, Burgundy. 25 acres, including Bâtard-Montrachet – 1.2 acres, Criots-Bâtard-Montrachet – 1.2 acres, Chassagne-Montrachet En Cailleret – 2.5 acres, La Maltroie – 1.2 acres, Morgeot (red and white) – 5 acres, Volnay Champans – 1 acre, Clos des Chênes – 1 acre and Pommard Les Rugiens – .5 acre. 60% of the estate was sold in 1979.

Deléger, Georges (F.)

An estate in Chassagne-Montrachet, Côte de Beaune, Burgundy. 12 acres, including Chevalier-Montrachet – .4 acre, Chassagne-Montrachet Les Chenevottes – .6 acre.

Deléger, Joseph (F.)

An estate in Chassagne-Montrachet, Côte de Beaune, Burgundy. 15 acres, including Criots-Bâtard-Montrachet – .6 acre, Chassagne-Montrachet En Cailleret – .6 acre, Santenay La Comme – 1.7 acres and some Puligny-Montrachet and St.- Aubin.

Delheim Estate EWO (S.Af.)   1941

An estate in the Stellenbosch district; produces a wide variety of wines including Cabernet, Pinot Noir, Shiraz, Riesling, Chenin Blanc and Gewürztraminer. 50,000 cases. 300 acres.

délicat (F.) *also* delikat (G.)

Delicate; fragile; low in alcohol.

Delicatessen (U.S.)

A red hybrid grape bred by Thomas Munson from a variety of grapes.

Delicato Vineyards (U.S.)   1935, 1976

A large winery in Manteca, San Joaquin Valley, California; produces mostly bulk and jug wines, and some varietal wines, from purchased grapes. 5 million cases.

Delor & Cie, A. (F.)   1865

A merchant in Bordeaux.

Demestica (Gr.)

A brand name for red and white wine made by Achaia Clauss.

demi (F.)

A half; a half-liter. *"Demie"* is a half-bottle.

demie-queue (F.)

An old term for a half-*queue* (a *queue* is an old Burgundian term for 2 *pièces* or barrels), therefore equal to one *pièce*, holding 228 liters.

demijohn (E.)

A large glass bottle with wicker wrapping having a 1-10 gallon capacity, used for storage and transport of wines. A corrupt form of *Dame-Jeanne*; also called carboy.

demi-sec (F.)

In Champagne it means sweet, with 4-6% added sugar solution. In still wines it means semi-dry, or slightly sweet.

Denominación de Origen (Sp.) 1926, 1972

Spanish for "Designation of Origin," the wine laws, begun in 1926 and centralized in 1972, designed to control quality and labeling of Spanish wines; abbreviated as DO.

Denominazione di Origine Controllata (I.)
1963

Italian for "Controlled Designation of Origin," the wine laws, passed in 1963, but not applied until 1966, controlling the quality and labeling of Italian wines; abbreviated as DOC.

Denominazione di Origine Controllata e Garantita (I.)
1980

A DOC designation upgraded with more rigorous standards of quality. The first wines selected for the DOCG enhancement were Barolo, Barbaresco, Brunello and Vino Nobile di Montepulciano; Chianti was added later.

Denominazione di Origine Semplice (I.)

Italian for "Designation of Simple Origin," part of the DOC laws controlling the district or regional wines of simpler character than the DOC wines; abbreviated as DOS.

densimeter

A device used for measuring the density of grape must.

deposit

A sediment consisting of solid particles precipitated in red wines and left in the bottom of the bottle after decanting. In white wines, deposits are tasteless crystals of tartaric acid.

déposito (P., Sp.)

A large storage or blending vat.

Derey Frères (F.)

An estate in Conchey, Côte de Nuits district, Burgundy. 25 acres, including Fixin Les Hervelets – 2.5 acres, Gevrey-Chambertin – 2.5 acres and Bourgogné Montre-Cul – 2.5 acres.

dérogation, droit de (F.)

The legal right to sell wine from a yield in excess of the normal legal limits. This is allowed in certain great vintages when the increased yield will not adversely affect the quality of the wine.

Derrière-la-Grange (F.)

A *Premier Cru* vineyard in Chambolle-Musigny, Côte de Nuits district, Burgundy. 10 acres.

Derrière Saint-Jean (F.)

A *Premier Cru* vineyard in Pommard, Côte de Beaune district, Burgundy. 3 acres.

Dervieux, Albert (F.)

An estate in Ampuis, Côte-Rôtie district, northern Rhône region. 7 acres.

Descombes, Jean (F.)

An estate in Villié-Morgon, Beaujolais district, Burgundy.

desengage (P.)

The separation of the stalks from the grapes.

Desmirail, Château (F.)

An estate in Margaux, Haut Médoc district, Bordeaux, originally part of Château Rauzan until the 18th century; classified in 1855 as a *Troisième Cru*, but had not produced wine for many years and was eventually sold to Château Palmer in 1957.

dessert wine

Any sweet, red or white wine, fortified or natural (Barsac, Sauternes, Vouvray, German *Auslese, Beerenauslese* and *Trokenbeerenauslese* wines, Port, Sherry, Madeira, etc.), served after a meal with or as dessert.

Dessilani & Figlio, Luigi (I.)
1924

An estate in Fara, Piedmont; produces Barbera, Bonarda, Caramino, Cornaggina, Fara, Gattinara and Spanna. 12,000 cases. 50 acres.

Deutsche Landwirtschafts Gesellschaft (G.)
1885

The German Agricultural Society, the organization that selects the wines that receive the *Bundesweinprämierung*, or National Wine Award.

Deutz & Geldermann (F.)   1838

A Champagne producer in Ay; the *cuvée de prestige* is Cuvée William Deutz. 650,000 bottles. 90 acres.

Deuxième Cru (F.)

Second Growth, the second tier from the top in the 1855 classification of red wines of the Médoc and white wines of Sauternes.

deuxième taille (F.)

The third (*sic*) pressing of wine in the Champagne region.

Devlin Wine Cellars (U.S.)   1978

A winery in Soquel, Santa Cruz County, California; produces Cabernet, Zinfandel, Chardonnay and Sauvignon Blanc wines from purchased grapes. 2,000 cases.

Devoy, Domaine du (F.)

An estate in St.-Laurent-des-Arbres, Lirac district, in the southern Rhône region; produces wine made from Grenache, Cinsault, Mourvèdre and Syrah grapes. 85 acres.

Dewetshof EWO *also* De Wetshof (S.Af.)

An estate in the Robertson district, well-known for its Riesling wine.

Deyrem-Valentin, Château (F.)

An estate in Soussans-Margaux, Haut Médoc district, Bordeaux; classified in 1932 as a *Cru Bourgeois*. 3,000 cases. 17 acres.

Dézaley (Sw.)

1. A district just southeast of Lausanne, on Lake Geneva, in the Lavaux district, Vaud region, which produces:

2. A white wine made from the Chasselas (called the Dorin) grape.

Dezat, André (F.)

An estate in Verdigny, Sancerre district, Upper Loire region; produces red and white wine. 30 acres.

Dezize-les-Maranges (F.)

A commune in the southern Côte de Beaune district, Burgundy; produces light red and white wines, usually blended with other *communes* and sold as Côte de Beaune-Villages; it has 1 *Premier Cru* vineyard: Les Maranges.

Dhron (G.)

A village in the Mosel-Saar-Ruwer region, Bereich Bernkastel, Grosslage Michelsberg. Since 1971 merged with Neumagen (see **Neumagen** for vineyard listing). 875 acres.

Diabetikerwein (G.)

Diabetic wine, a wine with a minimum of residual sugar – less than 4 grams per liter, considered safe for diabetics to drink.

Diablo Vista Winery (U.S.)   1977

A small winery in Benicia, Solano County, California; produces Cabernet, Zinfandel, Chardonnay and Malvasia wines; made from grapes purchased from Napa Valley, Sonoma County and Livermore Valley.

Diamond, *also* Moore's Diamond (U.S.)

A white hybrid grape – a cross of Iona and Concord grapes, developed by Jacob Moore in New York State in the 1860's.

Diamond Creek Vineyards (U.S.)   1972

A winery near Calistoga, on Diamond Mountain, Napa Valley, California; produces only Cabernet wines from 3 separate vineyards: Volcanic Hill – 8 acres, Red Rock Terrace – 7 acres and Gravelly Meadow – 5 acres. 3,000 cases. 20 acres.

Diamond Oaks Vineyard (U.S.)   1979

A label used by Manier Vineyards, Napa City, California, with a new winery in Sonoma; produces Cabernet and Chardonnay wines. 20,000 cases. 400 acres.

Diana (U.S.)

An early American red hybrid grape grown in New York and Ohio, developed to improve the Catawba grape.

diastase

A ferment with the ability to convert starch into dextrine, then into sugar.

Didiers, Les (F.)

A *Premier Cru* Vineyard in Prémeaux, Côte de Nuits district, Burgundy. 7 acres.

Diel auf Burg Layen, Schlossgut (G.)

An estate in Bad Kreuznach, Nahe region; owns vineyards in Burg Layen, Dorsheim and Münster. 45 acres.

Dienheim (G.)

A village in the Rheinhessen region, Bereich Nierstein, Grosslagen Krötenbrunnen and Güldenmorgen. The vineyards are Falkenberg, Herrenberg, Höhlchen, Kreuz, Siliusbrunnen and Tafelstein in Grosslage Güldenmorgen, and Herrengarten, Paterhof and Schloss in Grosslage Krötenbrunnen. 5 vineyards are shared with Oppenheim. 1,100 acres.

Digardi Winery (U.S.)   **1883, 1933**

A winery in Martinez, Contra Costa County, California; produces wines from purchased grapes.

Dijon (F.)

A city north of the Côte de Nuits district, and the largest city in Burgundy; it used to have good vineyards before they were destroyed by the growth of the city.

Dillon, Château (F.)

An estate in Blanquefort, Haut Médoc district, Bordeaux; classified in 1932 as a *Cru Bourgeois*; owned and run by the *École d'Agriculture*. 10,000 cases. 70 acres.

Dimiat *also* **Dimyat (Bul.)**

A local white grape; the same as the Smederevka grape grown in Yugoslavia.

Dimrit (T.)

A red grape grown in central Turkey.

Dingač (Y.)

Semi-sweet red wine from the Pelješac peninsula, north of Dubrovnik, in Dalmatia; made from semi-dried Plavac grapes

Diognières, Les (F.)

A vineyard section of Hermitage, northern Rhône region; produces red wines.

Diognières et Torras, Les (F.)

A vineyard section of Hermitage, northern Rhône region.

Dionysos (Gr.)

The ancient Greek God of Wine, who instituted the Bacchic rites; he was the son of Zeus and Semele.

Dioscorides (Gr.)

An ancient Greek author (1st century A.D.) who wrote *Materia Medica*, in which he discusses various wines.

dipping rod

A device used for measuring the contents of casks.

Dixie (U.S.)   **1976**

An American hybrid grape – a cross of Dog Ridge and *Vitis candicans*; it is beginning to replace the Scuppernong grape in the southeastern United States.

Dizy (F.)

A commune near Ay, in the Marne Valley district, Champagne region; produces a *Premier Cru* Champagne.

Dobrogeia (R.)

A region near the Black Sea, in southeastern Romania; produces Murfatlar wines, especially the sweet Muskat wine.

Döbülgen (T.)

A white grape.

Doçar (P.)

A red grape grown in the Vinho Verde region.

doce (P.)

Sweet.

Docteur Peste, Cuvée (F.)

A red wine from the Hospices de Beaune, Côte de Beaune district, Burgundy. The *cuvée* is composed of the following vineyards in Corton: Chaumes et Voirosses – 2.5 acres, Clos du Roi – 1 acre, Fiètre – 1 acre and Les Grèves – .25 acre.

Doepken, Schloss (U.S.) 1980, vines 1972

A winery in Ripley, Chautauqua region, New York; produces Chardonnay, Gewürztraminer, Riesling and other wines. 60 acres.

Dog Ridge (U.S.)

An American hybrid grape – a cross of *Vitis candicans* and *Vitis rupestis;* grown in Texas.

Doisy-Daëne, Château (F.)

An estate in Barsac, Sauternes district, Bordeaux; classified in 1855 as a *Deuxième Cru;* formerly a part of Château Doisy; produces sweet, white wine made from the Sémillon grape, also a dry, white wine from 50% Sémillon and 20% Sauvignon grapes with Muscadelle, Riesling and Chardonnay grapes. 2,000 cases sweet, 4,000 cases dry. 35 acres.

Doisy-Dubroca, Château (F.)

An estate in Barsac, Sauternes district, Bordeaux; classified in 1855 as a *Deuxième Cru;* formerly a part of Château Doisy, sold in 1880. 450 cases. 9 acres.

Doisy-Védrines, Château (F.)

An estate in Barsac, Sauternes district, Bordeaux; classified in 1855 as a *Deuxième Cru;* it is the original Château Doisy from which two other properties were separated. 5,700 cases. 75 acres.

Doktor *also* **Doctor (G.)**

A famous vineyard in Bernkastel, Bereich Bernkastel, Mosel-Saar-Ruwer region; owned by Dr. Thanisch, Dr. Deinhard and Dr. Lauerberg and more recently by 8 additional owners. Formerly 3.5 acres, presently 12.5 acres.

dolium, dolia (Lat.)

An ancient Roman earthenware storage vessel.

Dolan Vineyards (U.S.)   1980

A winery in Redwood Valley, Mendocino County, California; produces Cabernet and Chardonnay wines. 1,500 cases.

Dolceaqua DOC (I.)

1. A village and district around San Remo, in the western Liguria region, which produces:

2. A red wine made from the Rosesse grape.

Dolcetto DOC (I.)

1. A red grape grown in the Piedmont region of northern Italy.

2. A dry red wine from Acqui, Alba, Asti, Diano d'Alba, Ovado, Dogliani and Langhe Monregales, all DOC districts for Dolcetto, in the Piedmont region; made from the Dolcetto grape.

Dôle (Sw.)

A red wine from Sion, in the Valais region; made from the Gamay grape (called the Dôle grape) usually blended with the Pinot Noir grape, or from either grape by itself.

Dom (G.)

A cathedral.

Dom Pérignon (1639-1715) (F.)

1. A Benedictine Monk who, according to legend, perfected the method of making Champagne.

2. A famous, deluxe vintage Champagne made by Moët et Chandon.

domaine (F.)

An estate. See also **chateau,** and **clos.**

Domäne (G.)

An estate.

Domdechant (G.)

A Dean of a Cathedral.

Domecq S.A., Pedro (Sp.)   **1730**

A large Sherry producer in Jerez de la Frontera; produces several types of Sherry, especially famous for "La Ina" *(fino)* and "Celebration Cream"; also owns vineyards in Spain and Mexico.

Domecq Domain (Sp.)

A brand name for red and white wines made by Sociedad General de Viños S.A.

Domina (G.)

A red grape – a cross of Portugieser and Spätburgunder; developed at the Federal Research Institute, Geilweilerhof, Germany.

Dominique, Château La (F.)

An estate in St.-Émilion, Bordeaux; classified in 1955 as a *Grand Cru Classé*. 7,000 cases. 43 acres.

Dominodes, Les (F.)

A *Premier Cru* vineyard (also called Jarrons) in Savigny-lès-Beaune, Côte de Beaune district, Burgundy. 22 acres.

Don Alfonso (I.)

Red, white and rosé wines from the Isle of Ischia, in the Campania region.

Dona Branca (P., Sp.)

A white grape grown in the Dão and Colares regions of Portugal and in Galicia, northwestern Spain.

Donau Perle (Bul.)

A white wine from northeastern Bulgaria; made from a blend of the Fetiaska (the Fetească of Romania) and other white grapes.

Donna Maria Vineyards (U.S.)   **1974**
                                    1st wine 1980

A winery in Healdsburg, Sonoma County, California; produces Cabernet, Pinot Noir, Chardonnay, Sauvignon Blanc, Sémillon

and Gewürztraminer wines. 10,000 cases. 150 acres.

Donna Marzia (I.)

Red and white wines from Laverno, in the southern Apulia region. The red wine is made from the Negroamaro grape and the white wine is made from the Malvasia Bianca grape.

Donnaz DOC (I.)

1. A village and district in the southeastern Valle d'Aosta region of northern Italy, which produces:

2. A red wine made from the Nebbiolo grape, similar to Carema.

Donnici DOC (I.)   **since 1975**

1. A village and district south of Cosenza, in the western Calabria region, which produces:

2. A red wine made from Gaglioppo, Greco Nero, Malvasia Bianco and Mantonico Bianco grapes.

Donzelinho (P.)

A white grape used in making Port; one of 16 official "first quality" grapes.

Donzelinho Tinto (P.)

A red grape used in making Port, one of 16 official "first quality" grapes.

Dopff & Irion (F.)   **1945**

A large estate and merchant in Riquewihr, Haut-Rhin, Alsace region. 300 acres, including Amandiers vineyard – 7 acres (Muscat), Les Murailles (Schoenenberg) – 25 acres (Riesling), Les Sorcières – 27 acres (Gewürztraminer) and Domaine du Château de Riquewihr; now also owns Domaine Jux.

Dopff au Moulin (F.)

An estate in Riquewihr, Haut-Rhin, Alsace region. 185 acres, including Schoenenberg vineyard – 10 acres (Riesling) and Eichberg vineyard (Turckheim) – 10 acres (Gewürztraminer).

Dorgali, Cantina Sociale di (I.)

A co-op winery in Dorgali, Sardinia; produces Cannonau and other wines.

Dorin (Sw.)

1. A local name for the Chasselas grape.
2. A white wine from the Vaud region; made from the Chasselas grape.

Dorsheim (G.)

A village in the Nahe region, Bereich Kreuznach, Grosslage Schlosskapelle. The vineyards are Burgberg, Goldloch, Honigberg, Jungbrunnen, Klosterpfad, Laurenziweg, Nixenberg, Pittermännchen and Trollberg.

dosage (F.)

The final process in making Champagne, the addition of various amounts of sugar (from 0-10% depending on desired level of sweetness) which is mixed with Champagne and brandy; also called *liqueur d'expédition.*

double-magnum

A large bottle equal to 4 fifths, or about 100 ounces.

Doucillon (F.)

A white grape grown in Bandol and Cassis, in the Provence region; also called Grenache Blanc.

Doudet-Naudin (F.)   1849

An estate in Savigny-lès-Beaune, Burgundy. 12 acres, including Beaune Clos du Roi – 1.2 acres, Savigny Aux Guettes – 2.5 acres, Savigny Redrescuts – 2 acres, Corton Les Maréchaudes – 2.5 acres, Aloxe-Corton Les Bouttières – 2.5 acres and Pernand-Vergelesses Les Fichots – 1.6 acres.

Douro (P.)

1. A river which runs through the Douro and Vinhos Verdes regions in northern Portugal.
2. An important region in northern Portugal, along the Douro River, where the many grape varieties used in making Port wines are grown; also called Alto Douro and Upper Douro; divided into three districts: Baixo Corgo, Cima Corgo and Douro Superior.

Douro Superior (P.)

One of the three districts in the Upper Douro region.

doux (F.)

Sweet, in reference to still wines; very sweet, in reference to Champagne, with 8-10% added sugar solution *(dosage).*

Dover Vineyard (U.S.)   1934

A winery in Westlake, Ohio, near Cleveland; produces wines made from the Concord grape. 25 acres.

downy mildew

A crippling fungus disease of the vine, caused by *Plasmospora viticola;* it attacks the green portion of the vine before the grapes change color, causing an oily stain on the underside of the leaves; the stain later turns white and spreads; it can also appear on shoots, flowers and fruit. Also called false mildew.

Dow's Port (P.)   1798

A brand of Port wine made by Silva & Cosens Ltd., in Vila Nova de Gaia.

Draceno ((I.)

Red, white and rosé wines from Partanna, in western Sicily; the red and rosé wines are made from the Perricone grape and the white wine is made from the Catarratto grape.

Drăgăşani (R.)

A village and district in southwestern Romania, in the Wallachia region; produces various red and white varietal wines.

Drayton's Bellevue (Aus.)   1850

An old winery in Lower Hunter Valley, New South Wales; produces Cabernet, Shiraz, Chardonnay and Sémillon wines. 150 acres.

Dreher, S.A. (Br.)

A winery in Bento Goncalves, Rio Grande do Sul region, in southern Brazil; produces Cabernet and Barbera wines.

Dreimännerwein (G.)

German for "Three-man wine," a wine from the Baden region, so-called because it is considered to be so bad that to make a man drink it, it takes a second to hold him and a third to pour the wine down his throat.

droë (S. Af.)

Dry.

Droin-Baudoin, Paul; Droin-Mary, Marcel (F.)

An estate in Chablis, Burgundy. 15 acres, including Vaudésir -.8 acre, Grenouilles – 2.5 acres, Valmur – 2.5 acres, Les Clos – 2.5 acres and some Montée de Tonnerre, Montmains and Vaillons.

droit de dérogation (F.)

The legal right to sell wine from a yield in excess of the normal legal limits. This is allowed in certain great vintages when the increased yield will not adversely affect the quality of the wine.

Drouhin, Joseph (F.)   1880

A merchant and estate in Beaune, Burgundy. 115 acres, including Chambertin Clos de Bèze – .3 acre, Griotte-Chambertin – 1.2 acres, Bonnes Mares – .7 acre, Musigny – 1.6 acres, Chambolle-Musigny Les Amoureuses – 1.2 acres, Chambolle-Musigny *Premier Cru* - 3 acres, Clos de Vougeot – 2.4 acres, Grands Échézeaux – 1.2 acres, Échézeaux – 1 acre, Corton – 1.2 acres, Beaune Clos des Mouches (red and white) – 32 acres, *Premier Cru* - 6.7 acres, Volnay Clos des Chênes – .6 acre, Chablis *Grand Cru* - 5 acres, Chablis *Premier Cru* - 17 acres, Chablis – 30 acres; also makes, bottles and distributes Montrachet of Marquis de Laguiche – 5 acres and Puligny-Montrachet Clos du Cailleret of Dupard Aîné – 8.5 acres.

Drouhin, Cuvée Maurice (F.)

A red wine from the Hospices de Beaune, Côte de Beaune district, Burgundy. The *cuvée* is composed of the following vineyards in Beaune: Les Avaux – 2 acres, Les Boucherottes – 1.5 acres, Champs Pimont – 1.5 acres and Les Grèves – 1 acre. 675 cases.

Drouhin-Laroze, Domaine (F.)

An estate in Gevrey-Chambertin, Côte de Nuits, Burgundy. 37 acres, including Chambertin Clos de Bèze – 4 acres, Clos de Vougeot – 4 acres, Bonnes Mares – 5 acres, Latricières-Chambertin – 2 acres, Chapelle-Chambertin – 2.2 acres, Mazis-Chambertin – .6 acre, Gevrey-Chambertin *Premier Cru* - 5 acres and some Chambolle-Musigny and Morey-St.-Denis.

Drupeggio (I.)

A white grape grown in Orvieto, in the Umbria region.

dry

1. Not sweet, in reference to wine. Most red, white and rosé wines are made dry, although many are made in several styles, from dry to sweet. The following wines are always dry: all red Bordeaux, red and white Burgundy, almost all Rhône wine, all California Cabernet Sauvignon and Chardonnay wines (with one or two exceptions), almost all Alsatian wines, and in Italy, Barbaresco, Barolo, Chianti, Gattinara, Spanna, etc.

2. Unable by law to make, sell or drink alcoholic beverages; refers to a state or a county.

Dry Creek (U.S.)

A small district north of Healdsburg, west of the Russian River, along Dry Creek, in northern Sonoma County, California.

Dry Creek Vineyard (U.S.)   1972

A winery in Healdsburg, Dry Creek Valley, northern Sonoma County, California; produces Cabernet, Zinfandel, Chardonnay, Fumé Blanc, Chenin Blanc and Gewürztraminer wines. 35,000 cases. 50 acres.

Dubignon, Château (F.)

A former estate in Margaux, Haut-Médoc district, Bordeaux; classified in 1855 as a *Troisième Cru*, but absorbed by Château Malescot-St.-Exupéry.

Duboeuf, Georges (F.)

A merchant in Romanèche-Thorins, Beaujolais district, Burgundy; produces Beaujolais wines.

Dubois & Fils, Les Frères (Sw.)   1928

An estate in Cully, Lavaux district, Vaud region; produces Dorin, Pinot Noir, Pinot Gris and other wines. 5,000 cases. 15 acres.

Dubois et Fils, Robert (F.)

An estate in Prémeaux, Côte de Nuits district, Burgundy. 22 acres, including Nuits-St.-Georges Les Porrets – .7 acre and some Nuits-St.-Georges and Côte de Nuit-Villages.

Dubois-Goujon (F.)

An estate in Chorey-lès-Beaune, Burgundy. 15 acres, including Beaune Les Bressandes – 2 acres, Cent Vignes – .7 acre and some Savigny, Aloxe-Corton and Chorey.

Dubonnet (F.)

A brand of a red or white French apéritif made from a sweet wine base, with bitter bark and quinine added for flavoring.

Dubos Frères (F.)   1785

A merchant in Bordeaux.

Dubreuil-Bize, Paul (F.)

An estate in Savigny-lès-Beaune, Burgundy. 15 acres, including Savigny Les Vergelesses – 5 acres and Savigny Les Lavières – 2.5 acres.

Dubreuil-Fontaine Père et Fils, P. (F.)

An estate in Savigny-lès-Beaune, Côte de Beaune district, Burgundy. 43 acres, including Corton Clos du Roi – 2.5 acres, Bressandes – 4 acres, Perrières – 1.5 acres, Île de Vergelesses – 1.6 acres, Savigny Les Vergelesses – 6.2 acres, Corton-Charle-magne – 3 acres, Pommard Les Épenots – .4 acre and Pernand-Vergelesses Clos Berthet Monopole – 5 acres.

Duchesse (Br.)

A white grape grown in Brazil, probably the same as the Dutchess; also called Riesling de Caldas.

Duchet, Domaine (F.)

An estate in Beaune, Côte de Beaune district, Burgundy. 12 acres, including Corton-Charlemagne – .6 acre, Savigny Les Peuillets – 1 acre, Beaune Les Bressandes – 2.5 acres, Beaune Les Cent Vignes – 2.5 acres, Beaune Les Grèves – 1 acre, and Beaune Pertuisots, Les Teurons, and Blanchisserie and some Pommard.

Duckhorn Vineyards (U.S.)   1976

A winery in St. Helena, Napa Valley, California; produces Cabernet, Merlot, Sauvignon Blanc and Sémillon wines. 3,000 cases. 7 acres.

Ducru-Beaucaillou, Château (F.)

An estate in St.-Julien, Haut-Médoc district, Bordeaux; until the early 19th century it was Château Bergeron; classified in 1855 as a *Deuxième Cru*; owned by the Borie family since 1941. 110 acres. 15,000 cases.

Ducs, Clos des (F.)

A *Premier Cru* vineyard in Volnay, Côte de Beaune district, Burgundy. 6 acres.

Duff Gordon y Cía. S.A. (Sp.)   1768

A Sherry producer in Puerto de Santa Maria; produces several types, including "Club Dry" (*amontillado*), "El Cid" (*amontillado*) and Santa Maria Cream.

Dufort-Vivens, Château (F.)

An estate in Margaux, Haut Médoc district, Bordeaux; classified in 1855 as a *Deuxième Cru*; the Vivens was added in 1924. 8,000 cases. 100 acres.

Dufouleur Frères (F.)

A *négociant* and estate in Nuits-St.-Georges, Côte de Nuits district, Burgundy;

owns some Clos Vougeot, Musigny, Nuits-St.-Georges and Mercurey.

Duhart-Milon-Rothschild, Château (F.)

An estate in Pauillac, Haut-Médoc district, Bordeaux, classified in 1855 as a *Quatrième Cru;* it was called Duhart in 1855; the Rothschild (Lafite) family bought it in 1964. 100 acres. 12,000 cases.

Dujac, Domaine (F.)   1968

An estate, formerly the Domaine Graillet, in Morey-St.-Denis, Côte de Nuits district, Burgundy. 28 acres, including Clos St.-Denis – 4 acres, Clos de la Roche – 5 acres, Bonnes Mares – 1 acre, Échézeaux – 1.7 acres, Charmes-Chambertin – 1.7 acres, Gevrey-Chambertin – 1.7 acres, Gevrey-Chambertin Combottes – 2.5 acres, Morey-St.-Denis *Premier Cru* - 1 acre and Chambolle-Musigny *Premier Cru* - 1 acre.

dulce (Sp.)

1. Sweet.

2. The sweet wine which is added to dry Sherry to make a sweet Sherry.

Dulong, Pierre (F.)   1873

A merchant in Bordeaux.

Dumay, Cuvée Charlotte (F.)

A red wine from the Hospices de Beaune, Côte de Beaune district, Burgundy. The *cuvée* is composed of the following vineyards: Corton-Renardes – 5 acres, Corton-Les Bressandes – 2.5 acres and Corton-Clos du Roi – 1 acre. 575 cases.

Dumazet, Pierre (F.)

An estate in Limony, Condrieu district, northern Rhône region. Owns 1 acre.

dumb

A term used to describe a good wine which is still in a hard, unresolved stage of aging, thus obscuring the fruit and flavor.

dunkel (G.)

Dark; red, referring to a grape or a wine.

Dünweg, Weingut Otto (G.)

An estate and merchant in Neumagen-Dhron, Mosel-Saar-Ruwer region; owns vineyards in Neumagen, Dhron, Trittenheim and Piesport. 15 acres.

Dupard Aîné (F.)

An estate in Puligny-Montrachet, Côte de Beaune district, Burgundy. 25 acres, including Chevalier-Montrachet – 2.5 acres, Puligny-Montrachet Clos du Cailleret Les Demoiselles – 9 acres, Les Pucelles – 3 acres and Les Folatières – 1.7 acres.

Duplessis-Fabre, Château (F.)

An estate in Moulis, Haut-Médoc district, Bordeaux; classified in 1978 as a *Cru Bourgeois*. 30 acres. 7,000 cases.

Duplessis et Fils, Marcel (F.)

An estate in the Chablis district, Burgundy. 10 acres, including Les Clos – .8 acre and some Montée de Tonnerre, Montmains, Fourchaume and Châtain.

Duplessis-Hauchecorne, Château (F.)

An estate in Moulis, Haut-Médoc district, Bordeaux; classified in 1978 as a *Cru Grand Bourgeois*. 8,500 cases. 45 acres.

Duplin Wine Cellar (U.S.)   1975

A winery in Rose Hill, North Carolina; produces dry and sweet wines from Scuppernong, Carlos and Noble grapes. 75 acres.

Dupraz, Claude & Gilbert (Sw.)   1945

An estate in Geneva. 30 acres.

dur (F.)

Hard, not ready.

Duras (F.)

A local red grape grown in the Gaillac district of the Southwest region.

Durbach (G.)

A village in the Baden region, Bereich Ortenau, Grosslage Fürsteneck. The vineyards are: Bienengarten, Josephsberg,

Kapellenberg, Kasselberg, Kochberg, Öl-berg, Plauelrain, Schlossberg, Schloss Grohl and Steinberg.

Durban, Domaine (F.)

An estate in Beaumes-de-Venise, Rhône region; owns 22 acres of Muscat vines, some Gigondas and Côtes du Rhône-Villages.

Durbanville WO (S. Af.)

A city and district northeast of Capetown, in the southwestern Constantia region.

durchgegoren (G.)

Totally fermented, without any artificial interference of the fermentation process.

Durella *also* **Durello (I.)**

1. A white grape grown in the Veneto and Tuscany regions.
2. A white wine from Verona and Vicenza, in the Veneto region; made from the Durello grape.

Duresses, Les (F.)

A *Premier Cru* vineyard partly in Monthélie and partly in Auxey-Duresses, Côte de Beaune district, Burgundy. 20 acres total, 12 acres in Monthélie, 8 acres in Auxey-Duresses.

Duret, Cuvée Jacques (F.)

A wine from the Hospices de Nuits, Côte de Nuits district, Burgundy. The *cuvée* is composed of Nuit-St-Georges Didiers St.-Georges – 5 acres, which now also includes the Cuvée Cabet.

Durezza (F.)

A grape grown in the southern Rhône region.

Durieu, Domaine (F.)

An estate in Châteauneuf-du-Pape, Rhône region; produces red wine made from

Grenache, Syrah, Mourvèdre, Cinsault and Counoise grapes. 50 acres.

Duriff *also* **Durif (F.)**

A grape grown in the Rhône region, which is believed to be the same grape as the Petite Sirah grape of California.

Dürkheim, Bad (G.)

A village in the Rheinpfalz region, Bereich Mittelhaardt-Deutsche Weinstrasse, Grosslagen Feuerberg, Hochmess and Schenkenböhl. The vineyards are: Herrenmorgen, Nonnengarten and Steinberg in Grosslage Feuerberg; Hochbenn, Michelsberg, Rittergarten, and Spielberg in Grosslage Hochmess; and Abtsfronhof, Fronhof and Fuchsmantel in Grosslage Schenkenböhl. A considerable amount of red wine is made here from the Portugieser grape. 3,200 acres.

Durney Vineyard (U.S.)   **planted 1966 winery 1977**

A winery in Carmel, Monterey County, California; produces Cabernet, Gamay Beaujolais, Johannisberg Riesling and Chenin Blanc wines. 100 acres. 15,000 cases.

Dürnstein (A.)

A village, west of Krems, in the Wachau district, Lower Austria region.

Duroché (F.)

An estate in Gevrey-Chambertin, Côte de Nuits district, Burgundy. 18 acres, including Chambertin-Clos de Bèze – 1 acre, Charmes-Chambertin – 1 acre and Gevrey-Chambertin Lavaux St.-Jacques – 2.5 acres.

Durup, Jean (F.)

An estate in Maligny, Chablis district, Burgundy. 140 acres, including Domaine de l'Églantière, Château de Maligny, Domaine de la Paulière and Domaine de Valéry; also 32 acres in *Premier Cru* vineyards.

Dusemond (G.)

The former name of the village of Brauneberg, in the Mosel-Saar-Ruwer region.

Dutchess *also* Duchess (U.S.)

An American white hybrid grape – a cross of *Vitis labrusca* and *Vitis vinifera* grapes; developed in Marlboro, Dutchess County, New York (the site of the Benmarl Winery) by Andrew J. Caywood in 1867; also grown in Brazil.

Dutruch-Grand-Poujeau, Château (F.)

An estate in Moulis, Haut Médoc district, Bordeaux; classified in 1978 as a *Cru Grand Bourgeois Exceptionnel*. 8,500 cases. 45 acres.

E

Éts. (F.)

The abbreviation for *Établissements*, a business or company.

E.W.O. (S.Af.)   **1973**

The abbreviation for Estate Wines of Origin, an official designation for estate-produced wines of high quality.

Early Burgundy

In the U.S., another name for the Portugieser or Blauer Portugieser grape; also called Frühburgunder.

Early Niabell (U.S.)

A red hybrid grape – a cross of Niagara and Early Campbell; grown in California.

Easley Enterprises (U.S.)   **1970, 1977**

A winery in Indianapolis, Indiana, with vineyards at Cape Sandy, along the Ohio River; produces wines made from hybrid grapes. 20 acres.

East India (P.)

A Madeira wine shipped to its destination via the East Indies; the wine is matured and helped noticeably by the heat and motion of the journey.

Eastside Winery (U.S.)   **1934**

A large co-op winery in Lodi, San Joaquin Valley, central California; produces Ruby Cabernet, Chenin Blanc, Sémillon, Angelica, Emerald Riesling wines and Sherries; several hybrid grapes are also grown.

ebullioscope

A device for measuring the alcoholic content of wine and spirits by determining the boiling point.

Eburneo (I.)

A white wine from Arezzo, in the Tuscany region; made from Trebbiano and Chardonnay grapes.

Ecard-Guyot (F.)

An estate in Savigny-lès-Beaune, Côte de Beaune district, Burgundy. 30 acres, including Savigny Aux Serpentières – 7.5 acres, Les Jarrons, 2.5 acres and Les Narbantons – 4 acres.

Échanges, Aux (F.)

A vineyard in Chambolle-Musigny, Côte de Nuits district, Burgundy. 2.5 acres.

Échézeaux AOC (F.)

A group of 11 vineyards in the commune of Flagey-Échézeaux, Côte de Nuits district, Burgundy, officially and collectively rated as one *Grand Cru* vineyard of Vosne-Romanée; if the wine is not good enough it is declassified as Vosne-Romanée. Those vineyards are: Les Champs-Traversins, Les Cruots (or Vignes-Blanches), Les Échézeaux-de-Dessus, Les Loachausses, En Orveau, Les Poulaillières, Les Quartiers de Nuits, Les Rouges-du-Bas, Clos St.-Denis, Les Treux, and part of Les Beaux Monts (Bas). 75 acres.

l'Écho, Clos de (F.)

An estate in the Chinon district, Touraine region, Loire Valley. 35 acres.

echt (G.)

Unsugared, pure, natural, unadulterated.

Ecklé, Jean-Paul (F.)

An estate in Katzenthal, Haut-Rhin district, Alsace region. 25 acres.

135

Écloseaux (F.)

A *Premier Cru* vineyard in Rully, Côte Chalonnaise district, Burgundy.

École d'Agriculture Aoste (I.)

An agricultural school in Aosta, Valle d'Aosta region; produces Vin du Conseil, Gamay, Merlot, Malvoisie and other wines. 2,000 cases. 12 acres.

l'Écu, À (F.)

A *Premier Cru* vineyard in Beaune, Côte de Beaune district, Burgundy. 7.5 acres.

Écusseaux, Les (F.)

A *Premier Cru* vineyard (in part) in Auxey-Duresses, Côte de Beaune district, Burgundy. 16 acres.

Edelfäule (G.)

The *Botrytis cinerea* mold, or "noble rot," found on over-ripe grapes in the Rhine and Mosel regions in good or great vintages.

Edelkeur (S. Af.)   since 1973

A sweet white wine from the Nederburg estate, in the Stellenbosch district; made from over-ripe Steen grapes infected with *Botrytis*.

Edeloes (S. Af.)

A sweet white wine from the De Wetshof Estate, in the Robertson district, east of Paarl.

Edelwein (U.S.)

A sweet, white, Riesling wine infected with *Botrytis*; made by Freemark Abbey Winery, Napa City, California; first made in 1973.

Edelweiss (U.S.)

A white hybrid grape grown in Minnesota, developed by Elmer Swenson.

Edelweisser (I.)

A white wine from Tramin, in the northern Trentino-Alto Adige region, made from the De Vite grape.

Edelzwicker (F.)

In Alsace, a wine blended mostly from various noble grapes: Riesling, Gewürztraminer, Sylvaner and Muscat.

Eden (U.S.)

An American red grape, a variety of *Vitis rotundifolia*.

édes (H.)

Sweet.

Edmeades Vineyards (U.S.)   1969

A winery in Philo, Anderson Valley, in Mendocino County, California; produces Cabernet, Zinfandel, Pinot Noir, Chardonnay, Gewürztraminer, French Colombard and Rain wine, a blended white wine made from their own and purchased grapes. 20,000 cases. 35 acres.

Edna Valley (U.S.)

A district in southern San Luis Obispo County, California.

Edna Valley Vineyard (U.S.)   1979
vines 1973

A winery in San Luis Obispo, San Luis Obispo County, California; partly owned and run by Chalone Vineyard; produces Pinot Noir, Chardonnay and Johannisberg Riesling wines. 20,000 cases. 600 acres.

eelworms

Nematodes, parasitic worms which puncture roots, eventually killing the vines.

effer-soet (S. Af.)

Semi-sweet.

effervescence

A sparkle, consisting of rising bubbles, caused by the presence of carbon dioxide gas in the Champagne or other sparkling wine.

Efringen-Kirchen (G.)

A village in the Baden region, Bereich Markgräflerland, Grosslage Vogtei Rötteln. The vineyards are: Oelberg, Kirchberg, Sonnhohle and Steingässle.

Eger (H.)

A village and district in northeastern Hungary, famous for the red Egri Bikavér wine.

L'Églantière, Domaine de (F.)

An estate in Chablis, Burgundy. 125 acres, including Fourchaume – 25 acres, Montée de Tonnerre – 2.5 acres, Montmains – 1.3 acres and some Vaucoupin, Chablis and Petit Chablis.

l'Église, Clos (F.)

An estate in Pomerol, Bordeaux. 12 acres. 2,000 cases.

l'Église, Domaine de (F.)

An estate in Pomerol, Bordeaux. 16 acres. 2,000 cases.

l'Église-Clinet, Château (F.)

An estate in Pomerol, Bordeaux. 10 acres. 1,500 cases.

égrappage (F.)

The process of separating the stalks from the grapes prior to pressing in order to avoid the bitter and harsh elements contained in the stalks.

égrappoir (F.)

A device used to remove the stems from grapes before fermentation; a stemmer.

Egri Bikavér (H.)

Hungarian for "Bull's Blood of Eger," a red wine from Eger, made from a blend of Kadarka, Pinot Noir, Merlot and other grapes. Classified as red wine of Excellent Quality.

Egypt

A country in northeastern Africa; produces some wines from west of the Nile delta; the best vineyard is Mariout. 1.3 million gallons.

Ehrenfelser (G.)

A white grape – a cross of Riesling and Sylvaner; developed at the State Teaching and Research Institute, Geisenheim, Germany in 1929; similar to the Müller-Thurgau grape.

Eichberg (F.)

A famous vineyard in Eguisheim, Haut-Rhin district, Alsace region.

Eichberg (F.)

A vineyard, a part of the Brand vineyard, in Turckheim, Haut-Rhin district, Alsace region.

Eimer (G.)

A keg, or small barrel; a wine measure of various sizes, from 12-15 gallons.

Einaudi, Luigi (I.)   1907

An estate in Dogliani, Piedmont region; produces Barbera, Barolo, Dolcetto and Nebbiolo wines. 13,000 cases. 60 acres.

Einzellage (G.)

An individual vineyard site, or *"climat."*

Eisele Vineyard (U.S.)

A vineyard near Calistoga, Napa Valley, California; produces Cabernet grapes for Joseph Phelps and Nyers wineries, and formerly for Conn Creek, Ridge and Souverain wineries. 20 acres.

Eisenthal (G.)

A village in the Baden region, Bereich Ortenau, Grosslage Schloss Rodeck. The vineyards are: Betschgräbler and Sommerhalde.

Eiswein (G.)

A wine made from frozen grapes.

Eitelsbacher Karthäuser-Hofberg (G.)

The famous Carthusian Monastery in Trier, Grosslage Römerlay, on the Ruwer River, Bereich Saar-Ruwer, in the Mosel-Saar-Ruwer region. The Karthäuserhofberg vineyards are Burgberg, Kronenberg,

Orthsberg, Sang and Stirn; Marienholz is another of its vineyards in Trier. 185 acres.

El Bierzo (Sp.)

A district in western León region, in northern Spain; produces red, white and rosé wines made from Mencia and Alicante grapes for the red and rosé, and Palomino grapes for the white wines.

El Condado de Rosal (Sp.)

A district in the Galicia region of northwestern Spain; produces red wine from Tintarrón, Caiño and Espadeiro grapes, and white wine from the Albariño grape.

El Dorado County (U.S.)

An important region in the Sierra foothills of northeastern California, especially for Zinfandel wines.

elaboracion (Sp.)

The production of wine, from fermentation to final blending and clearing.

Elan, Château (U.S.)   1982

A winery in Braselton, Georgia; *vinifera* grapes have been planted. 250 acres.

Elat (Is.)

A dry white wine from Judea, in the Ascalon district; made from the Sauvignon Blanc grape.

Elba DOC (I.)

1. An island and district off the coast of the southern Tuscany region, which produces:
2. Red and white wines, the red wine made mostly from the Sangioveto (Sangiovese) grape, and the white wine made from the Procanico (Trebbiano) grape.

Elbling (G.)

A white grape grown in the Upper Mosel and Luxembourg; low in sugar, high in acidity, thin in body, no bouquet; it has a very prolific yield and is good for blending. Also called Alben, Kleinberger, Klemperich (on the Mosel), and is the same grape as the Pedro Ximénez in Spain.

Elefantenwein (G.)

German for "Elephant Wine," a wine from the Württemberg region, made from grapes supposedly so hard that only an elephant could crush them.

élevage (F.)

The "bringing up" of wine: the maturing of wine, which includes choosing, blending, aging and bottling, usually accomplished by a shipper or wine merchant.

éleveur (F.)

A wine merchant who "brings up" the wine (as above).

Elfenhof, Weingut (A.)   1680

A merchant and estate in Rust, Burgenland region. 13,000 cases.

Elk Cove Vineyards (U.S.)   1977
vines 1972

A winery in Gaston, Willamette Valley, northwestern Oregon; produces Pinot Noir, Chardonnay and Riesling wines. 5,000 cases. 25 acres.

Elliott's (Aus.)   1893

An old winery in Pokolbin, Lower Hunter Valley, New South Wales; produces earthy, red wines and rich, white wines, including Shiraz and Sémillon.

Eltville (G.)

A village in the Rheingau region, Bereich Johannisberg, Grosslage Steinmächer. The vineyards are Langenstuck, Rheinberg, Sandgrub, Sonnenberg and Taubenberg. It is also a wine-trading center. 600 acres.

Eltz, Schloss (G.)

A famous estate in Eltville, Rheingau region; now broken up and dispersed among several owners. 100 acres.

Elvira (U.S.)

An American white hybrid grape developed in Missouri in the late 19th century; used for making white wines, especially sparkling wines.

Elzenbaum, Von (I.)   **16th cent.**

An estate in Tramin, Trentino-Alto Adige region; produces Alto Adige, Edelweisser, Gewürztraminer and Blauburgunder wines. 40 acres.

embotellado (Sp.)

Bottled.

Emerald Dry (U.S.)

A white wine made from the Emerald Riesling grape; produced by Paul Masson Winery.

Emerald Riesling (U.S.)

1. A white grape – a cross of Johannisberg Riesling and Muscadelle de Bordelais; developed in California by Dr. Harold Olmo.
2. A white wine made from the Emerald Riesling grape.

emfialosis (Gr.)

Bottled.

Emilia-Romagna (I.)

A region north of the Tuscany region, in central Italy; produces one-sixth of the nation's wine; famous for Lambrusco wines. The principal grapes grown are: Sangiovese, Lambrusco, Trebbiano, Barbera, Bonarda and Albana di Romagna.

Emir (T.)

A white grape grown in central Turkey.

l'En de l'El (F.)

A local white grape grown in Gaillac, Southwest region.

En Ergot (F.)

A *Premier Cru* vineyard in Gevrey-Chambertin, Côte de Nuits district, Burgundy. 3 acres.

en primeur (F.)

The youngest wine, or first wine of the year, usually applied to very young Beaujolais wines, released and shipped no earlier than November 15.

en vaso (Sp.)

The *gobelet* method of vine-training and pruning, using 3 main stems, each with 2 grafted shoots and each bearing 2 bunches of grapes.

en virgen (Sp.)

In wine-making, fermenting without the presence of stems, skins or pips, as when making white wine.

en vrac (F.)

In bulk, as opposed to bottled.

encépagement (F.)

The selection and blending of grape varieties used in making a wine.

l'Enclos, Château (F.)

An estate in Pomerol, Bordeaux. 3,000 cases. 18 acres.

Encruzado (P.)

A white grape grown in the Dão region.

Enfer d'Arvier DOC (I.)

Italian for "Inferno of Arvier," a red wine from Arvier, in the Valle d'Aosta region of northwestern Italy; made from the Petit Rouge grape.

engarrafado (P.)

Bottled.

Engel, Domaine René (F.)

An estate in Vosne-Romanée, Côte de Nuits, Burgundy. 17 acres, including Clos de Vougeot – 3 acres, Grands Échézeaux – 1.2 acres and Vosne-Romanée Les Brûlées – 6 acres.

England and Wales

Countries of the British Isles, where weather conditions and birds make wine production difficult. There are about 700 small vineyards in southern England, Wales and the Channel Islands; the average size is 7 acres, the largest is about 30 acres. Grapes grown are mostly German and French white hybrids, including

Müller-Thurgau, Seyval Blanc, Huxelrebe and Reichensteiner.

English Black Hamburg

Another name for the Trollinger grape.

English Cuvée (E.)

Very dry Champagne, blended to suit the British taste for dry wines.

Enkirch (G.)

A village in the Mosel-Saar-Ruwer region, Bereich Bernkastel, Grosslage Schwarzlay. The vineyards are: Batterieberg, Edelberg, Ellergrub, Herrenberg, Monteneubel, Steffensberg, Weinkammer and Zeppwingert. 500 acres.

Enofriulia (I.)   1967

An estate in Capriva del Friuli, Friuli-Venezia Giulia region; produces a large selection of varietal wines.

enoteca, *plur.* enoteche (I.)

A wine library; a collection of many or all wines from a region or country, frequently providing opportunities to taste the wines. There is an extensive one at the Italian Wine Center, in N.Y.C.

Enoteca Braida (I.)

An estate in Rocchetta Tanaro, near Asti, Piedmont region; produces Barbaresco, Barbera, Barolo, Brachetto, Dolcetto, Grignolino and Moscato wines.

Ensenada, Vinícola de (Mex.)

A large winery in Ensenada, Baja California region; produces a large number of different wines.

Enterprise Wines (Aus.)   1976

A winery in Clare, Clare-Watervale district, South Australia; owned by Tim Knappstein, formerly of the Stanley Wine Company; produces Cabernet, Shiraz, Gewürztraminer and Rhine Riesling wines. 10,000 cases. 140 acres.

Entre-Deux-Mers AOC (F.)

1. French for "Between two Seas," a large area southeast of Bordeaux, in the Bordeaux region, so-called because it lies between the two rivers, the Garonne and the Dordogne; produces red and white wines under several AOC designations: Cadillac, Côtes de Bordeaux St.-Macaire, Entre-Deux-Mers, Graves-de-Vayres, Loupiac, Premières Côtes de Bordeaux, Ste.-Croix-du-Mont and Ste.-Foy-Bordeaux.

2. The AOC designation for white wine from most of the Entre-Deux-Mers area of Bordeaux, made from Sauvignon, Sémillon, Muscadelle, Colombard and other grapes.

enveloppe (F.)

A cylindrical casing, made of straw and/or cardboard, used to protect expensive bottles of wine.

Enz Vineyards (U.S.)   vineyards 1895
                                winery 1973

An old vineyard and recent winery in Hollister, San Benito County, California; produces Zinfandel, Pinot St. George, Fumé Blanc and French Colombard wines. 30 acres. 5,000 cases.

enzyme

A large protein produced by organisms to catalyze chemical reactions; sometimes isolated and purified and added to crushed grapes to facilitate fermentation.

Épen(e)aux, Domaine Clos des (F.)

An estate in Pommard, Côte de Beaune district, Burgundy; owns Pommard Clos des Épen(e)aux Monopole – 13 acres.

Épenots, Les *also* Épen(e)aux *also* Grands Épenots (F.)

A *Premier Cru* vineyard in Pommard, Côte de Beaune district, Burgundy. 25 acres.

Épenots, Clos des *also* Épen(e)aux (F.)

A *Premier Cru* vineyard (in part) in Pommard, Côte de Beaune district, Burgundy. 13 acres.

Épenottes, Les (F.)

A *Premier Cru* vineyard in Beaune, Côte de Beaune district, Burgundy. 25 acres.

Épernay (F.)

An important city in the Champagne region, containing offices and cellars of most of the Champagne producers.

Épinottes, Les (F.)

A *Premier Cru* vineyard in Chablis, Chablis district, Burgundy; usually included as part of the Mélinots vineyard.

d'Epiré, Château (F.)   1640

An estate in St.-Georges-sur-Loire, Savennières district, Anjou region, Loire Valley; produces Savennières and other Anjou wines. 25 acres.

Episcopio (I.)   1860

An estate in Ravello, Campania region; produces red, white and rosé wines.

epitrapezio (Gr.)

Table wine.

épluchage (F.)

The selective picking or sorting of grapes to remove damaged or spoiled fruit.

Equipe Trentina Spumanti (I.)

A producer of *spumante* wines in Mezzolombardo, Trentino-Alto Adige region; produces Equipe 5 sparkling wines. 17,000 cases.

Erbach (G.)

A village in the Rheingau region, Bereich Johannisberg, Grosslage Deutelsberg. The vineyards are: Hohenrain, Honigberg, Marcobrunn, Michelmark, Schlossberg, Siegelsberg, and Steinmorgen. 675 acres.

Erbaluce (I.)

A white grape grown north of Torino, in the Piedmont region.

Erbaluce di Caluso DOC (I.)

1. A district around Caluso, north of Torino, in the Piedmont region, which produces:
2. A dry white wine and a sweet *passito* wine, sometimes fortified; made from the Erbaluce grape.

Erbarola (I.)

Another spelling of the white Albarolo grape, grown in the Liguria region.

Erben (G.)

Heirs.

Erden (G.)

A village in the Mosel-Saar-Ruwer region, Bereich Bernkastel, Grosslage Schwarzlay. The vineyards are: Busslay, Herrenberg, Prälat and Treppchen. 300 acres.

erinose

A microscopic mite which causes blisters on leaves, grapes and flower clusters.

Ermitage *also* Hermitage (Sw.)

A white wine from the Valais region made from the Marsanne grape.

Ermitage (F.)

An old spelling of Hermitage, in the Rhône region.

L'Ermite (F.)

One of the important vineyards in the Hermitage district, northern Rhône region.

Erzeugerabfüllung (G.)

Estate-bottled.

esca

See **apoplexy.**

Eschen (U.S.)

A vineyard in Fiddletown, Amador County, California; produces Zinfandel grapes for the Carneros Creek and Ridge wineries. 20 acres.

Eschenauer, Louis (F.)   1821

A merchant in Bordeaux; owns Châteaux La Garde, Olivier, Rausan-Segla and Smith-Haut-Lafitte.

Escherndorf (G.)

A village in the Franken region, Bereich Maindreieck, Grosslage Kirchberg. The vineyards are: Berg, Fürstenberg and Lump.

Esgana-Cão (P.)

A white grape, one of 16 classified as a First Quality grape used to make Port wine.

Esganoso (P.)

A white grape used to make Vinho Verde.

esmagamento (P.)

The crushing of grapes.

Espadeiro (P., Sp.)

A red grape grown in the Vinhos Verdes and Carcavelos regions of Portugal, and in Galicia, Spain.

espalier (F.)

A method of vine-training in which the arms are trained flat, against a wall or on wires in an even, symmetrical pattern.

Espar (F.)

Another name for the Mourvèdre grape.

l'Esparrou, Château de (F.)

An estate in Canet-Plage, Roussillon region; produces Côtes du Roussillon and other wines. 60,000 cases. 250 acres.

Esperanza, Château (U.S.)   1979

A winery in Bluff Point, on the northern tip of Lake Keuka, Finger Lakes region, New York; produces Chardonnay, Chancellor Noir, Pinot Noir, Riesling and Ravat wines from purchased grapes. 6,000 cases.

espumante (P.)

Sparkling.

espumantes naturais (P.)

Sparkling wines made by the Champagne method.

espumoso (Sp.)

Sparkling.

Essencia *also* **Eszencia (H.)**

The rare essence of Tokaji wine from the Tokaji district, in northeastern Hungary; made from the free-run juice of uncrushed, overripe, botrytis-infected grapes, fermented and aged very slowly.

Esslingen (G.)

A village in the Württemberg region, Bereich Remstal-Stuttgart, Grosslage Weinsteige. The vineyards are Ailenberg, Kirchberg, Lerchenberg and Schenkenberg.

Est! Est!! Est!!! di Montefiascone DOC (I.)

A famous dry white wine from Montefiascone, in the northern Latium region; made from Trebbiano, Malvasia and Rossetto grapes.

estágio (P.)

A resting period for Madeira wines after they are heated.

L'Estagnol, Château de (F.)

An estate in Suze-la-Rousse, in the Côtes du Rhône district, southern Rhône region.

estate

A property or piece of land planted with grapes, owned by a person, family or company, for the purpose of making wine; a vineyard, often with a wine-making facility.

estate-bottling

The practice of individual vineyard owners producing and bottling wine from their own grapes, grown on the property, as in château-bottled wine of Bordeaux. Indication of this practice on labels include: *Mise en Bouteilles au Château, Mis du Domaine, Mise au Domaine, Mise du Propriétaire, Mise à la Propriété;* in German the indication was *Original-Abfüllung* and is now *Erzeuger-abfüllung* or *Aus eigenem Lesegut;* the English term is Estate-bottled.

Estate Wines of Origin, *or* EWO (S. Af.)
1973

The official designation of estate-produced wines of high quality in South Africa. There are 40 estates with this designation.

Esterhazy'sche Schlosskellerei (A.)
17th cent.

An historic estate in Eisenstadt, Burgenland; owns vineyards in Rust, Grosshöflein, Eisenstadt, St. Georgen and St. Margaretten. 28,000 cases. 100 acres.

esters

Groups of ethyl compounds produced from the alcohols reacting with the acids in wine. They are partially responsible for the sweet, fruity aroma of wine.

Estienne, Cuvée (F.)

A red wine from the Hospices de Beaune, Côte de Beaune district, Burgundy; produced until 1968, thereafter partly absorbed into the Cuvée Dames Hospitalières.

Estrella River Winery (U.S.)
1973
1st wine 1977

A winery in Paso Robles, San Luis Obispo County, California; produces Cabernet, Zinfandel, Barbera, Syrah, Chardonnay, Chenin Blanc, Sauvignon Blanc and Muscat wines. 70,000 cases. 600 acres.

estufa, *plural* estufades (P.)

A large heating chamber or cask for heating Madeira and similar wines.

étampé (F.)

Branded, in reference to corks.

ethers

Chemical compounds in wines, partially responsible for the aroma.

Etikett (G.)

A label.

etiqueta (Sp.)

A label.

étiquette (F.)

A label.

Etna DOC (I.)
1968

1. A district on the eastern slopes of Mt. Etna, in eastern Sicily, which produces:

2. Red, white and rosé wines; the red and rosé wines made from 80% Nerello Mascalese, up to 20% Nerello Cappuccio and other grapes and the white wine made from 60% Carricante, up to 40% Catarratto and Trebbiano, Minella Bianco and other grapes.

Étoile AOC (F.)

A village in the Jura region; produces white wines made from Savagnin, Chardonnay and Poulsard grapes, and is also made as a *vin mousseux*.

Étournelles (F.)

A *Premier Cru* vineyard in Gevrey-Chambertin, Côte de Nuits district, Burgundy. 5 acres.

eudemis

A species of moth, the larvae of which is destructive to vine leaves.

Eugenia (Lat.)

An ancient grape grown in Latium; mentioned by Cato.

Eumelan (U.S.)

A red grape grown in the eastern United States.

Euxinograd (Bul.)

A white wine from the Black Sea region of eastern Bulgaria; made from a blend of Dimiat, Misket and Wälschriesling grapes.

L'Évangile, Château (F.)

An estate in Pomerol, Bordeaux. 3,500 cases. 32 acres.

Evensen Vineyards and Winery (U.S.) 1979

A winery in Oakville, Napa Valley, California; produces Gewürztraminer wine. 1,000 cases. 20 acres.

extra dry

Semi-dry, in reference to Champagne; with 1-2% added sugar solution, or *dosage*.

extra-sec

Extra dry, in reference to Champagne; actually semi-dry, with 1-2% added sugar solution or *dosage*.

Extremadura (Sp.)

A large region in southwestern Spain, extending to the Portuguese border.

Extrísimo Bach (Sp.)

A sweet, white wine made by Masía Bach 2050in Barcelona, Catalonia region.

Eyrie Vineyard (U.S.) 1970, vines 1965

A small winery in Dundee, Willamette Valley, northwestern Oregon; produces mainly Pinot Noir and Chardonnay, also Pinot Gris, Pinot Meunier, White Riesling and Muscat Ottonel. 6,000 cases. 25 acres.

Ezerjó (H.)

1. A white grape grown in Hungary.
2. A white wine from Mór, near Budapest; made from the Ezerjó grape.

F

Faber (G.)

A white grape – a cross of Weissburgunder and Müller-Thurgau; developed in 1929 at the State Research Institute in Alzey, in the Rheinhessen region.

Fabrini, Attilo (I.)   1969

An estate in Serrapetrona, the Marches region; produces Colli Maceratesi, Verdicchio, Vernaccia and other wines, some in both still and sparkling versions. 8,000 cases.

Façonnières, Les (F.)

A *Premier Cru* vineyard in Morey-St.-Denis, Côte de Nuits district, Burgundy. 2.5 acres.

Factory House (P.)

A famous eighteenth century building in Oporto, Portugal, used as a club for the owners of the thirteen British Port shippers.

Fagon, Cuvée (F.)

A red wine from the Hospices de Nuits, Côte de Nuits district, Burgundy. The *cuvée* consists of the following vineyard: Nuits-St. Georges Didier Monopole – 2.5 acres.

Fairview Estate EWO (S. Af.)   1974

An estate in the southwestern Paarl district; produces a wide variety of varietal and blended wines. 300 acres.

Faiveley, J. (F.)

A large estate in Nuits-St.-Georges, Côte de Nuits district, Burgundy. 280 acres, including Chambertin Clos de Bèze – 3 acres, Latricières-Chambertin – 4 acres, Mazis-Chambertin – 4 acres, Gevrey-Chambertin Combe aux Moines – 2.5 acres, Premier Cru – 7.5 acres, Musigny – 4 acres, Bonnes Mares – 1.2 acres, Chambolle-Musigny Les Amoureuses – 1.2 acres, Premier Cru – 4 acres, Échézeaux – 2.5 acres, Clos de Vougeot – 4 acres, Nuits-St.-Georges Clos de la Maréchale Monopole – 24 acres, Les St.-Georges – 1.2 acres, Les Porets – 5 acres, Premier Cru – 4 acres, Corton Clos des Cortons Monopole, Mercurey Clos des Myglands Monopole – 7.5 acres and Mercurey – 44 acres.

Falanghino (I.)

A white grape grown in the Campania and Latium regions, used in making Falerno wines.

Falchini, Riccardo (I.)

An estate in San Gimignano, Tuscany region; produces Chianti, Vernaccia and Vin Santo wines. 15,000 cases. 50 acres.

Falcon Crest (U.S.)

A second label of Spring Mountain Vineyards, St. Helena, Napa Valley, California.

Falconi, Il (I.)

A red wine from Castel del Monte DOC district, in the northern Apulia region; made from Montepulciano grapes, with some Uva de Troia and Bombino Nero grapes.

Falerio dei Colli Ascolani DOC (I.)

1. A district around Ascoli Piceno, in the southern Marches region, which produces:

2. A white wine made from 80% Trebbiano Toscana grapes with Passerina, Verdicchio, Malvasia Toscana and Pecorino grapes.

145

Falernian *also* Falernum (Lat.)

A sweet, white wine, the most famous wine of Ancient Rome, from the slopes of Monte Massico, between Rome and Naples; mentioned by Horace and Pliny.

Falerno (I.)

1. Red and white wines from Mondragone, in the northwestern Campania region of southwestern Italy. The red wine is made from the Aglianico grape and the white wine is made from the Falanghina grape.

2. Red and white wines from southern Latium. See **Falernum**.

Falernum *also* Falerno (I.)

1. Red and white wines from southern Latium. The red wine is made from Aglianico, Negroamaro, San Giuseppe Rosso, Falanghino and other grapes and the white wine is made from Falanghino, Negroamaro and Cicienello grapes.

2. The Latin name for the ancient Roman wine, Falernian.

Faller et Fils, Robert (F.)

An estate in Ribeauvillé, Haut-Rhin district, Alsace region. 25 acres, including 3 acres of the Giesberg vineyard.

false mildew

See **downey mildew**.

fan leaf

See **court noué**.

Far Niente Winery (U.S.)   1979

An old, rebuilt winery in Oakville, Napa Valley, California; produces Cabernet and Chardonnay wines. 12,000 cases. 20 acres.

Fara DOC (I.)

1. A village and district north of Novara, in the northeastern Piedmont region, which produces:

2. A red wine made from Nebbiolo, Vespolina and Bonarda grapes.

Faranan (Alg.)

A white grape.

Färbertraube (G.)

A coloring grape, or *teinturier*, a grape with dark juice used to darken light red wines.

Farfelu Vineyard (U.S.)   1976

A winery in Flint Hill, Virginia; produces Seyval Blanc and other wines from French hybrid grapes. 13 acres.

Fargues, Château de (F.)

An unclassified estate in Fargues, Sauternes district, Bordeaux; under the same ownership as Château d'Yquem. 1,600 cases. 24 acres.

Faro DOC (I.)

A red wine from Messina, in northeastern Sicily; made from Nerello Mascalese, Nocera, Nerello Cappuccio and some Calabrese, Gaglioppo and Sangiovese grapes.

Fartó (Sp.)

A white grape grown in the Alicante district of southeastern Spain.

Fass, *plur.* Fässer (G.)

A cask.

Fassatti (I.)

An estate in Pieve di Sinalunga, Tuscany; produces Chianti, Chianti Classico and Vino Nobile di Montepulciano wines.

Fasschen (G.)

A small cask.

Fassle (G.)

A little barrel; a 5-liter wooden cask, used with a tube, or *Spitzle*, inserted through the cork, as a drinking vessel; *porrón*, in Spanish.

fassweise (G.)

On draught; from the barrel, by the barrel, or in barrels.

fattoria (I.)

A farm, estate, or winery with vineyards.

Faugères AOC (F.)   1982

1. A village and district northwest of Béziers, in the Languedoc region of the Midi, which produces:

2. Red and white wines, the red made from Carignan, Grenache and Cinsault grapes, and the white from Clairette grapes.

Faurie-de-Souchard, Château (F.)

An estate in St.-Émilion, Bordeaux; classified in 1955 as a *Grand Cru Classé*. 4,500 cases. 21 acres.

Faustino Martinez, Bodegas (Sp.)   1860

A winery in Oyón, in the Rioja Alta; produces red and white wines from the Rioja Alavesa region from their own and purchased grapes. 300,000 cases. 600 acres.

Faustus, Azienda Vinicola Grotta (I.)

A winery in Palermo, Sicily; produces red, white and rosé wines.

Favonio (I.)

Red and white wines from east of Foggia, in the northern Apulia region. The red wines are made from Cabernet Franc and Pinot Nero grapes as separate varietals, and the white wines from Pinot Blanc, Trebbiano and Chardonnay grapes as varietals.

Favonio, Attilo Simonini (I.)   1970

An estate in Foggia, Apulia region; produces Cabernet Franc, Chardonnay, Pinot Bianco, Pinot Rosato and Trebbiano wines. 25,000 cases. 40 acres.

Favorita (I.)

1. A white grape grown in an area around Alba and Dogliani, in the southern Piedmont region, which produces:

2. A dry white wine.

Favre, Les Fils de Charles (Sw.)   1944

A merchant in Sion, in the Valais region; produces Fendant, Dôle and Arvine wines from their own and purchased grapes. 6 acres.

Fay Vineyard (U.S.)   c. 1960

A vineyard in Yountville, Napa Valley, California, owned by the Fay family; grows Cabernet grapes for Cabernet wines made by Heitz, Caneros Creek and Vichon wineries. 100 acres.

Fayolle et ses Fils, Jules (F.)

An estate in Gervans, Hermitage district, northern Rhône region; produces Hermitage – 3 acres, and Crozes-Hermitage – 18 acres.

Fazi-Battaglia Titulus (I.)

A winery in Castelplanio Stazione, in the Marches region; produces Rosso Cònero, Rosso Piceno, Sangiovese and Verdicchio wines from their own and purchased grapes. 300,000 cases. 550 acres.

Federweisser (G.)

German for "feather white," a young, white wine, fermented for about 4 days, sold in taverns on tap. Also called *Sauser*.

Fedrigotti, Conti Bossi (I.)   c. 1860

An estate in Rovereto, Trentino-Alto Adige region; produces Foianeghe, Teroldego, Trentino and other wines. 30,000 cases. 75 acres.

Fefiñanes Palacio (Sp.)

A white wine from the Fefiñanes Palace, in Cambados, on the western shore of the Gallicia region of northwestern Spain; made from the Albariño grape.

Féguine, Clos de la (F.)

A *Premier Cru* vineyard (a part of Aux Cras) in Beaune, Côte de Beaune district, Burgundy; a *monopole* of Jacques Prieur.

Fehér (H.)

White.

Fehér Szagos (H.)

A white grape; also grown in California.

Fehérbor (H.)

A white wine made from the Fehér Szagos grape.

Fehérburgundi (H.)

Another name for the Pinot Blanc grape.

Felluga, Livio (I.)

A winery in Brazzano di Cormons, Friuli-Venezia Giulia region; produces Collio and Colli Orientali wines. 70,000 cases. 300 acres.

Felluga, Marco (I.)   1956

A winery in Gradisca d'Isonzo, Friuli-Venezia Giulia region; produces Collio wines from their own and purchased grapes. 60,000 cases. 170 acres.

Felton-Empire Vineyard (U.S.)   1976

A winery in Felton, Santa Cruz County, California; formerly the old Hillcrest Vineyard; produces Cabernet, Pinot Noir, Zinfandel, Johannisberg Riesling, Gewürztraminer and Chenin Blanc wines. 20,000 cases. 60 acres.

Fendant (Sw.)

1. A white grape grown in the Valais region, the same as the Chasselas of France, Gutedel of Germany and Chasselas Doré of California; also called Sweetwater.

2. A white wine from the Valais region; made from the Fendant grape.

Fenestra Winery (U.S.)   1976

A small winery in Livermore, Alameda County, California; produces Cabernet, Petite Sirah, Zinfandel, Chardonnay, Chenin Blanc and Sauvignon Blanc wines. 2,000 cases.

Fenn Valley Vineyard (U.S.)   1974

A winery in Fennville, southwestern Michigan; produces Riesling and Gewürztraminer wines and wines made from from hybrid grapes. 60 acres.

Fenton Acres Winery (U.S.)   1979

A winery in Healdsburg, Sonoma County, California; produces Pinot Noir and Chardonnay wines. 1,500 cases. 100 acres.

Fer *also* Ferservadou *also* Fer Servadou (F.)

A red grape grown in the Southwest region of France; also called the Pinenc and Couabort.

Féraud, Domaine des (F.)

An estate in Vidauban, in the Provence region.

Fermade, La (F.)

An estate in Lirac, southern Rhône region. 50 acres.

fermage (F.)

The practice of renting a vineyard for cash, instead of part of the harvest. See **métayage**.

ferme (F.)

Closed, firm; not opened up yet, and therefore, not ready to drink.

Ferme Blanche, Domaine de la (F.)

An estate in Cassis, in the Provence region.

ferment

1. To bring about the fermentation of a liquid substance.

2. An agent cabable of causing fermentation, such as any number of different yeasts, and other enzymes or organisms.

fermentation

The process of turning grape juice into wine; it is set in motion by yeasts, which cause sugar to be converted into alcohol and carbonic gas; in addition, a number of side-products are formed, including high alcohols, nitrogenous compounds and glycerin.

Fernão Pires (P.)

A white grape grown in central Portugal.

Ferral (Arg.)

A red grape.

Ferrando, Luigi (I.)

An estate in Ivrea, Piedmont region; produces Carema, Donnaz, Enfer d'Avrier and Erbaluce di Caluso wines.

Ferrar, Bodegas José L. (Sp.)

A winery in Binisalem, Majorca Island; produces red and white wines made from Spanish grapes. 370 acres.

Ferrari (I.)   1902

A producer of sparkling wines in Trento, Trentino-Alto Adige region.

Ferreira, A.A. (P.)   1761

A Port producer in Vila Nova de Gaia; owns Quinta do Vesuvio, Quinta do Vale de Meão and Quinta do Roriz; also produces Ferreirinha and Barca Velha table wines. 4,000 acres.

Ferren (Sp.)

A red grape grown in Galicia.

Ferrero Ranch (U.S.)

A vineyard in the Shenandoah Valley, Amador County, California; produces Zinfandel grapes for Monterey Peninsula Winery and San Martin Winery. 20 acres.

Ferrière, Château (F.)

An estate in Margaux, Haut-M;édoc district, Bordeaux; classified in 1855 as a *Troisième Cru*, although the wine is made at Château Lascombes. 1,000 cases. 12 acres.

Ferro-Lazzarini, Villa del (I.)

An estate in San Germano dei Berici, Veneto region; produces several red and white wines. 20 acres.

Ferrucci, Francesco (I.)   1931

An estate in Castelbolognese, Emilia-Romagna region; produces Albana, Sangiovese and Trebbiano wines.

Ferservadou (F.)

See **Fer.**

Fesles, Château de (F.)

An estate in Thouarcé, Anjou region, Loire Valley; produces Bonnezeaux and other wines. 260 acres, including 30 acres of Bonnezeaux.

Fête des Vignerons (Sw.)

A great wine festival held in the village of Vevey since the 17th century.

Fetească (R.)

A white grape, the same as the Leányka grown in Hungary.

Fetească Albă *and* Fetească Regală (R.)

Two strains of the Fetească grape, both white.

Fetească Neagră (R.)

A red strain of the Fetească grape, grown in eastern Romania.

Fetiaska (Bul.)

A white grape, the same as the Fetească of Romania and the Leányka of Hungary.

Fetzer Vineyards (U.S.)   1968

A winery north of Ukiah, Mendocino Valley region, California; produces Cabernet, Petite Sirah, Zinfandel, Sémillon, Pinot Blanc, Gewürztraminer, Sauvignon Blanc and Johannisberg Riesling wines; several wines have single vineyard designations. The 2nd label is Bel Arbres. 400 acres. 400,000 cases.

feuilliette (F.)

A cask, containing anywhere from 114-136 liters; used in the Burgundy region.

Fèves, Les (F.)

A *Premier Cru* Vineyard in Beaune, Côte de Beaune district, Burgundy. 11 acres.

Fèvre, Bernard (F.)

An estate in Saint-Romain, Côte de Beaune district, Burgundy. 12.5 acres, including 10 acres of St.-Romain and 2.5 acres of Auxey-Duresses.

Fèvre, Maurice (F.)

An estate in the Chablis district, Burgundy. 10 acres, including 3.2 acres of Les Clos, 3.2 acres of Valmur, 1.6 acres of Les Preuses and some Fourchaume; now part of Domaine de la Maladière.

Feytit-Clinet, Château (F.)

An estate in Pomerol, Bordeaux. 1,500 cases. 15 acres.

Fiano (I.)

A grape grown in Avellino, near Naples, in the Campania region of southern Italy.

Fiano di Avellino DOC (I.)

A white wine from Avellino, in the central Campania region; made from the Fiano grape.

fiasco (I.)

Italian for "flask," a straw-covered bottle of varying sizes used for inexpensive wines, especially Chianti wines.

ficeleur (F.)

In Champagne, one who binds the cork to the bottle with wire.

Fichots, Les (F.)

A *Premier Cru* vineyard in Pernand-Vergelesses, Côte de Beaune district, Burgundy; may be sold as Aloxe-Corton. 27.5 acres.

Ficklin Vineyards (U.S.)   1946

A winery in Madera, San Joaquin Valley, Madera County, California; produces vintage and non-vintage Port-style wines made from Ruby Cabernet, Tinta Madeira, Tinta Cão and Tinta Souzão grapes. 10,000 cases.

field-budding *also* **field-grafting**

A method of grafting vines by planting the phyloxera-resistant stock in the proper place in the vineyard, then cutting off the top when the bud has been established;

the scion is then grafted or budded in its place.

**Field Stone Winery (U.S.)   grapes 1966,
                                        winery 1977**

A winery in Healdsburg, Alexander Valley, northern Sonoma County, California; produces Cabernet, Cabernet Rosé, Petite Sirah, Johannisberg Riesling, Chenin Blanc and Gewürztraminer wines; the winery is built into a hillside and uses field-crushed grapes. 10,000 cases. 150 acres.

Fiètres, Les (F.)

A *Grand Cru* vineyard, part of the Corton vineyard, in Aloxe-Corton, Côte de Beaune district, Burgundy. 3.5 acres.

Fieuzal, Château (F.)

An estate in Léognan, Graves district, Bordeaux; classified in 1959 as a *Cru Classé* for red wine only. 53 acres.

Figari (F.)

A village and district in southern Corsica; produces red, white and rosé wines, the red and rosé made from Niellucio and Sciacarello grapes and the white from Vermentino grapes.

Figeac, Château (F.)

An estate in St.-Émilion, Bordeaux; classified in 1955 as a *Premier Grand Cru*; next to and at one time a part of Cheval Blanc, in the Graves section. 35% Cabernet Sauvignon, 35% Cabernet Franc, 30% Merlot. 15,000 cases. 85 acres.

Filhot, Château (F.)

An estate in Sauternes, Sauternes district, Bordeaux; classified in 1855 as a *Deuxième Cru*; owned by the Lur-Saluces family for many generations until c.1980. 70% Sémillon, 25% Sauvignon, 5% Muscadelle. 10,000 cases. 130 acres.

Filippi Vintage Company, J. (U.S.)   1934

A large winery in Mira Loma, Cucamonga district, San Bernadino County, in southern California; produces 35 different wines and champagnes; uses the Château Filippi label. 10,000 cases. 300 leased acres.

fillette (F.)

French for "little girl," a slang term for a half-bottle, especially in the Anjou region, Loire Valley.

Filliatreau, Paul (F.)

An estate in Chaintres, Saumur-Champigny district, Anjou region, Loire Valley. 65 acres.

film yeast

Flor, as in Sherry. See **flor.**

Fils D'Antonin Guyon (F.)

An estate in Savigny-lès-Beaune, Côte de Beaune district, Burgundy; bottles under various domaine names, including Domaine des Héritiers D'Hyppolite Thévenot, Domaine de la Guyonnière and Domaine du Village de Chambolle. 33 acres, including 1.2 acres of Corton-Charlemagne, 1.8 acres of Corton Clos du Roi, 2.5 acres of Les Bressandes, .7 acre of Le Corton, 2.5 acres of Volnay Clos des Chênes, 1.2 acres of Meursault Les Charmes, 5 acres of Gevrey-Chambertin, 5 acres of Aloxe-Corton, 5 acres of Pernand-Vergelesses and 5 acres of Beaune.

Filsinger Vineyards (U.S.)   **1980**

A winery in Temecula, Riverside County, California; produces Chardonnay, Emerald Riesling, Fumé Blanc, Petite Sirah and Zinfandel wines. 25 acres. 5,000 cases.

filtering

The clarification or clearing of wine by passing it through a filter or similar screening device, the purpose of which is to remove suspended solid particles.

finage (F.)

In Burgundy, a commune or parish.

Fine Champagne (F.)

Fine Cognac; a blend of Cognac from the Grande Champagne and Petite Champagne districts.

Fines-Roches, Château des (F.)

An estate in Châteauneuf-du-Pape, southern Rhône region. 117 acres.

Finger Lakes (U.S.)

An important region in New York State named after the 11 long, narrow lakes southwest of Syracuse which, on a map, look like the fingers of a hand; Lakes Keuka, Cayuga, and Seneca are the most important for wine production. The others are Canadice, Canandaigua, Conesus, Hemlock, Honeoye, Otisco, Owasco, and Skaneateles.

Finger Lakes Wine Cellar (U.S.)   **1981**

A winery in Branchport, on the northwestern shore of Lake Keuka, in the Finger Lakes region, New York; produces wines made from hybrid and *lambrusca* grapes. 75 acres.

Finkenauer, Weingut Carl (G.)

An estate in Bad Kreuznach, in the Nahe region; owns vineyards in Kreuznach, Winzerheim and Roxheim. 70 acres.

fino (Sp.)

The driest type of Sherry.

finos de mesa (Sp.)

Fine table wines.

Fior di Mosto (I.)

A rosé wine from north of Perugia, in the Colli Altotiberini district, northern Umbria region; made from Sangiovese and Merlot grapes.

Fiorano (I.)

Red and white wines from the Appian Way, just north of Rome, in the Latium region. The red wine is made from Merlot and Cabernet grapes and the white wine is made from Malvasia di Candida and Sémillon grapes.

Fiorano (I.)   **1946**

A small estate in Divino Amore, near Rome, in the Latium region; produces Fiorano Bianco and Rosso wines. 5 acres.

Fiore di Pigato (I.)

A white wine from Albenga, in the western Liguria region; made from the Pigato grape.

Fiorita, La (I.)   1970

An estate in Macchie di Castiglione del Lago, Umbria region; produces Colli del Trasimeno, Rosé and Sangue di Miura wines. 370 acres.

Firestone Vineyard (U.S.)   vines 1973
                                1st wine 1975

A winery in Los Olivos, Santa Ynez Valley, Santa Barbara County, California; produces Cabernet, Pinot Noir, Merlot, Rosé of Cabernet, Rosé of Pinot Noir, Chardonnay, Johannisberg Riesling and Gewürztraminer wines. 300 acres. 65,000 cases.

Firnewein (G.)

A fine wine that is at its peak condition of age; an aged wine.

Fischer, Weingüter Dr. (G.)

An estate in Ockfen-Wawern, Saar district, Mosel-Saar-Ruwer region; owns vineyards in Ockfen, Saarburg and Wawern. 60 acres.

Fisher Vineyards (U.S.)   1974

A winery in Santa Rosa, Sonoma County, California; produces Cabernet and Chardonnay wines. 18 acres, and 50 acres in Napa Valley. 5,000 cases.

Fitou AOC (F.)

1. A village and district including several additional *communes* south of Narbonne, in the Languedoc region, which produces:

2. A red wine made from Carignan, Grenache, Cinsault, Mourvèdre, Syrah and other grapes.

Five Roses (I.)

A rosé wine from Salice Salentino, south of Brindisi, in the southern Apulia region, made from Negroamaro grapes.

fixed acidity

The presence of natural acids, mainly tartaric, malic and citric, giving an agreeable taste to the wine.

Fixin AOC (F.)

The northernmost AOC commune in the Côte de Nuits district, Burgundy; produces only red wines. The *Premier Cru* vineyards are: Clos de la Perrière, Clos du Chapitre, Aux Cheusots (Clos Napoléon), Les Meix Bas, Les Arvelets and Les Hervelets; most of the wine is usually sold as Côte de Nuits; 105 acres sold as Fixin.

Flagey-Échézeaux (F.)

A commune in the Côte de Nuits, Burgundy, but not an AOC place name. It contains 2 *Grand Cru* vineyards: Grands-Échézeaux and Échézeaux. In poor years the wines can be declassified and sold as Vosne-Romanée; wines from any of the other vineyards are also sold as Vosne-Romanée.

flagon

A large metal or ceramic vessel with a handle, a spout and a lid.

Flame Tokay (U.S.)

A white *vinifera* grape grown in California; used to make sherries and blended wines. Also called Ahmeur bou Ahmeur.

flat

1. A term used to describe wine that is dull, uninteresting, or lifeless.

2. Of Champagne, having lost its effervesence.

flétri (Sw.)

French for dried; late-picked, in reference to grapes used in the Valais regon to make sweet wines.

fleur (F.)

See **mycoderma**.

Fleur du Cap (S. Af.)

Red and white varietal wines from the Stellenbosch district; produced by the Bergkelder.

Fleur Milon, Château La (F.)

An estate in Pauillac, Haut-Médoc district, Bordeaux; classified in 1978 as a *Cru Grand Bourgeois*. 50 cases. 32 acres.

Fleurie AOC (F.)

A commune and a *Cru Beaujolais* wine, in the Beaujolais district, Burgundy. 1,700 acres.

Fleurie, Château de (F.)

An estate in Fleurie, Beaujolais district, Burgundy.

Fleurot-Larose, Domaine (F.)

An estate in Santenay, Côte de Beaune, Burgundy. 43 acres, including .8 acre of Montrachet, .4 acre of Bâtard-Montrachet, 17 acres of Chassagne-Montrachet Abbaye de Morgeot (red and white), 7.5 acres of Santenay Clos du Passe-Temps and 5 acres of Clos Rousseau.

fliers

Small, clear, tasteless particles which sometimes appear in wine, especially white wine; caused by cold temperature, they usually disappear when the wine is warmed up.

flor (Sp.)

Spanish for "flower," a thick, white layer of yeast (*Saccharomyces*) which forms on the top of fermenting vats of some sherries and some wines of the Montilla and Manzanilla districts of Spain, and in the Jura region of France and imparts to those wines a characteristic nutty taste and aroma. Sherry with the *flor* formation is called *Fino* and without it is called *Oloroso*.

Flora (U.S.)

A white grape – a cross of Gewürztraminer and Sémillon; developed at the University of California by Dr. Harold Olmo in 1938, released in 1958. Parducci makes a varietal wine and Schramsburg makes a *demi-sec* champagne from this grape.

Flora Springs Wine Company (U.S.)   1978

A winery in St. Helena, Napa Valley, California; produces Cabernet, Chardonnay, Sauvignon Blanc, Chenin Blanc and Johannisberg Riesling wines. 8,000 cases. 250 acres.

floraison (F.)

The flowering of the grape vine.

Florence Red (E.)

A 13th century name in England for red wine from the Florence district (now Chianti); also called Vermiglio.

Florental (U.S.)

A red hybrid grape – a cross of Gamay Noir à Jus Blanc and S. 8365; grown in the eastern and midwestern U.S.

Florimont (F.)

A vineyard in Ingersheim, Haut-Rhin district, Alsace region.

Florio (I.)   1883

A winery in Marsala, Sicily; produces several types of Marsala wine. 300,000 cases.

Florita (Aus.)

A light, delicate, Sherry-like wine from Château Leonay Winery, in the Barossa Valley, South Australia.

Flörsheim-Dahlsheim (G.)

A village in the Rheinhessen region, Bereich Wonnegau, Grosslage Burg Rodenstein. The vineyards are: Bürgel, Frauenberg, Goldberg, Hubacker, Sauloch and Steig.

fluid ounce

A 1/16 of a standard U.S. pint. 957 centiliters; in Britain 841 centiliters.

Flurbereinigung (G.)

German for "land re-arrangement," a program of vineyard rebuilding and reorganization begun after World War II, which utilized bulldozing on a large scale.

flûte (F.)

1. A tall, narrow bottle traditionally used in Alsace and Germany for Rhine or Mosel wines.

2. A tall, narrow glass for serving Champagne.

Foch (F.)

A red, early-ripening, hybrid grape developed in Alsace by Eugène Kuhlman; known as Kuhlmann 188.2. Also called Maréchal Foch; grown in the eastern and midwestern U.S.

Focşani (R.)

A town and district in the province of Moldavia, in eastern Romania. Includes the towns of Focşani, Coteşti (red and white wines), Odobeşti (white wines) and Nicoreşti (red wines). The red wines are made from Pinot Noir, Merlot and Cabernet grapes and the white wines are made from Wälschriesling, Muscat, Fetească, Traminer, Furmint and Aligoté grapes.

Fogarty Winery, Thomas (U.S.)   1982

A winery in Portola Valley, San Mateo County, California; produces Cabernet, Chardonnay and Pinot Noir wines. 5,000 cases.

Foianeghe Rosso (I.)

A red wine from Rovereto, in the southern Trentino-Alto Adige region; made from Cabernet, Cabernet Franc and Merlot grapes.

Folatières, Les (F.)

A *Premier Cru* vineyard (in part) in Puligny-Montrachet, Côte de Beaune district, Burgundy. 8.5 acres.

Folgosão (P.)

A white grape, one of 16 officially rated First Quality grapes used in making Port wine.

Folha de Figo (Br.)

Portuguese for "fig leaf," the name of a grape in Brazil.

Folie, Domaine de la (F.)

An old estate in Rully, Côte Chalonnaise district, southern Burgundy. 45 acres.

Folle Blanche (F.)

A white grape grown widely in France, primarily important in making Cognac; also called Gros Plant and Picpoul; also used as a varietal wine by the L. Martini winery, in California.

Folle Noir (F.)

A local red grape grown in Bellet, in the Provence region.

Folonari, Fratelli (I.)   1825

A merchant in Brescia, Lombardy region; produces Bardolino, Soave, Valpolicella and other wines. 4 million cases.

Fombrauge, Château (F.)

An estate in St.-Émilion, Bordeaux, classified in 1955 as a *Grand Cru*. 100 acres. 20,000 cases.

Fonbadet, Château (F.)

An estate in Pauillac, Bordeaux; classified in 1932 as a *Cru Bourgeois*. 10,000 cases. 75 acres.

Fondillón (Sp.)

A red wine from Monovar, in the Alicante district, the Levante region, in southeastern Spain; made from the Monastrell grape.

Fonpiqueyre, Château (F.)

An estate in St.-Sauveur, Haut-Médoc district, Bordeaux; classified in 1978 as a *Cru Bourgeois*.

Fonplégade, Château (F.)

An estate in St.-Émilion, Bordeaux; classified in 1955 as a *Grand Cru Classé*. 8,500 cases. 40 acres.

Fonréaud, Château (F.)

An estate in Listrac, Haut-Médoc district, Bordeaux; classified in 1978 as a *Cru Bourgeois*. 18,000 cases. 100 acres.

Fonroque, Château (F.)

An estate in St.-Émilion, Bordeaux; classified in 1955 as a *Grand Cru Classé*. 8,000 cases. 45 acres.

Fonsalette, Château de (F.)

An estate in Lagarde-Paréol, in the Côtes du Rhône district, southern Rhône region; produces red and white wines, the red wine made from Grenache, Syrah and Cinsault grapes, and the white from Clairette and Grenache Blanc grapes. Owned by Château Rayas of Châteauneuf-du-Pape. 37 acres.

Fonscolombe, Château de (F.)   1720

An estate in Le Puy-Ste.-Réparade, in the Coteaux-d'Aix-en-Provence district, Provence region; produces red, white and rosé wines. 50,000 cases. 230 acres.

Fonseca (P.)

A Port producer in Vila Nova de Gaia. The wines are shipped by Guimaraens.

Fonseca, J.M. de (P.)   1834

A merchant in Lisbon; produces Moscatel de Setúbal, Lancers Rosé, Periquita, Camarate and Terras Atlas Dãos (the last three are red wines).

Fontafredda (I.)   1878

A winery in Serralunga d'Alba, Piedmont region; produces Barbaresco, Barolo, Barbera, Dolcetto and sparkling wines; made from their own and purchased grapes. 300,000 cases. 250 acres.

Fontana Candida (I.)

A large winery and estate in Monteporzio Catone, Latium region; produces Frascati wines. 350,000 cases.

Fontanelle (I.)

A white wine from Cossignano, near Ascoli Piceno, in the southern Marches region; made from the Verdicchio grape.

Fontblanche, Château de (F.)

An estate in Cassis, in the Provence region.

Fontegal (P.)

A white grape grown in northern Portugal.

Fonteny, Le (F.)

A *Premier Cru* vineyard in Gevrey-Chambertin, Côte de Nuits district, Burgundy. 9 acres.

Fonterutoli, Castello di (I.)   1435

An estate in Castellina in Chianti, Tuscany region; produces Chianti Classico and Bianco della Lega wines. 18,000 cases. 80 acres.

Fontesteau, Château (F.)

An estate in St.-Sauveur, Haut-Médoc district, Bordeaux; classified in 1978 as a *Cru Grand Bourgeois*. 5,000 cases. 40 acres.

Fontsainte, Domaine de (F.)

An estate in Boutenac, Corbières district, Languedoc region; produces red and rosé wines. 40,000 cases. 100 acres.

Foppiano Winery (U.S.)   1896

A large, old winery in Healdsburg, Russian River Valley, Sonoma County, California; produces Cabernet, Petite Sirah, Pinot Noir, Zinfandel, Chenin Blanc, French Colombard, Fumé Blanc and jug blends from own and purchased grapes. 200 acres. 200,000 cases.

Forastera (I.)

A white grape grown on the island of Ischia, in the Campania region.

Forcadière, Domaine de la (F.)

An estate in Tavel, southern Rhône region. 105 acres; also 50 acres in Lirac.

Forchetière, Domaine de (F.)

An estate in Courcoué-sur-Logne, Muscadet region, Loire Valley; produces Muscadet wine. 18 acres.

Forêts, Les (F.)

A *Premier Cru* vineyard in Chablis, Chablis district, Burgundy; usually included as as part of the Montmains vineyard.

Forêts, Clos des (F.)

A *Premier Cru* vineyard in Prémeaux (sold as Nuits-St.-Georges), Côte de Nuits district, Burgundy. 17 acres.

Forgeot, Robert (F.)

An estate in the Chablis district, Burgundy; owns a vineyard in Bernouil, near Tonnerre; produces Bourgogne AOC wine.

Forgeron Vineyard (U.S.) 1977, vines 1970

A winery in Elmira, Willamette Valley, northwestern Oregon; produces Pinot Noir, Chardonnay, Riesling, Gewürztraminer and Pinot Gris wines. 2,000 cases. 25 acres.

Formex-Ybarra (Mex.)   1957

A winery in Guadalupe Valley, northeast of Ensenada, Baja California; produces Terrasola wines and brandy. 800 acres.

formic acid

One of several acids naturally present in small amounts in wine.

Formosa Dourada (P.)

A white grape grown in southern Portugal.

Forneret, Cuvée (F.)

A red wine from the Hospices de Beaune, Côte de Beaune district, Burgundy. The *cuvée* is composed of the following vineyards in Savigny: Les Vergelesses – 2.5 acres and Aux Gravains – 1.5 acres.

Forrester Vinhos Lda., Offley (P.)   1737

A Port producer in Vila Nova de Gaia; owns Quinta do Bõa Vista and Quinta do Cachucha. 200 acres.

Forst (G.)

An important village in the Rheinpfalz region, Bereich Mittelhaardt-Deutsche Weinstrasse, Grosslagen Mariengarten and Schnopfenflug an der Weinstrasse. The vineyards are: Elster, Freundstück, Jesuitengarten, Kirchenstück, Musenhang, Pechstein and Ungeheuer in Grosslage Mariengarten; and Bischofsgarten, Stift and Süsskopf in Grosslage Schnepfenflug an der Weinstrasse. 500 acres.

Fort Vauban, Château (F.)

An estate in Cussac, Haut-Médoc district, Bordeaux; classified in 1978 as a *Cru Bourgeois*. 100 acres. 12,000 cases.

Forta (G.)

A white grape – a cross of Madeleine Angevine and Sylvaner, developed at the Federal Research Institute, in Geilweilerhof, Germany.

Fortana (I.)

A red grape grown in the eastern part of the Emilia-Romagna region. Also called Uva d'Oro.

Fortet, Clos (F.)

An estate in St.-Émilion, Bordeaux; classified in 1955 as a *Premier Grand Cru*. 25% Cabernet Sauvignon, 25% Cabernet Franc, 50% Merlot. 7,000 cases. 50 acres.

Fortia, Château (F.)   1763

An estate in Châteauneuf-du-Pape, southern Rhône region; produces red wine made from 80% Grenache, 10% Syrah, 3% Mourvèdre, 2% Counoise, 5% Roussanne, Grenache Blanc and Clairette grapes combined; some white wine is also made. 7,500 cases. 70 acres.

fortified

Made stronger by the addition of brandy to a wine, especially Port, Sherry, Madeira,

Marsala, and VDN, thus raising the alcohol content to 18-20%.

Fortino Winery (U.S.)   **1970**

A winery in Gilroy, Santa Clara County, California; formerly the Cassa Winery; produces varietal wines, including Barbera, Charbono, Petite Syrah, Cabernet, Carignan, and jug wines. 10,000 cases.

Forts de Latour, Les (F.)   **1966**

The second wine of Château Latour, made since 1966.

forzato (I.)

Vinified from the must of semi-dried or over-ripe grapes.

Foscara (I.)

A grape grown in the Tuscany region.

Fosse, La (F.)

A *Premier Cru* vineyard in Rully, Côte Chalonnaise district, Burgundy.

Fossi (I.)

An estate in Florence, Tuscany region; produces Chianti Classico wine. 5,000 cases.

foudre (F.)

A large cask for storing or transporting wine. Also called *Fuder*, in German.

foulées (F.)

Grapes that have been separated from their stalks.

foulograppe (F.)

A machine for separating the stalks from the grapes before fermentation. Also called *égrappoir*.

fouloir (F.)

A beater, or crusher, used to extract the first juice before the main crushing.

fouloir-égrappoir (F.)

A machine that separates the stalks from the grapes and crushes them as well; hence, a crusher-stemmer.

Fouquerand, Cuvée (F.)

A red wine from the Hospices de Beaune, Côte de Beaune district, Burgundy. The *cuvée* is composed of the following vineyards in Savigny: Basses Vergelesses – 2.5 acres, Les Talmettes – 1.5 acres, Aux Gravains – 1 acre and Aux Serpentières – .3 acre.

Fourcas-Dupré, Château (F.)

An estate in Listrac, Haut Médoc district, Bordeaux; classified in 1978 as a *Cru Grand Bourgeois Exceptionnel*. 15,000 cases. 100 acres.

Fourcas-Hosten, Château (F.)

An estate in Listrac, Haut-Médoc district, Bordeaux; classified in 1978 as a *Cru Grand Bourgeois Exceptionnel*. 14,000 cases. 90 acres.

Fourchaume (F.)

A *Premier Cru* vineyard in the *communes* of La Chapelle-Vaupelteigne, Fontenay, Maligny and Poinchy, in the Chablis district, Burgundy; it usually also includes the following vineyards: Vaulorent, Côte de Fontenay, Vaupulent and L'Homme Mort.

Fourmone, Domaine La (F.)

An estate in Vacqueyras, Côtes du Rhône-Villages district, southern Rhône region. 40 acres, and 22 acres in Gigondas.

Fourneaux, Aux (F.)

A *Premier Cru* vineyard (in part) in Savigny-lès-Beaune, Côte de Beaune district, Burgundy. 20 acres.

Fourneaux, Clos des (F.)

A *Premier Cru* vineyard in Mercurey, Côte Chalonnaise district, Burgundy.

Fourneaux, Les (F.)

A *Premier Cru* vineyard in Fleys, Chablis district, Burgundy; it usually also includes the following vineyards: Morein and Côtes des Près-Girots.

Fournier, Jean (F.)

An estate in Marsannay-la-Côte, Côte de Nuits district, Burgundy. 15 acres, including 1.6 acres of Gevrey-Chambertin and some Côtes de Nuits-Village and Marsannay.

Fournières, Les (F.)

A *Premier Cru* vineyard in Aloxe-Corton, Côte de Beaune district, Burgundy. 15 acres.

Fousselottes, Les (F.)

A *Premier Cru* vineyard in Chambolle-Musigny, Côte de Nuits district, Burgundy. 10 acres.

foxy

A term used to describe wines which have a strong, wild, grapey taste and aroma, especially applied to wines made from the native American grapes of the *Vitis labrusca* species.

Fraccaroli, Fratelli (I.)

An estate in Peschiera del Garda, Veneto region; produces Lugana wines. 8,000 cases.

franc de goût (F.)

Honest, straightforward and clean-tasting.

Franc-Mayne, Château (F.)

An estate in St.-Émilion, Bordeaux; classified in 1955 as a *Grand Cru Classé*. 3,000 cases. 16 acres.

Francavilla (I.)

A white grape grown in the southern Apulia region.

France

A county in northwestern Europe; produces about 2 billion gallons of wine annually, 265 million gallons are AOC wines. Annual export is more than 100 million gallons and annual import is more than 200 million gallons. 2.8 million acres of vineyards. The principal regions are: Alsace, Bordeaux, Burgundy, Champagne, Corsica, the Jura, Languedoc, the Loire Valley regions of Anjou, Muscadet, Touraine and the Upper Loire, Provence, Rhône, Roussillon, Savoie and the Southwest.

France, Château La (F.)

An estate in Blaignan, Médoc district, Bordeaux; classified in 1978 as a *Cru Bourgeois*. 4,000 cases. 15 acres.

Franciacorta DOC (I.)

1. A district around Cortefranca, northwest of Brescia, in the Lombardy region, which produces:

2. Red, white and sparkling wines; the red wines are made from Cabernet Franc, Barbera, Nebbiolo and Merlot grapes, the white wines are made from the Pinot Bianco grape and the sparkling wines are made from Pinot Nero, Pinot Grigio and Pinot Bianco grapes.

Franciscan Vineyards (U.S.)   **1975**
vines 1971

A large winery in Rutherford, Napa Valley, California; produces Cabernet, Zinfandel, Merlot, Chardonnay and Johannisberg Riesling wines. 200,000 cases. 900 acres in Napa, Sonoma and Lake Counties.

Franco Españolas S.A., Bodegas (Sp.)

A large winery in Logroño, Rioja Alta region; produces Diamante and other wines made from their own and purchased grapes. 650,000 cases.

François, Château (Aus.)   **1970**

A small, award-winning winery in Lower Hunter Valley, New South Wales; produces Cabernet Sauvignon, Shiraz, Pinot Noir, Chardonnay and Sémillon wines.

François de Salins, Cuvée (F.)

A white wine from the Hospices de Beaune, Côte de Beaune district, Burgundy. The *cuvée* is composed of the following vineyard in Corton: Corton-Charlemagne – .5 acre. 75 cases.

Franconia *also* **Franken (G.)**

A region in central Germany; produces red wines from the Spätburgunder grape and white wines from Sylvaner, Müller-Thurgau, Riesling and Traminer grapes; the most famous wine is the Steinwein of Würtzburg. All or most of Franconian wines are sold in a flat bottle called a Bocksbeutel. 10,000 acres.

Franconia (I.)

1. A red grape grown in the Collio district, southeastern Friuli-Venezia Giulia region, which produces:

2. A red wine made from the Franconia grape.

Franken *also* **Franconia (G.)**

A region (*Anbaugebiet*) around Würtzburg, in central Germany; contains 3 *Bereiche:* Mainviereck, Maindreieck and Steigerwald.

Franken Riesling (G.)

See **Frankentraube.**

Frankentaler (G.)

In Germany, another name for the Trollinger grape.

Frankentraube (G.)

Another name for the Sylvaner grape. Also called Franken Riesling.

Frankenwein (G.)

Wine from the Franconia region, formerly called *Steinwein.*

Frankovka (Cz.)

A red grape grown in Moravia.

Fransdruif *also* **Frans (S. Af.)**

Another name for the Palomino grape.

Franzia Brothers Winery (U.S.)   1906

A large winery in Ripon, San Joaquin Valley, central California; produces over 30 different wines and champagnes under several brand names. 4,200 acres. 350,000 cases.

Frappato (I.)

Another name for Cerasuolo di Vittoria DOC wine of Sicily.

Frappato di Vittoria (I.)

A red grape grown in Sicily.

Frascati (I.)

1. A town southeast of Rome, in the Castelli Romani district, Latium region, which produces:

2. Dry and sweet white wines made from Malvasia Bianca, Malvasia del Lazio, Greco, Trebbiano Toscano, Bellone and Bonvino grapes.

frasche *also* **fraschette (I.)**

Young wines, or new wines from the Latium region; when available for public consumption, laurel branches are hung outside various establishments; similar to Austria's *Heurige* wines.

frasco (P., Sp.)

A flask.

Frasinetti and Sons (U.S.)   1897

A winery in Sacramento, Sacramento County, California; produces various generic wines. 40,000 cases.

**Fratelli Valsangiacomo du Vittore (Sw.)
1831**

An estate and merchant in Chiasso, Ticino region; produces red and rosé wine made from their own and purchased grapes. 30,000 cases. 35 acres.

Frecciarossa DOC (I.)

An estate near Casteggio, in the Oltrepò Pavese district, Lombardy region; produces red, rosé and white wines. 50 acres.

Fredonia (U.S.)

An American red grape, closely related to the Concord grape; grown mainly in New Jersey.

Fredonia Products Company (U.S.)   1933

A winery in Fredonia, Chautauqua region, New York; produces sweet Kosher wines for Manischewitz made from the Concord grape. The winery recently planted hybrids and other *labrusca* grapes. 500 acres.

Fred's Friends (U.S.)

Still white wines made from the second pressing of the grapes used to make the sparkling wines of Domaine Chandon; made from Chardonnay or Pinot Noir grapes. 5,000 cases.

Fredson Winery, Chris A. (U.S.)   1885

A large winery in Geyserville, Sonoma County, California; produces wine for the Charles Krug Winery.

free-run

An term describing juice that has been expressed from the grapes during loading or de-stemming, but that has not been pressed or crushed mechanically; it is the best quality juice and is frequently fermented separately.

Freemark Abbey Winery (U.S.) 1895, 1967

An old winery (but not an Abbey) in St. Helena, Napa Valley, California; produces Cabernet, Pinot Noir, Petite Syrah, Chardonnay, Riesling and Edelwein (a sweet, botrytis-infected Riesling). 600 acres. 25,000 cases.

Freiberg (F.)

A vineyard in Barr, Bas-Rhin district, Alsace region; produces Gewürztraminer and Tokay grapes.

Freiburger Jesuitenschloss
Staatliches Weinbauinstitut (G.)   1920

A school and estate in Freiburg, Baden region; owns vineyards in Freiburg, Müllheimer, Ihringen, Heckling and Durbach; also owns the Blankenhornsberg estate in Ihringen. 155 acres.

Freiherr, Freiherrlich (G.)

A Baron, and Barony, respectively.

Freisa (I.)

1. A red grape grown in the Piedmont region, which produces:

2. Red wines from Asti, Chieri and Alba, in the Piedmont region, made from the Freisa grape.

Freisa d'Asti DOC (I.)

A dry, semi-sweet, or sparkling red wine made around Asti, in the Piedmont region, from the Freisa grape.

Freisa di Chieri DOC (I.)

A dry, sweet or sparkling red wine from Chieri, southeast of Turin, in the Piedmont region, made from the Freisa grape.

Freisamer (G.)

A white grape – a cross of Sylvaner and Ruländer; developed at the State Viticultural Institute, Freiburg im Breisgau, Germany in 1916.

Freixenet S.A. (Sp.)   1915

A large winery in San Sadurní de Noya, west of Barcelona, Catalonia region; produces several still and sparkling wines.

Fremières, Les (F.)

A *Premier Cru* vineyard in Morey-St.-Denis, Côte de Nuits district, Burgundy. 6 acres.

Fremiers, Les (F.)

A *Premier Cru* vineyard in Pommard, Côte de Beaune district, Burgundy. 12 acres.

Fremiets, Les (F.)

A *Premier Cru* vineyard in Volnay, Côte de Beaune district, Burgundy. 16 acres.

French Colombard *also* Colombard (U.S.)

1. A white grape grown in California, the Colombard grape from France.

2. A white wine made by several wineries in California; made from the French Colombard grape.

Frères Dubois & Fils, Les (Sw.)   1928

An estate in Cully, Lavaux district, Vaud region; produces Dorin, Pinot Noir, Pinot Gris and other wines from their own and purchased grapes. 5,000 cases. 15 acres.

Frescobaldi, Marchesi de' (I.)   1300

A large estate in Florence, Tuscany region; produces Chianti Rufina (including Castello di Nipozzano), Montesodi, Poggio a Remole, Galestro, Nuovo Fiore, Pomino Bianco, Villa di Corte Rosé and Vin Santo wines. 1,300 acres.

Fretter Wine Cellars (U.S.)   1977

A small winery in Berkeley, Alameda County, California; produces Cabernet, Merlot, Pinot Noir, Gamay, Gamay Rosé, Chardonnay, Sémillon and Sauvignon Blanc wines from purchased grapes. 1,000 cases.

Frey Vineyards (U.S.)   1979, vines 1966

A winery in Redwood Valley, Mendocino County, California; produces Cabernet, Chardonnay, French Colombard and Grey Riesling wines. 30 acres. 2,000 cases.

Frick Winery (U.S.)   1976

A small winery in Soquel, Santa Cruz County, California; produces Pinot Noir, Zinfandel, Petite Sirah, Gewürztraminer and other wines. 5 acres.

Frickenhausen (G.)

A village in the Franken region, Bereich Maindreieck (but no *Grosslage*). The vineyards are Fischer, Kapellenberg and Markgraf Babenberg. 160 acres.

Friedrich-Wilhelm-Gymnasium, Stiftung Staatliches (G.)

An estate in Trier, Mosel-Saar-Ruwer region; owns vineyards in Ockfen, Oberemmler, Pellingen and Falkenstein in the Saar district and Trittenheim, Bernkastel, Graach, Neumagen and Mehring in the Mosel district. 110 acres.

Frîncuşa (R.)

A white grape grown in the Cotnari district, in northeastern Romania.

Frionnes, Les (F.)

A *Premier Cru* vineyard in St.-Aubin, Côte de Beaune district, Burgundy. 2.5 acres.

Fritz Cellars (U.S.)   1979

A winery in Cloverdale, Dry Creek, Sonoma County, California; produces Char-

donnay, Sauvignon Blanc and Zinfandel wines. 8,000 cases. 45 acres.

Fritz-Ritter, Weingut K. (G.)

An estate in Bad Dürkheim, Rheinpfalz region; owns vineyards in Dürkheim, Wachenheim and Ungstein. 50 acres.

Friuli-Venezia Giulia (I.)

A region northeast of Venice, in northeastern Italy, with three important DOC districts: Collio Goriziano, Colli Orientali del Friuli and Grave del Friuli. 26.5 million gallons.

frizzante (I.)

Semi-sparkling; slightly effervescent.

Frog's Leap Vineyard (U.S.)   1981

A winery in St. Helena, Napa Valley, California; produces Chardonnay, Sauvignon Blanc and Zinfandel wines. 2,500 cases. 5 acres.

Froichots, Les (F.)

A *Premier Cru* vineyard in Morey-St.-Denis, Côte de Nuits district, Burgundy. 5 acres.

Fromentin (I.)
See **Furmentin.**

Fronsac AOC (F.)

A town and district northwest of Libourne, in the Bordeaux region; formerly known as Côtes de Fronsac, and is designated for red wines only, made from Cabernet Sauvignon, Cabernet Franc and Merlot grapes.

Frontenac Point Vineyard (U.S.)   1982

A winery in Trumansburg, on the western shore of Lake Cayuga, in the Finger Lakes region, New York; produces wines made from Chardonnay, Pinot Noir, Riesling and hybrid grapes. 20 acres.

Frontignac (S. Af.)

A white grape.

Frontignan (F.)

1. A town south of Montpellier, in the Languedoc region, famous for the production of Muscat de Frontignan wine (VDN).

2. Another name for the Ugni Blanc grape in the Blaye district of Bordeaux.

3. A term sometimes used for a 75-centiliter bottle.

Frühburgunder (G.)

A red grape; a variant of the Spätburgunder grape; ripens very early; also called Early Burgundy and Blauer Portugieser.

fruity

A term used to describe certain wines, especially young wines and sweet wines, that have a grapey, fresh fruit aroma and taste.

Fruška Gora (Y.)

A hilly district in the Province of Vojvodina, north of Serbia; produces mostly white varietal wines made from several different grapes.

Fruškogorski Biser (Y.)

A sparkling wine from the Fruška Gora district, province of Vojvodina, north of Serbia.

Fruttano (I.)

A red grape grown in the Colli Piacentini district, in the Emilia-Romagna region.

Fuder (G.)

A large cask with a 1,000-liter (264-gallon) capacity.

Fuées, Les (F.)

A *Premier Cru* vineyard in Chambolle-Musigny, Côte de Nuits district, Burgundy. 15.5 acres.

Fuelle Noir (F.)

A red grape grown in Bellet, Provence region.

Fuflans

An ancient Eutruscan wine God.

Fuissé (F.)

A commune in the Mâconnais district of Burgundy, one of four *communes* that make up the Poilly-Fuissé AOC designation for white wines.

Fuissé, Château (F.)

An estate in Pouilly-Fuissé, Mâconnais district, Burgundy.

Fumé Blanc (U.S.)

A dry, white wine from California; made from the Sauvignon Blanc grape; the name is derived from the Pouilly-Fumé district of France.

Funchal (P.)

A port and principal town of Madeira, where much of the Madeira wine is stored, aged and shipped.

furfural

An aldehyde present in heated sweet wines, such as Marsala and Madeira.

Furmentin *also* Fromentin (I.)

A dry, white wine made near Alba, in the Piedmont region; made from the Furmint grape.

Furmint (H.)

An important white grape; used to make Tokaji wine and other white wines; also grown in northern Italy.

Fürst, Fürstlich (G.)

Prince, Princely.

Furstentum (F.)

A *Grand Cru* vineyard in Kientzheim and Sigolsheim, Haut-Rhin district, Alsace region.

fût (F.)

A cask, or barrel.

Fux, Alfonse (F.)

An estate in Zellenberg, Haut-Rhin district, Alsace region. 10 acres.

G

G.A.E.C. (F.)

The abbreviation for *Groupement Agricole d'Exploitation en Commun* (Agricultural Association for Mutual Development), a kind of co-op of vineyards.

G.A.E.C. Lamé-Delille-Boucard (F.)

A co-op estate in Ingrandes-de Touraine, Bourgueil district, Touraine region, Loire Valley. 60 acres.

G.A.E.C. St.-Fulrade (F.)   **1966**

A co-op estate in St.-Hippolyte, northern Haut-Rhin district, Alsace region. 25 acres.

G.A.E.C. de la Syrah (F.)

A co-op estate in Chanos-Curson, Crozes-Hermitage district, Rhône region; owns Crozes-Hermitage – 25 acres of Syrah grapes and 6 acres of Marsanne and Roussanne grapes.

GmbH (G.)

The abbreviation for *Gesellschaft mit beschränkter Haftung,* a company with limited liability.

Gabbiano, Castello di (I.)

An estate in Mercatale Val di Pesa, Tuscany region; produces Chianti Classico wines. 25,000 cases.

Gabiano DOC (I.)

1. A village north of Asti, in the Piedmont region, which produces:

2. A red wine made from the Barbera grape.

Gabiano, Castello di (I.)

An estate in Gabiano Monferrato, Piedmont region; produces Barbera d'Asti, Gabiano and Grignolino d'Asti wines.

Gaensbroennel, Clos (F.)

A vineyard in Barr, Bas-Rhin district, Alsace region; owned by Willm; 18 acres of Gewürztraminer vines.

Gaffelière, Château La (F.)

An estate in St.-Émilion, Bordeaux; classified in 1955 as a *Premier Grand Cru;* in one family for 300 years. 65% Merlot, 25% Cabernet Franc, 10% Cabernet Sauvignon. 9,500 cases. 50 acres.

Gaggiarone Amaro (I.)

A red wine from Rovescala, south of Pavia, in the Oltrepò Pavese district, southern Lombardy region; made mostly from Bonarda grapes with some Barbera grapes.

Gaglioppo (I.)

A red grape grown in Calabria. Also called Magliocco and Arvino.

Gagnard, Jean-Noël (F.)

An estate in Chassagne-Montrachet, Côte de Beaune district, Burgundy. 17 acres, including Bâtard-Montrachet – .8 acre, Chassagne-Montrachet Clos de la Maltroie – .8 acre, Morgeot – 2.5 acres and Santenay Le Clos de Tavannes – .8 acre.

Gagnard-Delagrange (F.)

An estate in Chassagne-Montrachet, Côte de Beaune district, Burgundy. 11 acres, including Montrachet – .2 acre, Bâtard-Montrachet – .6 acre, Chassagne-Montrachet La Boudriotte – 3 acres, Morgeot (red and white) – 2.5 acres, Clos St. Jean – .8 acre and Volnay Champans – 1 acre.

Gai, Château (C.)   1890

A winery near Niagara Falls, Ontario; produces a variety of wines from purchased grapes.

Gaibola (I.)

White varietal wines from south of Bologna, in the Emilia-Romagna region; made from various local grapes.

Gaillac AOC (F.)

1. A city and district in the Southwest region, which produces:

2. Red, white (dry, sweet and sparkling) and rosé wines under several Gaillac AOC designations, including Gaillac Doux (sweet white wine), Gaillac Mousseux (sparkling) and Gaillac Perlé (slightly sparkling); the red and rosé wines are made from Duras, Fer, Gamay, Syrah, Cabernet Franc, Cabernet Sauvignon, Merlot and other grapes, and the whites made from Mauzac, L'En de l'El, Ondenc, Sémillon, Sauvignon and Muscadelle grapes.

Gaillac Premières Côtes AOC (F.)

A designation for dry or sweet white wine from the Gaillac district, but with an additional 1.5% minimum alcohol.

Gaillard, Le Château (F.)

A *Premier Cru* vineyard in Monthélie, Côte de Beaune district, Burgundy. 2 acres.

Gaillard, Ferdinand (1821-1905) **(F.)**

A hybridizer from Brignais, in the Rhône department, active in the late 19th century with his nephew, Girard.

Gaja, Angelo (I.)   1859

An estate in Barbaresco, Piedmont region; produces Barbaresco, Barbera, Dolcetto and Nebbiolo wines. 20,000 cases. 135 acres.

Galbenă (R.)

A grape grown in the Focşani district, in eastern Romania.

Galego Dourado (P.)

A white grape grown in the Carcavelos district, near Lisbon.

Galestro (I.)   since 198(

A white wine from the Chianti district, ir the Tuscany region; made from Trebbiano, Sauvignon, Chardonnay and Pinot Bianco grapes; 10.5% maximum alcohol.

Galgenwein (G.)

German for "Gallow's wine," a wine sc harsh and strong, it is said, that when i goes down the throat it can choke the drinker as effectively as a gallows rope.

Galibert (F.)

A French hybridizer from St. Christol, ir the Hérault department, active from 1937- 55.

Galicia (Sp.)

A region in the northwestern corner of Spain; it has two DO districts: Valdeorras and Ribeiro.

Galissonnière, Château de la (F.)

An estate in Le Pallet, Muscadet region, Loire Valley; also controls Château de la Jannière and Château de la Maisdonnière. 75 acres.

Gallais-Bellevue, Château (F.)

An estate in Potensac, Médoc district, Bordeaux; classified in 1978 as a *Cru Bourgeois*, same ownership as Château Potensac. 3,000 cases.

Galleano Winery (U.S.)   1933

A winery in Mira Loma, Cucamonga district, San Bernardino County, southern California; produces Zinfandel, Mission Rosé and generic wines. 80,000 cases.

Gallization (G.)

Another term for chaptalizing. Also called *Verbessernung* and *Anreicherung*, in German. See **chaptalization**.

allo, E.and J. (U.S.)　　　　　1933

huge winery complex in Modesto, San oaquin Valley, Stanislaus County, California, with additional wineries in Livingson, Fresno and Healdsburg; mass-roduces generic wines in jugs and varietal ines. Labels include: Carlo Rossi, Thunerbird, Ripple, André Champagne, oone's Farm and Spañada. 250 million allons. 5,000 acres.

allo nero (I.)　　　　　　　　　1924

alian for "black rooster," a symbol used n the neck band of wines from the Chianti lassico district, Tuscany region, whose roducers are members of the consortium f growers of that district and who set their wn minimum standards of quality; origiated in 1924.

allon

. In the United States, a measure equal to 31 cubic inches, or 3.78 liters, or 128 unces.

. In Britain, an imperial gallon equal to 77.27 cubic inches, which is 1.2 U.S. galons, or 4.54 liters, or 160 ounces.

Gamay (F.)

. A common grape grown in Burgundy nd several other regions, especially used o make Beaujolais wines; it was probably amed after the village of Gamay in the Côte de Beaune; also called Gamay Noir à us Blanc.

.. A commune in the southern part of the Côte de Beaune, Burgundy, in the hills bove Chassagne-Montrachet and Puigny-Montrachet.

Gamay Beaujolais (U.S.)

A red grape, and the wine made from it; not the true Gamay grape, but a clone or train of the Pinot Noir grape; grown in California. The Napa Gamay is now hought to be the Valdiguié grape of southrn France.

Gamay Blanc (F.)

A local name for the Chardonnay grape in he Jura region.

Gamay au Jus Coloré (F.)

A red grape with red juice grown in France; also called Gamay Teinturier.

Gamay de Liverdun (F.)

A red grape grown in the Lorraine region.

Gamay Noir (U.S.)

A red grape grown in the Napa Valley, California; it was previously thought to be a late-ripening clone of the true Gamay grape, but is now considered to be the Valdiguié grape of southern France; also called Napa Gamay.

Gamay Noir à Jus Blanc (F.)

The Gamay grape, the principal red grape of the Beaujolais district.

Gamay Teinturier (F.)

A red grape with red juice, also called Gamay au Jus Coloré.

Gamay de Toul (F.)

A red grape grown in the Lorraine region.

Gamay della Valle d'Aosta (I.)

Red wine from Aosta, in the Valle d'Aosta region; made from the Gamay grape; like a Beaujolais, dry and fruity.

Gambellara DOC (I.)

1. A district northeast of Soave, in the Veneto region, which produces:

2. Several types of white wine made from the Garganega grape with a little Trebbiano grape.

Gamza (Bul.)

1. A red grape grown in northern Bulgaria (in Hungary known as the Kadarka), which produces:

2. A red wine, light in body, similar to Beaujolais wine.

Gancia, Fratelli (I.)　　　　　1850

A producer of sparkling wines and vermouth in Canelli, Piedmont region. 1 million cases.

Garbellotto e Figlia, G.B. (I.)

A famous firm in Conegliano, in the Veneto region, which makes wine barrels and vats.

Garcinières, Domaine des (F.)

An estate in Cogolin, in the Provence region.

Garda (I.)

A lake in the eastern Lombardy region; the area around the lake produces several DOC wines with names ending with "del Garda."

Garde, Château la (F.)

An unclassified estate in Martillac, Graves district, Bordeaux; produces mostly red wine and some white wine. 20,000 cases red, 2,500 cases white. 115 acres.

Gardine, Château de la (F.)

An estate in Châteauneuf-du-Pape, southern Rhône region. 130 acres.

Garenne, La (F.)

A *Premier Cru* vineyard in Puligny-Montrachet, Côte de Beaune district, Burgundy. 26 acres.

Garennes, Domaine des (F.)

An estate in Chadoux-Verdigny, Sancerre district, Upper Loire region. 25 acres.

Garganega *also* Garganego (I.)

A white grape grown in the Veneto region, the principal grape of Soave wines.

Gargarin Blue (U.S.S.R.)

A red grape grown in Russia.

Garnacha de Alicante (Sp.)

A red grape grown in the Galicia region.

Garnacha Paluda (Sp.)

A red grape grown in the Catalonia region.

Garnacho Blanco (Sp.)

A white grape grown in the Rioja regio the same grape as the Grenache Blanc France.

Garnacho Tinto (Sp.)

A red grape grown in the Rioja region; a proved for DO wines. The same as th Grenache of the Rhône region of Franc also called Tinto Aragonés.

Garofoli (I.)   18

A winery in Loreto, the Marches regio produces Rosso Cònero and Verdicch wines from their own and purchase grapes. 130,000 cases. 125 acres.

Garonnais *also* Garonnet (F.)

A red hybrid grape, also called Seyve-Vi lard 18283 – a cross of S. 7053 and S. 6905

garrata (P.)

A bottle.

garrafeira (P.)

A producer's special quality wine, usuall well-aged in cask and bottle; similar t *reserva*.

Garrido Fino (Sp.)

A white grape grown in the Huelva di trict, in the Extremadura region of sout western Spain.

Garrigue, Domaine de la (F.)

An estate in Vacqueyras, in the Côtes d Rhône-Villages district, Rhône region.

Garrigues, Les (F.)

An estate in Roquemaure, Lirac distric Rhône region. 90 acres.

Garrigues, Les (F.)

An estate in Gigondas, Côtes du Rhône Villages, Rhône region.

Garvey S.A. (Sp.)   178

A famous Sherry producer in Jerez d Frontera; produces several types of Sherr especially San Patricio (*fino*). 750 acres.

Gaschy, Antoine (F.)

An estate and merchant in Wettolsheim, Haut-Rhin district, Alsace region. 16 acres, including Steingrubler vineyard – 2 acres (Riesling) and Pfersigberg vineyard in guisheim – 1.5 acres (Gewürztraminer).

Gassman, Rolly (F.)

An estate in Rorschwihr, northern Haut-Rhin district, Alsace region. 37 acres in Rorschwihr, Bergheim and Rodern.

Gatão (P.)

A sweet white wine from the Lima district, Vinho Verde region.

Gattinara DOC (I.)

1. A village north of Novara, in the northeastern Piedmont region, which produces:
2. A famous red wine made from the Nebbiolo (Spanna) grape and up to 10% Bonarda grapes.

Gattungslage (G.)

A term used prior to the 1971 wine laws denoting a generic site, now called *Grosslage*.

Gaudichots, Les (F.)

A *Premier Cru* vineyard in Vosne-Romanée, Côte de Nuits district, Burgundy; sometimes legally blended in with La Tâche. 15 acres.

Gaunoux, François (F.)

An estate in Meursault, Côte de Beaune district, Burgundy. 25 acres, including Meursault La Goutte d'Or – 2.5 acres, Les Genevrières – .8 acre, Puligny-Montrachet Les Folatières – .8 acre, Bâtard-Montrachet – 1.7 acres, Pommard *Premier Cru* - 2.5 acres, Beaune Le Clos des Mouches – 2.5 acres, Les Épenottes – 2.5 acres and Volnay Clos des Chênes – 3 acres.

Gaunoux, Domaine Michel (F.)

An estate in Pommard, Côte de Beaune district, Burgundy. 30 acres, including Pommard Les Grands Épenots – 7.5 acres, Les Rugiens Bas – 2.5 acres, Les Arvelets – .2 acres, Les Charmots – .8 acre, Beaune *Premier Cru* - 2 acres and Corton-Renardes – 4 acres.

Gautherin, Raoul (F.)

An estate in the Chablis district, Burgundy. 21 acres, including Les Clos – .5 acre, Grenouilles – .5 acre and some Séchet, Butteaux, Lys and Mellinot.

Gauthey, Le Clos (F.)

A *Premier Cru* vineyard in Monthélie, Côte de Beaune district, Burgundy. 5 acres.

## Gauthier, Laurent (F.)					1898

A small estate in Savigny-lès-Beaune, Côte de Beaune district, Burgundy; owns some Savigny Les Lavières.

Gautronnières, Domaine des (F.)

An estate in La Chapelle-Heulin, Muscadet region, Loire Valley; produces Muscadet de Sèvre-et-Maine sur lie and other wines. 50 acres.

Gauvain, Cuvée (F.)

A red wine from the Hospices de Beaune, Côte de Beaune district, Burgundy. The *cuvée* is composed of the following vineyards in Volnay: Les Santenots – 4 acres, Les Pitures – 1 acre. 425 cases.

Gavi *also* Cortese di Gavi DOC (I.)

1. A village southeast of Alessandria, in the southeastern Piedmont region, which produces:
2. A white wine made from the Cortese grape.

Gavi dei Gavi (I.)

An expensive white wine from Gavi, in the Piedmont region; made from the Cortese grape; produced by La Scolca.

Gavilan Cellars (U.S.)

A label used by Chalone winery, California, for French Colombard wine made from purchased grapes.

Gay, Château le (F.)

An estate in Pomerol, Bordeaux. 2,000 cases. 20 acres.

Gay, Maurice (Sw.)   **1883**

A merchant in Sion, Valais region; produces Fendant, Amigne, Chasselas, Dôle and other wines from their own and purchased grapes. 40 acres.

Gay-Lussac (1778-1850) (F.)

The French chemist and physicist who produced the classic formula for the fermentation process.

gaz carbonique (F.)

Carbon dioxide gas.

gazéifié (F.)

Sparkling wine that is artificially carbonated.

Gaziantep (T.)

1. A city in southeastern Turkey, which produces:
2. A red wine made from the Sergikarasi grape.

Gazin, Château (F.)

An estate, the largest one in Pomerol, Bordeaux. 60 acres. 8,000 cases.

Geantet-Pansiot, E. (F.)

An estate in Gevrey-Chambertin, Côte de Nuits, Burgundy. 10 acres, including Charmes-Chambertin – 1 acre, Gevrey-Chambertin *Premier Cru* Poissenot – 1.2 acres.

Gebiet *also* **Anbaugebiet (G.)**

A region, of which there are eleven in Germany.

Gebiets-Winzergenossenschaft Deutsches Weintor (G.)

A large co-op winery in Ilbesheim, Rheinpfalz region; over 1,200 member growers; produces wines from Morio-Muskat, Müller-Thurgau, Silvaner, Kerner and other grapes. 28,000 acres.

Geierberg (I.)

A red wine from Nals, near Bolzano, in th Trentino-Alto Adige region; made from th Schiava grape.

Geisberg (F.)

A *Grand Cru* vineyard in Ribeauvillé, Haut Rhin district, Alsace region; produce Riesling grapes.

Geisenheim (G.)

A village in the Rheingau region, Grossla gen Erntebringer and Burgweg. The vine yards are: Fuchsberg, Mäuerchen Monchspfad and Rothenberg in Grosslag Erntebringer; and Kilzberg, Klaus, Kläus erweg and Schlossgarten in Grosslag Burgweg. It is the home of an important vi ticultural school. 1,000 acres.

Geissbühl (F.)

A vineyard in Zimmerbach, Haut-Rhi district, Alsace region.

Geisweiler et Fils (F.)   **180**

A shipper and grower in Nuits-St. Georges, Côte de Nuits district, Burgundy owns 50 acres of Nuits-St.-Georges and 17 acres of Hautes-Côtes de Nuits, in Bevy.

Gelin, Domaine Pierre (F.)

An estate in Fixin, Côte de Nuits district Burgundy. 40 acres, including 1.6 acres o Chambertin Clos de Bèze, 1 acre of Mazis Chmbertin, 5 acres of Fixin Clos Napoléon Monopole, 1.2 acres of Fixin Les Hervelet and 12 acres of Fixin Clos du Chapitre.

Gem City Vineland (U.S.)   **185**

A vineyard and winery in Nauvoo, west ern Illinois; produces labrusca wines. 12(acres.

Gemarkung (G.)

A wine town or village, now officiall called a *Weinbauort*, or *Gemeinde*. Als called a *commune*, in French.

Gemeinde (G.)

See **Gemarkung.**

Gemello Winery (U.S.)   1934

A winery in Mountain View, Santa Clara County, California; produces Cabernet, Zinfandel, Pinot Noir, Petite Sirah, Chardonnay, Chenin Blanc, white Pinot Noir and white Zinfandel wines. 8,000 cases.

Général Muteau, Cuvée (F.)

A red wine from the Hospices de Beaune, Côte de Beaune district, Burgundy. The *cuvée* is composed of the following vineyards in Volnay: Le Village – 2 acres, Carelle sous la Chapelle – 1 acre, Cailleret Dessus – .5 acre, Fremiets – .5 acre and Taille Pieds – .5 acre. 450 cases.

generic wine

1. A regional wine, or a blended wine with no specific district, village or grape designated on the label.

2. A type of wine, such as dessert, apéritif, fortified, etc.

générique (F.)

Generic (wine); a general or regional wine, i.e. Côtes du Rhône, Bourgogne, Bordeaux Supérieur, Vin Rouge, Vin de Table, etc.

generoso (P.)

High in alcohol, usually in reference to a dessert wine or an apéritif.

Genestière, Domaine de la (F.)

An estate in Tavel, with vineyards also in Lirac, in the southern Rhône region; produces rosé wine made from 50% Grenache, 20% Cinsault and Carignan, Clairette, Picpoul and Bourboulenc grapes. 2nd label is Domaine Longval. 85 acres in Tavel and 25 acres in Lirac.

Genêt, En (F.)

A *Premier Cru* vineyard in Beaune, Côte de Beaune district, Burgundy. 12 acres.

Geneva White (U.S.)

An American white hybrid grape – a cross of Seyval Blanc and Schuyler. Also called Cayuga White.

Geneva Agricultural Experiment Station (U.S.)   1882

A research institute run by Cornell University in Geneva, Finger Lakes region, New York; engaged in wine research, grape breeding and vineyard science.

Genevrières, Les (F.)

A *Premier Cru* vineyard in Morey-St.-Denis, Côte de Nuits district, Burgundy. 7.5 acres.

Genevrières Dessous, Les (F.)

A *Premier Cru* vineyard (in part) in Meursault, Côte de Beaune district, Burgundy; usually sold as Les Genevrières. 13 acres.

Genevrières Dessus, Les (F.)

A *Premier Cru* vineyard (in part) in Meursault, Côte de Beaune district, Burgundy; usually sold as Les Genevrières. 20 acres.

Genièvres, Les (F.)

A white wine from Lugny, Mâconnais district, Burgundy; produced by L. Latour.

Genovesella (F.)

A grape grown in Corsica.

Gentil (F.)

The Alsatian name for the Riesling grape.

Gentile (I.)

A red grape grown around Lake Garda, in the Lombardy region.

Geoffroy Père et Fils (F.)

An estate in Gevrey-Chambertin, Côte de Nuits district, Burgundy. 12 acres, including Mazis-Chambertin – .3 acre and Gevrey-Chambertin Clos-Prieur – 2.5 acres.

Geografico, Agricoltori del Chianti (I.)

A co-op winery in Gaiole in Chianti, Tuscany region; produces Chianti Classico wine. 100,000 cases.

Georgia (U.S.S.R.)

A republic of the Soviet Union; produces mostly sparkling wines as well as red wines made from Mukuzani, Seperavi and Napareuli grapes and white wines from Tsinandali and Gurdzhaani grapes.

Georgia (U.S.)

A state in the southeastern United States; Scuppernong and other muscadine grapes are grown here as well as the Concord grape; it has only one winery, the Monarch Wine Company in Atlanta. 1,000 acres.

Georgics (Lat.)

The famous poem by Vergil, written in 30 B.C., in which vineyards, grape varieties and wines are discussed.

Geproklameerde Gebiede van Oorsprung (S.Af.)

Proclaimed Areas (Regions) of Origin, the system of wine laws similar the the French AOC laws.

gerebelt (A.)

A term found on Austrian wine labels, meaning hand-picked.

Geregistreerde Landgoedere (S. Af.)

Registered Estate, one which grows its own grapes and makes and bottles its wine.

gerente (Sp.)

A bodega manager.

Germain, Domaine (F.)

An estate in Chorey-lès-Beaune, Côte de Beaune, Burgundy, also including Château de Chorey and Domaine de Saux. 37 acres, including Beaune Teurons – 5 acres, Beaune Cras – 4 acres, Vignes Franches – 2.5 acres, Boucherottes – 2.5 acres, Cent Vignes – 1.2 acres, Chorey-lès-Beaune Château de Chorey Monopole – 2.5 acres, Pernand-Vergelesses and Bourgogne Château Germain.

Germain ECVF, Sélection Jean (F.)　1972

An estate and merchant in Meursault, Côte de Beaune district, Burgundy; owns 1 acre of Puligny-Montrachet Grands Champs and 1 acre of Meursault.

Germany

A country in Europe divided into 11 regions (Gebiete), mostly around the Rhine River and its tributaries; produces 85% white wines. 225 million gallons. 250,000 acres.

geropiga also jeropiga (P.)

Boiled grape juice or syrup used to sweeten wines, especially Port wines.

Geschein (G.)

A pannicle; a cluster of buds on a vine.

Gevrey-Chambertin AOC (F.)

1. A village in the Côte de Nuits district Burgundy; produces the famous Chambertin wine; it has 8 Grand Cru and 24 Premier Cru vineyards. 1,400 acres.

2. The village AOC designation for red wine from Gevrey-Chambertin.

Gewächs (G.)

A growth of; grown by; vintage; also Wachstum and Kreszenz; these terms have not used since 1971.

Gewann (G.)

In Baden and Württemberg, a site, or plot Also called Lage.

Gewürztraminer

1. A white grape grown in Alsace, Germany and northern Italy, but also in Australia, California and other regions; a spicier version of the Traminer grape which it has replaced, for the most part.

2. A white varietal wine made from this grape.

Geyser Peak Winery (U.S.)　　1880, 1972

A large, old winery in Geyserville, Dry Creek district, northern Sonoma County, California; produces many varietal and sparkling wines, also makes the Summit label jug wines. 600 acres. 2 million cases.

Ghemme DOC (I.)

1. A village north of Novara, in the northeastern Piedmont region, which produces

2. A red wine made from 60-85% Nebbiolo grapes with some Vespolina and Bonarda grapes; very similar to Gattinara.

Ghiaie della Furba (I.)

A red wine from Carmignano, northwest of Florence, in the Tuscany region; made from Cabernet, Cabernet Franc and Merlot grapes.

Giacobazzi (I.)

A large winery in Nonantola, Emilia-Romagna region; produces several Lambrusco wines and other wines.

Giacosa, Bruno (I.)   1890

A winery in Neive, Piedmont region; produces Barbaresco, Barbera, Dolcetto, Freisa, Arneis, Grignolino and Nebbiolo wines from purchased grapes.

Gibson Wine Company (U.S.)   1945

A large co-op winery in Sanger, east of Fresno, San Joaquin Valley, California; produces jug wines. 6 million gallons.

Gigondas AOC (F.)   since 1971

1. A commune in the Côtes du Rhône district, southern Rhône region, which produces:

2. Red, white and rosé wines, the red and rosé made principally from the Grenache grape as well as the Syrah, Cinsault, and Mourvèdre and very little white made from Clairette, Bourboulenc, Grenache Blanc and Picpoul grapes. 3,000 acres.

Gilbey de Loudenne (F.)

A merchant in St.-Yzans, Médoc district, Bordeaux; owns Château Loudenne.

Gilette, Château (F.)

An unclassified estate in Preignac, Sauternes district, Bordeaux. 3,000 cases. 35 acres.

gill (E.)

A quartern; a quarter-pint.

Gilles, Henri (F.)

An estate in Comblanchien, Côte de Nuits district, Burgundy. 17 acres, including Nuits-St.-Georges Les Brulées – 4 acres, Corton Renardes – .7 acre and Côte de Nuits-Villages.

Ginestet (F.)   1899

A merchant in Bordeaux.

Ginger Wine (E.)

Not a true wine; a beverage made from ginger, yeast, sugar, lemon rind, raisins and water and fortified with spirits.

Gioia del Colle (I.)

1. A village south of Bari, in the central Apulia region, which produces:

2. A dry red wine made from the Primitivo grape; 14-16% alcohol. Also called Primitivo di Gioia.

Girard, Cuvée Arthur (F.)

A red wine from the Hospices de Beaune, Côte de Beaune district, Burgundy. The *cuvée* is composed of the following vineyards in Savigny: Les Peuillets – 2.5 acres and Les Marconnets – 2 acres.

Girard, Michel (F.)

An estate in Verdigny, Sancerre district, Upper Loire region. 12 acres.

Girard Winery (U.S.)   vines 1974
                                  winery 1980

A winery in Oakville, Napa Valley, California; produces Cabernet, Chardonnay and Chenin Blanc wines; the second wine uses the Stevens label. 10,000 acres. 40 acres.

Girardi, Villa (I.)

An estate in San Pietro Incariano, Veneto region; produces Amarone, Bardolino, Soave and Valpolicella wines. 85 acres.

girasol (Sp.)

Spanish for "sunflower," a mechanical riddler, a large octagonal-shaped frame mounted on an inverted pyramid holding about 500 bottles; its purpose is to gradually rotate the bottles of sparkling wine to work the sediment of the 2nd fermentation down to the neck of the bottle; replaces the *pupitre*, or hand-riddling system.

Giraud, Domaine Charles (F.)

An estate in Meursault, Côte de Beaune district, Burgundy. 22 acres, including Pommard La Refène – .6 acre, Volnay Clos des Chênes – .6 acre, Meursault Les Genevrières – 4 acres, Les Charmes – .6 acre, Les Perrières – .5 acre and Côte de Beaune-Villages.

Girò (I.)

A red grape grown in Sardinia.

Girò di Cagliari DOC (I.)

Dry or sweet red wines from Cagliari, in southwestern Sardinia, made from the Girò grape; 14-18% alcohol.

Giscours, Château (F.)

An estate in Labarde-Margaux, Haut Médoc district, Bordeaux; classified in 1855 as a *Troisième Cru;* was active as early as 1552, when it was sold. 190 acres. 30,000 cases.

Gisselbrecht, Louis (F.)   1936

An estate and merchant in Dambach-la-Ville, Bas-Rhin district, Alsace region. 50,000 cases. 15 acres.

Gisselbrecht et Fils, Willy (F.)   1936

An estate and merchant in Dambach-la-Ville, Bas-Rhin district, Alsace region. 100,000 cases. 30 acres.

Gitton, Marcel (F.)   1945

An estate in Sancerre, Upper Loire region. 50 acres in Sancerre and 22 acres of Pouilly-Fumé.

Giumarra Vineyards (U.S.)   1946

A large winery in Bakersfield, San Joaquin Valley, Kern County, California; produces generic jug wines and varietal wines. 8,000 acres. 1 million cases.

Givry AOC (F.)

1. A commune in the Côte Chalonnaise district, Burgundy; known as early as 1390, and produces:

2. Red and white wines. There are no *Grand Cru* or *Premier Cru* vineyards.

Glana, Château du (F.)

An estate in St.-Julien, Haut-Médoc district, Bordeaux; classified in 1978 as a *Cru Grand Bourgeois Exceptionnel.* 30,000 cases. 175 acres.

Glantenay, Georges (F.)

An estate in Volnay, Côte de Beaune district, Burgundy. 15 acres, including Pommard Rugiens – .6 acre, Volnay Les Santenots – .8 acre and Les Brouillards – 2.5 acres.

Glantenay, Louis (F.)

An estate in Volnay, Côte de Beaune district, Burgundy. 20 acres, including Volnay Clos des Chênes – 1.2 acres, Caillerets, – .6 acre, Les Santenots – 1.7 acres and Pommard Les Rugiens – .6 acre.

Glasscock Vineyard (U.S.)   1977

A vineyard and projected winery on Blue Mt., southeast of El Paso, near Fort Davis, Texas; grows Cabernet, Merlot, Sauvignon Blanc, Chenin Blanc and other *vinifera* grapes. 35 acres.

Glen Ellen Winery (U.S.)   1979

A small winery in Glen Ellen, Sonoma County, California; produces Cabernet, Chardonnay, Sauvignon Blanc and other wines. 32 acres.

Glen Oak Hills Winery (U.S.)   1978

A small winery in Temecula, Riverside County, southern California.

Glenora Wine Cellars (U.S.)   1977

A winery near Dundee, on the southwestern shores of Lake Seneca, Finger Lakes region, New York; grows mostly hybrid grapes and some Riesling and Chardonnay grapes. 20,000 cases. 500 acres.

Glenvale Vineyards (N.Z.)　　　1933

A winery in Hawkes Bay, North Island; produces Cabernet, Merlot, Pinotage, Riesling Sylvaner, Gewürztraminer, Müller-Thurgau and fortified wines. 150 acres.

glög *also* glögg (Sweden)

A hot wine drink made with red wine, brandy, nuts, raisins and spices, a traditional Swedish winter drink.

Gloeckelberg (F.)

A *Grand Cru* vineyard in Rodern, northern Haut-Rhin district, Alsace region.

Gloria (G.)

A white grape – a cross of Silvaner and Müller-Thurgau; developed at the Federal Research Institute, Geilweilerhof, Germany.

Gloria, Château (F.)　　　c. 1945

An unclassified estate in St.-Julien, Haut Médoc district, Bordeaux; made up of parts of several classified *châteaux* (Leoville-Poyferré, Gruaud-Larose, St.-Pierre and Duhart-Milon). 20,000 cases. 110 acres.

Glottertal (G.)

A village in the Baden region, Bereich Breisgau, Grosslage Burg Zahringen. The vineyards are Eichberg and Roter Bur.

glucometer

An instrument for testing the sugar content of must.

glycerin *also* glycerine

Glycerol; a sweet, syrupy, liquid form of trihydroxy alcohol present in wine.

Gnangara Wines (Aus.)

A small winery in the Margaret River district, Western Australia; produces red wines from a blend of Cabernet and Shiraz grapes.

gobelet (F.)

One of several methods of training grape vines, in which a single trunk terminates in 2 or more arms rising in the shape of a goblet.

goblet

A drinking glass, having a stem and a foot.

Godello (Sp.)

A white grape grown in the Galicia region.

Goede Hoop EWO (S. Af.)

An estate in the Stellenbosch district; produces red wines.

Goisses, Clos des (F.)

A vineyard in Mareuil-sur-Ay, Champagne region; grows Pinot Noir and Chardonnay grapes; produced by Philipponat.

Gold (U.S.)

A white grape – a double cross of Muscat Hamburg and Sultanina with Muscat Hamburg and Scolokertek Kiralyroje; developed in southern California by Harold Olmo.

Gold Seal (U.S.)　　　1865

A large winery and vineyard near Hammondsport, on Keuka Lake, Finger Lakes region, New York; produces Catawba, *labrusca* and various blended wines; it was the first commercial winery to produce *vinifera* wines in New York (Chardonnay and Johannisberg Riesling). It was originally the Urbana Wine Company. 600,000 cases. 500 acres.

Golden Chasselas (U.S.)

In California, another name for the Palomino grape.

Golden Muscat (U.S.)

An American white hybrid grape – a cross of Muscat Hamburg and Diamond; grown in California and New Hampshire.

Golden Rain Tree Winery (U.S.)   1975

A winery in Wadesville, southwestern Indiana; grows hybrid grapes.

Goldert (F.)

A *Grand Cru* vineyard in Gueberschwihr, Haut-Rhin district, Alsace region.

Gols (A.)

A village in the Burgenland region, near the Neusliedlersee, in eastern Austria; produces white wines.

gönc, *plur.:* **gönci (H.)**

A wooden cask, about 140-liter or 35-gallon capacity, in which Tokaji wine is slowly fermented over a period of 5 to 6 years. A bung-like hole is left open in the cask and a thin film of flor-like fungus grows on the surface of the wine, adding a nutty flavor to the Tokaji wines.

Gonzalez Byass, Ltd. (Sp.)   1835

A famous Sherry producer in Jerez de Frontera; produces several well-known types of Sherry: Tio Pepe *(fino)*, La Concha *(amontillado)*, Alfonso Dry *(oloroso)*, San Domingo (pale cream) and Nectar (cream). 2 million cases.

Gordo Blanco (Aus.)

A white grape.

Goron (Sw.)

A light, red wine from the Valais district, made from a blend of Gamay and Pinot Noir grapes, similar to Dôle, but of lower quality.

Gosset (F.)   16th cent.

A Champagne producer in Ay; also owns Philipponat. 200,000 bottles.

Gothe (Br.)

A grape grown in Brazil.

Gouachon, Domaine du Général (F.)

An estate in Prémeaux, Côte de Nuits district, Burgundy. 15 acres, including Nuits-St.-Georges Clos des Corvées Monopole –

12.5 acres and Clos des Argillières – 2 acres.

Goubert, Domaine des (F.)

An estate in Gigondas, southern Rhône region. 13 acres.

Goud de Beaupuis, Domaine (F.)   1787

An estate in Chorey-lès-Beaune, Côte de Beaune district, Burgundy. 30 acres, including Pommard Les Épenots – .6 acre, Pommard La Chanière – 1.2 acres, Beaune Clos des Vignes Franches – 4.4 acres, Grèves – 4 acres, Toussaints – .6 acre, Savigny Les Vergelesses – .8 acre, Aloxe-Corton Valozières – .6 acre and some Ladoix, Chorey and Bourgogne Château des Montots.

Gouges, Henri (F.)

An estate in Nuits-St.-Georges, Côte de Nuits district, Burgundy. 25 acres, including Nuits-St.-Georges Les St.-Georges – 2.5 acres, Les Vaucrains – 2.5 acres, Clos des Porets St.-Georges Monopole – 9 acres, Les Pruliers – 6.6 acres, La Perrière – 1.2 acres and Les Chaignots – .8 acre.

Goujan, Château de (F.)

An estate in Murviel, St.-Chinian district, Languedoc region; produces Coteaux de Murviel, St.-Chinian and Cabernet rosé wines.

Goulaine, Marquis de (F.)

An estate in Haute-Goulaine, Muscadet de Sèvre-et-Maine district, Muscadet region, Loire Valley. 95 acres.

Gould, Campbell (P.)

A Port producer in Vila Nova de Gaia; shipped by Smith, Woodhouse and Co. Lda.

Goulet, Georges (F.)   1867

A Champagne producer in Reims; Cuvée du Centenaire is the *cuvée de prestige;* also produces still wines. No vineyards. 1 million bottles.

Goulots, Les (F.)

A *Premier Cru* vineyard in Gevrey-Chambertin, Côte de Nuits district, Burgundy. 4.5 acres.

Goundrey Wines (Aus.)   1970's

An estate in the Mount Barker district, Western Australia; produces award-winning Cabernet wine.

Goureau, Cuvée (F.)

A white wine from the Hospices de Beaune, Côte de Beaune district, Burgundy. The *cuvée* is composed of the following vineyards in Meursault: Le Poruzot .8 acre, Les Pitures – .8 acre and Les Cras – .5 acre. 225 cases.

gourmet (F.)

The Alsatian name for a wine-broker.

Gouron, René (F.)

An estate in Cravant-lès-Coteaux, Chinon district, Touraine region, Loire Valley. 5,000 cases. 45 acres.

Gouroux, Henri (F.)

An estate in Flagey-Échézeaux, Côte de Nuits district, Burgundy. 8 acres, including Grands Échézeaux – 1 acre, Clos de Vougeot – .8 acre and Vosne-Romanée Les Suchots – .8 acre.

Gouroux, Louis (F.)

An estate in Flagey-Échézeaux, Côte de Nuits district, Burgundy. 10 acres, including Clos de Vougeot – .7 acre, Grands Échézeaux – 1.2 acres and Échézeaux – 5 acres.

goût de capsule (F.)

French for "taste of the capsule," a hard, somewhat metallic taste present in some red wines, notably Bordeaux wines.

goût de pierre à fusil (F.)

French for "taste of gunflint," used to describe a characteristic taste of some very dry white wines made from grapes grown in chalky limestone soil, particularly Chablis; a flinty taste.

goût de terroir (F.)

French for "taste of the earth," used to describe a taste reminiscent of soil in certain red and white wines, especially Burgundy wines.

Goutte d'Or, La (F.)

A *Premier Cru* vineyard in Meursault, Côte de Beaune district, Burgundy. 14 acres.

Gouveio (P.)

A white grape, one of 16 official first-quality grapes used to make Port wine; also known as Verdelho.

governo all'uso Toscano (I.)

A practice of adding partially fermented dried grapes to new wine, causing a secondary fermentation; the finished wine has a fresh taste and a slight sparkle; this method is especially used in making Chianti wines, though less often now.

Graach (G.)

A famous village in the Mosel-Saar-Ruwer region, Bereich Bernkastel, Grosslage Münzlay. The vineyards are: Abtsberg, Domprobst, Himmelreich and Josefshöfer. 250 acres.

Graben (G.)

A vineyard in Bernkastel, Bereich Bernkastel, Grosslage Badstube, Mosel-Saar-Ruwer region; often blended with the Doktor vineyard and bottled as "Doktor und Graben."

Graber, Weingut Karl (A.)   1950

An estate in Gumpoldskirchen, south of Vienna; produces Gumpoldskirchner wines. 30 acres.

Grâce-Dieu, Château La (F.)

An estate in St.-Émilion, Bordeaux; classified in 1955 as a *Grand Cru*. 6,000 cases. 30 acres.

grächen (Lux.)

Ordinary wine, common table wine; bottled under the name Vin de la Moselle Luxembourgeoise, without the grape name.

Graciano (Sp.)

A local red grape grown in the Rioja region, an approved DO grape.

Gradnik, Gradimir (I.)

An estate in Plessiva di Cormons, Friuli-Venezia Giulia region; produces Collio wines. 6,000 cases. 25 acres.

Graecula (Gr.)

An ancient Greek grape mentioned by Cato.

Graf (G.)

A Count; a noble title.

Gragnano (I.)

1. A town south of Naples, in the Campania region, which produces:

2. A red wine, also sparkling, made from Aglianico, Piedirosso, Olivella and other grapes.

Graham & Co., W. & J. (P.)   1820

A Port producer in Vila Nova de Gaia. Owns Quinta dos Malvedos, sometimes bottled as a single quinta wine.

grains (F.)

Raisins; the individual grape berries.

graisse (F.)

A malady of white wines produced by certain bacteria which cause the wine to become thick, to lose sugar and to increase volatile acidity, producing a gummy deposit.

Gramont, Domaine Machard de (F.)

An estate in Nuits-St.-Georges, Côte de Nuits district, Burgundy. 75 acres, including Clos de Vougeot, Nuits-St.-Georges – 15 acres, Vosne-Romanée, Chambolle-Musigny, Aloxe-Corton, Pommard – 20 acres, Savigny-lès-Beaune, Volnay, Beaune and Clos des Topes Bizot (a Côte de Beaune *Monopole*) – 11 acres.

Gramp's (Aus.)

An old winery in the Barossa Valley district, South Australia. See **Orlando.**

Gran Nero (Sp.)

A red grape grown in the Galicia region.

Grancey, Château Corton (F.)

An estate and a vineyard in Aloxe-Corton, Côte de Beaune district, Burgundy; classified as a *Grand Cru*; built in 1749, owned by Louis Latour and used as his vineyard designation of red Corton.

Grand-Barrail-Lamarzelle-Figeac, Château (F.)

An estate in St.-Émilion, Bordeaux; classified in 1955 as a *Grand Cru Classé*. 15,000 cases. 80 acres.

Grand'Boise, Château (F.)

An estate in Trets-en-Provence, in the Provence region; produces red, rosé and sparkling wines. 20,000 cases. 100 acres.

Grand Chemarin, Le (F.)

A vineyard in Bué, Sancerre district, Upper Loire region. 50 acres.

Grand-Corbin-Despagne, Château (F.)

An estate in St.-Émilion, Bordeaux; classified in 1955 as a *Grand Cru Classé*. 16,000 cases. 60 acres.

Grand-Corbin-Pécresse, Château (F.)

An estate in St.-Émilion, Bordeaux; classified in 1955 as a *Grand Cru Classé*. 6,500 cases. 30 acres.

Grand Cour, Domaine de la (F.)

An estate in Fleurie, Beaujolais district, Burgundy. 20 acres.

Grand Cru *also* **Grand Cru Classé (F.)**

1. An official classification of a vineyard or *château* considered to be in the top class or of the highest quality; this applies to the following: red wines of the Médoc (Haut-Médoc) classified in 1855, sweet white wines of Sauternes and Barsac, classified

in 1855, red wines of St.-Émilion, classified in 1955, certain vineyards in Alsace, certain vineyards that are rated 100% in Champagne, certain vineyards, or *climats,* in the Côte d'Or of Burgundy, two vineyards in Savennieres, and two vineyards in Coteaux-du-Layon (these last four in the Loire Valley).

2. An unofficial ranking of some wines that may or may not merit such a distinction. The official *Cru Classé* red and white wines of Graves were labeled *Grand Cru Classé* until recently; the 9 *Crus* of Beaujolais are sometimes referred to as the *Grands Crus* of Beaujolais.

Grand Cru Vineyards (U.S.)   1886, 1970

An old winery in Glen Ellen, Sonoma County, California with vineyards at Alexander Valley and Dry Creek; produces Cabernet, white Zinfandel, Gewürztraminer, Chenin Blanc, Sauvignon Blanc and sparkling wines from own and purchased grapes. 40,000 cases. 30 acres.

Grand Duroc Milon, Château (F.)

An estate in Pauillac, Haut-Médoc district, Bordeaux; classified in 1978 as a *Cru Bourgeois.*

Grand-Mayne, Château (F.)

An estate in St.-Émilion, Bordeaux; Classified in 1955 as a *Grand Cru Classé.* 7,000 cases. 45 acres.

Grand Moulin, Château (F.)

An estate in St.-Seurin-de-Cadourne, Haut Médoc district, Bordeaux; classified in 1978 as a *Cru Bourgeois.* 22,000 cases. 75 acres.

Grand Pacific Vineyard (U.S.)   1975

A small winery in St. Rafael, Marin County, California; produces Merlot and Chardonnay wines from Sonoma County grapes. 8,000 cases.

Grand-Pontet, Château (F.)

An estate in St.-Émilion, Bordeaux; classified in 1955 as a *Grand Cru Classé.* 6,000 cases. 33 acres.

Grand-Puy-Ducasse, Château (F.)

An estate in Pauillac, Haut-Médoc district, Bordeaux; classified in 1855 (under the name of Artique-Arnaud) as a *Cinquième Cru;* includes 1/3 of the original Château Grand Puy (since the 15th century); this estate tripled in size in 1971. 80 acres. 15,000 cases.

Grand-Puy-Lacoste, Château (F.)

An estate in Pauillac, Haut-Médoc district, Bordeaux; classified in 1855 as a *Cinquième Cru;* a part of the original Château Grand Puy. 85 acres. 15,000 cases.

Grand River Wine Company (U.S.)   1971

A new winery near Madison, Ohio; produces Pinot Noir, Gamay Beaujolais Rosé, Chardonnay and French hybrid wines. 30 acres.

Grand Roussillon (F.)

The former name of the AOC Côtes du Roussillon.

Grand Roussillon VDN (F.)

The designation for sweet red, white and rosé fortified wines from the Roussillon region made from Grenache, Maccabéo, Malvoisie and Muscat grapes. See **VDN.**

Grand Rue, La (F.)

A *Premier Cru* vineyard in Vosne-Romanée, Côte de Nuits district, Burgundy; can be legally blended in with La Tâche. 2.5 acres.

Grand Travers, Château (F.)   1974

A vineyard and winery near Traverse City, northern Michigan; produces White Riesling and Chardonnay wines. 50 acres.

Grand Vin (F.)

1. In Alsace, a legal designation for superior quality wines made from noble grape varieties: Riesling, Gewürztraminer, Muscat and Tokay d'Alsace (Pinot Gris); *Grand Cru* designation is also used legally. Must contain 11% alcohol.

2. Great Wine, a term often freely used on lesser-quality wines in other parts of France.

Grande Champagne (F.)

The best district in the Charentes region; produces wines used in making Cognac.

Grandes-Lolières (F.)

A *Premier Cru* vineyard in Ladoix-Serrigny, Côte de Beaune district, Burgundy; may be sold as Aloxe-Corton. 7.5 acres.

Grandes-Murailles, Château (F.)

An estate in St.-Émilion, Bordeaux; classified in 1955 as a *Grand Cru Classé*. 800 cases. 5 acres.

Grandes Ruchottes, Les (F.)

A *Premier Cru* vineyard in Chassagne-Montrachet, Côte de Beaune district, Burgundy. 7.5 acres.

Grandes-Vignes, Clos des (F.)

A *Premier Cru* vineyard (in part) in Prémeaux, Côte de Nuits district, Burgundy. 5.5 acres.

Grands Champs, Les (F.)

A *Premier Cru* vineyard in Auxey-Duresses, Côte de Beaune district, Burgundy. 11 acres.

Grands Devers, Domaine des (F.)

An estate in Valréas, Côtes du Rhône district, southern Rhône region.

Grands-Échézeaux AOC (F.)

A *Grand Cru* vineyard in Flagey-Échézeaux, Côte de Nuits district, Burgundy; when declassified it is labeled as Vosne-Romanée; partly owned by the Société Civil de la Romanée-Conti. 4,500 cases. 22.5 acres.

Grands Épenots, Les *also* Les Épenots (F.)

A *Premier Cru* vineyard in Pommard, Côte de Beaune district, Burgundy. 25 acres.

Grands Liards, Aux (F.)

A *Premier Cru* vineyard (in part) in Savigny-lès-Beaune, Côte de Beaune district, Burgundy. 25 acres.

Grands Murs, Les (F.)

A *Premier Cru* vineyard in Chambolle-Musigny, Côte de Nuits district, Burgundy. 2.5 acres.

Granfiesta (Aus.)

A *fino* sherry-style wine from the Quelltaler Winery, in the Clare-Watervale district, South Australia.

Grange Hermitage (Aus.)

A famous red wine from Penfold's Winery, Magill, South Australia; made from the Shiraz grape.

Grangeneuve, Domaine de (F.)

An estate in Rasteau, in the Côtes du Rhône district, southern Rhône region; produces red, white and rosé Cotes du Rhône wines and VDN wines.

Grangeneuve, Domaine de (F.)   vines 1965 wine 1974

An estate in Roussas, in the Coteaux du Tricastin district, southern Rhône region; produces mostly red wine, with a little rosé and white wine. 240 acres.

Grangier, Cuvée (F.)

A red wine from the Hospices de Nuits, in Nuits-St.-Georges, Côte de Nuits district, Burgundy.

Granja União (Br.)

A brand name for the better red and white wines produced by Vinícola Riograndense, in Caxias.

Granjo (P.)

A sweet, white wine made from late-picked grapes, produced by the Real Companhia Vinícola do Norte de Portugal.

grano (Sp.)

A grape berry.

Granval (U.S.)

The second wine of the Clos Du Val winery, Napa Valley, California.

rape

A fruit of the vine from which wine is made. A grape consists of skin, about 20% by weight, pulp, 75% and 1-6 seeds, or pips, 5%; the pulp consists of: water – 70-80%, extract – 10-25%, sugars – 15-25%, pectins – .1-1.0%, pentosans – .01-0.05%, inositol – .02-.08%, malic acid – .1-.8%, tartaric acid – .2-1.0%, citric acid – .01-.05%, tannin – 0-.2%, nitrogen – .01-.2% and ash – .2-.6%.

ras (F.)

Fat, velvety, a term applied to a wine.

Gras-Moutons, Domaine de (F.)

An estate in Saint-Fiacre, Muscadet de Sèvre-et-Maine district, Loire Valley. 20 acres.

Grasă *also* **Grasă de Cotnari (R.)**

A white grape grown in the Cotnari district of northeastern Romania.

Graševina *also* **Grašica (Y.)**

The local name for the Wälschriesling, or Italian Riesling grape.

Gratien, Alfred (F.)   1864

A Champagne producer in Épernay. 200,000 bottles.

Gratien-Meyer (F.)   1864

A producer of sparkling wines in the Saumur district, Anjou region, Loire Valley; produces still and sparkling wines from their own and purchased grapes. 1.5 million bottles. 120,000 cases. 50 acres.

Gratiesti (U.S.S.R.)

A sweet, white wine from Moldavia SSR; made from the Rcatsitelli grape.

Grattamacco (I.)

Red and white wines made southeast of Livorno, in the western Tuscany region. The red wine is made from Colorino, Sangiovese and other grapes and the white wine is made from Trebbiano, Malvasia and other grapes.

Gravains, Aux (F.)

A *Premier Cru* vineyard in Savigny, Côte de Beaune district, Burgundy. 16.5 acres.

Grave del Friuli DOC (I.)

A large district covering the plains of the Tagliamento River, in the southwestern part of the Friuli-Venezia Giulia region; produces varietal wines made from the two Cabernet grapes, Merlot, Pinot Bianco, Pinot Grigio, Refosco, Tocai and Verduzzo grapes.

Grave-Trigant-de-Boisset, Château La (F.)

An estate in Pomerol, Bordeaux. 2,100 cases. 20 acres.

Graves AOC (F.)

1. A district in the Bordeaux region of southwestern France; the vineyard areas surround the city of Bordeaux; produces red and white wines; the best growths, or *châteaux*, were classified in 1953 and 1959 simply as *Crus Classés*. The red wine of Château Haut-Brion, a top growth, was the only Graves wine included in the 1855 classification of the Médoc wines, and was rated a *Premier Cru*.

2. The AOC designation for unclassified red and white wines of the Graves district.

Graves (F.)

A section of the St.-Émilion district near Pomerol, and which forms a flat, gravely, sandy plateau, producing fuller, richer wines, more like those of Pomerol. Cheval Blanc and Figeac are in this section.

Graves de Vayres AOC (F.)

A district in the Entre-Deux-Mers section of the Bordeaux region; Vayres is the main commune; produces red and white wines.

Graves Supérieures AOC (F.)

A designation for blended white wine from the Graves district, Bordeaux. 12% alcohol.

Gravières, Les (F.)

A *Premier Cru* vineyard (in part) in Santenay, Côte de Beaune district, Burgundy. 72 acres.

Gray Riesling *also* Grey Riesling (U.S.)

A white grape grown in California; not a Riesling at all, but actually, the Chauché Gris grape of France.

Great Plain (H.)

A region east of the Danube River, containing about half of Hungary's vineyards; produces ordinary red and white wines. Also called Alföld. 200,000 acres.

Great Wall (China)

A white wine from Hebei, eastern China; made from the native Loong Yan (Dragon's Eye) grape.

Great Western (Aus.)

A district in western Victoria; known for sparkling wines made by Colin Preece as well as his Cabernet and Shiraz wines, now owned by Seppelt.

Grecanico (I.)

A white grape grown in Sicily.

Grechetto, Grechetto Bianco *also* Greco (I.)

A white grape grown in the Tuscany region (where it is also called Pulcinculo), in Latium (where it is also called Trebbiano Giallo), and in the Umbria and Calabria regions.

Grechetto di Gradoli (I.)

1. A red grape grown in the Latium region, which produces:

2. A red wine from Gradoli, north of Lake Bolsena, in the northern Latium region; made from Grechetto and Sangiovese grapes.

Greco (I.)

1. A white grape, a strain of the Erbaluce, which produces:

2. A white wine from the Piedmont region; made from the Greco grape.

Greco di Bianco DOC (I.)

A new name for Greco di Gerace, a high-quality sweet, white wine from Bianco, in the southwestern Calabria region; made from the Greco grape. 17-19% alcohol.

Greco di Gerace DOC (I.)

See **Greco di Bianco DOC.**

Greco di Tufo DOC (I.)

A dry, white wine from Tufo, north of Avellino, in the central Campania region; made from the Greco grape with up to 20% of the Coda di Volpe grape.

Greece

A country in southeastern Europe on the Mediterranean Sea, ranks 13th in the world for wine production; known for Retsina and Mavrodaphne wines. 475,000 acres.

green

Young; too acidic; raw or harsh.

Green and Red Vineyards (U.S.)   1977

A small winery in St. Helena, Napa Valley, California; produces Zinfandel wine. 3,000 cases. 7 acres.

Green Grape (S. Af.)

The Sémillon grape. Also called Groendruif.

Green Hungarian (U.S.)

1. A white *vinifera* grape grown in California.

2. A white wine made from the Green Hungarian grape.

Greenwood Ridge Vineyards (U.S.)   1972

A small winery and vineyard in Philo, Mendocino County, California; produces Cabernet and Johannisberg Riesling wines. 2,000 cases. 8 acres.

Greffieux (F.)

An important vineyard in Hermitage, in the northern Rhône region; produces red wines.

Grenache (F.)

A sweet, red grape with a distinctive bouquet; wine made from this grape generally has a high alcohol content. It is used in the Rhône and Roussillon regions (where it is known as Carignane Rousse and Alicante Pinto) and in the Provence region for red and rosé wines; also grown in California for rosé wines; also called Alicante or Garnacha in Spain.

Grenache Blanc (F.)

A white grape grown in the Rhône and Provence regions.

Grenache Gris (F.)

A white grape grown in the Rhône region.

Grenache Noir (F.)

Another name for the Grenache grape.

Grenache-rouge (F.)

Another name for the Grenache grape.

Grenouille, Domaine de la (F.)

An estate in Chablis, Burgundy; owned by the Testut family since 1966. 25 acres of the Grenouilles vineyard.

Grenouilles (F.)

One of 7 *Grand Cru* Vineyards in Chablis, Chablis district, Burgundy.

Greppo (I.)

A red wine from Montalcino, in the Tuscany region; made from the young Brunello vines.

Grésigny (F.)

A *Premier Cru* vineyard in Rully, Côte Chalonnaise district, Burgundy.

Gressier Grand Poujeaux, Château (F.)

An estate in Moulis, Haut Médoc district, Bordeaux; classified in 1932 as a *Cru Bourgeois*; it has been in the same family since 1724. 5,000 cases. 35 acres.

Grèves, Les (F.)

A *Grand Cru* vineyard in Aloxe-Corton, Côte de Beaune district, Burgundy, when used with Corton; otherwise, a *Premier Cru* vineyard. 5 acres.

Grèves, Les (F.)

A *Premier Cru* vineyard in Beaune, Côte de Beaune district, Burgundy. 79 acres.

Grèves Vigne de l'Enfant Jésus, Les (F.)

A section of the Grèves vineyard in Beaune, Côte de Beaune district, Burgundy, a *monopole* owned by Bouchard Père et Fils. 10 acres.

Grey, Terrence (F.)

An estate in Tain-L'Hermitage, northern Rhône region; owns Hermitage Domaine de l'Hermite – 8 acres.

Grey Riesling *also* Gray Riesling (U.S.)

1. A white grape grown in California. Also called Chauché Gris in France (grown around Poitiers).

2. A white wine from California; made from the Grey Riesling grape.

grey rot

See **pourriture grise.**

Greysac, Château (F.)

An estate in Bégadan, Médoc district, Bordeaux; classified in 1978 as a *Cru Grand Bourgeois*. 130 acres. 20,000 cases.

Grgich Hills Cellar (U.S.)   1977

A winery in Rutherford, Napa Valley, California; produces Cabernet, Zinfandel, Chardonnay, Johannisberg Riesling and Fumé Blanc wines. 10,000 cases. 140 acres.

Grignolino (I.)

A red grape grown in northern Italy and California.

Grignolino d'Asti AOC (I.)

1. A district around Asti, in the Piedmont region, which produces:

2. A red wine made from Grignolino and some Freisa grapes.

Grignolino del Monferrato Casalese DOC (I.)

1. A district around Casale, northeast of Asti, in the eastern Piedmont region, which produces:

2. A red wine made from Grignolino and some Freisa grapes.

Grillet, Château AOC (F.)

A famous vineyard and estate in St. Michel-sur-Rhône, Condrieu district, northern Rhône region; it has its own AOC; produces a famous white wine made from the Viognier grape. 4.2 acres (recently enlarged to 7.4 acres).

Grillo (I.)

1. A white grape grown in Sicily.

2. A red grape grown in California, possibly a red version of #1.

Gringet (F.)

A local white grape grown in the Savoie region.

Grinzing (A.)

A northern suburb of Vienna, where the *Heurige* wine (new wine) is drunk in special cafés called *Heurigen*.

Griotte-Chambertin AOC (F.)

One of 9 *Grand Cru* vineyards in Gevrey-Chambertin, Côte de Nuits district, Burgundy. 8 acres.

Gripa, Bernard (F.)

An estate in Mauves, St.-Joseph district, northern Rhône region; produces red and white St.-Joseph wines. 10 acres.

Grippat, Jean-Louis (F.)

An estate in Tournon, St.-Joseph district, Rhône region; owns 8.5 acres of St.-Joseph and 4 acres of Hermitage.

Gris, Château (F.)

A *Premier Cru* vineyard (part of Aux Crots vineyard) in Nuits-St.-Georges, Côte de Nuits district, Burgundy; a *monopole* owned by Lupé-Cholet. 10 acres.

Gris de Boulaouane (Mor.)

A well-known rosé wine from the Boulaouane district, southwest of Casablanca; made from the Grenache grape.

Grivault, Cuvée Albert (F.)

A white wine from the Hospices de Beaune, Côte de Beaune district, Burgundy. The *cuvée* is composed of the following vineyard: Meursault Les Charmes Dessus – 1.2 acres. 225 cases.

Grivault, Domaine Albert (F.)

An estate in Meursault, Côte de Beaune district, Burgundy. 8.5 acres, including Meursault Clos des Perrières Monopole – 2.5 acres, Les Perrières – 4 acres and Pommard Clos Blanc – 2.5 acres.

Grivelet, Domaine (F.)

An estate in Chambolle-Musigny, Côte de Nuits district, Burgundy; 12.5 acres, including Chambolle-Musigny les Amoureuses – .3 acre, Les Charmes – 1.6 acres, Aux Beaux-Bruns – 1 acre and Les Hauts Doix – .3 acre.

Grivelet, Émile (F.)

An estate in St.-Romain, Côte de Beaune district, Burgundy. 20 acres, including St.-Romain (red and white) and Auxey-Duresses (red and white).

Grivot, Jean (F.)

An estate in Vosne-Romanée, Côte de Nuits district, Burgundy. 30 acres, including Clos de Vougeot – 5 acres, Échézeaux – 1.2 acres, Vosne-Romanée Les Beaumonts – 2.4 acres, Les Suchots – .5 acre, *Premier Cru* - .7 acre, Nuits-St.-Georges aux Boudots – 2.4 acres and some Chambolle-Musigny.

Grk *also* Gerk (Y.)

1. A white grape grown in Dalmatia.

. A dry, white wine from Dalmatia, in Croatia, made from the Grk grape.

Groendruif (S. Af.)

The Sémillon grape of France; also called Green Grape.

Groenesteyn, Schloss (G.)

A famous estate in Kiedrich, Rheingau region. See **Schloss Groenesteyn.**

Groffier, Domaine Robert (F.)

An estate in Morey-St.-Denis, Côte de Nuits district, Burgundy. 17 acres, including Chambertin-Clos de Bèze – 1 acre, Bonnes Mares – 2.5 acres and Chambolle-Musigny Les Amoureuses – 2.5 acres.

Grolleau *also* **Groslot (F.)**

A red grape grown in the Anjou region, Loire Valley; used for making rosé wines. Also called Pineau de Saumur.

Groot Constantia EWO (S. Af.) 1685, 1975

An important estate in Constantia, in the Cape district, owned by the government; produces Cabernet, Pinot Noir, Pinotage, Shiraz, Heerenrood (a blended red wine), Chenin Blanc, Kerner and Riesling wines. 30,000 cases. 280 acres.

Groppello (I.)

1. A red grape grown in the Lombardy and Trentino-Alto Adige regions.

2. A red wine from Brescia, west of Lake Garda, in the Lombardy region; made mostly from the Groppello grape.

Gros Bouchet (F.)

In St.-Émilion and Pomerol, another name for the Cabernet Franc grape. Also called Bouchet.

Gros Frère et Soeur, Domaine (F.)

An estate in Vosne-Romanée, Côte de Nuits district, Burgundy. 18 acres, including Richebourg – 2.5 acres, Clos de Vougeot – 4 acres (the section formerly known as Les Musigny du Clos Vougeot) and some Vosne-Romanée.

Gros Manseng (F.)

A white grape grown in the Jurançon district, in the Southwest region.

Gros Noiren (F.)

In Arbois, in the Jura region, another name for the Pinot Noir grape.

Gros Père et Fils (F.)

An estate in Vosne-Romanée, Côte de Nuits district, Burgundy; formerly part of Domaine Gros-Renaudot, now run by Jean and François Gros. 30 acres, including Richebourg – 2.5 acres, Clos de Vougeot – 2.5 acres, Vosne-Romanée Clos des Réas Monopole – 5 acres and some Chambolle-Musigny and Vosne-Romanée.

Gros Plant (F.)

In the Loire Valley, another name for the Folle Blanche grape.

gros rouge (F.)

Ordinary red wine from the Midi, in southern France.

Gros Vien (I.)

A red grape grown in the Valle d'Aosta region; used in making Chambave Rouge wine.

Gros des Vignes, Le (F.)

A vineyard section of Hermitage, northern Rhône region; produces red wine.

Groseilles, Les (F.)

A *Premier Cru* vineyard in Chambolle-Musigny, Côte de Nuits district, Burgundy. 3 acres.

Gross Highland Winery (U.S.)   1934

A winery in Absecon, north of Atlantic City, New Jersey; produces sparkling wines and red, white and rosé wines from Maréchal Foch, Noah, Dutchess, Niagara and Ives grapes. The name was changed to Bernard d'Arcy Wine Cellars in 1982. 80 acres.

Gross-Vernatsch (G.)

The German name for the Trollinger grape.

Grosse Vidure (F.)

Another name for the Cabernet Franc grape.

Grosskohlausen (F.)

A vineyard in Voegtlinshoffen, Haut-Rhin district, Alsace region.

Grosslage (G.)

A large area of several vineyards within a *Bereich*, or district, legally joined because of similarities of taste and style.

Groslot *also* Grolleau (F.)

A red grape, also called Pineau de Saumur, grown in the Anjou region, Loire Valley.

Grosso Nero (I.)

A local red grape grown in Sicily.

Groth Vineyards (U.S.)   1982

A winery in Oakville, Napa Valley, California; produces Cabernet, Chardonnay and Sauvignon Blanc wines. 130 acres. 10,000 cases.

Grover Gulch Winery (U.S.)   1979

A small winery in Soquel, Santa Cruz County, California; produces Cabernet, Zinfandel, Petite Sirah and Carignane wines.

growth (F.)

A *cru;* a vineyard, *château* or winery.

Gruaud-Larose, Château (F.)

An estate in St.-Julien, Haut Médoc district, Bordeaux; classified in 1855 as a *Deuxième Cru*. It was formed in 1757 from three properties and was called Fonbedeau, later changed to Gruau or Gruaud, the Larose added in 1778, when it was inherited by the new owner. It was divided into two properties in 1867 (Gruaud-Larose-Faure and Gruaud-Larose-Sarget), and re-united in 1934. 190 acres. 30,000 cases.

Gruenchers, Les (F.)

A *Premier Cru* vineyard in Chambolle-Musigny, Côte de Nuits district, Burgundy. 5 acres.

Gruenchers, Les (F.)

A *Premier Cru* vineyard in Morey-St.-Denis, Côte de Nuits district, Burgundy. 7.5 acres.

Grumello DOC (I.)

A red wine from the Valtellina DOC district, in the northern Lombardy region; made from at least 95% Nebbiolo (known here as Chiavennasca) grapes.

Grüner Veltliner (A.)

An important white grape grown in northeastern Austria.

Guadalupe (Mex.)

A district in Baja California, 50 miles south of the California border.

Guadet-St.-Julien, Château (F.)

An estate in St.-Émilion, Bordeaux; classified in 1955 as a *Grand Cru Classé*. 2,000 cases. 13 acres.

Guarnaccia (I.)

A red grape grown in the Campania region, southern Italy, to make red Ischia wine.

Guarnaccia Bianca (I.)

A white grape grown in the Calabria region.

Guérets, Les (F.)

A *Premier Cru* vineyard in Aloxe-Corton, Côte de Beaune district, Burgundy. 6 acres.

Guérin, Domaine René (F.)

An estate in Puligny-Montrachet, Côte de Beaune district, Burgundy. 22 acres, including Puligny-Montrachet Hameau de Blagny – 1.2 acres, Blagny – 2 acres, Les Chalumeaux – 1.2 acres and Champs Gain – 4 acres.

Guerrouane (Mor.)

An important district southwest of Meknès, which produces red and rosé wines from Carignane, Cinsault and Grenache grapes.

Guerry, Château (F.)

An estate in Bourg, Côtes de Bourg district, Bordeaux.

Guettes, Aux (F.)

A *Premier Cru* vineyard (in part) in Savigny, Côte de Beaune district, Burgundy. 53 acres.

Guettes, Domaine du Clos des (F.)

An estate in Aloxe-Corton, Côte de Beaune district, Burgundy; run by La Reine Pédauque. Owns 6 acres of Savigny Clos des Guettes.

Guglielmo Winery, Emilio (U.S.) 1925

A winery in Morgan Hill, Santa Clara County, California; produces mostly jug wines and some red varietals. 40,000 cases. 150 acres.

Guigal, La Maison (F.) 1946

An estate and merchant in Ampuis, Côte-Rôtie district, Rhône region. Owns 7 acres of Côte-Rôtie, including La Mouline and La Landonne vineyards. 12,000 cases from their own and purchased grapes.

Guigone de Salins, Cuvée (F.)

A red wine from the Hospices de Beaune, Côte de Beaune district, Burgundy. The *cuvée* is composed of the following vineyards in Beaune: Les Bressandes – 2.5 acres, En Senrey – 2 acres and Champs Pimont – 1.5 acres. 500 cases.

Guihoux, Marcel-Joseph (F.)

An estate in Mouzillon, Muscadet de Sèvre-et-Maine district, Loire Valley. 60 acres.

Guild Winery and Distillers (U.S.) 1937

A large co-op winery with wineries in Lodi, Fresno and Ukiah; uses the brand names of Cribari, Roma, Cresta Blanca, Tavola and Winemaster; over 100 different wines, mostly generic jug wines.

Guillemard, Domaine Jules (F.)

An estate in Pommard, Côte de Beaune district, Burgundy. 20 acres, including Pommard Les Rugiens – 1.2 acres, Les Epenots – 1.2 acres, La Platière – 2.5 acres, Beaune Le Clos des Mouches – 1.2 acres and Les Épenottes – 1.2 acres.

Guillemot, Pierre (F.)

An estate in Savigny-lès-Beaune, Côte de Beaune district, Burgundy. 12 acres, including 3 acres of Savigny Aus Serpentières.

Guimaraens Vinhos SARL (P.) 1822

A Port producer in Vila Nova de Gaia; shipper of Fonseca's wines. Owns Quinta do Cruzeiro and Quinta Santo Antonio. 300 acres.

Guimonière, Château de la (F.)

An estate in Rochefort-sur-Loire, Coteaux du Layon-Chaume district, Anjou region, Loire Valley. 40 acres.

Guindon, Jacques (F.)

An estate in Saint-Géréon, Muscadet des Coteaux de la Loire district, Loire Valley; produces Muscadet sur lie and Coteaux d'Ancenis wines. 20,000 cases. 60 acres.

Guiraud, Château (F.)

An estate in Sauternes, Sauternes district, Bordeaux; classified in 1855 as a Premier Cru; it was formerly called Château Bayle in 1855. 70% Sémillon and 30% Sauvignon grapes. 135 acres. 7,000 cases. Also makes a dry red and dry white wine.

Guiraud-Cheval Blanc, Château (F.)

An estate in St.-Ciers-de-Canessé, Côtes de Bourg district, Bordeaux.

Guita, La (Sp.)

A well-known sherry wine (a *manzanilla posada*) made by Hijos de Rainera Pérez Marín in Sanlucar de Barrameda; also the popular name of the *bodega*.

Gumpoldskirchen (G.)

1. A town and district south of Vienna, in the Lower Austria region, which produces:

2. Dry and sweet white wines made from Grüner Veltliner, Spätrot, Zierfändler and Rotgipfler grapes, and sometimes Gewürztraminer and Riesling grapes.

Gundlach-Bundschu (U.S)   1858, 1973
first wine 1976

An old, re-opened winery southeast of Sonoma City, Sonoma County, California; produces Cabernet, Pinot Noir, Merlot, Zinfandel, Gewürztraminer, Johannisberg Riesling, Kleinberger (Elbling) and Sylvaner wines. 300 acres. 25,000 cases.

gunflint

An element not actually present in certain white wines, but a term used to describe a characteristic taste. Wines said to taste of gunflint are made from grapes grown in chalky subsoils; Chablis is the best example; called *goût de pierre à fusil*, in French.

Guntersblum (G.)

A village in the Rheinhessen region, Bereich Nierstein, Grosslagen Krötenbrunnen and Vogelsgärten. The vineyards are: Eiserne Hand, Sankt Julianenbrunnen, Sonnenberg, Sonnenhang and Steinberg in Grosslage Krötenbrunnen; and Authental, Bornpfad, Himmelthal, Kreuzkapelle and Steig-Terressen and Teufelskopf in Grosslage Vogelsgärten. 1,500 acres.

Guntrum, Louis (G.)   1824

An estate and merchant in Nierstein, Rheinhessen region; owns important vineyards in Nierstein, Oppenheim and Dienheim. 160 acres.

Gurdzhaani (U.S.S.R.)

A white wine from the republic of Georgia SSR.

Gurgue, Château La (F.)

An estate in Margaux, Haut-Médoc district, Bordeaux; classified in 1932 as a *Cru Bourgeois*. 3,500 cases. 25 acres.

Gutedel (G.)

A white or pink grape grown mostly in the Baden region; low in acid; makes light, fresh wines with low alcohol content. Also called Chassalas Doré in California, Chasselas in France, Fendant in Switzerland and Sweetwater.

Gutenborner (G.)

A white grape – a cross of Müller-Thurgau and Chasselas Napoléon; developed at the State Technical and Research Institute, Geisenheim, Germany.

Gutsname (G.)

A wine estate.

Gutsverwaltung (G.)

A vineyard management company.

Gutturnio dei Colli Piacentini DOC (I.)

A red wine from the southwestern hills of Piacenza, in the western Emilia-Romagna region; made from 60% Barbera and 40% Bonarda grapes.

Guyard de Changey, Cuvée (F.)

A red wine from the Hospices de Nuits, Nuits-St.-Georges, Côte de Nuits district, Burgundy. The *cuvée* is composed of Nuits-St.-Georges Les Murgers – .5 acre.

Guyon (F.)

See **Fils D'Antonin Guyon.**

guyot (F.)

A method of vine-training in which the canes of one arm emanating from the trunk are trained on wires; used in the Médoc district and in Burgundy.

Guyot, Domaine de L'Héritier (F.)

See **Héritier Guyot.**

Gyöngyös-Visonta (H.)

1. A district in the Matraalja region of northeastern Hungary, which produces:

2. Red, white and sparkling wines.

gyropalette (F.)
A square-shaped device that acts as a mechanical riddler, used in Champagne; holds up to 500 bottles. Also called *champanex* (hexagonal-shaped) and in Spain, *girasol*.

H

HMR (U.S.)

Hoffman Mountain Ranch, a winery in Paso Robles, San Luis Obispo County California.

Hnos. (Sp.)

The abbreviation for *Hermanos* (Brothers).

Habersham Vineyards (U.S.)   **1983**

A winery in Baldwin, Georgia; planted with *vinifera* grapes. 30 acres.

habzó (H.)

Sparkling.

Hacienda Wine Cellars (U.S.)   **1973**

A winery in Sonoma, Sonoma Valley, Sonoma County, California; produces Cabernet, Pinot Noir, Zinfandel, Chardonnay, Gewürztraminer, Johannisberg Riesling and Chenin Blanc wines. 18,000 cases. 110 acres.

Hagelberg (F.)

A vineyard in Voegtlinshoffen, Haut-Rhin district, Alsace region.

Hagnau (G.)

An important village in the Baden region, Bereich Bodensee, Grosslage Sonnenufer. The only vineyard is Burgstall.

Hahnenberg (F.)

A vineyard in Châtenois, southern Bas-Rhin district, Alsace region.

Hahnhof, Weingut (G.)

An estate and merchant in Deidesheim, Rheinpfalz region; owns vineyards in Deidesheim, Forst and Ruppertsberger. 60 acres.

Haight Vineyards (U.S.)   **1978**

A winery in Litchfield, Connecticut; produces Chardonnay, Riesling and Foch wines. 2,000 cases. 20 acres.

Hainfeld (G.)

A village in the Rheinpfalz region, Bereich Südliche Weinstrasse, Grosslage Ordensgut. The vineyards are Kapelle, Kirchenstück and Letten.

Hajós (H.)

A town in the Mecsek district, in southwestern Hungary; produces red wine from the Cabernet grape.

Halbrot (Sw.)

A Swiss term for rosé wine.

Halbstück (G.)

A cask used for storing and aging wines from the Rheingau region; 600-liter or 66-case capacity.

halbtrocken (G.)

Half-dry or semi-dry; sweeter than *trocken*, but drier than *Kabinett*.

Hallereau, Joseph (F.)

An estate in Vallet, Muscadet de Sèvre-et-Maine district, Loire Valley. 45 acres.

Hallet, Château (F.)

An unclassified estate in Barsac, Sauternes district, Bordeaux. 2,200 cases. 25 acres.

Hallgarten, Arthur (G.)   **1898**

A merchant in Geisenheim, Rheingau region; markets estate and regional wines.

Hallgarten (G.)

A village in the Rheingau region, Bereich Johannisberg, Grosslage Mehrholzchen. The vineyards are Hendelberg, Jungfer, Schönhell, and Würzgarten. 520 acres.

Hambledon (E.)   1951

A vineyard (one of the first new vineyards in modern England) in Mill Down, Hambledon, Hampshire; grows Chardonnay, Pinot Noir and Pinot Meunier grapes. 5 acres.

hameau (F.)

A hamlet; a little village.

Hameau de Blagny (F.)

A *Premier Cru* vineyard in Puligny-Montrachet, Côte de Beaune district, Burgundy. 10 acres.

Hamlet Hill Vineyard (U.S.)   1980
                                                        planted 1975

A winery in Pomfret, northeastern Connecticut; produces wines made from hybrid grapes. 15 acres.

Hammel, G. (Sw.)   1920

An estate, winery and merchant in Rolle, La Côte district, Vaud region; produces many wines from their own and other domaines. 60 acres.

Hammurabi, Code of

An ancient document (Babylon, c. 1,750 B.C.) which cites the conditions for the sale of wine and the punishment for selling fraudulant wine.

Hanepoot (S. Af.)

The South African name for the Muscat d'Alexandre grape.

Hannappier, Léon (F.)   1816

A merchant in Bordeaux.

Hanteillan, Château (F.)

An estate in Cissac, Haut-Médoc district, Bordeaux; classified in 1978 as a *Cru Grand*

Bourgeois; combined with Château Larrivaux in 1979. 15,000 cases. 95 acres.

Hanwood Port (Aus.)

Sweet, red dessert wine, Port-style, from McWilliams winery, in the Riverina district, New South Wales.

Hanzell (U.S.)   1952, 1st wine 1956

A small winery just north of Sonoma City, Sonoma County, California; famous for Chardonnay (first produced in 1956) and Pinot Noir (first produced in 1965) wines. 35 acres, and 5 acres planted with Cabernet Sauvignon. 2,000 cases.

Haraszthy, J.J. and Son (U.S.)   1975, 1978

A small winery in Glen Ellen, Sonoma County, California; produces Pinot Noir, Zinfandel, Chardonnay, Johannisberg Riesling and Gewürztraminer wines from purchased grapes and/or wine. 6,000 cases.

Harbor Winery (U.S.)   1972

A small winery in Sacramento, Sacramento County, California; produces Cabernet, Zinfandel, Chardonnay and Mission wines from purchased grapes. 1,200 cases.

hard

A term used to describe wine that has excessive tannin, a sign that the wine is too young to drink.

Hardt, *also* Harth (F.)

A vineyard in Colmar, Haut-Rhin district, Alsace region.

Hardy's (Aus.)   1857

A large winery in McLaren Vale, near Adelaide, Southern Vales district, South Australia; also has vineyards in the Barossa Valley; known for Port-style wines made from Shiraz grapes, Cabernet, blended from various regions as well as other red and white wines; some from purchased grapes. 800,000 cases. 750 acres.

Hargrave (U.S.)   1973, 1st wine 1975

The first commercial winery on Long Island, in the town of Cutchogue, on the North Fork, Suffolk County, New York State; produces Cabernet, Chardonnay, Merlot, Pinot Noir, Riesling and Sauvignon Blanc wines. 40 acres.

Haro (Sp.)

A city in the Rioja region, the center of the wine trade in that region.

Harriague (Ur.)

A grape grown in Uraguay, the same as the Tannet grape of France.

Hárslevelü (H.)

Hungarian for "lime leaf," a grape used to made Debröi Hárslevelü wine; it is also used in some Tokaji wines.

Hart Winery (U.S.)   1980

A small winery in Temecula, Riverside County, southern California; produces Cabernet, Merlot, Petite Sirah, Gamay Beaujolais and Sauvignon Blanc wines. 1,500 cases. 10 acres.

Harth, *also* Hardt (F.)

A vineyard in Colmar, Haut-Rhin district, Alsace region.

Harvey & Sons (España) Ltd., John (Sp.)
1796, 1970

A famous English company, this branch in Jerez de la Frontera; blends and markets many types of Sherries, including the famous Bristol Milk and Bristol Cream. Since 1970 owns vineyards and *bodegas* in the Sherry region.

Hasandede (T.)

A white grape grown in central Turkey.

Hatschbourg *also* Hatschburg (F.)

A *Grand Cru* vineyard mostly in Voegtlinshoffen, and partly in Hattstatt, Haut-Rhin district, Alsace region.

Hattenheim (G.)

A village in the Rheingau region, Bereich Johannisberg, Grosslage Deutelsberg. The vineyards are Engelmannsberg, Hassel, Heiligenberg, Mannberg, Nussbrunnen, Pfaffenberg, Schützenhaus, Steinberg (an Ortsteil – does not use the Hattenheim name) and Wisselbrunnen. 575 acres.

Hauller et Fils, Jean (F.)

An estate in Dambach-la-Ville, Alsace region. 45 acres, including vines in Châtenois, Hahnenberg and Scherwiller.

Hauptlese (G.)

The main harvest of the grape-picking, as opposed to late-harvest or early-harvest.

haut *also* haute (F.)

High, in reference to direction, and not to quality; i.e. upstream, or up river, or on higher ground.

Haut-Bages-Libéral, Château (F.)

An estate in Pauillac, Haut-Médoc district, Bordeaux; classified in 1855 as a *Cinquième Cru*; the wine was made at Château Pontet-Canet until 1972; it is now Château-bottled. 55 acres. 8,000 cases.

Haut-Bages-Monpelou, Château (F.)

An estate in Pauillac, Haut-Médoc district, Bordeaux; classified in 1978 as a *Cru Bourgeois*. 4,500 cases. 25 acres.

Haut-Bailly, Château (F.)

An estate in Léognan, Graves district, Bordeaux; classified in 1959 as a *Cru Classé* for red wine. 5,000 cases. 60 acres.

Haut-Batailley, Château (F.)

An estate in Pauillac, Haut-Médoc district, Bordeaux; classified in 1855 as a *Cinquième Cru*; was part of Château Batailley until 1924; the wine was made at Ducru-Beaucaillou until 1974. 50 acres. 6,500 cases.

Haut-Beaujolais (F.)

The northern half of the Beaujolais district, containing the 9 *Crus* Beaujolais and the villages that make up Beaujolais-Villages;

more granite and manganese in the soil results in higher-quality wines than those of the southern half, or Bas-Beaujolais.

Haut-Bénauge AOC (F.)

A sweet, white wine from the Entre-Deux-Mers, Bordeaux region, under the *Bordeaux Supérieur* designation; made from Sauvignon, Sémillon and Muscadelle grapes.

Haut-Beychevelle Gloria, Château (F.)

An unclassified estate in St.-Julien, Haut-Médoc district, Bordeaux; owned by Château Gloria.

Haut-Bommes, Château (F.)

An unclassified estate in Bommes, Sauternes district, Bordeaux. 1,400 cases. 18 acres.

Haut-Brion, Château (F.)

A famous estate in Pessac, Graves district, Bordeaux; the red wine was included in the 1855 classification of the Médoc as a *Premier Cru*; the red and white wines were classified in 1959 and 1960, respectively, as *Crus Classés* of the Graves district. The second wine is labeled Bahans-Haut-Brion. 100 acres red, 10 acres white. 12,000 cases.

Haut-Cadet, Château (F.)

An estate in St.-Émilion, Bordeaux; classified in 1955 as a *Grand Cru*. 3,600 cases. 32 acres.

Haut-Canteloup, Château (F.)

An estate in Couquèques, Médoc district, Bordeaux; classified in 1978 as a *Cru Bourgeois*. 70 acres. 20,000 cases.

Haut-Comtat VDQS (F.)

A designation for red and rosé wine from Nyons, in the Côtes du Rhône district, Rhône region; made from Grenache grapes, with some other Rhône grapes.

Haut-Corbin, Château (F.)

An estate in St.-Émilion, Bordeaux; classified in 1969 as a *Grand Cru Classé*. 2,000 cases. 10 acres.

Haut-Dahra (Alg.)

A red wine district east of Oran, in the Oran region.

Haut-Garin (F.)

An estate in Bégadan, Médoc district, Bordeaux; classified in 1978 as a *Cru Bourgeois*. 15 acres. 5,000 cases.

Haut-Marbuzet, Château (F.)

An estate in St.-Estèphe, Haut-Médoc district, Bordeaux; classified in 1978 as a *Cru Grand Bourgeois Exceptionnel*. 20,000 cases. 100 acres.

Haut-Médoc AOC (F.)

The southern and higher (up river) part of the Médoc district just north of Bordeaux city, in the Bordeaux region. The best *communes* in the district are found here, including Margaux, Pauillac, St.-Julien and St.-Estèphe, and which contain most of the great châteaux of the entire region. The AOC designation may include lesser growths and blended red wines from this district.

Haut-Montravel AOC (F.)

The designation for sweet white wine from a few select villages in the hills of the Montravel district, west of Bergerac, in the Southwest region; the other villages in the hills are under the Côtes de Montravel AOC; made from Sémillon, Sauvignon and Muscadelle grapes.

Haut Mornag (Tun.)

Red, white and rosé wines produced by a union of co-ops.

Haut-Padarnac, Château (F.)

An estate in Pauillac, Haut-Médoc district, Bordeaux; classified in 1978 as a *Cru Bourgeois*.

Haut-Peyraguey, Clos (F.)

An estate in Bommes, Sauternes district, Bordeaux; classified as a *Premier Cru*; in 1855 it was part of Château Peyraguey but was separated in 1879. 35 acres. 2,500 cases.

Haut-Rhin (F.)

The southern half of the Alsace region, producing wines generally believed to be of better quality than those of the Bas-Rhin, in the north.

Haut-Sarpe, Château (F.)

An estate in the commune of St. Christophe des Bardes, St.-Émilion, Bordeaux; classified in 1969 as a *Grand Cru Classé*. 25 acres. 6,000 cases.

Hautes Cornières, Domaine des (F.)

An estate in Santenay, Côte de Beaune district, Burgundy. 30 acres, including Corton – 1.2 acres, Santenay Les Gravières – 5 acres, La Comme – 2.5 acres, Chassagne-Montrachet Morgeot – 5 acres and Aloxe-Corton – 7.5 acres.

Hautes-Côtes de Beaune AOC (F.)

A district covering the hills behind the Côte de Beaune, Burgundy. The AOC designation is Bourgogne-Hautes-Côtes de Beaune; produces red, white and rosé wines.

Hautes-Côtes de Nuits AOC (F.)

A district covering the hills behind the Côte de Nuits, Burgundy. The AOC designation is Bourgogne-Hautes-Côtes de Nuits; produces red, white and rosé wines.

Hauts-Doix, Les (F.)

A *Premier Cru* vineyard in Chambolle-Musigny, Côte de Nuits district, Burgundy. 2.5 acres.

Hauts-Jarrons (F.)

A *Premier Cru* vineyard in Savigny-lès-Beaune, Côte de Beaune district, Burgundy. 15 acres.

Hauts-Marconnets (F.)

A *Premier Cru* vineyard in Savigny-lès-Beaune, Côte de Beaune district, Burgundy. 23 acres.

Hauts-Pruliers, Les (F.)

A *Premier Cru* vineyard in Nuits-St.-Georges, Côte de Nuits district, Burgundy. 11 acres.

Hawk Crest (U.S.)

The second label of Stags Leap Wine Cellars, Napa Valley, California.

Haywood Nursery (U.S.)   1980

A winery in Sonoma City, Sonoma County, California; produces Cabernet, Zinfandel, Chardonnay and Johannisberg Riesling wines. 7,000 cases. 100 acres.

Healdsburg Wine Company (U.S.)   1979

A winery in Healdsburg, Sonoma County California; produces Cabernet, Pinot Noir and Chardonnay wines. 4,000 cases.

Hecker Pass Winery (U.S.)   1972

A winery in Gilroy, Santa Clara County, California; produces numerous varietal and generic wines. 15 acres. 3,500 cases.

hectare (F.)

A European metric measure of land equal to 100 ares, or 10,000 square meters, or 2.47 acres.

hectolitre (F.)

A European metric measure equal to 100 liters, or 26.4 U.S.gallons, or 22 imperial gallons.

Heerenrood (S. Af.)

A blended red wine from the Groot Constantia estate, in the Constantia district.

Heidebodenhof, Weingut (A.)

An estate and merchant in Pamhagen, Burgenland region; owns vineyards in Seewinkel. 40 acres.

Heidsieck, Charles (F.)   1851

A champagne producer in Reims; La Royale (first vintage, 1955, released in 1963) is the *cuvée de prestige*; owns no vineyards. 3.5 million bottles.

Heidsieck & Co. Monopole (F.) 　　1785

A Champagne producer in Reims; Diamant Bleu is the *cuvée de prestige*. 2 million bottles. 265 acres.

Heilbronn (G.)

A village in the Württemberg region, Bereich Württembergisch Unterland, Grosslagen Kirchenweinberg and Staufenberg. The vineyards are Altenberg and Sonnenberg in Grosslage Kirchenweinberg and Stahlbühl, Stiftsberg and Wartberg in Grosslage Staufenberg.

Heiligenkreuz (A.)

A Cistercian monastery in Thallern, near Gumpoldskirchen, south of Vienna; famous for its white wines from the Wiege vineyard. See **Thallern, Freigut.**

Heim, Alfred (F.)

An estate and merchant in Westhalten, Haut-Rhin district, Alsace; 12 acres, including Strangenberg vineyard – 2.5 acres (Pinot Blanc).

Heineman Winery (U.S.) 　　1896

A winery in the village of Put-in-Bay, South Bass Island, in Lake Erie, Ohio; produces a dry white Catawba and other wines made from American grapes. 20 acres.

Heitz Wine Cellars (U.S.) 　　1961

A famous winery in St. Helena, Napa Valley, California; produces Cabernet, Pinot Noir, Barbera, Grignolino, Chardonnay, Gewürztraminer and Angelica wines, mostly from purchased grapes. The best known wines are: Martha's Vineyard Cabernet, Fay Vineyard Cabernet and Bella Oaks Cabernet. 30,000 cases. 40 acres.

Helbon *also* **Chalybon (Gr.)**

An ancient white wine of Syria or Lebanon; a favorite of Persian kings; mentioned in the *Bible (Ezekial).*

Helfensteiner (G.)

A red grape – a cross of Frühburgunder and Trollinger; developed at the State

Teaching and Research Institute, Weinsberg, Germany; grown in the Württemberg region.

Hemus (Bul.)

A sweet, white wine from Karlovo, in central Bulgaria; made from the Misket grape.

Hengst (F.)

A *Grand Cru* vineyard in Wintzenheim, Haut-Rhin district, Alsace region.

Henriot (F.) 　　1808

A Champagne producer in Reims; the special *cuvées* are Réserve Baron Philippe de Rothschild (since 1973) and Souverain (since 1966). 1.5 million bottles. 270 acres.

Henriques & Henriques (P.)

A producer of Madeira wines.

Henry Winery (U.S.) 　　1972

A winery in Umpqua, Umpqua Valley, southwestern Oregon; produces Pinot Noir, Chardonnay and Gewürztraminer wines. 15 acres.

Henschke (Aus.) 　　c. 1850

A winery and vineyard in Keyneton, Barossa Valley district, South Australia; produces well-known reds: Hill of Grace and Mount Edelstone, from Old Shiraz vines and some whites: Rhine Riesling and Sémillon. 30,000 cases. 250 acres.

Heppenheim (G.)

A village in the Hessische Bergstrasse region, Bereich Starkenburg, Grosslage Schlossberg. The vineyards are Eckweg, Guldenzoll, Maiberg, Steinkopf, Stemmler and Zentgericht.

Herbanges, Domaine (F.)

An estate in the Muscadet region, Loire Valley. 50 acres.

Herbemont (U.S.)

A red hybrid grape – a cross of *Vitis vinifera* and *Vitis aestivalis* varieties; developed in Columbia, South Carolina by Nicholas

Herbemont, c.1820; grown in the eastern U.S. and in Brazil.

L'Héritier Guyot, Domaine de (F.) 1845

An estate in Vougeot, Côte de Nuits district, Burgundy. 13 acres, including Clos de Vougeot – 2.5 acres, Clos Blanc de Vougeot Monopole – 7.5 acres and Vougeot *Premier Cru* - 2.5 acres.

Hermanos (Sp.)

Brothers.

Hermitage AOC (F.)

A famous district in the northern Rhône region; famous for fine red and white wines from the slopes above the village of Tain-l'Hermitage; the red wine is made from the Syrah grape, sometimes bottled under vineyards names such as: Les Bessards, Le Méal, L'Hermite and La Chapelle. The white wines are made from Marsanne and Roussanne grapes. 375 acres.

Hermitage (S.Af.)

A red grape grown in South Africa, the same as the Cinsault grape.

Hermitage *also* Ermitage (Sw.)

A white wine from the Valais region made from the Marsanne grape.

L'Hermitage, Domaine (F.)

An estate in Bouzeron, Côte Chalonnaise district, southern Burgundy. 55 acres, including Bouzeron – 20 acres, Rully – 30 acres and Mercurey – 5 acres.

hermitaged

A term applied to red Bordeaux wines which, in the past, had been strengthened with wines from the Hermitage district, in the Rhône region. This process is no longer used.

L'Hermite (F.)

A vineyard section of Hermitage, in the northern Rhône region; grows red grapes.

Heroldrebe (G.)

A red grape – a cross of Portugieser and Lemberger; developed at the State Teaching and Research Institute, Weinsberg, Germany, named after the breeder.

Heron Hill Vineyard (U.S.) 1977

A winery in Hammondsport, on Lake Keuka, Finger Lakes region, New York; produces Chardonnay, Riesling, Aurora, Seyval Blanc and Ravat wines. 8,000 cases. 40 acres.

Herrenweg (F.)

A vineyard in Turckheim, Haut-Rhin district, Alsace region.

Herrschaft *also* Bundner Herrschaft (Sw.)

A district in eastern Switzerland, near Liechtenstein.

Hervelets, Les (F.)

A *Premier Cru* vineyard in Fixin, Côte de Nuits district, Burgundy. 9 acres.

Hesiod (Gr.)

An ancient Greek poet, c. 700 B.C., who wrote the poem *Works and Days*, which describes vine-growing.

Hessische Bergstrasse (G.)

One of 11 *Anbaugebiet* (regions) in Germany. It is the smallest, containing only 2 *Bereiche*: Starkenburg and Umstadt, and including only 10 villages. 900 acres.

Hessisches Weingut, Landgräflich (G.)

An estate in Johannisberg, Rheingau region; owns vineyards in Rüdesheim, Geisenheim, Johannisberg, Winkel, Eltville and Kiedrich. 75 acres.

Heurige (A.)

1. German for "the new wine," a local, home-made, young, white wine sold by the glass and pitcher in special wine restaurants or taverns in Grinzing, Neustift, Sievering, Nussdorf and Kahlenberg, suburbs of Vienna.

2. The name for the establishment that makes and sells the *Heurige* wine.

Heyl zu Herrnsheim, Weingut Freiherr (G.)

An estate in Nierstein, Rheinhessen region; owns vineyards in Nierstein and Dienheim. 70 acres.

Hidalgo (Mex.)

Premium wines from the Cavas de San Juan Winery, north of Mexico City, San Juan district; made from Cabernet, Pinot Noir, Gamay, Chardonnay and other grapes.

Higgins (U.S.)

A white muscadine grape; grown in Florida and Texas.

Highland Manor Winery (U.S.)   1980

A winery near Nashville, Tennessee; grows hybrid, *vinifera* and native American grapes. 7 acres.

High Tor Vineyard (U.S.)   1954, 1981

A well-known estate near New City, Hudson River region, New York; grows only French hybrids. 15 acres. 2,500 cases. The winery closed down after the 1976 vintage and re-opened in 1981.

hijos (Sp.)

Sons.

Hill, Cavas (Sp.)   1660

An old winery in Moja-Vilafranca del Penedès, Catalonia region; produces several still and sparkling wines.

Hill Winery, William (U.S.)   1980

A winery in Napa City, Napa Valley, California; produces Cabernet and Chardonnay wines. 8,000 cases. 700 acres.

Hillcrest Vineyard (U.S.)   1963

A winery and vineyard near Roseburg, Umpqua Valley, southwestern Oregon; produces Cabernet, Pinot Noir, Zinfandel, Riesling, Chardonnay, Gewürztraminer,

Sémillon and Sauvignon Blanc wines. 10,000 cases. 30 acres.

Hinzerling Vineyard (U.S.)   1971 first wine 1976

A winery in Prosser, Yakima Valley district, in southern Washington; produces Cabernet, Merlot, Pinot Noir, Chardonnay, Gewürztraminer and Johannisberg Riesling wines. 20 acres.

Hippocras

A wine made in the Middle Ages with honey and spices added, and filtered through a wool filter.

Hirpinia *also* Irpinia (I.)

1. A district in the central Campania region, which produces:

2. Red and rosé wines from Sanginoso, Olivella, Aglianico, Sangiovese, Piedirosso and Barbera grapes and white wines from Coda di Volpe, Malvasia, Greco and Trebbiano grapes.

Hirtzberger, Weingut Franz (A.)

A small estate in Spitz, Wachau region; produces Grüner Veltliner and other wines. 4,000 cases. 20 acres.

Hochheim (G.)

An important village on the Main River, 10 miles east of the Rhine river, in the Rheingau region, Bereich Johannisberg, Grosslage Daubhaus. The vineyards are: Berg, Domdechaney, Herrnberg, Hofmeister, Hölle, Kirchenstück, Königen Victoriaberg, Reichestal, Sömmerheil, Stein and Stielweg. 520 acres.

hock (E.)

The British term for wine from the Rheingau region of Germany; also loosely applied to all Rhine wines; derived from Hochheim, a village in the Rheingau region.

Hof, Hof- (G.)

A court; a manor-house.

Hoffman Mountain Ranch
also **HMR (U.S.)**   **1964**
A winery in Paso Robles, San Luis Obispo County, California; produces Cabernet, Pinot Noir, Zinfandel, Chardonnay, Johannisberg Riesling, Chenin Blanc, and Sylvaner wines. 40,000 cases. 180 acres.

Hoffman's (Aus.)
A winery in the Barossa Valley district, South Australia; known for sweet Muscat, Cabernet and Shiraz wines.

Hofstätter, J. (I.)   **1907**
A winery in Tramin, Trentino-Alto Adige region; produces Alto Adige, Caldaro, De Vite and Kolbenhofer wines; made from their own and purchased grapes. 85 acres.

hogshead
A cask for shipping wines and spirits, varying in size from 55 gallons in Bordeaux and Burgundy to 72 gallons for brandy.

Holdenried (U.S.)
A vineyard in Kelseyville, Lake County, California. 350 acres.

hollejo (Sp.)
A grapeskin.

Homburg (G.)
A village in the Franken region, Bereich Maindrieck; there is no *Grosslage*. The vineyards are Edelfrau and Kallmuth. 115 acres.

L'Homme (F.)
A vineyard section of Hermitage, northern Rhône region; grows red grapes.

L'Homme Mort (F.)
A *Premier Cru* vineyard in La Chapelle-Vaupelteigne, in the Chablis district, Burgundy; usually included as part of the Fourchaume vineyard.

Honig Cellars, Louis (U.S.)   **1981**
A winery in Rutherford, Napa Valley, California; produces only Sauvignon Blanc wine; uses the HNW label. 50 acres. 6,000 cases.

Hop Kiln Winery (U.S.)   **1975**
A winery in Healdsburg, Russian River Valley, northern Sonoma County, California; produces Johannisberg Riesling, French Colombard, Chardonnay, Gewürztraminer, Petite Sirah and Zinfandel wines. 70 acres. 6,000 cases.

Horace (65-8 B.C.) **(Lat.)**
An ancient Roman author who discusses wines in his *Odes* and *Satires*.

Horgazuela (Sp.)
The local name for the Palomino grape in Puerta de Santa Maria, Sherry region.

Horizon Winery (U.S.)   **1977**
A small winery in Santa Rosa, Sonoma County, California; produces only Zinfandel wines. 1,500 cases.

Horozkarasi (T.)
A red grape grown in southeastern Turkey.

hors classé (F.)
In a class by itself; outstanding.

hors ligne (F.)
Outstanding; first-rate; out of the ordinary.

Hörstein (G.)
A village in the Franken region, Bereich Mainviereck, Grosslage Reuschberg. The only vineyard in Abtsberg. 100 acres.

Hospices, Clos des (F.)
A *Grand Cru* vineyard in Chablis, in the Chablis district, Burgundy, a part of Les Clos vineyard; at one time owned by the Hospices de Chablis, now owned by J. Moreau. 6 acres.

Hospices de Beaujeu (F.)
The Hospital at Beaujeu, Beaujolais district, Burgundy; owns vineyards mostly in Beaujolais-Villlages and some in Brouilly.

The best is the Cuvée Pissevielle, in Brouilly. 150 acres.

Hospices de Beaune (F.)   1443

The charity hospital in the city of Beaune, Côte de Beaune district, Burgundy; owns many fine parcels of vines, which were donated and are produced under it's own label by various wine-making firms. The wines are auctioned the 3rd Sunday in November at a very prestigeous affair, which sets the prices for Burgundy wines. Founded in 1443 by Nicolas Rolin and his wife, Guigone de Salins, who also donated their vineyards to the Hospices; first gift was in 1459. There are 32-34 *cuvées*, one of which is a parcel of Mazis-Chambertin (Côte de Nuits), since 1977. 37,000 gallons (75% red). 137 acres.

Hospices de Nuits (F.)   1692

Fourteen parcels of *Premier Cru* vines, owned by the hospital of Nuits-St.-Georges, Côte de Nuits district, Burgundy, are auctioned every year since 1961, as at the Hospices de Beaune. Cuvees: Guyard de Changey, Antide Midan, Mesny de Boisseaux, Fagon, Camille Rodier, Saint-Laurent, Cabet, Jacques Duret, des Sires de Vergy, Poyon, Guillaume Labye, Soeurs Hospitalières, Grangier, Mignotte, Didiers (entirely owned by the Hospices de Nuits – 9 acres) and St.-Georges. Total: 30 acres.

Hospices de Romaneche-Thorins (F.)

A hospital in Romaneche-Thorins, Beaujolais district, Burgundy, which owns 20 acres of Moulin-à-Vent.

hotte (F.)

A long, back-basket for carrying grapes while picking in the vineyard.

Houbanon, Château also Hourbanon (F.)

An estate in Prignac, Médoc district, Bordeaux; classified in 1978 as a *Cru Bourgeois*. 3,000 cases. 15 acres.

Houghton (Aus.)   1859

A famous winery in Swan Valley, Western Australia; one of three wineries taken over by Hardy's Winery; famous for white Burgundy (made from the Chenin Blanc grape) and for Tokay, Rhine Riesling and Cabernet wines. 150,000 cases. 800 acres.

Houissant, Château (F.)

An estate in St.-Estèphe, Haut-Médoc district, Bordeaux; classified in 1932 as a *Cru Bourgeois*. 8,500 cases. 50 acres.

Hourtin-Ducasse, Château (F.)

An estate in St.-Sauveur, Haut-Médoc district, Bordeaux, classified in 1978 as a *Cru Bourgeois*. 40 acres. 6,000 cases.

Hudelot et ses Fils, Paul (F.)

An estate in Chambolle-Musigny, Côte de Nuits district, Burgundy. 30 acres, including Bonnes Mares – .3 acre and Chambolle-Musigny Les Charmes – 5 acres.

Hudelot-Noëllat, Alain (F.)

An estate in Chambolle-Musigny, Côte de Nuits, Burgundy. 25 acres, including Richebourg – .6 acre, Romanée St.-Vivant – 1.2 acres, Clos de Vougeot – 1 acre, Vosne-Romanée Les Malconsorts – .6 acre, Les Suchots – 1 acre, Nuits-St.-Georges Les Murgers – 2 acres and some Chambolle-Musigny.

Hudson River Valley (U.S.)

The oldest wine region in the United States, situated on the west bank of the Hudson River between Newburgh and Kingston, New York; vines planted since 1677; first commercial winery in 1827; produces red, white and rosé wines made from Catawba, Delaware and other American and hybrid grapes. 12 wineries. 1,200 acres.

Hudson Valley Wine Company (U.S.)1907

A winery in Highland, Hudson River Valley region, New York; produces still and sparkling wines from *labrusca* and hybrid grapes. 100,000 cases. 200 acres.

Huelva DO (Sp.)

A town and district in the southwestern corner of Spain; produces Sherry-style wines, much of which goes to Jerez for blending.

Huet, Gaston (F.)

An estate in Vouvray, Touraine region, Loire Valley; produces dry and sweet Vouvray wines; owns the vineyards Les Haut-Lieu – 20 acres, Le Mont – 17 acres and Clos du Bourg – 15 acres.

### Hugel et Fils (F.)							1639

An estate inRiquewihr, Haut-Rhin district, Alsace region. 60 acres, mostly in Riquewihr, including Sporen vineyard – 16 acres (Tokay, Riesling, Gewürztraminer and Muscat).

Huguenot, Roger (F.)

An estate in Marsannay-la-Côte, Côte de Nuits district, Burgundy. 24 acres, including Charmes-Chambertin – .5 acre, Gevrey-Chambertin *Premier Cru* - 3 acres, Fixin – 10.5 acres and Marsannay.

Hugues et Louis Betault, Cuvée (F.)

A red wine from the Hospices de Beaune, Côte de Beaune district, Burgundy. *The cuvée* is composed of the following vineyards in Beaune: Les Grèves – 2.2 acres, La Mignotte – 1.2 acres, Les Aigrots – 1 acre, Les Sizies – 1 acre and Les Vignes Franches – .5 acre. 875 cases.

### Hultgren and Samperton (U.S.)				1978

A winery in Healdsburg, Russian River Valley district, Sonoma County, California; produces Cabernet, Petite Sirah, Gamay and Chardonnay wines from purchased grapes. 10,000 cases.

Humagne (Sw.)

One of several old white grapes grown in the Valais region.

Humbolt, Cuvée Jehan (F.)

A white wine from the Hospices de Beaune, Côte de Beaune district, Burgundy. The *cuvée* is composed of the following vineyards in Meursault: Le Poruzot – 1.5 acres and Grands Charrons – .3 acre. 300 cases.

Hungary

A country in eastern Europe; includes 4 regions: Great Plain (Alföld), Northern Transdanubia, Southern Transdanubia and Northern Hungary; famous for Tokaji Aszú wine. 130 million gallons. 400,000 acres.

### Hungerford Hill (Aus.)						1967

A winery in Coonawarra, South Australia; also owns in Hunter Valley and Riverlands districts; produces Cabernet, Shiraz, Rhine Riesling, Sémillon, Chardonnay and other wines. 50,000 cases. 350 acres plus 250 acres in the Hunter Valley district.

Hunt (U.S.)

An American red muscadine grape, grown in the southeast U.S. and in Texas.

Hunter Riesling (Aus.)

The former name for a white wine made from the Sémillon grape in Australia, especially in the Hunter Valley district, in New South Wales.

Hunter Valley (Aus.)

An important district of New South Wales, in the northeastern part of the region, north of Sidney, near Pokolbina and Cessnock; divided into Upper (northern) and Lower (southern) Hunter Valley; produces Shiraz, Cabernet, Pinot Noir, Sémillon and Chardonnay wines.

### Huntington Estate (Aus.)					1969

A famous winery in the Mudgee district, New South Wales; produces Cabernet, Sémillon and Chardonnay as well as Pinot Noir, Shiraz, Merlot and Sauvignon Blanc wines. 100 acres. 12,000 cases.

Hurolaie, La (F.)

An estate in Benais, Bourgueil district, Touraine region, Loire Valley. 2,500 cases. 25 acres.

### Husch Vineyards (U.S.)						1968

A winery in Philo, Anderson Valley, Mendocino County, California; produces Cabernet, Pinot Noir, Chardonnay,

Gewürztraminer and Sauvignon Blanc wines. 7,000 cases. 35 acres.

Huxelrebe (G.)

A white grape – a cross of Gutedel and Courtillier Musqué; developed at the State Research Institute, Alzey, in the Rheinhessen region in 1927.

hybrid

A grape which was developed by crossing American and European varieties in order to develop a hardy and disease-resistant vine with fruit of *Vitis vinifera* quality. Examples are Baco, Couderc, Seibel, etc. Any cross of two different species is considered a hybrid, whether by design or by an accident of Nature. Crosses between two varieties of the same species are known as crosses, or crossbreeds (*métis*, in French). Some experts, however, suggest that the product of any cross is a hybrid.

hydrometer

An instrument for measuring the percentage of the sugar content of must.

Hymettus (Gr.)

1. A town in the Attica region, near Mount Hymettus, which produces:

2. A light, red or white wine made from Mavroudi or Rhoditis grapes for red, and Savatiano grapes for white.

I

I.N.A.O. (F.)

The abbreviation for *Institut National des Appellations d'Origine des Vins et Eaux-de-Vie* (National Institute of Names of Origin of Wines and Spirits), the regulatory body for the wines of France.

I.N.D.O. (Sp.) 1972

The abbreviation for *Instituto Nacional de Denominaciones de Origen*, a governmental body in Madrid which supervises the controlling activities of the *Consejos Reguladores* (regulatory council) of each region.

I Piani (I.)

A red wine from Alghero, in northwestern Sardinia; made from the Carignano grape.

Iasi (R.)

An important city in the province of Moldavia, northeastern Romania; produces the famous sweet, white Cotnari wines.

ice wine

A sweet, white wine made from frozen grapes; *Eiswein*, in German.

Idaho (U.S.)

A state in the mid-western United States; a few wineries existed before Prohibition; recent planting began in 1969; produces Concord, hybrid and *vinifera* wines. Over 400 acres. There is only one commercial winery of importance: Ste. Chapelle.

Idyll (Aus.) 1966

A renovated winery in Geelong, southwest of Melbourne, southern Victoria; produces Cabernet and Traminer wines.

Ihringen (G.)

A village in the Baden region, Bereich Kaiserstuhl-Tuniberg, Grosslage Vulkanfelsen. The vineyards are Castellberg, Doktorgarten, Fohrenberg, Kreuzhalde, Schlossberg, Steinfelsen and Winklerberg.

Il Falcone (I.)

A red wine from Castel del Monte DOC district, in the northern Apulia region; made from Montepulciano grapes, with some Uva de Troia and Bombino Nero grapes.

Île des Vergelesses (F.)

A *Premier Cru* vineyard partly in Pernand-Vergelesses and partly in Savigny-lès-Beaune, Côte de Beaune district, Burgundy; may use the AOC Aloxe-Corton. 28 acres.

imbottigliato dal produttore all'origine (I.)

Bottled by the producer at the source. Other similar designations include: *imbottigliato dal viticoltore* – bottled by the grower, *imbottigliato dalla cantina sociale* – bottled by the co-op, *imbottigliato dalla cooperative* – bottled by the co-op, *imbottigliato dai produttori riuniti* – bottled by an organization of united producers, and *imbottigliato nella zona di produzione* – bottled in the production zone (i.e., *not* estate-bottled).

imperial (F.)

A large bottle used for long keeping of fine Bordeaux wines and other fine wines; 6-liter (8 fifths) capacity.

Impigno (I.)

A local, white grape grown in the southern Apulia region.

incrustation

The formation of a crust in wines, especially Ports.

Indiana (U.S.)

A state in the midwestern United States. A new law was enacted in 1971, modeled on the laws in Pennsylvania of 1968, favoring small wineries. Indiana now has about a dozen wineries.

Inferno DOC (I.)

A red wine from the Valtellina district, in the northern Lombardy region; made from 95% Nebbiolo grapes.

Infernot (I.)

A special Barbaresco *riserva* wine made from the Nebbiolo grape, produced by Gaja.

Ingelheim (G.)

A village, known for its red wine, in the Rheinhessen region, Bereich Bingen, Grosslage Kaiserpfalz. There are 15 vineyards, of which the most well-known are Burgweg, Höllenweg, Horn, Pares, Rheinhöhe and Steinacker. One-third of the production is red wine made from Pinot Noir and Portugieser grapes. 1,700 acres.

Inglenook Vineyards (U.S.)   1879   winery 1887

A famous, old winery in Rutherford, Napa Valley, California; the wines are made at Oakville; produces many varietal and generic wines including "Cask" Cabernet wines; the Navalle label is for second-quality wines. 1.5 million cases. 1,500 acres.

Ingoldby (Aus.)

A winery in the Southern Vales district, South Australia; produces red and white wines.

injerto (Sp.)

A graft.

Inniskillin (C.)   1974

A winery in Queenstown, Ontario; produces White Riesling, Gamay Teinturier, Gamay Noir, Seyval Blanc and Gewürztraminer wines. 25 acres.

Insignia (U.S.)

A premium red wine of Joseph Phelps Winery in St. Helena, Napa Valley, California; made from varying blends of Cabernet, Cabernet Franc and Merlot grapes.

Institut National des Appellations d'Origine des Vins et Eaux-de-Vie (F.)   1935

The National Institute of Names of Origin of Wines and Spirits (INAO), created in 1935, the organization which sets the standards for, and the regulation of, all French wines and spirits.

Institute of Masters of Wine (E.)

An organization developed in 1955 in London by 12 Masters of Wine (MW's); conducts tastings, seminars, wine trips and a series of examinations leading to the awarding of the MW.

Instituto Agrario Provinciale San Michele all'Adige (I.)

See **San Michele**.

Instituto do Vinho do Porto (P.)   1933

The regulating body which governs the production of Port wine; it has 2 sub-divisions: *Casa do Douro*, which supervises the vineyards and *Gremio dos Exportadores do Vinho do Porto*, which controls the shipping of the wines.

Internacionales S.A., Bodegas (Sp.)   1974

A Sherry producer in Jerez de la Frontera; produces many types of Sherry; also ages wines for several other producers.

invecchiato (I.)

Aging, growing old; semi-aged.

Inzolia (I.)

A white grape grown in Sicily.

Iona (U.S.)

An American, red hybrid grape named after the Iona Island, in the Hudson River, near Peekskill; developed in New York State, it produces a dry, white wine.

owa (U.S.)

A state in the mid-western United States; very little wine is produced there, and most of it is Rhubarb wine.

Iphofen (G.)

A village in the Franken region, Bereich Steigerwald, Grosslage Burgweg. The vineyards are Julius-Echter-Berg, Kalb and Kronsberg. 600 acres.

Ippolito, Vincenzo (I.)   **1845**

An estate in Cirò Marina, Calabria region; produces red, white and rosé Cirò wines. 60,000 cases. 175 acres.

Irancy (F.)

A village southwest of Chablis, in Burgundy, once famous for its wines; it now produces red and rosé wines made from Pinot Noir grapes and some César and Tressot grapes under the Bourgogne AOC.

Irakara (T.)

A red grape grown in Turkey.

Iron Horse Vineyard (U.S.)   **1979**

A winery in Sebastopol, Russian River Valley, Sonoma County, California; produces Cabernet, Pinot Noir, Zinfandel, Chardonnay, Sauvignon Blanc and sparkling wines. 15,000 cases. 135 acres.

Irouléguy AOC (F.)

1. A village and small district south of Bayonne, in the Southwest region, which produces:

2. Red, white and rosé wines, the red and rosé made from Tannet, Fer, and other grapes, and the white from Manseng, Courbu and other local grapes. 100 acres.

Irpinia (I.)

See **Hirpinia**.

Isabella (U.S.)

An American red *labrusca* grape mainly used for blending in New York State; found in South Carolina c. 1815; known as Americano in Switzerland.

Ischia DOC (I.)   **DOC since 1966**

1. An island and district off the coast of Naples, in the Campania region, which produces:

2. Light red and white wines, the red wines made from 50% Guarnaccia, 40% Per'e Palummo and 10% Barbera grapes and the white wines are made from 50% Forastera, 40% Biancolella and 10% San Lunardo grapes.

isinglass

A white, almost transparent gelatinous substance, derived from sturgeon and other freshwater fish bladders; used for fining or clarifying wine and beer.

Iskra (Bul.)

A white, sweet, sparkling wine from northern Bulgaria; a small amount is made by the *méthode Champenoise*.

Island Belle (U.S.)

A North American red grape used in the state of Washington for making red wine. Also called Campbell's Early.

Island View Farm (U.S.)   **1978**

A winery in Culpeper, northern Virginia; produces Riesling and Chardonnay wines.

Isonzo DOC (I.)

A small district along the Isonzo River, south of Gorizia, in the sousteastern Friuli-Venezia Giulia region; produces varietal wines made from Cabernet, Cabernet Franc, Malvasia, Merlot, Pinot Bianco, Pinot Grigio, Riesling Renano, Sauvignon, Tocai, Traminer and Verduzzo grapes.

Isoz, Robert (Sw.)   **1929**

An estate in Yvorne, Chablais district, Vaud region; produces Pinot Noir, Pinot Gris and Gewürztraminer wines. 12 acres.

Israel

A country in western Asia which produces Kosher wines of all types, mostly from *vinifera* grapes and some hybrid and local varieties. 10,000 acres. 9.3 million gallons.

d'Issan, Château (F.)

An estate in Cantenac-Margaux, Haut-Médoc district, Bordeaux; classified in 1855 as a *Troisième Cru*; it was known as Château Lamothe de Cantenac in the 13th century; the present Château was built in the 17th century. 12,000 cases. 80 acres.

Issarts (F.)

A *Premier Cru* vineyard in Gevrey-Chambertin, Côte de Nuits district, Burgundy; also called Plantigione. 4 acres.

Istria (Y.)

A peninsula and region, formerly part of Italy, in northwestern Yugoslavia; produces red wines from Teran (Refosco), Cabernet, Gamay, Merlot and Pinot Noir grapes and white wines from Malvasia and Muscat grapes.

Italian Swiss Colony (U.S.)   1887

A large, old winery in Asti, south of Cloverdale, northern Sonoma County, California; produces varietal and jug wines; also has wineries in Fresno and Lodi; the name on the label has been changed to Colony. 8 million gallons.

Italy

A country in southern Europe, and now the largest producer and exporter of wine in the world. 1.7 billion gallons, 20% of which is exported. DOC began in 1963. 3.3 million acres of vineyards. There are 20 regions, which correspond to the 20 political regions of the country.

Iund Vineyard (U.S.)

A vineyard in the Carneros district, southern Napa Valley, California; produces Pinot Noir grapes for Acacia Winery.

Ives (U.S.)

An American red *labrusca* grape grown in the eastern U.S.

J

J.N.V. (P.)   **1937**

The abbreviation for *Junta National do Vinho*, the official organization regulating all wines in Portugal except Port wines.

Jaboulet Aîné, Paul (F.)   **1834**

An estate and merchant in Tain-L'Hermitage, northern Rhône region. 160 acres, including 62 acres of Hermitage, 85 acres of Crozes-Hermitage; also produces Côte-Rôtie, Châteauneuf-du-Pape, Tavel and other Rhône wines; also uses the Jaboulet-Isnard label. 80,000 cases.

Jaboulet-Vercherre (F.)   **1834**

An estate and merchant in Beaune, Côte de Beaune, Burgundy. 22 acres, including Pommard Clos du Château de la Commaraine Monopole – 4 acres, Pommard Clos Blanc – 5 acres, Volnay Caillerets – .6 acre, Beaune Clos de L'Écu Monopole – 7 acres, Corton Les Bressands – 1.2 acres, Clos de Vougeot – .8 acre and Chambertin – .6 acre.

Jacob, Domaine Louis (F.)

An estate in Savigny-lès-Beaune, Côte de Beaune, Burgundy. 40 acres, 5ncluding Savigny Vergelesses – 5 acres, Savigny – 15 acres, Beaune Premier Cru - 1.6 acres, Aloxe Corton, Pernand-Vergelesses and Hautes-Côtes de Beaune – 15 acres.

Jacobins, Clos des (F.)

An estate in St.-Émilion, Bordeaux; classified in 1955 as a *Grand Cru Classé*. 4,500 cases. 20 acres.

Jacobsdal EWO (S. Af.)

An estate in the southwestern Stellenbosch district; produces red wines.

Jacquère (F.)

A white grape grown in the Savoie region of southeastern France.

Jacques, Château des (F.)

An estate in Romanèche-Thorins (Moulin-à-Vent), Beaujolais district, Burgundy. 85 acres.

Jacques Gaillard (Br.)

A grape grown in Brazil.

Jacqueson, Henri et Paul (F.)

An estate in Rully, Côte Chalonnaise district, southern Burgundy. 16 acres in Rully and Mercurey.

Jacquesson et Fils (F.)   **1798**

A Champagne producer in Épernay. 500,000 bottles. 50 acres.

Jacquez (U.S.)

An American red hybrid grape developed in South Carolina in 1829; grown in Europe and the U.S. Also called Black Spanish and Lenoir.

Jaculillo (I.)

A red grape grown in the Campania region, southern Italy; it is used to make Gragnano wine.

Jade Mountain Winery (U.S.)   **1974**

A winery in Cloverdale, Russian River Valley, northern Sonoma County; produces Cabernet and Johannisberg Riesling wines. 1,000 cases. 30 acres.

Jadot, Louis (F.)   **1859**

An estate and *négociant* in Beaune, Côte de Beaune district, Burgundy. 63 acres, including Corton Pougets – 6 acres, Corton-Charlemagne – 4 acres, Pernand-Verge-lesses en Caradeux Clos de la Croix de Pierre Monopole – 5 acres, Beaune Clos du Roi – 1.2 acres, Les Teurons – 2.5 acres, Les Bressandes – 4 acres, Les Vignes Franches – 1.2 acres, Clos des Ursules Monopole, Les Boucherottes – 7.5 acres and Chevalier-Montrachet Les Demoiselles – 1.2 acres.

Jaen (P.)

A red grape grown in the Dão region.

Jaén (Sp.)

Various red and white grapes grown in the La Mancha and Old Castile regions: Jaén Blanco, Jaén Tinto and Jaén Doradillo.

Jaffelin (F.)   1816

An estate in Beaune, Côte de Beaune district, Burgundy. 10 acres, including Clos de Vougeot – 1.6 acres, Beaune Les Bressandes – 6 acres and Les Avaux – 1.2 acres; owned by Drouhin.

Jamek, Weingut Josef (A.)   1912

An estate and merchant in Joching, Wachau region; produces Grüner Veltliner, Rheinriesling, Weissburgunder and other wines from their own and purchased grapes. 14,000 cases. 45 acres.

James (U.S.)

An American muscadine grape grown in the southern United States.

Jampal (P.)

A white grape grown in central Portugal.

Japan

A country in eastern Asia; most of the wine is produced around Kofu, in the province of Yamanashi, west of Tokyo; some wine is also made in the provinces of Osaka and Yamagata. European, American and native Koshu grapes are grown. 5 million gallons. 75,000 acres of vines, including table grapes.

jardinage (F.)

A system of replacing each individual vine after it has reached its maximum age.

Jarollières, Les (F.)

A *Premier Cru* vineyard in Pommard, Côte de Beaune district, Burgundy. 8 acres.

Jarrons, Les (F.)

A *Premier Cru* vineyard in Savigny, Côte de Beaune district, Burgundy; also called Les Dominodes. 22 acres.

Jasmin, Georges (F.)

An estate in Ampuis, Côte-Rôtie district, Rhône region; owns 7 acres of Côte-Rôtie.

Jasnières AOC (F.)

A semi-sweet, white wine from L'Homme and Ruille-sur-Loir, in the Coteaux du Loir district, north of Tours, in the Touraine region, Loire Valley; made from the Chenin Blanc grape.

Jau, Château de (F.)

An estate in Cases de Péné, Rivesaltes district, Roussillon region; produces Côtes du Roussillon, Muscat and other wines.

Jaun Ibañez (Sp.)

A red grape grown in the Aragón region of northern Spain.

Javillier, Raymond (F.)

An estate and merchant in Meursault, Côte de Beaune district, Burgundy. 12.5 acres, including Meursault Clos du Cromin and Tillets.

Jean-Faure, Château (F.)

An estate in St.-Émilion, Bordeaux; classified in 1955 as a *Grand Cru Classé*. 5,000 cases. 40 acres.

Jeanniard, Domaine Georges (F.)

An estate in Nuits-St.-Georges, Côte de Nuits district, Burgundy. 19 acres, including Nuits-St.-Georges Les Pruliers – 5.5 acres, Les Perrières – 2.5 acres and Les Argillats – 1.6 acres.

ekel Vineyard (U.S.)   1972, winery 1978

A winery in Greenfield, Monterey County, California; produces Cabernet, Pinot Noir, Pinot Blanc, Chardonnay and Johannisberg Riesling wines. 30,000 cases. 160 acres.

ehan de Massol, Cuvée (F.)

A red wine from the Hospices de Beaune, Côte de Beaune district, Burgundy. The *cuvée* is composed of the following vineyard in Volnay: Les Santenots – 4 acres. 675 cases.

ehan Humbolt, Cuvée (F.)

A white wine from the Hospices de Beaune, Côte de Beaune district, Burgundy. The *cuvée* is composed of the following vineyards in Meursault: Le Poruzot – 1.5 acres and Grands Charrons – .3 acre. 300 cases.

ennelotte, La (F.)

A *Premier Cru* vineyard in Blagny, but sold as Meursault, Côte de Beaune district, Burgundy. 13 acres.

Jerez de la Frontera (Sp.)

A city in the Andalucia region of southern Spain, the center of the Sherry trade and from which the word "Sherry" is derived.

Jermann (I.)   1880

An estate in Villanova di Farra, Friuli-Venezia Giulia region; produces Collio, Picolit and Tunina wines. 5,000 cases.

jeroboam

A large bottle of various sizes. In Portugal and Champagne it is equal to 4 bottles; in Bordeaux, 5 or 6 bottles and in England, usually 6 bottles.

jeropiga *also* **geropiga (P.)**

A grape syrup used to sweeten Port.

Jeruzalem (Y.)

A famous vineyard in the Ljutomer district, in the northeastern Slovenia region.

Jessiaume Père et Fils (F.)   1880

An estate in Santenay, Côte de Beaune district, Burgundy. 25 acres, including Santenay Les Gravières – 12 acres and Beaune Les Cent Vignes – 3 acres.

Joannès-Seyve 26-205 (F.)

Another name for the red hybrid Chambourcin grape, bred by Joannès Seyve.

João de Santarém (P.)

A red grape grown in the Bairrada region.

Joguet, Charles (F.)

An estate in Sazilly, Chinon district, Anjou region, Loire Valley. 25 acres.

Johannisberg (G.)

1. The name of the only *Bereich* in the Rheingau region.

2. A famous village in the Rheingau region, Grosslage Erntebringer. The vineyards are Schloss Johannisberg (an *Ortsteil*), Goldatzel, Hasenberg, Hölle, a part of Klaus, Mittelhölle, Schwarzenstein and Vogelsang. 260 acres.

Johannisberg (Sw.)

A white wine from the Valais region made from the Sylvaner grape.

Johannisberg, Schloss (G.)

A famous estate in Johannisberg, Rheingau region; owned by Fürst von Metternich-Winneburg. 27,000 cases. 85 acres.

Johannisberg Riesling (G.)

1. The complete name of the Riesling grape when referring to the one grown in Germany; grown in the United States and other countries as well; also called White Riesling.

2. A white wine made from the Johannisberg Riesling grape.

Johanniswein (G.)

St. John's wine, a bottle of wine which is taken to Mass on St. John's Day for a special blessing. It is supposed to bring health, fertility and peace; used at weddings and funerals in various parts of Germany.

Johnson Estate (U.S.)   1961

A winery in Westfield, Chautauqua region, New York; produces Seyval Blanc, Chancellor Noir and blends from hybrid grapes as well as wines from *labrusca* varieties. 10,000 cases. 125 acres.

Johnson-Turnbull Vineyards (U.S.)   1979

A small winery in Oakville, Napa Valley, California; produces Cabernet wine. 20 acres. 1,500 cases.

Johnson's Alexander Valley Wines (U.S.)
1975

A winery in Healdsburg, Alexander Valley, northern Sonoma County, California; produces Cabernet, Pinot Noir, Zinfandel, Chardonnay, Johannisberg Riesling, Gewürztraminer and Chenin Blanc wines. 45 acres. 10,000 cases.

Johnston, Nathaniel (F.)   1734

A merchant in Bordeaux.

Joliot, Domaine Jean et Fils (F.)

An estate in Nantoux, Côte de Beaune district, Burgundy. 18 acres, including Hautes-Côtes de Beaune – 16 acres, Pommard – 2.5 acres, Meursault – 5 acres and some Beaune Boucherottes.

Joly, A. (F.)

An estate in Savennières, Anjou region, Loire Valley. Owns Coulée de Serrant – 17 acres and Clos de la Bergerie (part of La Roche-aux-Moines).

Jonicole Vineyard (U.S.)   1973

A winery in Roseburg, Umpqua Valley, southwestern Oregon; vines originally planted in 1968; produces Cabernet wine from their own and purchased grapes. 3,000 cases. 5 acres.

Jordan and Ste. Michelle Cellars (C.) 1921

The largest winery in Canada, in Jordan, near Niagara Falls and St. Catherine, Ontario; produces rosé, sparkling and sherry-style wines. 10 million gallon capacity.

Jordan Vineyard (U.S.)   1972
1st wine 1976

A winery in Healdsburg, Alexander Valley, northern Sonoma County, California; produces Cabernet and Chardonnay wines and some Merlot for blending; first estate-bottled Cabernet in 1978. 50,000 cases. 300 acres.

Josephshof (G.)

A famous vineyard in Gràach, Grosslage Munzlay, Bereich Bernkastel, Mosel-Saar-Ruwer region, owned by Von Kesselstatt; seen on labels as Josefshöfer. 15 acres.

Jouan-Marcillet (F.)

An estate in Nuits-St.-Georges, Côte de Nuits district, Burgundy. 12.5 acres, including Nuits-St.-Georges Clos des Perrières Monopole – 2.5 acres and Aux Crots – 1.6 acres.

Jouchère, Domaine La (F.)

An estate in the Chablis district, Burgundy. 135 acres, including Chablis Vaillons – 12 acres, Beauroy – 3.5 acres, Vaudevey – 28 acres and some Chablis and Petit Chablis; controlled by négociant Bacheroy-Josselin.

journal *plur.*: journeaux (F.)

An old Burgundian measure of land equal to 1/3 *hectare*, or .8 acre.

Journets, Domaine des (F.)

An estate in Chénas, Beaujolais district, Burgundy.

Jübiläum (G.)

A new white hybrid grape.

Juge, Marcel (F.)

An estate in Cornas, northern Rhône region; produces Cornas and St.-Péray wines.

Juillot, Domaine Michel (F.)

An estate in Mercurey, Côte Chalonnaise district, southern Burgundy. 42 acres.

Juliénas AOC (F.)

A village and a *Cru* Beaujolais in the northern Beaujolais district, Burgundy. 1,200 acres.

Juliénas, Château de (F.)

An estate in Juliénas, Beaujolais district, Burgundy.

Juliusspital-Weingut (G.)   1576

A hospital estate in Würtzburg, Franken region; owns vineyards in Würtzburg, Randersacker and other villages. 375 acres.

July Muscat

A white muscat grape.

Jumilla DO (Sp.)

A district west of Alicante, in the Levante region of southeastern Spain; produces mostly strong red wine from the Monastrell grape.

Junfark (H.)

Hungarian for "Lamb's tail," a white grape.

Junta National do Vinho (JNV) (P.)   1937

National Council of Wine, the official organization which regulates all wine in Portugal except Port wines; headquarters are in Lisbon.

Jura (F.)

A region between Burgundy and Switzerland; produces an enormous variety of wines, including red, white, rosé, sparkling, *vins de paille* (straw wines) and *vins jaunes* (yellow wines). The most famous wine is Château-Châlon. 2,500 acres.

Jurançon AOC (F.)

1. A district around Pau, in the Southwest region, which produces:

2. A sweet white wine made only from old local grapes including Gros Manseng, Petit Manseng, Courbu, Camaralet and Lauzet grapes; a dry version is also made. 400,000 gallons of sweet wines; 50,000 gallons of dry wine.

Jurançon Blanc (F.)

A white grape grown in the Cognac region; also called Pineau des Charentes.

Jurançon Noir (F.)

A red grape grown in Gaillac, in the Southwest region.

Justice, Clos de la (F.)

An unclassified vineyard in Gevrey-Chambertin, Côte de Nuits district, Burgundy, a *monopole* of Pierre Bourée. 5 acres.

Justino (P.)

A producer of Madeira wines.

Juvenal (Lat.)

The ancient Roman satirist (c. A.D.100), who wrote about wine.

Juvinière, Domaine de la (F.)

An estate in Aloxe-Corton, Côte de Beaune district, Burgundy; controlled by La Reine Pédauque. 60 acres, including Clos de Vougeot – 2.5 acres, Corton Clos du Roi, Corton Pougets, Corton Combes, Clos des Langres Monopole – 17 acres, Savigny, Pommard and Aloxe-Corton.

Jux, Charles (F.)

An estate in Colmar (now owned by Dopff et Irion), Haut-Rhin district, Alsace region. 200 acres, including 75 acres of the Harth vineyard.

K

K.

The abbreviation for Kuhlmann, a hybrid grape.

K.G. (G.)

The abbreviation for *Kommanditgesellschaft,* Limited Partnership.

K.M.W. (A.)

Klosterneuberger Mostwaage (Klosterneuberger Must Weight), the Austrian measurement of sugar content in must.

K.W.V. (S. Af.)   **since 1918**

The abbreviation for *Ko-operatieve Wijnbouwers Vereniging van Zuid-Afrika Beperkt* (the Co-operative Wine Growers Association of South Africa, Ltd.).

Kaapse Riesling (S. Af.)

The South African name for the Wälschriesling, or Italian Riesling grape or vine.

Kabarcik (T.)

A white grape grown in Turkey.

Kabinett (G.)

A designation for a *QmP* wine which, by law, is estate-bottled, unsugared, and which is the driest wine in this category (though still somewhat sweet); formerly, *Cabinet.*

Kadarka (H.)

An important red grape grown in Hungary and Bulgaria; in Romania the same grape is spelled Cadarcă, or Cadarkă.

Kaefferkopf (F.)

A famous *Grand Cru* vineyard in Ammerschwihr, Haut-Rhin district, Alsace region; produces Riesling and Gewürztraminer grapes. 155 acres.

Kahlenberg (A.)

A northern suburb of Vienna; produces *Heurige* wines.

Kaiser-Stuhl (Aus.)

1. The highest hill in the Barossa Valley, north of Adelaide, South Australia.

2. The name for the Barossa Cooperative Winery; specializes in Cabernet, Shiraz and Rhine Rieslings, especially the Purple Ribbon Auslese; now owned by Penfolds.

Kaiserstuhl-Tuniberg (G.)

A *Bereich,* one of 7 in the Baden region; the two *Grosslagen* are Attilafelsen and Vulkanfelsen. 10,000 acres.

Kalecik (T.)

A red grape grown in central Turkey.

Kalin Cellars (U.S.)   **1977**

A small winery in Novato, Marin County, California; produces Cabernet, Merlot, Pinot Noir, Chardonnay, Johannisberg Riesling and Sémillon wines; made from grapes from Sonoma, Mendocino and Santa Barbara Counties. 3,000 cases.

Kallstadt (G.)

A town in the Rheinpfalz region, Bereich Mittelhaardt/Deutsche Weinstrasse, Grosslagen Feuerberg, Kobnert and Saumagen. The vineyards are: Annaberg and Kreidkeller in Grosslage Feuerberg, Kronenberg and Steinacker in Grosslage Kobnert, and Horn, Kirkenstück and Nill in Grosslage Saumagen. 875 acres.

Kalolehorio (Cyp.)

A village south of Mt. Olympus, on the Island of Cyprus; one of the three villages which produce Mavrodaphne wine.

Kalte Ente (G.)

German for "Cold Duck," a popular drink made from white wine or sparkling wine, lemon and sugar, similar to a Champagne punch; the red version is called *Turkenblut*. It is a precursor of the American "Cold Duck."

Kalterersee (I.)

See **Lago di Caldaro.**

Kamp *also* Kamptal (A.)

A river and valley in the Langenlois district, northwest of Vienna, in the Lower Austria region.

Kan-k-Komet (Egypt)

An ancient vineyard of Rameses III (1198-1166 B.C.).

Kanne, *plur.* Kannen (G.)

A liter.

Kanonkop Estate EWO (S. Af.)   1973

A large estate in the Stellenbosch district; known for Cabernet, Pinotage and Pinot Noir wines. 12,000 cases. 300 acres.

Kanzem (G.)

A village in the Mosel-Saar-Ruwer region, Bereich Saar-Ruwer, Grosslage Scharzberg. The vineyards are Altenberg, Hörecker, Schlossberg and Sonnenberg. 185 acres.

Kanzler (G.)

A white grape – a cross of Müller-Thurgau and Sylvaner; developed at the State Research Institute, Alzey, Germany in 1927. The name means "Chancellor."

Kanzlerberg (F.)

A *Grand Cru* vineyard in Bergheim, northern Haut-Rhin district, Alsace region; produces Riesling and Gewürztraminer grapes.

Kappelrodeck (G.)

A village in the Baden region, Bereich Ortenau, Grosslage Schloss Rodeck. The only vineyard is Hex vom Dasenstein.

Karalahna (T.)

A red grape grown in Turkey.

Karasakiz (T.)

A red grape grown in Turkey.

Karst & Söhne, Weingut Johannes (G.)

An estate and merchant in Bad Dürkheim, Rheinpfalz region; owns vineyards in Dürkheim. 25 acres.

Karthaüserhof Gutverwaltung Werner Tyrell (G.)

An estate in Trier, Mosel-Saar-Ruwer region, formerly of H.W. Rautenstrauch; owns vineyards in Eitelsbach, in the Ruwer district. 50 acres.

Kasel (G.)

A village in the Mosel-Saar-Ruwer region, Bereich Saar-Ruwer, Grosslage Römerlay. The vineyards are Dominikanerberg, Herrenberg, Hitzlay, Kehrnagel, Nieschen, Paulinsberg and Timpert. 220 acres.

Kastelberg (F.)

A *Grand Cru* vineyard in Andlau, Bas-Rhin district, Alsace region.

Kavadarka (Y.)

A red grape grown in Macedonia.

Kay Brothers (Aus.)   1890

An old winery in the McLaren Vale district South Australia; produces Shiraz and Sauvignon Blanc wines. 125 acres.

ecskemét (H.)

A town and district southeast of Buda-
est, in the Great Plain region, which
roduces:

Red and white wines, made from Ka-
arka and Olasz (Italian) Riesling grapes,
spectively.

**eenan Winery, Robert (U.S.)   1904-37,
1977**

remodeled winery on Spring Mountain,
St. Helena, Napa Valley, California; pro-
uces Cabernet and Chardonnay wines.
000 cases. 45 acres.

eg

small barrel or cask with usually less
an a 10-gallon capacity.

ékfrankos (H.)

red grape, the same as the Gamay grape;
e name means "blue French."

éknyelü (H.)

A white grape grown in the Badacsony
istrict. The name means "blue stalk." It
roduces:

A white wine.

elch (G.)

goblet, cup, or chalice.

eller (G.)

cellar.

ellerabfüllung *also* **Kellerabzug (G.)**

ottled in the cellar; bottled in the cellar
f...; used on German wine labels prior to
971; also called *Kellerabzug* ("drawn off in
e cellar of..."); estate-bottled. Since 1971
ese terms have been replaced by *Erzeu-
rabfüllung,* which has the same meaning.

ellerabzug (G.)

ee **Kellerabfüllung.**

**elleramt Chorherrenstift
losterneuburg (A.)   1108**

large, historic estate in Klosterneuburg,
orth of Vienna; owns vineyards in Klos-

terneuburg, Kahlenbergerdorf and Tatten-
dorf; produces many red and white wines
and a *Sekt;* also uses purchased grapes. 250
acres.

Kelter (G.)

A wine press.

Kendermann OHG, Hermann (G.)

A merchant in Bingen; markets estate and
generic wines.

Kennedy Wines, Kathryn (U.S.)   1973

A small winery in Saratoga, Santa Clara
County, California; produces Cabernet
and Pinot Noir wines. 10 acres. 2,000 cases.

Kentucky (U.S.)

A state in the eastern U.S. The wine laws
were revised in 1976 and the first commercial wines since Prohibition were produced
in 1977, from the Colcord Winery in Paris.
There are 2 or 3 other wineries as well.

Kenwood Winery (U.S.)   1905, 1070

An old winery in Kenwood, southern Sonoma County, California; formerly the Pa-
gani Winery; produces Cabernet, Pinot
Noir, Zinfandel, Chardonnay, Sauvignon
Blanc, Chenin Blanc, Gewürztraminer and
Johannisberg Riesling wines from their
own and purchased grapes. 45,000 cases.
20 acres.

Kenworthy Vineyards (U.S.)   1978

A small winery in Plymouth, Amador
County, California; produces Cabernet,
Zinfandel and Chardonnay wines. 1,000
cases. 7 acres.

Kerner (G.)

A white grape – a cross of Trollinger and
Riesling, developed at the State Teaching
and Research Institute, Weinsberg, Germany, a replacement for the Sylvaner in the
Rheinhessen; named after Justinus Kerner,
a physician. It is a spicy, fruity grape with
high acidity.

Kesselstatt, Reichsgraf von (G.)

An estate in Trier, Mosel-Saar-Ruwer region; owns 9 smaller estates and vineyards in Piesport, Zelting, Dhron, Graach, Bernkastel, Wilting and elsewhere. 200 acres.

Kesten (G.)

A village in the Mosel-Saar-Ruwer region, Bereich Bernkastel, Grosslage Kurfürstlay. The vineyards are Herrenberg, Paulinsberg and Paulinshofberg. 300 acres.

Kettmeir (I.)   1908

A large winery in Caldaro, Trentino-Alto Adige region; produces many still and sparkling wines from their own and purchased grapes. 260,000 cases.

Kevedinka (Y.)

A white grape grown in Serbia.

Kiedrich (G.)

A village in the Rheingau region, Bereich Johannisberg, Grosslage Heiligenstock. The vineyards are Gräfenberg, Klosterberg, Sandgrub, and Wasserros. 430 acres.

Kientzler et Fils (F.)

An estate in Ribeauvillé, Haut-Rhin district, Alsace region. 25 acres, including Giesberg – 3 acres (Muscat) and Osterberg – 1.5 acres (Chasselas).

Kipperlé also Knipperlé (Fr.)

A white grape grown in the Alsace region; called Räuschling in Germany and Switzerland.

Kir (F.)

A well-known drink made from white Burgundy wine with Cassis liqueur added. It was named after Canon Félix Kir, the mayor of Dijon and a leader in the French Resistance.

Kirchberg (F.)

A vineyard in Barr, Bas-Rhin district, Alsace region.

Kirchthal Schneckenberg (F.)

A section of the Brand vineyard, in Turkheim, Haut-Rhin district, Alsace region.

Kirigin Cellars (U.S.)   1976

A rebuilt winery north of Gilroy, Santa Clara County, California; formerly the Louis Bonesio Winery; produces Cabernet, Pinot Noir, Zinfandel, French Colombard and Malvasia wines. 15,000 cases. 48 acres.

Kirwan, Château (F.)

An estate in Cantenac-Margaux, Haut-Médoc district, Bordeaux; classified in 1855 as a *Troisième Cru*; château-bottled only since 1967. 80 acres. 9,000 cases.

Kisalföld (H.)

A region in northwestern Hungary, also called the Small Plain; produces red wines, especially from Sopron.

Kistler Vineyards (U.S.)   1978

A winery in Glen Ellen, in the Mayacamus Mountains, Sonoma County, California; produces Cabernet, Pinot Noir and Chardonnay wines. 6,000 cases. 40 acres.

Kitterlé, (F.)

A vineyard in Guebwiller, Haut-Rhin district, in the Alsace region; produces Riesling and Gewürztraminer grapes; 37 acres are owned by Schlumberger.

Klävner (G.)

One of the various spellings of the Klevner, or Pinot Noir grape; also called Klebrot, Klevener, Clevner, and Blauer Spätburgunder; also loosely used as a general name for the Pinot grape of any color.

Klebrot (G.)

See **Klävner.**

Klein Karoo WO (S. Af.)

A large district east of Capetown, around Montagu and further east, known for dessert wines made from the Muscat grape.

Kleinberger (G.)

A white grape, also called Elbling and Albern in Germany, Klemperich in the Mosel; also grown in California.

Klemperich (G.)

See Elbling and Kleinberger.

Klevener de Heiligenstein (F.)

1. A rare, red grape grown in Heiligenstein, Barr, Goxwiller and Gertwiller, Bas-Rhin district, in the Alsace region; only 35 acres planted. Also called Savagnin Rose.

2. A white wine made from the above grape.

Klevner, Klevener, Klävner also Clevner (G.,Sw.)

1. The German and Swiss name for the Pinot Noir grape.

2. The Alsatian name for the Pinot Blanc grape.

Klingelberger (G.)

In the Baden region, near Oftenburg, another name for the Riesling grape.

Klingenberg (G.)

A village in the Franken region, Bereich Mainviereck. The vineyards are Hochberg and Schlossberg. 60 acres.

Klingshirn Winery (U.S.)   1935

A winery in Avon Lake, Ohio; grows mostly Concord grapes. 10 acres.

Klipfel, Domaine (F.)

A merchant in Barr, Bas-Rhin district, Alsace region. 80 acres, including Freiberg – 7 acres (Gewürztraminer and Tokay) and Clos Zisser – 12 acres (Gewürztraminer). 10,000 cases.

Klöch (A.)

A village in the Styria region, southeastern Austria.

Kloster Eberbach (G.)   1116

A famous Cistercian monastery founded in 1116 in Hattenheim, Rheingau region, now owned by the state. Important wine auctions are held there. The famous Steinberg vineyard belongs to the Kloster.

Kloster Marienthal, Statliche Weinbaudomän (G.)

An estate in Bad Neuenahr-Ahrweiler, Ahr region; owns vineyards in Marienthal, Walporzheim and Ahrweil; produces red wine from the Spätburgunder, Portugieser and other grapes. 50 acres.

Klosterberg (G.)

A Grosslage, the only one in Bereich Walporzheim/Ahrtal, in the Ahr region.

Klosterkeller (Bul.)

A white wine made from the Sylvaner grape.

Klosterneuburg (A.)

1. A town and district north of Vienna, in the Lower Austria region.

2. The monastery in Klosterneuburg.

3. A wine from Klosterneuburg.

Klosterneuburger Mostwaage (A.)

Klosterneuburger Must Weight, a measurement of the sugar content in must, expressed in percentage: 10 degrees *KMW* – 10% sugar.

Klüsserath (G.)

A village in the Mosel-Saar-Ruwer region, Bereich Bernkastel, Grosslage Sankt Michael. The vineyards are Brüderschaft and Königsberg. 900 acres.

Knight's Valley (U.S.)

A district in northeastern Sonoma County, just east of Alexander's Valley, California.

Knipperlé (F.)

A white grape grown in Alsace. Also called Kipperlé, Kleinberger and Kleiner Räuschling.

Knudsen-Erath (U.S.)   1976

The combined wineries of Knudsen and Erath in Dundee, Willamette Valley, northwestern Oregon; sometimes labeled under either individual name or under both names; produces Pinot Noir, Chardonnay and Riesling wines. Erath started in 1967 and Knudsen in 1973. 20,000 cases. 135 acres.

Knyphausen, Weingut Freiherr zu (G.)

An estate in Eltville, Rheingau region. 43 acres, including vineyard holdings in Erbach, Hattenheim, Kiedrich, Eltville and Rauenthal.

Kocher-Jagst-Tauber (G.)

A *Bereich*, one of 3 in the Württemberg region. The *Grosslagen* are Kocherberg and Tauberberg.

Koehler-Ruprecht, Weingut (G.)

An estate in Kallstadt, Rheinpfalz region; owns vineyards in Kallstadt. 20 acres.

Kofu (J.)

A city and district west of Tokyo, Yamanashi Prefecture, in central Japan.

Kokkineli (Cyp., Gr.)

A dry rosé wine from Cyprus or Greece made from the Mavron grape, usually resinated.

Kokur Niznegorsky (U.S.S.R.)

A dry white wine from the Crimea region of the Ukraine SSR.

Kolbenhofer (I.)

A red wine from Tramin (Termeno), south of Bolzano, in the Trentino-Alto Adige region, made from the Schiava grape.

Kolor (G.)

A red grape – a cross of Spätburgunder and Färbertraube, developed at the State Viticultural Institute, Freiburg, Germany.

Königen Victoria Berg (G.)

See **Victoria Berg.**

Königheim (G.)

A village in the Baden region, Bereich Badisches Frankenland, Grosslage Tauberklinge. The sole vineyard is Kirchberg.

Königsbach (G.)

A village in the Rheinpfalz region, Bereich Mittelhaardt-Deutsche Weinstrasse, Grosslage Meerspinne. The vineyards are Idig, Jesuitgarten, Oelberg and Reiterpfad.

Königshofen (G.)

A village in the Baden region, Bereich Badisches Frankenland, Grosslage Tauberklinge. The vineyards are Kirchberg, Turmberg and Walterstal.

Konocti Cellars (U.S.)   1974

A co-op winery of 35 members in Kelseyville, Lake County, California; produces Cabernet, Zinfandel, Sauvignon Blanc and Johannisberg Riesling wines. 20,000 cases. 400 acres.

Konvict (G.)

A seminary, or a hostel.

Kopke, C.N. & Company (P.)   1638

The oldest Port company, located in Vila Nova de Gaia; owns Quinta São Luiz; founded in 1638 by Christian Kopke, the first Consul-General for the Hanseatic League of Free Towns. 500 acres.

Konsumwein (G.)

Ordinary wine.

Ko-operatieve Wijnbouwers Vereniging van Zuid-Afrika, Beperkt (S. Af.)   1918

The Co-operative Wine Growers Association of South Africa, Limited; consisting of some 5,700 members, located in Paarl.

Koopmanskloff Estate EWO (S. Af.)

A large estate in the Stellenbosch district; the wines are bottled by the Bergkelder part of the Oude Meester Group.

Corbel (U.S.)   1886

A winery in Guerneville, northwest of Santa Rosa, Russian River Valley, Sonoma County, California; produces sparkling wines: Natural, Brut, Extra Dry, Sec, Blanc de Noirs, Blanc de Blancs, and a semi-dry Rosé; also makes brandy as well as some table wines. 500,000 cases. 600 acres.

Corčula (Y.)

An island off the Dalmatia coast, in the Adriatic Sea; produces Pošip wine, one of the better white wines, Grk wine and other white wines.

Cornell Champagne Cellars, Hanns (U.S.)   1958

A large winery in St. Helena, Napa Valley, California; formerly the old Larkwood Vineyard; produces champagnes from purchased wines in Brut, Extra-dry, Sec, Demi-Sec, Rouge, Rosé, and Sehr Trocken styles, mostly from the Riesling grape, and Muscat of Alexandria; all are bottle-fermented. 100,000 cases.

Kosher wine

Wine made according to Rabbinical law for use during Jewish religious services. It must be pure, natural, and made under the supervision of a Rabbi. Sugar may be added, though more dry Kosher wines are now available.

Koshu (J.)

A native white grape.

Kosmet (Y.)

A province and district in the republic of Kosovo, south of Serbia; produces mostly red varietal wines from Cabernet, Cabernet Franc, Pinot Noir and Merlot grapes.

Kotisfalo *also* Kotisphalo (Gr.)

A red grape grown in Crete.

Krajina (Y.)

A district in eastern Serbia; produces mainly red wines, especially from Gamay grapes; the word means "borderland."

Krampen (G.)

A section of the Mosel-Saar-Ruwer region from Cochem to Eller, so-called because of a bend or "cramp" in the river.

Krasnostok (U.S.S.R.)

A white grape grown in the Rostov district of Russia SSR.

krater (Gr.)

A wide, flat bowl from ancient Greece, used for mixing wine and water.

Kratosija (Y.)

A traditional red wine from Macedonia.

Krems (A.)

1. An important town and district of the Lower Austria region, northwest of Vienna.

2. A wine from Krems.

Kressman (F.)   1871

A merchant in Bordeaux; owns Château La Tour-Martillac (Graves).

Kretzer (I.)

A dialectic German word for rosé in the Alto Adige, Trentino-Alto Adige region, Italy.

Bad Kreuznach (G.)

A village in the Nahe region, Bereich Kreuznach, Grosslage Kronenberg, the regional center of the wine trade. The vineyards which are considered the best of 38 vineyards are: Hinkelstein, Krötenpfuhl, Brückes, Narrenkappe, St. Martin, Mollenbrunnen and Rosenheck.

Kreuznach (G.)

A *Bereich*, one of 2 in the Nahe region; the *Grosslagen* are: Kronenberg, Pfarrgarten, Schlosskapelle and Sonnenborn.

Kröv (G.)

A village in the Mosel-Saar-Ruwer region, Bereich Bernkastel, Grosslage Nacktarsch. The vineyards are Burglay, Herrenberg,

Kirchlay, Letterlay, Paradies and Steffensberg. 875 acres.

Krug (F.)   **1843**

A Champagne producer in Reims; makes
only two Champagnes: Grande Cuvée -
non-vintage and vintage. 500,000 bottles.
40 acres.

Krug Winery, Charles (U.S.)   **1861**

A large, old winery in St. Helena, Napa
Valley, California, actually C. Mondavi and
Sons; produces many varietal and jug (CK
brand) wines. The Vintage Selection Cabernet is considered the best. 1,200 acres in
various parts of Napa Valley. 1.8 million
cases.

Kruse, Thomas (U.S.)   **1971**

An unusual winery in Gilroy, Santa Clara
County, California; produces Cabernet,
Zinfandel, Sauvignon Blanc, French Colombard wines and a varietal made from
Thompson Seedless grapes; also a bottle-
fermented sparkling wine made from Grignolino and Zinfandel grapes. 3,000 cases.

Kuehn (F.)   **1675**

An estate and merchant in Ammerschwihr, Haut-Rhin district, Alsace region. 20 acres, including 12 acres of
Kaefferkopf (Riesling).

Kuentz-Bas (F.)   **1919**

An estate and merchant in Husseren-lès-
Châteaux, Haut-Rhin district, Alsace region. 30 acres.

Kuhlmann, Eugene (1858-1932) **(F.)**

A French hybridizer who developed Maréchal Foch (K.188.2) and Léon Millet
(K.194.2), both red grapes grown in the
eastern U.S.

Kuntra (T.)

A red grape grown in Turkey.

Kurfürstlay (G.)

A *Grosslage*, one of 10 in Bereich Bernkastel, in the Mosel-Saar-Ruwer region. It contains 11 villages, including part of
Bernkastel and all of Brauneberg. 42
vineyards.

kylix (Gr.)

A shallow goblet from ancient Greece.

L

L.

The abbreviation for Landot, a hybrid grape.

L.B.V. (P.)

The abbreviation for Late Bottled Vintage, a Port wine of a single vintage aged in casks for 3-6 years.

Lda. (P., Sp.)

Licenciada (licensed).

Ltda. (P.)

Limitada (ldt., limited).

La Mancha DO (Sp.)

A large region in central Spain; includes the following DO districts: Almansa, Mancha, Manchuela, Méntrida and Valdepeñas. 1.8 million acres.

La Morra (I.)

A village in the Barolo district, Piedmont region.

La Sabla (I.)

A red wine from Aymaville, in the Valle D'Aosta region of northwestern Italy; made from the Petit Rouge grape.

La Vigna (U.S.) 1977

A winery in Anthony, Mesilla Valley, southern New Mexico; grows *vinifera* grapes. 50 acres.

Labat, Château de (F.)

An estate in St.-Laurent, Haut-Médoc district, Bordeaux; classified in 1978 as a *Cru Bourgeois*.

Labégorce, Château (F.)

An estate in Margaux, Haut-Médoc district, Bordeaux; classified in 1932 as a *Cru Bourgeois*. 13,000 cases. 74 acres.

Labégorce-Zédé, Château (F.)

An estate in Soussans-Margaux, Haut-Médoc district, Bordeaux; classified in 1932 as a *Cru Bourgeois*. 10,000 cases. 52 acres.

Labouré-Roi (F.) 1832

An estate in Nuits-St.-Georges, Côte de Nuits district, Burgundy; owns Nuits-St.-Georges Bellecroix and Tribourg – 6.3 acres; also handles the René Manuel estate of 15 acres: Meursault Bouches Chères – 4 acres, Les Poruzots – 3 acres and Clos de la Baronne Monopole (red) – 6.3 acres.

Labrusca (I.)

A pink *spumante* wine from Correggio, near Reggio Emilia, in the Emilia-Romagna region; made from Lambrusco grapes.

labrusca (U.S.)

A species of grape – the *Vitis labrusca*, native to North America; produces wines with a so-called foxy taste, better suited for making semi-sweet than dry wines. Grape varieties which belong to this species are: Concord, Catawba, Delaware, Niagara, Dutchess, and Ives.

Labye, Cuvée Guillaume (F.)

A red wine from the Hospices de Nuits, Nuits-St.-Georges, Burgundy. The *cuvée* is composed of *Premier Cru* vineyard parcels in Nuit-St.-Georges.

Lacarelle, Domaine de (F.)

An estate in St.-Etienne-des-Oullières, Beaujolais-Villages district, Burgundy. 350 acres.

lacrima (I.)

Italian for "teardrop," a system of vinification utilizing very soft crushing; used in the Apulia region of southern Italy.

Lacroix, Albert (F.)

An estate in Savigny-lès-Beaune, Côte de Beaune district, Burgundy. 6 acres, including Savigny Aux Serpentières – 1.2 acres and Les Rouvrettes – 1.2 acres.

Lacryma Christi del Vesuvio DOC (I.)

Red, white and rosé wines from the slopes of Mt. Vesuvio, in the Campania region; the red and rosé made from Aglianico, Olivella and Piedirosso grapes, and the white from Coda di Volpe, Falanghina, Greco del Vesuvio and other grapes.

Lacrymarosa d'Irpinia (I.)

A rosé wine from the Vesuvio district, in the Campania region; made from Piedirosso, Olivella and Aglianico grapes.

Ladoix-Serrigny AOC (F.)

A commune just north of Aloxe-Corton, Côte de Beaune district, Burgundy; several vineyards are considered *Grands Crus* when used with the Corton designation preceding the vineyard name: Les Vergennes, Le Rognet en Corton, Les Carrières, etc.; the *Premier Cru* vineyards may also be sold as Aloxe-Corton: Les Basses Mourettes, La Coutière, Les Grandes Lolières, La Maréchaude, Les Petites Lolières and La Toppe-au-Vert. Other wines are sold as Côte de Beaune-Villages. 850 acres.

Ladoucette, de (F.)

An estate in Pouilly-sur-Loire, Pouilly-Fumé district, Upper Loire Valley; also uses the Baron de Ladoucette label (his best wine). 80,000 cases. 150 acres.

Lafarge, Michel (F.)

An estate in Volnay, Côte de Beaune district, Burgundy. 20 acres, including Volnay Clos des Chênes – 2.5 acres, Beaune Les Grèves – 1.2 acres and Meursault – 1.2 acres.

Lafaurie-Peyraguey, Château (F.)

An estate in Bommes, Sauternes district, Bordeaux; classified in 1855 as a *Premier Cru*; it was called Château Peyraguey in 1855 and is now divided into 2 properties, the other being Clos Haut-Peyraguey; produces sweet white wine and some dry white wine. 4,800 cases. 50 acres.

Lafite-Rothschild, Château (F.)

A famous estate in Pauillac, Haut-Médoc district, Bordeaux; classified in 1855 as a *Premier Cru*. Owned by Gombaud de Lafite in 1234, bought by the Rothschild family in 1868. The name Lafite comes from *"lahite"* – a corruption of *"la hauteur,"* which means the height, or knoll. The second wines are Carruades de Château Lafite (made as early as 1878, last vintage in 1967) and Moulin des Carruades, the second wine since 1974, but which used to be a third wine, made only in excellent years. The old spellings used were *Laffite*, *Lafitte* and *Laffitte*. 22,000 cases. 225 acres.

Lafleur, Château (F.)

An estate in Pomerol, Bordeaux. 1,200 caes. 10 acres.

Lafleur-Gazin, Château (F.)

An estate in Pomerol, Bordeaux. 1,200 cases. 10 acres.

Lafleur-Pétrus, Château (F.)

An estate in Pomerol, Bordeaux, next to Château Pétrus. 3,500 cases. 22 acres.

Lafões (P.)

A small district north of the Dão region and south of the Douro River; produces mostly red and some white wines.

Lafon, Château, (F.)

An unclassified estate in Sauternes, Sauternes district, Bordeaux. 2,000 cases. 15 acres.

Lafon, Château (F.)

An estate in Listrac, Haut-Médoc district, Bordeaux; classified in 1978 as a *Cru Grand Bourgeois*. 3,000 cases. 17 acres.

Lafon, Domaine des Comtes (F.)

An estate in Meursault, Côte de Beaune district, Burgundy. 30 acres, including Montrachet – .8 acre, Meursault Les Charmes – 4 acres, Les Perrières – 2 acres, Les Genevrières – 2 acres, La Goutte d'Or – 1.2 acres, Clos de la Barre Monopole – 5 acres, Volnay Les Santenots – 6 acres, Clos des Chênes – 1.2 acres and Champans – 2.5 acres.

Lafon-Rochet, Château (F.)

An estate in St.-Estèphe, Haut-Médoc district, Bordeaux; classified in 1855 as a *Quatrième Cru*; formerly Château Rochet. 110 acres. 15,000 cases.

Lafouge-Clerc et Fils, F. (F.)

An estate in Auxey-Duresses, Côte de Beaune district, Burgundy. 20 acres, including Auxey-Duresses La Chapelle – 2.5 acres, Les Duresses – .6 acre and some Meursault.

lagar, *plur.:* lagare (P., Sp.)

A large wooden or stone trough used for crushing grapes by foot in making Madeira and other wines; also, an old-style winepress.

Lage (G.)

A vineyard; a site or vineyard plot, formed by nature, continuous in extent and relatively uniform. Also called *Gewann* in the Baden and Württemberg regions; also called *Weinberg* and *Weingarten*. It may be divided into several vineyard parcels or holdings.

Lage im Alleinbesitz (G.)

A *monopole*; a single-owned vineyard site.

Lageder, Alois (I.)   1855

A winery in Bolzano, Trentino-Alto Adige region; produces Alto Adige, Caldara, Santa Maddalena and Terlano wines; made from their own and purchased grapes. 450,000 cases. 50 acres.

Lagniappe, Château (U.S.)

Wines from the Cedar Hill Winery, Cleveland, Ohio; made from Pinot Noir, Chancellor and Chambourcin grapes.

Lago di Caldaro DOC *also* Caldaro *also* Kalterersee (I.)

1. A lake and district southwest of Bolzano, in the Trentino-Alto Adige region in northeastern Italy, which produces:

2. A light red wine made from Schiava Grossa, Schiava Gentile and Schiava Grigia grapes.

Lagrange, Château (F.)

An estate in St.-Julien, Haut-Médoc district, Bordeaux; classified in 1855 as a *Troisième Cru*; it was known in 1287; formerly 750 acres (250 of vines) in the middle 19th century. 18,000 cases. 130 acres.

Lagrange, Château (F.)

An estate in Pomerol, Bordeaux. 2,500 cases. 20 acres.

Lagrein *also* Lagrina (I.)

A local red grape grown in the northern Trentino-Alto Adige region; used to make red and rosé wines; the red is called Lagrein Scuro or Lagrein Dunkel, and the rosé is called Lagrein Rosato or Lagrein Kretzer.

Lágrima (Sp.)

Spanish for "tear," a sweet, fortified Málaga wine.

lágrima (Sp.)

A method of obtaining must from grapes without mechanical means but rather from the weight of the grapes gently pressing out the juice.

Lagrina (I.)

A native red grape grown in the Alto Adige region. The same as *Lagrein* in German.

Laguiche et ses Fils, Marquis de (F.)

An estate in Chassagne-Montrachet, Côte de Beaune district, Burgundy. 12 acres, including Montrachet – 5 acres (made and bottled by Joseph Drouhin) and Chassagne-Montrachet Morgeot white – 4.2 acres, and red – 2.5 acres.

Laguna (Mex.)

A district around the cities of Torreón, Lerdo and Gómez Palacio; produces red, rosé and sherry-style wines.

Lagune, Château La (F.)

An estate in Ludon, Haut-Médoc district, Bordeaux; classified in 1855 as a *Troisième Cru*; originally planted in 1724; known in the 19th century as Grand-La-Lagune; became well-known after 1828. 20,000 cases. 140 acres.

Laidière, La (F.)

An estate in Bandol, in the Provence region.

Laira Vineyards (Aus.)   1966

An estate in the Coonawarra district, South Australia, owned by Eric Brand; produces Cabernet, a Cabernet-Malbec-Shiraz blend and Shiraz wines. 55 acres.

Laird and Company Virginia Wine Cellars (U.S.)

An old winery in North Garden, Virginia; produces *labrusca* wines.

Lairén (Sp.)

A white grape grown in the Montilla district, used in making sherry-like wines and white Valdepeñas wine; also called Airén.

Lake County (U.S.)

A region east of Mendocino County, and north of Napa County, California. 2,500 acres.

Lake Erie (U.S.)

A lake and district in Ohio, including the islands in the lake as well as the mainland; produces red, white and sparkling wines made from Catawba and Delaware grapes.

Lake Sylvia Vineyard (U.S.)   1976

A small winery in Maple Lake, northwest of Minneapolis, Minnesota; produces wines made from French hybrid grapes and from Variety 439. 5 acres.

Lake's Folly (Aus.)   1963

A winery in Pokolbin, north of Sidney, Lower Hunter Valley, New South Wales; produces mostly Cabernet, Shiraz and Chardonnay wines. 3,500 cases. 75 acres.

Lakespring Winery (U.S.)   1980

A winery in Napa City, Napa County, California; produces Cabernet, Merlot, Chardonnay, Chenin Blanc and Sauvignon Blanc wines from their own and purchased grapes. 7 acres. 15,000 cases.

Lalande, Armand (F.)   1844

A merchant in Bordeaux; a former owner of several fine *Châteaux*.

Lalande-de-Pomerol AOC (F.)

A village and district, which also includes Néac, north of Pomerol, in Bordeaux; produces red wine similar to Pomerol.

Laleure-Piot (F.)

An estate in Pernand-Vergelesses, Côte de Beaune district, Burgundy. 17 acres, including Pernand-Vergelesses Île des Vergelesses – 1.2 acres, Corton Bressandes – .8 acre, Beaune Les Blanches Fleurs – .8 acre, Savigny Vergelesses – .8 acre and Corton-Charlemagne – 2 acres.

Lamarche, Domaine Henry (F.)

An estate in Vosne-Romanée, Côte de Nuits district, Burgundy. 32 acres, including Grands Échézeaux – 1.2 acres, Échézeaux – 1.2 acres, Clos de Vougeot – 2.5 acres, Vosne-Romanée la Grande Rue Monopole – 4 acres, Aux Malconsorts – 2.5

acres, Les Suchots – 2 acres, Pommard Les Épenots- 4 acres and Pommard – 7.5 acres.

Lamarque, Château (F.)

An estate in Lamarque, Haut-Médoc district, Bordeaux; classified in 1978 as a *Cru Grand Bourgeois*. 25,000 cases. 115 acres.

Lamb Winery, Ronald (U.S.)   1976

A small winery in Morgan Hill, Santa Clara County, California; produces Zinfandel, Gamay Beaujolais, Chardonnay, Chenin Blanc and Johannisberg Riesling wines made from single-vineyard purchased grapes from Monterey, Sonoma and Amador counties. 1,000 cases.

Lamberhurst Priory (E.)   1972

A winery in Turnbridge Wells, Kent, the largest winery in England; produces white wine made from Müller-Thurgau, Seyval Blanc, Reichensteiner and Schönburger grapes. 35 acres.

Lambert Bridge (U.S.)   1976

A winery in Healdsburg, Dry Creek Valley, northern Sonoma County, California; produces Cabernet and Chardonnay wines. 10,000 cases. 80 acres.

Lamberti (I.)

A large winery in Lazize sul Garda, Veneto region; produces Bardolino, Soave, Valpolicella and sparkling wines made from their own and purchased grapes. 1.5 million cases.

Lambertins, Domaine des (F.)

An estate in Vacqueyras, Côtes du Rhône-Villages district, southern Rhône region.

Lamblin et fils (F.)   1920

An estate in the Chablis district, Burgundy. 17 acres, including Valmur – 1.6 acres and some Mont-de-Milieu, Beauroy and Fourchaume.

Lambrays, Clos des (F.)

A *Grand Cru* vineyard (official in 1981) in Morey-St.-Denis, Côte de Nuits district, Burgundy; also called Les Larrets. 20 acres.

Lambrusco (I.)

1. A red grape grown in the Emilia-Romagna region, frquently called by a local or variant name (L. di Sorbara, L. Grasparossa, L. Salamino), which produces:

2. Light, fizzy, red, white or rosé wines, sweet or dry, made around Reggio and Modena, in the central Emilia-Romagna region.

Lambrusco Bianco (I.)

A white version of Lambrusco made by separating the dark grape skins before fermenting and then made into a sparkling wine by the Charmat process.

Lambrusco Grasparossa di Castelvetro DOC (I.)

One of the 4 DOC designations for Lambrusco wine, from several villages south of Modena.

Lambrusco Reggiano DOC (I.)

One of the 4 DOC designations for Lambrusco wine, from the area around Reggio Emilia, northwest of Modena.

Lambrusco Salamino di Santa Croce DOC (I.)

One of the 4 DOC designations for Lambrusco wine, from Santa Croce and other villages around Carpi, northeast of Modena.

Lambrusco di Sorbara DOC (I.)

One of the 4 DOC designations for Lambrusco wine, from Sorbara and other villages northeast of Modena; produces what is considered to be the best Lambrusco wine.

Lamé-Delille-Boucard, G.A.E.C. de la (F.)

See under **G.A.E.C.**

Lamezia DOC (I.)

1. A village and district around Lamezia Terme and other villages near Catanzaro, in the southwestern Calabria region, which produces:

2. A red wine from made from Nerello Mascalese, Nerello Cappuccio, Gaglioppo and Greco Nero grapes.

Lamothe, Château (F.)

An estate in Sauternes, Sauternes district, Bordeaux; classified in 1855 as a *Deuxième Cru*. Château Lamothe-Bergey was once part of this *château*. 20 acres. 2,000 cases.

Lamothe, Château (F.)

An estate in Cissac, Haut-Médoc district, Bordeaux; classified in 1978 as a *Cru Grand Bourgeois*. 15,000 cases. 70 acres.

Lamothe-de-Bergeron, Château (F.)

An estate in Cussac, Haut-Médoc district, Bordeaux; classified in 1978 as a *Cru Bourgeois*. 15,000 caes. 100 acres.

Lamothe-Bergey, Château (F.)

An estate in Sauternes, Sauternes district, Bordeaux; classified in 1855 as a *Deuxième Cru*. It was once a part of Château Lamothe but is now separated. 1,500 cases.

Lampia (I.)

One of several clones of the Nebbiolo grape, DOC approved.

Lamy, Hubert (F.)

An estate in Saint-Aubin, Côte de Beaune district, Burgundy; split from the Jean Lamy estate; owns some Puligny-Montrachet, Chassagne-Montrachet and St.-Aubin.

Lamy et ses Fils, Jean (F.)

An estate in St.-Aubin, Côte de Beaune district, Burgundy. 55 acres, including Chassagne-Montrachet, Puligny-Montrachet, Santenay, Bâtard-Montrachet, St.-Aubin, Côte de Beaune-Villages and Aligoté. The estate has been split up between the two sons.

Lamy, René (F.)

An estate in Chassagne-Montrachet, Côte de Beaune district, Burgundy; split from the Jean Lamy estate; owns some Bâtard-Montrachet, Chassagne-Montrachet Clos

St.-Jean and Morgeot, Santenay and St.-Aubin.

Lan, Bodegas (Sp.)   1969

A winery in Fuenmayor, Rioja Alta region; produces red and white wines. 175 acres.

Lancers (P.)

A brand of slightly sparkling rosé wine made by J.M. de Fonseca; also makes a white (*branco*) and a red (*rubeo*).

Landal

A red hybrid grape – a cross of Seibel 5.455 and Seibel 2.816; also called Landot 244.

Landat, Château Le (F.)

An estate in Cissac, Haut-Médoc district, Bordeaux; classified in 1978 as a *Cru Bourgeois*. 15 acres. 2,500 cases.

landgoed (S. Af.)

An estate.

Landgräflich (G.)

Belonging to a landgrave.

Landmark Vineyards (U.S.)   1974

A winery in Windsor, Russian River Valley, Sonoma County, California; produces Cabernet, Zinfandel, Pinot Noir, Chardonnay, Johannisberg Riesling and Gewürztraminer wines. 80 acres in Russian River Valley and Alexander Valley. 15,000 cases.

Landon, Château (F.)

An estate in Bégadan, Médoc district, Bordeaux; classified in 1978 as a *Cru Bourgeois*. 15,000 cases. 62 acres.

Landonne, La (F.)

The best vineyard in the Côte Brune, Côte-Rôtie district, northern Rhône region; owned by Guigal.

Landot, Pierre (1900-42) (F.)

A French hybridizer from Conzieu, Ain Department; developed several hybrid grapes, including L. 244, or Landal (red),

L. 2281 (red), and L. 4511, or Landot Noir (red).

Landskroon Estate EWO (S. Af.)   1974

An estate in the Paarl district; produces Port-style wines, Pinot Noir, Shiraz, Cinsault and Cabernet wines. 500 acres.

Landwein (G.)   1982

A new official designation for regional wines, a step higher than *Tafelwein* but below QbA.

Lanessan, Château (F.)

An estate in Cussac, Haut-Médoc district, Bordeaux; classified in 1966 as a *Cru Grand Bourgeois Exceptionnel*; not classified in 1978. 12,500 cases. 75 cases.

Langenbach & Co. (G.)

A merchant in Worms; markets estate and generic wines.

Langenlois (A.)

A village and district just northeast of Krems, in the Lower Austria region; produces white wine made from the Grüner Veltliner grape.

Langenlonsheim (G.)

A village in the Nahe region, Bereich Kreuznach, Grosslage Sonnenborn. The vineyards are: Bergborn, Königsschild, Lauerweg, Löhrer Berg, Rothenberg, St. Antoniusweg and Steinchen.

Langenzug (F.)

A vineyard in Rouffach, Haut-Rhin district, in the Alsace region.

Langoa-Barton, Château (F.)

An estate in St.-Julien, Haut-Médoc district, Bordeaux; classified in 1855 as a *Troisième Cru;* known as Pontet-Langlois until Hugh Barton bought it in 1821; was a part of Château Léoville until the sub-division occurred in 1826; château-bottled only since 1969. 50 acres. 8,000 cases.

Languedoc (F.)

A large region of the Midi, in southern France, sometimes joined with Roussillon as one immense region. There are numerous VDQS districts and a few AOC districts as well, covering red, white, rosé and sparkling wines. The principal grapes grown are Carignan, Cinsault, Grenache, Clairette and Bourboulenc.

Languettes, Les (F.)

A *Grand Cru* vineyard (in part) in Aloxe-Corton, Côte de Beaune district, Burgundy, when the name appears after Corton. Part of the vineyard is a *Premier Cru*. 20 acres.

Laniotte, Château (F.)

An estate in St.-Émilion, Bordeaux; classified in 1969 as a *Grand Cru Classé*. 2,500 cases. 13 acres.

Lanson Père et Fils (F.)   1760, 1838

A Champagne-producing firm in Reims; Noble Cuvée, a *cuvée de prestige*, was added in 1982. 5 million bottles. 550 acres.

Lanzac, de (F.)

An estate in Tavel, southern Rhône region.

Larcis-Ducasse, Château (F.)

An estate in St.-Émilion, Bordeaux; classified in 1955 as a *Grand Cru Classé*. It is one of 2 *châteaux* not in St.-Émilion village, but in St. Laurent des Combes. 6,000 cases. 25 acres.

Larmande, Château (F.)

An estate in St.-Émilion, Bordeaux; classified in 1955 as a *Grand Cru Classé*. 5,000 caes. 30 acres.

Laroche, Domaine (F.)

An estate in the Chablis district, Burgundy. 55 acres, including Chablis Blanchot – 12 acres, Les Clos – 2.5 acres, Bougros – 1 acre, Fourchaume – 17 acres, Vaillons – 2.5 acres and Montmains – 2.5 acres. Controlled by *négociant* Bacheroy-Josselin.

Larose Trintaudon, Château (F.)   1965

An estate in St.-Laurent, Haut-Médoc district, Bordeaux; classified in 1978 as a *Cru Grand Bourgeois*. 70,000 cases. 390 acres.

Laroze, Château (F.)

An estate in St.-Émilion, Bordeaux; classified in 1955 as a *Grand Cru Classé*. 10,000 cases. 70 acres.

Larrets, Les (F.)

Another name for the Clos des Lambrays vineyard in Morey-St.-Denis, Côte de Nuits district, Burgundy. 20 acres.

Larrey (F.)

A commune in the northern Côte de Nuits district, Burgundy, that was known for its wines in the 19th century.

Larrivaux, Château (F.)

An estate in Cissac, Haut-Médoc district, Bordeaux; classified in 1932 as a *Cru Bourgeois*. It was combined with Château Hanteillan in 1979. 1,900 cases. 12 acres.

Larrivet-Haut-Brion, Château (F.)

An unclassified estate in Léognan, Graves district, Bordeaux. 5,500 cases. 35 acres.

Lartigue de Brochon, Château (F.)

An estate in St.-Seurin-de-Cadourne, Haut-Médoc district, Bordeaux; classified in 1978 as a *Cru Bourgeois*. 30 acres. 8,000 cases.

Lascombes, Château (F.)

An estate in Margaux, Haut-Médoc district, Bordeaux; classified in 1855 as a *Deuxième Cru*. 35,000 cases. 250 acres.

Laski Rizling (Y.)

The Yugoslavian name for the Wälschriesling, or Italian Riesling grape.

Lassalle, Cru (F.)

An estate in Potensac, Medoc district, Bordeaux; classified in 1978 as a *Cru Bourgeois*, actually a part of Château Potensac.

Lasserre, Château *also* La Serre (F.)

An estate in St.-Émilion; Bordeaux; classified in 1955 as a *Grand Cru Classé;* at the end of the 19th century it was a part of a large vineyard which included part of Château Pavie. 4,000 cases. 18 acres.

late-bottled vintage Port (P.)

A vintage Port kept in wood for about 5 years, blended from different vineyards.

Latisana DOC (I.)

A town and small district in the southern part of the Friuli-Venezia Giulia region; produces varietal wines made from Cabernet, Merlot, Pinot Bianco, Pinot Grigio, Refosco, Tocai and Verduzzo grapes.

Latium *also* Lazio (I.)

A region in southwestern Italy around Rome; the most well-known wines are Castelli Romani, Frascati, Est! Est!! Est!!! and Colli Albani.

Latour, Château (F.)

A famous estate in Pauillac, Haut-Médoc district, Bordeaux; classified in 1855 as a *Premier Cru;* 70% Cabernet, the rest is Merlot, Cabernet Franc and Petit Verdot grapes; well-known for requiring exceptionally long aging in good vintages and for making good wines in poor vintages; the second wine is Les Forts de Latour, made principally from younger vines, since 1966. 20,000 cases. 150 acres.

Latour, Henri (F.)

An estate in Auxey-Duresses, Côte de Beaune district, Burgundy. 15 acres, including Auxey-Duresses La Chapelle – 1.2 acres and Les Grands Champs – 1.2 acres.

Latour, Louis (F.)   1797

An estate and *négociant* in Beaune, Côte de Beaune district, Burgundy. 115 acres, including Chambertin – 2.5 acres, Romanée-Saint-Vivant Quatre Journaux – 2.5 acres, Corton (Château Corton-Grancey) – 40 acres, Corton Clos de la Vigne au Saint Monopole – 6.6 acres, Corton-Charlemagne – 17 acres, Aloxe-Corton Les Chailts – 11 acres, Pernand-Vergelesses Île des ergelesses – 2 acres, Les Vignes Franches 6.6 acres, Les Perrières – 2.5 acres, Clos u Roi – 1.2 acres, Les Grèves – .5 acre, ommard Les Épenots- 1.2 acres, Volnay es Mitans – 2.5 acres and Chevalier-Monachet Les Demoiselles – 1.2 acres.

atour Blanche, Château (F.)

n estate in St.-Émilion, Bordeaux; classi-ed in 1955 as a *Grand Cru*. 400 cases. 3 cres.

atour-à-Pomerol, Château (F.)

n estate in Pomerol, Bordeaux. 3,500 ases. 22 acres.

atricières-Chambertin AOC (F.)

ne of 9 *Grand Cru* vineyards in Gevrey-Chambertin, Côte de Nuits district, Bur-undy. 15 acres.

audun (F.)

commune of the Côtes du Rhône-Vil-ages district, southern Rhône region; pro-duces red, white and rosé wines.

auerburg, Weingut L. (G.) 1700

small estate in Bernkastel, Mosel-Saar-Ruwer region; owns vineyrds in Bernkas-el, Wehlen and Graach. 10 acres.

auffen (G.)

village in the Württemberg region, Be-eich Württembergisch Unterland, Gross-age Kirchenweinberg. The vineyards are: ungfer, Katzenbeisser, Nonnenberg and Riedersbückele.

augel, Michel (F.)

merchant in Marlenheim, Bas-Rhin dis-rict, Alsace region. 300,000 cases. 25 acres Pinot Noir).

aujac, Château (F.)

n estate in Bégadan, Médoc district, Bor-deaux; classified in 1978 as a *Cru Grand Bourgeois*. 14,000 cases. 60 acres.

Laurel Glen Vineyards (U.S.) 1980

A winery in Santa Rosa, Sonoma County, California; produces Cabernet wine. 25 acres. 5,000 cases.

Laurence, L., Courtier et Viticulteur (F.)

An estate and merchant in Dezize, Côte de Beaune district, Burgundy; owns Santenay Les Gravières – 2.5 acres and some Pu-ligny-Montrachet and Côte de Beaune-Villages.

Laurets, Château des *or* les (F.)

An estate in Puissequin-St.-Émilion, Bor-deaux. 37,500 cases. 175 acres.

Laurier, Domaine (U.S.) 1978

A winery in Forestville, Russian River Val-ley, Sonoma County, California; produces Cabernet, Pinot Noir, Chardonnay, Sau-vignon Blanc and Johannisberg Riesling wines. 6,000 cases. 30 acres.

Lauzet (F.)

A white grape grown in the Jurançon dis-trict, in the Southwest region.

Lauzières, Domaine de (F.)

An estate in Mouriès, in the Provence region.

Lavalière, Château (F.)

An estate in St.-Cristoly, Médoc district, Bordeaux; classified in 1978 as a *Cru Bour-geois* Being Reconstituted. 40 acres. 11,000 cases.

Lavaut (F.)

A *Premier Cru* vineyard in Gevrey-Cham-bertin, Côte de Nuits district, Burgundy. 23 acres.

Lavaux (Sw.)

A district along the northern shore of Lake Geneva, in the eastern Vaud region; pro-duces white wines made from the Chas-selas grape.

Lavières, Les (F.)

A *Premier Cru* vineyard in Savigny, Côte de Beaune district, Burgundy. 45 acres.

Laville-Haut-Brion, Château (F.)

An estate in Talence, Graves district, Bordeaux; classified in 1959 as a *Cru Classé* for white wine only; owned by Château La Mission Haut-Brion. 50% Sauvignon, 50% Sémillon grapes. 1,800 cases. 12 acres.

Lavrottes, Les (F.)

A *Premier Cru* vineyard in Chambolle-Musigny, Côte de Nuits district, Burgundy. 2.5 acres.

Lawrence Winery (U.S.)   1979

A large winery in San Luis Obispo, San Luis Obispo County, California; produces varietal and bulk wines. 200,000 cases.

Lazio (I.)

The Italian name for the Latium region.

Leacock & Co. (P.)   1754

A producer of Madeira wines.

Leányka (H.,R.)

Hungarian for "young girl," a white grape grown in Hungary and Romania.

Leasingham (Aus.)

A brand of wine from the Stanley Wine Company, Clare/Watervale district, South Australia; includes Cabernet and Riesling wines made from purchased grapes.

Lebaron, François (F.)

A merchant in Beaune, Côte de Beaune district, Burgundy.

Lebelin, Cuvée (F.)

A red wine from the Hospices de Beaune, Côte de Beaune district, Burgundy. The *cuvée* is composed part of one vineyard in Monthélie: Les Duresses – 2 acres. 225 cases.

lebrija (Sp.)

A special local clay used to fine or clarify the new wines of the Montilla district, in southern Spain.

Leconfield (Aus.)   1970

A small winery in the Coonawarra district, in South Australia; produces Cabernet and Rhine Riesling wines. 5,000 cases.

Ledia (I.)

A red grape grown in the northern Trentino-Alto Adige region; also called Mittervernatsch.

Lee Vineyard (U.S.)

A vineyard in the Carneros district, southern Napa Valley, California; produces Pinot Noir for Acacia Winery.

Leelanau Wine Cellars (U.S.)   1975

A winery in Omena, Lake Leelanau, north of Traverse City, northern Michigan; produces wines from *vinifera* and hybrid grapes. 60 acres.

lees

The sediment left at the bottom of the vat after fermentation and racking.

Leeuwin (Aus.)   1974

A large winery in Margaret River, Western Australia; produces Cabernet, Pinot Noir, Shiraz, Chardonnay, Rhine Riesling and Gewürztraminer wines. 30,000 cases. 225 acres.

Leeward Winery (U.S.)   1978

A small winery in Oxnard, Ventura County, California; produces Cabernet, Zinfandel and Chardonnay wines from purchased grapes. 4,000 cases.

lefkos (Gr.)

White.

Leflaive, Domaine (F.)

An estate in Puligny-Montrachet, Côte de Beaune district, Burgundy. 45 acres, including Chevalier-Montrachet – 2.5 acres, tard-Montrachet – 5 acres, Bienvenues-tard-Montrachet – 2.5 acres, Puligny-ontrachet Clavoillons – 12.5 acres, Les ombettes – 1.7 acres, Les Pucelles – 7.5 res and Blagny (red) – 4 acres.

·iser (G.)

village in the Mosel-Saar-Ruwer region, ereich Bernkastel, Grosslagen Kurfür-lay and Beerenlay. The vineyards are: chlossberg in Grosslage Kurfürstlay; and iederberg-Helden, Rosenlay and Süssen-erg in Grosslage Beerenlay. 500 acres.

eiwen (G.)

village in the Mosel-Saar-Ruwer region, ereich Bernkastel, Grosslage Sankt Mi-nael. The vineyards are Laurentiuslay and lostergarten. 1,100 acres.

ejeune, Domaine (F.)

n estate in Pommard, Côte de Beaune istrict, Burgundy. 20 acres, including ommard Les Rugiens – 2.5 acres, Les Ar-illières – 4 acres, Les Poutures – 2.5 acres, ras – 4 acres and Les Chaponnières – 1.2 cres.

emberger *also* Limberger (G.)

small, red, late-ripening, very produc-ive grape grown in Württemberg; it nakes a full-bodied red wine; it is often lended with Trollinger or Portugieser rapes. Also called Blaufränkischer in Austria.

embo Vineyard (U.S.)   1977

winery in Lewistown, Pennsylvania; roduces Seyval Blanc, Chelois and de Chaunac wines. 6 acres.

emmon Ranch (U.S.)

vineyard in St. Helena, Napa Valley, Cal-fornia; owned by Beringer winery; pro-luces Cabernet grapes. 18 acres.

emnos, *also* Limnos (Gr.)

n island in the Aegean Sea, south of Thrace; produces a well-known Muscat vine.

Leneuf, Héritiers Raoul (F.)

An estate in Pommard, Côte de Beaune district, Burgundy. 10 acres, including some Pommard and Beaune.

Lenoir

A red hybrid grape, originated in South Carolina in 1829. Also called Jacquez and Black Spanish.

Lenz, Peter (U.S.)   planted 1979
first wine 1983

A winery in Peconic, North Fork district, Long Island region, N.Y.; produces Char-donnay, Cabernet, Merlot, Pinot Noir and Gewürztraminer wines. 4,000 cases. 30 acres.

León (Sp.)

A city and district in the Old Castile region, near the northeastern corner of Portugal, in northwestern Spain; produces old and new style red wines made from Prieto Pi-cudo, Tempranillo and Mencia grapes, and some white wines made from Verdejo and Jerez Palomino grapes.

León S.A., Jean (Sp.)   1964

An estate in Plá de Penedès, Penedès dis-trict, Catalonia region; produces only Ca-bernet Sauvignon and Chardonnay wines. 17,000 cases. 275 acres.

Léon Millot

A red hybrid grape. Also called Kuhlmann 194-2; grown in New York State, U.S.A.

Leonay, Château (Aus.)

A winery in the Barossa Valley, South Aus-tralia, with vineyards in the Clare/Water-vale district as well; produces a renowned Rhine Riesling wine as well as sherry-style Florita and some red wines. It is now owned by Lindeman's.

Leone de Castris (I.)   1929

A large winery in Salice Salentino, Apulia region; produces Locorotondo, Salice Sal-entino and a wide range of red, white and rosé wines; made from their own and pur-chased grapes. 1,000 acres.

Léoville-Barton, Château (F.)

An estate in St.-Julien, Haut-Médoc district, Bordeaux; classified in 1855 as a *Deuxième Cru;* bottled at Château Langoa-Barton; one of the three sections of the original Château Léoville, split up c. 1820. 15,000 cases. 85 acres.

Léoville-Las-Cases, Château (F.)

An estate in St.-Julien, Haut-Médoc district, Bordeaux; classified in 1855 as a *Deuxième Cru;* one of the three sections of the original Château Léoville, split up c. 1820. The second wine is sold as Clos du Marquis. 25,000 cases. 200 acres.

Léoville-Poyferré, Château (F.)

An estate in St.-Julien, Haut-Médoc district, Bordeaux; classified in 1855 as a *Deuxième Cru;* one of the three sections of the original Château Léoville, split up in c. 1820. The second wine is Château Moulin-Riche. 20,000 cases. 130 acres.

Lepe (Sp.)

1. A village in the Huelva district, in the southern Extremadura region, in the southwestern corner of Spain, which produces:

2. A Sherry-like wine that is famous because it is mentioned in Chaucer's *Canterbury Tales* (The *Pardoner's Tale.*)

Lepitre, Abel (F.)   1924

A Champagne producer in Reims; the special *cuvées* are Crémant Blanc de Blancs and Prince A. de Bourbon Parme. 1 million bottles. No vineyards.

Lequin-Roussot, Domaine (F.)   1734

An estate in Santenay, Côte de Beaune district, Burgundy. 36 acres, including Bâtard-Montrachet – .8 acre, Corton – 1 acre, Chassagne-Montrachet Morgeot – 3 acres, Santenay La Comme – 5 acres, Le Passe-Temps – 3 acres and Petit Clos Rousseau – .6 acre.

Leroy, Établissements (F.)   1868

An estate in Auxey-Duresses, Côte de Beaune district, Burgundy; also co-owner of Domaine de La Romanée-Conti. 15 acres, including Chambertin – 1.7 acres, Clos de Vougeot – .8 acre, Musigny – 1 acre, Pommard – 2 acres, Meursault – 5.5 acres and Auxey-Duresses – 4 acres.

Lesbian (Gr.)

An ancient, sweet Greek wine, mentioned by Athenaeus.

Lese (G.)

The harvest; the vintage.

Lesegut (G.)

A wine estate.

Lessona DOC (I.)

1. A small district in the northern Piedmont region, which produces:

2. A red wine made from Nebbiolo, Vespolina and Bonarda grapes.

Lestage, Château (F.)

An estate in Listrac, Haut-Médoc district, Bordeaux; classified in 1978 as a *Cru Bourgeois.* 18,000 cases. 120 acres.

Lettere (I.)

1. A village, south of Naples, near Sorrento, in the western Campania region, which produces:

2. A red wine made from Aglianico, Olivella, and Per'e Palummo grapes.

Leu Winery, Château De (U.S.)   1981

A winery in Suisun, Solano County, California; produces Petite Sirah, Gamay, Chardonnay, Fumé Blanc, Chenin Blanc and French Colombard wines. 20,000 cases.

Leutershausen (G.)

A village in the Baden region, Bereich Badische Bergstrasse/Kraichgau, Grosslage Rittersberg. The vineyards are Kahlberg and Staudenberg.

Leverano DOC (I.)

1. A village and district in the southwestern Apulia region, which produces:

230

Red, white and rosé wines, the red and
sé wines made from the Negroamaro
pe and the white wines made from Mal-
sia Bianca, Bombino Bianco and Trebbi-
o Toscano grapes.

ure (F.)

ast.

yvraz & Stevens (Sw.)   **1905**

estate in Geneva; produces Chasselas,
may and Pinot Noir wines. 125 acres.

atiko *also* **Liatico (Gr.)**

red grape grown in Crete.

bertas, Château (S. Af.)

red wine from Stellenbosch Farmers Wi-
ry; made from a blend of Cabernet,
iraz and Cinsault grapes.

berty School (U.S.)

e second wine of Caymus Vineyard, in
utherford, Napa Valley, California; in-
udes Cabernet Sauvignon, Zinfandel and
hardonnay wines.

brandi (I.)   **1950**

n estate in Cirò Marina, Calabria; pro-
uces Cirò wines. 65,000 cases. 125 acres.

ichine & Co., Alexis (F.)

merchant in Bordeaux; owns Château
rieuré-Lichine.

e (F.)

he lees, or sediment produced by fermen-
tion of the must; it contains solid parti-
es, skins, pips, etc.

iebfraumilch (G.)

Originally the white wine of the Liebfrau-
nkirche in Worms, then called Liebfraunstift (after the name of the vineyard);
ow it refers to any German wine of good
uality made from any of the usual grapes
rown in the particular region of origin.
he name has been used since 1744. Be-
ween 1910 and 1971 it was used only for
heinhessen wines; since 1982 it refers
nly to a *Qualitätswein* from the Nahe,

Rheinhessen or Rheinpfalz regions, the
wine from each region kept separate from
each other.

Liebfraunstift (G.)

The vineyard and wine of the Liebfrauen-
kirche, in Worms, Grosslage Liebfrauenmorgen, Bereich Wonnegau, in the
Rheinhessen region.

lieblich (G.)

Slightly sweet.

Liechtenstein

A small country nestled between Switzerland and Austria; known mostly for the
light red Vaduzer wine.

Liechtenstein'sches Weingut, Prinz (A.)
      1813

A merchant in the Steiermark region; produces Schilcher rosé wine and other wines;
made from their own and purchased
grapes. 80,000 cases. 15 acres.

lieu-dit (F.)

A local vineyard site, or neighborhood.

Liger-Belair, Abbé (F.)

An estate in Vosne-Romanée, Côte de
Nuits district, Burgundy; also called Château de Vosne-Romanée. 3.6 acres, including La Romanée Monopole – 2 acres and
Vosne-Romanée Les Reignots – 1.6 acre;
the wines are handled by Bouchard Père et
Fils.

Liger-Belair et Fils (F.)   **1720**

An estate in Nuits-St.-Georges, Côte de
Nuits district, Burgundy. 9 acres, including
Richebourg – 1.3 acres, Clos de Vougeot – 2
acres, Nuits-St.-Georges Les St.-Georges –
5.7 acres and the Domaine du Vivier
(Beaujolais).

light wine (U.S.)

A wine with a low alcohol content, 7-9%,
therefore, with fewer calories for diet-con-
scious consumers. It was first introduced
around 1981-1982.

Lignier et Fils, G. (F.)

An estate in Morey-St.-Denis, Côte de Nuits district, Burgundy. 37 acres, including Clos de la Roche – 5 acres, Clos St.-Denis – 5 acres and Morey-St.-Denis Clos des Ormes – 12 acres.

Liguria (I.)

A region in northwestern Italy, on the Italian Riviera; white wine production predominates here but some red is also produced. Genoa is the center. 10.6 million gallons.

Lillet (F.)

A semi-sweet, red or white apéritif made from wine, brandy and flavorings.

Lilliano (I.)

An estate in Castellina in Chianti, Tuscany region; produces Chianti Classico wines. 22,000 cases.

Limberger *also* **Lemberger (G.)**

A red grape grown in Germany and Austria; also called Blaufränkischer, Bleufrancs and Franconia.

Limnio (Gr.)

A red grape grown in Macedonia.

Limoux (F.)

A village near Carcassonne, in the southwestern Languedoc region; produces a white wine called Vin de Blanquette and Blanquette de Limoux, a sparkling wine.

Lindeman's Ben Ean (Aus.)　　　1870

A large winery with vineyards all over Australia. Ben Ean vineyard is in Lower Hunter Valley, New South Wales; Leo Buring vineyard is in the Barossa Valley and Rouge Homme vineyard is in Coonawarra. 500,000 cases. 1,400 acres.

Linderos, Viña (Ch.)

A vineyard and winery in the Maipo Valley, central Chile; produces mainly Cabernet Sauvignon wine, and some Sémillon, Riesling and Chardonnay wines. 250 acres.

Linero Bianco (I.)

A dry white wine from La Spezia, in the southeastern Liguria region, made from Vermentino, Malvasia and Trebbiano grapes.

Linero Rosso (I.)

A red wine from La Spezia, in the southeastern Liguria region, made from Sangiovese, Vermentino, and Nebbiolo grapes with some Cabernet and Merlot grapes.

Liot, Château (F.)

An unclassified estate in Barsac, Sauternes district, Bordeaux. 3,000 cases. 28 acres.

Lipovina (Cz.)

A grape grown in eastern Czechoslovakia, used in making a Tokay-style wine along with Furmint and Muscatel grapes.

liqueur d'expédition (F.)

Dosage; a mixture of sugar, Champagne and brandy which is added to the Champagne after *dégorgement* in various amounts (from 0-10%), depending on the desired sweetness.

liqueur de tirage (F.)

A mixture of cane sugar dissolved in wine, sometimes with a little citric acid added; this is added to each bottle of wine, in the Champagne region, in order to induce a second fermentation. This is the process which causes the production of CO_2 gas, which remains in the bottle.

Liquière, Château de la (F.)

An estate in Cabrerolles, Faugères district, Languedoc region; produces red, white and rosé wines.

liquoreux (F.)

Rich and sweet, referring to a wine; having the qualities of a liqueur.

liquoroso (I.)

Liqueur-like; sweet, and sometimes fortified, as a dessert wine.

irac AOC (F.)

A village and district near Tavel, in the outhern Rhône region, including Lirac, oquemaure, St.-Laurent-des-Arbres and t.-Geniès-de-Comolas, which produces:

. Red and rosé wines made mostly from he Grenache and also Cinsault, Syrah and Mourvèdre grapes, and white wine from Clairette and Maccabéo grapes. 1,200 acres f AOC Lirac, 3,700 acres of Côtes du Rhône wines.

Lisbon Port (P.)

A port-like wine from Lisbon.

Lisini (I.)

A small estate in Montalcino, Tuscany region; produces Brunello and Rosso wines. 5,000 cases. 25 acres.

Listán (Sp.)

Another name for the Palomino grape grown in the Sherry region; also grown in Argentina.

Listrac AOC (F.)

A commune in the Haut-Médoc district, Bordeaux; produces red wines which are classified as *Cru Bourgeois* and *Cru Grand Bourgeois*. 750 acres.

liter

A standard liquid metric measure equal to 100 centiliters, or 33.8 fluid ounces, or 1.06 quarts.

Little Karoo WO *also* Klein Karoo (S. Af.)

A district around Montagu, east of Cape Town; known for producing a dessert wine from the Muscat grape.

Live Oaks Winery (U.S.)   1912

A winery in Gilroy, Santa Clara County, California; produces jug wines. 18,000 cases.

Livermore Valley (U.S.)

A district in Alameda County, east of San Francisco, California; produces primarily white wines.

Livermore Valley Cellars (U.S.)   1978

A winery in Livermore, Livermore Valley, Alameda County, California; produces Pinot blanc, French Colombard, Grey Riesling and Golden Chasselas wines. 35 acres. 5,000 cases.

Liversan, Château (F.)

An estate in St.-Sauveur, Haut-Médoc district, Bordeaux; classified in 1978 as a *Cru Grand Bourgeois*. 18,000 cases. 110 acres.

Livran, Château (F.)

An estate in St. Germain-d'Esteuil, Médoc district, Bordeaux; classified in 1932 as a *Cru Bourgeois*. 16,000 cases. 100 acres.

Ljutomer *also* Lutomer (Y.)

1. A famous district and town in eastern Slovenia, which produces:

2. Varietal white wines made from several grapes, including Riesling, Sylvaner, Traminer, Šipon, Sauvignon, etc.

Llano Estacado (U.S.)   1971

A winery in Lubbock, in northwestern Texas, also known as the Staked Plain Winery; produces wines made from numerous hybrid, *vinifera* and muscadine grapes. 15 acres.

Llords and Elwood (U.S.)   1955

A wine company based in Los Angeles which uses leased facilities in San José and partly in Weibel Vineyards, Warm Springs, Alameda County, California; produces Sherry, Port, Johannisberg Riesling and Pinot Noir wines from purchased grapes. 20,000 cases.

Locorotondo DOC (I.)

1. A village and district in the southern Apulia region, which produces:

2. A white wine made from Verdeca and Bianco di Alessano grapes; a spumante version is also made.

lodge *also* loja (P.)

An above-ground warehouse for storing and aging Port wines, mostly situated along the River Douro.

Lohr, J. (U.S)   1974

The label used for wines made by the Turgeon and Lohr Winery in San José, Santa Clara County, California.

Loire (F.)

An important river, valley and very large region in northwestern France and usually divided into the following regions: Muscadet, Anjou (or Anjou-Saumur), Touraine and Upper Loire. The region produces numerous red and rosé wines from the Cabernet Franc, Gamay and Pinot Noir grapes and white wines from Chasselas, Chenin Blanc, Muscadet and Sauvignon Blanc grapes.

loja (P.)

A lodge; an above-ground warehouse where wine is stored in barrels.

Lolle (Sp.)

A local red grape from the Canary Islands.

Lolonis (U.S.)

A vineyard in Ukiah, Mendocino County; produces Zinfandel grapes for Fetzer Vineyards. 100 acres.

Loma, La (U.S.)

A vineyard south of Napa, Carneros district, in Napa Valley, California, owned by the L. Martini winery; produces mostly Pinot Noir and Gamay Beaujolais and some Chardonnay grapes. 340 acres.

Lombardy (I.)

A region in northern Italy, east of the Piedmont region; the largest districts are Valtellina (planted with Nebbiolo grapes), Lugana and Oltrepò Pavese.

Lomelino Lda. (P.)   1820

A producer of Madeira wines.

London Vineyard, Jack (U.S.)

A vineyard in Glen Ellen, Sonoma County; grows Cabernet grapes for Château St Jean and Kenwood wineries.

Lônes, Domaine des (F.)

An estate in the Coteaux du Tricastin district of the southern Rhône region.

Long-Dépaquit, Domaine A. (F.)

An estate in the Chablis district, Burgundy. 63 acres, including some Les Clos, Vaudésir, Les Preuses, Vaillons, Lys and Beugnons; distributed by Bichot, of Beaune.

Long Island (U.S.)   1975

A new region on the eastern end of Long Island, New York, divided into the North Fork and South Fork districts; almost all the grapes and wines produced are *vinifera* varieties. Since 1975 4 wineries and about 30 vineyards have been established. Hargrave Vineyard made the first L.I. wine in 1975.

Long Vineyards (U.S.)   1978

A winery on Pritchard Hill, in St. Helena, Napa Valley, California; produces Cabernet, Chardonnay and Johannisberg Riesling wines. 1,500 cases. 20 acres.

Loong Yan (China)

A white grape grown in Hebei, eastern China; used to make Great Wall Wine. The name means "Dragon's Eye."

Lopez de Heredia Viña Tondonia S.A., R. (Sp.)   1877

A well-known winery in Haro, Rioja Alta region; produces several wines including Viña Tondonia, Viña Bosconia, Viña Cubillo, Viña Gravonia, etc.; made from their own and purchased grapes. 90,000 cases.

Loppin, Cuvée (F.)

A white wine from the Hospices de Beaune, Côte de Beaune district, Burgundy. The *cuvée* is composed of only one vineyard in Meursault: Les Criots – 1.3 acres. 175 cases.

Lorenz, Gustave (F.)

An estate and merchant in Bergheim, northern Haut-Rhin district, Alsace region. 200,000 cases. 60 acres.

orenz, Jerôme (F.)

An estate in Bergheim, northern Haut-
hin district, Alsace region. 25 acres.

orraine (F.)

A small region in northeastern France; it
ncludes the Côtes de Toul VDQS district,
which produces mostly *vin gris* (light rosé)
nd Vins de la Moselle VDQS, which pro-
uces mostly light rosé and white wines.

os Alamos Winery (U.S.)   1972

A vineyard and winery in Los Alamos,
anta Barbara County, California; pro-
uces Chardonnay and Zinfandel wines.
50 acres.

os Hermanos (U.S.)

A label used for second-quality varietal
nd generic jug wines made by Beringer
Vineyards, Napa Valley, California.

os Monteros (Sp.)

A red wine from the Valencia district, in
astern Spain, made entirely from the
Monastrell grape.

os Reyes (Mex.)

1. A town near Mexico City.
2. A well-known red wine from Los Reyes
nade by the Pedro Domecq Winery.

os Tercios (Sp.)

A district in the Sherry region, west of
erez.

ost Hills Vineyards (U.S.)   1976

A winery in Lost Hills, Kern County, Cal-
fornia; produces varietal and generic
wines. 100,000 cases. 1,500 acres.

ote (P.)

A selected lot of new Port wine taken from
he *quinta* to rest and age.

Loudenne, Château (F.)

An estate in St.-Yzans, Médoc district,
Bordeaux; classified in 1978 as a *Cru Grand
Bourgeois*. 15,000 cases. 80 acres.

Louisiana (U.S.)

A state in the southern United States; there
are no commercial wineries here except
those that produce orange wine.

Loupiac AOC (F.)

1. A commune in the Bordeaux region on
the right bank of the River Garonne, across
from the Sauternes district, which
produces:
2. A sweet white wine made from Sauvignon, Sémillon and Muscadelle grapes,
similar to wine from neighboring St.-
Croix-du-Mont.

Loureiro (P.)

A white grape grown in the Vinho Verde
region.

Louvière, Château La (F.)

A large unclassified estate in Léognan,
Graves district, Bordeaux; produces red
and white wines. 25,000 cases. 125 acres.

Lovedale (Aus.)

A vineyard of the McWilliams Winery in
Lower Hunter Valley, New South Wales;
produces white wine from the Sémillon
grape.

Lower Lake Winery (U.S.)   1977

A winery in Lower Lake, Lake County,
California; produces Cabernet and Sauvignon Blanc wines from purchased grapes.
4,000 cases.

Loyse, Château de (F.)

An estate in the Beaujolais district, Burgundy; produces white Beaujolais wine;
owned by Thorin. 15 acres.

Lucas Vineyards (U.S.)   1980

A winery in Interlaken, on Cayuga Lake,
Finger Lakes region, New York; produces
several varietal wines from hybrid grapes.
23 acres.

Lucas Winery (U.S.)   1978

A winery in Lodi, San Joaquin Valley, California; produces dry and sweet Zinfandel
and Tokay wines. 30 acres.

Lugana DOC (I.)

1. A district south of Lake Garda, in the Lombardy region, which produces:

2. A dry white wine made from the Trebbiano di Lugana grape, with a little Vernaccia grape.

Lumassina (I.)

1. A grape, also called Buzzetto, grown in the Liguria region, which produces:

2. A white wine made from the Lumassina grape.

Lung Yen (China)

A famous ancient vineyard in Peking; some wine is still made there.

Lungarotti, Giorgio (I.)   1960

A large estate in Torgiano, Umbria region; produces Cabernet Sauvignon, Chardonnay, Rosciano, Rubesco Solleone, Torgiano and other wines. 130,000 cases. 500 acres.

Luparello (I.)

A light red wine from Pachino, in southeastern Sicily; made from the Calabrese grape.

Lupé-Cholet et Cie. (F.)   1903

An estate in Nuits-St.-Georges, Côte de Nuits district, Burgundy; owns Nuits-St.-Georges Château Gris Monopole (part of *Premier Cru* Aux Crots) – 10 acres and Clos de Lupé (Bourgogne AOC) – 5 acres.

Lurets, Les (F.)

A *Premier Cru* vineyard (in part) in Volnay, Côte de Beaune district, Burgundy. 5 acres.

Lussac-St.-Émilion AOC (F.)

A commune just northeast of St.-Émilion, in Bordeaux; produces red wines similar to St.-Émilion wines.

Lust, Weingut Josef (A.)

An estate in Retz, in the Lower Austria region, in northeastern Austria; produces mostly red wines. 45 acres.

Lustau S.A., Emilio (Sp.)   1896

A Sherry producer in Jerez de la Frontera; produces several types of Sherry, including "Dry Lustau," a dry *oloroso*.

Lutomer, *also* Ljutomer (Y.)

1. A famous district and town in eastern Slovenia, which produces:

2. Several white varietal wines made from Riesling, Sylvaner, Traminer, Šipon and Sauvignon grapes.

Lützelsachsen (G.)

A village in the Baden region, Bereich Badische Bergstrasse/Kraichgau, Grosslage Rittersberg. The only vineyard is Stephansberg.

Luxembourg

A country in northern Europe which produces white wines similar to those from Alsace, using similar grapes (mostly Riesling and Müller-Thurgau) grown on the left bank of the Moselle River. The best-known *communes* are: Ehnen, Grevenmacher, Remich, Schengen, Wasserbillig, Wellenstein and Wintringen; it produces some sparkling wine as well. 4 million gallons. 3,000 acres.

Luze, de (F.)   1820

A merchant in Bordeaux.

Lycée Viticole (F.)   1884

An estate in Beaune, Côte de Beaune district, Burgundy, a viticultural school. 58 acres, including Beaune Champs Pimont, Montée Rouge, Les Bressandes, Les Aigrots, Les Perrières, Côte de Beaune, Chorey-lès-Beaune, Puligny-Montrachet and Bourgogne Passe-Tout-Grains.

Lyeth Vineyard (U.S.)   1982

A winery in Asti, Russian River Valley, Sonoma County, California; produces Cabernet wine and a blend of Sauvignon and Sémillon. 100 acres.

Lynch-Bages, Château (F.)

An estate in Pauillac, Haut-Médoc district, Bordeaux; classified in 1855 as a *Cinquième*

Cru; originally owned by Lynch, an Irish mayor of Bordeaux; first listed in 1846 as Jurine à Bages; owned by M. Jurine in 1855. 24,000 cases. 170 acres.

Lynch-Moussas, Château (F.)

An estate in Pauillac, Haut-Médoc district, Bordeaux; classified in 1855 as a *Cinquième Cru;* formerly owned by Lynch, an Irish mayor of Bordeaux. 80 acres.

Lys, Les (F.)

A *Premier Cru* vineyard in Chablis, Chablis district, Burgundy, usually included as part of the Vaillons vineyard.

Lytton Springs Winery (U.S.)   **1975**

A winery in Healdsburg, Russian River Valley, northern Sonoma County, California; formerly, it was a vineyard, supplying grapes for other wineries; produces Zinfandel wines. 10,000 cases. 50 acres.

M

M.E.V. (U.S.)

A second label of the Mount Eden Vineyards winery, in Saratoga, California, for wines made from purchased grapes. 3,000 cases.

M.I.A. (Aus.)

Murrumbidgee Irrigation Area, a part of the Riverina district, near Griffeth, west of Sidney, in New South Wales.

M.W. (Eng.)   1953

Master of Wine; a title awarded by the Institute of Masters of Wine, London, to those who are engaged in the wine trade and pass a 13-hour examination; first given in 1953. Well-known MW's include Serena Sutcliffe, Michael Broadbent and David Peppercorn.

Maby, Domaine (F.)

An estate in Tavel, southern Rhône region; produces Tavel, Lirac and Côtes du Rhône wines. 220 acres.

Mac-Carthy, Château (F.)

An estate in St.-Estèphe, Haut-Médoc district, Bordeaux; classified in 1978 as a *Cru Grand Bourgeois*. 2,000 cases. 14 acres.

MacCarthy-Moula, Château (F.)

An estate in St.-Estèphe, Haut-Médoc district, Bordeaux; classified in 1978 as a *Cru Bourgeois*. 2,500 cases. 16 acres.

Macabeo (Sp.)

In Catalonia, another name for the white Viura grape; the same as the French Maccabéo grape; also called Alcanon and Alcanol.

macaco (P.)

A wooden paddle used to keep the *manta*, or cap, submerged in the fermenting vat.

Maccabéo (F.)

A white grape grown in the Midi and in Algeria; the same as the Spanish Macabeo grape.

Maccarese (I.)

Red and white wines from north of Rome, in the Latium region. The red wine is made from Montepulciano, Cesanese and Merlot grapes and the white wine is made from Malvasia, Trebbiano, and some Sauvignon and Sémillon grapes. See **Castel San Giorgio.** .

Macedonia (Y.)

A republic of Yugoslavia, in the southern part of the country; produces red wines from the Procupac grape and more recently from Cabernet, Merlot and Pinot Noir grapes, and white wine from Smederevka and Zilavka grapes.

Maceratino (I.)

A white grape grown in the Marches region.

Machard de Gramont, Domaine (F.)

An estate in Nuits-St.-Georges, Côte de Nuits district, Burgundy. 75 acres. See **Gramont, Domaine Machard de.**

Macharnudo (Sp.)

A district north of Jerez, in the Sherry region.

Macherelles, Les (F.)

A *Premier Cru* vineyard in Chassagne-Montrachet, Côte de Beaune district, Burgundy; produces red and white wine. 20 acres.

Mâcon AOC *also* Mâcon-Villages AOC (F.)

1. An important city and center of the Mâconnais district of Burgundy.

2. Red and white wines from the Mâconnais region; the name of a village may be added (there are more than 40 villages: Fuissé, Lugny, Prissé, Viré, etc.); the red wine is made from Gamay or Pinot Noir grapes and the white wine from the Chardonnay grape, with some Pinot Blanc.

Mâconnais (F.)

A district in the southern Burgundy region; produces mostly white wine and some red and rosé wine. The AOC designation applies to Mâcon and Mâcon Supérieur red, white and rosé wines. The best-known communnal wines are Pouilly-Fuissé, Pouilly-Loché, Pouilly-Vinzelles, St. Veran, Mâcon-Viré, Mâcon-Prissé, Solutré, Chaintre and Mâcon-Lugny. The vineyards are planted with 60% Chardonnay, 30% Gamay and 10% Pinot Noir grapes. 15,000 acres of AOC vines.

Maculan (I.)   1937

An estate in Breganze, Veneto region; produces Breganze, Cabernet Sauvignon, Torcolato and other wines. 10,000 cases. 75 acres.

Madeira (P.)

1. An island off the coast of Portugal, discovered in 1419.

2. A wine from the island of Madeira. The wines are dry or sweet, fortified with brandy, then heated for 6 months and rested for 18 months; most Madeira wines are blends of different vintages and matured in a *solera* system like Sherry. The wines were originally not fortified until the mid-18th century but are now fortified to 18% alcohol. They have the longest aging capability of any wine. Formerly the grapes used included Negra Mole, Mosca-

tel and Terrantez; now the grapes used are Sercial, Verdelho, Bual and Malmsey. The four types of Madeira are: Sercial - dry, Verdelho - semi-sweet, Bual (Boal) - fuller and sweeter and Malmsey - rich and sweet. The wine was being exported to Europe by 1460 and became very popular in the end of the 18th century in England.

Madeleine, Clos La (F.)

A small estate in St.-Émilion, Bordeaux; classified in 1955 as a *Grand Cru Classé*. 500 cases. 4 acres.

Madeleine-Angevine (E.)

A white *vinifera* grape grown in England.

Madeleine Collignon, Cuvée (F.)   1977

A red wine from the Hospices de Beaune, Côte de Beaune district, Burgundy. The *cuvée* is composed of one vineyard in Gevrey-Chambertin (the only *cuvée* from the Côte de Nuits): Mazis-Chambertin - 4 acres. 675 cases.

Madère (F.)

The French name for Madeira wine.

maderization

A premature browning of white wine caused by oxidation, producing a color and taste somewhat like Sherry or Madeira wine; it is considered unpleasant in most dry white wines but it is an asset to Château-Châlon, Sherry, Marsala, etc.

Madiran AOC (F.)

1. A town and district north of Pau and Tarbes, and just south of the Armagnac district, in the Southwest region, which produces:

2. A full-bodied red wine made from Tannet, Fer, Cabernet, Cabernet Franc (called Bouchy) and Pinenc or Couhabort grapes. The white wine from this area is called Pacherenc du Vic Bilh AOC.

Madre, Viña (U.S.)   1978, vines 1972

A winery in Roswell, Pecos Valley, in southern New Mexico; produces wines rom several *vinifera* grapes, including Barbera, Cabernet and Zinfandel. 40 acres.

Madroña Vineyard (U.S.)　　　1980

A winery in Camino, El Dorado County, California; produces Cabernet, Chardonnay, Riesling and Zinfandel wines. 35 acres. 5,000 cases.

Magdelaine, Château La (F.)

An estate in St.-Émilion, Bordeaux; classified in 1955 as a *Premier Grand Cru Classé*; made from 80% Merlot grapes. 4,000 cases. 25 acres.

Magence, Château (F.)

An estate in St. Pierre-de-Mons, Graves district, Bordeaux; produces white wine. 5,000 cases. 30 acres.

Magenta, Domaine du Duc de (F.)

An estate in Chassagne-Montrachet, Côte de Beaune district, Burgundy. 30 acres, including 4.8 acres of Puligny-Montrachet Clos de La Garenne Monopole, 2 acres of Meursault, 2.5 acres of Auxey-Duresses Les Bretterins and Chassagne-Montrachet Abbaye de Morgeot Clos de la Chapelle Monopole (red and white) - 12 acres.

Magliocco (I.)

A local red grape grown in the Calabria region - a cross of Gaglioppo and Arvino.

Magliocco Canino (I.)

A local red grape grown in the Calabria region.

Magnolia (U.S.)

A white, muscadine grape which is replacing the Scuppernung grape in the southeastern United States.

magnum

A bottle size equal to two fifths, 1.5 liters, or 50 ounces.

Mähler-Besse (F.)　　　　　1890's

A merchant in Bordeaux; part-owner of Château Palmer.

Maïana (I.)

Red and rosé wine from the Salice Salentino DOC, in the southern Apulia region; made mostly from the Negroamaro grape.

Maillard-Diard, Daniel (F.)

An estate in Chorey-lès-Beaune, Côte de Beaune district, Burgundy. 25 acres, including 2.5 acres of Aloxe-Corton Les Lolières and some Beaune, Savigny and Chorey.

Maimbray, Château de (F.)

An estate in Sury-en-Vaux, Sancerre district, Upper Loire region; produces red, rosé and white Sancerre wine. 28 acres.

Maindreieck (G.)

A *Bereich*, one of 3 in the Franken region. The *Grosslagen* are: Burg, Ewig Leben, Hofrat, Honigberg, Kirchberg, Ravensberg and Rosstal.

Mainviereck (G.)

A small *Bereich* in the Franken region. The *Grosslagen* are Heiligenthal and Reuschberg.

Maipo Valley (Ch.)

A region in central Chile, just south of Santiago; produces red wines from Cabernet, Cabernet Franc and Malbec grapes and white wines from Sauvignon Blanc, Sémillon, Riesling, Chardonnay and Pinot Gris grapes.

Maire et Fils (F.) 1780

A merchant in Beaune, Burgundy, which handles the wines of Domaine P. Labet (Beaune *Premier Cru*) and Domaine du Château de la Tour (Clos de Vougeot).

Maison Blanche (F.)

A vineyard section of Hermitage, northern Rhône region.

Maison Brûlée (F.)

A *Premier Cru* vineyard in Morey-St.-Denis, Côte de Nuits district, Burgundy. 3 acres.

Maître, Paul (F.)

An estate in Benais, Bourgeuil district, Touraine region, Loire Valley. 5,000 cases. 30 acres.

maître de chai (F.)

In Bordeaux, the head cellerman in charge of vinification and aging of the wine; also called *caviste* in other regions.

Maja, Château (U. S.)

The second wine of Conn Creek Winery, St. Helena, Napa Valley, California.

Majărcă (R.)

A white grape grown in the Banat region.

Malá Trňa (Cz.)

An important town in southeastern Slovakia; produces a Tokay wine similar to Hungarian Tokaji made from the same grapes.

Maladière, La (F.)

A *Premier Cru* vineyard in Santenay, Côte de Beaune district, Burgundy. 33 acres.

Maladière, Domaine de la (F.)

An estate in Chablis, Burgundy. 62 acres, including 8 acres of Les Clos, 13 acres of Bougros, 5 acres of Les Preuses, 4 acres of Vaudésir, 4.5 acres of Valmur, 1.2 acres of Grenouilles and some Vaulorent, Vaillons, Montée de Tonnerre, Lys, Forêts and others.

Málaga (Sp.)

1. A city and district in southeastern Spain, which produces:

2. A sweet red wine made from 60% Pedro Ximénez, 20% Lairén, 15% Moscatel and other grapes. 14-23% alcohol; much of the wine is not fortified; matured by the *solera* system with must obtained by the *lagrima* method. 1.5 million gallons. 12,500 acres.

Malartic-Lagravière, Château (F.)

An estate in Léognan, Graves district, Bordeaux; classified in 1959 as *Cru Classé* for red and white wine. Red wine - 6,000 cases, 35 acres; white wine - 800 cases, 5 acres.

Malbec (F., Arg.)

A red grape grown in Bordeaux, the Southwest and other regions of France; the same grape as the Cot, Cahors or Auxerrois in Cahors, the Cot in the Loire Valley, and Pressac in St.-Émilion; also grown in Argentina, where it accounts for ⅔ of the country's red wine.

Malconsorts, Les (F.)

A *Premier Cru* vineyard in Vosne-Romanée, Côte de Nuits district, Burgundy. 15 acres.

Maldant-Pauvelot et Fils (F.)

An estate in Chorey-lès-Beaune, Côte de Beaune district, Burgundy. 28 acres, including 10 acres of Savigny, 10 acres of Aloxe-Corton and 7.5 acres of Chorey.

Malescasse, Château (F.)

An estate in Lamarque, Haut-Médoc district, Bordeaux; classified in 1932 as a *Cru Bourgeois*. 10,000 cases. 80 acres.

Malescot-Saint-Exupéry, Château (F.)

An estate in Margaux, Haut-Médoc district, Bordeaux; classified in 1855 as a *Troisième Cru*. It was acquired by Simon Malescot in 1697, then by the Counts of St.-Exupéry in 1827 when the Exupéry name was added. 65-80% Cabernet Sauvignon and Cabernet Franc, 30% Merlot and 5% Petit Verdot. 12,000 cases. 75 acres.

Malfatti, Baroni (I.)

An estate in Veglie, Apulia region; produces Salice Salentino and other white, red and rosé wines. 140,000 cases. 370 acres.

Mali Plavac (Y.)

A red grape grown in the province of Dalmatia, Croatia.

malic acid

One of three acids (tartaric and citric are the other two) found in wine and in unripe grapes.

Malijay, Château (F.)   15th cent.

An estate in Jonquières, Côtes du Rhône district, southern Rhône region; produces red and rosé wines made from Grenache, Cinsault, Carignan, Counoise, Syrah, Mourvèdre and Clairette grapes. 450 acres.

Mallard, Michel (F.)

An estate in Ladoix-Serrigny, Côte de Beaune district, Burgundy. 22 acres, including 1.2 acres of Corton and some Aloxe-Corton, Côte de Beaune and Côte de Nuits.

Mallard-Gaullin (F.)   1875

An estate in Beaune, Côte de Beaune district, Burgundy. 55 acres, including 4 acres of Corton-Renardes, 4 acres of Corton-Charlemagne and some Aloxe-Corton Premier Cru.

Malle, Château de (F.)

An estate in Preignac, Sauternes district, Bordeaux; classified in 1855 as a *Deuxième Cru*. 70% Sémillon, 25% Sauvignon, 5% Muscadelle grapes. Also produces dry red and dry white wines. 13,000 cases. 110 acres.

Malleret, Château (F.)

An estate in Le Pian, Haut-Médoc district, Bordeaux; classified in 1978 as a *Cru Grand Bourgeois*. 10,000 cases. 55 acres.

Malmesbury WO (S. Af.)

A town and district north of Capetown.

Malmsey (P.)

A type of Madeira wine made from the Malvasia grape, originally a corruption of Monemvasia (Greek), Malvagia (Spanish) and Malvoisie (French).

malolactic fermentation

The transformation by bacteria of malic acid into lactic acid and CO_2 during a second fermentation. It lowers the acid content.

Malte, Domaine du Clos de (F.)

An estate in Santenay, Côte de Beaune, Burgundy; owns Santenay Clos de Malte Monopole – 17 acres.

Maltroie, La (F.)

A *Premier Cru* vineyard in Chassagne-Montrachet, Côte de Beaune district, Burgundy; produces red and white wine. 23 acres.

Maltroie, Château de la *also* **Maltroye (F.)**

An estate in Chassagne-Montrachet, Côte de Beaune district, Burgundy. 33 acres, including .8 acre of Bâtard-Montrachet, 1.2 acres of Chassagne-Montrachet Grands Ruchottes, 4 acres of Vigne Blanche, .8 acre of Clos St.-Jean, 5 acres of Santenay La Comme and 6 acres of Chassagne-Montrachet Clos du Château de la Maltroie Monopole (red and white).

Malvasia

A white grape originally grown in Greece, now grown all over the world; used in making Malmsey, a sweet Madeira wine. The same as Monemvasia in Greek, Malvoisie in French and Malvagia in Spanish. It is approved for DO wines in the Rioja region of Spain.

Malvasia di Bosa DOC (I.)

A white wine, dry or sweet, from Bosa, in northwestern Sardinia; made from the Malvasia di Sardegna grape. 15-18% alcohol.

Malvasia di Cagliari DOC (I.)

A white wine from Cagliari, in southwestern Sardinia; made from the Malvasia di Sardegna grape. 14-18% alcohol.

Malvasia di Casorzo d'Asti DOC (I.)

A sweet, red wine, usually sparkling, from Casorzo, northeast of Asti, in the Piedmont region; made from the Malvasia Rossa grape.

Malvasia di Castelnuovo Don Bosco DOC (I.)

A sweet, sparkling, red wine from Castelnuovo Don Bosco, near Turin, in the Piedmont region; made from the Malvasia Rossa grape.

Malvasia Fina (P.)

A white grape, one of 16 first-quality grapes used to make Port wine.

Malvasia del Lazio (I.)

A white grape grown in the Latium region; also called Puntinata.

Malvasia delle Lipari DOC (I.)

1. A local white grape grown on the Lipari Islands.

2. A sweet white wine from the Lipari or Aeolian Islands, north of Messina, Sicily; made from Malvasia di Lipari and Corinto Nero grapes. 12-20% alcohol.

Malvasia di Planargia (I.)

A dry, white wine from Bosa, in northwestern Sardinia; made from the Malvasia Sardegna grape.

Malvasia Rei (P.)

A white grape, one of 16 first-quality grapes used to make Port wine.

Malvasia Rossa (I.)

A red grape grown in the Latium and Piedmont regions. In the Frascati district of the Latium region, another name for the Malvasia Bianca di Candia grape.

Malvasia Sarda (I.)

An important strain of the white Malvasia grape grown on the island of Sardinia; also called Malvasia di Sardegna.

Malvazÿa (Y.)

The Yugoslavian spelling of the Malvasia grape.

Malvoisie (F.)

The Malvasia grape.

Malvoisie de Cossan (I.)

A semi-sweet, white wine from Cossan, in the Valle d'Aosta region; made from the Pinot Gris (Malvoisie) grape.

Malvoisie de Nus (I.)

A sweet, white wine from Nus, east of Aosta, in the Valle d'Aosta region; made from the Pinot Gris (Malvoisie) grape.

Mambourg *also* Mamburg (F.)

A vineyard in Sigolsheim, northern Haut-Rhin district, Alsace region. 220 acres.

Mamertine (Lat.)

An ancient Roman wine made near Messina, in northeastern Sicily. It is still made there as Mamertino.

Mamertino (I.)

Once a famous ancient wine, now a dry, sweet or semi-sweet white wine from Messina, in northeastern Sicily; made from semi-dried Catarratto, Inzolia, Grillo and some Pedro Jimenez grapes.

Mammolo (I.)

A red grape grown in the Tuscany region; used in Vino Nobile di Montepulciano.

mana (Cyp.)

An old system used in Cyprus for making Commandaria wine, in which the oldest jar of wine is never empty, but is constantly refilled with younger wine, similar to the Spanish *solera* system.

Mancha DO (Sp.)

A large district in the La Mancha region of central Spain; it accounts for about half of the wine production of La Mancha.

Manchuela DO (Sp.)

A district in the La Mancha region, just east of the Mancha district, in central Spain; produces red and white wines.

Mandelberg (F.)

A vineyard in Mittelwihr, Haut-Rhin district, Alsace region; produces Gewürztraminer, Riesling and Muscat grapes.

Mandelot, Domaine du Château de (F.)

An estate in Beaune, Côte de Beaune district, Burgundy; the wines are made by Bouchard Père et Fils. 15 acres, including 5.6 acres of Bourgogne Hautes-Côtes de Beaune, 4.5 acres of Bourgogne Passe-Tout-Grains and 4.2 acres of Bourgogne Aligoté.

Mandement (Sw.)

A district west of Geneva, in the canton of Geneva; produces red and white wines.

Mandilaria (Gr.)

A red grape grown in Crete.

Mandrolisai DOC (I.)   1979

1. A district around Sorgono, in central Sardinia, named after a part of the Gennargentu Mountains, which produces:

2. Red and rosé wines made from Bovale, Muristellu, Cannonau, Monica and Girò grapes.

manganese

A mineral which is present in all wine, especially red wine; it comes mostly from the pips.

Maniar Vineyards (U.S.)   1980

A winery in Napa City, Napa Valley, California; produces Cabernet, Chardonnay, Fumé Blanc and Johannisberg Riesling wines; bottled under Diamond Oaks Vineyard label. 20,000 cases.

Manière-Noirot (F.)

An estate in the Côte de Nuits district, Burgundy. See **Noirot, Albert.**

Manischewitz (U.S.)

A brand name for sweet Kosher wines produced by the Monarch Wine Company, New York, New York.

Manissy, Château de (F.)

An estate in Tavel, southern Rhône region, owned by the religious order of Sainte Famille. 70 acres.

mannequin (F.)

A large basket used to collect grapes at harvest time in the Champagne region; also called *caque*.

mannitic fermentation

A disease of wine caused by too high a temperature in the fermenting vat, which kills yeasts and allows bacteria to attack the sugar. Mannite, a sweet, non-fermentable substance, is produced and the wine becomes cloudy and develops a bittersweet taste.

manta (P.)

The cap, the mass of skins, pips, etc. which rises to the top of the fermenting must when making red wines; called *chapeau*, in France.

Manteudo (P.)

A white grape grown in southern Portugal.

Mantey Vineyard (U.S.)   1880

An old winery near Sandusky, Ohio; produces Catawba, Johannisberg Riesling, Baco Noir and Seyval Blanc wines.

Mantinea *also* Mantinia (Gr.)

A white wine from central Peloponnese, made from the Moschofilero grape.

Mantlerhof, Weingut (A.)   1814

An estate in Gedersdorf Bei Krems; produces Grüner Veltliner, Roter Veltliner, Müller-Thurgau and Rheinriesling wines. 16,000 cases. 25 acres.

Mantonico Bianco (I.)

A white grape grown in the Calabria region.

Mantonico di Bianco (I.)

A semi-sweet, white wine from Bianco, in the southwestern Calabria region; made from the Montonico Bianco grape. Up to 16% alcohol.

Mantúa (Sp.)

A white grape grown in the Huelva district, in the Extremadura region, southwestern Spain.

Manzanilla (Sp.)

A dry wine from Sanlúcar de Barrameda, northwest of Jerez de la Frontera, in the Sherry region, sold as a type of *fino* Sherry, sometimes fortified.

Maranges (F.)

A *Premier Cru* vineyard shared by three communes in the southernmost part of the Côte de Beaune district, in Burgundy; they are Cheillley-les-Maranges, Dezize-les-Maranges and Sampigny-les-Maranges. 200 acres.

Maraština (Y.)

1. A white grape grown in the province of Dalmatia.

2. A white wine from the northern Dalmatia province, made from the Maraština grape.

Maratheftika (Cyp.)

A red grape grown in Cyprus.

Marbuzet, Château de (F.)

An estate in St.-Estèphe, Haut-Médoc district, Bordeaux; classified in 1978 as a *Cru Grand Bourgeois Exceptionnel*. 5,000 cases. 30 acres.

marc (Fr., E.)

1. Grape pressings; the skins and seeds left in the press after the wine has been extracted; pomace.

2. Brandy distilled from *marc*; called *eau-de-vie marc*.

Marcarini, Poderi (I.)

An estate in La Morra, Piedmont region; produces Barbera, Barolo, Dolcetto and Freisa wines.

Marches (I.)

A region in east central Italy, well-known for Verdicchio wine.

Marchesi di Barolo (I.)   1861

A winery in Barolo, Piedmont region; produces Asti Spumante di Gavi, Barolo, Barbaresco, Cortese, Greisa, Dolcetto and Nebbiolo wines; made from their own and purchased grapes. 100 acres.

Marcilly, Clos- (F.)

A *Premier Cru* vineyard in Mercurey, Côte Chalonnaise district, Burgundy.

Marcilly Frères, P. de (F.)   1849

An estate in Beaune, Côte de Beaune district, Burgundy; 38 acres, including some Chassagne-Montrachet Clos St.-Jean, Morgeot, La Conière, Beaune Les Grèves and Premier Cru, Bâtard-Montrachet, Les Criots-Bâtard-Montrachet and Chambertin; usually all blended together and declassified as Bourgogne.

Marconnets, Les (F.)

A *Premier Cru* vineyard in Beaune, Côte de Beaune district, Burgundy, contiguous with the vineyard of the same name in Savigny-lès-Beaune. 22 acres.

Marconnets, Les (F.)

A *Premier Cru* vineyard in Savigny-lès-Beaune, Côte de Beaune district, Burgundy, contiguous with the vineyard of the same name in Beaune. 23 acres.

marcottage (F.)

Layering, a method of propagating grape vines by allowing vine shoots to droop down to the ground and grow roots of their own in the earth, thus forming new plants, which are separated when they are strong enough.

Mare, Clos de la (E.)

A white wine from Blayney Vineyards, Jersey, Channel Island; made from Müller-Thurgau, Huxelrebe and Reichensteiner grapes.

Maréchale, Clos de la (F.)

A *Premier Cru* vineyard in Prémeaux, Côte de Nuits district, Burgundy. 25 acres.

Maréchal, Jean (F.)

An estate in Mercurey, Côte Chalonnaise district, southern Burgundy. 22 acres.

Maréchal Foch (F.)

An red hybrid grape, also called Foch, and Kuhlmann 188.2, bred in Alsace, France by Eugène Kuhlmann.

Maréchaudes, Les (F.)

A *Premier Cru* vineyard in Ladoix-Serrigny, Côte de Beaune district, Burgundy; may use Aloxe-Corton AOC, and is contiguous with the vineyard of the same name in Aloxe-Corton. 3 acres.

Maréchaudes, Les (F.)

A *Grand Cru* vineyard (in part) in Aloxe-Corton, Côte de Beaune district, when used with Corton. The other part of the vineyard is *Premier Cru*; contiguous with the vineyard of the same name in Ladoix-Serrigny. 13 acres.

Marègia (I.)

A white wine from Marzeno di Brisighella, in the eastern Emilia-Romagna region; made from Albana, Trebbiano and Pinot Bianco grapes.

Maremma (I.)

Red, white and rosé wines from the Maremma hills, in the southwestern Tuscany region. The red and rosé wines are made from Sangiovese and other grapes and the white wines are made from Procanico (Trebbiano), Ansonica and Vermentino grapes.

Mareotic (Egypt)

An ancient, sweet, white Egyptian wine from Alexandria; later known in Rome and mentioned by Horace.

Marey-Monge, Domaine (F.)

An estate in Vosne-Romanée, Côte de Nuits district, Burgundy; owns 14 acres of

Romanée-St.-Vivant; handled by Domaine de la Romanée-Conti.

Marfil (Sp.)

A white grape grown in southwestern Spain.

Margaret River (Aus.)

A river and district south of Perth, in Western Australia.

Margaux AOC (F.)

An important commune in the Haut-Médoc district, Bordeaux; the AOC also includes Arsac, Soussans, Cantenac and Labarde.

Margaux, Château (F.)

A famous estate in Margaux, Haut-Médoc district, Bordeaux; classified in 1855 as a *Premier Cru;* known in the 5th century as Lamothe. A white wine is also made (since 1847), called Pavillon Blanc de Château Margaux, made from Sauvignon grapes. 200 acres. 16,000 cases red, 4,000 cases white.

Margoté (F.)

A *Premier Cru* vineyard in Rully, Côte Chalonnaise district, Burgundy.

Maria Gomes (P.)

A white grape grown in the Bairrada region; accounts for 80% of the white wines produced there.

Marie-Jeanne (F.)

A large bottle equal to 3.5 fifths, or approximately 84 ounces.

Marienberg (Aus.)   1968

A small, distinctive winery in the hills near Adelaide, in South Australia; produces red and white wines made from Shiraz, Cabernet and Rhine Riesling grapes. 25 acres.

Mariensteiner (G.)

A white grape - a cross of Silvaner and Rieslaner; developed at the State Viticultural Institute, Würzburg-Veitshöchheim, Germany.

Marietta Cellars (U.S.)   1980

A small winery in Healdsburg, Sonoma County, California; produces Cabernet and Zinfandel wines. 5,000 cases.

Marin County (U.S.)

A new region just north of San Francisco, California; it has a few vineyards and wineries only since 1969.

Marino DOC (I.)

1. A DOC village in the Castelli Romani district, south of Rome, in the Latium region, which produces:
2. A white wine made from Malvasia, Trebbiano and other grapes.

Marion, Domaine Dr. Henri (F.)

An estate in Beaune, Burgundy; the wines made by Bouchard Aîné et Fils, Beaune. 15 acres, including 4.8 acres of Chambertin Clos de Bèze, 3.3 acres of Fixin La Mazière and 7.5 acres of Côte de Nuits-Villages.

Marissou (F.)

A *Premier Cru* vineyard in Rully, Côte Chalonnaise district, Burgundy.

Mark West Vineyards (U.S.)   1972

A winery in Forestville, Russian River Valley, Sonoma County, California; produces Pinot Noir, Chardonnay and Gewürztraminer wines. 12,000 cases. 60 acres.

Markgräflerland (G.)

A *Bereich*, one of 7 in the Baden region. The *Grosslagen* are: Burg Neuenfels, Lorettoberg and Votgei Rötteln.

Markham Winery (U.S.)   1975
                 winery 1978

A winery in St. Helena, Napa County, California; produces Cabernet, Merlot, Gamay Beaujolais, Chardonnay, Johannisberg Riesling, Chenin Blanc and Muscat wines. 300 acres. 18,000 cases.

Markko Vineyard (U.S.)   1969

A winery near Conneaut, near Lake Erie, Ohio; produces Cabernet, Chardonnay and Johannisberg Riesling wines. 10 acres. 2,000 cases.

marl

A type of soil, a combination of crumbly calcium carbonate and clay.

Marlstone Vineyard (U.S.)

A vineyard in Alexander Valley, Sonoma County, California; produces Cabernet and Merlot grapes for Clos du Bois winery.

Marmilla (I.)

A new district in the hills above the Campidano Plains of southwestern Sardinia.

Marmilla, Cantina Sociale (I.)

A large co-op of 2,000 members in Sanluri, Sardinia; produces Cannonau, Malvasia, Monica, Nasco, Nuragus and other wines. 3 million cases. 13,000 acres.

Maronean (Gr.)

A wine from ancient Greece made near the Thracian shores. It was a dark wine and was mixed with water. Odysseus gave it to Polyphemus; mentioned by Homer and Pliny.

marque *also* marque déposé (F.)

A trade-mark or brand name; a registered trade-mark.

Marqués de Casa Concha (Ch.)

A red wine from the Maipo Valley, in central Chile; made from Cabernet grapes by Concha y Toro.

Marquês de Pombal (P.)

The founder of the Oporto Wine Company; in 1756 he improved conditions for making Port requiring the use of better brandy and eliminating the addition of elderberry juice and other foreign elements.

Marquis, Clos du (F.)

The second wine of Château Léoville-Las Cases.

Marquis d'Alesme-Becker, Château (F.)

An estate in Margaux, Haut-Médoc district, Bordeaux; classified in 1855 as a *Troisième Cru*. It has existed since at least 1616; in the 19th century it was known as Becker. 5,000 cases. 30 acres.

Marquis-de-Terme, Château (F.)

An estate in Margaux, Haut-Médoc district, Bordeaux; classified in 1855 as a *Quatrième Cru*. 15,000 cases. 100 acres.

Marsala DOC (I.)

1. A village and large district in western Sicily, which produces:

2. A white dessert wine made originally from the Grillo grape, now from Grillo, Catarratto and Inzolia grapes; fortified and matured in casks for 2-5 years; it has a burnt-sugar taste and is well-known for its use in making Zabaglione. It was developed in 1773 by John Woodhouse, an Englishman, by adding alcohol to Sicilian wine for export to England.

The three types of Marsala are: Marsala Fine - 17% alcohol, at least 4 months aging with *cotto* and *sifone*, Marsala Superiore - 18% alcohol, 2 years aging, of several styles, and Marsala Vergine - 18% alcohol, 5 years aging, dry and natural - no *cotto* or *sifone*. Marsala Speciale is a flavored product made with Marsala wine.

Marsala all'uovo (I.)

A drink made from Marsala wine mixed with an egg yolk and spirits.

Marsannay (F.)

A village on the northern end of the Côte de Nuits district, just south of Dijon, in Burgundy; produces red, white and rosé wines. The AOC designation is Bourgogne-Marsannay-la-Côte.

Marsanne (F.)

A white grape grown in the Rhône, Provence, and Savoie regions and in Algeria and other countries.

Marsanne, Jean (F.)

An estate in Mauves, St.-Joseph district, Rhône region; owns 5 acres of St.-Joseph.

Marshall, Domaine Tim (F.)

A small estate in Nuits-St.-Georges, Côte de Nuits district, Burgundy. 1.1 acres, including .6 acre of Nuits-St.-Georges Les Perrières and .5 acre of Les Argillats.

Martha's Vineyard (U.S.)　　　　1960

A famous vineyard in Oakville, Napa Valley, California; owned by Tom and Martha May; produces Cabernet grapes for wines made by Heitz Vineyard, St. Helena, Napa Valley, since 1966 (except 1971). 15 acres.

Martial *also* Martialis (c. 40-c.102 A.D.) (Lat.)

The ancient Roman satirist who wrote about wines.

Martin, Domaine (F.)

An estate in Travaillan, Côtes du Rhône district, Rhône region; produces red wines made from Grenache, Syrah, Cinsault, Mourvèdre, Carignan, Grenache Blanc and Clairette grapes. 85 acres.

Martin et Fils, Domaine Maurice (F.)

An estate in Chorey-lès-Beaune, Côte de Beaune district, Burgundy. 32 acres, including .6 acre of Beaune Teurons and some Aloxe-Corton, Savigny and Chorey.

Martina Franca DOC *also* Martina (I.)

1. A village and district near Locorotondo, in the central Apulia region, which produces:

2. Red, white and rosé wines, also *spumante;* the white is made from Verdeca and Bianco d'Alessano grapes, and the red and rosé from Negroamaro grapes.

Martinens, Château (F.)

An estate in Cantenac-Margaux, Haut-Médoc district, Bordeaux; classified in 1978 as a *Cru Grand Bourgeois*. 5,000 cases. 60 acres.

Martinet, Château (F.)

An unclassified estate in Sables-St.-Émilion, Bordeaux. 30 acres. 5,000 cases.

Martini, Conti (I.) 1977

An estate in Mezzocorona, Trentino-Alto Adige region; produces Müller-Thurgau, Pinot Grigio and Teroldego Rotaliano wines. 25 acres.

Martini and Prati Wines (U.S.) 1951

A large winery in Santa Rosa, Sonoma County, California; produces bulk wines and some varietals under the Fountaingrove label. 20,000 cases.

Martini & Rossi (I.) 1863

A major producer of sparkling wine and Vermouth in Torino, Piedmont region. Several million cases.

Martini Winery, Louis M. (U.S.) 1922
wines 1933, winery 1940

A famous, large winery in St. Helena, Napa Valley, California; produces Cabernet, Zinfandel, Merlot, Barbera, Gamay Beaujolais, Chardonnay, Johannisberg Riesling, Chenin Blanc, Folle Blanche, Gewürztraminer, Moscato Amabile and sherry-type wines; most wines are blended from different vineyards. 400,000 cases. 900 acres – Napa and Sonoma Counties.

Marufo (P.)

A red grape grown in northern Portugal.

Maryland (U.S.)

A state in the northeastern United States; it has about 7 commercial wineries, covering about 60 acres; grows *vinifera* and hybrid grapes.

Marzelle, Château La (F.)

An estate in St.-Émilion, Bordeaux; classified in 1955 as a *Grand Cru Classé*. 3,000 cases. 15 acres.

Marzemino (I.)

A red grape grown in the Lombardy and Trentino regions. In Brescia it is called Berzamino.

mas (F.)

The local name for a vineyard or farmhouse; used in the northern Rhône region (Hermitage), and in the Provence region.

Masada (Is.)

A sweet red wine from the Hadera district, Samaria; made from the Alicante grape.

Mascara (Alg.)

A district southeast of Oran, covering the same area as the finer Coteaux de Mascara; produces red, white and rosé wines.

Mascarello, Cantina (I.) 1919

An estate in Barolo, Piedmont region; produces Barolo wines.

Mascarello & Figlio, Giuseppe (I.) 1881

A winery in Monchiero, Piedmont region; produces Barbaresco, Barbera, Barolo, Dolcetto and Nebbiolo wines; made from their own and purchased grapes. 5,000 cases.

Masi (I.)

A winery in Gargagnago, Veneto region; produces Bardolino, Soave, Amarone, Valpolicella and other wines.

Masía Bach (Sp.) 1920

A winery in Sant Esteve Sesrovires, Penedès district, Catalonia region; produces red and white wines, especially Extrísimo Bach, a sweet, white wine.

Masianco (I.)

A white wine from Valpolicella, in the southwestern Veneto region; made from Garganega, Trebbiano and Durello grapes.

Massachusetts (U.S.)

A state in the northeastern United States; it has one vineyard on Martha's Vineyard since 1971; the fee for a winery license was reduced in 1977, thus encouraging more vineyards; there is now a second winery in Plymouth.

Massandra (U.S.S.R.)

A sweet, white wine from the southern Ukraine SSR, made from the Muskat grape; formerly, a famous estate.

Massol, Cuvée Jehan de (F.)

A red wine from the Hospices de Beaune, Côte de Beaune district, Burgundy. The *cuvée* is composed of the following vineyard in Volnay: Les Santenots – 4 acres. 675 cases.

Masson, Domaine Pierre-Yves (F.)

An estate in Meursault, Côte de Beaune district, Burgundy. 28 acres, including 2 acres of Vosne-Romanée Aux Malconsorts, 1.2 acres of Au-dessus des Malconsorts, 5.5 acres of Nuits-St.-Georges Premier Cru, 4 acres of Les Pruliers, 6.7 acres of Corton-Bressandes and 7 acres of Beaune Les Grèves.

Masson Vineyards, Paul (U.S.)   1852

An historic winery in Saratoga, Santa Clara County, California; produces numerous generic jug wines, and Pinot Noir, Cabernet, Zinfandel, Chardonnay, Chenin Blanc, Emerald Dry, Fumé Blanc, Champagne and Souzão Port wines. 6 million cases. 4,500 acres.

Mastantuono (U.S.)   1980

A winery in Paso Robles, San Luis Obispo County, California; produces Pinot Noir, Zinfandel, Carignane and Grenache wines. 10 acres. 3,000 cases.

Mastroberardino (I.)   1878

An estate in Atripalda, Campania region; produces Fiano di Avellino, Greco di Tufo, Lacryma Christi, Taurasi and other wines. 200 acres. 75,000 cases.

Matanzas Creek Winery (U.S.)   1978

A winery in Santa Rosa, Sonoma County; produces Cabernet, Merlot, Pinot Noir, Pinot Blanc, Chardonnay, Gewürztraminer and Sauvignon Blanc wines. 5,000 cases. 50 acres.

Mataro (F.)

Another name for the red Mourvèdre grape grown in southern France; also grown in Riverside County, California.

Materia Medica, Da (Gr.)

A book by the ancient Greek physician and author, Dioscorides (1st century, A.D.), in which various wines are described.

Mateus (P.)

Rosé and white wines made by SOGRAPE – Vinhos de Portugal SARL. The rosé wine is made from a blend of Bastardo, Touriga, Alvarelhão and Tinta Pinheira grapes grown in northern Portugal and the white wine is made from a blend of Arinto, Malvasia, Esgana Cão and Cercial grapes.

Mathouillet-Besancenot (F.)

An estate in Beaune, Côte de Beaune district, Burgundy. 15 acres, including 2.5 acres of Beaune Les Grèves, 2.5 acres of Clos du Roi, 7.5 acres of Les Cent Vignes and 1 acre of Corton-Charlemagne.

Matino DOC (I.)

1. A village and district near Lecce, in the southern Apulia region, which produces:

2. Red and rosé wines made from Sangiovese and Negroamaro grapes.

Mátraalja (H.)

A district in the Matra Mountains, near Eger and Gyöngyös, in northeastern Hungary; produces red wine made from the Kadarka grape and white wines from Wälschriesling, Leányka, Mézesfehér and other grapes. Debröi wines are made in this district. Rated white wine of Excellent Quality. 22,500 acres.

Matras, Château (F.)

An estate in St.-Émilion, Bordeaux; classified in 1969 as a *Grand Cru Classé*. 3,500 cases. 21 acres.

Matrot, Pierre (F.)

An estate in Meursault, Côte de Beaune district, Burgundy. 37 acres, including 2.5 acres of Meursault Les Charmes, .8 acre of

Les Perrières, 5 acres of Meursault Blagny, 2 acres of Puligny-Montrachet Les Chalumeaux, 5 acres of Blagny La Pièce sous le Bois and 4 acres of Volnay Les Santenots.

Matua Valley Wines (N.Z.)　　　**1974**

A winery in Waimauku, Aukland, North Island; produces Cabernet, Shiraz, Pinot Noir, Pinotage, Chardonnay, Muscat Blanc, Sauvignon Blanc, Chenin Blanc, Grey Riesling and other wines. 60 acres.

Maturana Blanca (Sp.)

A white grape grown in the Rioja region.

Maturana Tinta (Sp.)

A red grape grown in the Rioja region.

Matuschka-Greiffenclau, Weingut Graf (G.)

An estate in Winkel, Rheingau region; owner of the famous Schloss Vollrads.

Mau, Yvon (F.)

A merchant in La Récole, Bordeaux region.

Maucaillou, Château (F.)

An estate in Moulis, Haut-Médoc region; classified in 1932 as a *Cru Bourgeois*. 23,000 cases. 110 acres.

Mauerwein (G.)

A carafe wine from Baden-Baden, in the Baden region.

Mauffré, Henri (F.)

An estate in Morey-St.-Denis, Côte de Nuits district, Burgundy. 15 acres, including 1.2 acres of Clos de la Roche, 1.2 acres of Charmes-Chambertin and 4 acres of Morey-St.-Denis Clos des Sorbés.

Maufoux, Prosper (F.)　　　**1860**

A merchant in Santenay, Côte de Beaune, Burgundy; handles Domaine Saint-Michel in Santenay and Château de Viré (Mâcon-Viré AOC), and produces numerous *Grand Cru* and *Premier Cru* wines.

Maurice Drouhin, Cuvée (F.)

A red wine from the Hospices de Beaune, Côte de Beaune district, Burgundy. The *cuvée* is composed of the following vineyards in Beaune: Les Avaux – 2 acres, Les Boucherottes – 1.5 acres, Champs Pimont – 1.5 acres and Les Grèves – 1 acre. 675 cases.

Maury VDN (F.)

A village and district northwest of Perpignan, in the Roussillon region; produces red, white and rosé VDN and Vins de Liqueurs.

Mauvezin, Château (F.)

An estate in St.-Émilion, Bordeaux; classified in 1955 as a *Grand Cru Classé*. 1,000 cases. 10 acres.

Mauvezin, Château (F.)

An estate in Moulis, Haut-Médoc district, Bordeaux; classified in 1932 as a *Cru Bourgeois*. 150 acres. 20,000 cases.

Mauzac (F.)

A white grape used in Blanquette de Limoux sparkling wine and Vin de Blanquette, in the Languedoc region; also grown in the Southwest region.

mavro (Gr.)

Black; red (wine).

Mavrodaphne (Gr.)

1. A red grape. The name means "black laurel." In nearby countries it is also called Mavrud, or Mavroud.

2. A sweet, red wine from Patras, in northern Pelopponnese and other parts of Greece. 15% alcohol; made from the Mavrodaphne grape.

Mavron (Cyp.)

An important red grape grown in Cyprus; used to make red and dry rosé wine known as Kokkineli; also used to make Commandaria dessert wine when blended with the Xynisteri grape.

Mavroudi (Gr.)

1. A red grape.
2. A red wine from Delphi made from the Mavroudi grape.

Mavrud (Bul.)

1. A red grape grown mostly in southern Bulgaria; the name means "black."
2. A red wine from southern Bulgaria, especially from Asenowgrad, near Plovdiv; made from the Mavrud grape.

Maximin Grünhaus (G.)

A famous estate in Mertesdorf, Grosslage Römerlay, Bereich Saar-Ruwer, in the Mosel-Saar-Ruwer region; owned by the Von Schubert family. The vineyards are Abtsberg, Bruderberg and Herrenberg. 150 acres. See **Schubert, C. von.**

May wine (G.)

A traditional wine made in Germany from light Rhine wine flavored with the leaves of *Waldmeister* (woodruff). It is usually served from a bowl with strawberries floating in it.

Mayacamas Vineyard (U.S.)   1889, 1941

A winery in the Mayacamas Mountains, northwest of Napa City, Napa Valley, California, revitalized after abandonment in 1941; produces Cabernet, Zinfandel, Pinot Noir, Chardonnay and Sauvignon Blanc wines, some from purchased grapes. 5,000 cases. 50 acres.

Mayer, Weingut Franz (A.)   1683

An estate in Vienna; produces *Heurige* wine and several other red and white wines; owns vineyards in Grinzing, Alsegg and Nussberg. 13,000 cases. 60 acres.

Mazilly Père et Fils (F.)

An estate in Meloisey, in the Hautes-Côtes de Beaune, Burgundy. Owns 8 acres of Hautes-Côtes de Beaune, 2.5 acres of Pommard, 2 acres of Meursault and 1 acre of Beaune Premier Cru.

Mazoyères-Chambertin AOC (F.)

One of 9 *Grand Cru* vineyards in Gevrey-Chambertin, Côte de Nuits district, Burgundy; by law it may also be sold as Charmes-Chambertin. 46 acres.

Mazuelo (Sp.)

A red grape grown in the Rioja region; approved for DO wines. It may be the same as the Carignane grape of France.

Mazys-Chambertin AOC *also* Mazis- (F.)

One of 9 *Grand Cru* vineyards in Gevrey-Chambertin, Côte de Nuits district, Burgundy. 25 acres.

Mazza Vineyards (U.S.)   1972

A winery in the town of North East, Pennsylvania; the vineyards grow hybrid, *vinifera* and native grapes; also produces Riesling, Traminer, Chardonnay, Pinot Gris and Cabernet wines from a nearby vineyard.

Mazziotti, Italo (I.)

An estate in Bolsena, Latium region; produces Bolsena Rosso and Est! Est!! Est!!! wines. 60 acres.

McDowell Valley Vineyards (U.S.)   1978

A winery in Hopland, Mendocino County, California; produces Cabernet, Zinfandel, Petite Sirah, Chardonnay, Chenin Blanc, Sauvignon Blanc, French Colombard and Grenache wines. 360 acres. 40,000 cases.

McGregor Vineyard (U.S.)   1980

A winery south of Penn Yan, on the eastern shore of Lake Keuka, Finger Lakes region, New York; produces Chardonnay, Gewürztraminer, Pinot Noir and Riesling wines. 20 acres.

McHenry Vineyards (U.S.)   1980

A small winery in Santa Cruz City, Santa Cruz County, California; produces Pinot Noir and Chardonnay wines. 5 acres.

McLester (U.S.)   1979

A winery in Inglewood, Los Angeles County, California; produces Cabernet and Zinfandel wines from grapes purchased in San Luis Obispo County. 1,500 cases.

McWilliams (Aus.)   1880

A large company with wineries in the Hunter Valley and Riverina districts. Mount Pleasant, Lovedale and Rosehill are three of the well-known vineyards; produces a vast array of wines with special designations and names, including Cabernet, Rhine Riesling, Chardonnay, Sauvignon Blanc, Traminer, Sémillon, blends of Riesling and Traminer wines and port-style wines from their own and purchased grapes. 2 million cases. 650 acres.

McWilliams Wines (N.Z.)   1944

Originally a branch of McWilliams of Australia, now a large, separate winery in Hawkes Bay, North Island; has 14 vineyards and 3 wineries; produces Cabernet, Chardonnay, Riesling, Sylvaner, Müller-Thurgau, hybrid and fortified wines, some from purchased grapes. 900 acres.

Méal, Le (F.)

A vineyard in Hermitage, northern Rhône region; grows red grapes.

meal-moth (pyralid, *or* pyralis)

One of several moths whose larvae feed on grape leaves and fruit.

méchage (F.)

Fumigation of a wine vat or barrel with burning sulphur to destroy bacteria and unwanted yeasts. The wick used to burn the sulphur is called *mèche*.

Mechin (Sp.)

In the Rioja region, the local name for the Monastrel grape.

Mecsek (H.)

A district in the southern Transdanubia region, southwestern Hungary; produces red and white wines from 6 villages, the best-known of which is Pécs; made from Wälschriesling, some Furmint and other grapes. The white wine is officially rated

White Wine of Excellent Quality. 4,000 acres.

Meddersheim (G.)

A village in the Nahe region, Bereich Schloss Böckelheim, Grosslage Paradiesgarten. The vineyards are: Altenberg, Edelberg, Liebfrauenberg, Präsent and Rheingrafenberg.

Médoc AOC (F.)

1. A famous district north of Bordeaux city, in the Bordeaux region, southwestern France; produces some of the finest red wines in the world. It is divided into Médoc (formerly, Bas-Médoc), in the north and Haut-Médoc, in the south.

2. The northern section of the Médoc district, as distinguished from the southern, or Haut-Médoc section, which is of higher quality and more famous.

3. A red AOC wine from the entire Médoc district made from Cabernet Sauvignon, Merlot, Cabernet Franc, Malbec and Petit Verdot grapes, in varying proportions.

Médoc Noir (H.)

In Hungary, the name (in French) for the Merlot grape.

Meerendal EWO (S. Af.)

An estate near Durbanville; produces red wines bottled by the Bergkelder.

Meerlust Estate EWO (S. Af.)   1776

An estate in the Stellenbosch district; produces a blend of Cabernet, Pinot Noir and Merlot wines, bottled by the Bergkelder. 25,000 cases. 600 acres.

Meersburg (G.)

A village in the Baden region, Bereich Bodensee, Grosslage Sonnenufer. The vineyards are: Bengel, Chorherrnhalde, Fohrenberg, Haltnau, Jungfernstieg, Lerchenberg, Rieschen and Sängerhalde.

Meffre, Gabriel (F.)   1930

A large estate and merchant in Gigondas, Rhône region. 2,000 acres, including Château de Vaudieu, in Châteauneuf-du-Pape, and extensive vineyards in Gigondas and other Côtes du Rhône villages.

Meier's Wine Cellars (U.S.)   1895

A winery in Cincinnati, the largest in Ohio, with vineyards in Sandusky, Silverton and Isle St. George, in Lake Erie; produces Catawba, Delaware and wines from hybrid grapes as well as White Riesling, Chardonnay, Gewürztraminer and sparkling wines.

Meikuishanputaochu (China)

A sweet, white wine from eastern China, similar to Muscat wine, made from a hybrid grape.

meio seco (P.)

Medium-dry.

Meix, Les *also* Clos du Meix (F.)

A *Grand Cru* vineyard (in part) in Aloxe-Corton, Côte de Beaune district, Burgundy, when Corton precedes the name of the vineyard. The other part of the vineyard is *Premier Cru*. 5 acres.

Meix-Bas, Les (F.)

A *Premier Cru* vineyard in Fixin, Côte de Nuits district, Burgundy. 6 acres.

Meix-Bataille, Le (F.)

A *Premier Cru* vineyard in Monthélie, Côte de Beaune district, Burgundy. 6 acres.

Meix-Caillet (F.)

A *Premier Cru* vineyard in Rully, Côte Chalonnaise district, Burgundy.

Meix-Lallement, Les (F.)

A *Grand Cru* vineyard (in part) in Aloxe-Corton, Côte de Beaune district, Burgundy. The other part of the vineyard is *Premier Cru*.

Meix-Rentiers (F.)

A *Premier Cru* vineyard in Morey-St.-Denis, Côte de Nuits district, Burgundy. 3 acres.

Méjan-Taulier, Domaine (F.)

An estate in Tavel, southern Rhône region. 70 acres.

Meknes (Mor.)

A city and district east of Rabat; produces red wines made from Carignan, Cinsault and Grenache grapes.

Melesconera (N.Z.)

A red grape grown near Aukland, on the North Island.

Melini, Chianti (I.)   1705

A winery in Gaggiano di Poggibonsi, Tuscany region; produces Chianti, Chianti Classico, Orvieto, Vernaccia, Vin Santo, Vino Nobile de Montepulciano and other wines. 400 acres.

Mélinots *also* Mellinots (F.)

A *Premier Cru* vineyard in Chablis, Chablis district, Burgundy; it now usually includes Mélinots, Roncières and Les Épinottes.

Melissa DOC (I.)

1. A town and district south of Cirò, in the eastern Calabria region, which produces:

2. Red and white wines similar to Cirò wines; the red wines are made mostly from Gaglioppo grapes and the white wines are made from the Greco Bianco grape.

Melon (F.)

In the Loire Valley, another name for the Muscadet grape; also called Melon de Bourgogne.

Melon d'Arbois (F.)

In the Arbois district of the Jura region, another name for the Chardonnay grape.

Melon Blanc (F.)

A local French name for the Chardonnay grape.

Melon de Bourgogne (F.)

See **Melon**.

Mencía (Sp.)

A red grape grown in the León district, Old Castile region, in northern Spain and in the Galicia region, where it is also called Tintorera.

Mendocino County (U.S.)

A region north of Sonoma county, in northern California; includes the districts of: Anderson Valley, Ukiah Valley, McDowell Valley, Redwood Valley and Potter Valley.

Mendoza (Arg.)

An important province and city in west central Argentina; produces 2/3 of Argentina's wines made mostly from the Malbec grape; also red wines from Cabernet, Pinot Noir, Syrah, Lambrusco, Barbera and Tempranillo grapes and white wines from Pedro Ximénez, Chenin Blanc, Sémillon, Palomino, Moscatel, Chardonnay and Riesling grapes.

Ménétou-Salon AOC (F.)   1959

1. A village and small district of 300 acres north of Bourges, in the Upper Loire region, Loire Valley, which produces:

2. Red, white and rosé wines, the red and rosé made from the Pinot Noir grape, and the white from the Sauvignon grape.

Mennig (G.)

A village in the Mosel-Saar-Ruwer region, Bereich Saar-Ruwer, Grosslage Scharzberg. The vineyards are: Altenberg, Euchariusberg, Herrenberg and Sonnenberg. 275 acres.

Méntrida DO (Sp.)

A district southwest of Madrid, in the La Mancha region; produces ordinary red and white wines.

Menu-Pineau (F.)

See **Pineau Menu.**

Méo, Jean (F.)

An estate in Vosne-Romanée, Côte de Nuits district, Burgundy. 28 acres, including 7.5 acres of Clos de Vougeot, 1 acre of Richebourg, 5 acres of Vosne-Romanée Les Chaumes, 4 acres of Nuits-St.-Georges Aux Boudots and 1.6 acres of Aux Murgers.

Meraner Kurtraube (G.)

In Germany, another name for the Trollinger grape.

Meranese di Collina DOC *also* Meraner Hügel (I.)

A light red wine from Merano, in the the northern Trentino-Alto Adige region; made from the Schiava grape.

Mercey, Domaine du Château de (F.)

An estate in Cheilly, Côte de Beaune district, Burgundy. 100 acres, including 37 acres of Mercurey and 63 acres of Bourgogne Hautes-Côtes de Beaune.

merchant

A shipper, or *négociant;* also *éleveur.*

Mercian, Château (J.)

An estate-bottled red wine from the Yamanashi district.

Mercier (F.)   1858

A Champagne producer in Épernay; the *cuvée de prestige* is Réserve de l'Empereur. 5 million bottles. 500 acres.

Mercurey AOC (F.)

1. A village in the Côte Chalonnaise district, Burgundy region.

2. A red or white wine from Mercurey and the two nearby villages of St.-Martin-sous-Montaigu and Bourgneuf-Val-d'Or. The grapes are Pinot Noir and Chardonnay. There are five *Premier Cru* vineyards.

Meredyth Vineyard (U.S.)   1972

A winery near Middleburg, Virginia; produces red, white and rosé wines from hybrid grapes. 7,000 cases. 45 acres.

Merlot

An important red grape grown in France, Italy, California, Australia and elsewhere; the principal grape of Pomerol, and an important blending grape in most Bordeaux red wines; it ripens earlier than the Cabernet Sauvignon grape and produces softer, fleshier wine which matures sooner.

Merlot Blanc (F.)

The white Merlot grape, used in making Pineau des Charentes wine.

Mérode, Prince Florent de (F.)

An estate in Ladoix-Serrigny, Côte de Beaune district, Burgundy; also called Domaine de Serrigny. 26 acres, including 10 acres of Corton, 1.6 acres of Aloxe-Corton and 7 acres of Pommard Clos de la Platière; managed by Bitouzet of Savigny.

Merritt Estate Winery (U.S.)   1976

A winery in Forestville, Chautauqua region, southwestern New York; produces wines made from hybrid and *labrusca* grapes. 60 acres.

Merseguéra (Alg.)

A white grape, probably the Spanish Merzeguera grape, grown in Algeria.

Merxheim (G.)

A village in the Nahe region, Bereich Schloss Böckelheim, Grosslage Paradiesgarten. The vineyards are: Hunolsteiner, Römerberg and Vogelsang.

Merzeguera (Sp.)

A white grape grown in the Alicante district, in southeastern Spain.

Meslier (F.)

A white grape grown in small amounts in the Champagne and Southwest regions.

Mesnil (F.)

A village in the Côte des Blancs district, Champagne region; rated 99%.

Mesny de Boisseaux, Cuvée (F.)

A red wine from the Hospices de Nuits, Nuits-St.-Georges, Burgundy. The *cuvée* is composed of Nuits-St.-Georges Les Boudots - .5 acre.

Mesolone (I.)

A red wine from Brusengo, in the northern Piedmont region; made from Nebbiolo and Bonarda grapes.

Messapia (I.)

A red wine from Mesagne, near Brindisi, in the southern Apulia region.

Messias SARL (P.)

See **Sociedade Agricola...Messias SARL.**

Mestre Père et Fils (F.)

An estate in Santenay, Côte de Beaune, Burgundy. Owns 18 acres of Santenay Premier Cru, 6 acres of Aloxe-Corton, 1.5 acres of Corton and some Chassagne-Montrachet and Côte de Beaune.

Mestrezat-Preller (F.)   1814

A merchant in Bordeaux.

Métaireau, Louis (F.)

A co-op estate of ten growers in St.-Fiacre-sur-Maine, Muscadet de Sèvre-et-Maine district, Loire Valley; also owns the Domaine du Grand Mouton estate - 65 acres. 185 acres.

Metala (Aus.)

A vineyard in Longhorne Creek, south of Adelaide, South Australia; grows Cabernet and Shiraz grapes which are used to make red wine at Stonyfell Winery.

Metapontum (I.)

Red and white wines from Metaponto, in the Basilicata region. The red wines are made from Sangiovese, Negroamaro and Malvasia Nera grapes and the white wines are made from Malvasia Bianca, Trebbiano and Moscato di Terracina grapes.

métayage (F.)

The old practice of leasing of part of a vineyard or farm in exchange for a percentage of the produce; also called *vigneronnage*. See also **fermage.**

méthode Champenoise (F.)

The Champagne method, a traditional process of making a sparkling wine in each bottle, rather than using the bulk (or *Charmat*) process.

methuselah (F.)

A large bottle equal to eight 5ths, used in the Champagne region.

methyl anthranilate

An ester present in *labrusca* grapes which causes the so-called "foxy" or grapey taste.

métis (F.)

A cross between two grapes of the same species, as opposed to a hybrid, which is a cross of two grapes from different species.

metodo friulano (I.)

A method used in the Friuli-Venezia Giulia region of making fresh white wine by putting free-run must through a slow, low-temperature fermentation, allowing little or no contact with oxygen.

Metsovo (Gr.)

A red wine from Epirus (Ipiros), in northwestern Greece; made from the Cabernet Sauvignon grape.

Mettenheim (G.)

A village in the Rheinhessen region, Bereich Nierstein, Grosslagen Rheinblick and Krötenbrunnen. The vineyards are: Michelsberg and Schlossberg in Grosslage Rheinblick, and Goldberg in Grosslage Krötenbrunnen.

Meursault AOC (F.)

A village in the Côte de Beaune district, Burgundy region; it was known as early as 1102; the center of Côte de Meursault, which includes the communes of Chassagne, Puligny, Blagny and Meursault. Produces red and white wine; most of the red is sold as Volnay, and the wines of Blagny can be sold as Meursault. Including Blagny, there are 18 *Premier Cru* vineyards. 1,200 acres.

Meursault, Château de (F.)

An estate in Meursault, Côte de Beaune district, Burgundy. 25 acres, including vineyard parcels of Volnay Clos des Chênes - 9 acres, Meursault Les Perrières - 2.5 acres and Les Charmes - 12 acres. Controlled by Patriarche Père et Fils, in Beaune. See **Moucheron, Comte de.**

Mexico

A country in Central America. Wine has been produced mainly in the northern part of the country since the 16th century. The important regions are: Aguascalientes, northern Baja California, Delicias, Hermosillo, Saltillo-Parras-Torreon, San Juan del Río and Zacatecas. 100,000 acres.

Meyer et Fils, Joseph (F.)   1854

An estate and merchant in Wintzenheim, Haut-Rhin district, Alsace region. 30 acres, including the Hengst vineyard – 7 acres (Gewürztraminer and Riesling).

Meyney, Château (F.)

An estate in St.-Estèphe, Haut-Médoc district, Bordeaux; classified in 1978 as a *Cru Grand Bourgeois Exceptionnel*. 24,000 cases. 120 acres.

Meynieu, Château Le (F.)

An estate in Vertheuil, Haut-Médoc district, Bordeaux; classified in 1978 as a *Cru Grand Bourgeois*. 20 acres. 4,000 cases.

Meyzonnier, Domaine (F.)

An estate in Pouzols Minervois, Minervois district, Languedoc region. 3,000 cases. 13 acres.

Mézesfehér (H.)

A white grape. The name means "honey white."

Michel, Joseph et Robert (F.)

An estate in Cornas, northern Rhône region. 15 acres.

Michel et Fils, Louis (F.)

An estate in Chablis, Burgundy. 45 acres, including 2.5 acres of Vaudésir, 1.5 acres of

Grenouilles, 1.2 acres of Les Clos and some Montmain, Fourchaume, Vaillons, Butteaux, Montée de Tonnerre and Forêts.

Michelot, Bernard *also* Michelot-Buisson (F.)

An estate in Meursault, Côte de Beaune district, Burgundy. 50 acres, including 4 acres of Meursault Les Genevrières, 2.5 acres of Les Charmes, .6 acre of Les Perrières, 1.2 acres of Clos St.-Félix and some Puligny-Montrachet and Pommard.

Michelots, Domaine Héritiers Émile (F.)

An estate in Nuits-St.-Georges, Côte de Nuits district, Burgundy. 15 acres, including 5 acres of Nuits-St.-Georges Vaucrains, 1.2 acres of Les Porrets, .5 acre of Les St.-Georges, 1.2 acres of Aux Vignes Richemone and 3.6 acres of Premier Cru.

Michelsberg (G.)

A *Grosslage,* one of 10 in Bereich Bernkastel (Mittel-Mosel) in the Mosel-Saar-Ruwer region; it includes Piesport and Trittenheim. There are 29 vineyards.

Michet (I.)

A clone of the Nebbiolo grape, DOC approved.

Michigan (U.S.)

A state in the north central United States. It has about 20 wineries, mostly near Lake Erie and Lake Michigan. 12,000 acres.

Micot, Le Clos (F.)

A *Premier Cru* vineyard in Pommard, Côte de Beaune district, Burgundy. 7 acres.

micro-climate

A small area having a climatic condition that differs from the climate of the general region, thereby producing somewhat different wines.

Middelvlei Estate EWO (S. Af.)

An estate in the Stellenbosch district.

Midi (F.)

A large region in southern France, southwest of the Rhône region, including the Roussillon and Languedoc regions.

Midi Vineyard (U.S.)

A small winery in Lone Jack, western Missouri; produces wines made from hybrid grapes. 5 acres.

Migliorini, Valentino (I.)

An estate in Monforte d'Alba, Piedmont region. See **Rocche di Manzoni.**

Mignotte, Cuvée (F.)

A red wine from the Hospices de Nuits, in Nuits-St.-Georges, Burgundy. The *cuvée* includes parcels of *Premier Cru* vineyards in Nuit-St.-Georges.

Mignotte, La (F.)

A *Premier Cru* vineyard in Beaune, Côte de Beaune district, Burgundy. 6 acres.

Miguel del Arco (Sp.)

A red grape grown in the Rioja region.

Milano Winery (U.S.)   1977

A winery in Hopland, Mendocino County, California; produces Cabernet, Zinfandel, Petite Sirah, Gamay Beaujolais, Chenin Blanc and Sauvignon Blanc wines, mostly from purchased single vineyard grapes. 10,000 cases.

Mildara (Aus.)   1891

A large winery in Mildura, Murray River, northwestern Victoria; produces wines made from grapes grown in the Coonewarra district and from purchased grapes. 700 acres.

mildew

A fungus disease of vines; a mold. See **powdery mildew** and **downy (false) mildew.**

Mill Creek Vineyards (U.S.)   grapes 1965
                                              winery 1975

A winery in Healdsburg, Russian River

Valley, northern Sonoma County, California; produces Pinot Noir, Merlot, Gamay Beaujolais, Cabernet Blush (a Cabernet rosé), Chardonnay and Gewürztraminer wines. 10,000 cases. 65 acres.

Millandes, Les (F.)

A *Premier Cru* vineyard in Morey-St.-Denis, Côte de Nuits district, Burgundy. 10 acres.

millerandage (F.)

A condition consisting of the presence of some undeveloped, small green berries in otherwise ripe bunches of grapes, caused by unequal and incomplete flowering.

millésime (F.)

The date of the vintage; the vintage year; *millésimé* means vintaged, the product of a single year.

Milliand, René (F.)

An estate in St.-Péray, northern Rhône region. 16 acres.

Minervois VDQS (F.)

1. A large district northwest of Narbonne, in the Languedoc region, southern France, which produces:

2. Red and rosé wine made from Carignan, Grenache Noir and Cinsault grapes. 16 million gallons.

Minges, Weingut Ernst (G.)   1285

An estate and merchant in Edesheim, Rheinpfalz region; owns vineyards in Edesheim, Rhodt, Weyher and Edenkoben. 20 acres.

Ministrel (Sp.)

In the Rioja region, another name for the Monastrel grape.

Minnella Bianca (I.)

A white grape grown in eastern Sicily.

Minnesota (U.S.)

A state in the north-midwestern United States. Extremely cold winters prevent

much vine-growing, but there are a few vineyards planted with hardy hybrid grapes. 100 acres.

Minuty, Château (F.)

An estate in Gassin, in the Provence region; produces Cuvée de l'Orotaire. 22,000 cases. 100 acres.

Miraflores (Sp.)

A district northwest of Jerez, in the Sherry region.

Miramar (Aus.)   1974

A winery in Mudgee, New South Wales; produces Cabernet, Shiraz, Chardonnay, Sémillon and Port wines. 6,000 cases. 80 acres.

Mirassou (U.S.)   1854

A large, historic winery in San José, Santa Clara County, California; produces 20 or more varieties of still and sparkling wines. 300,000 cases. 1,400 acres.

Mirat, Château (F.)

An estate in Barsac, Sauternes district, Bordeaux; classified in 1855 as a *Deuxième Cru*; now spelled Château Myrat. The vines were uprooted in 1976.

Mireille, Clos (F.)

An estate in la Londe-Les-Maures, Provence region; owned by Domaines Ott; produces white wine made from Sémillon and Ugni Blanc grapes. 120 acres.

Mis en Bouteilles au Château (F.)

"Put in bottles at the Château," or château-bottled, a guarantee of authenticity, used mostly in Bordeaux. Equivalent designations are *Mis en Bouteilles au Domaine* and *Mis en Bouteilles à la Propriété*.

mise (F.)

Put (into bottles); bottled.

mise du château *also* mise au Domaine (F.)

Estate-bottled; bottled at the owner's property.

Mish (U.S.)

An American grape of the *Vitis rotundifolia*.

Misket (Bul.)

A red grape of the muscat family used to make red and white wines.

Misserey et Frère, P. (F.)   1904

An estate in Nuits-St.-Georges, Côte de Nuits district, Burgundy. 15 acres, including 5 acres of Nuits-St.-Georges Les Vaucrains, 2.5 acres of Les Cailles, 2.5 acres of Les St.-Georges, 2.5 acres of Aux Vignes Rondes and 2.5 acres of Aux Murgers.

Misset, Domaine P. (F.)

An estate in Gevrey-Chambertin, Côte de Nuits, Burgundy; owns Clos de Vougeot - 2.5 acres and Gevrey-Chambertin La Romanée (red); handled by Naigeon-Chaveau et Fils.

Mission (U.S.)

A red grape grown in California, the first *Vitis vinifera* grape grown in California. Also called Criolla in Mexico, where the grape originated.

Mission-Haut-Brion, Château La (F.)

An estate in Talence, Graves district, Bordeaux; classified in 1959 as a *Cru Classé* for red wine. It was part of the neighboring Haut-Brion estate until 1630. Laville-Haut-Brion (white) and La Tour-Haut-Brion (red) are under the same ownership. 65% Cabernet, 10% Cabernet Franc and 25% Merlot grapes. 6,000 cases. 35 acres.

Mission Vineyards (N.Z.)   1851

An historic winery in Taradale, Hawkes Bay, North Island, run by a religious order; produces Cabernet, Merlot, Sémillon, Gewürztraminer, Pinot Gris, Sauvignon Blanc and Chardonnay wines. 110 acres.

Mississippi (U.S.)

A state in the southeastern United States. The state prohibition law was repealed in 1966 and since then a few new wineries have opened; the muscadine grapes predominate.

Missouri (U.S.)

A state in the mid-western United States. It was an active wine producer until prohibition and there are now appoximately 20 wineries. 3,000 acres.

Missouri Riesling (U.S.)

A white hybrid grape – a cross of Taylor (*Vitis riparia*) and a *Vitis labrusca* grape, developed in 1860 by Nicholas Grein of Missouri; grown in the eastern U.S., and also called Elvira.

mist propagation

A method of vine propagation used in California in which mature canes are cut into one-bud pieces and grown in 83-degree chambers under an intermittant fine mist of water. After the buds have sprouted and leaves appear, the shoots are cut into pieces having one bud and one leaf; this is dipped into a growth hormone and rooted in the mist chamber; this way, a single 5-year-old vine can produce hundreds of new rootings in a year.

mistela (Sp.)

Must with spirits added to it to prevent fermentation; this is added to wines to sweeten and fortify them.

mistelle (F.)

A fortified wine made by adding spirits to the grape juice before fermentation, resulting in a sweet wine, since alcohol prevents the fermentation of sugar; used as a base for vermouth.

Mitan, Domaine (F.)

An estate in Vedène, Côtes du Rhône district, southern Rhône region; produces red and rose wines made from Grenache, Cinsault, Syrah and Mourvèdre grapes. 25 acres.

Mitans, Les (F.)

A *Premier Cru* vineyard in Volnay, Côte de Beaune district, Burgundy. 10 acres.

Mitchelton (Aus.)   1969

A winery in Mitchells Town, Nagambie, Victoria; produces Cabernet, Shiraz, Rhine Riesling, Trebbiano, Marsanne and Sémillon wines. 20,000 cases. 250 acres.

Mitrano (I.)

1. A village near Brindisi, in the southern Apulia region, which produces:

2. Red and rosé wines made from the Negroamaro grape.

Mittelhaardt (G.)

The central part of the Rheinpfalz region, now part of the Bereich Mittelhaardt-Deutsche Weinstrasse, where the most important wines of the district are produced.

Mittelhaardt-Deutsche Weinstrasse (G.)

A *Bereich*, one of 2 in the Rheinpfalz region, containing 17 *Grosslagen*.

Mittelheim (G.)

A village in the Rheingau region, Bereich Johannisberg, Grosslagen Erntebringer and Honigberg. The vineyards are: Edelmann and St. Nikolaus, partly in each *Grosslage*, and Goldberg, in Grosslage Erntebringer. 415 acres.

Mittelrhein (G.)

One of 11 *Anbaugebiete* (regions) north of the Rheingau region, from Rüdesheim north to Cologne, which produces ordinary wines, and which grows the northernmost vines in Europe. 60 miles long. 75% Riesling grapes. 2,500 acres.

Mittervernatsch (I.)

The German name for the red Ledia grape grown in Trentino-Alto Adige region.

moelleux (F.)

Soft, sweet, or mellow.

Moenchberg (F.)

A *Grand Cru* vineyard in Eichhoffen, Bas-Rhin district, Alsace region.

Moët et Chandon (F.)   1743

The largest Champagne producer, in Épernay; Dom Pérignon (since 1936) is the *cuvée de prestige*. 18 million bottles. 1,100 acres.

Mogen David (U.S.)   1932

A large producer of sweet, Kosher wines in Chicago, Illinois. 500 acres of vineyards in the Chautauqua region of New York as well as other vineyards in Michigan, Missouri and Pennsylvania; wines are made from Concord, hybrid and some *vinifera* grapes.

Moillard-Grivot (F.)   1850

A large estate, *négociant* and buyer of grapes in Nuits-St.-Georges, Côte de Nuits, Burgundy. 48 acres, including some Chambertin Clos de Bèze, Romanée-St.-Vivant and Clos de Vougeot, Vosne-Romanée Aux Malconsorts – 6 acres, Nuits-St.-Georges Clos de Thorey Monopole – 9 acres, Vosne-Romanée Les Beaumonts, Nuits-St.-Georges La Richemone, Les Grandes Vignes Monopole – 5 acres, Corton-Charlemagne, Corton Clos du Roi and Beaune Grèves; sole distributor of Corton Clos de Vergennes – 5 acres and Volnay Clos de la Barre - 2.5 acres, both *monopoles*.

Moldavia (U.S.S.R.)

A republic of Soviet Russia, formerly Bessarabia; produces Româneşti - a red wine made from Cabernet, Merlot and Malbec grapes, Negru de Purkar - a red wine from a blend of 5 grapes, Chumay - a sweet red made from the Cabernet grape and Grifesti - a sweet white made from the Muscat grape. 53 million gallons. 600,000 acres.

Molette (F.)

A white grape grown in Seyssel, Savoie region, for making sparkling wines.

Molinara (I.)

A red grape grown in the Veneto region; used in making Bardolino and Valpolicella wines.

Molinelli (I.)

1. A white grape grown in the Emilia-Romagna region.

2. A sweet, white wine made near Piacenza, in the western Emilia-Romagna region from from a rare, local grape of the same name. 15-16% alcohol.

Molinelli, Giancarlo (I.)

An estate in Ziano, Emilia-Romagna region; produces Barbera, Bonarda, Gutturnio, Malvasia, Molinelli and Müller-Thurgau wines.

Molise (I.)

A region in southeastern Italy, just south of the Abruzzi region; independent from Abruzzi since 1963; produces mostly varietal wines, but no DOC wines.

Mommessin, Domaine (F.)

An estate and *négociant* in La Grange St. Pierre, in the Mâcon district, Burgundy; owns Clos de Tart Monopole – 18 acres and some Beaujolais.

Monarch Wine Company (U.S.)

A winery in New York City; produces sweet Kosher wines mostly from purchased Concord grapes; added the name of Manischewitz around 1945.

Monarch Wine Company (U.S.)   1936

A winery in Atlanta, Georgia, the only commercial one in the state; produces wines from muscadine, Concord and other grapes as well as peach wine.

Monastrel (Sp.)

A red grape grown in Spain. Also called Valcarcelia, Monastel, Moraster, Ministrel, Negralejo and Mechín.

Monbadon (F.)

A white French grape known in California as the Burger grape.

Monbazillac AOC (F.)

1. A village and district south of Bergerac, in the Southwest region, which produces:

2. A sweet white wine from Monbazillac, as well as from Pomport, Rouffignac, Colombier and part of St.-Laurent-des-Vignes, made from Sémillon, Sauvignon and Muscadelle grapes.

Monbousquet, Château (F.)

An estate in St.-Émilion, Bordeaux; classified in 1955 as a *Grand Cru*. 14,000 cases. 75 acres.

Moncontour, Château (F.)

An estate in Vouvray, Touraine region, Loire Valley; produces sparkling and still Vouvray wines. 150 acres.

Mondavi Winery, Robert (U.S.)   1966

A famous winery in Oakville, Napa Valley, California; produces Cabernet, Zinfandel, Pinot Noir, Petite Sirah, Napa Gamay, Chardonnay, Johannisberg Riesling, Chenin Blanc, Fumé Blanc and other wines. 500,000 cases. 1,000 acres.

Mondeuse *also* Mondeuse Noir (F.)

A red grape grown in the Savoie and Rhône regions. Also called Refosco in northern Italy.

Mondeuse Blanche (F.)

A white grape grown in Bugey, in the Savoie region.

Monemvasia (Gr.)

A town in southern Peloponnese, southern Greece; produces Malvasia wines, historically, the first to do so.

Monfort Wine Co. (Is.)

A winery in Nathanya, Israel; produces Sauvignon Blanc, Grenache Rosé, French Colombard and other Kosher wines.

Monfortino (I.)

A red wine, similar to Barolo, from Monforte d'Alba, in the Piedmont region; made from the Nebbiolo grape.

Mongeard-Mugneret (F.)

An estate in Vosne-Romanée, Côte de Nuits district, Burgundy. 37 acres, including 1.6 acres of Clos de Vougeot, 2.5 acres of Grands Échézeaux, 7.5 acres of Échézeaux, 1.2 acres of Vosne-Romanée Les

Suchots, 1.2 acres of Nuits-St.-Georges Aux Boudots and 2.5 acres of Vougeot Premier Cru.

Monica (I.)

A red grape grown in Sardinia.

Monica di Cagliari DOC (I.)

A sweet, red wine from Cagliari, in southwestern Sardinia; made from 100% Monica grapes. 15-18% alcohol.

Monica di Sardegna DOC (I.)   1980

A red wine from Sardinia, DOC approved; made from the Monica grape.

Monimpex (H.)

The Hungarian State Export Agency, the official government export company for all wines and spirits.

Monis (S. Af.)

A famous winery in the Paarl district, well-known for sherry-style wines; mow a part of the Stellenbosch Farmers Wineries Group.

Monistrol, Marqués de (Sp.)   1882

A winery in San Sadurní de Noya, west of Barcelona, Catalonia region; produces still and sparkling wines. 750 acres.

Monnier, Domaine René (F.)

An estate in Meursault, Côte de Beaune district, Burgundy. 55 acres, including 5 acres of Meursault Les Charmes, 6 acres of Meursault Les Chevalières, 2 acres of Beaune Les Toussaints, 4 acres of Les Cent Vignes, 2 acres of Volnay Clos des Chênes, 2 acres of Puligny-Montrachet Les Folatières and 2 acres of Pommard.

Monnier, Jean (F.)   1720

An estate in Meursault, Côte de Beaune district, Burgundy. 37 acres, including .8 acre of Meursault Les Genevrières, 4 acres of Clos du Cromin, 1.7 acres of Les Charmes, 7.5 acres of Pommard Clos de Citeaux Monopole, 7.5 acres of Les Épenots, 1.7 acres of Les Argillières, .8 acre of Les

Fremiers, 1.7 acres of Beaune Les Montrev enots and 2.5 acres of Puligny-Montrachet

Monnot, André (F.)

An estate in Dezize, Côte de Beaune dis trict, Burgundy. 25 acres, including San tenay and Côte de Beaune-Villages.

Monnot, Henri (F.)

An estate in Volnay, Côte de Beaune district, Burgundy. 15 acres, including .5 acre of Volnay Caillerets, 7.5 acres of Premier Cru, .8 acre of Pommard Les Fremiets and .6 acre of Les Chanlins Bas.

monopole (F.)

A term used on certain wines as a designation of exclusive ownership, or monopoly; in Burgundy it means exclusive ownership of the vineyard; in blended wines it means exclusive use of the brand name of the wine.

Monpelou, Château (F.)

An estate in Pauillac, Haut-Médoc district, Bordeaux; classified in 1932 as a *Cru Bourgeois*. 20 acres. 5,000 cases. See, however, **Château Colombier Monpelou.**

Monsanto (I.)   1962

An estate in Barberino Val d'Elsa, Tuscany region; produces Chianti Classico wines, including one designated as Il Poggio. 30,000 cases. 125 acres.

Monsecco (I.)

A red wine from Gattinara, in the Piedmont region; made from the Nebbiolo grape by Conti Ravizza.

Monsedro (P.)

A red grape grown in southern Portugal.

Monstelo (Sp.)

A red grape grown in the Galicia region of northwestern Spain.

Mont Damnés (F.)

A vineyard in Verdigny and Chavignol, Sancerre district, Upper Loire region.

Mont de Milieu (F.)
See **Monts de Milieu.**

Mont-Olivet, Clos du (F.)
An estate in Châteauneuf-du-Pape, Rhône region. 2,000 cases. 42 acres.

Mont d'Or, Domaine du (Sw.)   1848
A well-known estate in Sion, Valais region; produces Johannisberg, Arvine, Fendant and Dôle wines. 50 acres.

Mont-Palais (F.)
A *Premier Cru* vineyard in Rully, Côte Chalonnaise district, Burgundy.

Mont-Redon, Domaine de (F.)
A large estate in Châteauneuf-du-Pape, Rhône region; produces red and white wine using all 13 grape varieties permitted. 235 acres.

Mont St. John Cellars (U.S.)   1979
A winery in Napa City, Napa Valley, California; produces Pinot Noir, Chardonnay, Johannisberg Riesling and other varietal wines. 160 acres in the Carneros district. 20,000 cases.

Mont Winery, La (U.S.)   1966, 1977
A winery in Lamont, San Joaquin Valley, Kern County, California; formerly Bear Mountain Winery; produces jug wines and some varietals. 6 million cases.

Montagliari, Fattoria di (I.)   17th cent.
An estate in Panzano, Tuscany region; produces Chianti Classico and Vin Santo wines; also owns La Quercia estate. 50,000 cases.

Montagne EWO (S. Af.)   1958
An estate in the northern Stellenbosch district; produces red wines, especially Cabernet and Shiraz. 6,000 cases. 300 acres.

Montagne, Château de la (Is.)
A dry white wine from the Carmel Winery; made from Sémillon and Sauvignon grapes.

Montagne de Reims (F.)
A district in the Champagne region, just south of Reims; planted mostly with Pinot Noir grapes.

Montagne-Saint-Émilion AOC (F.)
A commune north of St.-Émilion, in the Bordeaux region; the wines are similar to those of St.-Émilion.

Montagny AOC (F.)
1. A commune in the Côte Chalonnaise district of Burgundy, which produces:

2. A white wine from Montagny and three other nearby villages made from Chardonnay grapes. Red wines are sold under the Bourgogne AOC.

Montagu (S. Af.)
A town and district in the western Little Karoo region.

Montaiguillon, Château (F.)
An estate in Montagne-St.-Émilion, Bordeaux. 12,500 cases. 60 acres.

Montaigus, Clos des (F.)
A *Premier Cru* vineyard in Mercurey, Côte Chalonnaise district, Burgundy.

Montalbano, Castello di (I.)
A vineyard near Gattinara, in the Piedmont region; produces Spanna wine made by Vallana.

Montali Winery, R. (U.S.)   1982
A winery in Berkeley, Alameda County, California, using the equipment and stocks of the R. Carey Winery, which closed down in 1981. 40,000 cases.

Montana Wines (N.Z.)   1961
The largest winery in New Zealand, near Auckland, North Island with holdings at Mangatangi, Gisborne and 500 acres in Marlborough (South Island); produces Riesling, Gewürztraminer, Chardonnay, Cabernet and sparkling wines. 1,500 acres.

Montánchez (Sp.)

A village in the Cáceres district, in south-western Spain; produces a red and a white wine which produce a *flor* during fermentation, similar to Sherry wines.

Montbray Wine Cellars (U.S.)   1966

A winery in Silver Run, north of Westminster, Maryland; the first to make *vinifera* wines in the state (1971); produces Chardonnay, Riesling, Pinot Noir, Muscat Ottonel, Cabernet, Seyve-Villard white and Ravat red wines; also an ice wine in 1974. 20 acres.

Montchenot, Château (Arg.)

A red wine from Bodega Lopez, in Maipu, south of Mendoza City, in the northern Mendoza region; made from a blend of Cabernet and Malbec grapes.

Montclair Winery (U.S.)   1975

A winery in Piedmont, Alameda County, California; produces Cabernet, Zinfandel, Petite Sirah and French Colombard wines from grapes purchased from Dry Creek, Sonoma County. 1,200 cases.

Monte Antico (I.)

1. A village south of Siena, in the southern Tuscany region, which produces:

2. Red and white wine, the red made from Sangiovese Grosso and some Canaiolo, Colorino and Trebbiano grapes, and the white from Trebbiano and Malvasia grapes.

Monte Antico, Castello di (I.)

An estate in Civitella Marittima, Tuscany region; produces Castello di Monte Antico and Ardenghesca Bianco wines. 25,000 cases.

Monte Rosso (U.S.)

A vineyard in the Mayacamas Mts., north of Sonoma, Sonoma County, California, owned by the Louis Martini Winery; produces Cabernet Sauvignon, Zinfandel, Johannisberg Riesling and Muscat wines. 280 acres.

Monte Schiavo (I.)

An estate in Moie di Maiolati Spontini, the Marches region; produces Verdicchio wines. 24,000 cases. 70 acres.

Monte Venda (I.)

A white wine from the Colli Euganei district, in the Veneto region; made from Garganega, Serprina and Sauvignon grapes.

Monte Vertine (I.)

An estate in Radda, Tuscany region; produces Chianti Classico, Le Pergole Torte and Monte Vertine Bianco wines. 3,000 cases.

Montecarlo DOC (I.)

1. A village and district near Lucca, in the northwestern Tuscany region, which produces:

2. A white wine made from 60-70% Trebbiano grapes, and Sémillon, Pinot Bianco, Pinot Grigio, Vermentino, Sauvignon and Roussanne grapes.

Montecarlo, Fattoria di (I.)   1890

An estate in Montecarlo, Tuscany region; produces Montecarlo Bianco wine.

Montecompatri Colonna DOC (I.)

A white wine from Montecompatri and Colonna, making up one of 6 DOC designations of the Castelli Romani district, south of Rome, in the Latium region; made from Malvasia, Trebbiano and other grapes.

Montée de Tonnerre (F.)

A *Premier Cru* vineyard in Fyé, Chablis district, Burgundy; it also usually includes the Pied d'Aloup and Châpelot vineyards.

Montefalco DOC (I.)

1. A village and district in the central Umbria region, which produces:

2. A red wine made from Sangiovese, Sagrantino and Trebbiano grapes, and another red wine called Sagrantino di Montefalco, made from the Sagrantino grape, made in several styles.

Monteforcone (I.)

A village and the red and white wine it produces northwest of Perugia, in the Umbria region.

Montegiove (I.)

A red wine from the Orvieto district, in the Umbria region.

Montelena, Chateau (U.S.)   1882, 1968
                                                                        1st wine 1972

An historic and famous winery in Calistoga, Napa Valley, California; produces Cabernet, Zinfandel, Chardonnay and Johannisberg Riesling wines from Napa, Sonoma and Santa Barbara Counties. The second wine is Silverado Cellars. 30,000 cases. 100 acres in Napa Valley.

Montelle Vineyards (U.S.)   1973

A winery near Augusta, east central Missouri; grows hybrid grapes. 6 acres.

Montello e Colli Asolani DOC (I.)

A district north of Treviso, in the Veneto region; produces varietal wines from Cabernet and Merlot grapes.

Montenegro (Y.)

A state in southwestern Yugoslavia; produces a well-known varietal red wine made from the Vranac grape.

Montepulciano (I.)

1. An important village in the Tuscany region; produces Vino Nobile di Montepulciano and other red and white wines.

2. A red grape grown in Tuscany, Umbria, the Marches, Latium, Abruzzi, and other regions in the south.

Montepulciano d'Abruzzo DOC (I.)
                                                        DOC since 1967

1. A district north and south of Pescara, in the eastern Abruzzi region, which produces:

2. Red, white and rosé wines, the red (*rosso*) and rosé (*cerasuolo*) made from Montepulciano and 15% Sangiovese grapes. A white wine made here is called Trebbiano d'Abruzzo.

Monterey County (U.S.)

A coastal county, south of San Francisco, in California; the large vineyards of Masson, Almadén, Mirassou and Wente are located here.

Monterey Peninsula Winery (U.S.)   1974

A winery in Monterey City, Monterey County, California; produces Zinfandel, Cabernet and Chardonnay wines from purchased grapes. 15,000 cases.

Monterey Vineyard (U.S.)   1973

A large winery in Gonzales, Monterey County, California; produces special late-harvest Johannisberg Riesling, Sémillon, Sauvignon Blanc and Zinfandel wines. Also produces wine for other brand names (Taylor California Cellars). 140,000 cases, no vineyards.

Montericco (I.)

A red wine from the Valpolicella district, in the Veneto region; made from Valpolicella wine with the lees of *recioto* wine added for greater strength.

Monterosso Val d'Arda DOC (I.)

A sweet or dry white wine from the Arda River valley, southeast of Piacenza, in the eastern Emilia-Romagna region; made from Malvasia, Moscato, Trebbiano and Ortrugo grapes.

Monterrey (Sp.)

A district in the Galicia region of northwestern Spain; produces red wines from Alicante Negro, Garnacha, Tintorera (Mencía), Tinta Fina, Tinta de Toro and Monstelo grapes and white wines from Godello, Dona Branca and Xerez grapes.

Montescudaio DOC (I.)   1977

Red, white and *Vin Santo* wines from an area around Pisa, in the Tuscany region. The red wines are made from 65-85% Sangiovese, with other grapes, including Trebbiano and Malvasia, and the white wines are made from 70-83% Trebbiano, with some Malvasia and Vermentino grapes.

Monteviña (U.S.)   1973

A winery in Plymouth, Shenandoah Valley, Amador County, California; produces Zinfandel, Cabernet, Nebbiolo, Sauvignon and other wines. 150,000 cases. 160 acres.

Montézargues, Prieuré de (F.)

An estate in Tavel, Rhône region; produces rosé wines made from Grenache, Cinsault, Carignan and Picpoul grapes. 75 acres.

Monthélie AOC *also* **Monthélie-Côte de Beaune AOC (F.)**

A commune in the Côte de Beaune district, just behind Meursault, in Burgundy; produces mostly red and some white wines. The presence of vines have been recorded as early as the 9th century. 10 *Premier Cru* vineyards.

Monthélie-Douhairet, Domaine (F.)

An estate in Monthélie, Côte de Beaune district, Burgundy. 22 acres, including 2.5 acres of Volnay Champans, 1.6 acres of Volnay Clos des Chênes, 1.2 acres of Volnay Fremiet, .5 acre of Pommard Premier Cru, 1.6 acres of Meursault Les Santenots and some Monthélie.

Monthil, Château (F.)

An estate in Bégadan, Médoc district, Bordeaux; classified in 1978 as a *Cru Bourgeois*. 8,000 cases. 40 acres.

**Monticello Cellars (U.S.) 1980, vines 1970
                                    1st wine 1982**

A winery in Yountville, Napa Valley, California; produces Cabernet, Chardonnay, Gewürztraminer and Sauvignon Blanc wines. 200 acres.

Montilla-Moriles DO (Sp.)

1. A DO district north of Málaga, which includes the villages of Montilla and Moriles as well as several other villages in the Province of Córdoba, southwestern Spain. 40,000 acres.

2. Sherry-like wines from the Montilla-Moriles district; made from Pedro Ximénez and some Lairén, Baladí and Moscatel grapes.

Montille, Mme. François de (F.)

An estate in Volnay, Côte de Beaune district, Burgundy. 15 acres, including 2.5 acres of Pommard Les Rugiens, .6 acre of Les Épenots, 2.5 acres of Les Pézerolles, 2 acres of Volnay Taille-Pieds, 1.7 acres of Champans, 2.5 acres of Premier Cru and 2 acres of Les Mitans.

Montils (F.)

A white grape used to make Pineau des Charentes wine; also grown in Australia.

Montlouis AOC (F.)

1. A commune near Vouvray, in the Touraine region of the Loire Valley, which produces:

2. Dry, sweet and sparkling wines from Montlouis, Lussault and St.-Martin-le-Beau, made from Chenin Blanc grapes; similar to Vouvray.

Montmains (F.)

A *Premier Cru* vineyard in Chablis, Chablis district, Burgundy; it usually also includes the Les Forêts and Butteaux vineyards.

Montonech (Sp.)

A white grape grown in the Catalonia region; also called Parellada.

Montonico (I.)

A red grape grown in the Campania region; also grown in California.

Montoro, Castello di (I.)

An estate in Montoro di Narni, Umbria region; produces red, rosé and white wines.

Montouvert (I.)

An Ice-wine, a sweet, white wine from Villeneuve, in the Valle D'Aosta region, made from the Moscato grape.

Montpellier WO (S. Af.)   1970

An estate in the Tulbagh district; produces white wines, especially Riesling and Gewürztraminer. 30,000 cases. 350 acres.

Montpeyroux VDQS (F.)

1. A district west of Montpellier, in the Languedoc region, southern France, which produces:

2. Red and rosé wines made from Carignan, Grenache, Cinsault, Syrah and Mourvèdre grapes.

Montrachet AOC (F.)

A famous *Grand Cru* vineyard and the famous white wine from the communes of Puligny-Montrachet and Chassagne-Montrachet; there are 13 owners. 2,500 cases. 19 acres (10 in Puligny and 9 in Chassagne).

Montravel AOC (F.)

1. A district west of Bergerac, along the Dordogne River, in the Southwest region, which produces:

2. Sweet and dry white wine made from Sémillon, Sauvignon, Muscadelle, Chenin Blanc and Ugni Blanc grapes.

Montre-Cul (F.)

A vineyard in the Dijon district, Burgundy (Bourgogne AOC); growers are Derey Frères and Quillardet.

Montrevenots, Les (F.)

A *Premier Cru* vineyard (in part) in Beaune, Côte de Beaune district, Burgundy. 20 acres.

Montrose (Aus.)   1974

A winery in Mudgee, New South Wales; produces Cabernet, Shiraz, Sangiovese, Nebbiolo, Barbera, Chardonnay, Rhine Riesling and Gewürztraminer wines. 30,000 cases. 110 acres.

Montrose, Château (F.)

An estate in St.-Estèphe, Haut-Médoc district, Bordeaux; classified in 1855 as a *Deuxième Cru*. 20,000 cases. 140 acres.

Monts-Luisants (F.)

A *Premier Cru* vineyard in Morey-St.-Denis, Côte de Nuits district, Burgundy; produces white wine only. 7.5 acres.

Monts de Milieu (F.)

A *Premier Cru* vineyard in the communes of Fyé and Fleys, Chablis district, Burgundy.

Monts du Tessalah (Alg.)

A district south of Oran; produces red, white and rosé wines.

Monzingen (G.)

A village in the Nahe region, Bereich Schloss Böckelheim, Grosslage Paradiesgarten. The vineyards are: Frühlingsplätzchen, Halenberg and Rosenberg.

Moore's Diamond (U.S.)

An American white hybrid grape developed c. 1860 by Jacob Moore, in the Finger Lakes region, N.Y.; also called Diamond.

Moorilla Estate (Aus.)   1970

A winery in Berridale, Hobart, in Tasmania; produces Cabernet, Pinot Noir and Rhine Riesling wines. 3,000 cases. 20 acres.

Mór (H.)

A village and district in the hills west of Budapest, Transdanubia region, western Hungary; produces sweet and dry white wine made from the Ezerjó grape. Officially rated white wine of Excellent Quality. 2,700 acres.

Moraster (Sp.)

In the Rioja region, another name for the Monastrel grape.

Moravia (Cz.)

A province in central Czechoslovakia; includes the districts of Znojmo-Mikulov, Hustopeče-Hodonín and Bzenec-Strážnice. 30,000 acres.

Mörbisch (A.)

An important village south of Rust, in the Burgenland region of eastern Austria.

Moreau, Jean (F.)

An estate in Santenay, Cote de Beaune, Burgundy. 11 acres, including 2.5 acres of Santenay Clos des Mouches.

Moreau et Fils, J. (F.)   1814

A grower and shipper in Chablis, Burgundy; owns Chablis Les Clos – 20 acres, Valmur – 5 acres, Vaudésir – 2.5 acres, Vaillons – 22 acres and Chablis – 125 acres; sole owner of Clos des Hospices, which is part of Les Clos, in Chablis – 6 acres.

Moreau et Fils, Marcel (F.)

An estate in Chassagne-Montrachet, Côte de Beaune district, Burgundy. 16 acres, including .8 acre of Chassagne-Montrachet Grandes Ruchottes (white), 1.2 acres of Les Chenevottes (white) and Morgeot La Cardeuse Monopole (red) - 2 acres.

Morein (F.)

A *Premier Cru* vineyard in Fleys, Chablis district, Burgundy; usually included as part of Les Fourneaux vineyard.

Morellino di Scansano DOC (I.)   1978

A red wine from Scansano, south of Grosseto, in the southern Tuscany region; made from at least 85% Sangiovese grapes.

Morellone (I.)

A red grape grown in the southern Tuscany region.

Moresco, Enrico Giovannini (I.)

An estate in Treiso, Piedmont region; produces Barbaresco wine.

Moreto (P.)

A red grape grown in Bairrada, Algarve and other regions.

Morey, Éts André (F.)   1868

An estate in Beaune, Burgundy; owns 31 acres in Villié-Morgon (Beaujolais).

Morey, Berthe (F.)

An estate in Meursault, Côte de Beaune district, Burgundy. 25 acres, including 1.2 acres of Meursault Les Perrières, .6 acre of Meursault Les Charmes, .6 acre of Corton-Renardes, 2.5 acres of Pommard, 15 acres of Meursault and .6 acre of Volnay Les Santenots Clos de Grands Charrons Monopole.

Morey et Fils, Albert (F.)

An estate in Chassagne-Montrachet, Côte de Beaune district, Burgundy. 40 acres, including .4 acre of Bâtard-Montrachet, 2 acres of Chassagne-Montrachet En Cailleret, 2.5 acres of Les Embrazées, 1.2 acres of Morgeot (red and white), 3.3 acres of Beaune Les Grèves and 2 acres of Santenay Clos Rousseau.

Morey et Fils, Domaine Marc (F.)

An estate in Chassagne-Montrachet, Côte de Beaune district, Burgundy. 20 acres, including .4 acre of Bâtard-Montrachet, 1.7 acres of Chassagne-Montrachet En Cailleret (red), 5 acres of Les Chenevottes, .6 acre of Morgeot (red), 2 acres of Virondot, 1.2 acres of Puligny-Montrachet Les Pucelles and 1.2 acres of Beaune.

Morey-Saint-Denis AOC (F.)

A commune in the Côte de Nuits district of Burgundy, at one time sold at Gevrey-Chambertin or Chambolle-Musigny. It includes the following *Grand Cru* vineyards (all red): Bonnes-Mares – 4.5 acres (the other 34 acres are in Chambolle-Musigny), Clos Saint Denis – 16 acres, Clos De Tart - 18 acres, Clos de la Roche - 40 acres and Clos des Lambrays - 15 acres. Also 25 *Premier Cru* vineyards (red and white). 325 acres.

Morgan Winery (U.S.)   1982

A winery in Salinas, Monterey County, California; produces Chardonnay wine. 2,000 cases.

Morgeot (F.)

A *Premier Cru* vineyard (in part) in Chassagne-Montrachet, Côte de Beaune district, Burgundy; produces red and white wines. 10 acres.

Morgex (I.)

A village in the Vall d'Aosta region; produces Blanc de Morgex wine from the Blanc de Valdigne grape.

Morgon (F.)

A *Cru* Beaujolais in Villié-Morgon, Beaujolais district, Burgundy; the fullest in style, more like a Cote d'Or wine than any *Cru* Beaujolais. 2,000 acres.

Móri Ezerjó (H.)

A white wine, usually dry, but sometimes sweet, from Mór, west of Budapest, in the Transdanubia region; made from the Ezerjó grape.

Mori Vecio (I.)

A red wine from Mori, south of Trento, in the Trentino-Alto Adige region; made from Cabernet and Merlot grapes.

Morin, Château (F.)

An estate in St.-Estèphe, Haut-Médoc district, Bordeaux; classified in 1978 as a *Cru Grand Bourgeois*. 4,500 cases. 25 acres.

Morin Père et Fils (F.)   1822

An estate in Nuits-St.-Georges, Côte de Nuits district, Burgundy. 11 acres, including 5.5 acres of Nuits-St.-Georges Les Cailles, 2.5 acres of Les Pruliers and .7 acre of Les Vaucrains.

Morio-Muskat (G.)

A white grape - a cross of Silvaner and Weissburgunder; developed at the Federal Research Institute, Geilweilerhof, Germany, by Dr. Morio, in 1916. Grown in the Rheinpfalz region; gives a high yield and a strong muscat bouquet.

Morisca (Sp.)

A red grape grown in southwestern Spain.

Moro (I.)

An estate in Calerno di Sant'Illario d'Enza, Emilia-Romagna region; produces Ama-rone del Partitore, Lambrusco, Picòl Ross and Sauvignon wines.

Morocco

A country in North Africa, independent since 1956. All French-owned vineyards were nationalized in 1973; grapes planted include Carignan, Cinsault, Grenache, Alicante-Bouschet, Syrah, Mourvèdre, Cabernet, Clairette, Ugni Blanc, Pedro Ximénez, Muscat and other local varieties.

Morone (I.)

A grape grown in western Tuscany.

Moroni, Veuve Henri (F.)

An estate in Puligny-Montrachet, Côte de Beaune, Burgundy; owns .8 acre of Bâtard-Montrachet, .8 acre of Puligny-Montrachet Les Combettes, .5 acre of Les Pucelles and Puligny (red).

Morot, Albert (F.)   1820

An estate in Beaune, Côte de Beaune district, Burgundy. 17 acres, including 3.2 acres of Beaune Les Bressandes, 2.3 acres of Les Marconnets, 3.2 acres of Les Cent Vignes, 2.5 acres of Les Teurons, 2 acres of Les Toussaints and some Savigny Clos la Bataillère.

Morrastel (Alg.)

A red grape.

Morris Wines (Aus.)   1859

A winery in Rutherglen, northeastern Victoria; famous for sweet Muscat wines, Sémillon, Chardonnay, sherry- and port-style wines, Cabernet, Durif and Shiraz wines. 20,000 cases. 200 acres.

Morris Wineries, J.W. (U.S.)   1975

A winery in Emeryville, south of Berkeley, northern Alameda County, California; formerly J.W. Morris Port Works; produces Ports, Chardonnay, Sauvignon Blanc, Cabernet, Zinfandel, Pinot Noir and Angelica wines from grapes purchased in Sonoma, Monterey and Amador Counties. 30,000 cases.

Mortágua (P.)

A red grape, also called Camarete.

Mosbach (F.)

An estate and merchant in Marlenheim, Bas-Rhin district, Alsace region. 45 acres.

Mosbacher, Weingut Georg (G.)

An estate in Forst, Rheinpfalz region; owns vineyards in Forst, Deidesheim and Wachenheim. 20 acres.

Moscadelletto *also* Moscadello (I.)

1. A white grape grown in the Tuscany region; a relative of the Muscat grape.

2. A sweet, white, still or sparkling wine made from the Moscadelletto (Moscadello) grape.

Moscatel (Sp.)

A white grape, the same as the Muscat.

Moscatel Roxo (P.)

1. A red grape grown in Setúbal.

2. A sweet wine from Setúbal, made from the Moscatel Roxo grape.

Moscatel de Setúbal (P.)

1. A white grape used to make Moscatel de Setúbal wine. The same as Muscat d'Alexandria, grown in France and Italy, and Moscatel de Málaga, grown in Spain. Large clusters, large berries, thin skins, green to yellow-amber.

2. A sweet, fortified dessert wine from the Setúbal Peninsula, near Lisbon, made from Moscatel de Setúbal and (red) Moscatel Roxo grapes.

Moscatello (I.)

1. A white muscat grape, better known as Moscato di Canelli.

2. A white, semi-sparkling wine from the Liguria region; made from the Muscat grape. 8% alcohol.

Moscato (I.)

The Italian name for the Muscat grape or wine.

Moscato d'Asti DOC (I.)

A sweet, white wine, sometimes sparkling, from Asti, in the central Piedmont region; made from Moscato Bianco or Moscato di Canelli grapes.

Moscato di Cagliari DOC (I.)

A sweet, white wine from northeast of Cagliari, in southwestern Sardinia; made from the Moscato grape. 15-18% alcohol.

Moscato di Chambave (I.)

A dry, white wine from Chambave, in the Valle d'Aosta region, made from the Moscato grape.

Moscato Giallo (I.)

1. A white grape grown in the Trentino-Alto Adige region.

2. A sweet, white wine from the Trentino-Alto Adige region made from the Moscato Giallo grape.

Moscato Nobile del Cònero (I.)

A dry, white wine made near Mt. Cònero, south of Ancona, in the eastern Marches region, made from Moscato grapes.

Moscato di Noto DOC (I.)

A sweet, white wine from Noto, south of Siracusa, in southeastern Sicily, also made *spumante;* made from the Moscato Bianco grape. A *liquoroso* version is made with as high as 22% alcohol.

Moscato di Pantelleria DOC (I.)

A sweet, white wine from the Island of Pantelleria, a district of Sicily, off the coast of Tunisia; made from the Zibibbo grape; made also in *Passito* styles. 12-24% alcohol.

Moscato di Sardegna DOC (I.)   1980

A sweet, white wine (also sparkling) from anywhere in Sardinia with DOC approval; made from the Moscato grape.

Moscato di Siracusa DOC (I.)

A sweet, white wine from Siracusa, in southeastern Sicily; made from the Moscato Bianco grape; seldom made anymore. 17% alcohol.

Moscato di Sorso-Sennori DOC (I.)

A sweet, white wine from Sorso and Sennori, near Sassari, in northwestern Sardinia; made from the Moscato grape. 15-18% alcohol.

Moscato di Strevi (I.)

A sweet, sparkling wine from Strevi, near Acqui, in the southeastern Piedmont region, made from Moscato grapes.

Moscato di Terracina (I.)

A white grape grown in the Basilicata region of southern Italy.

Moscato di Trani DOC (I.)

A sweet, white wine from Trani, in the northern Apulia region; made from the Moscato Reale grape in two styles: *dolce naturale* - 15% alcohol and *liquoroso* - 18% alcohol.

Moschofilero (Gr.)

A white grape grown in Pelloponnese.

Mosel-Saar-Ruwer (G.)

One of 11 regions in West Germany, on the Mosel River and its 2 tributaries, the Saar and the Ruwer. The *Bereiche* are Bereich Obermosel (Upper Mosel), Bereich Bernkastel (formerly Middle Mosel), Bereich Zell (Lower Mosel) and Bereich Saar-Ruwer. 30,000 acres.

Moselblümchen (G.)

German for "little Mosel flower," a common table wine *(Tafelwein)* from the Mosel-Saar-Ruwer region, of a lower quality than Liebfraumilch.

Moser, Lenz (A.)   1929

A famous wine producer from the village of Rohrendorf, near Krems, in the Lower Austria region. 450 acres, mostly in Burgenland, but also in Retz.

Moss Wood (Aus.)   1969

A small estate in the Margaret River district, Western Australia; produces Cabernet, Pinot Noir, Sémillon and Chardonnay wines. 25 acres.

Mostar (Y.)

A city in southwestern Bosnia-Herzegovina; produces white Žilavka wine.

mosto (I., P., Sp.)

Must; unfermented grape juice.

mosto amuado (P.)

A concentrated must used to sweeten wine and to raise the alcohol level.

mosto cotto (I.)

Boiled must or grape juice, used as sweetening for dessert wines such as Marsala.

Möt Ziflon (I.)

A dry, red wine from Suno, in the northern Piedmont region, made from Nebbiolo, Bonarda and Freisa grapes.

Mother Lode (U.S.)

A region in the foothills of the Sierra Mountains, central California, including Amador, Calaveras, El Dorado and Placer Counties.

Moucheron, Comte de (F.)

An estate (known as Château de Meursault) in Meursault, Côte de Beaune district, Burgundy. 25 acres, including 9 acres of Volnay Clos des Chênes, 2.5 acres of Meursault Les Perrières and 12 acres of Les Charmes; controlled by Patriarche Père et Fils, in Beaune.

Mouches, Les Clos des (F.)

A *Premier Cru* vineyard in Beaune, Côte de Beaune district, Burgundy. 62 acres.

Moueix, Jean-Pierre (F.)

A merchant in Libourne, Bordeaux; part-owner of Château Pétrus, owner of Trotanoy, La Fleur-Pétrus and Lagrange, all in Pomerol, and Magdeleine, in St.-Émilion.

mouillage (F.)

The addition of water to wine.

Moulesne (F.)

A *Premier Cru* vineyard in Rully, Côte Chalonnaise district, Burgundy.

Moulin, Le (F.)

An estate in Cabestany, Roussillon region; produces Banyuls, Rivesaltes, Muscat and Côtes du Roussillon wines. 120 acres.

Moulin du Cadet, Château (F.)

An estate in St.-Émilion, Bordeaux; classified in 1955 as a *Grand Cru Classé*. 3,000 cases. 12 acres.

Moulin des Carruades (F.)

1. Formerly a 3rd wine of Château Lafite, made only in good years such as 1955, 1957, 1959, 1961 and 1964; made from young vines and 2nd pressings of Lafite.

2. The second wine of Château Lafite since 1974, replacing Les Carruades de Château Lafite.

Moulin des Costes (F.)

An estate in Bandol, Provence region.

Moulin aux Moines, Domaine de (F.)

An estate in St.-Romain, Côte de Beaune district, Burgundy; 16 acres controlled by Roland Thévenin. See **Thévenin.**

Moulin-Riche, Château (F.)

An estate in St.-Julien, Haut-Médoc district, Bordeaux; classified in 1932 as a *Cru Bourgeois Exceptionnel;* it is the second wine of Château Léoville-Poyferré. 1,600 cases.

Moulin de la Roque (F.)

A co-op winery in Bandol, Provence region.

Moulin Rouge, Château du (F.)

An estate in Cussac, Haut-Médoc district, Bordeaux; classified in 1978 as a *Cru Bourgeois.* 3,000 cases. 20 acres.

Moulin Touchais (F.)

A famous estate and merchant in Doué La Fontaine, Anjou region, Loire Valley; produces Anjou and Coteaux du Layon wines from the Chenin Blanc grape, and other red and white Anjou wines. 400 acres.

Moulin-à-Vent AOC (F.)

French for "windmill," one of the 9 *Crus* Beaujolais, in Romanèche-Thorins, in the Beaujolais district, Burgundy; it also includes part of Chénas. One of the fullest-bodied of the *Crus*, the wine can be aged.

Moulin-à-Vent, Château (F.)

An estate in Moulis, Haut-Médoc district, Bordeaux; classified in 1978 as a *Cru Grand Bourgeois.* 9,000 cases. 50 acres.

Moulin-à-Vent, Château du (F.)

An estate in Romanèche-Thorins, Beaujolais district, Burgundy; produces Moulin-à-Vent wine.

Moulin-à-Vent des Hospices (F.)

A red wine from the Hospices de Romanèche-Thorins, Beaujolais district, Burgundy. 20 acres of Moulin-à-Vent.

Mouline, La (F.)

A vineyard in the Côte Blonde section of the Côte-Rôtie district, northern Rhône region.

Moulinet, Château (F.)

An estate in Pomerol, Bordeaux region. 4,500 cases. 40 acres.

Moulis AOC (F.)

A commune northwest of Margaux, in the Haut-Médoc district, Bordeaux.

Mount Avoca (Aus.)   1970

A winery in Avoca, Victoria; produces Cabernet, Shiraz, Sémillon, Trebbiano, Chardonnay and Sauvignon Blanc wines. 50 acres.

Mount Barker (Aus.)

A town and district south of Perth, in the southwestern corner of Western Australia.

Mount Eden Vineyards (U.S.)   1972

A winery in Saratoga, Santa Clara County, California, originally part of the Martin Ray estate; produces Cabernet, with Merlot and Cabernet Franc, Chardonnay and Pinot Noir wines. The second label, using purchased grapes, is MEV. 30 acres. 3,000 cases.

Mount Elise Vineyard (U.S.)   1975

A winery in Bingen, southern Washington, formerly Bingen Wine Cellars; produces Chenin Blanc, Grenache, Pinot Noir and Gewürztraminer wines. 5,000 cases. 35 acres.

Mount Mary (Aus.)   1971

A winery in Lilydale, Yarra Valley district, Victoria; produces a Cabernet wine blended with Cabernet Franc; also Merlot, Pinot Noir and Chardonnay wines. 15 acres.

Mount Palomar Winery (U.S.)   1975

A winery in Temecula, Riverside County, southern California; produces Cabernet, Zinfandel, Petite Sirah, Sauvignon Blanc, Chenin Blanc and Johannisberg Riesling wines and sherry-style wines. 12,000 cases. 150 acres.

Mount Pleasant (Aus.)

A well-known vineyard owned by the McWilliams winery, in the Lower Hunter Valley region, New South Wales; produces Shiraz wine bottled under several different, special names.

Mount Pleasant Vineyard (U.S.) 1881, 1968

An old, restored winery in August, west of St. Louis, Missouri; grows hybrid and *labrusca* grapes. 25 acres.

Mount Veeder Winery (U.S.)   1973
vines 1965

A winery on Mt. Veeder, northwest of Napa City, Napa Valley, California; produces Cabernet, Zinfandel and Chenin Blanc wines. 4,000 cases. 20 acres.

Mountain House Winery (U.S.)   1980

A winery in Cloverdale, Mendocino County, California; produces Cabernet, Zinfandel and Chardonnay wines from purchased grapes from several regions. 3,000 cases. 5 acres.

Mountain View Winery (U.S.)   1980

A small winery in Mountain View, Santa Clara County, California; produces Chardonnay and Zinfandel wines from purchased grapes.

Mountain Winery (U.S.)

An historic winery of Paul Masson in the Santa Cruz Mountains, near Saratoga, Santa Clara Valley, California; it has vineyards 2,000 ft. high; the winery is not used except for aging wines and as a concert hall.

Mouraton (Sp.)

A red grape grown in the Galicia region of northwestern Spain.

Mourisco (P.)

An important red grape used to make Port. One of 16 First Quality grapes.

Mourvaison (F.)

A red grape grown in Bandol, in the Provence region.

Mourvèdre (F.)

A red grape grown in the Provence, Languedoc and southern Rhône regions; one of 13 used to make Châteauneuf-du-Pape wine; also grown in Algeria.

mousse (F.)

Foam, froth; effervescence; bubbles.

Mousse, Le Clos de la (F.)

A *Premier Cru* vineyard in Beaune, Côte de Beaune district, Burgundy. 8 acres.

Mousset, Société Louis (F.)

A large estate in Châteauneuf-du-Pape, southern Rhône region. 600 acres, including Château des Fines Roches and several other estates.

mousseux (F.)

Foaming; sparkling. The AOC *mousseux* wines are: Anjou Mousseux, Arbois Mousseux, Blanquette de Limoux, Bordeaux Mousseux, Bourgogne Mousseux (since 1980 called Crémant de Bourgogne), Clairette de Die Mousseux, Côtes du Jura Mousseux Crémant de Bourgogne (since 1980), Gaillac Mousseux, Montlouis Mousseux, St.-Péray Mousseux, Saumur Mousseux, Seyssel Mousseux, Touraine Mousseux, Vouvray Mousseux, Mousseux de Savoie, Mousseux de Savoie Ayze, and the VDQS Mousseux de Bugey.

Moussière, Domaine la (F.)

An estate in Sancerre, Upper Loire region. 80 acres.

moût (F.)

Must; the grape juice which is ready for fermentation.

Mouton d'Armailhacq, Château (F.)

The former name of Château Mouton-Baronne-Phillipe, in Pauillac, Bordeaux.

Mouton-Baronne-Phillippe, Château (F.)

An estate in Pauillac, Haut-Médoc district, Bordeaux; classified in 1855 as a *Cinquième Cru;* was part of Château Mouton until the 18th century; was called Mouton d'Armailhacq until 1956; and until 1975 was called Mouton-Baron-Phillippe. 16,000 cases. 125 acres.

Mouton-Rothschild, Château (F.)

A famous estate in Pauillac, Haut-Médoc district, Bordeaux; classified in 1855 as a *Deuxième Cru* and in 1973 as a *Premier Cru.* It was part of Château Lafite until 1730. The word "mouton" means "mound," from the old French, "mothon"; it also means "sheep"; called Brane-Mouton in the early 19th century. The wine is made

from 75-87% Cabernet grapes with Cabernet Franc and Merlot grapes. 22,000 cases. 175 acres.

Moutonne, La (F.)

In the 18th century it was a part of the Vaudésir vineyard in Chablis, Chablis district, Burgundy; later sold to the Long-Dépaqui family, who used Moutonne as a proprietary name; since 1950 used for a 5-acre vineyard, including part of Les Preuses as well as a section of the Vaudésir vineyard, and therefore, technically, a *Grand Cru* Chablis.

Moutonne, Domaine de la (F.)

An estate and owner of the Moutonne vineyard in the Chablis district, Burgundy; also known as Société Civile de la Moutonne. 5 acres. Wines distributed by Bichot and Drouhin.

Moyer, E. and E. (F.)   1825

An estate in Montlouis-sur-Loire, Vouvray district, Touraine region, Loire Valley. 35 acres.

Mtsvane (U.S.S.R.)

A local white grape grown in Georgia S.S.R.

Mudgee (Aus.)

A town and district, northwest of Sidney and Hunter Valley, in New South Wales.

Muerza, Bodegas (Sp.)   1882

A winery in San Adrian, Rioja region; produces several wines, including Rioja Vega, made from purchased grapes.

Muga S.A., Bodegas (Sp.)   1926

A winery in Haro, Rioja Alta region; produces several wines made from their own and purchased grapes. 35,000 cases. 70 acres.

Mugneret, René (F.)

An estate in Vosne-Romanée, Côte de Nuits district, Burgundy. 13.5 acres, including 1.6 acres of Échézeaux, .8 acre of

osne-Romanée Les Suchots and 1.2 acres
Nuits-St.-Georges Aux Boudots.

ugneret-Gibourg, A. (F.)

n estate in Vosne-Romanée, Côte de
uits district, Burgundy. 16 acres, includ-
g .8 acre of Clos de Vougeot, 3.4 acres of
chézeaux, 2.7 acres of Nuits-St.-Georges
nd some Vosne-Romanée.

ugneret-Gouachon, Bernard (F.)

n estate in Prémeaux, Côte de Nuits dis-
rict, Burgundy. 31 acres, including 5 acres
f Échézeaux, 3 acres of Vosne-Romanée,
ome Nuits-St.-Georges and 8.5 acres of
Juits-St.-Georges Aux Perdrix Monopole.

Muhlforst (F.)

A vineyard in Hunawihr, Haut-Rhin dis-
rict, Alsace region.

nuid (F.)

A pipe or cask, variable in size, from 260-
85 liters.

Mukuzani (U.S.S.R.)

A red wine from Georgia S.S.R.

mulled wine

A red wine which has been spiced, sweetened, and served hot.

Muller S.A., de (Sp.)   **1851**

A winery in Tarragona, Catalonia region;
produces several wines, including fortified
dessert wines and altar wines.

Müller-Scharzhof, Weingut Egon (G.)

An estate in Wiltingen, Saar district, Mosel-Saar-Ruwer region; owns 27 acres of
the Scharzhofberg vineyard.

Müller-Thurgau (G.)

An important white grape - a cross of Ries-
ling and Sylvaner, grown chiefly in Ger-
many; developed in 1882 by Hermann
Müller, at the State Teaching and Research
Institute in Geisenheim, it is the oldest
German crossbreed; named after Herr
Müller (from Thurgau, Switzerland); used
to made sweet, white wine; it is high in

yield, low in acid, early ripening, and
hardy. The grapes are oval, yellow-green
with a slight Muscat aroma; also grown in
Austria, California and Washington.

Müllerrebe (G.)

In Württemberg, another name for the red
Pinot Meunier, or Schwarzriesling grape, a
mutation of the Pinot Noir grape.

Multaner (G.)

A white grape - a cross of Riesling and Sylvaner; developed at the State Teaching and
Research Institute, Geisenheim, Germany.

Mumm, G.H. (F.)   **1827**

A Champagne firm in Reims; produces
Cordon Rouge Brut and Vintage Brut, etc.,
also René Lalou and Crémant de Cramant.
9 million bottles. 550 acres.

Mumm'sches Weingut, G.H. von (G.)

An estate in Johannisberg, Rheingau region; owns vineyards in Johannisberg, Rüdesheim, Assmannshausen, Geisenheim
and Winkel. 170 acres.

Münch (U.S.)

A red hybrid grape - a cross of Herbemont
and a wild grape from Missouri; developed
by Thomas Volney Munson in Texas, c.
1885.

Munson (U.S.)

The name for several red hybrid grapes
from Texas; developed by Thomas Volney
Munson.

**Munson, Thomas Volney (1843-1913)
(U.S.)**

An American hybridizer; developed several hybrid grapes in Denison, Texas, including the Delicatessen grape.

Münster-Sarmsheim (G.)

A village in the Nahe region, Bereich
Kreuznach, Grosslage Schlosskapelle. The
vineyards are Dautenpflanzer, Kapellenberg, Königsschloss, Liebehöll, Pitters-
berg, Rheinberg, Römerberg, Steinkopf
and Trollberg.

Münzlay (G.)

A *Grosslage*, one of 10 in Bereich Bernkastel (Mittel Mosel), in the Mosel-Saar-Ruwer region.

Murailles, Les (F.)

A vineyard in Riquewihr, Haut-Rhin district, Alsace region, owned by Dopff & Irion; produces Riesling grapes. 25 acres.

Muratie Estate EWO (S. Af.)   1926

An old estate in the Stellenbosch district known for Steen, red varietal, port-style and other wines. 160 acres.

Muré, A. & O. (F.)

An estate in Rouffach, Haut-Rhin district, Alsace. 42 acres, including Clos St. Landelin - 37 acres (Riesling, Gewürztraminer and others).

Murets, Les (F.)

A vineyard section of Hermitage, northern Rhône region; planted with red and white grapes.

Murfatlar (R.)

1. A town in the Dobrudja region of southeastern Romania, which produces:

2. A sweet, white wine made from the Muscat grape.

Murgers, Aux (F.)

A *Premier Cru* vineyard in Nuits-St.-Georges, Côte de Nuits district, Burgundy. 12.5 acres.

Murgers-des-Dents-de-Chien, Les (F.)

A *Premier Cru* vineyard in St.-Aubin, Côte de Beaune district, Burgundy; produces red and white wine. 7.5 acres.

Muri-Gries, Klosterkellerei (I.)

A monastic estate and winery in Bolzano, Trentino-Alto Adige region; produces Alto Adige, Malvasier, Santa Maddalena and Terlano wines.

Muristellu *also* Muristeddu (I.)

A red grape grown in Sardinia.

Murrão (P.)

A white grape grown in the Vinho Verd region.

Murray River *also* Murray Valley (Aus.)

A district on the border of South Austral and Victoria; produces Palomino an Pedro Ximénez grapes for making sherr type wines.

Murrieta, S.A. Marqués de (Sp.)   187

A winery in Ygay, Rioja Alta region; pro duces several wines, including Castill Ygay (red and white); made from their ow and purchased grapes. 280 acres.

Murrumbidgee (Aus.)

A district around Griffith, on the Murrum bidgee River, in New South Wales, als called MIA; also considered part of the Riv erina district; produces primarily fortifie wines.

Musar, Château (Leb.)   c. 193

An estate in Ghazir, north of Beirut, wit vineyards in the Bekka Valley; produce red wines made mostly from Caberne grapes, with some Cinsault and Syra grapes.

Muscadel (S. Af.)

A red grape of the Muscat family; used t make red, fortified dessert wines.

Muscadet (F.)

1. A region centered around Nantes, and also called the Nantais, in the wester Loire Valley, northwestern France, which produces:

2. A dry, white wine, sold under the AOC designations of Muscadet, Muscadet des Coteaux de la Loire, and Muscadet de Sèvre-et-Maine, made from:

3. An important white grape; also called Melon de Bourgogne.

muscadine (U.S.)

Any of several grape varieties of *Vitis rotundifolia* and *Vitis Munsoniana*, of the *subgenus Muscadiniae*, that are native to the

U.S., of which the Scuppernong grape is the most well-known.

Muscardin (F.)

A red grape used in making Châteauneuf-du-Pape wine.

Muscat

A white or red grape of the *Vitis vinifera* species, with many varieties grown all over the world, used mostly to make sweet, dessert wines except in Alsace, the western U.S. and Bulgaria, where dry muscat wines are also made.

Muscat d'Alexandria

1. A white grape of the muscat family.

2. A sweet, white wine made from the Muscat d'Alexandria grape.

Muscat d'Angelo (U.S.)

A sweet white wine from California, made from the Muscat grape.

Muscat de Beaumes-de-Venise VDN (F.)

See **Beaumes-de-Venise VDN.**

Muscat Blanc

A white muscat grape; also called Muscat Canelli and Muscat de Frontignan.

Muscat Canelli

A white grape of the muscat family; also called Muscat Blanc and Muscat de Frontignan.

Muscat de Frontignan (F., U.S.)

1. A white grape of the muscat family; also called Muscat Blanc and Muscat Canelli.

2. A famous sweet, white wine (VDN) from Frontignan, south of Montpellier, in the Languedoc region of France; made from the above grape.

3. A sweet, white wine made by Beaulieu Vineyards, California; made from the above grape.

Muscat Hamburg

A red grape of the muscat family, grown in California; also called Black Muscat.

Muscat de Lunel VDN (F.)

A sweet, fortified, white wine from Lunel, between Montpellier and Nîmes, in the Languedoc region; made from the Muscat grape.

Muscat de Miréval VDN (F.)

A sweet, fortified, white wine from Miréval, south of Montpellier, in the Languedoc region; made from the Muscat grape.

Muscat Ottonel *also* **Muscat Otonel**

A white grape of the muscat family, possibly a mutation of the Muscatel grape, grown in Austria, Yugoslavia, Romania, Alsace and New York State.

Muscat de Rivesaltes VDN (F.)

A sweet, fortified, white wine from Rivesaltes, northwest of Perpignan, in the Roussillon region; made from Muscat grapes.

Muscat de Saint-Jean-de-Minervois VDN (F.)

A sweet, fortified, white wine from St.-Jean-de-Minervois, west of Béziers, in the Languedoc region; made from Muscat grapes.

Muscat sec de Kelibia (Tun.)

A dry, white muscat wine from Kelibia, on Cap Bon, in northeastern Tunisia.

Muscatel

A sweet, white or red wine, usually fortified, made from muscat grapes.

muselage (F.)

The wire muzzle which serves as a clamp around the corks of Champagne bottles.

Musignano (I.)

Red and white wines from Città della Pieve, in the Umbria region.

Musigny, Les (F.)

A famous *Grand Cru* vineyard in Chambolle-Musigny, Côte de Nuits district, Burgundy; divided into 3 parts: Les Musigny, Les Petits Musigny and La Combe d'Orveau *(Premier Cru)*. Mostly red wine is made, but also some white wine, from 1.5 acres. 26.5 acres.

Muskat Sylvaner (G.)

The German name for the Sauvignon Blanc grape.

must

The term used for grape juice in the beginning stages of fermentation (with or without the crushed grapes).

Mustang

A wild, native grape grown in Texas, of the *Vitis candicans*.

mutage (F.)

The process of stopping a wine's fermentation before all the sugar is converted into alcohol. This is accomplished by the addition of sulfur dioxide or brandy.

muté (F.)

Muted; partially fermented wine, used in making apéritifs and in blending.

Muteau, Cuvee Général (F.)

A red wine from the Hospices de Beaune, Côte de Beaune district, Burgundy. The *cu-*

vée is composed of the following vineyard in Volnay: Le Village - 2 acres, Carelle sou la Chapelle - 1 acre, Cailleret Dessus - acre, Fremiets - .5 acre and Taille-Pieds - acre. 450 cases.

mycoderma(i)

An undesirable microbe which produces film on new wine; also called *fleur*, i French.

mycodermi aceti

A bacteria, called an acetobacter, whic causes the formation of vinegar in wine.

mycodermi vini

A yeast believed to be responsible for th formation of a film on certain wines, e.g *flor* in Sherry.

Myglands, Clos des (F.)

A vineyard in Mercurey, Côte Chalonnais district, Burgundy; owned by Faiveley produces red and white wines.

Myrat, Château *also* Mirat (F.)

An estate in Barsac, Sauternes district Bordeaux; classified in 1855 as a *Deuxièm Cru;* the vines were pulled up after the 197! vintage.

Mzwani (U.S.S.R.)

A white Russian grape of the *Vitis vinifer* species, also grown in New York an Massachusetts.

N

Nachf. (G.)

The abbreviation for *Nachfolger* (successor).

N.V.

Non-vintage; a blend of several vintages.

Nackenheim (G.)

A village in the Rheinhessen region, Bereich Nierstein, Grosslagen Gutes Domtal, Rehbach and Spiegelberg. The vineyards are: Engelsberg, in Grosslage Spiegelberg, Rothenberg, in Grosslage Rehbach, and Schmittskapellchen, in Grosslage Gutes Domtal. 375 acres.

Nacktarsch (G.)

A Grosslage, one of 10, in Bereich Bernkastel (Mittel Mosel), in the Mosel-Saar-Ruwer region. It includes only the six vineyards in Kröv.

Nahe (G.)

A river, a tributary of the Rhine, southwest of Bingen, and one of 11 regions (*Anbaugebiet*) in Germany. The best known villages are Bad Kreuznach, Niederhausen and Schloss Böckelheim. 11,000 acres.

Naigeon, Domaine Pierre (F.)

An estate in Gevrey-Chambertin, Côte de Nuits district, Burgundy. 2.5 acres, including 1.2 acres of Bonnes Mares and 1 acre of Gevrey-Chambertin Clos-Prieur; handled by Naigeon-Chauveau et Fils.

Naigeon-Chauveau et Fils (F.)   1890

A distributor of Domaine des Varoilles wines, in Gevrey-Chambertin, Côte de Nuits district, Burgundy. 25 acres, including 2.5 acres of La Romanée, 2.5 acres of Clos du Meix des Ouches, 1.2 acres of Clos

du Couvent, 1.5 acres of Charmes-Chambertin, 1.5 acres of Gevrey-Chambertin Champonnets and Clos des Varoilles Monopole – 15 acres; also handles wines of Domaine Pierre Naigeon – 2.5 acres, and Domaine P. Misset - 2.5 acres.

Nairac, Château (F.)

An estate in Barsac, Sauternes district, Bordeaux; classified in 1855 as a *Deuxième Cru*; was once a part of Château Broustet-Nérac. 90% Sémillon, 6% Sauvignon, 4% Muscat. 2,000 cases. 40 acres.

Nalys, Domaine de (F.)

An estate in Châteuneuf-du-Pape, southern Rhône region; produces red wine made from 55% Grenache, 18% Syrah, and several other grapes, and white wine made from Grenache Blanc, Clairette and other white varieties. 115 acres.

Nama (Gr.)

An ancient wine from Cyprus, made from semi-dried grapes; later named Commandaria; mentioned by Hesiod.

Naoussa (Gr.)

A red wine from Macedonia, northern Greece; made from the Xynomavro grape.

Napa (U.S.)

A city, county, river, and valley, and the most famous wine-producing region in the United States, located in northern California. Vines were first planted in 1836. It is 5 miles wide, 35 miles long. 26,000 acres.

Napa Creek Winery (U.S.)   1980

A winery in St. Helena, Napa Valley, California; produces Cabernet, Chardonnay, Johannisberg Riesling, Sauvignon Blanc,

Chenin Blanc and Gewürztraminer wines. 15,000 cases.

Napa Gamay (U.S.)

A red grape grown in the Napa region, California; previously believed to be a late-ripening clone of the true Gamay, now thought to be the Valdiguié grape of southern France. Also called Gamay Noir.

Napa Valley Co-operative Winery (U.S.) 1934

A large winery in St. Helena, Napa Valley, California; produces wines for sale in bulk to Gallo.

Napa Vintners (U.S.)　　　1978

A winery in Napa City, Napa Valley, California; produces Cabernet, Zinfandel, Chardonnay and Sauvignon Blanc wines. 10,000 cases.

Napa Wine Cellars (U.S.)　　　1975

A winery in Yountville, Napa Valley, California; produces Cabernet, Zinfandel, Chardonnay and Gewürztraminer wines mostly from purchased grapes. 12,000 cases. 3 acres.

Napareuli (U.S.S.R.)

A white wine from Georgia, S.S.R.

Napoléon, Clos (F.)

Another name for Aux Cheusots, a *Premier Cru* vineyard in Fixin, Côte de Nuits district, Burgundy. 4.5 acres.

Narbantons, Les (F.)

A *Premier Cru* vineyard in Savigny, Côte de Beaune district, Burgundy. 25 acres.

Nardò (I.)

A red wine from Lecce, in the southern Apulia region; made from Negroamaro and Malvasia Nera grapes.

Narince (T.)

A white grape grown in central Turkey.

Nasco (I.)

A local white grape grown in Sardinia.

Nasco di Cagliari DOC (I.)

A dry or sweet, white wine from Cagliari in southwestern Sardinia; made from semi-dried Nasco grapes. 14-18% alcohol.

natur, *also* naturrein (G.)

Natural, with no added sugar.

Naturalis Historia (Lat.)

A book by the ancient Roman author, Pliny the Elder (A.D. 23-79), in·which he discusses wine, and vine-growing and several wine writers.

naturbelassen (A.)

German for "made naturally," a term found on Austrian wine labels.

nature (F.)

1. Natural; having no additives which might affect the taste or strength of wine.

2. In sparkling wines, containing no *dosage*; bone-dry.

3. Still, a term formerly used in the Champagne region; the still wine from the Champagne region is now called Coteaux Champenois.

Naturé (F.)

In the Jura region, the local name for the Savagnin grape.

Naudin, Clos (F.)

An estate in Vouvray, Touraine region. 3,500 cases. 30 acres.

Navarra DO (Sp.)

A region in northern Spain, just north of the Rioja region; produces red and white wines. 100,000 acres.

Navarro Vineyards (U.S.)　　　1975

A winery in Philo, Anderson Valley, Mendocino County, California; produces Cabernet, Pinot Noir, Chardonnay, Gewürztraminer and Johannisberg Ries-ing wines from their own and purchased grapes. 4,000 cases. 35 acres

Navip (Y.)

A large co-op winery in Zenum, near Belgrade, Serbia; produces red and white varietal wines.

Naylor Wine Cellars (U.S.)   1978

A winery in Stewartstown, Pennsylvania; produces wines made from *vinifera* and hybrid grapes 18 acres.

Néac AOC (F.)

A commune just northeast of Pomerol, Bordeaux, and formerly (before 1954), a separate district; now it is mostly absorbed into the Lalande-de-Pomerol AOC.

Nebbiolo (I.)

1. An important red grape, grown throughout northern Italy, but mostly in the Piedmont and Lombardy regions. Subvarieties are the Michet, Lampia and Rosé; the Nebbiolo is also called Spanna, Picoutener (or Picutener) and Pugnet, and produces:

2. A red wine, usually a declassified Barolo or Barbaresco, from the Piedmont region.

Nebbiolo d'Alba DOC (I.)

A red wine, sometimes sweet, and also sometimes sparkling, made around Alba, in the southern Piedmont region; made from the Nebbiolo grape.

Nebbiolo di Gubbio (I.)

A red wine from Gubbio, in the northern Umbria region; made from the Dolcetto grape (*not* from the Nebbiolo grape).

Nebbiolo del Piemonte (I.)

A red wine from any of several DOC districts in the Piedmont region made from Nebbiolo grapes not up to DOC standards.

Nebraska (U.S.)

A state in the middle western United States; produces very little wine.

nebuchadnezzar (F.)

A large bottle used for Champagne equal to 20 fifths, or 16 liters.

nectar

A legendary drink of the ancient Greek gods; the term is often used to describe a fine wine when it is extraordinarily good.

Nederburg EWO (S. Af.)   1936

A well-known estate in the Paarl district; now part of the Stellenbosch Farmers Wineries; produces Riesling, Cabernet, Steen and Edelkeur wines. 1,800 acres.

Neethlingshof Estate (S.Af.)

A recently renovated estate in the Stellenbosch district; produces Cabernet, Pinotage, Riesling, Gewürztraminer and other wines. 5,000 cases. 700 acres.

négociant (F.)

A wine merchant or firm which buys, sells or stores wine, and who may may also own vineyards or parts of vineyards.

Negra Mole (P.)

A red grape once used to make Madeira wine (along with Moscatel and Terrantez grapes); it is now grown in the Algarve region for red and rosé wines.

Negralejo (Sp.)

Another name for the Monastrel grape in the Rioja region.

Négrette (F.)

A red grape grown near Toulouse, in the Côtes du Frontonnais; related to the Malbec grape, and may also be the same grape as the Pinot St. George grape of California.

Negri, Nino (I.)   1897

A winery in Chiuro, Lombardy region; produces Valtellina, Sfursat, Castel Chiuro, Inferno and other wines; made from their own and purchased grapes. 120,000 cases.

Negrino (I.)

A sweet, red dessert wine from Salice Sal-.entino, in the southern Apulia region; made from semi-dried Malvasia Nera and Negroamaro grapes. 16% alcohol.

Negroamaro (I.)

A red grape grown in the Apulia region.

Nègron (F.)

A red grape. Also called Mourvèdre.

Negru de Purkar (U.S.S.R.)

1. A district in Moldavia SSR, which produces:
2. A dry, red wine made from Cabernet, Merlot, Malbec, Saperavi and Rara Neagra grapes.

negus (E.)

A hot drink made with Port, sugar, lemon and spices, named after Col. Francis Negus, who first made the drink in the early 18th century.

Neipperg, Weingüter und Schlosskellerei Graf von (G.)   1248

An estate in Schwaigern Schloss, Württemberg region; owns vineyards in Neipperg and Klingenberg. 70 acres.

Neive, Castello di (I.)

An estate in Neive, Piedmont region; produces Barbaresco, Barbera, Dolcetto and Moscato wines.

Neive, Parroco di (I.)

An estate of S.S. Pietro and Paolo church in Neive, Piedmont region; produces Barbaresco, Barbera, Dolcetto and Moscato wines.

Nemea (Gr.)

1. A town and district in the eastern Peloponnese region, which produces:
2. A red wine made from the Aghiorgitiko grape.

Nemes Kadar (H.)

A semi-sweet, red wine from Szeksárd, in the southern Transdanubia region, southwestern Hungary; made from the Kadarka grape.

Nénin, Château (F.)

An estate in Pomerol, Bordeaux region. 7,500 cases. 50 acres.

Neoplanta (Y.)

A white grape – a cross of Smederevka and Traminer grapes.

Nera (I.)   1936

An estate in Chiuro, Lombardy region; produces Valtellina wines. 370 acres.

Nerello Cappuccio (I.)

A red grape grown in the Calabria region.

Nerello Mascalese (I.)

A red grape grown in the Calabria region.

Nero d'Avola (I.)

A red grape grown in Sicily.

Nero Buoni di Cori (I.)

A red grape grown in the southern Latium region.

Nerthe, Château de la (F.)   1599

An estate in Châteauneuf-du-Pape, southern Rhône region; produces red and white wines; the white is made from the Clairette grape. 120 acres.

Nervi & Figlio, Luigi (I.)

An estate in Gattinara, Piedmont region; produces Gattinara and Spanna wines.

Neuberger (A., Cz.)

A native white grape of Austria and Czechoslovakia.

Neuchâtel (Sw.)

1. A city and district in the northern Vaud region, which produces:

2. A white wine made from the Chasselas grape. A little red wine is also made from the Pinot Noir grape.

Neuenahr, Bad (G.)

A village in the Ahr region, Bereich Walporzheim/Ahrtal, Grosslage Klosterberg. The vineyards are: Kirchtürmchem, Schieferley and Sonnenberg; also produces some red wine.

Neumagen-Dhron (G.)

A village in the Mosel-Saar-Ruwer region, Bereich Bernkastel, Grosslage Michelsberg. The vineyards are: Engelgrube, Grafenberg, Grosser Hengelberg, Hofberger, Laudamusberg, Rosengärtchen, Roterd and Sonnenuhr. 875 acres.

Neusiedlersee (A.)

A large, shallow lake in the Burgenland region of eastern Austria, near the Hungarian border; produces sweet, white wines on the western side, and *Seewinkel* wines on the eastern side.

Neustift (A.)

A suburban village north of Vienna; produces *Heurige* wines.

Neuweier (G.)

A village in the Baden region, Bereich Ortenau, Grosslage Schloss Rodeck. The vineyards are Altenberg, Gänsberg, Heiligenstein, Mauerberg and Schlossberg.

Neva Munson (U.S.)

A red hybrid grape and wine from the St. James Winery, Missouri. See **Munson.**

New Hall (E.)

A vineyard in Chelmsford, Essex; produces white wine made from Huxelrebe and Müller-Thurgau grapes and experimental red wine from the Pinot Noir grape. 20 acres.

New Hampshire (U.S.)

A state in the New England region of the United States. White Mountain Vineyards in Belmont is the first and, as yet, the only winery, built in 1969.

New Jersey (U.S.)

A state in the northeastern United States. It has a few wineries and a wine glass museum in Egg Harbor City.

New Mexico (U.S.)

A state in the southwestern United States. It had many wineries until Prohibition; 12-15 reopened after Prohibition but only 5 remain open.

New South Wales (Aus.)

A state in southeastern Australia, the earliest state to produce wine. It is divided into three regions: Hunter Valley, Riverina or Murrumbidgee Irrigation Area (MIA) and Mudgee.

New York (U.S.)

A state in the northeastern United States, second in importance to California in wine production. Wine-producing areas include: Finger Lakes, Hudson River Valley, Chautauqua, Niagara County and eastern Long Island. The first commercial winery was in the Hudson Valley in 1839. Concord, hybrid and *vinifera* grapes are grown. 43,000 acres.

New York Muscat (U.S.)

A red hybrid grape – a cross of Muscat Hamburg and Ontario; used to make Muscatel wine.

New Zealand

An island country in the Pacific Ocean, southeast of Australia. It has 400 commercial wineries; 75% of the vineyards grow *vinifera* grapes, including Müller-Thurgau, which is the predominate grape, Palomino, Chardonnay, Grey Riesling, Pinot Gris, Chasselas, Chenin Blanc, Gewürztraminer, Rhine Riesling, Sauvignon Blanc, Traminer, Cabernet, Pinotage, Pinot Noir, Gamay, Malbec, Hermitage and Syrah. 10,000 acres.

Newlan Vineyards (U.S.)
**vines 1967
winery 1981**

A winery in Napa, Napa Valley, California; formerly, a vineyard supplying other wineries; produces Cabernet, Chardonnay, Pinot Noir and Sauvignon Blanc wines. 4,000 cases.

Newton Vineyard (U.S.)
**1978, first wine
1980**

A winery in St. Helena, Napa Valley, California, formerly the Forman Winery; produces Cabernet, Merlot, Cabernet Franc, Chardonnay and Sauvignon Blanc wines. 8,000 cases. 60 acres.

Neyers Winery (U.S.)
1980

A winery in St. Helena, Napa Valley, California; produces Cabernet blended with Merlot and Cabernet Franc (grapes from the Eisele Vineyard) and Chardonnay wines. 3,000 cases.

Niabell *also* Niobell (U.S.)

An American red hybrid grape – a cross of Niagara and Early Campbell; grown in California.

Niagara (U.S.)

An American white hybrid grape – a cross of Concord and Cassady; developed in Lockport, New York in 1868.

Niagara County (U.S.)

A region in northwestern New York, between Lake Erie and Lake Ontario. 2,800 acres.

Nicasio Cellars (U.S.)
1952

A small winery in Santa Cruz, Santa Cruz County, California; produces table wines and Champagne.

Nicastro (I.)

1. A village near Catanzaro, in the southwestern Calabria region, which produces:

2. Red and white wines, the red wine made mostly from Gaglioppo and Nerello grapes and the white wine from Malvasia Bianco or Annarella grapes.

Nichelini Vineyard (U.S.)
1890

A winery in St. Helena, Napa Valley, California with a vineyard nearby in Chiles Valley; produces Cabernet, Zinfandel, Gamay, Petite Sirah, Chenin Blanc and Sauvignon Vert wines. 6,000 cases. 50 acres.

Nicoreşti (R.)

A town in the Focşani district of Moldavia, in eastern Romania; produces red wines, and is especially known for the Băbească Neagră wine.

Niebaum-Coppola Estate (U.S.)
1978

A winery in Rutherford, Napa Valley, California; produces Cabernet blended with Merlot, Cabernet Franc, and Malbec grapes and Chardonnay wines. 5,000 cases. 100 acres.

Nièddera (I.)

1. A red grape grown in western Sardinia.

2. A red wine from the Tirso River Valley, near Oristano, in western Sardinia; made from the Nièddera grape.

Niederhausen (G.)

A village in the Nahe region, Bereich Schloss Böckelheim, Grosslage Burgweg. The most well-known of the 12 vineyards are: Hermannsberg, Hermannshöhle, and Steinberg.

Niederösterreich (A.)

The German name for Lower Austria, one of 4 regions in northeastern Austria; it includes 7 districts: Wachau, Krems, Langenlois, Weinviertel, Klosterneuburg, Baden and Vöslau. 80,000 acres.

Niéllon, Michel (F.)

An estate in Chassagne-Montrachet, Côte de Beaune district, Burgundy; owns some Chevalier-Montrachet, Bâtard-Montrachet, Chassagne-Montrachet Clos St.-Jean and Les Vergers.

Niellucio (F.)

A local red grape grown in Corsica.

Niepoort & Co. Ltd. (P.)   1842

A Port producer in Vila Nova de Gaia.

Nierstein (G.)

A *Bereich*, one of 3 in the Rheinhessen region. There are 11 *Grosslagen*.

Nierstein (G.)

A village in the Rheinhessen region, Bereich Nierstein, divided between Grosslagen Spiegelberg, Rehbach, Gutes Domtal and Auflangen. The best-known vineyards are: Brückchen, Hölle, Bildstock, Paterberg, Rosenberg, Findling, Klostergarten, in Grosslage Spiegelberg; Pettenthal, Brudersberg, Hipping, Goldene Luft (sold as Kufürstenhof) in Grosslage Rehbach; Krunzberg, Bergkirche, Ölberg, Orbel, Zehnmorgen, Heiligenbaum, Glöck and Schloss Schwabsburg in Grosslage Auflangen. Total number of vineyards is 23. 2,250 acres.

Noah (U.S.)

An American white, hybrid grape; developed in Illinois in the 19th century. Also called Nauvoo.

Nobilo Vintners (N.Z.)   1943

A winery in Huapai, Aukland, North Island; produces Cabernet, Pinotage, Estate Cabernet, Gewürztraminer, Chardonnay, Pinot Noir and Riesling Sylvaner wines. 200 acres.

noble

A term used to describe some wines, grapes, estates or districts as being superior, outstanding, or of highest quality.

Noble (F.)

A red muscadine grape grown in the southeastern U.S.

noble rot

Botrytis cinerea, a grape fungus which enhances the quality of sweet, white wines under the right climatic conditions.

Noblessa (G.)

A white grape – a cross of Madeleine Angevine and Sylvaner; developed at the Federal Research Institute, Geilweilerhof, Germany.

Nobling (G.)

A white grape – a cross of Silvaner and Gutedel; developed at the State Viticultural Institute, Freiburg im Breisgau, Germany, in 1939.

Nocera (I.)

A red grape grown in the Calabria region.

Noë, Château la (F.)

An estate in Vallet, Muscadet de Sèvre-et-Maine district, Loire Valley. 75 acres.

Noëllat, Charles (F.)

An estate in Vosne-Romanée, Côte de Nuits district, Burgundy. 45 acres, including 5 acres of Romanée-St.-Vivant, 2.5 acres of Richebourg, 7.5 acres of Clos de Vougeot, 5.3 acres of Vosne-Romanée Les Beaumonts, .3 acre of Aux Malconsorts, 1.2 acres of Les Suchots, 4 acres of Nuits-St.-Georges Aux Boudots and 1.6 acres of Aux Murgers.

Noëllat, Henri (F.)

An estate in Vosne-Romanée, Côte de Nuits district, Burgundy. 25 acres, including 1.2 acres of Clos de Vougeot, 4 acres of Vosne-Romanée Les Suchots, 5 acres of Les Beaumonts, 1.2 acres of Nuits-St.-Georges Aux Boudots and 5 acres of Chambolle-Musigny.

Noirien (F.)

Another name for the Pinot Noir grape.

Noirot et ses Fils, Albert (F.)

An estate in Vosne-Romanée, Côte de Nuits district, Burgundy. 12 acres, including .6 acre of Échézeaux, 4 acres of Vosne-Romanée Les Suchots and 2.5 acres of Nuits-St.-Georges Aux Boudots.

Noirots, Les (F.)
A *Premier Cru* vineyard in Chambolle-Musigny, Côte de Nuits district, Burgundy. 5 acres.

Nomentane (Lat.)
An ancient Roman grape grown in the Tuscany region; mentioned by Cato.

Nonini Winery, A. (U.S.)   1936
A winery in Fresno, Fresno County, California; produces many varietal wines, including Barbera, and various blended wines. 40,000 cases. 200 acres.

Nordheim (G.)
A village in the Franken region, Bereich Maindreieck, Grosslage Kirchberg. The vineyards are: Vogelein and Kreuzberg. 1,000 acres.

Norheim (G.)
A village in the Nahe region, Bereich Schloss Böckelheim. The vineyards are: Dellchen, Götzenfels, Kafels, Kirschheck, Klosterberg, Oberberg, Onkelchen and Sonnenberg.

Norman and Sons (Aus.)   1859
A winery near Adelaide, South Australia; produces a Cabernet/Shiraz blend, Pinot Noir, Gewürztraminer and Chenin Blanc wines. 15,000 cases. 150 acres.

North Carolina (U.S.)
A state in the southeastern United States; it has a few new wineries which produce wine from muscadine varieties, especially the Scuppernong grape, and some wines from *vinifera* and hybrid grapes. 3,000 acres.

Norton (U.S.)
An American red grape which produces full, balanced wines with very little of the foxy taste. Also called Cynthiana, in Missouri, and Virginia Seedling.

Norvin (U.S.)
A red, hybrid grape - a cross of Minnesota 78, a cold-resistant wild grape clone, and

Seibel 11803; developed in Wisconsin by Elmer Swenson. Also called Swenson's Red and Variety 439.

nose (U.S.)
Bouquet; the aroma of wine.

Nosiola (I.)
A white grape grown in the Trentino-Alto Adige region.

Nössel (G.)
A wine measure equal to a half-liter, or a pint.

Nostrano (Sw.)
A red wine from the Ticino region of eastern Switzerland; made from a blend of Bondola and other grapes.

Notar Domenico (I.)
A local red grape grown in the southern Apulia region.

nouveau (F.)
New, usually referring to a very young Beaujolais wine, shipped as early as November 15.

Nouveau Sierre, Caves de Riondaz (Sw.)   1943
An estate in Sierre, Valais region; produces Ermitage, Fendant, Johannisberg, Muscat, Pinot Noir, Rèze and other wines.

Nouvelles, Château de (F.)
An estate in Tuchan, Fitou district, Languedoc region (the Midi); produces Fitou and Rivesaltes wines. 200 acres.

Novitiate of Los Gatos Winery (U.S.)   1888
A historic, old Jesuit winery in Los Gatos, Santa Clara County, California; best-known for Black Muscat wine; also Cabernet, Pinot Noir, Pinot Blanc, Sherry, Chenin Blanc, Angelica and altar wines. 35,000 cases. 600 acres.

Nozay, Domaine du (F.)   1970

An estate in Sancerre, Sancerre district, Upper Loire region. 15 acres.

Nozzole (I.)

A large estate in Greve, Tuscany region; produces Chianti Classico and Bianco wines. 250 acres.

nu (F.)

A term used in the pricing of wine without the cost of the cask or bottle.

Nudant, André (F.)

An estate in Ladoix-Serrigny, Côte de Beaune district, Burgundy. 12.5 acres, including .8 acre of Corton-Charlemagne, some Aloxe-Corton La Coutière, La Toppe-au-Vert and Ladoix-Côte de Beaune.

Nuits-Saint-Georges AOC (F.)

1. An important city of the Côte de Nuits district, in Burgundy. It also includes the vineyards of Prémeaux. There are 38 *Premier Crus* (10 from Prémeaux). 265,000 gallons. 535 acres.

2. A red wine from Nuits-Saint-Georges, a full-bodied and long-aging wine; a small amount of white wine is also produced.

Nuovo Fiore (I.)

A red Vino Novello from the Chianti Rufina district, in the Tuscany region.

Nuraghe Majore (I.)

A white wine from Alghero, in northwestern Sardinia; made from the Clairette grape.

Nuragus (I.)

A white grape grown in Cagliari, Sardinia.

Nuragus di Cagliari DOC (I.)

A dry, white wine from the area north of Cagliari, in southwestern Sardinia, the largest DOC on the Island; made mostly from Nuragus grapes with some Trebbiano, Vermentino, Clairette and Semidano grapes.

Nussdorf (A.)

A village in the northern suburbs of Vienna; produces *Heurige* wines.

nutty

A term used to describe some wines, particularly Sherries, referring to a characteristic taste of nuts, especially hazelnuts.

O

O.H.G. (G.)

The abbreviation for *Offene Handelgesells-chaft*, an ordinary partnership.

O.I.V. (F.)   1924

Office International de la Vigne et du Vin (the International Office of Vine and Wine).

oak

The predominant wood used for barrels and casks for aging wine. The best oak is from Limousin and Nevers, France or from Yugoslavia. White oak from Tennessee is sometimes also used in the United States. The tannin in wine comes partly from the oak and adds to the wine's character.

Oak Knoll Winery (U.S.)   1970

A winery in Hillsboro, Willow Valley, northwestern Oregon; formerly produced rhubarb and berry wines; recently (1975) added *vinifera* wines.

Oakencroft Farm Winery (U.S.)   1983

A winery in Charlottesville, Virginia; produces wines made from *vinifera* and hybrid grapes. 7 acres.

Oakville Vineyards (U.S.)   1892, 1969

A winery in Oakville, Napa Valley, California, formerly the Madonna Winery; produces Cabernet, Sauvignon Blanc and Zinfandel wines. 265 acres. Closed down in 1977.

Obereisenheim (G.)

A village in the Franken region, Bereich Maindreieck, Grosslage Kirchberg. The only vineyard is Höll. 225 acres.

Oberemmel (G.)

A village in the Mosel-Saar-Ruwer region, Bereich Saar-Ruwer, Grosslage Scharzberg. The vineyards are: Agritiusberg, Altenberg, Hütte, Karlsberg, Raul and Rosenberg. 600 acres.

Oberhaardt (G.)

Formerly, the name of the southern district of the Rheinpfalz region; changed in 1971 to Bereich Südliche Weinstrasse.

Oberkirch (G.)

A village in the Baden region, Bereich Ortenau, Grosslage Fürsteneck. The only vineyard in Renchtäler.

Obermosel (G.)

A *Bereich*, one of 4 in the Mosel-Saar-Ruwer region. The *Grosslagen* are Gipfel and Königsberg.

Oberrotweil (G.)

A village in the Baden region, Bereich Kaiserstuhl-Tuniberg, Grosslage Vulkanfelsen. The vineyards are: Eichberg, Henkelberg, Käsleberg, Kirchberg and Schlossberg.

Oberwesel (G.)

A village in the Mittelrhein region, Bereich Rheinburgengau, Grosslage Schloss Schönburg. The vineyards are: Bernstein, Bienenberg, Goldenmund, Ölsberg, Römerkrug, St. Martinsberg and Sieben Jungfrauen.

Obester Winery (U.S.)   1977

A winery in Half Moon Bay, San Mateo County, California; produces Cabernet, Johannisberg Riesling and Sauvignon Blanc wines from purchased grapes. 4,000 cases.

Occhio di Pernice (I.)

A red grape grown in the Tuscany region.

Öchsle *also* Oechsle (G.)

A scale, similar to Balling and Brix, used to determine the amount of sugar in must, expressed in degree numbers; this is further used to determine the potential alcohol content of wines. The Öchsle degree number is divided by 8 to get the alcohol percentage number.

Öchsle, Ferdinand (1774-1852) *also* Oechsle (G.)

A German physicist and inventor from Pforzheim, in the Baden region; he invented a device, a calibrated hydrometer, for measuring the sugar content of must.

Ockfen (G.)

A village in the Mosel-Saar-Ruwer region, Bereich Saar-Ruwer, Grosslage Scharzberg. The vineyards are Bochsten, Geisberg, Heppenstein, Herrenberg, Kupp, Neuwies and Zickelgarten.

octave

A small cask equal to 1/8 of a pipe (both of which vary in size), or 14-21 gallons; usually listed as 17 gallons.

Oddero, Fratelli (I.)   1870

An estate in La Morra, Piedmont region; produces Barbaresco, Barbera, Barolo, Dolcetto, Freisa and Nebbiolo wines. 16,000 cases. 50 acres.

Odobeşti (R.)

A town in the Focşani district, province of Moldavia, in eastern Romania; produces mostly white wines from a variety of grapes.

Oechsle, Ferdinand (G.)

See Öchsle, Ferdinand.

oeil de perdrix (F.)

French for "eye of partridge," a pinkish tint characteristc in certain white wines which are made from red grapes; similar in color to the eye of a partridge.

oenologist

A wine scientist; one who studies and practices wine-making.

oenology

The science of wine and wine-making.

oesjaar (S. Af.)

The vintage.

Oesterreicher (G.)

Another name for the Sylvaner or Franken Riesling grape.

Oestrich (G.)

A village in the Rheingau region, mostly in Grosslage Gottesthal. The vineyards are: Doosberg, Klosterberg, Lenchen and Schoss Reichartshausen (an estate, or *Ortsteil*, which does not use the village name). 1,100 acres.

Office International de la Vigne et du Vin (F.)   1924

The International Office of the Vine and Wine, an information and research service, which also advises member nations and attempts to influence and consolidate wine laws and practices.

Oggau (A.)

A village south of Vienna, in the Burgenland region.

Ogier et Fils, A. (F.)   1824

A merchant in Sorgues, Châteauneuf-du-Pape district, southern Rhône region; blends and bottles many Rhône wines from purchased wines; mostly known for Châteauneuf-du-Pape.

Ohio (U.S.)

A state in the central United States; important in the 19th century for Catawba wines, which it still mostly produces. 3,000 acres.

oïdium (F.)

Powdery mildew, a fungus disease which affects the leaves, young shoots and grapes producing a white, dusty covering; kept in control by the application of Bordeaux mixture.

oinoparagogas (Gr.)

A wine producer.

oinopoieion (Gr.)

A winery.

oinos (Gr.)

Wine.

Ojo de Liebre (Sp.)

In Catalonia, one of several names for the red Tempranillo grape; also called Cencibel in La Mancha.

Okanagan Valley (C.)

A district south of Okanagan Lake, in British Columbia. 2,500 acres.

Oklahoma (U.S.)

A state in the south central U.S. There is very little commercial wine-making or grape-growing here.

Öküzgözü *also* Öküz Gözü (T.)

A red grape grown in eastern Turkey; used to make Buzbağ wine.

Olarra S.A., Bodegas (Sp.)   1972

A winery in Logroño, Rioja Alta region; produces wines made from purchased grapes, such as Cerro Añon and others.

Olasz Rizling (H.)

The Italian Riesling or Wälschriesling grape; not the true Johannisberg Riesling.

Old South Winery (U.S.)   1979

A new winery in Natchez, Mississippi; produces muscadine wines. 12 acres.

Oleron's disease

A bacterial blight of vines, causing stains on leaves and flower clusters; almost disappeared in Europe, but still exists in South Africa.

Olive Farm Winery (Aus.)   1829

A small, old winery in Perth, Western Australia; produces Cabernet, Chenin Blanc, Muscat and Chardonnay wines as well as a white Burgundy from Tokay and Sémillon grapes; some purchased grapes. 8 acres.

Olivella (I.)

A red grape grown in the Campania region. Also locally called Sciascianoso.

Oliver Winery (U.S.)   1972

A winery in Bloomington, Indiana; the first of the new wineries since a new wine law was passed in 1971 in Indiana; grows French hybrid grapes. 40 acres.

Olivier, Château (F.)

An estate in Léognan, Graves district, Bordeaux; classified in 1959 as a *Cru Classé* for red and white wines. 10,000 cases, mostly white. 80 acres.

Ollwiller (F.)

A *Grand Cru* vineyard and estate in Wuenheim, southern Haut-Rhin district, Alsace region. 40 acres.

Olmo, Dr. Harold (U.S.)

An oenologist from Davis (U.C.), California; he found what he believes to be the original wild *Vitis vinifera* grape in 1948 at the border of Iran and Afganistan; developed the Ruby Cabernet, Emerald Riesling, Carnelian, Centurian and Carmine, all hybrid grapes.

Oloroso (Sp.)

A style of Sherry that is nutty in flavor, not quite as dry as *Fino*; made dry without developing a *flor*, and later sweetened.

Oltrepò Pavese DOC (I.)

A large district south of Pavia, in the southwestern Lombardy region; produces several red and white varietal and other wines: Barbacarlo, Barbera, Bonarda, Buttafuoco, Cortese, Moscato, Pinot, Riesling, Rosso and Sangue di Giuda.

Omar Khayyam (Egypt)

A sweet, white wine made mostly from the Muscat grape.

Ondarrubi Beltza (Sp.)

A red grape grown in the Chacolí district, Basque region, northeastern Spain.

Ondarrubi Zuria (Sp.)

A white grape grown in the Chacolí district, Basque region, northeastern Spain.

Ondenc (F.)

A white grape grown mostly in the Southwest region.

O'Neale S.A., Rafael (Sp.)   1924

A small Sherry producer in Jerez de la Frontera; produces several types of Sherry.

Ontario (C.)

A province of Canada, the most important wine region in the southeast; grows French hybrids, *labrusca* and *vinifera* grapes.

Opimian wine (Lat.)

An ancient Roman wine from the time of Opimius (121 B.C.)

Opol (Y.)

A rosé wine from the province of Dalmatia; made from the Plavač grape.

Oporto (P.)

A port city in northern Portugal, at the mouth of the River Douro; by law, any wine labeled Port must be shipped from Oporto.

Oppenheim (G.)

A famous village in the Rheinhessen region, Bereich Nierstein, Grosslagen Güld-enmorgen and Krötenbrunnen. The vineyards are: Daubhaus, Gutleuthaus, Herrenberg, Kreuz, Sackträger, Schützenhütte and Zuckerberg in Grosslage Güldenmorgan; and Herrengarten, Paterhof, Schloss and Schlossberg in Grosslage Krötenbrunnen. Several vineyards are shared with the village of Dienheim. 560 acres.

Opthalma (Cyp.)

A red grape grown in Cyprus.

Optima (G.)

A white grape – a cross of Sylvaner and Riesling crossed with Müller-Thurgau; developed at the Federal Research Institute, Geilweilerhof, Germany; similar to but considered better than the Bacchus grape.

Opus 1 (U.S.)   1979

The first red wine of the combined Mondavi-Rothschild winery, Napa Valley, California; made from Cabernet and other Bordeaux varieties.

Orange Muscat (U.S.)

A white grape of the muscat family with the aroma of orange blossoms; used by Quady Winery, in California to make a dessert wine.

l'Oratoire, Clos de (F.)

An estate in St.-Émilion, Bordeaux; classified in 1969 as a *Grand Cru Classé*. 3,500 cases. 20 acres.

l'Oratoire des Papes, Clos de (F.)

An estate in Châteauneuf-du-Pape, southern Rhône region. 100 acres.

l'Oratoire St.-Martin (F.)

An estate in the commune of Cairanne, Côtes du Rhône-Villages district, southern Rhône region. 85 acres.

ordinaire (F.)

A term used to describe common, ordinary wines, for everyday drinking.

Oregon (U.S.)

A state in the northwestern United States, an important wine region, especially Willamette, Umpqua, Roque and Tualatin Valleys; there are presently 30 wineries, 200 growers. State laws require that the wine be made from 90% of the grape named on the label except for Cabernet Sauvignon, which has a 75% minimum. 1,200 acres.

Orfila (Arg.)

An estate in San Martin, Mendoza region; produces Chardonnay and Cabernet Sauvignon wines. 700 acres.

organoleptic

Referring to an impression of a wine made by the organs of taste, smell and sight.

Original Abfüllung *also* Originalabzug (G.)

A term meaning estate-bottled, used prior to 1971; the present term is *Erzeugerabfüllung.*

Orlando (Aus.)   1847

An large, old winery in the Barossa Valley, South Australia; produces well-known individual vineyard bottlings, especially Rhine Riesling as well as Cabernet, Gewürztraminer, Chardonnay, sweet sparkling and fortified wines. Some purchased grapes. 280 acres.

l'Orme, En (F.)

A *Premier Cru* vineyard in Beaune, Côte de Beaune district, Burgundy. 5 acres.

l'Ormeau, En (F.)

A *Premier Cru* vineyard in Volnay, Côte de Beaune district, Burgundy. 11 acres.

Ormes, Le Clos des (F.)

A *Premier Cru* vineyard (in part) in Morey-St.-Denis, Côte de Nuits district, Burgundy. 10 acres.

Ormes de Pez, Château Les (F.)

An estate in St.-Estèphe, Haut-Médoc district, Bordeaux; classified in 1978 as a *Cru Grand Bourgeois.* 14,000 cases. 70 acres.

Ormes-Sorbet, Château Les (F.)

An estate in Couqueques, Bordeaux; classified in 1978 as a *Cru Grand Bourgeois.* 10,000 cases. 40 acres.

Orsat, Alphonse (Sw.)   1874

A large winery and merchant in Martigny, Valais region; produces Fendant, Johannisberg, Ermitage, Dôle and other wines. 1 million cases.

Ortega (G.)

A white grape – a cross of Müller-Thurgau and Siegerrebe, developed at the State Viticultural Institute, Würzburg-Veitshöchheim, Germany.

Ortenau (G.)

A *Bereich,* one of 7 in the Baden region. The two *Grosslagen* are Fürsteneck and Schloss Rodeck.

Ortenberg (G.)

A village in the Baden region, Bereich Ortenau, Grosslage Fürsteneck. The vineyards are: Andreasberg, Franzensberger, Freudental and Schlossberg.

Ortrugo (I.)

A local white grape grown in the western Emilia-Romagna region.

Ortsteil (G.)

A suburb or a section of a community; a famous vineyard or estate which may use its name without the village name on the label: Scharzhofberg, Maximin Grünhaus, Eitelsbach, Schloss Johannisberg, Schloss Reichartshausen, Schloss Vollrads, Steinberg and a few others.

orujo (Sp.)

The lees, or residue of skins, pips, etc. after the fermentation of the must is completed.

Orvieto, Orvieto Classico DOC (I.)

1. A town and district including 15 other villages, in the southwestern Umbria region, which produces:

2. A famous white wine (now mostly dry, but formerly, semi-sweet) made from 50-65% Trebbiano, 15-25% Verdello, and the remainder Grechetto, Drupeggio and Malvasia grapes. The Classico designation is for wine only from Orvieto village.

Osaka (J.)

A large city and one of the main wine-producing districts in southern Japan.

Osborn D'Arenberg Wines (Aus.) 1912

A winery in McLaren Vale, near Adelaide, Southern Vales district, South Australia; produces Shiraz, Cabernet, Grenache, Palomino, Pedro Ximénez, Rhine Riesling and blended wines. 40,000 cases. 150 acres.

Osborne y Cía S.A. (Sp.) 1772

A Sherry producer in Puerta de Santa Maria; also owns wineries in the Rioja region, Mexico and Portugal.

Osey *also* Aussey (E.)

An ancient wine from Alsace or Auxerre, west of the Chablis district, shipped to England in the 13-16th centuries and mentioned in *Piers Plowman* and by Shakespeare.

Osiris (G.)

A white grape – a cross of Riesling and Rieslaner; developed at the State Viticultural Institute, Würzburg-Veitshöchheim, Germany.

Osterberg (F.)

A vineyard in Ribeauvillé, Haut-Rhin district, Alsace region; produces mostly Riesling grapes.

Österreich (A.)

The German name for Austria. 165,000 acres of vines, mostly in the eastern part of the country.

Österreicher (G.)

Another name for the Sylvaner grape. Also called Frankentraube.

Osthofen (G.)

A village in the Rheinhessen region, Bereich Wonnegau, Grosslagen Gotteshilfe and Pilgerpfad. The vineyards are: Goldberg, Hasenbiss, Lockzapfen and Neuberg in Grosslage Gotteshilfe; and Kirchberg, Klosterberg, Liebenberg and Rheinberg in Grosslage Pilgerpfad.

Ostuni DOC (I.)

1. A town and district northwest of Brindisi, in the southern Apulia region, which produces:

2. Light red or white wine. The red wine is made from Ottavianello grapes with some Negroamaro, Malvasia Nera, Notar Domanico and Sussumariello grapes and is called Ottavianello; the white wine is made from Impigno grapes with some Francavilla and Verdeca Bianco d'Alessano grapes.

Othello (U.S.)

An American red hybrid grape – a cross of Clinton and Black Hamburg; grown in the eastern and mid-western U.S.

Othello (Cyp.)

A brand of dry, red wine from Cyprus.

Ott, Domaines (F.) 1896

An estate in La Londe-les-Maures, in the Provence region. 350 acres, including Château de Selle, Clos Mireille and Château Romasson; produces white and rosé wines. 45,000 cases.

Ottavianello (I.)

1. A red grape grown in the southern Apulia region.

2. A red wine from the Ostuni DOC district, in the southern Apulia region; made from the Ottavianello and other grapes.

Oude Libertas (S. Af.)

A brand name for red and white wines from the Stellenbosch Farmers Winery, in the Stellenbosch district.

ouillage (F.)

1. Ullage, the evaporation or leaking of wine from a bottle or barrel.

2. The topping up of a wine barrel with wine to compensate for evaporation; this is done repeatedly during long aging and storing. Also called *remplissage*.

Oujda (Mor.)

A town and district in northeastern Morocco; produces dry rosé wines from Grenache grapes and sweet Muscat wines.

ouvrée (F.)

An old Burgundian land measure equal to 1/24 of a *hectare* or 1/8 of a *journal*, or about 1/10 of an acre. It is still seen on some vineyard names.

overcropping

Allowing vines to bear too much, thus lowering the quality of the grapes and the wine produced from such vines.

Overgaauw Estate EWO (S. Af.)   1906

An estate in the Stellenbosch district; produces Cabernet, Pinotage, Merlot, Chenin Blanc, Sylvaner and other wines. 10,000 cases. 150 acres.

oxidation

Exposure to air caused by leakage or from over-aging in the cask or bottle; it occurs in white or rosé wines; it spoils the taste and causes the wine to turn brown. Also called maderization.

P

P.D. (F.)

Producteur Directe (Direct Producer), a vine grown on its own roots, i.e. not grafted onto another root-stock.

P.X. (P.)

The abbreviation for the Pedro Ximénez grape.

Prüf. Nr. (G.)

The abbreviation of Prüfungsnummer, the testing number printed on German quality-wine labels. See **A.P.**

Paarl WO (S. Af.)

A city and district northeast of Cape Town; famous for the Nederburg vineyard, east of Paarl city.

Pacheco Ranch Winery (U.S.)   **1979**
vines 1971

A small winery in Ignacio, Marin County, California; produces Cabernet, Rosé of Cabernet and Chardonnay wines. 1,000 cases. 15 acres.

Pacherenc du Vic Bihl AOC (F.)

A dry, or semi-sweet, white wine from the Madiran district, north of Pau and Tarbes, in the Southwest region; made from Ruffiat, Manseng, Courbu, Sémillon and Sauvignon Blanc grapes.

Padeiro (P.)

A red grape grown in the Vinho Verde region.

Padouen, Château (F.)

An unclassified estate in Barsac, Sauternes district, Bordeaux. 2,000 cases. 25 acres.

Pagadebit (I.)

A dry, or sweet, white wine from Bertinoro, south of Ravenna, in the eastern Emilia-Romagna region; made from the Pagadebit Gentile grape.

Pagadebito *also* **Pagadebit Gentile (I.)**

A rare, local, white grape grown in the eastern Emilia-Romagna region.

Page Mill Winery (U.S.)   **1976**

A small winery in Los Alto Hills, Santa Cruz Mountains, Santa Clara County, California; produces Cabernet, Merlot, Zinfandel and Chardonnay wines mostly from purchased grapes from Napa Valley. 2,000 cases. 1 acre.

Pagliarese (I.)

An estate in Castelnuovo Berardenga, Tuscany region; produces Chianti Classico, Vin Santo and Bianco wines; made from their own and purchased grapes. 30,000 cases. 75 acres.

paglierino (I.)

Straw-colored, referring to a white wine.

Païen (Sw.)

A local, white grape grown in the Valais region.

País (Ch.)

1. A red grape of Spanish origin, similar to the Mission grape; 70% of all grapes grown in Chile are País.

2. A red wine made from the País grape.

pajarete (Sp.)

In Málaga, a term denoting sweet or semi-sweet wines.

Pajarilla (Sp.)

A white wine from the Cariñena village and district, Aragón region, in northeastern Spain; made from the Garnacho Blanco grape.

Palace Hotel do Buçaco (P.)

An estate in Luso, Barraida region, owned by the hotel; produces red, white and rosé wines. 35 acres.

Palais, Château Les (F.)

An estate in St. André de Cabrerisse, Corbières district, Languedoc region (the Midi). 55,000 cases. 250 acres.

Palatinate (G.)

The English term for the Rheinpfalz region of Germany.

Palette AOC (F.)

1. A small district east of Aix-en-Provence, in the Provence region, which produces:

2. Red, white and rosé wines, the red and rosé made from Grenache, Cinsault and Mourvèdre grapes, and the white mainly from Clairette grapes.

Pallières, Domaine des (F.)

An estate in Gigondas, southern Rhône region. 62 acres.

palma cortado (Sp.)

A *fino* Sherry with body, almost as full as an *amontillado*.

Palmer, Château (F.)

An estate in Cantenac-Margaux, Haut-Médoc district, Bordeaux; classified in 1855 as a *Troisième Cru*; originated from a division of Château d'Issan in 1748, and known as Château de Gascq. 40% Cabernet, 40% Merlot, 10% Cabernet Franc, 10% Petit Verdot. 12,000 cases. 90 acres.

palo cortado (Sp.)

A Sherry wine with characteristics of both *amontillado* and *oloroso*.

Palombina (I.)

In Vesuvio, Campania region, another name for the Piedirosso grape.

Palomino (Sp.)

A white grape grown in Jerez, the primary grape used to make Sherry; large yield, low acidity. Also called: Listán, Horgazuela, Palomina, Ojo de Liebre, Temprana, Albán and, in South Africa, the Frandsdruift.

Palomino Negro (Sp.)

A red grape grown in southwestern Spain.

Palomino & Vergara S.A. (Sp.)　　　1765

A Sherry producer in Jerez de la Frontera.

Palumbo (I.)

A local white grape grown in the Apulia region.

palus (F.)

The low-lying land near the primary rivers in the Bordeaux region; produces ordinary wines.

Pamid (Bul.)

1. A red grape grown in southern Bulgaria. Also called Plovdina, which produces:

2. Red and rosé wines.

Pampanino (I.)

A white grape grown in the Apulia region. Also called Pampanuto.

Panciu (R.)

A town in the Focşani district, province of Moldavia, in eastern Romania; produces white wines.

panicle

A cluster of buds on a vine.

Panigon, Château (F.)

An estate in Civrac, Médoc district, Bordeaux; classified in 1978 as a *Cru Bourgeois*. 9,000 cases. 50 acres.

ansa Blanca (Sp.)

white grape grown in the Catalonia region. Also called Xarel-lo.

ansa Rosada (Sp.)

red grape grown in the Catalonia region.

antelleria, Agricoltori Associati di (I.)

A co-op winery on the Island of Pantelleria, south of Sicily; produces Moscato, olimano, Tanit and other wines. 1,000 growers.

aola di Mauro (I.)

An estate in Marino, Latium region; produces Colle Picchioni Rosso and Marino wines. 2,200 cases. 8 acres.

apagni Vineyards (U.S.)   1973

A winery in Madera, San Joaquin Valley, Madera County, California; produces Cabernet, Zinfandel, Alicante Bouchet, Chardonnay, Chenin Blanc, Sauvignon Blanc, Muscats and sparkling wines (*Charmat process*). 125,000 cases. 2,000 acres.

Papazkarsi (T.)

A red grape.

Pape-Clément, Château (F.)

An estate in Pessac, Graves district, Bordeaux; classified in 1959 as a *Cru Classé* for red wine only; planted in 1300 by Bertrand de Goth, Archbishop of Bordeaux, who later became Pope Clément V. 10,000 cases. 65 acres.

Papes, Clos des (F.)

An estate in Châteauneuf-du-Pape, southern Rhône region, the old Papal vineyard; produces red wine from Grenache, Syrah, Muscardin and Vaccarèse grapes and some white wine. 75 acres.

Papillon, Clos du (F.)

A vineyard in Savennières, near La Roche aux Moines vineyard, in the Anjou region, Loire Valley. 10 acres.

Para Liqueur (Aus.)

A famous Port wine from Seppelt Winery, in the Barossa Valley, South Australia.

Paradis, Domaine de (F.)

An estate in Saint-Amour, Beaujolais district, Burgundy. 20 acres.

Paradiso (I.)

A sweet, white wine from the Emilia-Romagna region; made from the Picolit grape.

Paradiso, Fattoria (I.)   1880

An estate in Capocolle di Bertinoro, Emilia-Romagna region; produces Albana, Barbarossa, Cagnina, Pagadebit, Sangiovese and Trebbiano wines. 13,000 cases. 60 acres.

paragogi (Gr.)

Produced.

Paraza, Château de (F.)

An estate in Lézignan, Minervois district, Languedoc region; produces red and rosé wines. 37,000 cases. 175 acres.

Pardillo (Sp.)

A white grape grown in the La Mancha region.

Parducci Wine Cellars (U.S.)   1933

A winery in Ukiah, Mendocino County, California; produces Merlot, Cabernet, Pinot Noir, Petite Sirah, Carignane, French Colombard and jug wines from their own and purchased grapes. 300,000 cases. 400 acres.

Parent, Domaine (F.)

An estate in Pommard, Côte de Beaune, Burgundy. 29 acres, including 2 acres of Pommard Les Chaponnières, 6 acres of Les Épenots, .8 acre of Les Chanlins Bas, 5 acres of Beaune Les Épenottes and 1.2 acres of Les Boucherottes.

Paris (F.)

The capital of France. Wine was made here in the 13th century; surprisingly, some is still made in Montmartre.

Paris, Domaine des (F.)

An estate in St. Tropez, Provence region.

Parnay, Château de (F.)

An estate in Parnay, Coteaux-de-Saumur district, Anjou region, Loire Valley. 30 acres.

Paros (Gr.)

1. An island southeast of Athens.

2. A red wine from Paros made from the Mandilari grape.

parra (Mex.)

A grapevine.

parral (Arg., Ch.)

A system of vine-training used in the province of San Juan, Argentina and in Chile. It allows 25-30 buds per plant with very little pruning; produces very high yields (up to 150 *hectolitres* per *hectare*).

Parras (Mex.)

A district west of Saltillo, in the state of Coahuila, north central Mexico. The first winery in Mexico was built there in the 16th century.

Parrina, La DOC (I.)

1. A small district in the southern end of the Tuscany region, which produces:

2. Red and white wines; the red wine is made from mostly Sangiovese and Canaiolo grapes with some Morellone and Colorino and the white wine is made mostly from Procanico (Trebbiano) grapes with some Ansonica and Malvasia .

Parsac-Saint-Émilion AOC (F.)

A commune east of St.-Émilion, in the St.-Émilion district, Bordeaux; mostly sold as Montagne-St.-Émilion.

Parsons Creek Winery (U.S.)   197

A winery in Ukiah, Mendocino County California; produces Chardonnay, Johann isberg Riesling and Gewürztraminer wine from purchased grapes from various re gions. 10,000 cases.

Parsons Winery, Michael (U.S.)

A small winery in Soquel, east of Sant Cruz City, Santa Cruz County, California produces Cabernet wines. 500 cases. acre.

Partom (Is.)

A sweet, red wine from Israel.

pas dosé (F.)

Natural, with no *dosage* added; refers to a very dry, sparkling wine.

pasado (Sp.)

Maderized.

Pascal et Fils, Domaine Jean (F.)

An estate in Puligny-Montrachet, Côte de Beaune district, Burgundy. 20 acres, including 2 acres of Pommard, 1 acre of Volnay and 10 acres of Puligny-Montrachet.

Pascal Blanc (F.)

A white grape grown in Cassis, in the Provence region.

Pascal S.A. (F.)

A merchant in Vacqueyras, southern Rhône region; produces Côtes du Rhône, Côtes du Rhône-Villages, Côtes du Ventoux, Gigondas and Vacqueyras wines; made from their own and purchased grapes. 80,000 cases. 10 acres.

Pascale (I.)

A local red grape grown in Sardinia.

Pasmodos (P.)

A red wine from the Setúbal region of southern Portugal; made from a blend of various grapes from the Alentejo region.

Pasolini Dall'Onda (I.)   16th c.

An estate in Montericco di Imola, Emilia-Romagna region and also in the Tuscany region; produces Albana, Chianti, Sangiovese and Trebbiano wines. 65,000 cases. 200 acres.

Pasqua, Fratelli (I.)

A winery in Verona, Veneto region; produces Amarone, Bardolino, Soave, Valdadige and Valpolicella wines.

Pasquero-Elia Secondo (I.)

An estate in Bricco di Neive, Piedmont region; produces Barbaresco and Dolcetto wines.

Passe-Temps, Le (F.)

A *Premier Cru* vineyard in Santenay, Côte de Beaune district, Burgundy. 31 acres.

Passe-Tout-Grains *also* Passetoutgrains (F.)

A red or rosé wine from the Burgundy region, made from at least 1/3 Pinot Noir grapes and the rest Gamay grapes. The AOC designation is Bourgogne Passe-Tout-Grains.

passerillage (F.)

In Jurançon and other districts, the late harvesting of overripe, shriveled grapes, which, therefore, contain a more concentrated juice, used for making sweet wines.

Passerina (I.)

A white grape grown in the Marches and Abruzzo regions.

passito (I.)

1. A process in which the harvested grapes are allowed to dry in the sun or in hot, well-ventilated attics before pressing in order to obtain stronger, sweeter wines.
2. A style of Italian wine made from dried grapes; usually sweet and high in alcohol. Also called *vino da meditazione*.

Passito di Chambave (I.)

A sweet, white wine from Chambave, in the Valle d'Aosta region; made from dried Moscato grapes.

Passito Liquoroso di Caluso DOC (I.)

A sweet, white wine from Caluso, northeast of Turin, in the Piedmont region; made from selected, dried Erbaluce grapes; aged 5 years, 16% alcohol.

Passover wine

Kosher wine for the Jewish festival of Passover; traditionally very sweet, but more dry wines are now being made Kosher for Passover.

Pasteur, Louis (1822-95) (F.)

The French chemist who discovered the process of pasteurization and isolated the micro-organisms which cause grape juice to ferment into wine.

pasteurization

The process of sterilizing liquids by heating quickly and briefly to 130-150 degrees farenheit (54-66 degrees centigrade), thus killing most of the harmful bacteria. Wine is pasteurized by heating it to 130 degrees F. (54 degrees C.); sweet wines are generally pasteurized before or during bottling at 180 degrees F. (82 degrees C.) for 1 minute or at 130 degrees F. (54 degrees C.) for a longer period. The shorter the heating time the less change of quality in the wine.

Pastori Winery (U.S.)   1st wines 1975

A winery in Geyserville, Sonoma County, California; produces generic, Cabernet and Zinfandel wines. 9,000 cases. 60 acres.

pastoso (I.)

Semi-sweet.

Patache d'Aux, Château (F.)

An estate in Bégadan, Médoc district, Bordeaux; classified in 1978 as a *Cru Grand Bourgeois*. 25,000 cases. 80 acres.

Paternel, Domaine du (F.)

An estate in Cassis, Provence region.

Paternina S.A., Federico (Sp.)   1896

A large winery in Haro, Rioja Alta region; produces wines from their own and purchased grapes: Banda Azul, Banda Dorada and reserva wines. 800,000 cases. 600 acres.

Patras (Gr.)

A city and district in northern Peloponnese; produces Mavrodaphne and Muscat wines as well as light red wines.

Patriarche Père et Fils (F.)   1780

A large company in Beaune, Côte de Beaune district, Burgundy. 30 acres, including Beaune Les Fèves, Les Grèves, Les Bressandes, Les Avaux, Clos du Roi, Les Blanches Fleurs, Les Cent Vignes, Les Toussaints and Château du Meursault; also produces Kriter sparkling wine.

Patrimonio AOC (F.)

Red, white and rosé wines from Patrimonio and Bastia, in northern Corsica; the red and rosé wines are made from Niellucio and Grenache grapes and the whites (dry and sweet) from Vermentino, Rossola, Ugni Blanc, Malvoisie and Muscat grapes. The AOC is Vin de Corse Patrimonio.

Pau Ferro (P.)

A red grape grown in southern Portugal.

Pauillac AOC (F.)

The most important commune in the Haut-Médoc district of Bordeaux, and the home of the famous Châteaux Lafite, Latour and Mouton-Rothschild.

Paul Chanson, Cuvée (F.)

A white wine from the Hospices de Beaune, Côte de Beaune district, Burgundy. The *cuvée* is composed of one vineyard in Corton: Corton-Vergennes – .7 acre. 68 cases.

Paul Robert (Alg.)

A well-known red wine from the Haut-Dahra district, west of Algiers; now called Taughrite.

Pauland, En *also* Les Paulands (F.)

A *Grand Cru* vineyard (in part) in Aloxe-Corton, Côte de Beaune district, Burgundy

when the name is preceded by "Corton." The other part is *Premier Cru*. 6 acres.

Paulsen Vineyard, Pat (U.S.)   1980

A small winery in Cloverdale, Russian River Valley, northern Sonoma County, California; produces Cabernet, Muscat, Sauvignon Blanc and Chardonnay wines. 8,000 acres. 35 acres.

Paveil de Luze, Château (F.)

An estate in Soussans-Margaux, Bordeaux; classified in 1978 as a *Cru Grand Bourgeois*. 4,000 cases. 35 acres.

Pavelot-Glantenay (F.)

An estate in Savigny-lès-Beaune, Côte de Beaune district, Burgundy. 20 acres, including 3.2 acres of Savigny La Dominode, 2.5 acres of Les Peuillets and 2.8 acres of Aux Guettes.

Pavie, Château (F.)

An estate in St.-Émilion, Bordeaux; classified in 1955 as a *Premier Grand Cru*. 16,000 cases. 80 acres.

Pavie-Decesse, Château (F.)

An estate in St.-Émilion, Bordeaux; classified in 1955 as a *Grand Cru Classé*. 3,500 cases. 20 acres.

Pavie-Macquin, Château (F.)

An estate in St.-Émilion, Bordeaux; classified in 1955 as a *Grand Cru Classé*. 3,000 cases. 25 acres.

Pavillon-Cadet, Château (F.)

An estate in St.-Émilion, Bordeaux; classified in 1955 as a *Grand Cru Classé*. 1,200 cases. 7 acres.

Pavy, Gaston (F.)

A small estate in Saché, Touraine Azay-le-Rideau district, Touraine region, Loire Valley. 8 acres.

Pazo (Sp.)

A brand of red, white and rosé wines from the Galicia region of northwestern Spain.

'eaceful Bend Vineyard (U.S.)   **1972**

A winery in Steelville, near St. James, in
entral Missouri; produces wines from hy-
orid grapes.

'écharmant AOC (F.)

. A village and district northeast of Ber-
;erac, in the southwest region, which
>roduces:

!. A red wine made from the two Cabernet
;rapes, Merlot and Malbec grapes, similar
n style to the lesser wines of St.-Émilion.

'ecorello (I.)

A red grape grown in the Calabria region.

Pecorino (I.)

A white grape grown in the Calabria
region.

Pecota Winery, Robert (U.S.)   **1978**

A winery in Calistoga, Napa Valley, California; produces Cabernet, Gamay, Beaujolais, Sauvignon Blanc and French
Colombard wines. 15,000 cases. 40 acres.

Pécoui-Touar (F.)

A red grape grown in Bandol, in the Provence region.

Pécs (H.)

The best-known town in the Mecsek dis-
trict, Transdanubia region, southwestern
Hungary; produces white wines made
from Wälschriesling, Furmint, Müller-
Thurgau, Zierfändler, Chardonnay, Pinot
Blanc and other grapes.

pecsenyebor (H.)

Dessert wine.

Pedernã (P.)

A white grape grown in the Vinho Verde
region.

Pédesclaux, Château (F.)

An estate in Pauillac, Haut-Médoc district,
Bordeaux; classified in 1855 as a *Cinquième
Cru*. 8,000 cases. 55 acres.

Pedregal (U.S.)

The second label for Cabernet and Chardonnay wines made by Stag's Leap Vineyards, Napa Valley, California.

Pedrizzetti Winery (U.S.)   **1919**

A winery in Morgan Hill, Santa Clara
County, California; produces generic
wines and Cabernet, Barbera, Petite Sirah,
Zinfandel, French Colombard, Chenin
Blanc and Barbera Bianca wines from purchased grapes. Other labels used are Morgan Hill Cellars and Crystal Springs.
80,000 cases.

Pedro Luis (Sp.)

A white grape grown in the Huelva district
of southwestern Spain.

Pedro Ximénez (Sp.)

A white grape used in making the sweet
Sherry and Málaga wines, and the dry
Montilla-Moriles wines; also called Elbling.

Pedroncelli Winery, J. (U.S.)   **1904**

An old winery in Geyserville, Alexander
Valley, northern Sonoma County, California; produces Cabernet, Pinot Noir, Zinfandel, Zinfandel rosé, Chardonnay,
Gewürztraminer and Chenin Blanc wines
from their own and purchased grapes.
130,000 cases. 135 acres.

Peel Estate (Aus.)   **1974**

A small winery near Mandurah, Western
Australia; produces Cabernet, Shiraz, Zin-
fandel, Verdelho, Chardonnay and Chenin
Blanc wines. 3,000 cases. 30 acres.

Pegazzera, Tenuta (I.)

An estate in Casteggio, Lombardy region;
produces Oltrepò Pavese wines. 13,000
cases. 55 acres.

Peixotto, Château *also* **Pexotto (F.)**

Formerly, an estate in Bommes, Sauternes
district, Bordeaux; classified in 1855 as a
Deuxième Cru; now a part of Château Rabaud-Promis.

Pelaquié, Domaine (F.)

An estate in Laudun, in the Côtes du Rhône-Villages district, southern Rhône region.

Pelaverga (I.)

1. A red grape grown in the Piedmont region.
2. A rosé wine from Saluzzo, north of Cuneo, in the Piedmont region; made from the Pelaverga grape.

Péléat (F.)

A vineyard section of Hermitage, northern Rhône region; planted with white grapes.

pelin (R.)

A Romanian drink made from wine and herbs, served cold with ice.

Pellaro (I.)

1. A village in the southwestern end of the Calabria region, which produces:
2. Red and rosé wines made mostly from the Alicante grape.

Peloponnese (Gr.)

A large peninsula and region in southwestern Greece; produces 1/3 of all Greek wine; known for Mavrodaphne wine from Patras.

pelure d'oignon (F.)

French for "onion skin," the reddish-brown color seen in some rosé wines and in some very old red wines.

Peñafiel (Sp.)

A town and district east of Valladolid, in northwestern Spain; produces red and rosé wines made from the Tinto Fino grape.

Penamcor (P.)

A red grape grown in the Dão region. Also called Rufete and Tinta Pinheira.

Pendelton Winery (U.S.)   1977

A winery in San José, Santa Clara County, California; produces Cabernet, Zinfandel,

Pinot Noir, Chardonnay and Chenin Blanc wines from purchased grapes. 6,000 cases

Penedès DO (Sp.)

A district west of Barcelona, in the Catalonia region of northeastern Spain; the 3 sub-divisions are Bajo Penedès, Medio Penedès and Alto Penedès; grows Garnacha, Tempranillo, Viura, Cariñena, Monastrell (red), and Parellada (white) grapes as well as French and German varieties, limestone soil.

Penfolds (Aus.)   1844

A famous, large winery centered in Adelaide, South Australia; known for red Grange Hermitage and St. Henri Claret wines; also numbered Bin wines including Bin 707 – Cabernet Sauvignon, Bin 389 – a blend of Cabernet and Shiraz from different areas and Bin 28 – Shiraz; also Port-style wines and some whites. Several thousand acres.

Penn-Shore Vineyards (U.S.)   1969

A winery in the town of North East, near Erie, Pennsylvania; produces numerous wines from native and *vinifera* grapes. 125 acres.

Pennsylvania (U.S.)

A state in the northeastern U.S.; it has 12,000 acres of vines; grows mostly Concord grapes for grape juice; new laws in 1968 made it possible to operate and sell wine and there are several new wineries.

Pepe, Emilio (I.)

An estate in Torano Nuovo, Abruzzi region; produces Montepulciano and Trebbiano wines. 3,000 cases.

Pepi Winery, Robert (U.S.)   1981
                                                    vines 1970

A winery in Oakville, Napa Valley, California; produces Cabernet, Chardonnay, Sauvignon Blanc and Sémillon wines. 50 acres. 5,000 cases.

erdido Vineyards (U.S.)   **1972**

A winery in Perdido, northeast of Mobile, the only one in Alabama; grows Scuppernong, other muscadine grapes and some hybrids. 50 acres.

erdrix, Aux (F.)

A *Premier Cru* vineyard in Prémeaux, Côte de Nuits district, Burgundy. 8.5 acres.

er'e Palummo (I.)

A red grape grown in Ischia, in the Camania region; a local name for the Piedirosso grape.

ère Caboche, Domaine du (F.)   **1772**

An estate in Châteauneuf-du-Pape, Rhône region; produces red wine made from 70% Grenache and 10% Syrah grapes and white wine made from Clairette, Grenache Blanc and Bourboulenc grapes. 75 acres.

ère Clément, Clos du (F.)

An estate in Visan, southern Rhône region; produces only red wine.

erelli-Minetti Winery (U.S.)   **1922, 1936**

A large winery in Delano, southern San Joaquin Valley, Kern County, California; owns many brands of the former California Wine Association, which was formed in 1894, including Guasti, Eleven Cellars, Greystone, etc. 12,000 cases. 1,500 acres.

erez Marín, Aijos de Rainera (Sp.)   **1850**

A Sherry producer in Sanlúcar de Barrameda; produces *manzanilla* sherries, especially "La Guita" (a *manzanilla pasada*).

ergola (I., P.)

A kind of horizontal trellis for vines used in northern Italy and in the Vinho Verde region in Portugal; it has the affect of cooling the grapes by allowing greater circulation of air.

ergole Torte, Le (I.)

A red wine from Radda, in the Chianti Classico district, Tuscany region; made from the Sangiovese grape.

pergole trentine (I.)

Inverted L-shaped supports for new vine shoots used in the Trentino-Alto Adige region of northeastern Italy.

Periquita (P.)

1. A red grape grown in central and southern Portugal; grows well in sand; the name means "little parrot."
2. A red wine from the Setúbal district; made from the Periquita grape.

Perla (R.)

A white wine from the Tîrnave district, Transylvania, in central Romania; made from Italian Riesling, Fetească and Muscat Ottonel grapes.

Perla Vineyard, La (U.S.)

A 1,500 ft. high mountain vineyard on Spring Mountain, near St. Helena, Napa Valley, California; it once was part of the former La Perla Winery, replanted c. 1970.

perlage (F.)

A slight effervescence.

Perlan (Sw.)

In the Mandement district west of Geneva City, another name for the Chasselas grape.

perlant *also* **perlé (F.)**

Slightly sparkling; literally, beady, or forming beads.

Perle (G.)

A white grape – a cross of Gewürztraminer and Müller-Thurgau; developed at the Alzey and Würzburg Institutes; grown only in the Franken region.

Perlwein (G.)

Sparkling wine, usually made by artificial carbonation; not as effervescent as true sparkling wine.

Pernand-Vergelesses AOC (F.)

A commune in the Côte de Beaune district, Burgundy; produces red and some white wines; contains 5 *Premiers Crus*, some of which are sold as Aloxe-Corton. 350 acres.

Pernod, Fernand (F.)

An estate in Gevrey-Chambertin, Côte de Nuits district, Burgundy. 17 acres, including .7 acre of Griotte-Chambertin, 2.4 acres of Gevrey-Chambertin Clos St.-Jacques, 1.2 acres of Combe aux Moines and .7 acre of Les Champeaux.

Peronospora

A genus of fungi which are harmful to vine leaves.

Perricone (I.)

A red grape grown in Scalani, Sicily.

Perrier, Joseph (F.)   1825

A Champagne producer in Châlons-sur-Marne; Cuveé de Cent Cinquantenaire NV Brut is the *cuveé de prestige*. 600,000 bottles. 50 acres.

Perrier, Laurent (F.)   1812

A Champagne producer in Tours-sur-Marne, east of Épernay; Grand Siècle NV and Ultra Brut (1981) are the *cuvées de prestige;* also makes a Coteaux Champenois. 6 million bottles. 220 acres.

Perrier, Laurent (U.S.)   1981

A winery in San José, California; produces Chardonnay wine.

Perrier-Jouët (F.)   1811

A Champagne producer in Épernay; Blason de France and Belle Époque (Fleur de Champagne) are the *cuvées de prestige*. 2.2 million bottles. 300 acres.

Perrière, La (F.)

A *Premier Cru* vineyard in Gevrey-Chambertin, Côte de Nuits district, Burgundy. 6 acres.

Perrière, La (F.)

A *Premier Cru* vineyard in Nuits-St.-Georges, Côte de Nuits district, Burgundy. 8 acres.

Perrière, La *or* Clos de la (F.)

A *Premier Cru* vineyard in Fixin, Côte d Nuits district, Burgundy. 12 acres.

Perrière, La (F.)

A vineyard in Verdigny, Sancerre distric Upper Loire region, Loire Valley.

Perrière, Clos de la (F.)

A *Premier Cru* vineyard in Vougeot, Côte d Nuits district, Burgundy. 3.5 acres.

Perrière, Domaine de la (F.)   12th cen

An old 12th century estate in Fixin, Côt de Nuits district, Burgundy. Owns Fixi Clos de la Perrière Monopole – 12.5 acre distributed by Moillard, Reine Pédauqu and Dufouleur.

Perrière-Noblet, En La (F.)

A *Premier Cru* vineyard (in part) in Nuit St.-Georges, Côte de Nuits district, Bu gundy. 5 acres.

Perrières, Les (F.)

A *Grand Cru* vineyard in Aloxe-Corton Côte de Beaune district, Burgundy, whe the name Corton precedes the vineyar name. 23 acres.

Perrières, Les (F.)

A *Premier Cru* vineyard in Beaune, Côte d Beaune disfrict, Burgundy. 8 acres.

Perrières, Les (F.)

A *Premier Cru* vineyard in Meursault, Côt de Beaune district, Burgundy; divided int several sections, which may bottle win separately or together. 42 acres total – a Perrières vineyards.

Perrières, Clos des (F.)

A *Premier Cru* vineyard in Meursault, Côt de Beaune district, Burgundy; a *monopole* Domaine Albert Grivault; considered to b the finest vineyard plot in Meursault. 2 acres.

rrières Dessous, Les (F.)

Premier Cru vineyard in Meursault, Côte
Beaune district, Burgundy. 42 acres total
all Perrières vineyards.

rrières Dessus, Les (F.)

Premier Cru vineyard in Meursault, Côte
Beaune district, Burgundy. 42 acres total
all Perrières vineyards.

rrum (P.)

white grape grown in southern Portugal.

rsan (F.)

red grape grown in the Savoie region.

rtuisots (F.)

Premier Cru vineyard in Beaune, Côte de
eaune district, Burgundy. 14 acres.

ru

country in South America. Vines have
rown there since 1566; produces wines
ear Lima, Cuzco, Artquipa and Mo-
uega, in the southern part of the country;
ie wines are similar to those of Spain. 2
iillion gallons. 35,000 acres.

senti Winery (U.S.)   **vines 1923**
                             winery 1934

winery in Templeton, San Luis Obispo
ounty, California; produces many varietal
nd dessert wines. 30,000 cases. 65 acres.

essac (F.)

commune in the Graves district of the
ordeaux region; Haut-Brion and Pape-
lément are the most well-known Châ-
eaux there.

este, Cuvée Docteur (F.)

red wine from the Hospices de Beaune,
ôte de Beaune district, Burgundy. The *cu-
ée* is composed of the following vineyards
i Corton: Chaumes et Voirosses – 2.5
cres, Clos du Roi – 1 acre and Les Grèves
.3 acre.

Petaluma (Aus.)   **1976**

A small winery near Adelaide, South Australia; produces Chardonnay, Riesling and
Cabernet wines from purchased grapes.
20,000 cases.

Petaluma Cellars (U.S.)

A second label for La Crema Viñera winery, Petaluma, Sonoma County,
California.

pétillant (F.)

Slightly sparkling.

pétillement (F.)

A slight sparkle; crackling.

Petit Barbaras, Domaine du (F.)

An estate in Bouchet, Côtes-du-Rhône district, southern Rhône region; produces red
wine made from Grenache, Cinsault,
Syrah and Carignan grapes. 70 acres.

Petit Chablis AOC (F.)

A white wine from the Chablis district,
Burgundy, the lowest classification of
Chablis wines; made from the Chardonnay
grape with some minor grapes; frequently
sold in bulk (barrels); some of the better
wine is sold in bottles. 300 acres.

Petit-Faurie-de-Souchard, Château (F.)

An estate in St.-Émilion, Bordeaux; classified in 1955 as a *Grand Cru Classé*. 3,000
cases. 20 acres.

Petit Manseng (F.)

An old, white grape grown in the Jurançon
district, Southwest region.

Petit Rouge (I.)

1. A red grape of French origin, grown in
the Valle d'Aosta region of northern Italy,
which produces:

2. A red wine made from the above grape.

Petit Verdot *also* **Verdot (F.)**

A red grape grown in the Bordeaux region;
used for blending with Cabernet and Merlot grapes.

Petit Vidure (F.)

Another name for the Cabernet Sauvignon grape.

Petit-Village, Château (F.)

An estate in Pomerol, Bordeaux. 4,000 cases. 25 acres.

Petite Arvine (I., Sw.)

A white grape grown in the Valle d'Aosta region, in Italy and in the Valais region, in Switzerland.

Petite Champagne (F.)

The second highest rated vineyards in the Cognac, or Charente region, situated south of the town of Cognac. The soil contains less limestone than the higher rated Grande Champagne vineyards.

Petite Chappelle (F.)

A *Premier Cru* vineyard in Gevrey-Chambertin, Côte de Nuits district, Burgundy; also called Champitennois. 10 acres.

Petite Dôle (Sw.)

A Dôle wine from the Valais region; made from the Pinot Noir grape only. Dôle is made from the Gamay grape or a blend of Gamay and Pinot Noir.

Petite Sirah (U.S.)

1. A red grape grown in California; it is believed to be either a relative of the Syrah grape or the Durif grape.
2. The red wine made from the Petite Sirah grape.

Petites Lolières (F.)

A *Premier Cru* vineyard in Ladoix-Serrigny, Côte de Beaune district, Burgundy; may also be sold as Aloxe-Corton. 3 acres.

Petitjean, Pierre, (F.)

An estate in Savigny-lès-Beaune, Côte de Beaune district, Burgundy. 37 acres, including 2.5 acres of Savigny Aux Serpentières, 2.5 acres of Les Lavières, 2.5 acres of Les Charnières, 2.5 acres of Aux Gravains, 1.2 acres of Hauts Jarrons, .8 acre of Beaune Avaux, .8 acre of Les Bressande .8 acre of Champimonts and 1.2 acres Corton-Renardes.

Petits-Épenots, Les *also* Petits-Épenaux, Les (F.)

A *Premier Cru* vineyard (in part) in Pommard, Côte de Beaune district, Burgund 50 acres.

Petits Godeaux (F.)

A *Premier Cru* vineyard (in part) in Savign Côte de Beaune district, Burgundy. 1 acres.

Petits Liards, Aux (F.)

A *Premier Cru* vineyard (in part) in Savign Côte de Beaune district, Burgundy. c. acres.

Petits-Monts, Les (F.)

A *Premier Cru* vineyard in Vosne-Romané Côte de Nuits district, Burgundy. 9 acres.

Petits Musigny, Les (F.)

One of 3 sections of the Les Musigny vin yard in Chambolle-Musigny, Côte de Nui district, Burgundy.

Petits-Vougeots, Les (F.)

A *Premier Cru* vineyard in Vougeot, Côte d Nuits district, Burgundy. 13 acres.

Petri Wines (U.S.)

A label for jug wines from United Vintne made in Escalon, San Joaquin Valle California.

Petronius Arbiter (died c. 66 A.D.) (Lat.)

The Roman satirist, author of the *Satyrico* in which various wines are discussed.

Pétrus, Château (F.)

A famous estate in Pomerol, Bordeaux considered to be one of the greates growths in Bordeaux. 95% Merlot, wit some Cabernet Franc. It received a gol medal at the Paris Exhibition in 1878. E panded from 2,000 to 4,000 cases and fror 17 to 28 acres.

...tures, Les (F.)

Premier Cru vineyard in Meursault, Côte ... Beaune district, Burgundy. 27 acres.

...tures, Les (F.)

Premier Cru vineyard in Volnay, Côte de ...aune district, Burgundy; red wine only. 10 acres.

...uillets, Les (F.)

Premier Cru vineyard (in part) in Savigny, ...ôte de Beaune district, Burgundy. 53 ...res.

...wsey Vale (Aus.)

... vineyard owned by the Yalumba winery, ... the Barossa Valley district, South Aus-...alia; produces Rhein Riesling wine.

...xem (P.)

... red grape, one of the approved varieties ...sed to make rosé wine.

...ymartin, Château (F.)

...n estate in Ordonnac, Médoc district, ...ordeaux; classified as a *Cru Bourgeois*; ...ow owned by Château Gloria. 8,000 ...ses. 37 acres.

...ynaud, Émile (F.)

... famous Oenologist; the former director ...f *Station Oenologique* of the University of ...ordeaux; consultant to many Châteaux of ...e Bordeaux region as well as other re-...ions all over the world.

...yrabon, Château (F.)

...n estate in St.-Sauveur, Haut-Médoc dis-...ict, Bordeaux; classified in 1978 as a *Cru ...rand Bourgeois*. 12,000 cases. 80 acres.

...ez, Château de (F.)

...n estate in St.-Estèphe, Haut-Médoc dis-...ict, Bordeaux; classified in 1932 as a *Cru ...ourgeois*. 15,000 cases. 100 acres.

...eza (Gr.)

... district near Heraklion, Crete; produces ...ed wine.

Pézerolles, Les (F.)

A *Premier Cru* vineyard in Pommard, Côte de Beaune district, Burgundy. 15 acres.

Pfarrkirche, Weingut der (G.)

An estate in Bernkastel, Mosel-Saar-Ru-wer region; owns vineyard parcels of Gra-ben, Lay, Bratenhofchen, Schlossberg and Johannisbrünnchen in Bernkastel and Graacher Himmelreich. 25 acres.

Pfeffingen, Weingut (G.)

An estate in Bad Dürkheim, Rheinpfalz re-gion; owns vineyards in Ungstein. 25 acres.

Pfersigberg (F.)

A vineyard in Eguisheim, Haut-Rhin dis-trict, Alsace region.

Pfingstberg (F.)

A vineyard in Orschwihr, Haut-Rhin dis-trict, Alsace region; produces Riesling and Gewürztraminer grapes.

Phélan-Ségur, Château (F.)

An estate in St.-Estèphe, Haut-Médoc dis-trict, Bordeaux; classified in 1978 as a *Cru Grand Bourgeois Exceptionnel*. 20,000 cases. 120 acres.

Phelps, Joseph (U.S.)   1972, 1st wine 1974

A winery in St. Helena, Napa Valley, Cali-fornia; produces Cabernet, Cabernet Franc and Merlot blends under the Insignia label, Cabernet, Syrah, Zinfandel, Gewürztra-miner, Johannisberg Riesling, Sauvignon Blanc and Chardonnay wines; second label is Le Fleuron. 50,000 cases. 240 acres.

Philippe le Bon, Cuvée (F.)

A white wine from the Hospices de Beaune, Côte de Beaune district, Bur-gundy. The *cuvée* is composed of the fol-lowing vineyards in Meursault: Les Genevrières Dessus – .5 acre and Les Ge-nevrières Dessous – 1 acre. 200 cases.

Phillipponat (F.)

A Champagne producer in Mareuil-sur-Ay, owned by Gosset (since 1980); Clos des

Gloisses is the *cuvée de prestige*. 1 million bottles. 25 acres.

phylloxera

A plant louse, *Phylloxera vastatrix,* native to the U.S., which devastated Europe's vineyards in the 1870's when accidentally brought there.

Piada, Château (F.)

An unclassified estate in Barsac, Sauternes district, Bordeaux; 2,800 cases. 30 acres.

Piani, I (I.)

A red wine from Alghero, in northwestern Sardinia; made from the Carignano grape.

Piave DOC (I.)

1. A river and district in the northeastern Veneto region, which produces:

2. Red and white varietal wines: Cabernet, Merlot, Pinot Bianco, Pinot Grigio, Pinot Nero, Tocai, Verduzzo and *Spumante*.

Pibarnon, Domaine de (F.)

An estate in Bandol, in the Provence region.

Pibran, Château (F.)

An estate in Pauillac, Haut-Médoc district, Bordeaux; classified in 1978 as a *Cru Bourgeois*. 4,000 cases. 22 acres.

Pic, Albert (F.)

A *négociant* in Chablis, Burgundy; marketed by A. Regnard et Fils.

Pic-Saint-Loup VDQS (F.)

1. A district northwest of Montpellier, in the Languedoc region, which produces:

2. Red, white and rosé wines.

Picard, Lucien (F.)

An estate in Bué, Sancerre district, Upper Loire region. 20 acres, including 5 acres of Clos du Chêne Marchand and 3 acres of Clos du Roy.

Picardan

A red grape, one of 13 grapes used to ma Châteauneuf-du-Pape wine.

Picatum, Picatus (Lat.)

An ancient Roman wine, containing pitc or resin; mentioned by Pliny.

Piccone (I.)

A red wine from Lessona, west of Gat nara, in the northern Piedmont regio made from Nebbiolo, Bonarda and Vesp lina grapes.

pichet (F.)

A pitcher.

Pichon-Longueville Baron, Château (F.)

An estate in Pauillac, Haut-Médoc distri Bordeaux; classified in 1855 as a *Deuxiè Cru;* was originally joined with Château I chon-Lalande as a single property in t 17th century. Cabernet, Merlot, and M bec grapes. 10,000 cases. 75 acres.

Pichon-Longueville, Comtesse de Laland Château (F.)

An estate in Pauillac, Haut-Médoc distri Bordeaux; classified in 1855 as a *Deuxier Cru;* was originally joined with Château I chon-Baron as a single property in the 17 century. Cabernet Sauvignon, Caberm Franc, Merlot and Petit Verdot grapes. 1 acres. 18,000 cases.

Pick, Château du (F.)

An unclassified estate in Preignac, Sa ternes district, Bordeaux. 6,000 cases. acres.

Picòl Ross (I.)

A dry version of Lambrusco wine fro Sant'Illario d'Enza, southeast of Reggio, the central Emilia-Romagna region.

Picolit (I.)

1. A rare, white grape grown in northeas ern Italy, especially in the Friuli-Venez Giulia region.

A sweet, white wine made from the Pi-olit grape; may contain up to 10% of other rapes; minimum of 15% alcohol; famous the 18th and 19th centuries.

icoutener (I.)

Donnaz and Carema, Piedmont region, nother name for the Nebbiolo grape. Also alled Pugnet.

icpoul *also* Picpoule *and* Picquepoul (F.)

. A white grape, grown in the Languedoc nd Rhône regions, one of 13 used to make háteauneuf-du-Pape wine.

. In Armagnac and the Midi, another ame for the Folle Blanche grape; called villo in Spain.

icpoul de Pinet VDQS (F.)

. A small district around Pinet, northeast f Béziers, in the Languedoc region of outhern France, which produces:

. A light, dry white wine made from Pic-oul, Clairette and Terret Blanc grapes.

icpoule Noir (F.)

A red grape.

iece (F.)

A barrel size used in Burgundy equal to 28 liters or 24 cases; the same as a *barrique* sed in Bordeaux.

ièce-sous-le-Bois, La (F.)

A *Premier Cru* vineyard in Blagny (but sold s Meursault), Côte de Beaune district, urgundy. 28 acres.

ied-d'Aloup (F.)

A *Premier Cru* vineyard in Fyé, Chablis dis-rict, Burgundy; usually included as part of he Montée de Tonnerre vineyard.

ied-Rouge (F.)

A local name for the Cot grape.

ied-Tendre (F.)

n the Charente region, another name for he Colombard grape. Also called Bon lanc and Blanquette.

Piede di Palumbo (I.)

A red grape grown in the Campania re-gion; used to make Gragnano wine.

Piedirosso (I.)

A red grape grown in the Campania re-gion; used to make Ischia wine. Also called Per'e Palummo and in the Vesuvio district, Palombina.

Piedmont *also* Piemonte (I.)

A famous region in northwestern Italy; contains 36 DOC zones, or districts; fa-mous for Barolo, Barbaresco, Gattinara, Spanna and Asti Spumanti wines. Grapes grown include Nebbiolo (called Spanna), various Muscats, Barbera, Bonarda, Freisa, Brachetto, Cortese, Dolcetto, Erbaluce and Grignolino. 135 million gallons.

Piedmont Vineyard (U.S.)   1978

A winery in Middleburg, Virginia; grows Seyval Blanc, Chardonnay and Sémillon grapes. 25 acres.

Pierce (U.S.)

An American red grape of the *Vitis labrusca* species.

Pierce's disease (U.S.)

In California, a disease caused by the mi-croorganism rickettsia, in which the leaves turn yellow, the edges burn, dwarfed shoots appear, the fruit colors prematurely and wilts and the vines die in a few years.

Pieropan (I.)

An estate in Soave, in the western Veneto region; produces Soave and Riesling Italico wines.

Pierre Virely, Cuvée (F.)

A red wine from the Hospices de Beaune, Côte de Beaune district, Burgundy. The *cu-vée* is composed of the following vineyard in Beaune: Les Cent Vignes; not made sep-arately since 1968.

Pierrelle, La (F.)

A vineyard section of Hermitage, northern Rhône region; produces red wine.

313

Pierres, Les (F.)

A *Premier Cru* vineyard in Rully, Côte Chalonnaise district, Burgundy.

Pierreux, Château de (F.)

An estate in Odénas (Brouilly), Beaujolais district, Burgundy. 175 acres.

Piesport (G.)

A village in the Mosel-Saar-Ruwer region, *Bereich* Bernkastel (Mittel Mosel), Grosslage Michelsberg. The vineyards are: Goldtröpfchen, Domherr, Falkenberg, Gärtchen, Günterslay, Schubertslay and Treppchen. 1,250 acres.

Pigato (I.)

1. A white grape grown in the Liguria region.
2. A white wine from Albenga, in the Liguria region; made from the Pigato grape.

pigeage (F.)

In Burgundy, the old practice of mixing the "cap" (*chapeau*) with the must by utilizing human feet to break up the cap.

Pigna, Villa (I.)

A large estate in Offida, the Marches region; produces Falerio dei Colli Ascolani, Rossote in Greve in Chianti, Tuscany region; produces Chianti Classico wine.

Pignoletto *also* **Pignolino** *also* **Pignulein (I.)**

A white grape grown in the Colli Bolognesi district, in the Emilia-Romagna region.

Pile e Lamole (I.)

An estate in Greve in Chianti, Tuscany region; produces Chianti Classico wine.

Pillot (F.)

A *Premier Cru* vineyard in Rully, Côte Chalonnaise district, Burgundy.

Pillot, Domaine Alphonse (F.)

An estate in Chassagne-Montrachet, Côte de Beaune district, Burgundy. 16 acres, including 2.5 acres of Chassagne-Montrachet

Mórgeot (red and white) and some Le Chenevottes.

Pillot, Paul (F.)

An estate in Chassagne-Montrachet, Côte de Beaune district, Burgundy. 25 acres, including 1.2 acres of Chassagne-Montrachet La Romanée, .4 acre of Grandes Ruchotte and 5 acres of Clos St. Jean.

Pilongo (P.)

A red grape grown in the Dão region. Also called Alvarelhão.

pinard (F.)

Army slang for ration wine issued to soldiers; a slang word for cheap, red wine.

Pindar Vineyards (U.S.)   grapes 198
                                first wine 198

A winery in Peconic, North Fork district Long Island, New York; produces Cabernet, Chardonnay, Cayuga White, Gewürztraminer, Riesling, Merlot, Pinot Noir Muscat Canelli and Seyval Blanc wines. 11 acres. 20,000 cases.

Pindefleurs, Château (F.)

An estate in St.-Émilion, Bordeaux; classified in 1955 as a *Grand Cru*. 3,000 cases. 2 acres.

Pine Ridge Winery (U.S.)   197

A winery in Napa City, Napa Valley, California; produces Cabernet, Chardonnay and Chenin Blanc wines from grape grown in various districts in Napa Valley 15,000 cases. 120 acres.

Pineau des Charentes (F.)

A sweet, white or rosé, fortified wine from the Cognac region; usually served as a apéritif. 16-22% alcohol.

Pineau d'Aunis (F.)

A red grape grown in the Anjou region used to make rosé wine; also called Chenin Noir.

Pineau de la Loire (F.)

1. In the Loire Valley, and sometimes in California, another name for the Chenin Blanc grape.
2. A white wine made from the Chenin Blanc grape.

Pineau Menu (F.)

A white grape grown in the Touraine region, Loire Valley; also called Arbois and Menu Pineau.

Pineau de Saumur (F.)

Another name for the Groslot (or Grolleau) grape grown in the Anjou region and used to make rosé wines.

Pinela (Y.)

A white grape grown in Slovenia.

Pinenc (F.)

A grape grown in Madiran, in the Southwest region; also called Couhabort, Fer and Fer Servadou.

Pinget, Gérard (Sw.)

A small estate in Rivaz, Vaud region; produces Dézaley and other wines. 4 acres.

Pinnacles Vineyard (U.S.)

A large vineyard in Slainos Valley, Monterey County, California; owned by Paul Masson Winery; first planted in 1962. 1,000 acres.

Pinon, Jean-Baptiste (F.)

An estate in Lhomme, Jasnières district, Touraine region; produces Jasnières and other wines.

Pinot Beurot (F.)

In Burgundy, another name for the white Pinot Gris grape.

Pinot Bianco (I.)

A dry, white wine from the Piedmont region; made from the Pinot Blanc grape; also the name in Italy for the Pinot Blanc grape.

Pinot Blanc (F.)

A white grape grown in Burgundy and California; not actually in the Pinot family, according to some experts; related to the Pinot Blanc, according to other experts.

Pinot Chardonnay-Mâcon AOC (F.)

A designation for white wine from the Mâcon district, in Burgundy; made from the Pinot Blanc or the Chardonnay grape.

Pinot Grigio (I.)

A white grape, the same as the Pinot Gris of France; also the white wine made from the Pinot Grigio grape.

Pinot Gris (F.)

A white grape (but with a greyish-rose tint) of the Pinot family. Also called Pinot Grigio, Pinot Beurot, Fauret, Ruländer, Tokay (in Alsace), Malvoisie and Auxerrois Gris.

Pinot Meunier (F.)

A red grape used in making Champagne. *Meunier* means "miller" in French and the grape is so named because the underside of the leaves is powdery white, like flour.

Pinot Nero (I.)

The Pinot Nero grape.

Pinot Noir (F.)

The famous red grape used to make dry, red wine and white sparkling wines; grown in Burgundy, Champagne, Italy, California, etc. Also called Noirien, Savagnin Noir and other names in France, Spätburgunder and Blauer Burgunder in Germany, Rotclevner in Switzerland and Pinot Nero in Italy. Also Blauburgunder, Blauklevner and Schwarzeklevner.

In Burgundy, various clones have developed and are distinguished as follows: Pinot fin, classique or tourdo; Pinot droit; Pinot Liebalt; there are more than 150 other sub-varieties known throughout France.

Pinot St. George (U.S.)

1. A red grape (not a Pinot, but possibly, the Negrette) grown in California, fre-

quently used for root-stock and as a varietal wine.

2. A red wine from California made from the Pinot St. George grape.

Pinotage (S. Af.)

1. A red grape – a cross of Pinot Noir and Cinsault (or Hermitage); developed at the University of Stellenbosch by Professor Peroldt in 1922; not planted until 1952.

2. A red wine from South Africa, made from the Pinotage grape.

Pinson, Louis (F.)

An estate in the Chablis district, Burgundy. 10 acres, including 2.5 acres of Les Clos and some Monts de Milieu, Forêts and Montmains.

pip

The seed of a grape.

pipe (E.)

A large cask with tapered ends varying in size and used mostly for shipping and aging Port wine. In Madeira = 418 liters, Marsala = 423 liters, Port = 523 liters.

Piper-Heidsieck (F.)　　　　　　1785

A Champagne producer in Reims. The *cuvée de prestige* is Brut Sauvage (with the smallest *dosage*), made since 1980 and Florens-Louis; owns no vineyards; 2nd label is Becker. 5 million bottles.

Piper-Sonoma (U.S.)　　1980, 1st wine 1982

A winery in Windsor, Sonoma County, California; jointly run by Sonoma Vineyards and Piper-Heidsieck, of France; produces several Champagnes. 100,000 cases.

Pipers Brook (Aus.)　　　　　　1974

A small winery in Launceston, Tasmania; produces Cabernet, Pinot Noir, Merlot, Cabernet Franc, Chardonnay, Rhine Riesling and Gewürztraminer wines. 25 acres. 5,000 cases.

pipette (F.)

A tube for removing wine from a large cask.

piqué (F.)

Vinegary, a term used to describe a spoiled wine.

piquette (F.)

1. Wine made by adding water to the *marc* (pressed grape skins), which results in a wine that is low in alcohol, tart and thin.

2. Any poor, thin, or mediocre wine.

piqûre (F.)

Acescence or acetification; excessive acetic acid in wine.

Piros Cirfandli (H.)

A white grape.

Pissevielle, Cuvée (F.)

The best-known vineyard of the Hospices de Beaujeu, in Brouilly, Beaujolais district, Burgundy.

pitching

The process of adding yeast to grape juice in order to start fermentation.

Piteşti (R.)

An important city in the Argeş district, in the Wallachia region of central Romania.

pithoi (Gr.)

Ancient Greek fermenting jars.

Pitsilia (Cyp.)

A district near Mt. Olympus; produces white wines from the Xynesteri grape.

Pitures Dessus (F.)

A *Premier Cru* vineyard in Volnay, Côte de Beaune district, Burgundy. 9 acres.

Pizay, Château de (F.)

An estate in Villié-Morgon, Beaujolais district, Burgundy.

Plan Dei (F.)

An estate in Gravaillan, Côtes du Rhône district, Rhône region; produces wine made from 65% Grenache, 25% Mourvèdre and 10% Counoise grapes; second label wine is La Vignonnerie. 35 acres.

Plantagenet Wines (Aus.)　　　　　1968

An estate in the Mount Barker district, Western Australia; produces award-winning Rhine Riesling wine; also Cabernet, Shiraz, Chardonnay and Chenin Blanc wines. 5,000 cases. 85 acres.

Plantes, Les (F.)

A *Premier Cru* vineyard in Chambolle-Musigny, Côte de Nuits district, Burgundy. 5 acres.

Plantes de Maranges (F.)

A *Premier Cru* vineyard in Cheilly-les-Maranges, Côte de Beaune district, Burgundy.

Plantet

A red hybrid grape; also called Seibel 5455.

Plantey, Château (F.)

An unclassified estate in Pauillac, Haut-Médoc district, Bordeaux. 40 acres.

Plantey de la Croix (F.)

An estate in St. Seurin-de-Cadourne, Haut-Médoc district, Bordeaux; classified in 1978 as a *Cru Bourgeois*.

Plantigone (F.)

A *Premier Cru* vineyard in Gevrey-Chambertin, Côte de Nuits district, Burgundy. Also called Issarts. 4.5 acres.

plastering

The process of adding gypsum or calcium sulfate (plaster of Paris) to low-acid wines in order to raise their acid levels.

Platière, La (F.)

A *Premier Cru* vineyard (in part) in Pommard, Côte de Beaune district, Burgundy. 14 acres.

Platres (Cyp.)

A village in the foothills of Mt. Olympus, in the Afames district; produces red wines.

Plavac (Y.)

1. A red grape grown in Dalmatia.
2. A red wine from Dalmatia; made from the Plavac grape.

Plavina (Y.)

A red grape grown in the province of Dalmatia.

Pleasant Valley Winery (U.S.)　　　1860

A winery near Hammondsport, on Lake Keuka, in the Finger Lakes region, New York, one of the oldest in the state; introduced hybrids to the Finger Lakes region in 1964; produces Great Western Champagne; now owned by the Taylor Winery.

Plemenka (Y.)

A white grape grown in Serbia.

Pletchistik (U.S.S.R.)

A white grape grown in the Rostov district, Russia S.S.R.

Plince, Château (F.)

An estate in Pomerol, Bordeaux. 2,000 cases. 20 acres.

Pliny the Elder (Lat.)

An ancient Roman author (A.D. 23-79); he wrote *Naturalis Historia* (Bk. XIV) in which he discusses vine-growing and wines.

Ploussard *also* Poulsard (F.)

A red grape grown in the Arbois district of the Jura region.

Plovdina (Y.)

A red grape grown in Serbia.

Plozner (I.)

An estate in Spilimbergo, Friuli-Venezia Giulia region; produces Chardonnay, Grave, Pinot Nero and Traminer wines.

podere (I.)

A farm, or estate.

Poggio alle Mure (I.)

An estate in Montalcino, Tuscany region; produces Brunello, Chianti Colli Senesi, Moscadello and Vin Santo wines. 125 acres.

Poggio Reale Spalletti Valdisieve (I.)   1912

An estate in Rufina, Tuscany region; produces Chianti Poggio Reale wines. 27,000 cases. 125 acres.

Poggione, Tenuta Il (I.)   1890

An estate in Montalcino, Tuscany region; produces Brunello, Moscadelletto, Rosso and Vin Santo wines. 10,000 cases. 135 acres.

Pointe, Château La (F.)

An estate in Pomerol, Bordeaux. 7,000 cases. 50 acres.

point de fraîcheur (F.)

In Alsace, a term used for the faint sparkle found in very young wines.

Pointes d'Angles, Les (F.)

A *Premier Cru* vineyard in Volnay, Côte de Beaune district, Burgundy. 4 acres.

poios (P.)

Small, terraced plots of vineyard land on Madeira Island.

Poisot, Henri (F.)

An estate in Aloxe-Corton, Côte de Beaune district, Burgundy. 16 acres, including 2.5 acres of Corton-Charlemagne, 2.5 acres of Bressandes, 2.5 acres of Languettes; managed by Michel Voarick.

Poissenot (F.)

A *Premier Cru* vineyard in Gevrey-Chambertin, Côte de Nuits district, Burgundy. 5.5 acres.

Pojer & Sandri (I.)   1975

An estate in Faedo, Trentino-Alto Adige region; produces Chardonnay, Müller-Thurgau, Nosiola, Pinot Nero, Schiava and Vin de Molini wines. 15 acres.

Pokal (G.)

A goblet; a large wine glass with a cone-shaped stem; also called Römer.

Pol Roger (F.)   1849

A Champagne producer in Épernay. The *cuvée de prestige* is Blanc de Blancs (since 1959). 1.3 million bottles. 150 acres.

Polcevera (I.)

A delicate, white wine from Genoa, in the central Liguria region.

Polgazão (P.)

A white grape grown in northwestern Portugal.

Pollino DOC (I.)

A red wine from the Pollino hills near Castrovillari, in the northwestern Calabria region; made from Gaglioppo, Greco Nero and some Malvasia Bianco, Mantonico Bianco and Guarnaccia Bianco grapes.

Pollio (Lat.)

An ancient wine from Sicily, praised by the Greek poet Hesiod (8th cent. B.C.) and by Pliny.

polsuho (Y.)

Medium dry.

Polychrosis viteana

One of several species of moths whose larvae feed on grape bunches.

pomace

Crushed grape skins, etc. which are left after the juice has been extracted; the same as *marc*, in French.

Pombal, Marquês de (P.)

The founder of the Oporto Wine Company; in 1756 he improved conditions for making

Port requiring the use of better brandy and eliminating the addition of elderberry juice and other foreign elements to the wine.

Pomerol AOC (F.)

A small commune and district in Bordeaux, northeast of Libourne, on the right bank of the Dordogne River, next to St.-Émilion; produces red wines mostly from Merlot grapes, with some Cabernet Franc, Cabernet Sauvignon and Malbec grapes. No official classification of the numerous estates has ever been made; Château Pétrus is the most famous. 1,750 acres.

Pomije, Château (U.S.)

A vineyard and projected winery in New Alsace, Indiana; grows *vinifera* grapes. 20 acres.

Pomino Bianco (I.)

A white wine from the Chianti Rufina district, in the Tuscany region; made from Pinot Bianco, Pinot Grigio, Chardonnay and Sauvignon grapes.

Pommard AOC (F.)

A commune in the Côte de Beaune district, Burgundy. It has 26 *Premier Cru* vineyards; Épenots and Rugiens are the most famous. 265,000 gallons. 750 acres.

Pommard, Château de (F.)　　　　1726

An estate in Pommard (from 1726), Côte de Beaune district, Burgundy; the largest, single-owned Clos in Burgundy. 50 acres.

Pommeraie Vineyards (U.S.)　　　1979

A small winery in Sebastopol, Sonoma County, California; produces Cabernet and Chardonnay wines from purchased grapes. 2,000 cases.

Pommery & Greno (F.)　　　　　1836

A Champagne producer in Reims. The *cuvées de prestige* are Avize Blanc de Blancs and Prestige de Pommery (since 1983). 4 million bottles. 740 acres.

Poniatowski, Prince (F.)

An estate in Vouvray, Touraine region. 50 acres, including 44 acres of Clos Baudoin and some Aigle Blanc. 7,000 cases.

Ponnelle, Pierre, (F.)　　　　　1875

An estate and merchant in Beaune, Côte de Beaune district, Burgundy. 14 acres, including some Beaune Clos du Roi, Vougeot Domaine du Prieuré, Clos de Vougeot, Chambolle-Musigny, Charmes-Chambertin, Bonnes Mares and Musigny.

Ponsot, Domaine (F.)

An estate in Morey-St.-Denis, Côte de Nuits district, Burgundy. 20 acres, including 9 acres of Clos de la Roche, 4 acres of Morey-St.-Denis Monts-Luisants *Blanc*, .8 acre of Latricières-Chambertin, some Gevrey-Chambertin and Chambolle-Musigny.

Pont, Michel (F.)

An estate in Volnay, Côte de Beaune district, Burgundy. 62 acres, including 5 acres of Auxey-Duresses Le Val, 2.5 acres of Les Duresses, 4 acres of Monthélie Les Champs Fulliot, 2.5 acres of Sous Roches, 1.2 acres of Meursault Les Chevalières, 1.2 acres of Volnay Caillerets, 2.5 acres of Volnay Clos des Chênes, 2.5 acres of Pommard Les Chanlins Bas, 4 acres of Bourgogne Clos du Chapitre Monopole, 2.5 acres of Le Clos du Roy and 4 acres of Le Chapitre (these last three in Chenôve).

Pontet, Château (F.)

An estate in Blaignan, Médoc district, Bordeaux; classified in 1978 as a *Cru Bourgeois*. 5,000 cases. 20 acres.

Pontet-Canet, Château (F.)

An estate in Pauillac, Haut-Médoc district, Bordeaux; classified in 1855 as a *Cinquième Cru;* château-bottled only since 1972. 40,000 cases. 180 acres.

Pontoise-Cabarras, Château (F.)

An estate in St.-Seurin-de-Cadourne, Haut-Médoc district, Bordeaux; classified in 1978 as a *Cru Grand Bourgeois*. 13,000 cases. 45 acres.

Ponzi Vineyards (U.S.)   1974, grapes 1970

A winery in Beaverton, Willamette Valley, northwestern Oregon; produces Chardonnay, Johannisberg Riesling, Pinot Gris and Pinot Noir wines from their own and purchased grapes. 10 acres. 4,000 cases.

pop wine (U.S.)

A fruit-flavored wine from California, first made in the 1950's and containing up to 7 lbs. of pressure per square inch of carbonation, so as to produce a "pop" sound when opened; made mostly from Thompson Seedless grapes and fruit flavors.

Pope Valley (U.S.)

A district northeast of St. Helena, in Napa Valley, California.

Pope Valley Winery (U.S.)   1909, 1972

A winery in the Pope Valley district, northeast of St. Helena, Napa Valley, California; produces Cabernet, Zinfandel, Petite Sirah, Chardonnay, Chenin Blanc, Johannisberg Riesling and Sauvignon Blanc wines from purchased grapes. 12,000 cases.

Poplar Ridge Vineyards (U.S.)   1981

A winery in Lodi, on the eastern shore of Lake Seneca, in the Finger Lakes region, New York; produces wines made from hybrid grapes. 20 acres.

Pornassio Ormeasco (I.)

A red wine from Pornassio, in the western Liguria region, made from Dolcetto grapes.

Porrets, Les also Porets (F.)

A *Premier Cru* vineyard in Nuits-St.-Georges, Côtes de Nuits district, Burgundy. 17.5 acres.

porrón (Sp.)

A round-bellied glass or ceramic drinking vessel with a narrow spout, for pouring a thin stream of wine that one can drink without one's mouth touching the spout.

Port (P.)

1. A sweet red wine from the Upper Douro region, in northeastern Portugal, fortified by Portuguese grape brandy and shipped only from Oporto; made from a blend of several of over 40 red and white grape varieties, including Bastardo, Mourisco, Rufete, Sousão, Tinto Cão and Tinta Francisca grapes. Some white port is made from Verdelho, Malvasia, Rabigato and other grapes. Contains up to 20% alcohol. 13 million gallons. 62,500 acres.

2. A sweet, red wine from other countries, made in a similar style from the same grape varieties or from other grapes, such as Cabernet and Zinfandel.

Port Wine Shippers Association (E.)

An organization of 42 shippers of Port; includes all of the well-known firms such as Calem, Cockburn, Croft, Dow, Graham, Quinta do Noval, Sandeman, Taylor and Warre.

Portland (U.S.)

An American white hybrid grape.

Porto Carras, Domaine de (Gr.)

A large company in Sithonia, Khalkidhiki; produces many wines from local and French grapes. 100,000 cases. 4,000 acres.

Portugal

A country in southwestern Europe, famous for Port, Vinho Verde, Dão, Colares and Moscatel de Setúbal wines. 290 million gallons table wines, 13 million gallons fortified wines, 1.3 million gallons Madeira. 900,000 acres (7,000 acres Madeira).

Portugieser (G.)

A red grape grown in the Ahr region; not known in Portugal, regardless of the name, but came to Germany from Austria; big, densely berried dark-blue grapes, very prolific, early ripening; it is used to make inexpensive German red wine.

Portulano (I.)

A red wine from Alezio, in the southern Apulia region; made from Negroamaro and Malvasia Nero grapes.

Poruzot, Le *also* **Porusot (F.)**

A *Premier Cru* vineyard (in part) in Meursault, Côte de Beaune district, Burgundy. 10 acres.

Poruzot Dessus, Le *also* **Porusot Dessus (F.)**

A *Premier Cru* vineyard in Meursault, Côte de Beaune district, Burgundy. 17 acres.

Pošip (Y.)

1. A white grape grown on the island of Korčula, off the coast of Dalmatia.

2. A white wine from Korčula made from the Pošip grape.

Possum Trot Farm (U.S.)   1967

A winery northeast of Bloomington, Indiana; grows hybrid grapes. 30 acres.

Post Winery (U.S.)   1880

A large, old winery in Altus, northwestern Arkansas; produces blended, sparkling and varietal wines made from muscadine, *labrusca*, and hybrid grapes. 185 acres.

Postup (Y.)

A semi-sweet, red wine from the province of Dalmatia; made from the Plavač grape; similar to Dingač wine.

pot (F.)

A small bottle equal to about a half liter (17 oz.) or 2/3 of a fifth; frequently used in Beaujolais.

Potensac, Château (F.)

An estate in Potensac, Médoc district, Bordeaux; classified in 1978 as a *Cru Grand Bourgeois*. 30,000 cases. 115 acres.

Pothier-Rieusset, Domaine V. (F.)

An estate in Pommard, Côte de Beaune district, Burgundy. 20 acres, including 2 acres of Pommard Les Rugiens, .5 acre of Les Épenots, 2.5 acres of Clos de Verger and 1.2 acres of Beaune Les Boucherottes.

Potinet-Ampeau (F.)

An estate in Monthélie, Côte de Beaune district, Burgundy. 28 acres, including 2 acres of Volnay Clos des Chênes, 5 acres of Les Santenots, 1.2 acres of Pommard Premier Cru, .8 acre of Meursault Les Perrières, 1.2 acres of Les Charmes and some Monthélie.

Potter Valley (U.S.)

1. A district in Mendocino County, California; grapes grown here produce Johannisberg Riesling wines for Château St. Jean, Fetzer and Felton-Empire wineries.

2. The second label of Arroyo Sonoma Winery, Sonoma County; produces Chardonnay and other white wines.

pottle (E.)

An old English wine measure, equal to a half-gallon.

Pouget, Château (F.)

An estate in Cantenac-Margaux, Haut-Médoc district, Bordeaux; classified in 1855 as a *Quatrième Cru*. 2,500 cases. 30 acres.

Pougets, Les (F.)

A *Grand Cru* vineyard (in part) in Aloxe-Corton, Côte de Beaune district, when Corton precedes the name of the vineyard. The other part of the vineyard is *Premier Cru*. 25 acres.

Pouilly-Fuissé AOC (F.)

A white wine from the villages of Solutré-Pouilly, Pouilly, Fuissé, Chaintré and Vergisson, in the Mâconnais district, southern Burgundy; made from the Chardonnay grape; considered the best white wine of the district.

Pouilly-Fumé AOC *also* **Blanc Fumé de Pouilly AOC (F.)**

A dry, white wine from Pouilly-sur-Loire, in the Upper Loire region, Loire Valley; made from the Sauvignon Blanc grape.

Pouilly-Loché AOC (F.)

A dry, white wine from Loché, in the Mâconnais district, southern Burgundy; made from the Chardonnay grape, similar to Pouilly-Fuissé.

Pouilly-sur-Loire AOC (F.)

A dry, white wine from the same area as Pouilly-Fumé, in the Upper Loire region, but made from the Chasselas grape; considered inferior to Pouilly-Fumé.

Pouilly-Vinzelles AOC (F.)

A dry, white wine from Vinzelles, in the Mâconnais district, southern Burgundy; made from the Chardonnay grape.

Poujeaux, Château *also* Poujeaux-Theil (F.)

An estate in Moulis, Haut-Médoc district, Bordeaux; classified in 1932 and 1978 as a *Cru Grand Bourgeois Exceptionnel*. In 1544 it was known as La Salle de Poujeaux. 10,500 cases. 100 acres.

Poulet Père et Fils (F.)   1747

A large company in Beaune, Côte de Beaune district, Burgundy.

Poulette, Domaine de la (F.)

An old estate in Corgoloin, Côte de Nuits district, Burgundy. 42 acres, including .8 acre of Corton Renardes, 1.2 acres of Vosne-Romanée Les Suchots, 2.5 acres of Nuits-St.-Georges Les St.-Georges, 5 acres of Les Vaucrains, 2.5 acres of Les Poulettes and 5 acres of Côte de Nuits-Villages Les Langres.

Poulettes, Les (F.)

A *Premier Cru* vineyard in Nuits-St.-Georges, Côte de Nuits district, Burgundy. 5 acres.

Poulettes, Clos de (F.)

An estate in Juliénas, Beaujolais district, Burgundy.

Poulleau-Muet, G. (F.)

An estate in Gevrey-Chambertin, Côte de Nuits, Burgundy. 5 acres, including 1.2 acres of Gevrey-Chambertin and some Côte de Nuits-Villages.

Poulsard *also* Ploussard (F.)

A local red grape grown in the Arbois district of the Jura region.

pourridié (F.)

See **armillaria root-rot.**

pourriture grise (F.)

A fungus disease; the same as *Botrytis cinerea,* but undesirable when it affects unripe grapes and stalks. Also called grey rot.

pourriture noble (F.)

French for "noble rot," applied to the fungus *Botrytis cinerea* when it affects the right grapes at the right time; a fungus which attacks mostly white grapes by puncturing the skin and thus allowing water to evaporate, resulting in a rich, concentrated juice with a unique flavor.

Pousse d'Or *also* Bousse d'Or (F.)

Formerly, an alternate spelling of Bousse d'Or, a *Premier Cru* vineyard in Volnay, Côte de Beaune district, Burgundy. 5 acres. The name is now only allowed to be used for the *domaine,* or estate.

Pousse d'Or, Domaine de la (F.)

An estate in Volnay, Côte de Beaune district, Burgundy. 32 acres, including Volnay Bousse d'Or Monopole – 5.8 acres, Cailleret Dessous – 6 acres, Cailleret Dessus Clos des 60 Ouvrées Monopole – 6.5 acres, Clos d'Audignac Monopole – 2 acres, Pommard La Jarollières – 3.2 acres, Santenay Le Clos de Tavannes – 5 acres and Les Gravières – 5 acres.

Poutures, Les (F.)

A *Premier Cru* vineyard in Pommard, Côte de Beaune district, Burgundy. 11 acres.

Poveda Luz, Bodegas Salvador (Sp.)

An estate in Monóvar, Alicante region.

Poverella (Br.)

A white grape grown in Brazil.

owdery mildew

rue mildew. See **oïdium**.

oyen, Cuvée Claude (F.)

red wine from the Hospices de Nuits, in
Nuits-St.-Georges, Côte de Nuits district,
Burgundy.

radelle, Domaine de la (F.)

An estate in Chanos-Curson, Crozes-Hermitage district, Rhône region; owns
Crozes-Hermitage, 22 acres of Syrah
grapes and 7 acres of Marsanne; bottling
since 1978.

ramaggiore DOC (I.)

A village and district in the northeastern
Veneto region; produces red varietal wines
made from Merlot and Cabernet grapes,
each designated on the label.

ramnium *also* Pramnian (Gr.)

A famous ancient wine of Greece, mentioned by Homer, Dioscorides, Pliny, Ath-
naeus and Aristophanes.

réau (F.)

A *Premier Cru* vineyard in Rully, Côte Chalonnaise district, Burgundy.

recipitation

In red and white wines, the presence of
harmless crystals of bitartrate of potas-
sium (cream of tartar).

reiss-Henry (F.)   1535

An estate and merchant in Mittelwihr (or
now in Eguisheim), Haut-Rhin district, Alsace region. 100 acres, including 10 acres of
the Mandelberg vineyard (Riesling and
Gewürztraminer).

reiss-Zimmer, Jean (F.)

An estate in Riquewihr, Haut-Rhin district, Alsace region. 30 acres in Riquewihr,
including some of the Schoenenberg
vineyard.

Prémeaux (F.)

A village just south of Nuits-St.-Georges,
in the Côte de Nuits district, Burgundy;
the wines are always sold as Nuits-St.-
Georges; Prémeaux has ten *Premier Cru*
vineyards.

Premier Cru (F.)

1. In Bordeaux, certain classified Growths
or Estates officially ranked as First Growth;
they include: Châteaux Lafite, Latour,
Mouton-Rothschild (only since 1973, however), Margaux and Haut-Brion of the 1855
classification of Haut-Médoc wines, 12 estates of the Sauternes district, also classified in 1855, estates from St.-Émilion,
classified in 1955, including Châteaux Ausone and Cheval Blanc.

2. In Burgundy, (Côte d'Or, Chablis and
Côte Chalonnaise districts) a First Growth
vineyard and the wine from it, ranked just
below the *Grand Cru* (Great Growth).

3. In Champagne, a village and its vineyard rated between 90-99%, the second
highest rating, based on the highest price
(100%) paid for grapes from the very best
vineyards.

première taille (F.)

In Champagne, the second pressing of
wine, since the first pressing, giving the
best wine, is called *vin de cuvée*.

Premières Côtes de Blaye AOC (F.)

1. A district around Blaye, on the right
bank of the Gironde River, in the Bordeaux
region, covering the same area as Blaye (or
Blayais) AOC and Côtes de Blaye AOC,
which produces:

2. Mostly red (85%) and some white wines,
the red made from the two Cabernet
grapes, Malbec and Merlot grapes, and the
white (dry and sweet) from Sémillon and
Sauvignon grapes; considered the best
wines of the district.

Premières Côtes de Bordeaux AOC (F.)

1. A long, narrow district along the east
bank of the Garonne River, to the east and
south of the city of Bordeaux, in the Bordeaux region, which produces:

2. Red and white wines, the white made sweet and dry, made from the usual Bordeaux grape varieties.

prensa (Sp.)

A wine press.

Presque Isle Wine Cellars (U.S.)   1969

A winery in Moorheadville, near North East, Pennsylvania; produces Aligoté, Chardonnay, Gamay Beaujolais, Cabernet and hybrid wines. 20 acres.

Pressac (F.)

In St.-Émilion, the name for the Malbec grape.

Preston Vineyards (U.S.)   1975

A small winery in Healdsburg, Dry Creek Valley, northern Sonoma County, California; produces Cabernet, Zinfandel, Sauvignon Blanc and Chenin Blanc wines. 6,000 cases. 80 acres.

Preston Wine Cellars (U.S.)   1976

A winery in Pasco, Yakima Valley, Washington; produces Cabernet, Merlot, Chardonnay, Johannisberg Riesling, Gewürztraminer and Chenin Blanc wines. 60,000 cases. 180 acres.

Preto Mortágua (P.)

A red grape grown in the Dão region.

Preuses, Les (F.)

A *Grand Cru* vineyard in Chablis, Chablis district, Burgundy.

pricked wine

Acetic, vinegary wine.

Prieto Picudo (Sp.)

A red grape grown in the León district of northern Spain.

Prieur, Clos (F.)

A *Premier Cru* vineyard (in part) in Gevrey-Chambertin, Côte de Nuits district, Burgundy. 5 acres.

Prieur, Domaine Jacques (F.)

An estate in Meursault, Côte de Beaune district, Burgundy. 35 acres, including 2. acres of Chambertin, 2.5 acres of Musigny 3.2 acres of Clos de Vougeot, .8 acre of Vo nay Champans, Beaune Aux Cras Clos d la Féguine Monopole – 5 acres, Volnay Clo des Santenots Monopole – 2.5 acres, 2 acre of Volnay Les Santenots, Meursault Clos d Mazeray Monopole – 7.5 acres (red an white), .8 acre of Perrières, 4 acres of Pu ligny-Montrachet Les Combettes, 1.7 acre of Montrachet and .5 acre of Chevalie Montrachet; controlled by J. Calvet & C (Beaune) 1930-1975.

Prieur, G. (F.)   180

An estate in Santenay, Côte de Beaune di trict, Burgundy. 33 acres, including .3 acr of Bâtard-Montrachet, 1.2 acres of San tenay La Comme, 12 acres of La Maladière 2.5 acres of Meursault Les Charmes, acres of Chassagne-Montrachet Morgeo (red), .8 acre of Volnay Les Santenots an .5 acre of Pommard La Platière.

Prieuré, Château Le (F.)

An estate in St.-Émilion, Bordeaux; classi fied in 1955 as a *Grand Cru Classé*. 2,00 cases. 11 acres.

Prieuré, Domaine de (F.)

An estate in Rully, Côte Chalonnaise dis trict, Burgundy. 18 acres in Rully and Mercurey.

Prieuré-Lichine, Château (F.)

An estate in Cantenac-Margaux, Haut-Mé doc district, Bordeaux; classified in 1855 a a *Quatrième Cru;* was once the Priory of the Benedictine Monks of Cantenac; known a Château Cantenac-Prieuré until 1953 26,000 cases. 140 acres.

Prieuré de Montézargues (F.)

An estate in Tavel, southern Rhône region

Primaticcio (I.)

A red *vino novello* (new wine) from Alba, i the southern Piedmont region.

imitivo (I.)

n early maturing, sweet, red grape own in the southern Apulia region; be-ved to be related to the Zinfandel grape California.

imitivo di Gioia (I.)

red wine from Gioia del Colle, south of ari, in the east central Apulia region; ade from the Primitivo grape. 14-16% al-hol. Also called Gioia del Colle.

rimitivo di Manduria DOC (I.)

dry or sweet, red wine from Manduria, ist of Taranto, in the southern Apulia re-on; made from the Primitivo grape. Up to 3% alcohol.

rimor (Is.)

dry, red wine, similar in style to a urgundy.

rincic, Doro (I.)

n estate in Pradis di Cormons, Friuli-Ve-ezia Giulia region; produces Collio and ocai wines.

riorato DO (Sp.)

district in the Catalonia region, north-vest of Tarragona, in northeastern Spain; roduces strong, red wine made from Gar-acha Negra and Cariñena grapes and vhite wine from Garnacha Blanca, Maca-eo and Pedro Ximénez grapes; up to 18% lcohol.

rissey (F.)

A commune in the southern part of the Côte de Nuits, just south of Prémeaux, in Burgundy; produces red and white wines old as Côte de Nuits-Villages.

ritchard Hill (U.S.)

The 2nd wine of Chappellet Vineyards, in Napa Valley, California.

robstberg (G.)

A Grosslage, one of 10 in Bereich Bernkas-el, in the Mosel-Saar-Ruwer region. It in-ludes six villages, the most well-known of vhich is Longuich.

Procanico (I.)

On the Island of Elba, off the coast of Tus-cany, another name for the Trebbiano grape.

Procès, Les (F.)

A *Premier Cru* vineyard in Nuits-St.-Georges, Côte de Nuits district, Burgundy. 5 acres.

producteur direct (F.)

A direct producer, that is, a vine grown on its own roots, as opposed to a vine grafted onto a phylloxera-resistant American rootstock.

Productos de Uva (Mex.)   c. 1925

A winery in Tijuana, the first winery built by Angelo Cetto; uses the Chauvenet label of France; produces mostly bulk wines. There is another winery of the same name in Aguascalientes, owned by Cetto's brother, Ferruccio.

Produttori del Barbaresco (I.)   1894, 1958

A co-op winery of 50 growers in Barba-resco, Piedmont region; produces Barba-resco and Nebbiolo wines. 20,000 cases. 300 acres.

Prohibition (U.S.)   1920-1933

The 18th amendment (1920) to the United States Constitution which prohibited the manufacture, sale or transport of intoxicat-ing liquors for beverage purposes. It was repealed in 1933 by the 21st amendment. Individual states also enacted their own prohibition "dry" laws.

Prokupac (Y.)

1. An important red grape grown in Serbia and Macedonia, which produces:

2. A red wine made from the Prokupac grape.

Prolongeau (F.)

A red grape grown in the Blayais district, Bordeaux.

propionic acid

One of several volatile acids present in wine.

Prosecco (I.)

1. A white grape grown in the Treviso district, eastern Veneto region, which produces:

2. A dry or semi-sweet, white wine; also made sparkling.

Prosecco di Conegliano-Valdobbiadene DOC (I.)

1. A district around Conegliano and Valdobbiadene, in the northeastern Veneto region, which produces:

2. White wines of various styles made from the Prosecco grape.

Prosek (Y.)

A sweet, dessert wine from the province of Dalmatia; made from a blend of red and white grapes; up to 16% alcohol.

Protheau & Fils (F.)

An estate in Mercurey, Côte Chalonnaise district, southern Burgundy. 60 acres, mostly *Premier Cru*.

Provence (F.)

A region of southeastern France, on the Mediterranean Sea; primarily known for rosé wines; the most famous wines come from Bandol, Bellet, Cassis and Palette, all AOC wines. 160 million gallons.

provignage (F.)

Layering, a method of propagating vines by which an old vine is buried in earth with one shoot protruding; roots develop where the shoot is buried, producing a new vine when separated from the main plant.

Provins (Sw.)   1930

A large co-op winery (5,000 growers) in Sion, Valais region; produces Fendant, Dôle and other wines.

Prudence Island Vineyards (U.S.)   19

A winery on Prudence Island, Narraga sett Bay, Rhode Island; produces Caberne Chardonnay, Gamay Beaujolais, Gewür traminer, Merlot and Pinot Noir wines. : acres.

Prüfungsnummer (G.)

The official testing number of a particul wine, which is printed on the label. S A.P.

Prugnolo (I.)

A red grape grown in the Tuscany regio also called Sangiovese Grosso.

Pruliers, Les (F.)

A *Premier Cru* vineyard in Nuits-St Georges, Côte de Nuits district, Burgund 17.5 acres.

Prüm, Weingut J.J. (G.)

A famous estate in Wehlen, Mosel distric Owns vineyards in Wehlener Sonnenuh Klosterberg and Nonnenberg; in Graache Himmelreich and Domprobst; Zeltinge Sonnenuhr; Bernkasteler Bratenhöfche and Lay. 35 acres.

Prüm Erben S.A., Weingut (G.)

An estate in Bernkastel, Mosel distric Owns vineyards in Wehlener Sonnenuhr 5 acres, Klosterberg, Nonnenberg; Bern kasteler Badstube and Johannis brünnchen; Graacher Himmelreich an Domprobst; Zeltinger Schlossberg. 1 acres.

Prunier, Jean et Fils (F.)

An estate in Auxey-Duresses, Côte d Beaune district, Burgundy. 48 acres, in cluding Clos du Val Monopole – 2.5 acres .8 acre of Volnay Caillerets and some Meur sault, Pommard and Monthélie.

pruning

The process of trimming and cutting bacl some of the vine growth to control th amount of grape and foliage production thereby controlling the quality of the wine

unotto, Alfred (I.)   **1904**

estate in Alba, Piedmont region; pro-
ces Barbaresco, Barbera, Barolo, Dol-
tto and Nebbiolo wines.

t'ao Chiu (China)

ine that is made from grapes.

celles, Les (F.)

Premier Cru vineyard in Puligny-Mont-
chet, Côte de Beaune district, Burgundy.
acres.

glia (I.)

e Apulia region, as spelled in Italy.

gnet (I.)

Carema, in the Piedmont region, an-
her name for the Nebbiolo grape. Also
lled Picotener.

issequin-Saint-Émilion AOC (F.)

commune just northeast of St.-Émilion,
rdeaux; produces full, red wines similar
St.-Émilion.

ukhliakovsk (U.S.S.R.)

white grape grown in the Rostov district,
ussia S.S.R.

ulcianella (I.)

short, squat bottle covered with straw;
sed for Orvieto wine, in the Umbria
gion.

ulcinculo (I.)

white grape grown in the Tuscany re-
ion; also called Grechetto Bianco.

uligny-Montrachet AOC (F.)

n important commune in the southern
ôte de Beaune district (in the unofficial
ôte de Meursault); produces mostly dry
hite wine and very little red; the white
ine is considered to be some of the finest
 the world; includes 4 *Grand Cru* vine-
ards: Montrachet and Bâtard-Montrachet
both also partly in Chassagne-Mon-
achet), Chevalier-Montrachet, and Bien-

venues-Bâtard-Montrachet.   185,000
gallons. 580 acres.

**Puligny-Montrachet, Domaine de Château
de (F.)**

An estate in Saint-Romain, Côte de Beaune
district, Burgundy; controlled by Roland
Thévenin. 27 acres. See **Thévenin, R.**

punt

The indentation in the bottom of a wine
bottle, which serves to reinforce the bottle
and to collect the sediment.

Puntinata (I.)

A white grape grown in the Latium region;
also called Malvasia del Lazio.

pupitre (F.)

A special rack for holding bottles of Champagne with the neck down to ready them
for *dégorgement*.

Pusterla (I.)   **16th cent.**

An estate in Vigolo Marchese, Emilia-Romagna region; produces Gutturnio, Monterosso and other wines. 7,500 cases. 35 acres.

puttonyos (H.)

Baskets used in the Tokaji region for measuring amounts of specially selected, dried,
ripe grapes used in making Tokaji Aszú
wines, the labels indicating 3, 4, or 5
puttonyos.

Puy-Blanquet, Château (F.)

An estate in St.-Émilion, Bordeaux; classified in 1955 as a *Grand Cru*. 8,500 cases. 62
acres.

Py, Domaine du (F.)

An estate in Villié-Morgon, Beaujolais district, Burgundy. 33 acres.

Py, Vin de *or* Clos de (F.)

A famous section of the Morgon vineyard,
Beaujolais district, Burgundy.

pyralid, pyralis

The meal-moth, one of several moths
which feed on foliage and fruit.

Q

Q (I.)

A mark of quality appearing on wines from Sicily; awarded by the *Istituto Regionale della Vite e del Vino.*

Q.b.A. (G.)

An abbreviation for *Qualitätswein bestimmter Anbaugebiete,* German for "Quality wine from Specific Regions," an official designation for a good quality wine from a specific region, *Bereich* or village in Germany.

Q.m.P. (G.)

An abbreviation for *Qualitätswein mit Prädikat,* German for "Quality Wine with Distinction," an official designation for quality wine from a specific *Bereich,* village or vineyard in Germany. This is the highest classification of German wine, and can be further defined as to the village and vineyard, and as to the catagory of *Kabinett, Spätlese, Auslese, Beerenauslese, Trockenbeerenauslese* or *Eiswein.*

Quady (U.S.)   1977

A winery in Madera, Madera County, San Joaquin Valley, California; produces Port wines made from Zinfandel grapes and Essensia, a sweet, white wine made from the Orange Muscat grape. 3,500 cases.

Quail Ridge (U.S.)   1978

A winery in Napa City, Napa Valley, California; produces Cabernet, Chardonnay and French Colombard wines. 20 acres.

Qualitätswein bestimmter Anbaugebiet (G.)

See **Q.b.A.**

Qualitätswein mit Prädikat (G.)

See **Q.m.P.**

quart

1/4 of a gallon; 32 fluid ounces or 94.6 centiliters.

quart (F.)

A small carafe equal to about 1/4 liter, or a quarter-bottle (a split).

quarter-cask

Originally a cask equal to 1/4 of a pipe; equal to 113-160 liters or 30-42 gallons.

Quarterons, Clos des (F.)

An estate in St. Nicholas-de-Bourgeuil, Touraine region, Loire Valley. 2,500 cases. 35 acres.

quartier (F.)

In the Rhône region a term for a vineyard.

Quarto Vecchio (I.)

A full-bodied, red wine from Bevilacqua, southeast of Verona, in the south central Veneto region; made from Cabernet and Merlot grapes.

Quarts de Chaume AOC (F.)

A *Grand Cru* vineyard in Chaume, south of Angers, in the Coteaux du Layon district, Anjou region, Loire Valley; produces a sweet, white wine made from Chenin Blanc grapes. 125 acres.

Quatourze VDQS (F.)

A small district east of Narbonne in the Languedoc region of southern France (Midi); produces red and rosé wines made from Carignan, Cinsault, Grenache,

Mourvèdre and Terret Noir grapes; a small amount of white wine is also made.

Quatre Chemins, Cave des (F.)

An estate in Laudun, Côtes du Rhône-Villages district, southern Rhône region.

Quatre Journeaux, Les (F.)

A section of the Romanée-St.-Vivant vineyard (a *Grand Cru*), in Vosne-Romanée, Côte de Nuits district, Burgundy; owned by L. Latour. 2.5 acres.

Quatre Routes, Les (F.)

An estate in Maisdon-sur-Sèvre, Muscadet region. Loire Valley. 30 acres.

Quatrième Cru (F.)

Fourth Growth, one of the designations for red wines of the Haut-Médoc district, Bordeaux, from the 1855 classification.

Quattro Vicariati (I.)

A red wine from the Trentino-Alto Adige region; made from Cabernet and Merlot grapes.

Quelltaler Wines (Aus.)   1865

A winery in the Clare-Watervale district, South Australia; produces Fino Sherry, *"Granfiesta"* hoch wine, Rhine Riesling, Cabernet and Grenache wines. 600 acres.

Quenot Fils et Meuneveaux, Max (F.)

An estate in Aloxe-Corton, Côte de Beaune district, Burgundy. 16 acres, including 2.5 acres of Corton Bressandes, 1.6 acres of Perrières and .8 acre of Chaumes.

Querce, Fattoria La (I.)

An estate in Impruneta, Tuscany region; produces Chianti wine. 3,000 cases. 40 acres.

Querceto, Castello di (I.)

An estate in Lucolena, Tuscany region; produces Chianti Classico wine. 10,000 cases.

Querciolana, La (I.)

An estate in Panicale, Umbria region; produces Colli del Trasimeno and Grifo Boldrino wines.

Questa Vineyard, La (U.S.)   188

A famous, historic vineyard in Woodside San Mateo County, California; produces Cabernet wine until 1920; part of the vineyard was used by Woodside Vineyards which now bottles the wine.

queue (F.)

An old measure equal to anywhere from 216 to 894 liters (in Burgundy it equals 45 liters). A *queue* = 2 *pièces*, a *demi-queue* = pièces.

Queyrats, Château (F.)

An unclassified estate in St.-Pierre-de Mons, Graves district, Bordeaux; joined with Château St.-Pierre and Clos d'Uza 7,500 cases. 85 acres.

Quillardet, Charles (F.)

An estate in Marsannay-la-Côte, Côte de Nuits district, Burgundy. 43 acres, including 5 acres of Bourgogne Montre-Cul (Dijon), 5 acres of Gevrey-Chambertin, 2 acres of Marsannay and 5 acres of Côte de Nuits-Villages.

Quincy AOC (F.)

1. A village and district west of Bourges, in the Upper Loire Region, Loire Valley which produces:

2. A white wine made from the Sauvignon grape. 100,000 gallons. 550 acres.

Quinquina (F.)

An apéritif made from fortified wine flavored with quinine.

Quinta (P.)

An agricultural estate or property, the name of which sometimes appears on Port wine labels, indicating a single-vineyard designation.

Quinta da Aveleda (P.)

A well-known, white wine from the Vinho Verde region; estate grown and bottled; made from Loureivo, Trajadura and Pedernã grapes.

Quinta da Boa Vista (P.)

A single-vineyard Port wine made by Offley Forrester; the vineyard is northeast of Pesco da Régua.

Quinta do Bonfim (P.)

A single vineyard vintage Port wine made by Warre. The vineyard is located in Pinhão, on the Douro River.

Quinta da Corte (P.)

A single vineyard vintage Port wine made by Delaforce.

Quinta da Foz (P.)

A single vineyard vintage Port wine made by Cálem. The vineyard is located west of Pinhão, on the Douro River.

Quinta dos Malvedos (P.)

A single vineyard vintage Port wine made by Graham. The vineyard is located east of Pinhão, on the Douro River.

Quinta do Noval (P.)   1813

A Port producer in Vila Nova de Gaia; also owns Quinta do Silval. Both vineyards are north of Pinhão.

Quinta da Roeda (P.)

A single vineyard vintage Port wine made by Croft. The vineyard is located just east of Pinhão, on the Douro River.

Quinta de Vargellas (P.)

A single vineyard vintage Port wine made by Taylor. The vineyard is located east of Pinhão, on the Douro River.

Quinta do Vesúvio (P.)

A famous mansion and vineyard in the Douro region, owned by Ferreira.

Quintarelli, Giuseppe (I.)   1924

An estate in Negrar di Valpolicella, Veneto region; produces Amarone, Valpolicella and other wines. 25 acres.

Quiot, Domaine Pierre (F.)

An estate in Orange, Châteauneuf-du-Pape district, southern Rhône region; produces Châteauneuf-du-Pape, Côte du Rhône and Gigondas wines. 130 acres.

R

R (F.)

A dry, white wine made by Château Rieussec, Sauternes district, Bordeaux.

R.D. (F.)

Récemment dégorgé (recently disgorged), a term used in Champagne, referring to the practice of allowing the sediment of the second fermentation to remain in the the bottle until ready for shipment; it is then removed, or disgorged, and the Champagne recorked; this is done in order to produce a more full-bodied wine.

Rabaner (G.)

A white grape – a cross of Riesling and Riesling; developed at the State Teaching and Research Institute, Geisenheim, Germany.

Rabaud-Promis, Château (F.)

An estate in Bommes, Sauternes district, Bordeaux; classified in 1855 as a *Premier Cru* under the name of Château Rabeaud; it was divided into Rabaud-Sigalas and Rabaud-Promis in 1903, joined in 1929 and redivided in 1952. Château Peixotto, a *Deuxième Cru*, is now part of Château Rabaud-Promis. 5,000 cases. 75 acres.

Rabeaud, Château (F.)

A former estate in Bommes, Sauternes district, Bordeaux; classified in 1855 as a *Premier Cru*; it was divided in 1903 into Château Sigalas-Rabaud and Château Sigalas-Promis.

Rabelais (Alg.)

Formerly, a well-known red wine from the Haut-Dahra district, west of Algiers, now called Aïn Merane.

Rabigate (P.)

A white grape grown in the Vinho Verde region.

Rabigato (P.)

A white grape, one of 16 first-quality grapes used to make white Port.

Rabo de Ovelha (P.)

A white grape grown in the Bairrada region.

Raboso (I.)

1. A red grape grown east of Traviso, in the Veneto region, which produces:
2. A red wine made from the Raboso grape.

Rabourcé (F.)

A *Premier Cru* vineyard in Rully, Côte Chalonnaise district, Burgundy.

race (F.)

Distinction, breed; a term used to describe a fine wine.

racimo (Sp.)

A grape-bunch.

racking

The drawing off of the fermented wine into another vat in order to leave the lees and sediment behind. This is done 2-4 times before bottling. Also called *soutirage* (F.), *Abstich* (G.) and *travaso* (I.).

Raclot (F.)

A *Premier Cru* vineyard in Rully, Côte Chalonnaise district, Burgundy.

Radgona (Y.)

An important town in northeastern Slovenia; produces Radgonska Ranina, a sweet, white wine which is also known as Tigrovo Mljeko (Tiger's Milk); made from the Bouvier grape.

Radipan Vineyards (U.S.)   1981

A winery in Culpeper, Virginia; produces Riesling and Chardonnay wines. 200 acres.

Rafanelli Winery (U.S.)   1974

A winery and vineyard in Healdsburg, Dry Creek Valley, northern Sonoma County, California; produces Cabernet, Gamay Beaujolais and Zinfandel wines. 3,000 cases. 25 acres.

Raffault, Jean Maurice (F.)

An estate in Savigny-en-Véron, Chinon district, Touraine region. 6,000 cases. 70 acres.

Raffault, Olga (F.)

An estate in Savigny-en-Véron, Chinon district, Touraine region, Loire Valley. 35 acres.

Rafsai (Mor.)

A local white grape.

Raggio (I.)

A white wine from Gavi, in the southeastern Piedmont region; made from the Cortese di Gavi grape.

Ragose, Le (I.)   1969

An estate in Arbizzano, Veneto region; produces Amarone and Valpolicella wines. 25 acres.

Ragot, Domaine (F.)

An estate in Poncey, Côte Chalonnaise district, Burgundy; produces Givry wine (red and white). 20 acres.

Ragotière, Château de la (F.)

An estate in Vallet, Muscadet de Sèvre-et-Maine district, Muscadet region, Loire Valley. 60 acres.

Rahoul, Château (F.)

An unclassified estate in Portet, Graves district, Bordeaux. 5,000 cases of red and white wine. 35 acres.

Rainoldi (I.)

An estate in Chiuro, Lombardy region; produces Grumello, Sassella, Inferno, Valtellina and other wines.

Rainwater Madeira (P.)

A light Madeira wine made from a blend of grapes.

raisins entiers (F.)

Whole or uncrushed grapes, sometimes used in making wines.

Rajnski Rizling (Y.)

The Yugoslavian name for the Rhine Riesling grape or wine.

Ramage la Batisse, Château (F.)

An estate in St.-Sauveur, Haut-Médoc district, Bordeaux; classified in 1978 as a *Cru Bourgeois*. 20,000 cases. 110 acres.

Ramandolo DOC (I.)

1. A village in the Colli Orientali district, in the eastern Friuli-Venezia Giulia region, which produces:

2. A sweet, white wine made from Verduzzo grapes, semi-dried on straw mats.

Rameau-Lamarosse, Cuvée (F.)

A red wine from the Hospices de Beaune, Côte de Beaune district, Burgundy. The *cuvée* is composed of one vineyard in Pernand-Vergelesses: Les Basses Vergelesses – 1.3 acres.

rameur (F.)

A riddler, a specialist who shakes and turns the Champagne bottles in the cellar in preparation for *dégorgement*.

Ramisco (P.)

A red grape grown in the Colares region.

Ramitello (I.)

Red and white wines from Campomarino, in the Molise region; the red wine is made from Sangiovese and Montepulciano grapes and the white wine is made from Trebbiano and Malvasia grapes.

Ramonet, Claude (F.)

An estate in Chassagne-Montrachet, Côte de Beaune district, Burgundy. 15 acres, including 1.7 acres of Bâtard-Montrachet, .7 acre of Bienvenues-Bâtard-Montrachet, 3 acres of Chassagne-Montrachet Morgeot, .6 acre of Grandes Ruchottes, 1 acre of Clos St. Jean (red) and 1.7 acres of Clos de la Boudriotte (red).

Ramonet-Prudhon (F.)

An estate in Chassagne-Montrachet, Côte de Beaune district, Burgundy. 35 acres, including .8 acre of Bâtard-Montrachet, .8 acre of Bienvenues-Bâtard-Montrachet, 2.5 acres of Chassagne-Montrachet Grandes Ruchottes, 1.2 acres of En Cailleret, 12.5 acres of Morgeot, 2 acres of Clos de la Boudriotte and 1.7 acres of Clos St.-Jean.

Ramos-Pinto, Adriano (P.)   1880

A Port producer in Vila Nova de Gaia; owns Quinta Bom Retiro, Quinta Santa Maria and Quinta San Domingos. 200 acres.

Ranchita Oaks Winery (U.S.)   1979

A winery in San Miguel, San Luis Obispo County, California; produces Cabernet, Zinfandel, Petite Sirah and Chardonnay wines. 4,000 cases. 45 acres.

Rancho de Philo (U.S.)   1975

A small winery in Archibald, Cucamonga district, San Bernadino County, southern California; produces only Cream Sherry. 300 cases. 15 acres.

Rancho Sisquoc Winery (U.S.)   1977

A winery in Santa Maria, Santa Barbara County, California; produces Cabernet, Chardonny, Johannisberg Riesling, Sylva-ner and Sauvignon Blanc grapes. 2,000 cases. 200 acres.

Rancho Viejo (Mex.)

A district east of Ensenada, in the Baja California region.

rancio (F., Sp.)

Maderized; oxidized; a style of wine with an intentionally oxidized taste; made in Catalonia, Spain and in France (Banyuls, Château-Châlon, etc.).

Randersacker (G.)

A village in the Franken region, Bereich Maindreieck, Grosslage Ewig Leben. The vineyards are: Dabug (no *Grosslage*), Marsberg, Pfülben, Sonnenstuhl and Teufelskeller. 675 acres.

Rangen, Le (F.)

A vineyard in Thann, southern Haut-Rhin district, Alsace region.

Ranina Radgona (Y.)

A vineyard in Radgona, in northeastern Slovenia; produces Radgonska Ranina wine, a sweet, white wine known as Tigrovo Mljeko (Tiger's Milk), made from the Bouvier grape.

Raousset, Château de (F.)

An estate in Chiroubles, Beaujolais district, Burgundy. 100 acres (42 of Chiroubles).

rapé (F.)

The discarded grapes which are under- or over-ripe; also, the wine made from these grapes.

Rapet, Robert et Fils (F.)

An estate in Pernand-Vergelesses, Côte de Beaune district, Burgundy. 30 acres, including 2.5 acres of Corton and Corton Perrières, 4 acres of Corton-Charlemagne, 1.2 acres of Beaune Premier Cru, 6 acres of Pernand-Vergelesses les Vergelesses, 2.5 acres of Savigny Fourneaux and 7.5 acres of Aligoté.

Rapitalà (I.)

A white wine from Camporeale, southeast of Alcamo, in northwestern Sicily; made from Cattarratto, Damaschino, Grecanico and Trebbiano grapes.

Rapitalà (I.)

An estate in Camporeale, Sicily; produces Alcamo and Rapitalà Rosso wines. 120,000 cases. 500 acres.

Rappenhof, Weingut (G.)

An estate in Alsheim, Rheinhessen region; owns vineyards in Alsheim, Guntersblum, Dienheim and Nierstein; produces mostly dry wines. 75 acres.

Rapsani (Gr.)

A red wine from the province of Thessaly, near Mt. Olympus; made from a blend of several grapes.

Rara Neagra (U.S.S.R.)

A red grape grown in Moldavia SSR; one of several grapes used to make Negru de Purkar wine.

raspon (Sp.)

A grape-stalk.

Rasteau VDN *and* AOC (F.)

A commune in the southern Rhône region; produces white *Vin Doux Natural* and *Vin de Liquor* made mostly from the Grenache grape, and dry red, white and rosé wines. It is also one of the villages comprising the Côtes du Rhône-Villages.

Ratti, Renato (I.)   1962

A winery located in a 15th century abbey in La Morra, Piedmont region; produces Barbaresco, Barbera, Barolo, Dolcetto and Nebbiolo wines; made from their own and purchased grapes. 8,000 cases. 12 acres.

Rauenthal (G.)

A village in the Rheingau region, Bereich Johannisberg, Grosslage Steinmächer. The vineyards are: Baiken, Gehrn, Langen-stück, Nonnenberg, Rothenberg and Wülfen. 250 acres.

Rausan-Ségla, Château (F.)

An estate in Margaux, Haut-Médoc district, Bordeaux; classified in 1855 as a *Deuxième Cru*. 13,000 cases. 100 acres.

Räuschling (G.)

The German name for the Elbling grape; possibly the same grape as the Pedro Ximénez; also called Knipperlé, in Alsace.

Rautenstrauch Erben (G.)

The former owners of the famous Karthäuserhof Estate in Eitelsbach, Ruwer district, Mosel-Saar-Ruwer region. 50 acres. See **Karthäuserhof.**

Rauzan-Gassies, Château (F.)

An estate in Margaux, Haut-Médoc district, Bordeaux; classified in 1855 as a *Deuxième Cru*; was well-known by 1530. 10,000 cases. 75 acres.

Ravat, J.F. (d. 1940) (F.)

A French engineer and hybridizer from Marcigny, Saône-et-Loire; developed the following hybrid grapes: Ravat 6, also called Ravat Blanc – Chardonnay crossed with S. 5474, which is his best white grape; Ravat 34, white, early ripening and hardy, Ravat 51, white "Vignoles" – Pinot Noir crossed with S. 6,905; Ravat 262, also called Ravat Noir – a Pinot Noir crossed with S. 8,365, which is used in the U.S. for a wine similar to Beaujolais; and Ravat 578, white, early ripening and not hardy.

Ravat Blanc (F.)

A white, hybrid grape – a cross of Chardonnay and S. 5474; also called Ravat 6; developed by J.F. Ravat.

Ravat Noir (F.)

A red, hybrid grape – a cross of Pinot Noir and S. 8,365; also called Ravat 262; developed by J.F. Ravat.

Ravello (I.)

1. A village east of Sorrento, in the west central Campania region, which produces:

2. Red, white and rosé wines. The red and rosé wines are made from Per'e Palummo, Aglianico, Merlot and other grapes and the white wine is made from Coda di Volpe, San Nicola, Bianco Tenera, Greco and other grapes.

Ravenswood (U.S.)   1976

A winery in San Francisco, California; produces Cabernet, Zinfandel and Merlot wines from purchased grapes. 4,000 cases.

Ravineau, François (F.)

An estate in Chablis, Burgundy. 10 acres, including 1.2 acres of Les Clos, .8 acre of Blanchot, 2.5 acres of Montée de Tonnerre, 1.5 acres of Chapelot, 2.2 acres of Butteaux and .3 acre of Forêts.

Ray Vineyards, Martin (U.S.)   1943

A winery in the Santa Cruz Mountains, near Saratoga, Santa Clara County, California; produces Cabernet, Pinot Noir and Chardonnay wines and Champagne. Martin died in 1976 and the vineyards were split up; Mount Eden Vineyard owns most of Ray's land; Ray's son owns the remaining 5 acres and now uses the La Montaña label. Some purchased grapes. 5,000 cases.

raya (Sp.)

1. In the Sherry district, a coarse wine with no promise of improvement.

2. A system of marking Sherry butts to identify the style of the wine.

Rayas, Château (F.)   1894

An estate in Châteauneuf-du-Pape, southern Rhône region; produces red wine made from Grenache, Syrah and Cinsault grapes and white wine made from Grenache Blanc and Clairette grapes; also owns Château de Fonsalette, in the Côtes du Rhône district and Châteauneuf-du-Pape Pignan. 40 acres.

Raymond-Lafon, Château (F.)

An unclassified estate in Sauternes, Sauternes district, Bordeaux. 1,000 cases. 30 acres.

Raymond Winery (U.S.)   1975, vines 1971

A winery in St. Helena, Napa Valley, California; produces Cabernet, Zinfandel, Gamay, Merlot, Pinot Noir, Chardonnay, Chenin Blanc, Sauvignon Blanc and Johannisberg Riesling wines. 26,000 cases. 90 acres.

Rayne-Vigneau, Château (F.)

An estate in Bommes, Sauternes district, Bordeaux; classified in 1855 as a *Premier Cru*; originally called Château Vigneau; produces sweet, white wine, and some dry wine which is called Raynesec; also known for the semi-precious stones found in its soil. 15,000 cases. 150 acres.

Rayon d'Or (F.)

A French white hybrid grape; also called Seibel 4986.

Rcatsitelli *also* Rkatsitelli (Bul., U.S.S.R.)

A Russian white grape used to make dry or sweet, white wine in eastern Bulgaria; also grown in California.

Re Rustica, De (Lat.)

1. A book written by Marcus Terentius Varro (116-27 B.C.), in which he describes wine making; also called *Rerum Rusticarum Libri*.

2. A book written by Columella, c. 60 A.D., in which he describes vineyards.

3. A book written by Cato the Censor (234-149 B.C.), in which he describes vine growing and wine making; also called *De Agri Cultura*.

Real Tesoro S.A., Herederos de Marqués (Sp.)   19th cent.

A small Sherry producer in Jerez de la Frontera; produces several types of Sherry.

Reas, Clos de (F.)

A *Premier Cru* vineyard in Vosne-Romanée, Côte de Nuits district, Burgundy. 5.5 acres.

Rebe, -rebe (G.)

A vine; -*rebe* is used on endings of some grape varieties.

rebêche (F.)

In the Champagne region, the final pressing of the grapes; makes poor quality wine.

Rebgarten (F.)

A vineyard in Bennwihr, Haut-Rhin district, Alsace region; planted with Riesling grapes.

Rebholz, Weingut Ökonomierat (G.)

An estate in Seibeldingen, Rheinpfalz region; owns vineyards in Birkweil and Siebeldingen. 22 acres.

Rebula (Y.)

1. A white grape grown in western Slovenia.
2. A white wine from Brda, western Slovenia; made from the Rebula grape.

récemment dégorgé (F.)

See **R.D.**

recently disgorged

See **R.D.**

Recioto (I.)

A style of wine in which the grapes are picked from the upper portion of the clusters; these are the ones that are most exposed to the sun and they are called *recie* (from *orecchie*, meaning ears, since they tend to stick out). They are semi-dried and used to make sweet, sparkling, or dry Amarone wine; 13-17% alcohol. The word itself indicates sweet, semi-sweet and/or sparkling wine; when followed by the word *"Amarone"* it indicates a dry wine.

Recioto Bianco di Campociesa (I.)

A sweet, white wine from the Campociesa vineyard in Valgatara, north of Verona, in the Veneto region; made from semi-dried Garganega and Trebbiano grapes.

Recioto di Soave (I.)

A sweet, white wine from the Soave district, in the western Veneto region; made from Garganega and Trebbiano grapes, the same as those used to make Soave; 14% alcohol, 16% alcohol in the sweeter *liquoroso* version.

Recioto della Valpolicella (I.)

A fuller, sweeter version of a Valpolicella wine.

Recioto della Valpolicella Amarone (I.)

See **Amarone.**

récolte (F.)

The wine harvest or crop.

red spider

A red mite that builds webs and which causes premature browning of grape leaves.

Redbank Winery (Aus.)   1969

A winery in the Coonawarra district, South Australia; produces Cabernet and Shiraz wines; owned by Owen Redman of the Rouge Homme Estate.

Redbrook (Aus.)

A small vineyard of Gnangara Wines, Margaret River district, Western Australia; produces Bordeaux-style red wines.

Redde, Michel (F.)

An estate in Les Berthiers, Pouilly-Fumé district, Upper Loire region. 60 acres.

Redman (Aus.)   1966

A winery in the Coonawarra district, South Australia; produces Shiraz and Cabernet wines. 25,000 cases. 90 acres.

Redrescuts (F.)

A *Premier Cru* vineyard (in part) in Savigny, Côte de Beaune district, Burgundy. 2.5 acres.

Refène, La (F.)

A *Premier Cru* vineyard in Pommard, Côte de Beaune district, Burgundy. 6 acres.

Referts, Les (F.)

A *Premier Cru* vineyard in Puligny-Montrachet, Côte de Beaune district, Burgundy. 35 acres.

Refosco DOC (I.)

1. A local, red grape grown in the Friuli-Venezia Giulia region; in France known as the Mondeuse.

2. A red wine from the Colli Orientali district, in the Friuli-Venezia Giulia region; made from Refosco del Peduncolo Rosso and Refosco Nostrano grapes.

Regale (U.S.)

A red muscadine grape.

Regaleali (I.)

Red, white and rosé wines from Sclafani Bagni, southeast of Palermo, in north central Sicily. The red and rosé wines are made from Perricone, Nero d'Avola and Calabrese grapes and the white wine is made from Catarratto, Inzolia and some Sauvignon grapes.

Regaleali (I.) 　　　　　　　1835

An estate in Vallelunga Caltanissetta, Sicily; produces Regaleali and Rosso del Conte wines. 110,000 cases. 400 acres.

Região Demarcada (P.)

A Demarcated Region.

regional wine

A wine from any large region as opposed to a small district, commune or vineyard; essentially the same as a generic wine.

régisseur (F.)

The manager of a *château* or estate.

Regnard et Fils, A. (F.) 　　　　1870

A merchant in Chablis, Burgundy; makes Chablis Fourchaume from purchased must.

Regner (G.)

A white grape – a cross of Luglienca Bianca and Early Gamay; developed at the Institute in Alzey, Rheinhessen region, Germany, in 1929; named after a member of the Institute; similar to Müller-Thurgau, but considered better.

rehoboam (F.)

A large bottle used in Champagne, equal to 6 fifths or 162 ounces.

Reichartshausen, Schloss (G.)

A vineyard and estate (an *Ortsteil*) in Oestrich, Grosslage Gottesthal, in the Rheingau region. 10 acres.

Reichensteiner (G.)

A white hybrid grape – a cross of Müller-Thurgau crossed with Madeleine Angevine and Calabria; developed at the State Teaching and Research Institute, Geisenheim, Germany; named for the Reichenstein Castle, in Trechtingshausen, Mittelrhein region.

Reignots, Aux (F.)

A *Premier Cru* vineyard in Vosne-Romanée, Côte de Nuits district, Burgundy. 4 acres.

Reillanne, Domaine de (F.)

An estate in Cannet-des-Maures, Provence region.

Reims (F.)

A city in the Champagne region; one of 2 important centers of Champagne production.

Reina, La (U.S.)

A vineyard in Monterey, California; produces grapes for the J.W.Morris winery. 120 acres, half Pinot Noir and half Chardonnay grapes.

Reine Pédauque, La (F.)

A company in Aloxe-Corton, Côte de Beaune district, Burgundy; controls the following estates: Domaine de la Juvinière – 60 acres, Domaine Les Terres Vineuses – 63 acres, Domaine du Clos des Guettes – 7 acres, Domaine Viticole des Carmes – 45 acres. See under each *Domaine*.

Reinhart, Paul (F.)

An estate in Orschwihr, Haut-Rhin district, Alsace region. 12 acres, including Bollenberg vineyard – 7 acres (Riesling).

Reinhartshausen, Schloss (G.)

An estate in Erbach, in the Rheingau region; owns vineyards in Erbach, Hattenheim, Hallgarten, Kiedrich, Rauenthal and Rüdesheim; also owns part of Marcobrunn vineyard. The castle is in Erbach. Owned by the estate of Prince Heinrich Friedrich. 165 acres.

Remilly, En (F.)

A *Premier Cru* vineyard in St.-Aubin, Côte de Beaune district, Burgundy; produces red and white wines. 5 acres.

Remizières, Domaine des (F.)

An estate in Mercurol, Crozes-Hermitage district, Rhône region; owns 29 acres of Crozes-Hermitage.

Remoissenet Père et Fils (F.)   1879

An estate and large *négociant* in Beaune, Côte de Beaune district, Burgundy. 6 acres, including some Beaune Marconnets, Grèves, Toussaints and Bressandes.

remontage

The practice of drawing off must from the bottom of a vat during fermentation and pumping or spraying it over the cap or top of the vat.

Remoriquet, Henri (F.)

An estate in Nuits-St.-Georges, Côte de Nuits district, Burgundy. 10 acres, including .5 acre of Nuits-St.-Georges, .5 acre of Aux Damodes, 1 acre of Premier Cru, 2 acres of Les Allots and 2.5 acres of Hautes-Côtes de Nuits.

remplissage (F.)

The topping up of a cask or barrel with wine, to compensate for evaporation; also called *ouillage*.

Remstal-Stuttgart (G.)

A *Bereich*, one of 3 in the Württemberg region.

remuage (F.)

Shaking; riddling; this is done to bottles of Champagne to gradually shake and work the sediment of the 2nd fermentation to the neck of the bottle and up against the cork so it can be quickly removed without spillage. The bottles are turned in 1/4 turns and gradually shifted into an upside-down position in specially designed racks called *"pupitres."* For mechanical *remuage* devices, *see* **champanex, girasol** *and* **gyropalette.**

Rémy, Maison Henry (F.)

An estate in Morey-St.-Denis, Côte de Nuits district, Burgundy. 8 acres, including 2.5 acres of Chambertin, 4 acres of Latricières-Chambertin, 4 acres of Clos de la Roche, 2 acres of Chambolle-Musigny Les Fremières and some Derrière la Grange; formerly, the controller of Louis Rémy wines.

Renard, Domaine de la (F.)

An estate in Rully, Côte Chalonnaise district, southern Burgundy. 140 acres in Rully, 9 acres in Mercury, 11 acres in Givry, 4 acres in Bouzeron and 12 acres in La Rochepot.

Renarde, La (F.)

A *Premier Cru* vineyard in Rully, Côte Chalonnaise district, Burgundy.

Renardes, Les (F.)

A *Grand Cru* vineyard in Aloxe-Corton, Côte de Beaune district, Burgundy, when Corton precedes the name of the vineyard; part of the vineyard is a *Premier Cru*. 36 acres.

Renault (Alg.)

A vineyard in the Haut-Dahra district, east of Oran; produces red wine. It has been renamed Mazouna.

Renault Winery (U.S.)   1864

A winery in Egg Harbor City, New Jersey, the oldest and largest in the state; grows mostly *labrusca* grapes and some hybrid and *vinifera* grapes; produces blended wines (some blended with California wines) and sparkling wine. A famous wine glass museum in located here. 125 acres.

rendement (F.)

The yield of a vineyard, expressed as a ratio of *hectolitres* to *hectares*.

René, Clos (F.)

An estate in Pomerol, Bordeaux. 6,000 cases. 35 acres.

René Roy, Domaine (F.)

An estate in Auxey-Duresses, Côte de Beaune district, Burgundy. 25 acres, including .6 acre of Volnay Les Santenots, 2 acres of Auxey-Duresses Les Duresses and 12.5 acres of Le Val.

Renou, René (F.)

An estate in Thouracé, Anjou region, Loire Valley. 45 acres, including 15 acres of Bonnezeaux.

Renski Riesling (Y.)

Another name for the Rhine Riesling grape or wine.

Rentz, Marcel (F.)   1797

An estate in Zellenberg, Haut-Rhin district, Alsace region. 25 acres.

repeal (U.S.)   1933

In the United States, the 21st amendment to the Constitution, enacted in 1933, which ended the prohibition of alcoholic beverages; a repeal of the 18th amendment (1920).

Rerum Rusticarum Libri (Lat.)

A book written by Marcus Terentius Varro (116-27 B.C.), in which he describes wine making. Also called *De Re Rustica*.

reserva (Sp.)

Aged longer than usual; a special lot, cask or selection of wine.

reserve (U.S.)

An unofficial designation of a wine of special quality, from a special lot or cask, or made from the best or ripest grapes.

Réserve de la Comtesse (F.)

The 2nd wine of Château Pichon-Lalande, Haut-Médoc district, Bordeaux.

Réserve du Prieur Grenache (I.)

A sweet, white wine made at the Regional Agricultural School in Aosta, in the Valle d'Aosta region.

Restsüsse (G.)

The residual sugar in wine.

Retsina (Gr.)

White or rosé wines mainly from Attica, Peloponnese and Euboea Island made with the addition of resin from the Alep pine tree. Half of Greek wine is made with this resin, which is added to the must during fermentation and later removed, leaving the characteristic resinous taste.

Retz (A.)

An important town north of Krems, in the Weinviertel district, Lower Austria region.

Reugne (F.)

A *Premier Cru* vineyard in Auxey-Duresses, Côte de Beaune district, Burgundy. 8 acres.

Reugne, *known as* La Chapelle (F.)

A *Premier Cru* vineyard in Auxey-Duresses, Côte de Beaune district, Burgundy; a part of the vineyard formerly known as La Chapelle. 5 acres.

Reuilly AOC (F.)

A village and district west of Bourges, on the Arnon River, a tributary of the River Cher, in the Upper Loire region, Loire Valley; produces white wine from the Sauvignon grape and some red and rosé wines from the Pinot Noir grape. 26,500 gallons. 250 acres.

Reuter's Hill Vineyards (U.S.)   c. 1885

An old winery in Forest Grove, Tualatin Valley, northwestern Oregon, now joined with Charles Coury Vineyard; produces Riesling, Pinot Noir, Sylvaner, Gewürztraminer and Muscat Ottonel wines. 60 acres.

Reverdy, Bernard (F.)

An estate in Verdigny, Sancerre district, Upper Loire Region. 18 acres, including some La Perrière.

Reversées, Les (F.)

A *Premier Cru* vineyard in Beaune, Côte de Beaune district, Burgundy. 12 acres.

Reynella (Aus.)

An old winery near Adelaide, in the southern Vales district, South Australia; produces red wines, especially Cabernet and also Port, mostly from purchased grapes.

Reysson, Château (F.)

An estate in Vertheuil, Haut-Médoc district, Bordeaux; classified in 1978 as a *Cru Grand Bourgeois*. 18,000 cases. 110 acres.

Rèze (Sw.)

An old white grape grown in the Valais district, used in making *Vin du Glacier*.

Rhaetian *also* **Raetian (Lat.)**

An grape grown in the ancient Roman Empire; mentioned by Cato.

Rheinart Erben, Weingut Adolf (G.)

An estate in Longuich, Saar district, Mosel-Saar-Ruwer region; owns vineyards in Ockfen, Ayl and Wiltingen. 25 acres.

Rheinburgengau (G.)

A *Bereich*, one of 2 in the Mittelrhein region.

Rheingau (G.)

A famous region on the right bank of the Rhine river, from Assmannshausen east to Hochheim; the only *Bereich* is Bereich Johannisberg, with 10 *Grosslagen*, containing many of the finest vineyards and estates in Germany; produces mostly white wine from the Riesling grape and some red wine. 7,000 acres.

Rheinhessen (G.)

An important region on the left bank of the Rhine river, opposite the Rheingau; the *Bereiche* are Bingen, Nierstein and Wonnegau, with 24 *Grosslagen*; the most famous towns are Nierstein and Oppenheim; produces mostly white wines and some red wines. 58,000 acres.

Rheinpfalz (G.)

A region south of the Rheinhessen region, also known as the Palatinate. The two *Bereiche* are Südliche Weinstrasse and Mittelhaardt-Deutsche Weinstrasse; there are 26 *Grosslagen*. The most famous towns are Deidesheim and Forst. 55,000 acres.

Rhenish (E.)

An Old English term for Rhine wine or any German wine.

Rhode Island (U.S.)

A state in the northeastern United States. It has 3 new wineries since 1974.

Rhodes (Gr.)

A large island northeast of Crete; produces red and white wines, especially from the small island of Lindos, off the northwestern coast of Rhodes.

Rhoditis (Gr.)

A red grape grown in central Greece to make rosé wines.

Rhodt (G.)

A village in the Rheinpfalz region, Bereich Südliche Weinstrasse, Grosslage Ordensgut. The vineyards are: Klosterpfad, Rosengarten and Schlossberg.

Rhône (F.)

A region in southern France, along the Rhône river from Lyons south to Avignon, 140 miles long. The famous wines of Hermitage, Côte-Rôtie, Condrieu and Châteauneuf-du-Pape are from the Rhône region, as well as Tavel and Lirac. The important grapes are the Syrah, Grenache, Viognier, Roussanne, Marsanne and Clairette.

Ribatejo (P.)

A region north of Lisbon; produces red and white Serradayres wine and bulk wines.

Ribeauvillé (F.)

A village in the northern Haut-Rhin district, Alsace region.

Ribeiro DO (Sp.)

A district in the southern Galicia region; produces red wine from the Sonsón grape and white wine from Godello, Treixadura, Torrentés, Macabeo, Albilla and Loureira grapes.

Ribolla Giglia (I.)

1. A white grape grown in the Friuli-Venezia Giulia region.
2. A white wine from the Collio district, in the Friuli-Venezia Giulia region; made from the Ribolla Gialla grape.

Ricardelle de La Clape (F.)

An estate in La Clape, Coteaux du Languedoc district, Languedoc region.

Ricasoli, Barone (I.)   1141

An ancient estate in Florence, Tuscany region; produces Arbia, Brolio Bianco, Chianti, Chianti Classico, Galestro, Rosé, Torricella and Vin Santo wines. 165,000 cases. 600 acres.

Riccadonna, Ottavio (I.)   1921

A winery in Canelli, Piedmont region; produces Asti Spumante and several other sparkling wines, vermouth and Marsala.

Richards, Domaine des (F.)

An estate in Violès, Côtes du Rhône district, Rhône region; produces red, white and rosé wines made from Grenache, Syrah, Carignan and Ugni Blanc grapes. 45 acres.

Richard's Wine Cellar (U.S.)   1951

A winery in Petersburg, Virginia; also owns wineries in Canandaigua, New York, the Tenver Winery in South Carolina and the Mother Vineyard Winery of North Carolina, which recently moved to Palestine, Virginia.

Richebourg AOC (F.)

A famous *Grand Cru* vineyard in Vosne-Romanée, Côte de Nuits district, Burgundy. Around 1930 7.5 acres of the Véroilles vineyard were added. There are 8 owners, including the Domaine de la Romanée-Conti. 20 acres.

Richemone, La (F.)

A *Premier Cru* vineyard in Nuits-St.-Georges, Côte de Nuits district, Burgundy. 5.5 acres.

Richert and Sons (U.S.)   1953

A winery in Morgan Hill, Santa Clara County, California; produces Sherry and Port as well as Cabernet and Chardonnay wines. 5,000 cases.

Rico's Winery (U.S.)   1976

A renovated winery in Albuquerque, New Mexico, 6,000 feet high; produces Zinfandel and blended wines. 3 acres.

riddler

One who shakes and turns Champagne bottles in preparation for *dégorgement*, the release of sediment caused by the 2nd fermentation.

Riddoch (Aus.)

The first winery in the Coonawarra district, South Australia; now owned by Wynn's; produces red wines.

Ridge Vineyards (U.S.) 1960
first wine 1962

A famous winery in Cupertino, northwest of Saratoga, in the Santa Cruz Mountains, Santa Clara County, California; produces Cabernet, Zinfandel, Petite Sirah and Chardonnay wines, many from purchased grapes. The Montebello vineyard is the source of the estate-bottled Cabernet, Chardonnay, Zinfandel and Petite Sirah wines. 40,000 cases. 50 acres.

Riecine (I.) 1971

An estate in Gaiole, Tuscany region; produces Chianti Classico and Riecine Bianco wines.

Ried (A.)

A German word for vineyard, a term used in Austria.

Rieslaner (G.)

A white grape – a cross of Sylvaner and Riesling; developed at the State Viticultural Institute, Würzburg-Veitshöchheim in 1921; grown only in the Franken region.

Riesling

A white grape, the principal grape of Germany; also important in Alsace and Austria and grown in all the important wine-producing regions of the world; late-ripening, modest bearer, medium-sized grapes; also called Johannisberg Riesling and White Riesling.

Riesling de Caldas (Br.)

A grape grown in Brazil; also called Duchesse or Dutchess.

Rietvallei EWO (S. Af.)

An estate in the Robertson district; produces white wines, especially Muscat.

Rieussec, Château (F.)

An estate in Fargues, Sauternes district, Bordeaux; classified in 1855 as a *Premier Cru*; produces sweet, white wine and a dry wine called "R." 75% Sémillon, 22% Sauvignon, 3% Muscadelle. 8,500 cases. 130 acres.

Rincione (I.)

Red, white and rosé wines from Calatafimi, in western Sicily. The red wine is made from Nero d'Avola, Nerello Mascalese, Vernaccia Nera and Trebbiano grapes and the white wine is made from Catarratto, Inzolia and Trebbiano grapes.

Río Grande do Sul (Br.)

An important state in southern Brazil, where most of the country's wine is produced. 4.7 million gallons.

Río Negro (Arg.)

A river and province, south of Buenos Aires, and the southernmost wine region; produces red and white wines. 50,000 acres.

Rioja DO (Sp.)

A famous region of northern Spain, near the Ebro River; divided into 3 districts: Rioja Alta, Rioja Alavesa and Rioja Baja; produces red, white and rosé wines. The red wine is made from Garnacha, Tempranillo and Mazuelo grapes and is always blended; the white wine is made from Malvasía, Viura, Calagraño and Garnacha grapes. 110,000 acres.

Rioja, La (Arg.)

A city and region in west central Argentina; produces mostly white and rosé wines. 20,000 acres.

Rioja Alta S.A., La Bodegas (Sp.) 1890

A winery in Haro, Rioja Alta region; produces many wines from their own and purchased grapes. 600 acres.

Rioja Vega (Sp.)

A red wine from the Rioja region; produced by Bodegas Muerza.

Riojanas S.A., Bodegas (Sp.) 1890

A winery in Cenicero, Rioja Alta region; produces red and white wines from their own and purchased grapes. 80,000 cases. 500 acres.

Riotte, La (F.)

A *Premier Cru* vineyard in Morey-St.-Denis, Côte de Nuits district, Burgundy. 6 acres.

Riottes, Les (F.)

A *Premier Cru* vineyard in Monthélie, Côte de Beaune district, Burgundy. 2 acres.

Ripeau, Château (F.)

An estate in St.-Émilion, Bordeaux; classified in 1955 as a *Grand Cru Classé*. 12,000 cases. 75 acres.

Ripley (U.S.)

An American white hybrid grape developed at the New York State Agriculture Station in Geneva; used to make dry, white wine.

Riquewihr (F.)

An important village in the Haut-Rhin district, Alsace region; especially known for Riesling wine; includes the Sporen and Schoenenberg vineyards.

Riscal, S.A. Herederos de Marqués de (Sp.)   1860

A winery in Elciego, Rioja Alavesa region; produces wines from their own and purchased grapes, the red wine includes a varying percentage of Cabernet grapes. 250,000 cases.

riserva, riserva speciale (I.)

Reserve and special reserve, wine that is aged for a number of years in wood before bottling, usually a year longer than normal for *riserva*, and an additional 2-3 years longer for *riserva speciale*.

Riserva del Re (I.)

A red wine from Pierantonio, in the Colli Altotiberini district, northern Umbria region; made from Merlot and Sangiovese grapes.

Ritchie Creek Vineyard (U.S.)   1974, planted 1967

A small winery on Spring Mountain, St. Helena, Napa Valley, California; produces Cabernet and Chardonnay wines. 500 cases. 7 acres.

Riunite (I.)   1950

A large co-op group in Reggio Emilia, Emilia-Romagna region, with 10,000 growers; produces Lambrusco and white and rosé wines. 13 million cases.

Riva S.A., La (Sp.)

A Sherry producer in Jerez de la Frontera; produces several types of Sherry, including "Tres Palmas" (a *fino*).

River Oaks (U.S.)

The label used by a corporation for generic and varietal wines made from grapes grown in Alexander Valley, Sonoma County, California; made by several wineries, including Clos du Bois. 700 acres. 50,000 cases.

River Road Vineyards (U.S.)   1977

A winery in Forestville, Sonoma County, California; produces Zinfandel, Chardonnay, Fumé Blanc and Johannisberg Riesling wines. 7,000 cases. 120 acres.

River Run Vintners (U.S.)   1st wine 1978

A winery in Watsonville, Monterey County, California; produces Cabernet Sauvignon, Zinfandel, Pinot Noir, Chardonnay and Johannisberg Riesling wines from purchased grapes. 3,000 cases.

Rivera (I.)

A winery in Andria, Apulia region; produces Castel del Monte, Il Falcone, Locorotondo and Moscato wines. 80,000 cases.

Riverina (Aus.)

A district in central New South Wales, 250 miles west of Sidney; also includes the MIA district.

Riverland, The (Aus.)

A district along the Murray River, northeast of Adelaide, South Australia; produces mostly fortified wines.

Rivesaltes AOC (F.)

.1. A town and district northwest of Perpignan, in the Roussillon region, which produces:

2. Sweet, red, white and rosé VDN wines, some made in *rancio* style, made from Muscat, Grenache, Maccabéo and Malvoisie grapes.

Riviera del Garda Bresciano DOC (I.)

1. A large district around Lake Garda, east of Brescia, in the eastern Lombardy region, which produces:

2. Light, red and rosé (called *chiaretto*) wines made from Groppello, Sangiovese, Barbera and Marzemino grapes.

Rivière, Château La (F.)

An estate in Blaignan, Medoc district, Bordeaux; classified in 1978 as a *Cru Bourgeois*, but in 1978 listed as Being Reconstituted. 6,000 cases. 30 acres.

Rivière, Château la (F.)

An estate in La Rivière, Côtes de Fronsac district, Bordeaux. 20,000 cases. 120 acres.

Rivière-Le-Haut, Domaine de (F.)

An estate in La Clape, Coteaux du Languedoc district, Languedoc region; produces white wine made from the Bourboulenc grape.

Rizling (Y.)

The Italian Riesling grape or wine, not the true Johannisberg Riesling.

Rizzardi, Guerrieri (I.)

An estate in Bardolino, western Veneto region; produces Amarone, Bardolino, Soave, Valpolicello and San Pietro wines. 60,000 cases.

Robardelle (F.)

A *Premier Cru* vineyard (in part) in Volnay, Côte de Beaune district, Burgundy. 8 acres.

Robert, Paul (Alg.)

A well-known red wine from the Haut-Dahra district, west of Algiers; now called Taughrite.

Robertson WO (S.Af.)

A town and district east of Capetown and Stellenbosch; produces white wines made from Chenin Blanc, Palomino, Colombard and Muscat grapes; also dessert wines.

Robertson Bros. & Co. Lda. (P.)   1881

A Port producer in Vila Nova de Gaia; shipper of Rebello Valente ports; owns Quinta de la Rosa.

Robola (Gr.)

1. A white grape grown on the Island of Cephalonia.

2. A white wine from the Island of Cephalonia, off the coast of west central Greece; made from the Robola grape.

Robson (Aus.)   1972

A small winery in Hunter Valley, New South Wales; produces Chardonnay, Gewürztraminer, Sauvignon Blanc, Hermitage, Cabernet Sauvignon and Pinot Noir wines. 5,000 cases. 10 acres.

Roc, Château Le (F.)

An estate in St.-Estèphe, Haut-Médoc district, Bordeaux; classified in 1932 as a *Cru Bourgeois*. 500 cases. 3 acres.

Rocca Bernarda (I.)

An estate in Ipplis, Friuli-Venezia Giulia region; produces Colli Orientali and Picolit wines.

Rocca Rosso (I.)

A red wine from Angera, near Lake Maggiore, in the northwestern Lombardy region; made from Bonarda, Barbera and Nebbiolo grapes; also called Angera.

Rocche di Manzoni, Podere Valentino Migliorini (I.)

An estate in Monforte d'Alba, Piedmont region; produces Barbera, Barolo, Doletto, Bricco Manzoni and sparkling wines. 8,000 cases. 35 acres.

Roche AOC, Clos de la (F.)

A *Grand Cru* vineyard in Morey-St.-Denis, Côte de Nuits district, Burgundy. 40 acres.

Roché *also* **Rouchet (I.)**

1. A rare, red grape grown in Castagnole, northeast of Asti, in the central Piedmont region, which produces:

2. A red wine made from the Roché grape.

Roche-aux-Moines, La (F.)

A *Grand Cru* vineyard in Savennières, Anjou district, Loire Valley; has its own Savennières AOC. 17 acres.

Roches Gaudinières, Clos des (F.)

An estate in Mouzillon, Muscadet de Sèvre-et-Maine district, Loire Valléy. 45 acres.

Rochet, Château (F.)

The former name of Château Lafon-Rochet, a *Quatrième Cru* in St.-Estèphe, Haut-Médoc district, Bordeaux.

Rochette, Clos (F.)

An estate in Romanèche-Thorins (Moulin-à-Vent), Beaujolais district, Burgundy.

Rochette, Clos de la (F.)

An estate in Fleurie, Beaujolais district, Burgundy.

Roddis Cellar (U.S.)   1978

A small winery on Diamond Mountain, in Calistoga, Napa Valley, California; produces Cabernet Sauvignon wine. 5 acres.

Rodelsee (G.)

A village in the Franken region, Bereich Steigerwald, Grosslage Schlossberg. The vineyards are: Küchenmeister and Schwanleite. 240 acres.

Rodet, Antonin (F.)   1815

An estate and merchant in Mercurey, Côte Chalonnaise district,Burgundy. 50 acres,

including 7.5 acres of Mercurey Clos-du-Roi, 7.5 acres of Clos l'Éveque and 5 acres of La Mission Monopole.

Rodier, Cuvée Camille (F.)

A red wine from the Hospices de Nuits, in Nuits-St.-Georges, Burgundy. The *cuvée* is composed of .8 acre of Nuits-St.-Georges Rues de Chaux.

Roditis *also* **Roditys (Gr.)**

See **Rhoditis.**

Roederer, Louis (F.)   1765, 1827

A Champagne producer in Reims. The *cuvée de prestige* is Cristal vintage, made since 1876. 1.5 million bottles. 450 acres.

Rognet, Le (F.)

A *Grand Cru* vineyard in Ladoix-Serrigny, Côte de Beaune district, Burgundy; sold as Corton-Rognet; red and white wines. 25 acres.

Roi, Clos du (F.)

A *Premier Cru* vineyard in Mercurey, Côte Chalonnaise district, southern Burgundy.

Roi, Clos du (F.)

A *Grand Cru* vineyard (in part) in Aloxe-Corton, Côte de Beaune district, Burgundy. 25 acres.

Roi, Clos du (F.)

A *Premier Cru* vineyard (in part) in Beaune, Côte de Beaune district, Burgundy. 34 acres.

Rois, Clos des (F.)

A *Premier Cru* vineyard in Sampigny-les-Maranges, Côte de Beaune district, Burgundy.

Rolin, Nicolas (F.)

The Chancellor to the Duke of Burgundy, Philip the Good; he founded the Hôtel Dieu, or Hospices, in Beaune, Burgundy in 1443 and donated to the Hospices some of his vineyards.

Rolin, Cuvée Nicolas (F.)

A red wine from the Hospices de Beaune, Côte de Beaune district, Burgundy. The *cuvée* is composed of the following vineyards in Beaune: Les Cent Vignes – 4 acres, Les Grèves – 2 acres and En Genêt – 1 acre. 675 cases.

Rolle (F.)

A white grape grown in the Provence region.

Roma Wines (U.S.)

At one time an independent winery, now a part of Guild Wines, and a label for their generic jug wines. The old Roma winery is now Cribari & Sons, also a part of Guild Wines.

Romain (F.)

In the Auxerrois district, southwest of Chablis, another name for the red César grape.

Romain, Château (Alg.)

A red wine from the Zaccar district, west of Algiers.

Romanèche-Thorins (F.)

An important commune in the Beaujolais district of Burgundy, where the vineyards of Moulin-à-Vent, a *Cru* Beaujolais, are located. At one time, the wines of Romanèche-Thorins were made separately.

Romanée, La (F.)

A *Premier Cru* vineyard in Chassagne-Montrachet, Côte de Beaune district, Burgundy. 8 acres.

Romanée, La (F.)

An unclassified vineyard in Gevrey-Chambertin, Côte de Nuits district, Burgundy.

Romanée AOC, La (F.)

A *Grand Cru* vineyard in Vosne-Romanée, Côte de Nuits district, Burgundy; the smallest vineyard in Burgundy, situated just above Romanée-Conti; since 1976

made by Bouchard Père et Fils. 355 cases. acres.

Romanée-Conti AOC, La (F.)

A famous *Grand Cru* vineyard in Vosne-Romanée, Côte de Nuits district, Burgundy known from the 13th century, but as Romanée only since 1651; Conti was added 1760 when sold to Prince de Conti. Owned by the Société Civile de la Romanée-Conti it is a *monopole*, estate-bottled wine. Ungrafted, old vines were used to make the wine until 1946, when the old vines were uprooted and new, grafted vines were planted; the first vintage from the new vines was the 1952. 700 cases. 4.8 acres.

Romanée-Conti, Domaine de la (F.)

An estate in Vosne-Romanée, Côte de Nuits district, Burgundy. 63 acres, including Romanée-Conti Monopole - 4.8 acres, La Tâche Monopole - 15 acres, 8 acres of Richebourg, 13 acres of Romanée St.-Vivant, 9 acres of Grands Échézeaux, 11.5 acres of Échézeaux and 1.5 acres of Montrachet.

Romanée-Saint-Vivant AOC, La (F.)

A *Grand Cru* vineyard in Vosne-Romanée, Côte de Nuits district, Burgundy; it was once an Abbey. A part of the vineyard called Les Quatre Journeaux is owned by L. Latour. 4,000 cases. 23.5 acres.

Romănești (U.S.S.R.)

1. A district in Moldavia SSR, which produces:

2. A red wine made from Cabernet Sauvignon, Merlot and Malbec grapes.

Romania *also* Roumania *and* Rumania

A country in southeastern Europe; produces the well-known Cotnari, Murfatlar and Tîrnave wines. 200 million gallons (6th largest production in Europe). 800,000 acres.

Romassan, Château (F.)

An estate in Bandol, Provence region; a part of the Domaines Ott.

omefort, Château (F.)

n estate in Cussac, Haut-Médoc district, ordeaux; classified in 1978 as Being econstituted.

omeiko (Gr.)

. red grape grown in Crete.

ömer (G.)

. large wine goblet, with a cone-shaped tem, for drinking ordinary wine; also alled *Pokal*.

omer, Château (F.)

.n estate in Fargues, Sauternes district, ordeaux; classified in 1855 as a *Deuxième ru*. 50% Sémillon, 40% Sauvignon, 10% .luscat. 1,500 cases. 30 acres.

.omer-du-Hayot, Château (F.)

.n estate in Fargues, Sauternes district, ordeaux; classified in 1855 as a *Deuxième ru*; part of Château Romer, but bottled eparately, until 1977, when from then on ll the wine from both parts of the property as been bottled as Château Romer-du-Hayot. 30 acres. 1,500 cases.

.ömerlay (G.)

he only *Grosslage* in the Ruwer Valley, a ributary of the Mosel, Bereich Saar-Ruver, Mosel-Saar-Ruwer region.

.omorantin (F.)

.. A town southeast of Blois, in the eastern .oire Valley.

... A white grape grown in the Touraine region, Loire Valley.

.onceret (F.)

.. *Premier Cru* vineyard in Volnay, Côte de Beaune district, Burgundy. 5 acres.

.onchi di Cialla (I.)

.An estate in Prepotto, Friuli-Venezia Giulia region; produces Colli Orientali, Picolit, Schioppettino and Verduzzo wines.

Ronchi di Fornaz (I.)

An estate in Fornalis di Cividale, Friuli-Venezia Giulia region; produces Colli Orientali wines.

Roncière, La (F.)

A *Premier Cru* vineyard in Nuits-St.-Georges, Côte de Nuits district, Burgundy. 5.5 acres.

Roncières (F.)

A *Premier Cru* vineyard in Chablis, Chablis district, Burgundy; usually included as part of the Mélinots vineyard.

Ronco di Mompiano (I.)

A Red wine from Mompiano, near Brescia, in the eastern Lombardy region; made from Marzemino and Merlot grapes.

Roodeberg (S. Af.)

A blended red wine from the Paarl district; produced by the KWV.

Ropiteau Frères (F.)   1848

A merchant controlling 2 estates in Meursault, Burgundy:

1. Domaine A. Ropiteau-Mignon, with 2.5 acres of Meursault Les Genevrières, 1 acre of Les Charmes, .5 acre of La Goutte d'Or, 1.7 acres of Le Poruzot, .8 acre of Les Chevalières, 9 acres of Clous, 2.5 acres of Volnay Clos des Chênes, 3.4 acres of Pommard Les Chanlins, 2.5 acres of Monthélie Les Champs Fulliot, 3.3 acres of Les Duresses, 2.5 acres of Beaune Les Grèves and .8 acre of Clos Vougeot.

2. Domaine Maurice Ropiteau, with 3.2 acres of Meursault Les Perrières and 3.2 acres of Les Grands Charrons.

Roque de By, Château La (F.)

An estate in Bégadan, Médoc district, Bordeaux; classified in 1978 as a *Cru Bourgeois*.

Roques, Château des (F.)

An estate in Sarrians, Vacqueyras district, southern Rhône region.

Roquetaillade, Château de (F.)

An estate in Ordonnac-et-Potensac, Médoc district, Bordeaux; classified in 1932 as a *Cru Bourgeois*. 1,200 cases. 8 acres.

Rosa di Albenga (I.)

A dry, rosé wine from Albenga, southwest of Savona, in the western Liguria region; made from the Barbarossa grape.

Rosa del Golfo (I.)

A rosé wine from Alezio, in the southern Apulia region; made from Negroamaro and Malvasia Nero grapes.

Rosa de Perú (Mex.)

A grape grown in the Baja California region.

Rosacker (F.)

A vineyard in Hunawihr, Haut-Rhin district, Alsace region.

rosado (Sp., P.)

Rosé.

Rosaria (I.)

A grape grown in the northwestern Tuscany region.

Rosatello (I.)

A rosé wine from the Tuscany region; made from the Sangiovese grape.

Rosati Winery (U.S.)   c. 1937

A winery in Rosati, east of St. James, central Missouri; grows mostly Catawba grapes. 75 acres.

rosato (I.)

Rosé.

Rosato di Montanello (I.)

A rosé wine from Montanello, near Macerata, in the southeastern Marches region; made from Sangiovese and Montepulciano grapes.

Rosé (I.)

One of several clones of the Nebbiolo grap grown in the Barolo district. DOC approved.

rosé (F.)

Pink, rose-colored; a tinted white win made by allowing the skins from re grapes to ferment with the wine for 2-3 days, after which they are removed. *Vi gris* is a paler version of rosé.

Rosé di Alghero (I.)

A dry, rosé wine from Alghero, in north western Sardinia; made from Cannona and Sangiovese grapes.

Rose Marechale, Château de la (F.)

An estate in St. Seurin de Cadourne, Haut Médoc district, Bordeaux; classified in 1978 as a *Cru Bourgeois*.

Rose Pauillac, La (F.)   1933

A co-op estate in Pauillac, Haut-Médoc district, Bordeaux; added to the 1932 classification sometime later as a *Cru Bourgeois*. 30,000 cases. 275 acres.

Rosé des Riceys AOC (F.)

A still, pink wine from three *communes* with names starting with Riceys in the southern Champagne region: Riceys-Bas, Riceys-Haute and Riceys-Haut-Rive; made from Pinot Noir, Gamay and Savagnin Rose grapes.

Roseę (G.)

A new (1971) official German designation for rosé wines, formerly called Weisherbst.

Rosemount Estate (Aus.)   1969

A winery in Denman, Upper Hunter Valley, New South Wales; produces Rhine Riesling, including a TBA, Gewürztraminer, Sémillon and Chardonnay wines. 150,000 cases. 1,000 acres.

Rosenblume Cellars Winery (U.S.)   1978

A small winery in Oakland, Alameda County, California; produces Cabernet Sauvignon, Zinfandel, Petite Sirah, Chardonnay, Johannisberg Riesling, Chenin Blanc and Gewürztraminer wines from purchased grapes. 1,500 cases.

Rosenhügler (A.)

A white grape grown in the Krems district.

Rosenthaler Riesling (Bul.)

A white wine from the Karlovo district; made from Rhine Riesling and Italian Riesling grapes.

Rosette (F.)

A red hybrid grape; also called Seibel 1,000.

Rosette AOC (F.)

A semi-sweet, white wine from Bergerac, in the Southwest region; made from Sauvignon, Sémillon and Muscadelle grapes.

Ross-Kellerei (U.S.)   **1980**

A winery in Buellton, Santa Barbara County, California; produces blended and varietal wines from purchased grapes under the San Carlos de Jonata and Zaca Creek brands. 4,000 cases.

Rossese (I.)

A red grape grown in the Liguria region.

Rossese di Albenga (I.)

A red wine from Albenga, in the western Liguria region; made from the Rossese grape.

Rossese di Dolceacqua DOC (I.)

A red wine from Dolceacqua and several nearby villages in the western Liguria region; made from the Rossese grape. Also called Dolceacqua DOC.

Rossetto (I.)

A white grape grown in the Latium region; also called Trebbiano Giallo.

rosso (I.)

Red.

Rosso del Armentano (I.)

A red wine from south of Faenza, in the eastern Emilia-Romagna region; made from the Sangiovese grape with 30% Cabernet Sauvignon and 10% Pinot Nero grapes.

Rosso Barletta DOC (I.)

A red wine from the port city of Barletta, in the northern Apulia region; made from mostly Uva di Troia grapes and some Montepulciano, Sangiovese and Malbec grapes.

Rosso di Bellagio (I.)

A red wine from Bellagio, on Lake Como, in the northwestern Lombardy region; made from Malbec, Pinot Nero, Cabernet Sauvignon and Merlot grapes.

Rosso di Berchidda (I.)

A red wine from Berchidda, in northeastern Sardinia; made from mostly Pascale grapes with some Vermentino grapes.

Rosso della Bissera (I.)

A red wine from southwest of Bologna, in the Emilia-Romagna region; made from the Montepulciano grape.

Rosso Canosa DOC (I.)

A red wine from Canosa, northwest of Bari, in the northern Apulia region; made from 75% Uva di Troia grapes with Montepulciano and Sangiovese grapes. Also called Canusium.

Rosso di Cercatoia (I.)

A red wine from Montecarlo, near Lucca, northeast of Pisa, in the northwestern Tuscany region; made from Sangiovese and other grapes.

Rosso di Cerignola DOC (I.)

A red wine from Cerignola, in the northern Apulia region; made from a varying blend of Uva di Troia, Negroamaro, Sangiovese, Montepulciano, Malbec and Trebbiano Tosca grapes.

Rosso delle Colline Lucchesi DOC (I.)
1967

A red wine similar to Chianti, from the hills around Lucca, in the northwestern Tuscany region; made from Chianti grapes, with some Ciliegiolo and Vermentino grapes.

Rosso Cònero DOC (I.)

A red wine from Mt. Cònero, in the east central Marches region; made from the Montepulciano grape with up to 15% percent Sangiovese grapes.

Rosso di Corinaldo (I.)

A red wine from Corinaldo, near Jesi, in the east central Marches region; made from the Merlot grape.

Rosso dei Frati (I.)

A red, *frizzante* wine from the Lugana district, in the southeastern Lombardy region; made from Sangiovese, Groppello, Merlot and Corvina grapes.

Rosso Piceno DOC (I.)

1. A large district covering much of the southeastern Marches region, which produces:
2. A red wine made from 60% Sangiovese, up to 40% Montepulciano and/or up to 15% Trebbiano and Passerina grapes.

Rosso della Pusterla (I.)

A red wine from Vigolo Marchese, Colli Piacentini district, in the western Emilia-Romagna region; made from Barbera, Bonarda and Fruttano grapes.

Rosso del Roccolo (I.)

A red wine from Santa Maria della Versa, in the Oltrepò Pavese district, southern Lombardy region.

Rosso San Pietro (I.)

A red wine from Bardolino, in the southwestern Veneto region; made from semi-dried Corvina, Rondinella, Molinara and Negrara grapes.

Rosso di Sava DOC (I.)

A red wine from Sava, near Manduria, i the southern Apulia region; made from th Primitivo grape.

Rosso di Spicca (I.)

A red wine from Orvieto, in the Umbri region.

Rosso dei Vigneti di Brunello (I.)

A red wine from Montalcino, in souther Tuscany, made from the grapes of youn Brunello vines.

rot blanc (F.)

See **white rot.**

Rotberger (G.)

A red grape - a cross of Trollinger and Ries ling; developed at the State Teaching an Research Institute, Geisenheim, Germany

Rotgipfler (A.)

A red grape used to make red and whit wines in the Baden district, south o Vienna.

Rotgold (G.)

A rosé wine from the Baden region; mad from a blend of Pinot Noir and Pinot Gri grapes.

Rothbury Estate (Aus.)
196

A winery in the Lower Hunter Valley, New South Wales; produces Cabernet Sauvig non, Shiraz, Pinot Noir, Sémillon, Char donnay and Gewürztraminer wines 75,000 cases. 700 acres.

rôti (F.)

Roasted, parched, burnt, dried-out; *pas sito*, in Italian.

Rotling (G.)

A type of rosé wine made by blending red and white wine.

Rotluf (F.)

A vineyard in Barr, Bas-Rhin district, Alsace region.

oty, Domaine Joseph (F.)

recent estate in Gevrey-Chambertin, Côte de Nuits district, Burgundy; owns ome Charmes-Chambertin, Mazis-Chambertin, Griotte-Chambertin, Gevrey-Chambertin Clos Prieur and Les Fontenys.

oucaneuf (F., U.S.)

red hybrid grape; also called Seyve-Villard 12,309.

ouchet also Roché (I.)

. A local red grape grown around Asti, in he southern Piedmont region, which produces:

. A rare, red wine from high altitude vineyards in Castagnole, northeast of Asti.

oucoules, Les (F.)

A vineyard section of Hermitage, northern Rhône region; planted with white grapes.

ouden-Smith Vineyards (U.S.)   1972

A winery in Santa Cruz City, Santa Cruz County, California; produces Chardonnay, Pinot Blanc, Cabernet Sauvignon, Zinfandel and Petite Sirah wines from purchased grapes. 10,000 cases.

ouge (F.)

Red.

ouge Homme (Aus.)

A famous, old winery in Coonawarra, South Australia, named after Bill Redman; taken over by Lindeman's in 1965.

ougeau (F.)

A disease of the vine caused by a virus or a wound which interrupts the flow of sap. Also called leaf-reddening.

Rougeon

A red, hybrid grape. Also called Seibel 5898.

Rougeot, H. (F.)

An estate and merchant in Meursault, Côte de Beaune, Burgundy. 25 acres, including 2.5 acres of Meursault Les

Charmes, 2.5 acres of Volnay Les Santenots and some Ladoix-Côte de Beaune and Meursault.

Rouget, Château (F.)

An estate in Pomerol, Bordeaux. 3,000 cases. 30 acres.

Roulot et Fils, Guy (F.)

An estate in Meursault, Côte de Beaune district, Burgundy. 37 acres, including 15 acres of Meursault (some Perrières and Charmes), 6 acres of Auxey-Duresses (red), and some Beaune, Bourgogne and Aligoté.

Roumier et ses Fils, Domaine Georges (F.)

An estate in Chambolle-Musigny, Côte de Nuits, Burgundy. 40 acres, including .3 acre of Musigny, 5 acres of Bonnes Mares, 2.5 acres of Clos de Vougeot, 2.5 acres of Chambolle-Musigny Les Amoureuses and 6 acres of Morey-St.-Denis Clos de la Bussière Monopole.

Round Hill Cellars also Round Hill Vineyards (U.S.)   1978

A winery in St. Helena, Napa Valley, California; produces Cabernet Sauvignon, Zinfandel, Gewürztraminer, Fumé Blanc and other wines from purchased grapes from northern coast districts. Earlier wines were bottlings of purchased wines. Second label is Rutherford Ranch. 70,000 cases.

Roupeiro Cachado (P.)

A white grape grown in southern Portugal.

Rouquette-sur-Mer (F.)

An estate in La Clape, Coteaux de Languedoc district, Languedoc region; produces red, white and rosé wines.

Roussanne (F.)

A white grape used in making red and white Châteauneuf-du-Pape and other white wines from the Rhône region.

Rousseau, Domaine (F.)

An estate in Laudon, Côtes du Rhône-Villages district, southern Rhône region; also produces Lirac wines. 70 acres.

Rousseau-Deslandes, Cuvée (F.)

A red wine from the Hospices de Beaune, Côte de Beaune district, Burgundy. The *cuvée* is composed of the following vineyards in Beaune: Les Cent Vignes – 2.5 acres, Les Montrevenots – 1.5 acres, La Mignotte – 1 acre and Les Avaux – 1 acre. 450 cases.

Rousseau Père et fils, Domaine Armand (F.)

An estate in Gevrey-Chambertin, Côte de Nuits district, Burgundy; bottling since 1926. 32 acres, including 1.8 acres of Chambertin-Clos de Bèze, 2.5 acres of Chambertin, 2.5 acres of Chambertin Clos des Ruchottes Monopole, 8 acres of Gevrey-Chambertin Clos St.-Jacques, 1.2 acres of Charmes-Chambertin, 2 acres of Mazoyères-Chambertin, 1.2 acres of Mazis-Chambertin, 2 acres of Gevrey-Chambertin Cazetiers, 2 acres of Lavaux St.-Jacques and 3.7 acres of Morey-St.-Denis Clos de la Roche.

Roussette (F.)

A white grape of unknown origin grown in Seyssel, in the Savoie region, southeastern France, possibly related to the Roussanne grape. Also called Altesse.

Roussette de Savoie AOC (F.)

A dry white wine from the Savoie region; made from the Altesse grape and some Chardonnay and Mondeuse Blanc grapes.

Roussillon (F.)

A region in southern France, on the Mediterranean Sea, the southwestern part of what is called the Midi. Produces the VDN wines of Banyuls, Rivesaltes and Grand Roussillon, and Côtes du Roussillon AOC wines.

Rouvière, Mas de la (F.)

An estate in Bandol, in the Provence region. 70 acres.

Rouvrettes, Les (F.)

A *Premier Cru* vineyard (in part) in Savigny, Côte de Beaune district, Burgundy. 14.5 acres.

Roux, Château de (F.)

An estate in Cannet-des-Maures, Provenc region.

Roux, Les Fils de Hilarion (F.)

An estate in Gigondas, southern Rhône re gion; produces Gigondas wines. 6,50 cases. 60 acres.

Roux Père et Fils (F.)

An estate in Saint-Aubin, Côte de Beaun district, Burgundy. 25 acres, including . acre of Chassagne-Montrachet Clos St. Jean, .6 acre of Premier Cru, 3.4 acres o Santenay Premier Cru, .8 acre of Puligny Montrachet and 7.5 acres of St.-Aubin (rec and white).

Roxheim (G.)

A village in the Nahe region, Bereich Schloss Böckelheim, Grosslage Rosengar ten. The vineyards are: Berg, Birkenberg, Höllenpfad, Hüttenberg, Mühlenberg and Sonnenberg.

Roy, Clos du (F.)

A vineyard in Bué, Sancerre district, Upper Loire region. 35 acres.

Roy-Thévenin, Domaine (F.)

An estate in Montagny-Les-Buxy; produces white Montagny wine. 23 acres.

Royalty (U.S.)

A red *teinturier* (red-juiced) grape – a cross of Alicante Ganzin and Trousseau; developed in California by Harold Olmo in 1938. Grown in California as a blending wine and occasionally as a varietal wine.

Royat, Cordon de (F.)

A method of vine-training utilizing gobelet pruning and training the canes along wires.

Rozay, Château de (F.)

An estate in the Condrieu district, northern Rhône region. 400 cases. 4 acres.

Rozes Lda. (P.)   1853

A Port producer in Vila Nova de Gaia.

Rubesco DOC (I.)

A red wine from the Torgiano district, south of Perugia, in the central Umbria region; made from Sangiovese, Canaiolo, Montepulciano and Ciliegiolo grapes. Produced by Lungarotti.

Rubino (I.)

A red wine from the Colli Altotiberini district, in the northern Umbria region; made from Sangiovese and Merlot grapes.

Rubino (I.)

A red wine from the northern Abruzzi region; made from Montepulciano grapes with 20% Sangiovese grapes.

Rubino di Cantavenna DOC (I.)

A red wine from Cantavenna, north of Alessandria, in the east central Piedmont region; made from 75-90% Barbera grapes with Freisa and/or Grignolino grapes.

Rubired (U.S.)

A red *teinturier* (red-juiced) grape – a cross of Alicante Ganzin and Tinto Cão (or Mourisco); developed in 1938 by Harold Olmo, in California and grown there to make Port-style wines.

Ruby Cabernet (U.S.)

A red grape – a cross of Carignane and Cabernet Sauvignon; developed in California by Dr. Harold Olmo in 1946; grown extensively in California.

Ruby Port (P.)

A rich, sweet Port wine aged for 2 or more years in wood.

Ruchots, Les (F.)

A *Premier Cru* vineyard in Morey-St.-Denis, Côte de Nuits district, Burgundy. 6 acres.

Ruchottes-Chambertin AOC (F.)

A *Grand Cru* vineyard in Gevrey-Chambertin, Côte de Nuits district, Burgundy. 7.5 acres.

Rudd Cellars, Channing (U.S.)   1977

A small winery in Alameda, Alameda County, California; produces Cabernet, Petite Sirah, Zinfandel and other wines. 1,000 cases. 60 acres.

Rüdesheim (G.)

A village in the Rheingau region, Bereich Johannisberg, Grosslage Burgweg. The vineyards are: Berg Rottland, Berg Roseneck, Berg Schlossberg, Bischofsberg, Drachenstein, Kirchenpfad, Klosterberg, Klosterlay, Magdelenenkreuz and Rosengarten. 800 acres.

Rüdesheim (G.)

A village in the Nahe region, Bereich Schloss Böckelheim, Grosslage Rosengarten. The vineyards are Goldrube and Wiesberg.

Rue de Chau (F.)

A *Premier Cru* vineyard in Nuits-St.-Georges, Côte de Nuits district, Burgundy. 6 acres.

Rueda DO (Sp.)   1980

1. A village and district southwest of Valladolid, in north central Spain, which produces:

2. Sherry-like, white wines with *flor*, and dry, white wines made from Verdejo grapes with some Jerez Palomino and Viura grapes. 13-17% alcohol.

Ruedo (Sp.)

A dry, white wine from the Montilla-Moriles district, north of Málaga, in the Andalucia region. 14% alcohol.

Rufete (P.)

A red grape grown in the Dão region; also called Tinta Pinheira.

Ruffiat (F.)

A local white grape grown in the Pacher-
enc-du-Vic-Bihl district of the Southwest
region.

Ruffino, I.L. (I.)   1877

A large estate in Pontassieve, Tuscany region; produces Chianti, Chianti Classico,
Galestro, Orvieto and Rosatello wines;
made from their own and purchased
grapes. Riserva Ducale and Riserva Ducale
Gold Label are considered their best
Chianti Classico wines. 700 acres.

Rufina (I.)

A village east of Florence, in the northeastern Tuscany region, and which gives its
name to the Chianti Rufina district, which
is to the northeast of the Chianti Classico
district.

Rugiens-Bas, Les (F.)

A *Premier Cru* vineyard in Pommard, Côte
de Beaune district, Burgundy. 15 acres.
Usually appears on the label as Rugiens.

Rugiens-Hauts, Les (F.)

A *Premier Cru* vineyard (in part) in Pommard, Côte de Beaune district, Burgundy.
14 acres. Usually appears on the label as
Rugiens.

Ruinart Père & Fils (F.)   1729

A Champagne producer in Reims. The *cuvée de prestige* is Dom Ruinart Blanc de
Blancs. 1.2 million bottles. 35 acres.

Ruiz-Mateos S.A., Zoilo (Sp.)   1857

A Sherry producer in Jerez de la Frontera;
produces a full range of Sherries, especially the Don Zoilo brand. 600 acres.

Ruländer (G.)

A white (or greyish) grape which is named
after Johann Seger Ruland, from Speyer,
who introduced it to Germany from Burgundy in 1711; also called Pinot Gris,
Grauerburgunder and Tokaier.

Rulany (Cz.)

A white grape grown in Moravia, possib
the Ruländer grape.

Rully AOC (F.)

A commune in the Côte Chalonnaise di
trict, southern Burgundy; produces re
and white wines. 19 *Premier Cru* vineyard

Rumania

See **Romania.**

RUMASA (Sp.)

The name (coined from the *bodega* Ruiz M
teos S.A.) of a large conglomorate
Sherry producers under one managemen
now controlled by the Spanish goverr
ment. RUMASA owns: Garvey, Bodega
Internationales, Williams & Humber
Ruiz Mateos and other companies in Jere
Paternina, Franco Españoles, Berberan
Castelblanch, René Barbier and man
more, as well as banks, insurance, shi
ping, and hotels.

Rummy Port (Aus.)

A Port-style wine from Craigmoor winer
Mudgee district, New South Wales; ru
casks are used in the aging of the win
giving it a characteristic rum flavor.

Ruppertsberg (G.)

A village in the Rheinpfalz region, Bereic
Mittelhaardt/Deutsche   Weinstrass
Grosslage Hofstück. The vineyards ar
Gaisböhl, Hoheburg, Linsenbusch, Nus
bien, Reiterpfad and Spiess. 950 acres.

Rushing, The Winery (U.S.)   197

A winery in Merigold, northwestern Mis
issippi; produces muscadine wines. 3
acres.

Russia (U.S.S.R.)

A republic of the U.S.S.R. The distri
around the cities of Rostov and Anapa a
well-known for wine production, esp
cially for Tsimlyanskoye, a sweet, spa
kling red wine.

The nation as a whole is the third large
producer of wine in the world, with 3

illion acres producing some 800 million
llons, mostly sweet wines.

ssian River Valley (U.S.)

district which runs along the Russian
ver from the Pacific Ocean east, then
orth to Healdsburg, in northeastern Son-
ma County, California.

ssian River Vineyard (U.S.)   **1964**

winery in Forestville, northwest of Santa
osa, Sonoma County, California; in 1978 it
came Topolos at Russian River Vineyard,
id was enlarged. 25 acres.

ssiz, Villa (I.)   **1869**

n estate in Capriva del Friuli, Friuli-Vezia Giulia region; produces Collio and
colit wines. 13,000 cases. 60 acres.

stenburg (S. Af.)

n estate in the Stellenbosch district; con-
dered part of the Schoongezicht Estate;
roduces Cabernet Sauvignon and Pinot
oir wines.

ster Ausbruch (A.)

famous, sweet, white wine from Rust,
outheast of Vienna, in the Burgenland re-
ion; made mostly from the Furmint
rape.

stico (I.)

rustic, red wine from the Val Peligna, in
e central Abruzzi region; made from
fontepulciano and Sangiovese grapes.

utherford Hill Winery (U.S.)   **1972, 1976**

winery in St. Helena, Napa Valley, Cali-
rnia; formerly, Souverain of Rutherford,
ought in 1976 by the owners of Freemark
bbey; produces Cabernet Sauvignon,
ferlot, Pinot Noir, Zinfandel, Chardon-
ay, Gewürztraminer, Johannisberg Ries-
ng and Sauvignon Blanc wines. 100,000
ses. 600 acres.

Rutherford and Miles Lda. (P.)   **1814**

A producer of Madeira wines.

Rutherford Ranch Cellars (U.S.)

A second label of Round Hill Cellars, St.
Helena, Napa Valley, California; Produces
Cabernet, Zinfandel, Chardonnay and
Sauvignon Blanc wines. 5,000 cases.

Rutherford Vintners (U.S.)   **1976**

A winery in Rutherford, Napa Valley, California; produces Cabernet Sauvignon,
Pinot Noir, Merlot, Chardonnay, Johannisberg Riesling, and Muscat wines, some
from purchased grapes; also sells under
the Château Rutherford and Rutherford
Cellars labels. 30 acres. 15,000 cases.

Rutherglen (Aus.)

A well-known town and district in northeastern Victoria; produces fortified wines,
sweet wines and dry red wines.

Ruwer (G.)

A small tributary of the Mosel River, in the
Mosel-Saar-Ruwer region, Bereich Saar-
Ruwer. The only *Grosslage* is Römerlay; the
most well-known villages are Eitelsbach,
Kasel, Avelsbach and Mertesdorf, and the
famous estate of Maximin Grünhaus,
which is in Mertesdorf.

Ružica (Y.)

A rosé wine from Serbia; made from the
Prokupac grape.

Ryecroft (Aus.)

An important winery and vineyard in
McLaren Vale, part of the Southern Vales
district, South Australia; formerly owned
by Ingoldby; produces red wines. 250
acres.

Ryn Riesling (S. Af.)

Another name for the Rhine Riesling grape
or wine.

S

. (F.)

he abbreviation for Seibel, a French hybrid grape.

.A.

ociété Anonyme (F.), *Sociedad Anónima* (p.), *Societa Anonima* (I.), a corporation or mited company.

.A.R.L. (P.)

he abbreviation for *Sociedade Anônima de esponsabilidade Limitada* (joint stock company of limited liability).

.I.C.A. (F.)

he abbreviation for *Société Immobilière ommerciale et Agricole* (Association of ommercial and Agricultural Property).

.I.C.A.R.E.X. Méditerranée (F.)

he abbreviation for *Société d'Intérêt Collec- Agricole de Recherches Expérimentales*, a o-op in Le Grau-du-Roi, southern rance; promotes growing of the better rape varieties, experiments and produces ines under Domaine de l'Espiguette.

.p.A. (I.)

he abbreviation for *Società per Azioni*, a int-stock company.

.r.l. (I.)

he abbreviation for *Società a responsabilità mitata*, a limited partnership (Ltd.).

t. (F.)

aint (Holy; Saint).

te. (F.)

ainte (Holy; female Saint).

S.V.

The abbreviation for Seyve-Villard, a hybrid grape.

Saaleck (G.)

A village in the Franken region, Bereich Maindreieck, Grosslage Burg. The only vineyard is Schlossberg. 50 acres.

Saar (G.)

A tributary of the Mosel River. Grapes are grown in a small valley south of Trier, in the Mosel-Saar-Ruwer region, Bereich Saar-Ruwer, Grosslage Scharzberg. The important villages are Ayl, Okfen and Wiltingen. Scharzhofberg is the most famous estate on the Saar. 1,500 acres.

Saar-Ruwer (G.)

A *Bereich*, one of 4 in the Mosel-Saar-Ruwer region, which covers the wines of the Saar and Ruwer, two tributaries of the Mosel River.

Saarburg (G.)

A village in the Mosel-Saar-Ruwer region, Bereich Saar-Ruwer, Grosslage Scharzberg, the center of wine trade of the district. The vineyards are: Antoniusbrunnen, Bergschlösschen, Fuchs, Klosterberg, Kupp, Rausch, Schlossberg, and Stirn. 185 acres.

Sabla, La (I.)

A red wine from Aymaville village, in the Valle d'Aosta region of northwestern Italy; made from the Petit Rouge grape.

Sables du Golfe du Lion (F.)

A large district south of Montpellier on the Golfe du Lion, covering the sandy soil from

Agde east to Stes. Maries-de-la-Mer; produces red, white and rosé wines. The red and rosé wines are made from Cabernet Sauvignon, Cabernet Franc, Cinsault, Grenache, Carignan, Syrah and Merlot grapes and the white wine is made from Ugni Blanc, Clairette, Sauvignon, Carignan Blanc and Muscat grapes.

Sables-Saint-Émilion (F.)

A former commune just southeast of Libourne, in the Bordeaux region, now a part of St.-Émilion.

Sabon, Noël (F.)

An estate in Chante Cigale, Châteauneuf-du-Pape district, southern Rhône region; produces Châteauneuf-du-Pape wine. 100 acres.

Sabro (P.)

A white grape grown in southern Portugal.

sacador (Sp.)

A vineyard worker who carries grapes to the *bodega* for crushing.

saccharometer

See **mustimeter.**

Saccharomyces cereviseae

A natural yeast found on grapeskins, one of several varieties responsible for fermentation of wine.

Saccharomyces ellipsoideus

One of several yeasts responsible for fermentation of wine.

sack (E.)

An early English name for Sherry, derived from the Spanish *"sacar"* – to take out, export. Examples include Canary Sack and Málaga Sack; mentioned by Shakespeare.

sacramental wine

A wine, usually sweet, used for Christian and Jewish religious services.

Sacrantino *also* **Sacramentino (I.)**

Old names for red Sagrantino wine, fro Montefalco, in the Perugia hills, Umbria gion; made from the Sagrantino grape.

Sacy (F.)

A local white grape grown in the Auxerr district, west of Chablis, Burgundy; us primarily to make sparkling wines.

Sadova (R.)

A town in the Wallachia region, sout western Romania; produces red and ro wine made from Cabernet Sauvignon a Pinot Noir grapes.

Saering (F.)

A vineyard in Guebwiller, Haut-Rhin d trict, Alsace region.

Sagrantino (I.)

A red grape grown in the Umbria region

Sagrantino di Montefalco DOC (I.)

A red wine, usually sweet, from Mont falco, in the Perugia hills, northern Umbr region; made from the Sagrantino grap formerly known as Sacrantino a Sacramentino.

Saint-Amans, Domaine de l'Anci Prieuré de (F.)

An estate in Bizanet, Corbières distri Languedoc region. 7,000 cases. 28 acres.

St. Amant (U.S.)

A vineyard in Amador County, Californ produces Zinfandel grapes for Morris a Concannon wineries. 30 acres.

Saint-Amour AOC (F.)

A commune (called Saint Amour Bellevu and a *Cru* Beaujolais in the Beaujolais d trict, Burgundy; produces a red wine ma from Gamay grapes. 700 acres.

Saint-Amour, Château de (F.)

An estate in St.-Amour, Beaujolais distri Burgundy. 22 acres.

Saint-André-de-Figuière, Domaine (F.)

An estate in La Londe-les-Maures, Provence region.

St. Andrew's Winery (U.S.)   1980

A winery in Napa, Napa Valley, California; produces Chardonnay and Sauvignon Blanc wines. 80 acres.

Saint-Aubin AOC (F.)

A commune in the hills behind Puligny and Chassagne, in the Côte de Beaune district, Burgundy; produces red and white wines which may also be sold as Côte de Beaune-Villages. 8 *Premier Cru* vineyards. 9,500 gallons. 350 acres.

Saint-Bonnet, Château (F.)

An estate in Christoly, Médoc district, Bordeaux; classified in 1978 as a *Cru Bourgeois*. 10,000 cases. 80 acres.

Saint-Bris-le-Vineux VDQS (F.)

A village in the Chablis district, Burgundy; produces Sauvignon de Saint Bris wine (VDQS in 1974).

Saint-Chinian AOC (F.)

A large district west of Béziers, in the Languedoc region of the Midi, in southern France, which produces:

A red wine made from Carignan, Grenache and Cinsault grapes.

Saint Clair Vineyard (U.S.)

A vineyard in the Carneros district, Napa Valley, California; produces Pinot Noir wine made by the Acacia Winery.

Saint Clare (Aus.)   1973

A winery in the Clare-Watervale district, South Australia; produces Rhine Riesling and Cabernet Sauvignon wines.

St. Clement Vineyard (U.S.)   1975

A winery in St. Helena, Napa Valley, California; formerly the Spring Mountain Vineyard site; produces Cabernet Sauvignon, Chardonnay and Sauvignon Blanc wines. 4,000 cases.

St. Cyprien (Tun.)

A red-wine district near Tunis.

Saint-Denis AOC, Clos (F.)

A *Grand Cru* vineyard in Morey-St.-Denis, Côte de Nuits district, Burgundy. 16 acres.

Saint-Drézéry VDQS (F.)

A village north of Montpellier, in the Coteaux du Languedoc district, Languedoc region of the Midi, in southern France; produces red wine made from Carignan and other grapes.

St. Emiliana Cabernet (Ch.)

A red wine from the Maipo Valley in central Chile; made by Concha y Toro winery.

Saint-Émilion (F.)

A white grape grown in the Charentes region, a local name for the Ugni Blanc grape, used to make Cognac; in other regions it is called Clairette à Grains Ronds, Clairette de Vence, Graisse, Queue de Renard and Roussan; in Italy, Trebbiano; in Corsica, Rossola.

Saint-Émilion AOC (F.)

A town and district in the Bordeaux region, 18 miles east of the city of Bordeaux, across the Dordogne River from the Médoc district; the district also includes several surrounding communes. The wines were officially classified in 1955 into 12 *Premier Grand Crus Classés* vineyards and 72 *Grand Cru Classé* vineyards; in addition more than 500 growths are called *Grands Crus*. Châteaux Cheval Blanc and Ausone and considered to be the two best growths. The wines are red, made from Merlot, Cabernet Franc and a lesser amount of Cabernet Sauvignon grapes, as well as a little Malbec. 16,000 acres.

Saint-Estèphe AOC (F.)

A commune in the northern part of the Haut-Médoc district, Bordeaux region; classified in 1855; 2 *Deuxièmes Crus*, 1 *Troisième Cru*, 1 *Quatrième Cru* and 1 *Cinquième Cru*.

Saint-Estève, Château (F.)

An estate in Uchaux, in the Côtes du Rhône district, southern Rhône region; produces red and rosé wines made from Grenache, Syrah, Cinsault and Mourvèdre grapes and white wine made from Grenache Blanc, Roussanne, Clairette and Viognier grapes. 135 acres.

St. Francis Winery (U.S.)   1979

A winery in Kenwood, Sonoma County, California; produces Merlot, Pinot Noir, Chardonnay, Johannisberg Riesling and Gewürztraminer wines. 12,000 acres. 100 acres.

St.-Fulrade, G.A.E.C. (F.)   1966

A co-op estate in St.-Hippolyte, northern Haut-Rhin district, Alsace region. 25 acres.

Saint-Gayan, Domaine (F.)   1400

An estate in Gigondas, southern Rhône region. 35 acres.

Saint-Georges, Les (F.)

A *Premier Cru* vineyard in Nuits-Saint-Georges, Côte de Nuits district, Burgundy. 18.5 acres.

Saint-Georges, Château (F.)

An estate in St.-Georges-Saint-Émilion, Bordeaux; 25,000 cases. 120 acres.

St.-Georges-Côte-Pavie, Château (F.)

An estate in St.-Émilion, Bordeaux; classified in 1955 as a *Grand Cru Classé*. 2,100 cases. 15 acres.

St.-Georges-d'Orques VDQS (F.)

A village west of Montpellier, in the Coteaux du Languedoc district, Languedoc region of the Midi, in southern France; produces red wine made from Carignan, Cinsault and Granache grapes.

Saint-Georges-Saint-Émilion AOC (F.)

A commune north of St.-Émilion with wines similar to St.-Émilion.

St. Helena Wine Company (U.S.)

A co-op winery in St. Helena, Napa Valley California; produces wine for the Charle Krug Winery.

St. Henri Claret (Aus.)

A famous red wine from Penfolds Winer in Adelaide, South Australia; made fron the Shiraz grape.

St. Hubert's (Aus.)   196

A winery in the Yarra Valley district, Vic toria; produces red wines, especially Ca bernet Sauvignon as well as Shiraz an Pinot Noir and white wines, includin Rhine Riesling, Chardonnay and Trebb ano. 5,000 cases. 40 acres.

St. Hune, Clos (F.)

A vineyard in Hunawihr, Haut-Rhin dis trict, Alsace region, a *monopole* of Trimbach produces Riesling wines. 3 acres.

Saint-Jacques, Clos (F.)

A *Premier Cru* vineyard in Gevrey-Cham bertin, Côte de Nuits district, Burgundy. 1 acres.

St. James Winery (U.S.)   197

A winery in St. James, central Missour produces red, white and rosé wines, an bottle-fermented sparkling wines. 2 acres.

St. Jean, Château (U.S.)   197

A winery in Kenwood, southern Sonom County; produces Chardonnay, Johannis berg Riesling, Muscat, Gewürztramine Sauvignon Blanc and Cabernet Sauvigno wines in many different styles and vine yard bottlings, especially from the Rober Young Vineyard; also sparkling wines 70% purchased grapes. 90,000 cases. 10 acres.

Saint-Jean, Clos (F.)

A *Premier Cru* vineyard in Chassagne-Mor trachet, Côte de Beaune district, Bur gundy; produces red and white wines. 3 acres.

Saint-Jean, Domaine du Clos (F.)

An estate in Pommard, Côte de Beaune district, Burgundy. 18 acres, including 11 acres of Pommard and 1.7 acres of Meursault.

Saint-Jemms, Domaine (F.)

An estate in Mercurol, Crozes-Hermitage district, northern Rhône region; owns 25 acres of Syrah and 5 acres of Marsanne grapes.

St. Johannishof, Weingut (G.)

An estate in Bernkastel, Mosel-Saar-Ruwer region; owns vineyard parcels in Bernkasteler Doktor, Badstube, Graben and Lay, Graacher Himmelreich, Wellener Sonnennuhr, Ürziger Würzgarten, Erdener Treppchen and Prälat. 25 acres.

Saint-Joseph AOC (F.)   1956

A district around the town of Tournon, across the Rhône River from Hermitage, in the northern Rhône region, and includes 7 communes; produces mostly red and some white wines; the red wine is made from at least 90% Syrah grapes, the white from Marsanne and Roussanne grapes. 600 acres.

St. Julian Wine Company (U.S.)   1939

A large winery in Paw Paw, southeastern Michigan; formerly located in Detroit, and earlier in Windsor, Ontario; grows several *labrusca* and hybrid grapes.

Saint-Julien AOC (F.)

A commune in the Haut-Médoc district, Bordeaux; there are 5 *Deuxième Cru* vineyards, 2 *Troisième Cru* vineyards, 4 *Quatrième Cru* Vineyards. 1,600 acres.

St. Landelin, Clos (F.)

A vineyard in Rouffach, Haut-Rhin district, Alsace region; a *monopole* of Muré. 40 acres.

Saint-Laurent (G.)

A red grape grown in the Rheinhessen region; in Württemberg, a relative of the Clevner or Blauer Spätburgunder (Pinot Noir); also grown in Austria and Czechoslovakia.

Saint-Laurent, Cuvée (F.)

A red wine from the Hospices de Nuits, in Nuits-St.-Georges, Côte de Nuits district, Burgundy. The *Cuvée* is composed of Nuits-St.-Georges Corvées Paget – .8 acre.

Saint-Louis, Société Civile du Clos (F.)

An estate in Fixin, Côte de Nuits district, Burgundy. See **Société Civile du Clos St.-Louis.**

Saint-Marc, Le Clos (F.)

A *Premier Cru* vineyard in Prémeaux, Côte de Nuits district, Burgundy. 7 acres.

Saint Martin (F.)

An early patron saint of wine (c.345) in the Loire Valley.

Saint Martin, Château de (F.)

An estate in Taradeau, Provence region.

St.-Martin, Clos (F.)

An estate in St.-Émilion, Bordeaux; classified in 1955 as a *Grand Cru Classé*. 1,000 cases. 5 acres.

St.-Maur, Domaine de (F.)

An estate in Cogolin, southeastern Provence region.

Saint-Michel, Domaine (F.)

An estate in Santenay, Côte de Beaune district, Burgundy; partly run by Maufoux. 64 acres, including some Santenay Comme, Clos Rousseau, Puligny-Montrachet and 20 acres of Pouilly-sur-Loire.

Saint-Nicholas-de-Bourgueil AOC (F.)

A commune west of Tours, in the Touraine region of the Loire Valley, which produces red and rosé wine made from the Cabernet Franc grape; similar to Bourgueil wines. 35,000 acres.

St. Nicolaus Hopital (G.)

An estate in Bernkastel-Kues, Mosel-Saar-Ruwer region; owns vineyard parcels in Wehlener Sonnennuhr, Graacher Himmelreich, Bernkasteler Badstube, Bratenhöfchen and Lay and Brauneberger Juffer. 20 acres.

Saint-Paul, Clos (F.)

An unclassified vineyard in Givry, Côte Chalonnaise district, Burgundy.

Saint-Péray, Saint-Péray Mousseux AOC (F.)

1. A small commune across the Rhône River from Valence, in the northern Rhône valley, which produces:

2. Dry white wine and sparkling wine made from Roussanne and Marsanne grapes. 125 acres. 35,000 gallons.

St.-Pierre, Château (F.)

An estate in St.-Julien, Haut-Médoc district, Bordeaux; classified in 1855 as a *Quatrième Cru*; in 1892 was divided into St.-Pierre-Sevaistre and St.-Pierre-Bontemps, was re-united around 1946 as St.-Pierre-Sevaistre, while a parcel was sold to become part of Château Gloria. 6,000 cases. 40 acres.

Saint-Pierre, Château (F.)

An unclassified estate in St.-Pierre de Mons, Graves district, Bordeaux; produces red and white wines; also called Château Les Queyrats. 7,500 cases. 95 acres.

Saint-Pierre, Clos (F.)

An unclassified vineyard in Givry, Côte Chalonnaise district, Burgundy.

Saint-Pierre, Domaine (F.)

An estate in Violès, Côtes du Rhône district, southern Rhône region; produces wine made from Grenache, Syrah and Carignan grapes; also has vines in Gigondas and Vacqueyras. 60 acres.

Saint-Pierre, Domaine de (F.)

An estate in Verdigny, Sancerre district, Upper Loire region. 15 acres.

St.-Pierre-Sefivin (F.)

A large company in Châteauneuf-du-Pape, southern Rhône region; produces Châteauneuf-du-Pape wine under several labels. 500,000 cases.

Saint-Pierre-Sevaistre, Château (F.)

An estate in St.-Julien, Haut-Médoc district, Bordeaux; classified in 1855 as a *Quatrième Cru*; in 1693 it was known as Serançon; purchased by Baron St.-Pierre in 1767; divided into 2 sections from 1832-1946, St.-Pierre-Bontemps was the other section, half of which became Château Gloria. 6,000 cases. 40 acres.

Saint-Pourçain-sur-Sioule VDQS (F.)

A village south of Moulin, in central France, but considered a part of the Loire Valley; produces red, white and rosé wines, the red and rosé made from a blend of Pinot Noir and Gamay grapes, and the white wine from Tressalier (the Sacy grape), Chardonnay, Aligoté, Sauvignon and Saint-Pierre-Doré grapes.

Saint-Raphaël (F.)

A red or white, bitter-sweet apéritif made from fortified wine, quinine and other flavorings.

Saint-Roch, Domaine du Château (F.)

An estate in Roquemaure, Lirac district, southern Rhône region; produces 80% red, 19% rosé and 1% white wine; grows 40% Grenache, 23% Cinsault, 13% Syrah, 13% Mourvèdre and the rest white grapes. 100 acres.

Saint-Romain AOC (F.)

A commune in the Côte de Beaune district, Burgundy, in the hills behind Meursault, which produces red and white wines; can also be sold as Côte de Beaune-Villages when blended. There are no classified vineyards. 350 acres. 53,000 gallons.

Saint-Saphorin (Sw.)

A village in the Lavaux district, Vaud region.

Saint-Saturnin VDQS (F.)

A commune west of Montpellier, in the Coteaux du Languedoc district, Languedoc region of the Midi; produces red and rosé wine made from Carignan, Cinsault, Grenache, Mourvèdre and A vineyard in Dambach-la-Ville, Bas-Rhin district, Alsace region, a *monopole* of Hauller, producing Riesling and Gewürztraminer wines. 4 acres.

Saint-Sauveur, Domaine (F.)

An estate in Aubignan, Beaumes-de-Venise district, sourthern Rhône region; owns 15 acres of Muscat; also makes Côtes du Ventoux wines.

Saint-Sébastien, Cuvée (F.)

A vineyard in Dambach-la-Ville, Bas-Rhin district, Alsace region, a *monopole* of Hauller, producing Riesling and Gewürztraminer wines. 4 acres.

Saint-Trys, Château (F.)

An estate in the Beaujolais district, Burgundy.

Saint-Urbain, Clos (F.)

A parcel of the Rangen vineyard in Thann, southern Haut-Rhin district, Alsace region; produces Riesling and Tokay wines. 10 acres.

Saint-Vallerin (F.)

A commune in the Côte Chalonnaise district, Burgundy; sold as AOC Montagny.

Saint-Véran AOC (F.)   1971

A commune in the Mâconnais district, Burgundy, including several other villages both north and south of Pouilly-Fuissé; the village, formerly St.-Véran-des-Vignes, has been changed to St.-Vérand, so as not to be confused with the St.-Véran in the southwestern Beaujolais district; produces white wine similar to Pouilly-Fuissé.

Saint Vincent (F.)

The patron saint of *vignerons* in France. In Burgundy, his day is celebrated on January 22.

Sainte-Anne, Domaine (F.)

An estate in St.-Gervais, Côtes du Rhône-Villages district, southern Rhône region.

Sainte-Catherine, Clos de (F.)

An estate in Rochefort-sur-Loire, Coteaux du Layon district, Anjou region; Loire Valley; part of the Domaine de Baumard estate. 3.5 acres.

Ste. Chapelle Vineyards (U.S.)   1976

A large winery in Emmett, northwest of Boise, southwestern Idaho; produces White Riesling, Chardonnay, Gewürztraminer and Merlot wines. 60,000 cases. 420 acres.

Sainte-Croix-du-Mont AOC (F.)

A small district south of Bordeaux City, on the right bank of the Garonne River, across from the Sauternes district, in the Bordeaux region; produces sweet, white wines like Sauternes and made from the same grapes: Sémillon, Sauvignon and Muscadelle. 400,000 gallons.

Sainte-Foy-Bordeaux AOC (F.)

A district near Monbazillac, in the southeastern Bordeaux region; produces sweet, white wine made from Sémillon, Sauvignon and Muscadelle grapes and a little red wine from the usual Bordeaux red grapes.

Sainte-Magdeleine, Clos (F.)

An estate in Cassis, Provence region.

Ste. Michelle (C.)   1977

A large winery in Surrey, southeast of Vancouver, British Columbia; formerly the Grower's Winery in Victoria, B.C.; produces Chardonnay, Grey Riesling, Ruby Cabernet and blended wines.

Ste. Michelle, Château (U.S.)   1967

Formerly, the American Wine Growers, a leading winery producing *vinifera* wines, north of Seattle, Washington. Presently has vineyards in Cold Creek, east of Yakima and Grandview in the Columbia River Basin; produces Chardonnay, Sémillon, Riesling, Gewürztraminer, Muscat Canelli, Cabernet, Merlot and Grenache wines; also bottle-fermented sparkling wines. 3,000 acres.

Sainte-Odile, Clos (F.)

A vineyard in Obernai, Bas-Rhin district, Alsace region; produces Riesling, Gewürztraminer and Tokay wines. 25 acres.

Sainte-Roseline, Château (F.)

An estate in les Arcs-sur-Argens, eastern Provence region; produces rosé wine.

Sakonnet Vineyards (U.S.)   1976

A winery in Little Compton, near Newport, Rhode Island; grows hybrid and *vinifera* grapes. 7,000 cases. 40 acres.

Salem, Schloss (G.)

An estate in Salem, Baden region; owns vineyards in Birnau, Schloss Kirchberg and Bermatingen. 200 acres.

Sales, Château de (F.)

An estate in Pomerol, Bordeaux. 15,000 cases. 100 acres.

Salice Salentino DOC (I.)

A village south of Brindisi, in the southern Apulia region; produces red and rosé wines made mostly from Negroamaro grapes with up to 20% Malvasia Nera grapes.

Salins, Cuvée François de (F.)

A white wine from the Hospices de Beaune, Côte de Beaune district, Burgundy. The *cuvée* is composed of the following vineyard in Corton: Corton-Charlemagne – .5 acre. 75 cases.

Salins, Cuvée Guigone de (F.)

A red wine from the Hospices de Beaune, Côte de Beaune district, Burgundy. The *cuvée* is composed of the following vineyards in Beaune: Les Bressandes – 2.5 acres, En Senrey – 2 acres and Champs Pimont – 1.5 acres. 500 cases.

Salinas Valley (U.S.)

An important region in Monterey County, California, about 130 miles long, from Monterey to San Luis Obispo County.

Salishan Vineyards (U.S.)   1976

A winery in La Center, Washington, north of Portland, Oregon; produces Riesling, Pinot Noir and other wines from *vinifera* grapes. 12 acres.

Salle, Domaine de la (F.)

An estate in Lantignié, Beaujolais-Villages district, Burgundy; produces Kosher Beaujolais-Villages wine.

salmanazar (F.)

A large bottle equal to 12 fifths, 9.6 liters or 325 U.S. fluid ounces.

Saloman, Clos (F.)

An unclassified vineyard in Givry, Côte Chalonnaise district, Burgundy. 15 acres.

Salon le Mesnil (F.)   1911

A Champagne producer in Le Mesnil-sur-Oger, south of Épernay; produces only Blanc de Blancs. 30,000 bottles. 2 acres.

Saltillo (Mex.)

A city and district in northeastern Mexico.

Saltram (Aus.)   1859

A small, old winery in the Barossa Valley district; produces mostly red wines, including Mamre Brook Cabernet, Claret and Burgundy blends and Chardonnay, some from purchased grapes. 250 acres.

Salvador (U.S.)

A red hybrid grape grown in Central Valley, California; a *teinturier* grape used mostly for blending in jug wines.

Salvagnin (Sw.)

A red wine from the Vaud region, made from a blend of Gamay and Pinot Noir grapes; similar to Dôle wine.

Sambatyon (Is.)

A white, sparkling wine.

Samos (Gr.)

A small island east of Athens; famous for sweet, white Muscat wines.

Samperi (I.)

An estate in Marsala, Sicily; produces Vecchio Samperi wines. 1,200 cases. 37 acres.

Sampigny-les-Maranges (F.)

A commune in the southern Côte de Beaune district, Burgundy; the wines are mostly blended and sold as Côte de Beaune-Villages. There are two *Premier Cru* vineyards: Les Maranges and Clos des Rois. 110 acres.

Samtrot (G.)

A red grape, a variant of the Müllerrebe, which is a variant of the Blauer Spätburgunder (Pinot Noir); developed at the Viticultural Research Institute in Weinsberg, Württemberg region, Germany.

San Antonio Winery (U.S.)   1917

A winery in Los Angeles, southern California; produces 40 different wines from purchased grapes from Sonoma, Lodi and Cucamonga Counties. 300,000 cases.

San Benito County (U.S.)

A county near the central coast of California, east of Monterey County; vines planted since 1797; the large vineyards of Almadén (4,500 acres) are located here.

San Colombano al Lambro (I.)

1. A village and district around the Lambro River, southeast of Milan, in the southern Lombardy region, which produces:

2. Red and white wines, the red wines made from Barbera, Bonardo, Merlot, Cabernet Sauvignon and Malbec grapes and the white wine made from Verdea, Riesling, Tocai and Pinot Grigio grapes.

San Giocondo (I.)

A red *vino novello* from central Tuscany; produced by Antinori.

San Guido, Tenuta (I.)

An estate in Bolgheri, Tuscany region; produces Sassicaia, Rosé di Bolgheri and a white wine. 3,000 cases. 11 acres.

San Joaquin County (U.S.)

A county in central California; the wineries here produce mostly Sherry, Port and bulk wines from Zinfandel, Carignane and Flame Tokay grapes. Lodi and Sacramento are important cities in this region.

San Joaquin Valley (U.S.)

A large region in central California, 200 miles long, 30-50 miles wide, covering seven counties; produces a large proportion of California's jug wines and grows nearly all the grapes for Port, Sherry and brandy made in California.

San Juan (Arg.)

A city and province north of Mendosa, in west central Argentina; it has a hotter climate than Mendosa and the wines are richer. 20% of Argentina's wines come from there. 150,000 acres.

San Juan, Cavas de (Mex.)   1958

A winery in San Juan del Río, north of Mexico City; produces Cabernet, Hidalgo, Pinot Noir, sparkling and other wines. 600 acres.

San Juan del Río (Mex.)

A town and the southern most wine district in Mexico, 100 miles north of Mexico City.

San Leonardo (I.)

A red wine from Borghetto, south of Trento, in the Trentino-Alto Adige region; made from Cabernet Sauvignon and Merlot grapes by Tenuta San Leonardo.

San Leonardo, Tenuta (I.)   13th cent.

An estate in Borghetto all'Adige, Trentino-Alto Adige region; produces San Leonardo and Trentino Cabernet and Merlot wines. 35 acres.

San Lorenzo (Mex.) 1626

A large, historic winery and vineyard in the Parras district, north central Mexico, also called Casa Madero; produces red, rosé and sparkling wines made from Cabernet, Merlot, Zinfandel, Carignane, Grenache and Cinsault grapes. 1,000 acres.

San Luis Obispo (U.S.)

A city, county and region south of Monterey County, in California; Paso Robles, Shandon and Edna Valley are districts. 5,000 acres.

San Lunardo (I.)

A white grape grown in the western Campania region, including the island of Ischia.

San Marcos (Mex.)

A large winery and vineyard northeast of Aguascalientes, in the state of Aguascalientes; produces Cabernet, sparkling, and other wines.

San Marino (I.)

A small independent republic, and its capital city, in the southeastern Emilia-Romagna region, Italy; produces red wine made from Sangiovese grapes and a sweet Moscato wine.

San Marino Vineyards (N.Z.)

A winery in Kumeu, Auckland, North Island; produces Cabernet, Gewürztraminer, Riesling and Müller-Thurgau wines. 35 acres.

San Marten (I.)

A *vino novello* from Marzeno, south of Faenza, in the eastern Emilia-Romagna region; made from the Sangiovese grape by carbonic maceration.

San Martin (U.S.) 1892

A large winery in San Martin, Santa Clara County, California; produces numerous varietal wines from purchased grapes; spe-

cializes in making "soft" wines, containing only 8-10% alcohol. 300,000 cases.

San Mateo County (U.S.)

A small region south of San Francisco, California; it has only a few wineries and very few vineyards.

San Michele all 'Adige, Instituto Agrario Provinciale (I.)

An agricultural school in San Michele all'Adige, Trentino-Alto Adige region; produces Castel San Michele wine made from a blend of Cabernet Sauvignon and Merlot grapes. 100 acres.

San Nicola (I.)

A white grape grown in the Campania region.

San Pasqual Vineyards (I.) 1973

A winery in Escondido, San Diego County, southern California; produces Gamay, Sauvignon Blanc, Chenin Blanc, and Muscat wines and Champagne. 25,000 cases. 110 acres.

San Pedro (Ch.) 1865

A winery in Molina, central Chile; produces Cabernet Sauvignon and "Gato Bianco" wine, a blend of Sauvignon and Sémillon. 500,000 cases. 1,000 acres.

San Sadurní de Noya (Sp.)

An important town west of Barcelona, in the Catalonia region; produces Champagne-method sparkling wines; some of the largest *cavas* in the world are located here.

San Severo DOC (I.)

1. A town and district in the northern Apulia region, which produces:

2. Red, white and rosé wines; the red and rosé wines are made from Montepulciano and Sangiovese grapes and the white wine is made from Bombino Bianco, Trebbiano Toscano and some Malvasia Bianca and Verdeca grapes.

Sancerre AOC (F.)

1. A town and district in the Upper Loire region of the Loire Valley, which produces:

2. A dry, white wine made from the Sauvignon grape, and red and rosé wines made from the Pinot Noir grape; the best vineyards are considered to be in Bué, Champtin and Chavignol.

Sanchez Romale Hnos. (Sp.)   1781

A Sherry producer in Jerez de la Frontera; produces a wide range of sherries and brandy. 200 acres.

Sandbichler DOC (I.)

Red and white wines from the Alto Adige DOC district, in the northern Trentino-Alto Adige region; the red wine is made from the Pinot Nero grape and the white wine is made from the Riesling grape.

Sandelford (Aus.)   1840

A winery and vineyard in Caversham, Swan Valley district, Western Australia; produces varietal wines, especially Cabernet Sauvignon, Cabernet Rosé, Chenin Blanc, Verdelho and Rhine Riesling; also vineyards in the Margaret River District. 450 acres.

Sandeman & Co. Lda (P.)   1790

A Port and Sherry producer in Vila Nova de Gaia; owns Quinta de Confradeiro, Quinta de Celeirós and Quinta das Laranjeiras. 700 acres.

Sandeman Hermanos y Cía (Sp.)   1790

A famous Port and Sherry shipper in Jerez de la Frontera, only recently owning a *bodega* and vineyards; produces several sherry types: "Dry Dan" (*amontillado*), Apitiv (*fino*), "Armada Cream" and Imperial Corregidor (*oloroso*). 1,000 acres.

Sandweine (A.)

German for "Sand wine," a white wine made along the eastern shore of the Neusiedlersee, in the Burgenland region of eastern Austria, made from ungrafted vines planted in sandy soil where *phylloxera* can not survive. The wines are labeled Seewinkel followed by the grape name.

Sanford and Benedict Vineyards (U.S.)
1970

A winery in Lompoc, Santa Ynez Valley, Santa Barbara County, California; produces Cabernet Sauvignon, Merlot, Pinot Noir and Chardonnay wines. 10,000 cases. 110 acres.

Sang des Salasses (I.)

A red wine from Cossan, in the Valle d'Aosta region; made from the Pinot Nero grape by the École d'Agriculture Aoste.

Sanginoso (I.)

A red grape grown in the western Campania region.

Sangiovese (I.)

An important red grape grown in the Tuscany region, and throughout Italy; the Brunello and Prugnolo grapes are subvarieties.

Sangiovese dei Colli Pesaresi DOC (I.)

A red wine from Pesaro, in the northeastern Marches region; made from the Sangiovese Romagna grape.

Sangiovese di Romagna DOC (I.)

1. A red grape grown in the Emilia-Romagna region.

2. A red wine from the eastern half of the Emilia-Romagna region; made from the Sangiovese Romagna grape.

sangría (Sp.)

A wine punch made from red wine, citrus juice, sugar, soda or water and garnished with floating fruit.

Sangue di Giuda DOC (I.)

Italian for "Juda's Blood," a red, *frizzante* wine from Broni, southeast of Pavia, in the Oltrepò Pavese district, the southwestern Lombardy region; made from Croatina and other grapes.

Sankt Michael (G.)

A *Grosslage*, one of 10 in Bereich Bernkastel, in the Mosel-Saar-Ruwer region.

Sansonnet, Château (F.)

An estate in St.-Émilion, Bordeaux; classified in 1955 as a *Grand Cru Classé*. 3,000 cases. 15 acres.

Sant'Anna Isola di Capo Rizzuto DOC (I.)

1. A district in Isola di Capo Rizzuto, south of Crotone, in the southeastern Calabria region, which produces:

2. A red wine made from Gaglioppo, Nocera, Nerello Mascalese, Nerello Cappuccio, Malvasia Nera, Malvasia Bianca and Greco Bianca grapes. A non-DOC *bianco* wine is also made.

Sant'Elmo (I.)

A red wine from Vó, in the Colli Euganei district, southern Veneto region; made from Merlot, Cabernet Franc and Barbera grapes.

Santa Barbara Winery (U.S.)   1962

A winery in Santa Barbara, Santa Ynez Valley, Santa Barbara County, California; produces Cabernet Sauvignon, Zinfandel, Johannisberg Riesling, Chenin Blanc and Sherry wines. 10,000 cases. 40 acres.

Santa Carolina (Ch.)   1875

A large winery in Santiago; produces several Cabernet wines, sometimes blended with Merlot and a white wine made with Sémillon, Sauvignon and Chardonnay grapes.

Santa Clara County (U.S.)

A region south of San Francisco Bay, part of the Central Coast region, California; was once a flourishing vineyard region. 2,000 acres.

Santa Cruz (U.S.)

A city, a county and a mountain range south of San Francisco, on the coast of California.

Santa Cruz Cellars (U.S.)

The second wine of Bargetto Winery, Soquel, Santa Cruz County, California.

Santa Cruz Mountain Vineyard (U.S.)
vines 1970, 1st wine 1975

A small winery in Santa Cruz City, Santa Cruz County, California; produces estate-bottled Pinot Noir as well as Cabernet Sauvignon and Chardonnay wines from their own and purchased grapes. 3,000 acres. 15 acres.

Santa Helena (Ch.)

A winery in Santiago, central Chile; produces Sémillon, Riesling and Cabernet Franc wines.

Santa Maddalena DOC (I.)

1. A village north of Bolzano, in the Trentino-Alto Adige region, which produces:

2. A red wine made from the Schiava grape.

Santa Margherita (I.)

An estate in Fossalta di Portogruaro, Veneto region; produces Alto Adige, Chardonnay, Grave, Piave, Pinot, Pramaggiore, Pinot Grigio, Prosecco and Tocai wines.

Santa Maria (U.S.)

A town, river, and district in Santa Barbara County, California; produces Cabernet Sauvignon, Chardonnay and Johannisberg Riesling wines.

Santa Mavra (Gr.)

A red wine from the Island of Levkas, off the western coast of Greece; made from the Vertzami grape.

Santa Rita (Ch.)   1880

A winery in Buin, Maipo Valley, central Chile. 200,000 cases. 250 acres.

Santa Sofia (I.)

A winery in Pedemonte, Veneto region; produces Amarone, Bardolino, Bianco di Custoza, Soave and Valpolicella wines.

Santa Ynez Valley Winery (U.S.)   1976

A winery in Santa Barbara, Santa Ynez Valley, Santa Barbara County, California; produces Cabernet Sauvignon, Merlot, Chardonnay, Sauvignon Blanc, Johannisberg Riesling and Gewürztraminer wines, some from purchased grapes. 10,000 cases. 160 acres.

Santarem *also* João Santarem (P.)

A red grape grown in the Colares district.

Santenay AOC (F.)

A commune in the southern part of the Côte de Beaune district, Burgundy; produces mostly red wine, sometimes blended with other villages and sold as Côte de Beaune-Villages. 7 *Premier Cru* vineyards. 90,000 cases. 1,000 acres.

Santenots, Les (F.)

A *Premier Cru* vineyard in Volnay (red wine only), Côte de Beaune district, Burgundy. 20 acres.

Santenots Blancs, Les (F.)

A *Premier Cru* vineyard in Meursault, Côte de Beaune district, Burgundy. 7.5 acres.

Santenots du Milieu, Les (F.)

A *Premier Cru* vineyard in Meursault, Côte de Beaune district, Burgundy. 20 acres.

Santino Wines (U.S.)   1979

A winery in Plymouth, Amador County, California; produces Cabernet Sauvignon, Zinfandel, White Zinfandel and Sauvignon Blanc wines from purchased grapes. 8,000 cases.

Santo Tomás (Mex.)

1. A district south of Ensenada, in the Baja California region.

2. A vineyard and *bodega* in Ensenada, Baja California region; known for table wines made from Mission, Palomino, Grenache, Carignan, Cabernet Sauvignon, Pinot Noir, Johannisberg Riesling, Sémillon and Chenin Blanc grapes.

Santorin (Gr.)

1. An Island north of Crete, which produces:

2. Sweet and dry white wines made from Assyrtiko and other grapes. The name can also apply to wines made on the smaller Island of Thira.

Saperavi (U.S.S.R.)

A Russian red grape also grown in Bulgaria and New York State (Vinifera Wine Cellars); the same as the Serbian Plovdina and Bulgarian Pamid.

Sarah's Vineyard (U.S.)   1978

A winery in Gilroy, Santa Clara County, California; produces Cabernet Sauvignon, Zinfandel, Merlot, Petite Sirah, Chardonnay and Johannisberg Riesling wines, some from purchased grapes. 3,000 cases. 7 acres.

Saran (F.)

A white Coteaux Champenois wine from the Château de Saran vineyard in Chouilly, Champagne region; made by Moët & Chandon.

Saransot-Dupré, Château (F.)

An estate in Listrac, Haut-Médoc district, Bordeaux; classified in 1978 as a *Cru Bourgeois*. 1,500 cases. 10 acres.

Saratoga Cellars (U.S.)   1973

A label used by the Kathryn Kennedy Winery in Saratoga, Santa Clara County, California; produces Cabernet Sauvignon and Pinot Noir Wines.

Sardegna (I.)

The Italian spelling of Sardinia.

Sardinia *also* Sardegna (I.)

A large island off the western coast of central Italy; produces mostly varietal wines, the best-known of which are Vernaccia di Oristano DOC, Nuragus di Cagliari DOC and the many dessert wines made from Malvasia and Moscato grapes. 53 million gallons. 16 DOC wines.

Sardus Pater (I.)

A red or rosé wine from the Island of Sant'Antioco, off southwestern Sicily; made from the Carignano grape.

Sárgamuskotály (H.)

A white grape used in Tokaji wine; also called Yellow Muskat.

Sarrat (F.)

In the Jurançon district, southwestern France, another name for the Courbu grape.

Sarre (I.)

A village in the Valle d'Aosta region; produces La Colline de Sarre et Chesallet wine made from Petit Rouge and Gamay grapes.

Sarría, Señorio de (Sp.)   1952

A winery in Puente la Reina, Navarra region; produces several red, white and rosé wines from Spanish and some French grapes. 250 acres.

Sartène (F.)

A village and district in southwestern Corsica; produces red, whie and rosé wines under the Vin de Corse Sartène AOC.

Sasbachwalden (G.)

A village in the Baden region, Bereich Ortenau, Grosslage Schloss Rodeck. The vineyards are: Alter Gott and Klostergut Schelzberg.

Sassella DOC (I.)

A red wine from the Valtellina district, in the northern Lombardy region; made from 95% Nebbiolo grapes; considered the best wine of the district.

Sassicaia (I.)   1968

1. A vineyard of 11 acres in Bolgheri, south of Livorno, in the west central Tuscany region, owned by the Tenuta San Guido, which produces:

2. A red wine made from mostly Cabernet Sauvignon grapes with some Cabernet Franc grapes. 2,500 cases.

Sattui Winery, V. (U.S.)   1975

A winery in St. Helena, Napa Valley, California; formerly in San Francisco from 1894 to 1920; produces Cabernet Sauvignon, Zinfandel, Chardonnay and Johannisberg Riesling wines; red wines are made from grapes purchased in Amador County; lately, more wine is being produced from local grapes. 9,000 cases.

Satyricon (Lat.)   c. 66 A.D.

The famous writing by Petronius Arbiter (c. 66 A.D.), in which several wines are described.

Saumur AOC (F.)

A city and district in the eastern Anjou region of the Loire Valley; produces red, white and rosé wines, still and sparkling; the whites made mostly from Chenin Blanc grapes and the red and rosé from Cabernet Franc, Cabernet Sauvignon, Gamay, Cot, Groslot and Pineau d'Aunis grapes. The other AOC designations are Coteaux de Saumur (white), Cabernet de Saumur (rosé), Saumur-Champigny (red), Saumur Mousseux and Saumur Pétillant.

Saumur-Champigny AOC (F.)

A red wine from Champigny, Saumur district, in the Anjou region of the Loire Valley; made from the Cabernet Franc grape.

Sausal Winery (U.S.)   1973

A winery in Healdsburg, Alexander Valley, Sonoma County, California; produces Cabernet Sauvignon, Pinot Noir, Zinfandel, Gamay, Chardonnay and Sauvignon Blanc wines. 30,000 cases. 150 acres.

Sauser (G.)

"Rushing wine," a very young wine that has only fermented for about 4 days. Also called *Federweisser.*

Saussiles, Les (F.)

A *Premier Cru* vineyard in Pommard, Côte de Beaune district, Burgundy. 9.5 acres.

te bouchon (F.)

rk-popper, a wine that ferments a sec-
d time in the bottle in the spring and
ps the cork or breaks the bottle. Also
ed *vin diable* ("devil wine").

uternes AOC (F.)

An important commune and district in
e Bordeaux region, south of the city of
rdeaux, surrounded by the Graves dis-
ct; *communes* are Sauternes, Barsac,
mmes, Preignac, and Fargues. Château
Yquem is the most famous growth.
assified in 1855. It produces:

A natural, sweet white wine made from
erripe, botrytis-infected Sauvignon,
millon and Muscadelle grapes. 16-17%
ohol. Up to 6% residual sugar.

uvignon Blanc *also* Sauvignon (F.)

white grape used to make sweet or dry
hite wine in Bordeaux and in the Loire
lley; also known as Blanc Fumé in the
ire and Fumé Blanc in California.

uvignon de Saint-Bris VDQS (F.)   1974

white wine from Saint-Bris-le-Vineux,
hablis district, Burgundy; made from the
uvignon Blanc grape.

uvignon Vert (U.S.)

spicy, fruity, white grape grown in Cali-
rnia; also called Colombard.

uzet, Domaine Étienne (F.)

n estate in Puligny-Montrachet, Côte de
eaune, Burgundy. 30 acres, including
me Bâtard-Montrachet, Bienvenues-Bâ-
rd-Montrachet, 4 acres of Puligny-Mont-
chet Les Combettes, 4 acres of Champs
anet, 2 acres of Chassagne-Montrachet
nd 8 acres of Les Referts, Premier Cru and
los de Meix Monopole combined.

avagnin (F.)

white grape, believed to be the Traminer
rape, grown in the Jura region of eastern
rance.

Savagnin Noir (F.)

In some parts of France, another name for
the Pinot Noir grape.

Savagnin Rose (F.)

In France, another name for the red Gewürztraminer grape; also called Klevener
de Heiligenstein in the Alsace region.

Savatiano (Gr.)

A white grape grown in central Greece and
the Peloponnese region; used to make table
wines and liqueurs.

Savennières AOC (F.)

A commune in the Coteaux de la Loire district, Anjou region; produces dry and
semi-sweet, white wine, made from the
Chenin Blanc grape. The two *Grand Cru*
vineyards of Coulée-de-Serrant and Roche-
aux-Moines may be added to the Savennières name.

Savignola Paolina (I.)

An estate in Greve, Tuscany region; produces Chianti Classico and Bianco wines.
1,000 cases.

Savigny (F.)

The shorter name for the commune of Savigny-lès-Beaune, Côte de Beaune district,
Burgundy.

Savigny-lès-Beaune AOC (F.)

A commune in the Côte de Beaune district
near Beaune, Burgundy. 5 *Premier Cru*
vineyards. 900 acres.

Savoie *also* Savoy *also* Haute-Savoie (F.)

A region in eastern France; produces
mostly white wines, including Crépy,
Seyssel, and Roussette de Savoie, all AOC
designations. See **Vin de Savoie AOC.**

Savuto DOC (I.)

Red and rosé wines from the Savuto River
area, south of Cosenza, on the west coast
of the central Calabria region; made from
Gaglioppo, Greco Nero, Nerello, Cappuccio, Magliocco Canino, Sangiovese, Malvasia Bianca and Pecorino grapes.

Saxonvale (Aus.)   1971

A large winery in Fordwich, Lower Hunter Valley, New South Wales; produces Cabernet Sauvignon, Shiraz, Chardonnay, Sémillon and blended wines, especially Chardonnay with Sémillon. 800 acres.

Scacciadiavoli (I.)

Italian for "Devil chaser," a red wine from the Perugina hills, in the Umbria region; made from Barbera and Sangiovese grapes.

Scarpa, Antica Casa Vinicola (I.)
                                        19th cent.

A winery in Nizza Monferrato, Piedmont region; produces Barbaresco, Barbera, Barolo, Brachetto, Dolcetto, Freisa, Grignolino, Nebbiolo and Rouchet wines.

Scavino, Paolo (I.)

An estate in Castiglione Falletto, Piedmont region; produces Barbera, Barolo and Dolcetto wines.

scelto (I.)

Selected, choice.

Scharffenberger Cellars (U.S.)   1981

A winery in Ukiah, Mendocino County, California; produces sparkling Brut and Cuvée Pinot Noir from purchased grapes. 5,000 cases.

Scharzberg (G.)

The sole *Grosslage* in Bereich Saar-Ruwer, in the Mosel-Saar-Ruwer region. 17 villages, 80 vineyards.

Scharzhofberg (G.)

A famous vineyard in Wiltingen, Grosslage Scharzberg, Bereich Saar-Ruwer, in the Mosel-Saar-Ruwer region; an *Ortsteil* owned by Egon Müller, Hohe Domkirche and Von Kesselstatt. 60 acres.

Schaumwein (G.)

Sparkling wine, usually not bottle-fermented.

'sche(s) (G.)

The posessive ending, like *'s* in English.

Schenk (Sw.)   18⁖

A large estate and merchant in Rolle, ⁉ Côte district, Vaud region; owns sever estates and other companies in Franc Spain and Italy. 3.5 million cases. 6⁖ acres.

Scheurebe (G.)

A white grape – a cross of Silvaner ar Riesling; developed at the State Resear Institute at Alzey, in the Rheinhessen r gion, in 1916, named after Mr. Geor Scheu, the head of the Institute. It is a pr lific, late-ripening grape which makes full-bodied wine with a fruity bouque Also grown in California by Phelps ar Balverne wineries.

Schiava *also* Schiava Gentile (I.)

A red grape grown in the Lombardy ar northern Trentino-Alto Adige regions; als called Vernatsch.

Schiava di Faedo (I.)

A rosé wine from Faedo, north of Trent in the Trentino-Alto Adige region; mad from the Schiava grape.

Schiava Grigia (I.)

A red grape, also called Grauvernatsch grown in the northern Trentino-Alto Adig region.

Schilcher (A.)

A district in the Styria region, near Graz, i southeastern Austria; produces Schilcher wein, a spicy red wine.

Schilcherwein (A.)

A red wine from Stainz and Deutschlands berg, in the Styria region, southeaster Austria; made from the Blauer Wildbache grape.

Schiller Wine (G.)

A rosé wine from the Württemberg region made from a mixture of red and white grapes; similar to Siller wines.

hiopetto, Mario (I.)   **1969**

estate in Capriva del Friuli, Friuli-Vezia Giulia region; produces Cabernet uvignon, Collio, Merlot, Müller-Thuru and Riesling wines. 8,000 cases. 40 res.

hioppettino (I.)

A red grape, also called Ribolla Nera, own around Albana di Prepotto, in the olli Orientali district, eastern Friuli-Vezia Giulia region, which produces:

A red wine made from the Ribolla Nera, Schioppettino grape.

hlatter, Hans (Sw.)   **1931**

n estate and merchant in Zurich; produces Blauburgunder and Tokay wines. ,000 cases. 30 acres.

hlegelflasche (G.)

ne typical, slender, long-necked bottle sed in Germany and the Alsace region of ance.

hleimsäure (G.)

ime acid, oxidized glucose which can ter produce insoluble calcium salt crysls in bottles of wine.

chloss (G.)

castle; a wine estate.

chloss Böckelheim (G.)

Bereich, one of 2 in the Nahe region.

chloss Doepken (U.S.)   **1980**
                      vines 1972

winery in Ripley, Chautauqua region, Jew York; produces Chardonnay, Gerürztraminer, Riesling and other wines. 0 acres.

chloss Groenesteyn (G.)   **14th cent.**

well-known estate in Kiedrich, in the heingau region, which dates back to the 4th century and has been in the Von Ritter u Groenesteyn family since 1640. It owns ineyards in Kiedrich and Rüdesheim. 85 cres.

Schloss Johannisberg (G.)

A famous estate in Johannisberg, Grosslage Erntebringer, Bereich Johannisberg, in the Rheingau region; owned by Fürst (Prince) Von Metternich. 27,000 cases. 85 acres.

Schloss Reichartshausen (G.)

A vineyard and estate in Oestrich, Grosslage Gottesthal, in the Rheingau region. 10 acres.

Schloss Reinhartshausen (G.)

An estate in Erbach, in the Rheingau region; owns vineyards in Erbach, Hattenheim, Kiedrich, Rauenthal and Rüdesheim, and part of the Marcobrunn vineyard. The old castle is in Erbach; owned by the Estate of Prince Heinrich Friedrich. 160 acres.

Schloss Schönborn, Domänenweingut (G.)   **1349**

An estate in Hattenheim, Rheingau region; owns vineyards in Hattenheim, Erbach, Rauenthal, Hallgarten, Oesterich, Mittelheim, Winkel, Johannisberg, Geisenheim, Rüdesheim, Lorch and Hochheim. 160 acres.

Schloss Vollrads (G.)   **1335**

A famous estate in Winkel, Grosslage Johannisberg, Bereich Honigberg, in the Rheingau region, from 1335; owned by the Graf Matuschka-Greiffenclau family; qualifies as an *Ortsteil*; also handles the wines of Weingut Fürst Löwenstein estate (40 acres) in Hallgarten. 115 acres.

Schlossabzug (G.)

Estate-bottled, the same as Original Abfüllung, terms used before the new laws of 1971 disallowed their use.

Schlossberg (F.)

A *Grand Cru* vineyard in Kientzheim, Haut-Rhin district, Alsace region; grows mostly Riesling grapes. 148 acres.

Schlossböckelheim (G.)

A village in the Nahe region, Bereich Schloss Böckelheim, Grosslage Burgweg. The vineyards are: Felsenberg, Heimberg, In den Felsen, Königsfels, Kupfergrube, and Mühlberg.

Schluck (A.)

Ordinary, white wine from the Wachau region.

Schlumberger (F.)   1810

A large estate in Guebwiller, Haut-Rhin district, Alsace region; owns 37 acres of Kitterlé vineyard, (Gewürztraminer and Riesling). 300 acres.

Schlumberger, Weingut Robert (A.)   1842

An estate in Bad Vöslau; produces red wine made from St. Laurent, Cabernet Sauvignon, Merlot and Blauer Portugieser grapes. 35 acres.

Schmidt, René (F.)

An estate in Riquewihr, Haut-Rhin district, Alsace region; 22 acres, including 5 acres of Schoenenberg vineyard (Riesling).

Schmitt Söhne, Weinkellerei H. (G.)

A merchant in Longuich, Saar district, Mosel-Saar-Ruwer region; owns estates of G. Schmitt-Schenk'sches in Longuich, Weingut Petershof in Waldrach (Ruwer) and Adolf Rheinart Erbas (Saar).

Schmitt'sches Weingut, Gustav Adolf (G.)   1618

An estate and merchant in Nierstein, Rheinhessen region; owns vineyards in Nierstein, Dienheim and Oppenheim. 250 acres.

Schneider, Weingut Jacob (G.)

An estate in Niederhausen, Nahe region; owns vineyards in Niederhausen and Norheim. 30 acres.

Schoenenberg (F.)

A vineyard in Riquewihr, Haut-Rhin district, Alsace region; grows mostly Riesling grapes. 50 acres.

Scholtz Hermanos S.A. (Sp.)   1

A well-known *bodega* in Málaga; produ a wide range of Málaga wines includ very old *solera* wines ("Solera Sch 1885"). 200,000 cases.

Schönborn, Domänenweingut Schloss (G.)   1

An estate in Hattenheim, Rheingau gion; owns vineyards in Erbach, Geis heim, Hallgarten, Hattenheim, Ho heim, Johannisberg, Lorch, Mittelhei Oesterich, Rüdesheim and Winkel. acres.

Schönburger (G.)

A white grape – a cross of Spätburgun and an Italian table grape; developed at State Teaching and Research Institute, G senheim, Germany.

Schoongezicht EWO (S. Af.)   1

An estate in the Stellenbosch district; p duces red, white and rosé varietal a blended wines. 16,000 cases. 200 acres.

Schoppen (G.)

A German and Swiss wine measure eq to 1/2 liter or a little more than a pint; a called *Nössel*, or *Seidel*.

Schoppenwein (G.)

Carafe wine; ordinary table wine.

Schorlemer, Hermann Freiherr von (G.)

A large estate in Bernkastel-Kues, Mos Saar-Ruwer region; owns 5 other estat with vineyards in Bernkastel, Graach, Z tinger, Wehlen, Ockfen, Wiltingen ar other villages. 115 acres.

Schramsberg (U.S.)   1862, 19

An old winery in Calistoga, Napa Valle California, revived in 1965, 1st wine w Blanc de Blancs sparkling wine in 196 uses Chardonnay, Pinot Noir, Gama Pinot Blanc, Flora and Muscat grapes f Blanc de Blancs, Cuvée de Pinot, Blanc Noirs and Crémant (semi-sweet) Cha pagnes. 25,000 cases. 40 acres.

Schriesheim (G.)

A village in the Baden region, Bereich Badische Bergstrasse/Kraichgau, Grosslage Rittersberg. The vineyards are: Kuhberg, Madonnenberg, Schlossberg and Staudenberg.

Schröder & Schÿler (F.)   1739

A merchant in Bordeaux; owns Château Kirwan.

Schubert, C. von (G.)

An old estate in Trier, Ruwer district, Mosel-Saar-Ruwer region; known as Maximin Grünhaus; owns the Bruderberg, Herrensberg and Abtsberg vineyards. 80 acres.

Schuch, Weingut Geschwister (G.)   1817

An estate in Nierstein, Rheinhessen region; owns vineyards in Nierstein, Oppenheim and Dienheim. 40 acres.

Schug Cellars (U.S.)   1880, 1980

A winery in Calistoga, Napa Valley, California; formerly the old Jacob Grimm Winery; produces Pinot Noir and Scheurebe wines from purchased grapes. 2,000 cases.

Schuster and Son, John (U.S.)   1868

A winery in Egg Harbor, New Jersey.

Schuyler

A white hybrid grape – a cross of Ontario and Zinfandel.

Schwamberg, Weingut (A.)   1780

An estate and merchant in Gumpoldskirchen, Lower Austria region. 300,000 cases. 100 acres.

Schwarze Katz (G.)

1. The only *Grosslage* in Bereich Zell/Mosel, in the Mosel-Saar-Ruwer region; includes the village of Zell. It produces:

2. A well-known brand name of wine from Zell. The name means "Black Cat."

Schwarzlay (G.)

A *Grosslage*, one of 10 in Bereich Bernkastel, in the Mosel-Saar-Ruwer region.

Schwarzriesling (G.)

The German name for the Pinot Meunier, a red grape, therefore, not a Riesling grape at all. Also called Müllerrebe.

Sciaccarello (F.)

A red grape grown in Corsica.

Sciacchetrà (I.)

A sweet, white wine from Cinqueterre, in the Liguria region; made from dried Albarola, Bosco and Vermentino grapes.

Scialetti (I.)   1884

A small estate in Cologna Paese di Roseto, Abruzzi region; produces Montepulciano, Sammaro and Trebbiano wines. 5,000 cases.

Sciascianoso (I.)

A red grape grown in the northern Campania region.

scion

A section of a cane or shoot having one or more buds, usually grafted onto an American, disease-resistant stock. The resulting grapes take on qualities only from the scion plant.

Scolca, La (I.)

A small estate in Rovereto di Gavi, Piedmont region; produces Gavi wines. 12 acres.

scorrevole (I.)

Fluent, flowing, easy to drink, referring to a wine.

Scorza Amara (I.)

1. A red grape, similar to the Lambrusco grape, grown in the Emilia-Romagna region.

2. A red, *frizzante* wine from San Polo d'Enza, south of Parma, in the western Emilia-Romagna region; made from the Scorza Amara grape.

Scorzanera (I.)

A red, still version of Scorza Amara wine from north of Parma, in the northwestern Emilia-Romagna region; made from the Scorza Amara grape.

Scuppernong (U.S.)

1. An American white or bronze grape of the *Vitis rotundifolia* species, discovered on Roanoke Island, North Carolina, in 1584; also grown in Virginia.

2. A white wine made from the Scuppernong grape, sometimes with other grapes blended in.

scuro (I.)

Dark; red.

Seaview (Aus.)

A well-known vineyard and winery in the Southern Vales district, South Australia; produces Cabernet Sauvignon and Rhine Riesling wines.

Seaview Winery (U.S.)   1980

A winery in Casedero, Sonoma County, California; produces Pinot Noir, Zinfandel, Chardonnay and Sauvignon Blanc wines. 5,000 cases. 10 acres.

Sebastiani (U.S.)   1889

An old, established winery in Sonoma City, southern Sonoma County, California; produces Barbera, Cabernet Sauvignon, Pinot Noir, Gamay Beaujolais, Zinfandel, White Riesling, Chardonnay, Gewürztraminer and Pinot Noir Blanc (Eye of the Swan) wines; also jug blends; made the first U.S. *nouveau* wine from Gamay grapes. 4 million cases. 400 acres.

Sebennyticum *also* Sebennytic (Egypt)

An ancient Egyptian wine described by Pliny, a blend of Thasian, Soot grape and Pine Tree grapes.

Seberu (I.)

A white grape grown in northwestern Sardinia.

sec (F.)

1. Dry, when used to describe still wines

2. Semi-sweet, when used to descri Champagnes – 2-4% sugar solution add (*dosage*).

secchio (I.)

A wine measure equal to 2.37 gallons; pail, or bucket.

secco (I.)

Dry.

Secco-Bertani (I.)

A red Valpolicella wine, from the Vene region; made by the Bertani winery.

séché (F.)

Oxidized, flat, harsh, astringent.

Séché *also* Séchet (F.)

A *Premier Cru* vineyard in Chablis, Chabl district, Burgundy; usually considered part of the Vaillons vineyard.

seco (P.)

Dry.

second wine, second label

A wine with a different name and labe which is not up to the standards of the reg ular wine of that winery or *château*.

sediment

A deposit of solids, crystals, tartrates, etc that is found in bottles of aged wines o good quality, especially if the wine was no over-filtered.

Seeweine (G.)

"Lake wine," wine from the Bodensee dis trict, in the Baden region.

Seewinkel (A.)

An area that produces *Sandweine*, win from grapes grown in sand along the east ern shore of the Neusiedlersee, in the Burgenland region of eastern Austria.

Segarcea (R.)

A town and district in the Wallachia region of southwestern Romania; produces mostly red wine made from Cabernet Sauvignon and Pinot Noir grapes.

Segesta (I.)

A brand of red and white table wines from Marsala, in northwestern Sicily.

Ségriès, Château de (F.)

An estate in Lirac, in the southern Rhône region; produces 80% red wine and some rosé and white wines. 50 acres.

Seguin-Manuel (F.)   1720

An estate in Savigny-lès-Beaune, Côte de Beaune district, Burgundy; owns 5 acres of Savigny and 2.5 acres of Savigny Les Lavières.

Ségur, Château (F.)

An estate in Parempuyre, Haut-Médoc district, Bordeaux; classified in 1978 as a *Cru Grand Bourgeois*. 15,000 cases. 75 acres.

Seibel (F., U.S.)

French hybrid grapes grown in France and in the eastern U.S. The most important are: 1000, Rosette – Red; 4986, Rayon d'Or (s. 405 x s. 2007) – white; 5279, Aurora (Aurore) – white; 5455, Plantet – red; 5898, Rougeon – red; 7053, Chancellor – red; 8357, Colobel – red; 9110, Verdelet – white, perfumed, spicy; 9547, DeChaunac – red; 10713, Ambros – white; 10868, red; 10878, Chelois – red, spicy, fruity; 13053, Cascade – red, rosé, light; and 14596, Bellandais (Rhône Valley) – red.

Seibel, Albert Louis (1844-1936) (F.)

A French hybridizer from St.-Julien, in the Ardeche department; he developed hundreds of different hybrid grapes grown in France and the eastern U.S.

Seidel (A.,G.)

A wine measure equal to a half-liter; also called *Schoppen* and *Nössel*.

Seip, Heinrich (G.)

An estate in Nierstein, Rheinhessen region; owns vineyards in Nierstein, Oppenheim, Dienheim and Nackenheim. 85 acres.

Sekt (G.)

Sparkling wine.

Selak's Wines (N.Z.)

A winery in Kumeu, Aukland, North Island; produces Riesling Sylvaner and sparkling wines using the *méthode Champenoise*.

S'éleme (I.)

A light, dry, white wine from the Vermentino di Gallura district, in northeastern Sardinia; made from the Vermentino grape.

Sella & Mosca (I.)   1899

A large estate in Alghero, Sardinia; produces Anghelu Ruju, Cannonau, Torbato, Vermentino and other wines. 500,000 cases. 1,600 acres.

Sellari-Franceschini (I.)   1877

An estate in Scansano, Tuscany region; produces Biondello and Morellino wines.

Selle, Château de (F.)

An estate in Taradeau, in the Provence region; owned by Domaines Ott; produces red, white and rosé wines. 100 acres.

Selo de Origem (P.)

A seal of guarantee of origin, in the form of a numbered, narrow paper strip which is affixed to the cork and neck of the bottle before capsuling. It assures that the wine meets certain standards of origin and quality.

Seltz et Fils, A. (F.)

An estate and merchant in Mittelbergheim, Bas-Rhin district, Alsace region; owns Zotzenberg vineyard – 5 acres.

Semencière, Domaine de la (F.)

An estate in Les Milles, in the Provence region.

Semidano (I.)

A white grape grown in Sardinia.

Sémillon (F.)

A red grape grown principally in the Sauternes district, Bordeaux; used to make sweet or dry white wines, usually blended with the Sauvignon grape; also called Chevrier; also grown in most other districts of Bordeaux, as well as in California, South Africa (called Groensdruift, or the Green Grape), Australia and other regions of the world.

Senard, Daniel (F.)

An estate, also called Domaine des Meix, in Aloxe-Corton, Côte de Beaune district, Burgundy. 22 acres, including 1.2 acres of Corton Clos du Roi, 1.2 acres of Bressandes, 2 acres of Aloxe-Corton Valozières, 5 acres of Corton Clos des Meix Monopole, 2.4 acres of Corton, 7 acres of Aloxe-Corton and some Beaune and Côte de Beaune-Villages.

Sénéjac, Château (F.)

An estate in Le Pian, Haut-Médoc district, Bordeaux; classified in 1932 as a *Cru Bourgeois*. 7,000 cases. 40 acres.

Senoia (U.S.)

A red muscadine grape – a cross of Carlos and Higgins; developed in Georgia by B.O. Fry.

Sentiers, Les (F.)

A *Premier Cru* vineyard in Chambolle-Musigny, Côte de Beaune district, Burgundy. 10 acres.

Seppelt (Aus.)   1851

A winery centered in Adelaide, also in Barossa, Great Western, etc., South Australia; produces Champagne, dessert wine, Cabernet Sauvignon, Shiraz and numerous other wines. Also owns vineyards in Victoria and New South Wales. 3,000 acres.

Septimer (G.)

A white grape – a cross of Gewürztramine and Müller-Thurgau; developed at the State Research Institute, Alzey, Rheinhessen region, Germany by George Scheu in 1927.

Sequoia Grove Vineyards (U.S.)   198(

A winery in Oakville, Napa Valley, California; produces Cabernet Sauvignon and Chardonnay wines. 4,000 cases. 25 acres.

Serbia (Y.)

A republic in southeastern Yugoslavia, responsible for nearly half of all Yugoslavian wine production.

Sercial (P.)

1. A white grape grown in Madeira and used to make pale Madeira wines.
2. A dry, white wine from Madeira; made from the Sercial grape.

Sergikarasi *also* **Sergi Karasi (T.)**

A red grape grown in southeastern Turkey; used in making Gaziantep wine.

Sérine (F.)

In the Rhône region, the local name for the Syrah grape.

Serpentières, Aux (F.)

A *Premier Cru* vineyard (in part) in Savigny, Côte de Beaune district, Burgundy. 33.5 acres.

Serprina (I.)

A white grape grown in the Colli Euganei district, in the Veneto region.

Serradayres (P.)

Red and white wines from the Ribatejo region, just north of Lisbon.

serre (F.)

A pressing of grapes; the first, second and third pressings of grapes in Champagne, which give the best quality wine.

Serres S.A., Bodegas Carlos (Sp.)   1896

A winery in Haro, Rioja Alta region; produces numerous wines made from purchased grapes.

Serrig (G.)

A village in the Mosel-Saar-Ruwer region, Bereich Saar-Ruwer, Grosslage Scharzberg. The vineyards are: Antoniusberg, Heiligenborn, Herrenberg, Hoeppslei, König Johann Berg, Kupp, Schloss Saarsteiner, Schloss Saarfelser, Schlossberg, Vogelsang and Würtzberg. 230 acres.

Serrigny, Domaine de (F.)

An estate in Ladoix-Serrigny, Côte de Beaune district, Burgundy. 26 acres, including 10 acres of Corton, 1.6 acres of Aloxe-Corton and 8 acres of Pommard Clos de la Platière; managed by Bitouzet of Savigny.

Serristori, Conti (I.)

An estate in Sant'Andrea in Percussina, Tuscany region; produces Chianti, Chianti Classico, Galestro, Orvieto, Vin Santo, Vernaccia and other wines. 125,000 cases. 70 acres.

Servin, Marcel (F.)

An estate in Chablis, Burgundy. 30 acres, including 2 acres of Les Preuses, 2 acres of Bougros, 2.4 acres of Les Clos, 2.2 acres of Blanchots and some Montée de Tonnerre, Vaillons and Butteaux.

setier (F.)

An old wine measure equal to 1/18 of a *muid*, or about four gallons.

Setinus, Setine, Setian (Lat.)

An ancient Roman wine from Setia, now called Sezza, on the Appian Way, in the Latium region, a favorite of Augustus Caesar; mentioned by Pliny and Athanaeus.

Settesoli, Cantina Sociale (I.)   1958

A co-op winery of 1,200 members in Menfi, Sicily; produces Settesoli Bianco, Rosato and Rosso wines. 2 million cases. 8,000 acres.

Settlement Wine Company (Aus.)

A new winery in the Southern Vales district, South Australia; produces full, rich red wines and Port wines.

Setúbal (P.)

A town and district southeast of Lisbon, in southwest Portugal, famous for its Moscatel de Setúbal.

Seurey, Les (F.)

A *Premier Cru* vineyard in Beaune, Côte de Beaune district, Burgundy. 3 acres.

sève (F.)

Sap; a wine with *sève* has good body and a smooth, rich texture.

Sevenhill Cellars (Aus.)   1852

A winery run by St. Aloysius Jesuit College in the Clare/Watervale district, South Australia; produces Shiraz, Cabernet Sauvignon and Port wines. 12,000 acres.

Seville Estate (Aus.)   1962

A small winery in Seville, Victoria; produces Cabernet Sauvignon, Shiraz, Chardonnay and Riesling (including BA) wines. 1,000 cases. 8 acres.

sextarius (Lat.)

An old Roman "pint," equal to a half-liter, or 1/6 of a *congius*.

Seyssel AOC (F.)

A commune southwest of Geneva, Switzerland, in the Savoie region; produces white wine, still and sparkling, made from the Roussette grape; Molette and Chasselas grapes are also used to make the sparkling version. 150 acres.

Seyval Blanc

1. A white hybrid grape, also called Seyve-Villard 5276 – a cross of French and American grapes; very hardy, fruity, with very little foxy flavor; grown in the eastern United States and England.

2. A white wine from New York and other eastern states; made from the Seyval Blanc grape.

Seyve, Bertille (1864-1939) (F.)

A grape hybridizer from Bouge-Chambalud, in the Isère department; developed several hundred varieties some time after 1895. He had two sons, also hybridizers, Bertille and Joannes.

Seyve, Bertille (1895-1959) (F.)

A hybridizer, the son of Bertille Seyve. He married the daughter of Villard, another hybridizer, and developed the varieties called Seyve-Villard.

Seyve, Joannes (1900-1966) (F.)

A hybridizer, the son of Bertille Seyve; he took over his father's business and bred Joannes Seyve 26-205, also called Chambourcin.

Seyve-Villard (F.)

The name used for the grapes developed by Bertille Seyve, Jr., a hybridizer who developed hybrid grapes for hot climates. Red grapes: SV 5247, SV 13359, SV 18283 – Garonnais (Garonné, Garonnet) SV 18315 – Villard Noir, SV 23657; white grapes: SV 5276 – Seyval Blanc, SV 12309 – Roucaneuf, SV 12375 – Villard Blanc and SV 19287.

Sfursat also Sforzat also Sforzato DOC (I.)

A red wine from the Valtellina, in the Lombardy region; made from specially dried Nebbiolo grapes, with a required minimum of 14.5% alcohol.

Shafer Vineyards (U.S.)   1979

A winery in Napa City, Napa County, California; produces Cabernet Sauvignon, Zinfandel and Chardonnay wines. 8,000 cases. 40 acres in Stag's Leap area.

Shaw Vineyard and Winery, Charles F. (U.S.) 1979

A winery in St. Helena, Napa Valley, California; produces Napa Gamay, Zinfandel and Chenin Blanc wines. Second label is Bale Mill Cellars. 12,000 cases. 45 acres.

Shenandoah Valley (U.S.)

An old district in Amador County, California; produces mostly Zinfandel wine.

Shenandoah Vineyards (U.S.)   1977

A winery in Plymouth, Shenandoah Valley, Amador County, California; produces Zinfandel, Chenin Blanc, Black Muscat, Mission and Sauvignon Blanc wines, partly from purchased grapes. 8,000 cases. 30 acres of experimental plantings of unusual European varieties.

Sherrill Cellars (U.S.)   1973

A winery in Woodside, south of San Francisco, San Mateo County, California; produces Cabernet Sauvignon, Zinfandel and Petite Sirah wines from purchased grapes. 3,000 cases. 7 acres of Chardonnay and Johannisberg Riesling grapes nearby.

Sherry (Sp.)

1. A fortified white wine from the Jerez district centered around Jerez de la Frontera, in southwestern Spain; made mostly from Palomino grapes with some Pedro Ximénez, Mantúa, Albilla and Cañocaza grapes. 16-18% alcohol. It is made by a *solera* system of blending old and new wines. The different types are: Fino, Manzanilla, Palma, Amontillado, Oloroso, Palo Cortado, Raya, Amoroso and Cream. 21.2 million gallons. 27,500 acres.

2. The Jerez district, in southwestern Andalucia. 55,000 acres.

3. A wine similar to Sherry, but made in any of several other countries.

Shiraz

1. A city in southwestern Iran.

2. Formerly, the wine made in Shiraz, known by Marco Polo.

3. In Australia and South Africa, another name for the Syrah grape.

4. A red wine from Australia or South Africa; made from the Syrah grape, sometimes blended with Cabernet Sauvignon.

Shown and Sons Vineyards (U.S.)   1979

A winery in Rutherford, Napa Valley, California; produces Cabernet Sauvignon, Johannisberg Riesling and Chenin Blanc wines. 15,000 cases. 75 acres.

Sichel, Maison (F.)   1883
A merchant in Bordeaux.

Sichel Söhne, H. (G.)
A merchant in Alzey, Rheinhessen region; markets several wines, including the well-known Blue Nun Liebfraumilch.

Sicily (I.)
A large island off the southwestern coast of Italy, the largest region in Italy. Marsala DOC is the most important wine from this region; also produces Corvo, Etna DOC, Alcano, Cerasuolo, various Moscatos and Malvasia delle Lipari. 208 million gallons.

Sick-Dreyer (F.)
An estate in Ammerschwihr, Haut-Rhin district, Alsace region. 25 acres, including Kaefferkopf vineyard – 5 acres.

Sidi Larbi (Mor.)
A district south of Rabat; produces red wines.

Sidi Rais (Tun.)
A dry, rosé wine.

Sidi Tabet (Tun.)
An important red wine district.

Siegendorf, Klosterkeller (A.)   1860
An estate and merchant, formerly a monastery, in Siegendorf, Burgenland region; produces red and white wines. 80,000 cases. 80 acres.

Siegerrebe (G.)   1929
A white grape – across of Madeleine Angevine (a table grape) and Gewürztraminer; developed at the State Research Institute, Alzey, Germany in 1929; early-ripening, low acidity, good for blending.

Siegfried Riesling (G.)
A white hybrid grape grown in Germany and New York.

Sierra Vista Winery (U.S.)   1977
A small winery in Placerville, El Dorado County, California; produces Cabernet Sauvignon, Zinfandel, Petite Sirah, Syrah, Chenin Blanc, Chardonnay, Sauvignon Blanc and Fumé Blanc wines. 2,500 cases. 80 acres.

Sievering (A.)
A well-known northern suburb of Vienna; produces *heurige* wines.

Siffert et Fils, Louis (F.)
An estate in Orschwiller, southern Bas-Rhin district, Alsace region. 17 acres.

sifone (I.)
A mixture of sweet wine and wine alcohol, added to Marsala wine to produce various degrees of sweetness and alcoholic strength, usually in combination with *cotto*. Neither is used in Marsala Vergine.

Sigalas-Rabaud, Château (F.)
An estate in Bommes, Sauternes district, Bordeaux; classified in 1855 as a *Premier Cru*; owned by the de Rabaud family until 1660; it was Château Rabeaud in 1855; divided into 2 properties (the other being Rabaud-Promis) in 1903; reunited from 1929-1952 then divided again. 35 acres. 3,000 cases.

Siglo (Sp.)
A red or white wine from the Rioja region; produced by AGE, Bodegas Unidas S.A.

Signaux, Les (F.)
A vineyard section of Hermitage, northern Rhône region; produces red wine.

Sigognac, Château (F.)
An estate in St.-Yzans, Médoc district, Bordeaux; classified in 1978 as a *Cru Grand Bourgeois*. 18,000 cases. 100 acres.

Siklós (H.)
A town in the southern Transdanubia region, part of the Villány-Siklós district, in southwestern Hungary; produces red wine from Kadarka and Blauer Portugieser

grapes and some white wine from Wälsch-riesling and Hárslevelü grapes.

Siller Wine

A light, red wine made in central and southeastern Europe from red and white grapes, mixed before fermentation; skins are removed after a few days. It is similar to the Schillerwein of Württemberg, Germany.

Silva & Cosens Ltd. (P.)   1798

A producer of Dow's Port in Vila Nova de Gaia; owns Quinta do Bomfim and Quinta Santa Madalena.

Silvaner

See **Sylvaner.**

Silver Mountain Vineyards (U.S.)   1979

A winery in Los Gatos, Santa Cruz County, California; produces Zinfandel and Chardonnay wines, mostly from purchased grapes. 1,000 cases. 12 acres.

Silver Oak Cellars (U.S.)   1972

A winery in Oakville, Napa Valley, California; produces only 100% Cabernet Sauvignon wine, made from purchased grapes from Alexander Valley and Sonoma County. 6,000 cases.

Silverado Cellars (U.S.)

The second wine of Château Montelena, Calistoga, Napa Valley, California.

Silverado Vineyards (U.S.)   1981

A winery in Napa, Napa Valley, California; produces Cabernet, Chardonnay and Sauvignon Blanc wines. 180 acres. 10,000 cases.

Simard, Château (F.)

An estate in St.-Émilion, Bordeaux; classified in 1955 as a *Grand Cru.* 7,500 cases. 38 acres.

Simi Winery (U.S.)   1876, 1970

An old, refurbished winery (1970) north of Healdsburg, Alexander Valley, northern Sonoma County, California; produces Ca-bernet Sauvignon, Zinfandel, Pinot Noir, Gamay Beaujolais, Rosé of Cabernet, Chardonnay, Gewürztraminer and Chenin Blanc wines from purchased grapes. 135,000 cases.

Simmern'sches Rentamt, Freiherrlich Langwerth von (G.)   1464

An estate in Eltville, Rheingau region, with vineyards in Erbach, Eltville, Hattenheim and Rauenthal. 100 acres.

Simmonet-Febvre (F.)   1840

An estate in Chablis, Burgundy; owns 5 acres of Les Preuses and some Monts de Milieu.

Simone, Château (F.)

The only estate in Palette, near Aix-en-Provence, Provence region; produces red and white wines. 35 acres.

Simonsig Estate EWO (S. Af.)   1968

An estate in the Stellenbosch district; produces numerous red and white wines, especially Kerner, Weisser Riesling and Gewürztraminer. 100,000 cases.

Sion (Sw.)

A village in the Valais region; famous for Dôle and Fendant wines.

Šipon (Y.)

A native white grape grown in the republic of Slovenia; also known as Furmint.

Sipp, Jean (F.)

An estate in Ribeauvillé, Haut-Rhin district, Alsace region. 50 acres, including Clos du Schlossberg – 2 acres (Riesling, Gewürztraminer and Muscat).

Sipp, Louis (F.)

An estate and merchant in Ribeauvillé, Haut-Rhin district, Alsace region. 70 acres,

Sirah *also* Syrah (F.)

A red grape grown in the Rhône Valley, the principal grape of Côte-Rôtie and Hermitage wines; also grown in Australia and South Africa, where it is called Hermitage and Shiraz, and in California; in France it is also called Sirrac and Sérine.

Siran, Château (F.)

An estate in Labarde-Margaux, Haut-Médoc district, Bordeaux; classified in 1932 as a *Cru Bourgeois*. 10,000 cases. 75 acres.

Sires de Vergey, Cuvée des (F.)

A red wine from the Hospices de Nuits, in Nuits-St.-Georges, Burgundy. The *cuvée* is composed of 1.5 acres of Nuits-St.-Georges Les St.-Georges.

Sirrac (F.)

Another name for the Syrah grape.

Sirugue, Marcel (F.)

A grower in Couchey, Côte de Nuits district, Burgundy. 6 acres, including some Côte de Nuits-Villages.

Siskiyou Vineyards (U.S.)　　1978

A winery in Cave Junction, Rogue River Valley, southern Oregon; produces Cabernet Sauvignon, Pinot Noir and Gewürztraminer wines. 5,000 cases. 12 acres.

Sitges (Sp.)

A coastal town southwest of Barcelona, in the Penedès district of the Catalonia region; produces a sweet, white wine made from late-picked Malvasía and Moscatel grapes.

Sittman, Weingüter Carl (G.)

A large estate in Oppenheim, Rheinhessen region; owns vineyards in Nierstein, Oppenheim, Alsheim and Dienheim. 240 acres.

Sizeranne, La (F.)

1. A vineyard in Hermitage, northern Rhône region.
2. A brand name of red Hermitage wine made by Chapoutier.

Sizies, Les (F.)

A *Premier Cru* vineyard in Beaune, Côte de Beaune district, Burgundy. 21 acres.

Sizzano DOC (I.)

A village south of Gattinara, in the northeastern Piedmont region; produces a red wine made from 40-60% Nebbiolo grapes, with some Vespolino and Bonarda grapes.

Skadarka (Y.)

A red grape grown in the Republic of Serbia.

Sky Vineyards (U.S.)　　1979

A small winery in Glen Ellen, 2,000 feet up in the Mayacamas Mountains, Sonoma County, California; produces Zinfandel wine. 4,000 cases. 20 acres.

slatko (Y.)

Sweet.

Slavonia (Y.)

A province in the northeastern part of the Republic of Croatia; produces mostly white varietals from Wälschriesling (called Graševina), Sauvignon, Traminer, Sémillon, Pinot Blanc and Pinot Gris grapes.

Slovakia (Cz.)

An eastern province of Czechoslovakia; the important districts and towns are: Modra and Pezinok northeast of Bratislava; Nové Zámky and Hurbanovo, southeast of Bratislava; Skalica, Hlohovec and Trnava, further northeast of Brataslava; and Malá Trňa, in southeastern Slovakia.

Slovenia (Y.)

A republic of northern Yugoslavia, on the Austrian border; was once an Austrian province; Ljutomer is the most famous white wine from Slovenia.

Small Plain (H.)

A region in northwestern Hungary; produces red wines, especially Sopron. This region is also called Kisalföld.

Smederevka *also* Smedervka (Y.)

A white grape grown in Macedonia and Serbia; the same grape as the Bulgarian Dimiat.

Smith, Woodhouse & Co., Lda (P.)   1784

A Port producer in Vila Nova de Gaia; also a shipper of Gould, Campbell ports.

Smith-Haut-Lafite, Château (F.)

An estate in Martillac, Graves district, Bordeaux; classified in 1959 as a *Cru Classé* for red wine only, though some white wine is also made. 15,000 cases of red, 2,500 cases of unclassified Sauvignon Blanc. 120 acres.

Smith-Madrone Vineyards (U.S.)   1971
1st wine 1977

A winery on Spring Mountain, in St. Helena, Napa Valley, California; produces Cabernet Sauvignon, Pinot Noir, Chardonnay, Johannisberg Riesling and some Viognier wines. 4,000 cases. 50 acres.

Smothers (U.S.)   1977

A winery (Vine Hill Wines) in Santa Cruz City, Santa Cruz County, California; the site of the old Schermerhorn Vineyard; produces Cabernet Sauvignon, Zinfandel, Chardonnay, Gewürztraminer and Johannisberg Riesling wines from Vine Hill and Sonoma County grapes. 4,000 cases.

Soave DOC (I.)

1. A village and district, east of Verona, in the Veneto region which produces:
2. A white wine made from 70-90% Garganega grapes, with some Trebbiano di Soave grapes.

Sobrero & Figli, Filippo (I.)

An estate in Castiglione Falletto, Piedmont region; produces Barolo and Dolcetto wines. 800 cases.

Sociando-Mallet, Château (F.)

An estate in St.-Seurin-de-Cadourne, Haut-Médoc district, Bordeaux; classified in 1978 as a *Cru Grand Bourgeois*. 10,000 cases. 45 acres.

Sociedade Agricola e Comercial dos Vinhos Messias SARL (P.)   1926

A Port producer in Vila Nova de Gaia; owns Quinta do Cachão; also makes table wines in the Bairrada region. 250 acres.

Société Civile (F.)

A private company which owns and manages a wine estate.

Société Civile du Clos Saint-Louis (F.)

An estate in Fixin, Côte de Nuits district, Burgundy. 15 acres, including .3 acre of Fixin Les Hervelets and .3 acre of Gevrey-Chambertin.

Société Civile D'Exploitation du Château de Santenay (F.)

An estate in Santenay, Burgundy; owns 185 acres of Mercurey.

Société Civile du Domaine Thénard (F.)

An estate in Givry, Côte Chalonnaise district, Burgundy. 60 acres, including 4.5 acres of Montrachet, 2.5 acres of Corton Clos du Roi, 2.5 acres of Pernand-Vergelesses, .5 acre of Chassagne-Montrachet Clos St.-Jean, 2 acres of Mercurey, 5 acres of Givry Clos St.-Pierre Monopole, 12 acres of Cellier aux Moines and 28 acres of Bois-Chevaux.

Société d'Intérêt Collectif Agricole des Recherches Expérimentales (F.)

See **S.I.C.A.R.E.X.**

Soda Rock Winery (U.S.)   1980

A winery in Healdsburg, Sonoma County, California; produces Cabernet Sauvignon, Zinfandel, Chenin Blanc and Johannisberg Riesling wines.

soet (S. Af.)

Sweet.

Soeurs Hospitalières, Cuvée (F.)

A red wine from the Hospices de Nuits, in Nuits-St.-Georges, Côte de Nuits district, Burgundy. The *cuvée* is composed of Nuits-St.-Georges Les Fleurières.

soft

A term used to describe wine which is smooth, low in alcohol and usually somewhat sweet as well.

SOGRAPE – Vinhos de Portugal SARL (P.)   1942

A large firm in Porto; produces Mateus Rosé and Blanca, red and white Grão Vasco wine and *Garrafeira* wines. 3.5 million cases.

Sokol Blosser (U.S.)   1977, vineyards 1971

A large winery in Dundee, Willamette Valley, northwestern Oregon; the name is a combination of two family names; produces Pinot Noir, Merlot, Gewürztraminer, White Riesling, Chardonnay and other varietal wines and blends. 20,000 cases. 45 acres.

Solano County (U.S.)

A small region east of Napa Valley, in northern California; it has only a few wineries.

Solar de Samaniego (Sp.)

A red wine from the Rioja region, made by Bodegas Alavesas S. A.; made mostly from Tempranillo and some Viura grapes.

solera (Sp.)

A complex system of blending and aging Sherry and other wines by arranging a series of casks or butts from which the wine from the older butts is taken out for blending and replaced with wine from the younger butts; those butts are then replenished with younger wine, and so on.

Solitude, Domaine de la (F.)

A 16th century estate in Châteauneuf-du-Pape, southern Rhône region; produces red wine made from Grenache, Cinsault and Syrah grapes and white wine made from Clairette and Grenache Blanc grapes. 75 acres.

Solleone (I.)

A dry, Sherry-style wine from the Torgiano DOC district, in the Umbria region; made from Trebbiano and Grechetto grapes by the *solera* method. 18% alcohol.

Solopaca DOC (I.)

A town northeast of Caserta, in the northern Campania region, which produces red and white wines; the red wine is made from 40-60% Sangiovese grapes with some Piedirosso, Aglianico, Sciascianoso and others and the white wine is made from Trebbiano Toscano, Malvasia di Candia and some Malvasia Toscana and Coda di Volpe grapes.

Som (R.)

The Romanian name for the Furmint grape.

sombrero (Sp.)

The cap, consisting of skins, pips, stalks, etc., which rises to the surface of the vat during fermentation.

Somló (H.)

A district near Mt. Somló, north of Lake Balaton, in the Transdanubia region of northwestern Hungary; produces sweet and dry white wine made from Furmint, Riesling, Traminer and Ezerjó grapes. Officially rated white wine of Outstanding Quality. 1,000 acres.

sommelier (F.)

A wine steward or wine waiter, usually in charge of the wine cellar as well.

Sommelier Winery (U.S.)   1st wine 1976

A winery in Mountain View City, Santa Clara County, California; produces Cabernet Sauvignon, Zinfandel, Petite Sirah and Chardonnay wines from purchased grapes. 4,000 cases.

Sommerach (G.)

A village in the Franken region, Bereich Maindreieck, Grosslage Kirchberg. The vineyards are Katzenkopf and Rosenberg. 475 acres.

Sommerberg (F.)

A *Grand Cru* vineyard in Niedermorschwihr, Haut-Rhin district, Alsace region.

Sommerhausen (G.)

A village in the Franken region, Bereich Maindreieck, Grosslage is unassigned. The vineyards are Reifenstein and Steinbach.

Sonnenglanz (F.)

A vineyard in Beblenheim, Haut-Rhin district, Alsace region. 86 acres.

Sonnenküste (Bul.)

German for "Sunkissed," a white wine from the Black Sea region of eastern Bulgaria; made from Dimiat and Rcatsitelli grapes.

Sonoma (U.S.)

A city, valley, county, district and region north of San Francisco, in California, which runs from the Pacific Ocean, for the most part, east to Napa Valley. It is, along with Napa Valley, the leading region for premium wine production. The districts are: Russian River Valley, Alexander Valley, Dry Creek, Knight's Valley and Sonoma Valley. Over 100 wineries. 30,000 acres.

Sonoma-Cutrer (U.S.)   1973
first wine 1981

A former vineyard, and now a winery in Windsor, Sonoma County California; produces Chardonnay wine. 800 acres.

Sonoma Mountain Cellars (U.S.)

A second label of La Crema Viñera Winery in Petaluma, Sonoma County, California.

Sonoma Valley (U.S.)

A district in southeastern Sonoma County, north of San Francisco Bay.

Sonoma Vineyards (U.S.)   1960, 1970

A large winery in Windsor, Russian River Valley district, Sonoma County, California; also sells as Windsor Vineyards (mail orders, personalized labels); produces Cabernet Sauvignon, Zinfandel, Chardonnay, Johannisberg Riesling, Chenin Blanc, Ruby Cabernet, Petite Sirah, Gamay Beaujolais and sparkling wines; also single vineyard bottlings: Alexander's Crown Cabernet, Chalk Hill Chardonnay, River West Chardonnay and Zinfandel and Le Baron Johannisberg Riesling from their own and purchased grapes, some from purchased wine. 600,000 cases. 2,500 acres.

Sonsón (Sp.)

A red grape grown in the Galicia region of northwestern Spain; a highly perfumed grape.

Sopron (H.)

A town and district in the Small Plain region of northwestern Hungary, near the Austrian border; produces red wines made from Kékfrankos grapes (Gamay). Officially rated red wine of Excellent Quality. 3,000 acres.

Sorbés, Les (F.)

A *Premier Cru* vineyard in Morey-St.-Denis, Côte de Nuits district, Burgundy. 7.5 acres.

Sorbet, Clos *also* Clos Sorbés (F.)

A *Premier Cru* vineyard in Morey-St.-Denis, Côte de Nuits district, Burgundy. 6.5 acres.

Sorcières, Les (F.)

A vineyard in Riquewihr, Haut-Rhin district, Alsace region; a *monopole* of Dopff & Irion; produces Gewürztraminer wine. 27 acres.

sorì (I.)

In the Piedmont dialect, a piece of land with a southern exposure; a vineyard with a southern aspect.

Sorì San Lorenzo (I.)

A vineyard in Barbaresco, Piedmont region; owned by Gaja. 2 acres.

Sorì Tildin (I.)

A vineyard in Barbaresco, Piedmont region; owned by Gaja. 3 acres.

Sorni DOC (I.)

A town north of Trento, in the Trentino-Alto Adige region, which produces red, white and rosé wines; the red and rosé wine is made from Lagrein, Schiava and Teroldego grapes and the white wine is made from the Nosiola grape.

Sorrel, Henri (F.)

An estate in Tain-L'Hermitage, northern Rhône region; owns 8.5 acres of Hermitage (mostly in the vineyards of le Méal, Les Greffieux and Les Rocoules).

Sotoyome Winery (U.S.)　　　　1974

A small winery in Healdsburg, Russian River Valley district, northern Sonoma County, California; produces Cabernet Sauvignon, Gamay, Zinfandel and Petite Sirah wines. 8 acres. 6,000 cases.

souche (F.)

A vine-stock; a root stock; a single vine.

Soucherie, Domaine de la (F.)

An estate in Rochefort-sur-Loire, Coteaux du Layon district, Anjou, Loire region. 90 acres, including some Quarts des Chaume.

Soudars, Château (F.)

An estate in Avensan, Haut-Médoc district, Bordeaux; classified in 1978 as a *Cru Bourgeois*. 25 acres. 6,000 cases.

Sous le Dos d'Âne (F.)

A *Premier Cru* vineyard (in part) in Blagny, but sold as Meursault, Côte de Beaune district, Burgundy. 12 acres.

Sous le Puits (F.)

A *Premier Cru* vineyard in Blagny, Côte de Beaune district, Burgundy, but sold as Puligny-Montrachet. 17 acres.

Sousão *also* Souzão (P.)

A red grape used to make Port wine.

Soutard, Château (F.)

An estate in St.-Émilion, Bordeaux; classified in 1955 as a *Grand Cru Classé*. 7,000 cases. 45 acres.

South Africa

Vines were planted in 1654 and the first wine was produced in 1659. Wines of Origin laws were passed in 1973. The most important region is in the southwestern corner of the country. Important grapes are Pinotage, Cabernet, Cinsaut, Sémillon, Steen, Colombard and Clairette. 290,000 acres.

South Australia (Aus.)

A large province of south central Australia; in the southeastern part of the province are located the important vineyard districts, especially the Southern Vales, Barossa Valley and Clare/Watervale districts.

South Carolina (U.S.)

A state in the southern United States; grows muscadine, *labrusca* and hybrid grapes; it has a few commercial wineries. 2,000 acres.

South County Vineyards (U.S.)　1974

A winery in Slocum, Rhode Island, on the west side of Naragannsett Bay; the first winery in Rhode Island since Prohibition; grows *vinifera* grapes. 2 acres.

South Tyrol (I.)

A district in the northern part of the Trentino-Alto Adige region of northeastern Italy. Also called Alto Adige and Südtiroler (in German).

Southern Vales (Aus.)

A district, south of Adelaide, in South Australia; produces red wines, especially Cabernet Sauvignon, and fortified wines.

Southern Vales Co-op (Aus.)　　1965

A cooperative winery in McLaren Vale, Southern Vales district, South Australia; produces Cabernet Sauvignon, Rhine Riesling and other wines.

soutirage (F.)

Racking, drawing the wine off the lees or sediment after fermentation, usually performed several times, weeks or months apart.

Southwest region, the (F.)

See **Sud-Ouest.**

Souverain Cellars (U.S.)   1973

1. A co-op winery in Geyserville, Alexander Valley district, northern Sonoma County, California; produces numerous varietal wines and jug blends. 500,000 cases.

2. A winery in St. Helena, Napa Valley, California; re-named Burgess Cellars in 1972.

3. A winery in Rutherford, Napa Valley, California; re-named Rutherford Hill Winery in 1972.

Spain

A country in southwestern Europe. It contains 1/5 of all European vineyard land; most wine production is in the La Mancha, New Castile, Catalonia and Levante regions. The most well-known wines are from the Jerez, Rioja and Catalonia regions. A system of regulating the production of wine began in 1926, with the *Consejos Reguladores* formulating the *Denominaciones de Origen* rules for each region; these are now supervised by the *Instituto Nacional de Denominaciones de Origen*, formed in 1972. 900 million gallons. 4 million acres.

Spalletti (I.)

An estate in Savignano sul Rubicone, Emilia-Romagna region; produces Sangiovese and Rocca di Ribano wines. 100 acres.

Spalletti Valdisieve Poggio Reale (I.) 1912

A winery in Rufina, Tuscany region; produces Chianti, Orvieto and Vernaccia wines; made from their own and purchased grapes. 50,000 cases. 125 acres.

spalliera (I.)

Espalier, a method of vine-training in which vines are trained high on cement or wooden uprights and spread out on overhead wires; also called *tendone*.

Spanish earth

Aluminum silicate, used in fining or clearing wines of particle matter.

Spanna (I.)

1. In the Piedmont region, another name for the Nebbiolo grape.

2. A red wine (not DOC) made from the Nebbiolo grape.

sparkling

Effervescent; caused by CO_2 gas in the wine, which is a result of 1) a secondary fermentation in the bottle (*méthode Champenoise*) 2) fermentation in big tanks and bottling under pressure (*Charmat*, or bulk method) or 3) the addition of CO_2 gas to the wine, or artificial carbonation.

Sparr, Pierre (F.)

An estate and merchant in Sigolsheim, Haut-Rhin district, Alsace region. 75 acres, including Brand vineyard – 10 acres (Gewürztraminer), Mambourg – 15 acres (Gewürztraminer) and Altenbourg – 10 acres (Riesling).

Sparvo (I.)

A white, *spumante* wine from the Colli Bolognesi district of the Emilia-Romagna region; made from Pinot Bianco, Sauvignon, Riesling and Tocai grapes and bottle-fermented.

Spätburgunder (G.)

The German name for the Pinot Noir grape; grown mostly in the Ahr Region. Also called Blauer Spätburgunder, Clevner, Klävner and Klebrot.

Spätlese (G.)

Late harvest; a wine, usually sweet, made from late-picked, ripe grapes.

Spätrot (A.)

In Lower Austria, another name for the white Zierfändler grape.

Spiegel (F.)

A *Grand Cru* vineyard in Guebwiller, Haut-Rhin district, Alsace region.

Spier Estate EWO (S. Af.)   1969

An estate in the Stellenbosch district; produces red and white wines. 50,000 cases. 700 acres.

Spinello (I.)

A light, white wine from Pescara, in the eastern Abruzzo region; made from the Trebbiano grape.

Spitz (A.)

A village in the Wachau region of northeastern Austria.

Spitzenwein (G.)

A fine wine; quality wine; a "top" wine.

Spitzle (G.)

A tube which is inserted into the cork of a small barrel of about 5 liters called a *Fassle*, thereby rendering the barrel as a drinking vessel.

split

A 1/4 bottle of Champagne or wine, equal to about 6 ounces.

Sporen (F.)

A vineyard in Riquewihr, Haut-Rhin district, Alsace region. 25 acres.

Spring Mountain (U.S.)

A district on Spring Mountain, northwest of St. Helena, Napa Valley, California.

Spring Mountain Vineyards (U.S.)   1965
                                 new site 1974

A winery in St. Helena, on Spring Mountain, Napa Valley, California; since 1974 located at the renovated Miravalle mansion; produces Cabernet Sauvignon, Chardonnay and Sauvignon Blanc; some purchased grapes. 120 acres. 25,000 cases.

Spritzer (G.)

A summer drink made from Rhine or other wine and soda: 1 part wine to 2 parts soda, with ice.

spritzig (G.)

Slightly sparkling; *frizzante; perlé*.

spumante (I.)

Sparkling.

Squillace (I.)

1. A village southwest of Catanzaro, in the southwestern Calabria region, which produces:

2. A white wine made from Greco Bianco and Malvasia grapes.

Squinzano DOC (I.)

1. A town in the southern Apulia region, which produces:

2. Red and rosé wines made from Negroamaro and some Malvasia Nera and Sangiovese grapes.

Staatliche Lehr und Versuchsanstalt für Wein-und Obstbau Weinberg (G.)

An estate and wine school in Weinsberg, Württemberg region; owns vineyards in Abstatt, Weinsberg, Talheim and Gundelsheim. 110 acres.

Staatlichen Weinbaudomänen, Verwaltung der (G.)   1902

A state-owned estate in Niederhausen-Schloss Böckelheim; owns vineyards in Schloss Böckelheim, Niederhausen, Traisen, Altenbamberg, Dorsheim, Münster and other villages. 110 acres.

Staatlichen Weinbaudomänen, Verwaltung der (G.)

A state-owned estate in Trier; owns vineyards in Avelsbach, Ockfen, Serrig and Trier. 210 acres.

Staatlicher Hofkeller (G.)   **12th cent.**

An historic estate in Würtzburg, Franken region; owns vineyards in Würtzburg, Randersacker, Hörstein and Thüngersheim. 285 acres.

Staatsweingüter Eltville, Verwaltung der (G.)

A large, state-owned estate in Eltville, Rheingau region; owns vineyards in Assmannshausen, Rüdesheim, Hattenheim, Rauenthal, Eltville, Hochheim, Bensheim and Heppenheim, including all of Steinberg vineyard and the Kloster Eberbach monastery. 475 acres.

stabilimento (I.)

A firm or company.

Stag's Leap Vineyard *or* **Vintners (U.S.)**   **1888, new winery 1972**

A rebuilt historic winery in Napa City, Napa Valley, California; produces Petite Sirah, Pinot Noir, Merlot and Chenin Blanc wines. 10,000 cases. 100 acres.

Stag's Leap Wine Cellars (U.S.)   **1972 vines 1964, 1st wine 1973**

A winery near Napa City, Napa Valley, California; produces Cabernet Sauvignon, Merlot, Petite Sirah, Gamay Beaujolais, Chardonnay and Johannisberg Riesling wines, some from purchased grapes. 20,000 cases. 40 acres.

stahlig (G.)

Steely, hard, a term usually applied to Saar wines.

Staiger, P. and M. (U.S.)   **1973**

A small winery in Boulder Creek, Santa Cruz County, California; produces Cabernet Sauvignon, Zinfandel and Chardonnay wines. 500 cases. 6 acres.

Staked Plain Winery (U.S.)

See **Llano Estacado.**

stalky

Having the taste of grape stalks that were pressed with the grapes; tannic.

Stanley Wine Company (Aus.)   **1894**

A winery in the Clare/Watervale district, South Australia; produces different styles of dry Rhine Riesling, Cabernet Sauvignon and blended red wines; uses bin numbers: Bin 49 – Cabernet Sauvignon, Bin 56 – Cabernet and Malbec, Bin 5 and 7 – Rhine Riesling; mostly from purchased grapes. Also makes the Leasingham label.

Stanton and Killeen (Aus.)   **1925, 1970**

An old, revived winery in Rutherglen, Victoria; produces Cabernet Sauvignon, Shiraz, Muscats and Port wines. 6,000 cases.

Stanusina (Y.)

A red grape grown in Macedonia.

Starkenburg (G.)

A *Bereich*, one of 2 in the Hessische Bergstrasse region; the sole *Grosslage* is Schlossberg.

Steen *also* **Steendruif (S. Af.)**

The South African name for the Chenin Blanc grape.

Steiermark *also* **Styria (A.)**

A region in southeastern Austria. The capital is Graz; produces white and rosé wines; known for *Heurige*, or May wines, *Schilcherwein* and *Steinwein*. 5,000 acres.

Steigerwald (G.)

A *Bereich*, one of 4 in the Franken region.

Steinbach (G.)

A village in the Baden region, Bereich Ortenau, Grosslage Schloss Rodeck. The vineyards are: Stich den Buben and Yburgberg.

Steinberg (G.)

A famous vineyard estate in Hattenheim, Grosslage Deutelsberg, Bereich Johannisberg, in the Rheingau region. It is an *Ortsteil*, bottled only under the vineyard name; owned by the German state. 80 acres.

Steingarten (Aus.)

A vineyard of the Orlando Winery, Barossa Valley district, South Australia.

Steinglitz (F.)

A section of the Brand vineyard in Turckheim, Haut-Rhin district, Alsace region.

Steingrubler (F.)

A vineyard in Wettolsheim, Haut-Rhin district, Alsace region.

Steinschiller (R.)

A white grape grown in the Banat district, Transylvania.

Stein wine *also* Steinwein (G.)

"Stone wine," a white wine from the Franconia region in Germany and the Styria region in Austria; it is bottled in a flat, oval flask known as a *Bocksbeutel*; it legally applies only to wine from certain parts of a rocky hill in the town of Würzburg.

Stellenbosch WO (S. Af.)

An important town and district in the Cape province, the home of a Government Research Institute for Viticulture and Enology; also contains some of the best estates in South Africa; produces white wines from Chenin Blanc, Clairette Blanche, Riesling, Colombard and other grapes.

Stellenbosch Farmers' Winery SFW (S. Af.)   1935

The largest winery in South Africa; produces Lieberstein – an inexpensive table wine, Zonnebloem – a top quality wine, Oude Libertas – light style wines and Château Libertas – a blend of Cabernet Sauvignon, Shiraz and Cinsault grapes. Owns some vineyards but mostly buys grapes and wine for blending.

Steltzner Vineyard *and* Winery (U.S.)   vines 1967 / winery 1977

A vineyard in Yountville, Stag's Leap area, Napa Valley, California; produces Cabernet and Riesling grapes for Burgess Cellars, Veedercrest and Carneros Creek wineries. 50 acres.

Stemmler Winery, Robert   1978

A winery in Healdsburg, Dry Creek Valley, northern Sonoma County, California; produces Cabernet Sauvignon, Chardonnay and Fumé Blanc wines. 5 acres. 5,000 cases.

Steri (I.)

Red and white wines from Agrigento, in southwestern Sicily. The red wine is made from Nero d'Avola, Barbera and Lambrusco grapes and the white wine is made from Trebbiano, Inzolia and Vernaccia di San Gimignano grapes.

Sterling Vineyards (U.S.)   1964 / winery 1973

A famous, large winery on a high hill near Calistoga, Napa Valley, California; produces Cabernet Sauvignon, Merlot, Pinot Noir, Zinfandel, Chardonnay, Sauvignon Blanc and Gewürztraminer wines. 80,000 cases. 400 acres.

Steuben (U.S.)

An American, red muscadine grape.

Steuk Wine Company (U.S.)   1855

An old winery in Venice, near Sandusky, Ohio; produces sparkling Catawba and wines from hybrid grapes. 4 acres.

Stevenot Winery (U.S.)   1978

A winery in Murphys, Calaveras County, south of Amador County, in northeastern California; prodruces Zinfandel, Petite Sirah, Chardonnay, Johannisberg Riesling and Chenin Blanc wines; some from purchased grapes. 10,000 cases. 20 acres.

still wine

A wine that has no sparkle or effervescence.

stock

A vine with roots on to which another scion of a different species or variety is grafted.

Stoltz Vineyard Winery (U.S.)   1968

A winery near St. James, central Missouri;

produces wines mostly from hybrid grapes. 130 acres.

Stone Hill Winery (U.S.)   **1847, 1965**

A winery in Hermann, Missouri; once thriving until Prohibition, revived in 1965; produces Missouri Riesling and Catawba wines from native grapes. 50 acres.

Stonecrop Vineyard (U.S.)   **1980**
                                       vines 1977

A winery in Stonington, northeastern Connecticut; produces wines made from hybrid grapes. 8 acres.

Stonegate Winery (U.S.)   **1973**

A winery in Calistoga, Napa Valley, California; produces Cabernet Sauvignon, Pinot Noir, Merlot, Chardonnay, Sauvignon Blanc and French Colombard wines. 12,000 cases. 45 acres.

Stoneridge (U.S.)   **vines 1971**
                               1st wine 1975

A small winery in Sutter Creek, Amador County, California; produces Zinfandel and Ruby Cabernet wines. 3.5 acres.

Stony Hill Vineyard (U.S.)   **1951**

A winery in St. Helena, Napa Valley, California; produces Chardonnay, Sémillon, Johannisberg Riesling and Gewürztraminer wines. 4,000 cases. 36 acres.

Stony Ridge (U.S.)   **1883, 1975**

A winery in Pleasanton, Livermore Valley, Alemeda County, California, on the site of the old Ruby Hill Vineyard (1883). Produces Cabernet, Chardonnay, Petite Sirah, Sémillon and Zinfandel wines. 35,000 cases. 200 acres.

Stonyfell (Aus.)

A famous, old winery near Adelaide, South Australia; produces a well-known red wine made from Cabernet and Shiraz grapes from Metala Vineyard and a Port-style wine from the Cabernet Sauvignon grape.

stoup (E.)

1. An old English term for a drinking vessel, cup, flagon or tankard.
2. A draught of wine.

Stover (U.S.)

A white, hybrid grape – a cross of Mantey and Roucaneuf; developed in Florida by Loren Stover.

strain

A clone, or a closely related variety.

Strangenberg (F.)

A vineyard in Westhalten, Haut-Rhin district, Alsace region; produces Pinot Noir and Pinot Blanc wines.

stravecchio (I.)

Very old; aged for a longer period of time than normal.

Stravecchio Siciliano (I.)

A dry, white wine from Vittoria, in southeastern Sicily; made from the Cerasuolo grape; also called Perpetuo; similar to Sherry and aged for a very long time, up to 35 years or more.

straw wine (F.)

In the Jura region, a wine made from ripe grapes dried on straw mats in the sun; called *vin de paille*, in French.

Strohwein (G.)

Straw wine; *vin de paille*, in French.

Stück (G.)

A cask equal to 1,200 liters, 317 gallons or 1,656 bottles. It is used in the Rheinpfalz and Rheinhessen regions.

stuck wine

Wine which has stopped fermenting before all the sugar has been converted to alcohol.

Stuttgart (G.)

A city in the Württemberg region, Bereich Remstal-Stuttgart, Grosslage Weinsteige.

The vineyards are: Kriegsberg, Monchberg and 16 other vineyards in various *Ortsteilen*.

Styria *also* Steiermark (A.)

A region in southeastern Austria. The capital is Graz; produces white and rosé wines; known for *Heurige* wines, *Schilcherwein* and *Steinwein*. 5,000 acres.

Suau, Château (F.)

An estate in Barsac, Sauternes district, Bordeaux; classified in 1855 as a *Deuxième Cru*. 15 acres. 1,300 cases.

suave (P.)

Sweet.

Subotička Pešcara (Y.)

A district in the province of Vojvodina, in the northern part of the Republic of Serbia; produces red and white varietal wines.

Suchots, Les (F.)

A *Premier Cru* vineyard in Vosne-Romanée, Côte de Nuits district, Burgundy. 33 acres.

Sud-Ouest (F.)

The Southwest, a region in southwestern France, excluding Bordeaux; the principal districts are: Bergerac, Gaillac, Monbazillac, Montravel, Madiran and Jurançon.

Südliche Weinstrasse (G.)

A *Bereich*, one of 2 in the Rheinpfalz region.

Südtiroler (I.)

The German name for the northern, mountainous part of the Trentino-Alto Adige region in northeastern Italy. In Italy it is called Alto Adige, or South Tyrol.

Suduiraud, Château (F.)

An estate in Preignac, Sauternes district, Bordeaux, adjoining Château d'Yquem; classified in 1855 as a *Premier Cru*. 95% Sémillon, 5% Sauvignon grapes. 10,000 cases. 200 acres.

süffig (Sw.)

A Swiss term used to describe slightly sweet wines.

suho (Y.)

Dry.

sulfur dioxide

A gas or compressed liquid chemical used to sterilize wines and equipment; it kills unwanted and harmful yeasts and bacteria; the usual method is to burn sulfur wicks.

sulfurization

The process of sulfurizing wine or must with sulfur dioxide (SO_2) or sulfurous acid (H_2SO_3) in order to kill harmful bacteria and yeasts.

Sullivan Vineyards Winery (U.S.)   1979

A vineyard and winery in Rutherford, Napa Valley, California; produces Cabernet Sauvignon, Zinfandel, Chenin Blanc and Chardonnay wines. 5,000 cases. 30 acres.

Sultanina

Another name for the Thompson Seedless grape.

Sulzfeld (G.)

A village in the Franken region, Bereich Maindreieck, Grosslage Hofrat. The vineyards are: Cyriakusberg and Maustal.

Summarello (I.)

A red grape grown in the northern Apulia region; also calle Uva di Troia.

Summerhill Vineyards (U.S.)   1917, 1980

A large winery in Gilroy, Santa Clara County, California; formerly the old Bertero Winery; produces Cabernet Sauvignon, Barbera, Grignolino, Pinot Noir, Zinfandel, Sherries and Port wines mostly from purchased wines. 40,000 cases.

Sumoll Tinto (Sp.)

A red grape used in making sparkling wines.

Sunrise Winery (U.S.)   1902, 1976

A re-established, old winery in Santa Cruz, Santa Cruz County, California; formerly the Locatelli Winery; produces Cabernet Sauvignon, Pinot Noir, Zinfandel and Chardonnay wines from purchased grapes grown in various regions of the state. 3,000 cases.

Sur Gamay (F.)

A *Premier Cru* vineyard in St.-Aubin, Côte de Beaune district, Burgundy. 35 acres.

Sur-les-Grèves (F.)

A *Premier Cru* vineyard in Beaune, Côte de Beaune district, Burgundy. 10 acres.

Sur Lavelle *also* Sur La Velle (F.)

A *Premier Cru* vineyard in Monthélie, Côte Chalonnaise district, Burgundy. 15 acres.

sur lie (F.)

"On the lees," a term applied to a wine that is left for a short time on the lees, or sediment left after fermentation, to give the wine a certain fruity freshness before bottling; practiced especially in Muscadet.

Sur le Sentier du Clou (F.)

A *Premier Cru* vineyard in St. Aubin, Côte de Beaune district, Burgundy. 30 acres.

sur souche (F.)

"On the vine," wine that is sold before the harvesting of the grapes.

surdo *also* vinho surdo (P.)

Sweet must with added alcohol, used to adjust the sweetness of Madeira wines.

Suremain, Hugues de (F.)

An estate in Mercurey, Côte Chalonnaise district, southern Burgundy. 30 acres.

Suremain, Robert de (F.)

An estate in Monthélie, Côte Chalonnaise district, Burgundy. 20 acres, including some Château de Monthélie (red) and Rully Premier Cru (white).

Surin (F.)

In the Loire Valley, another name for the Sauvignon Blanc grape.

surmaturité (F.)

French for "overripeness of grapes," used to made rich, sweet, white wines, especially Vouvray.

Suronde, Château de (F.)

An estate in Rochefort-sur-Loire, Anjou district, Loire region; produces Quarts de Chaume and Coteaux du Layon wines. 65 acres.

Süssdruck (Sw.)

The Swiss equivalent of the German *Auslese*; selected bunches of grapes.

Süssreserve (G.)

Sweet reserve, a sweet grape must added to wine before bottling to add freshness and to bring it up to the desired degree of sweetness.

Sussumariello (I.)

A red grape grown in Ostuni, in the southern Apulia region.

Sutter Home (U.S.)   1890, 1947

An old winery in St. Helena, Napa Valley, California; formerly in Howell Mountain until 1906; produces Zinfandel, White Zinfandel, and Muscato Amabile wines from purchased grapes grown in Amador County. 100,000 cases.

Svetinje (Y.)

A famous vineyard in the Ljutoner district, in the northeastern part of the Republic of Slovenia; produces Beli Burgundec (Pinot Blanc) wine.

Swan Valley (Aus.)

A district north of Perth, in the southwestern corner of Western Australia.

Swan Vineyards, Joseph (U.S.) 1969

A small winery in Forestville, northwest of Santa Rosa, southern Sonoma County, California; produces Zinfandel from purchased grapes; also Chardonnay and Pinot Noir wines. 10 acres. 2,000 cases.

Swartland WO (S. Af.)

A district north of Cape Town around the towns of Riebeck and Malmesbury; produces mostly white wine and some red and Port-style wines. The best known estate is Allesverloren.

sweet

Having the presence and taste of sugar, known as residual sugar, noticeable starting at around 1% sugar. The most well-known natural sweet wines are Sauternes, Barsac, Muscats, Vouvray, German *Spätlese*, *Auslese*, *Beerenauslese* and *Trokenbeerenauslese* wines, Hungarian Tokaji, and other similar wines from other countries. The sweet, fortified wines are Port, Sherry, Madeira, Marsala, VDN wines, etc. Actually, any wine from almost any grape can be vinified as dry, semi-sweet and sweet, as many are in France, Italy, California (even Chardonnay, Cabernet and Zinfandel) and Australia.

Sweetwater (Aus.)

Another name for the Chasselas grape; also called Gutedel, Fendant and Chasselas Doré.

Swellendam WO (S. Af.)

A town and district east of Cape Town, just south of Little Karoo; produces white wines and dessert wines.

Switzerland

A central European country with 30,000 acres of vines; the well-known wines are made in the west, around Lake Neuchâtel, Lake Geneva and along the Rhône River in the southeast. The principal wines are Dôle, Dorin, Fendant, Dézaley and Neuchâtel.

Sycamore Creek Vineyards (U.S.) 1976

A winery in Morgan Hill, Santa Clara County, California; produces Cabernet Sauvignon, Zinfandel, Zinfandel Rosé, Johannisberg Riesling, Chardonnay and Gewürztraminer wines. 15 acres. 4,000 cases.

Sylvaner *also* Silvaner (G.)

A white grape grown in the Alsace region of France and in Germany, as well as in California, U.S. and other countries; early-ripening, large yield, dense clusters of round, greenish berries, slightly acid, good for crossing. Also called Franken Riesling.

Symphony (U.S.) 1982

A white grape – a cross of Muscat Alexander and Grenache; developed in Davis, California by Dr. Harold Olmo.

Syrah *also* Sirah (F.)

An important red grape grown in the Rhône region; also grown in California, Australia, South Africa and Switzerland; the grape used in making Hermitage, Côte-Rôtie and Châteauneuf-du-Pape wine; also called Sérine and Sirrac, and in Australia and South Africa, Shiraz, or Hermitage.

Szamorodni (H.)

Polish for "such as it was grown" or "self-made," in reference to the ordinary grapes used in Tokaji wines, i.e. not *Aszú* (dried grapes); it can be made sweet or dry.

száraz (H.)

Dry.

Szeged (H.)

A city and district in south central Hungary.

Szekszárd (H.)

A town and district in the southern Transdanubia region of southwestern Hungary;

produces red wine from the Kadarka grape. Officially rated red wine of Excellent Quality. 4,500 acres.

Szemelt (H.)

Selected bunched of grapes. The same as *Auslese* in Germany.

Szilváni (H.)

The Hungarian name for the Sylvaner grape.

Szürkebarát (H.)

"Grey Friar," a white grape, related to the Pinot Gris.

T

TBA (G.)

Trockenbeerenauslese (a selection of dried berries), usually, a very intense, sweet wine.

table wine

Wine that is to be drunk with food, usually not sweet, sparkling or fortified, and usually under 14% alcohol.

Tabor Hill Vineyard (U.S.)   1970

A winery in Baroda, southwestern Michigan; produces Chardonnay, Riesling, Baco Noir, Maréchal Foch, Vidal Blanc and other wines. 20 acres.

Tâche, La (F.)

A famous *Grand Cru* vineyard in Vosne-Romanée, Côte de Nuits district, Burgundy; the wine was allowed to include that of the adjoining vineyards, Les Gaudichots and La Grand Rue, as of a 1936 law, and sometime later most of Les Gaudichots was absorbed into La Tâche. La Tâche is now a *monopole* (since 1933) owned by the Société Civile de la Romanée-Conti. 1,700 cases. Formerly 3.5 acres, now 15 acres.

Taeniotic (Egypt)

An ancient Egyptian wine, white, sweet, and aromatic; it was considered to be even better than the famous Mareotic wine. Mentioned by Athanaeus, c. A.D. 200.

Tafelwein (G.)

Table wine; an official designation for an ordinary wine, ranked below the *Qualitätswein*; usually sold in 1-liter bottles.

taglio (I.)

Cutting, or blending, referring to a wine used for that purpose.

Tahbilk, Château (Aus.)   1860

An old, historic estate and winery in central Victoria, north of Melbourne; produces long-lived red wines, especially Shiraz and Cabernet Sauvignon and some white wines, including Rhine Riesling, Marsanne and white Hermitage. 35,000 cases. 125 acres.

Taillan, Château du (F.)

An estate in Le Taillan, Haut-Médoc district, Bordeaux; classified in 1978 as a *Cru Grand Bourgeois*. 4,000 cases. 30 acres.

taille (F.)

Pruning.

taille-gobelet (F.)

A system of vine training in a bush form around one stake, used in the southern Rhône region.

Taille-Pieds (F.)

A *Premier Cru* vineyard in Volnay, Côte de Beaune district, Burgundy. 22 acres.

Taillefer, Château (F.)

An estate in Pomerol, Bordeaux. 4,300 cases. 25 acres.

Tain-l'Hermitage (F.)

An important town in the northern Rhône region, north of Valence; the famous Hermitage wines are made from grapes grown in the surrounding hill vineyards.

Taittinger (F.)   1734, 1932 as Taittinger

A Champagne producer in Reims; the *cuvées de prestige* are Comtes de Champagne (a vintage *blanc de blancs*) and Brut Absolu (with no *dosage*), made since 1982. 4 million bottles. 600 acres.

Talbot, Château (F.)

An estate in St.-Julien, Haut-Médoc district, Bordeaux; classified in 1855 as a *Quatrième Cru*; named after John Talbot, 1st Earl of Shrewsbury (d. 1453). Also makes a dry white wine called Caillou Blanc. 35,000 cases. 215 acres.

Talmettes, Les (F.)

A *Premier Cru* vineyard (in part) in Savigny, Côte de Beaune district, Burgundy. 7.5 acres.

Taltarni (Aus.)   1972

A winery in Victoria owned by the Portet Family of France; produces long-lived red wines, including Cabernet Sauvignon, Shiraz and Merlot as well as Rhine Riesling, Chardonnay and other wines. 25,000 cases. 250 acres.

Tamarez (P.)

A white grape grown in southern Portugal.

Tamianka (Bul.)

A sweet, white dessert wine from Stara Zagora, in central Bulgaria.

Tămîioasa Romînească (R.)

A white, muscat type of grape grown in the Cotnari district.

Tañama (Mex.)

A district in the northern Baja California region, near Tecate.

Tanit (I.)

A sweet, white wine in *passito* style from Sicily; made from the Moscato grape; produced by Agricoltura Associati di Pantelleria.

Tannat *also* Tannet (F.)

A red grape grown in Madiran, in the Southwest region; considered to be the same as the Harriagne grape grown in Uraguay.

tannin

Tannic acid, a desirable component of wine, especially red wine, derived from the skins, pips, stems and the oak barrels in which the wine is aged; it produces a harsh, astringent taste in a young wine and is responsible for the long aging capabilities of many red wines.

Tarczal, de (I.)

An estate in Marano d'Isera, Trentino-Alto Adige region; produces Cabernet, Merlot, Marzemino, Schiava and Teroldego wines.

tardive *also* tardif (F.)

Late, referring to the harvest (*vendage tardive*); used in Alsace for sweet, late-harvest white wines, similar to the German *Spätlese*.

tarefa de barro (P.)

A large clay vat used for fermenting must.

Targé, Château de (F.)   1655

An estate in Parnay, Saumur-Champigny district, Anjou region; produces red and white wines. 12 acres.

Tarragona DO (Sp.)

One of 5 DO districts in the Catalonia region, around the city of Tarragona; best-known for sweet, dessert wines.

Tarrantez *also* Terrantez (P.)

A white grape formerly used in making a Mádeira wine of the same name; now grown in the Ribatejo and Vinho Verde regions.

Tart AOC, Clos de (F.)

A *Grand Cru* vineyard in Morey-St.-Denis, Côte de Nuits district, Burgundy; prior to 1141 it was called Climat de la Forge; sold in that year to a Cistercian order of nuns called Bernadines de l'Abbaye de Notre-Dame de Tart; a *monopole* owned by Monmessin. 17.5 acres.

tartrates

Tartar, or tartaric acid, in the form of crystalline salt deposits, which, found in some wines, are harmless and tasteless.

Tastet et Lawton (F.)   1740

A merchant in Bordeaux.

tastevin (F.)

A traditional tasting cup, usually small and made of silver; used especially in Burgundy.

Tastevinage (F.)

1. A special label appearing on certain Burgundy wines that have been approved by a tasting panel of the *Confrérie du Tastevin*, a wine fraternity based in the *château* of Clos de Vougeot.

2. The annual tasting of Burgundy wines each year held by the *Confrérie des Chevaliers du Tastevin* in order to determine which wines will receive the Tastevinage label of approval.

Tatachilla (Aus.)

A large vineyard in McLaren Vale, South Australia.

Tauberbischofsheim (G.)

A village in the Baden region, Bereich Badisches Frankenland, Grosslage Tauberklinge; the vineyards are Edelberg and Silberquell.

Taupine, La (F.)

A *Premier Cru* vineyard in Monthélie, Côte Chalonnaise district, Burgundy. 11 acres.

Taurasi DOC (I.)

1. A town in the central Campania region, northeast of Avellino, which produces:

2. A red wine made mostly from Aglianico grapes with up to 30% Piedirosso, Sangiovese and Barbera grapes.

Tavannes, Le Clos des (F.)

A *Premier Cru* vineyard (in part) in Santenay, Côte de Beaune district, Burgundy. 66 acres.

Tavel AOC (F.)

1. A commune and district northwest of Avignon, in the southern Rhône region, which produces:

2. A rosé wine made usually from 60% Grenache and 15% Cinsault grapes with some Clairette, Bourboulenc, Syrah and other grapes. 2,000 acres.

Tawny Port (P.)

A Port wine, a blend of different vintages, aged up to 10 years in wood, making a paler, more aromatic, but not a full-bodied wine. Once bottled, unlike Vintage Port, it does not improve with age. Also known as a wood Port.

Tayac, Château (F.)

An estate in Soussans-Margaux, Haut-Médoc district, Bordeaux; classified in 1978 as a *Cru Bourgeois*. 10,500 cases. 50 acres.

Taylor California Cellars (U.S.)   1979

A large winery in Gonzalez, Monterey County, California; produces jug blends and varietal wines from purchased wines. 10 million cases.

Taylor Fladgate & Yeatman (P.)   1692

A famous Port producer in Vila Nova de Gaia; owns Quinta de Vargellas, Quinta do Panascal and Quinta de Terrafeita. 1,500 acres.

Taylor Winery (U.S.)   1880

A winery in Hammondsport, New York, the largest in the eastern U.S.; produces various styles of wine made from hybrid and *labrusca* grapes. 1,200 acres.

Tazzalenga *also* Tacelenghe (I.)

A red wine from Buttrio, in the Colli Orientali district of the Friuli-Venezia Giulia region; made from the Refosco grape.

Te Mata Estate (N.Z.)   1896, 1978

A revived winery in Havelock North, Hawkes Bay, North Island, the oldest in New Zealand; produces Cabernet Sauvignon, Merlot, Chardonnay, Gewürztraminer, Furmint and Sauvignon Blanc wines. 30,000 cases. 80 acres.

Téa (Sp.)

A district in the Galicia region of northwestern Spain; produces red wine from Tintarrón, Caiño and Espadeiro grapes and white wine from the Albariño grape.

Tébourba (Tun.)

A town and district west of Tunis; produces red wines.

Tedeschi Vineyard (U.S.)   1977, vines 1974

A vineyard and winery near Ulupalakua, on the island of Maui, Hawaii; produces Chardonnay, Chenin Blanc, Carnelian and a pineapple wine called Maui Blanc. 20 acres.

Tegea (Gr.)

A light rosé wine from the Peloponnese region.

Tegna (Lat.)

The ancient Roman name for Tain-l'Hermitage, in the northern Rhône region, France.

Tegolato (I.)

A red wine from the Chianti district, in the Tuscany region; aged by exposing the wine to extreme temperatures on roof tiles (*tegole*); made from Canaiolo and Sangiovese grapes.

teinturier (F.)

A tinting or coloring grape; a red grape with red juice, such as Alicante-Bouchet; it is used to give color to pale wines.

Tejon Ranch (U.S.)   1971

A large, privately owned vineyard in southeastern Kern County, California. 7,000 acres.

Tekirdag (T.)

1. A village in the Trakya (Thrace) region, in northwestern Turkey, which produces:

2. A semi-sweet, white wine made from the Yapincak grape.

Tempier, Domaine (F.)

An estate in Bandol, Provence region; produces red and white wines. 60 acres.

Tempranillo (Sp.)

A red grape grown in the Rioja region; also called Ull de Llebre, Ojo de Liebre and Cencibel.

tendone (I.)

A method of vine-training in which vines are trained high and horizontally on an arbor or on wires, similar to espalier; also called *spalliera*.

tenimento (I.)

A farm.

Tenner Brothers (U.S.)

A winery in Patrick, South Carolina; produces wines from muscadine and *labrusca* grapes. 300 acres.

Tennessee (U.S.)

A state in the southern United States; there are no commercial wineries; however, some muscadine, Riesling, Chardonnay, Pinot Noir and hybrid grapes are grown in various parts of the state.

Tent wine (E.)

Formerly, the English name for Spanish red wine from the Alicante region and for red wine from Madeira; also called "Tinto."

tenuta (I.)

A farm.

Tepusquet Vineyard (U.S.)

A large vineyard in Santa Maria, San Luis Obispo and Santa Barbara Counties, California; almost 2,000 acres of numerous varieties. The vineyard has supplied Riesling grapes for Bargetto and Felton-Empire, Chardonnay for Monteviña and Zaca Mesa, and Cabernet for Caparone.

Teran (Y.)

In the Istria region, the name for the Refosco grape.

Terciona, Villa (I.)

An estate in Mercatale Val di Pesa, Tuscany region; produces Chianti Classico and Terciona Bianco wines.

Terlano *or* **Terlaner DOC (I.)**

1. A village and district northwest of Bolzano, in the Trentino-Alto Adige region, which produces:

2. White varietal wines from various grapes: Müller-Thurgau, Pinot Bianco, Riesling Italico, Riesling Renano, Sauvignon and Sylvaner.

Terme, Château Marquis de (F.)

See **Marquis-de-Terme, Château.**

Termeno Aromatico (I.)

The Italian name for the Gewürztraminer grape; also called Traminer Aromatico.

Teroldego (I.)

A red grape grown in the Campo Rotaliano plain, northwest of Trento, in the south central Trentino-Alto Adige region.

Teroldego Rotaliano DOC (I.)

A red or rosé wine from the Campo Rotaliano Plain, northwest of Trento, in the south central Trentino-Alto Adige region; made from the Teroldego grape.

Terra Calda Scorza Amara (I.)

A dark red Lambrusco wine from Reggio Emilia, in the Emilia-Romagna region; made from the Lambrusco grape.

Terra Rossa (Aus.)

A small area of red soil in the Coonawarra district, South Australia, where some of the most famous red wines in Australia are made.

Terrano del Carso (I.)

A red wine from Trieste, in the southeastern Friuli-Venezia Giulia region; made from various local red grapes; low in alcohol.

Terrantez *also* **Tarrantez (P.)**

A white grape formerly used in making a Madeira wine of the same name; now grown in the Ribatejo and Vinho Verde regions.

Terre del Barolo (I.)

A co-op winery in Castiglione Falletto, Piedmont region; produces Barbera, Barolo, Dolcetto and Nebbiolo wines.

Terre Ferme, Domaine de la (F.)

An estate and merchant in Bédarrides, Châteauneuf-du-Pape district, Rhône region; produces red and white Châteauneuf-du-Pape and Côtes du Rhône wines.

Terre Rosse, Vallania (I.)   **1965**

An estate in Zola Predosa, Emilia-Romagna region; produces Cabernet Sauvignon, Chardonnay, Colli Bolognese, Malvasia and Pinot Grigio wines. 11,000 cases. 50 acres.

Terres Vineuses, Domaine les (F.)

An estate in Aloxe-Corton, Côte de Beaune district, Burgundy; operated by La Reine Pédauque. 63 acres, including some Corton Clos du Roi, Corton Renardes, Aloxe-Corton Premier Cru, Ladoix Clos les Chagnots Monopole – 11 acres, and Corton-Charlemagne.

Terret Blanc (F.)

A white grape grown in the Rhône and Languedoc regions.

Terret-Bourret (F.)

A white grape grown in Palette, Provence region.

Terret Noir (F.)

A red grape grown in the Rhône and Languedoc regions; it is one of 13 grapes used to make Châteauneuf-du-Pape wine.

Terry S.A., Fernando A. de (Sp.)   1883

A Sherry producer in Puerto de Santa Maria; produces a full range of sherries.

Tertre, Château Du (F.)

An estate in Arsac-Margaux, Haut-Médoc district, Bordeaux; classified in 1855 as a *Cinquième Cru*. "Tertre" means a hilloch or a rise. 15,000 cases. 120 acres.

Tertre-Daugay, Château (F.)

An estate in St.-Émilion, Bordeaux; classified in 1955 as a *Grand Cru Classé*. 5,000 cases. 35 acres.

Teruzzi & Puthod Ponte a Rondolino (I.)   1975

An estate in San Gimignano, Tuscany region; produces Chianti Colli Senesi, Galestro and Vernaccia wines. 15,000 cases. 50 acres.

Tesch, Weingut Erbhof (G.)   1723

An estate in Langenlonsheim/bei Bingen/Rhein, Nahe region; owns vineyards in Laubenheim and Langenlonsheim. 100 acres.

Testucchio (I.)   since 1973

A red wine from Montespértoli, southwest of Florence, in the Tuscany region; made from Sangiovese, Occhio di Pernice, Mammolo, Ciliegiolo and Prugnolo grapes.

Testut (F.)

An estate in the Chablis district, Burgundy; owns Domaine de la Grenouille – 25 acres of the Grenouilles vineyard.

Testuz, Jean & Pierre (Sw.)   1845

An estate in Treytorrens-Cully, Dézaley, Lavaux district, Vaud region; produces red and white wines under several *Domaine* labels. 500 acres.

Tête, Louis (F.)

A merchant in St.-Didier sur Beaujeu, Beaujolais district, Burgundy; produces Beaujolais wines.

tête de cuvée (F.)

"Best of the crop," an unofficial designation used on some wine labels to indicate a superior quality wine; formerly it was synonymous with *Grand Cru*, especially in Burgundy.

Teurons, Les (F.)

A *Premier Cru* vineyard in Beaune, Côte de Beaune district, Burgundy. 36 acres.

Tewksbury Wine Cellars (U.S.)   1979

A winery in Oldwick, New Jersey; produces Chardonnay and Gewürztraminer wines and wines made from hybrid grapes. 17 acres.

Texas (U.S.)

A state in the southwestern United States, the largest in the country; grew Mission grapes in 1662 and had dozens of wineries before Prohibition; 100 new wineries have been established since the late 1960's but less than 1,000 acres of vines.

Thallern (A.)

A village in the Lower Austria region of eastern Austria, just south of Vienna; home of the Heiligenkreuz monastery where the famous Wiege vineyard in located.

Thallern, Freigut (A.)   1141

An historic, Cistercian estate in Gumpoldskirchen; owns vineyards in Gumpoldskirchen, including the *Ried* Wiege, and elsewhere. 235 acres.

Thanisch, Weingut Wwe. Dr. H. (G.)

A famous estate in Bernkastel-Kues, Mosel-Saar-Ruwer region; owns vines in Bernkasteler Doktor, Badstube and Lay, Braueberger Juffer and Sonnenuhr, Graacher Himmelreich and Lieserer Schlossberg.

Thasian (Gr.)

A rich, pink, ancient Greek wine; mentioned by Theophrastus.

Thébaud, Gabriel (F.)

A merchant in St.-Fiacre-sur-Maine, Muscadet region, Loire Valley; owns the Domaine de la Hautière.

Thénard, Domaine (F.)

An estate in Givry, Burgundy. See **Société Civile du Domaine Thénard.**

Theophrastus (371-287 B.C.) (Gr.)

A Greek philosopher, a pupil of Plato and Aristotle, and an important writer on botany; also wrote about grapes and wine.

Theuniskrall EWO (S. Af.)   1962

An estate in the Tulbagh district; produces white wines, especially Riesling and Gewürztraminer. 50,000 cases. 400 acres.

Thévenin, Domaine René (F.)   1868

An estate in St.-Romain, Côte de Beaune district, Burgundy. 30 acres, including some Volnay, Beaune, Meursault, Monthélie and St.-Romain.

Thévenin, Roland (F.)   1856

An estate in St.-Romain, Côte de Beaune district, Burgundy; owns the Domaine du Château de Puligny-Montrachet – 28 acres, including Montrachet – .5 acre, Puligny-Montrachet Les Folatières – 7.5 acres, La Garenne – 2 acres, Champs Gain – 2 acres, Clos de Chaniot – 1.2 acres, Nosroyes – 2.5 acres and Meursault Casse-Têtes – 1.2 acres; Domaine du Moulin aux Moines – 16 acres, including Auxey-Duresses Clos du Moulin aux Moines Monopole – 7 acres, Les Écusseaux – 5.7 acres; Domaine de la Corgette – 17 acres, including Saint-Romain Clos des Ducs Monopole – 2.5 acres, Clos de la Branière – 4 acres, Beaune Les Teurons – 1 acre, Les Perrières – 2 acres and some Pommard.

Thévenot-Le-Brun et Fils (F.)

An estate in Marey-Les-Fussey, Côte de Beaune district, Burgundy. 37 acres, including Hautes-Côtes de Nuits – 27 acres and some Passe-tout-grains, Aligoté perlé and Pinot Gris.

Théviot, Germain (F.)

An estate in St.-Romain, Côte de Beaune, Burgundy. 12.5 acres, including 5 acres of Monthélie and 7.5 acres of St.-Romain.

thief

A tube, or *pipette*, for withdrawing wine, etc. from a barrel; made of glass or silver.

thin

Lacking in body, alcohol and flavor.

Thivin, Château de (F.)

An estate in Côte de Brouilly, Beaujolais district, Burgundy.

Thomas (U.S.)

An American red muscadine grape grown in the southeastern U.S.

Thomas-Bassot (F.)   1850

An estate in Gevrey-Chambertin, Côte de Nuits district, Burgundy. 27 acres, including 2 acres of Ruchottes-Chambertin, 4.6 acres of Griotte-Chambertin, 8 acres of Mazis-Chambertin and 7.4 acres of Gevrey-Chambertin Premier Cru.

Thompson Seedless (U.S.)

A white *vinifera* grape, also called Sultanina, grown in California for blending (Chablis, etc.), as a base for inexpensive Champagne, brandy and pop wines and occasionally as a varietal wine. It was discovered and planted by an Englishmen, William Thompson, in 1872 in Yuba City, Sacramento, California.

Thompson Vineyard and Winery (U.S.)   1963

A winery in Monee, south of Chicago, Illinois; produces wines from French hybrid grapes as well as Delaware, Catawba and some Riesling, Chardonnay and sparkling wines. 30 acres.

Thorey, Aux (F.)

A *Premier Cru* vineyard in Nuits-St.-Georges, Côte de Nuits district, Burgundy. 15 acres.

Thorin, Domaine J. (F.)

A merchant in Pontanevaux, Beaujolais district, Burgundy; operates Château de Jacques (Moulin-à-Vent) and Château de Loyses, a Beaujolais Blanc.

Thousand Oaks Vineyard (U.S.)   1978

A winery in Starkville, near Columbus, Mississippi; produces wines from local muscadine, hybrid, and some *vinifera* grapes. 25 acres.

Thüngersheim (G.)

A village in the Franken region, Bereich Maindreieck, Grosslage Ravensburg. The vineyards are: Johannisberg and Scharlachberg. 625 acres.

Tibouren (F.)

A red grape grown in Bandol, Provence region.

Ticino (Sw.)

The Italian region of Switzerland, in the southeast; produces red and white wines, including Nostrano and Viti.

Tiegs Winery (U.S.)   1980

A small winery in Lenoir City, Tennessee; produces wines from French hybrid grapes.

Tielandry (F.)

A *Premier Cru* vineyard in Beaune, Côte de Beaune district, Burgundy; also called Clos Landry. 5 acres.

Tierra de Barros DO (Sp.)

Red and white wines from the Badajoz district, in the Extremadura region of southwestern Spain; the red wine is made from Almendralejo, Garnacho and Morisca grapes and the white wine is made from the Cayetán Blanca grape.

Tierra Rejada (U.S.)   1972

Spanish for "furrowed earth," a large vineyard in Paso Robles, San Luis Obispo County, California; produces Zinfandel and Merlot grapes. 500 acres.

Tierra del Vino (Sp.)

A district southwest of Valladolid, in nortl central Spain; includes the villages o Rueda, Serrada, La Seca and Nava del Rey

Tifernum (I.)

Red and rosé wines from Petrella Tifer nina, in the Molise region; made from Montepulciano, Sangiovese and Aglianic grapes.

Tiger's Milk *or* Tigrovo Mljeko (Y.)

A sweet, white wine from Radgona, i1 northeastern Slovenia; made from the Bou vier grape.

Tignanello (I.)   since 197

A red wine from the Chianti Classico dis trict, in the Tuscany region; made from Sangiovese, Canaiolo and 10% Caberne Sauvignon grapes. The first vintage of th(wine also had some Malvasia grapes; mad(by Antinori.

Tigrovo Mljeko (Y.)

"Tiger's Milk," a sweet, white wine from Radgona, in northeastern Slovenia; mad(from the Bouvier grape.

Tillets, Les (F.)

An unclassified vineyard in Meursault Côte de Beaune district, Burgundy.

Timişoara (R.)

A city and district in the Banat region, wes central Romania; produces red wine mad(from Cabernet Sauvignon, Merlot and Ca darka grapes and white wine made from the Fetească grape.

Timna (Is.)

A dry, red wine from the Gadera district ir Judea; made from the Carignan grape; solc under the Camel Brand label.

Timok (Y.)

A district in the eastern part of the Repub lic of Serbia; produces mainly red wines including a Gamay wine.

najes *also* **tinajas (Sp.)**

pecial jars made of concrete or earthenware from the Montilla-Moriles district, in
outhern Spain; they are used to fine new
rines; the old style was amphora-shaped,
 meters high.

no (Sp.)

 large, rectangular vat with up to a 32,000
ter capacity; usually made of oak with
oncrete legs.

inta (E.)

n Victorian England, the term for a strong,
ed wine from the Island of Madeira; made
rom the Negra Mole grape; it was also
alled "Tent wine," a name also used then
or similar wines from southern Spain.

inta *also* **Tinto (P.)**

 group of red grapes of different varieties
sed to make Port wine; some are also
rown in the U.S.

inta Amarela (P.)

 red grape grown in the Dão region.

inta Carvalha (P.)

 red grape grown in the Douro region.

inta Francisca (P.)

 red grape; one of 19 first quality grapes
sed to make Port wine; similar to the
inot Noir grape.

inta Madeira (P.)

 red grape used to make Port wine; also
rown in California.

inta Miuda (P.)

 red grape grown in the Ribatejo and
orres Vedras regions of the southwest;
sed to made red and rosé wines.

inta Pinheira (P.)

 red grape grown in the Dão region, pos-
ibly a strain of the Pinot Noir grape; also
alled Rufete and Penamcor.

Tinta Roriz (P.)

A red grape; one of 16 first quality grapes
used to make Port wine.

Tinta de Toro (Sp.)

A red grape grown in the Galicia region of
northwestern Spain.

Tintara (Aus.)

An old vineyard of Hardy's Winery in the
Southern Vales district, South Australia;
grows mainly Shiraz and Cabernet Sauvignon grapes.

Tintarrón (Sp.)

A red grape grown in the Galicia region of
northwestern Spain.

tinto (P., Sp.)

Red, usually full-bodied.

Tinto (Sp.)

Another name for the Mourvèdre grape
grown in northern Spain.

Tinto Aragonés (Sp.)

In the Rioja region, another name for the
Garnacho Tinto grape.

Tinto Cão (P.)

A red grape; one of 16 first quality grapes
used to make Port wine.

Tinto Fino (Sp.)

A red grape grown in the Galicia region of
northwestern Spain.

Tintore (I.)

A red grape grown in Capri, in the Campania region.

Tintorera (Sp.)

Another name for the red Mencía grape.

tirage (F.)

The process of drawing off wine from barrels, usually into bottles.

Tîrnave (R.)

A district on the Tîrnave river, in Transylvania, central Romania; includes the town of Blaj; produces mainly white wines including Wälschriesling, Traminer, Muscat Ottonel, Alba, Regala, Ruländer, Sauvignon and Perla, a blended white wine.

Tirnovo (Bul.)

A sweet, red dessert wine.

Tischwein (A., G.)

German for common wine or table wine; *vin ordinaire*, in French.

Tisdall (Aus.)   1979

A winery in Echuca, north central Victoria; produces Rhine Riesling, Chenin Blanc and Colombard wines mostly from grapes grown in other areas (Picola and Mt. Helen); also Merlot, Cabernet Sauvignon, Pinot Noir and others. 50,000 cases. 300 acres.

Tizzano, Fattoria di (I.)

An estate in San Polo in Chianti, Tuscany region; produces Chianti Classico wines. 8,000 cases.

Tobía (Sp.)

In the Rioja region, another name for the white Malvasía grape.

Tocai *also* Tocai Friulano (I.)

1. A white grape (no relation to Hungarian Tokaji) grown in the Friuli-Venezia Giulia, Lombardy, Veneto and Tuscany regions.

2. A white wine from the Collio district, in the Friuli-Venezia Giulia region; made from the Tocai grape.

Tocai Rosso *also* Tocai Nero (I.)

A rare, red version of the Tocai grape grown in the Veneto and Friuli-Venezia Giulia regions of northeastern Italy.

Tocai di San Martino della Battaglia DO (I.)

A dry, white wine from San Martino, south of Lake Garda, in the Lombardy region; made from the Tocai Friulano grape

Todhunter International (U.S.)   197

A winery in West Palm Beach, Florida; produces wines sold in bulk.

Tokaier (G.)

In Germany, another name for the Pinot Gris grape; also called Ruländer and Grauerburgunder.

Tokajhegyalja (H.)

The Hungarian name for the district in northeastern Hungary, where the famous Tokay wines are made from Furmint, Hárslevelü and Sárgamuskotály grapes, named after the village of Tokaji. Rated white wine of Outstanding Quality. 16,000 acres.

Tokaji *also* Tokay (H.)

1. A town and district in northeastern Hungary, which produces:

2. A sweet, white wine of the following types: Furmint, Szamorodni, Aszú, Máslás, Forditás, Eszencia and Pecsenyebor from 29 villages, the best of which are considered to be: Tallya, Tarcal, Tokaj, Olaszliszka, Mád, Erdöbenye, Tolcsva, Satoraljaujhely and Sárospatak; made from Furmint, Hárslevelü and Sárgamuskotál grapes. 5.3 million gallons.

Tokaji Aszú (H.)

A sweet, white wine from the Tokaji district, in northeastern Hungary; made from Furmint, Hárslevelü and Sárgamuskotál grapes with varying stated degrees of sweetness, depending on the number of *puttonos*, or *puttonyos* (which are 25-liter baskets), of a paste made from specially selected, late-harvested, dried grapes (usually botrytis-infected) that are added to each 140-liter barrel (*gönc*) containing wine made from normal grapes.

Tokaji Edes Szamorodni (H.)

The sweet version of Tokaji Szamorodni.

Tokaji Eszencia *or* Essencia (H.)

A rare essence of Tokaji, made from un-pressed *Aszú* (dried) grapes, fermented and aged for many years; now seen as Aszú Essencia, a lesser version of the true Essencia.

Tokaji Forditás (H.)

A wine which is made by adding fresh must to the lees of Tokaji Aszú and allow-ing the new mixture to ferment.

Tokaji Furmint (H.)

A semi-sweet, or dry, white wine from the Tokaji district, in northeastern Hungary; made from the Furmint grape.

Tokaji Máslás (H.)

A Tokaji wine made by adding Tokaji Sza-morodni wine to the lees of Tokaji Szamo-rodni or Aszú in a *gönc* (barrel) and allowing the wine to stand for several months, resulting in a stronger wine.

Tokaji Pecsenyebor (H.)

The lowest quality of Tokaji wine.

Tokaji Szamorodni (H.)

A Tokaji wine without added *Aszú* (or dried) grapes; made dry or sweet, accord-ing to the condition of the Furmint, Hár-slevelü and Sárgamuskotály grapes. Szamorodni is Polish for "just as it is."

Tokay d'Alsace (F.)

The Alsatian name for the Pinot Gris grape.

Tokmak (T.)

A red grape.

Tollana (Aus.)   1858

A winery in Nuriootpa, Barossa Valléy, South Australia; once known for Brandy, now produces red wines, Rhine Riesling and Gewürztraminer wines as well as sin-gle-vineyard wines from the Woodbury Es-tate. 1,200 acres.

Tollot-Beaut et Fils, Domaine (F.)   1880

An estate in Chorey-lès-Beaune, Côte de Beaune district, Burgundy. 50 acres, in-cluding 2.5 acres of Corton Les Bres-sandes, 1.7 acres of Le Corton, 2.5 acres of Beaune Clos du Roi, 1.8 acres of Les Grèves, 3.2 acres of Savigny Les Lavières, 4 acres of Champ Chorey Monopole and some Aloxe-Corton and Chorey-lès-Beaune.

Tollot-Voarick, Domaine (F.)

An estate in Chorey-lès-Beaune, Côte de Beaune district, Burgundy. 55 acres, in-cluding 1.2 acres of Beaune Clos du Roi, 2 acres of Pernand-Vergelesses Île des Hautes Vergelesses, 8.5 acres of Aloxe-Corton, 2 acres of Savigny and some Chorey, Ladoix, and Côte de Nuits-Villages.

Tomasello Winery (U.S.)   1888, 1937

A winery in Hammonton, New Jersey. 80 acres.

Tommasi (I.)

An estate in Pedemonte, Veneto region; produces Amarone, Bardolino, Bianco di Custoza, Soave and Valpolicella wines.

Tondonia, Viña (Sp.)

See **Lopez de Heredia Viña Tondonia.**

tonel, *plur.* toneis (P.)

A very large wooden barrel or cask.

tonelada (Sp.)

A metric ton; 1,000 kilograms, or about 10 hectoliters.

tonneau (F.)

1. A large barrel.

2. In Bordeaux, a standard measure equal to 4 *barriques* (barrels) or 237 gallons or 900 liters. Formerly, one *tonneau* was equal to 96 cases of 730 ml. bottles. Since 1977, one *tonneau* is equal to 100 cases of 750 ml. bottles.

tonnelier (F.)

In the northern Rhône region, a barrel-maker.

Topolos at Russian River Vineyards (U.S.)   1964, 1978

A winery in Forestville, Sonoma County, California; produces Cabernet Sauvignon, Zinfandel, Pinot Noir, Petite Sirah, Chardonnay and Gewürztraminer wines. 6,000 cases. 115 acres.

Toppe au Vert (F.)

A *Premier Cru* vineyard in Ladoix-Serrigny, Côte de Beaune district, Burgundy; may be sold as Aloxe-Corton. 5 acres.

Torbato (I.)

A white grape grown in Sardinia.

Torbato di Alghero (I.)

A white wine from Alghero, in northwestern Sardinia; made from the Torbato grape.

Torbolino (I.)

A sweet, white wine from the Collio district, west of Gorizia, in the Friuli-Venezia Giulia region of northeastern Italy; made from the Ribolla Gialla grape.

torchio (I.)

A wine press.

Torcolato (I.)

A sweet, white wine from Breganze, in the Veneto region; made from semi-dried Vespaiolo, Garganega and Tocai grapes.

Torgiano DOC (I.)

1. A town and district south of Perugia, in the central Umbria region, which produces:

2. Red and white wines. The red wines are labeled Rubesco and are made from Sangiovese, Canaiolo, Montepulciano and Ciliegiolo grapes and the white wines are labeled Torre di Giano and are made from Trebbiano and Grechetto grapes.

Torkel (G.)

In southeastern Germany, the word for wine-press.

Torna-Viagem (P.)

A very old wine, similar to Madeira, made in Azeitao, south of Lisbon, and shipped across the equator and back, as is done with Madeira wine.

Toro (Sp.)

1. A village and district, west of Valladolid, in north central Spain along the River Douro, which produces:

2. A red wine made from Jaén, Valencia, Tinto Aragonés, Albillo and Tempranillo grapes.

Torok, Ladislaus (A.)   1626

An estate in Rust, Burgenland region; produces red and white wines. 8,000 cases. 15 acres.

Torrantel (Ch.)

A native white grape grown in central Chile.

Torre Alemanna (I.)

A red wine from Cerignola, in the northern Apulia region; made from Malbec, Negroamaro and Uva di Troia grapes.

Torre Ercolana (I.)

A red wine from Anagni, in the southeastern Latium region, from a 2-acre vineyard; made from Cesanese, Cabernet Sauvignon and Merlot grapes.

Torre di Giano (I.)

A white wine from the Torgiano DOC district, in the central Umbria region; made mostly from Trebbiano and some Grechetto grapes.

Torre in Pietra (I.)

A red wine from Torre, northwest of Rome, in the northern Latium region; made from Sangiovese, Montepulciano and other grapes.

Torre Quarto (I.)   1847

1. An estate in Cerignola, Apulia region; produces Rosso di Cerignola, Torre Quarto and other wines made from their own and purchased grapes. 120,000 cases. 150 acres.

2. Red, white and rosé wines from Cerignola, in the northern Apulia region. The red and rosé wine is made from Malbec and Uva di Troia grapes and the white wine is made from Bombino Bianco, Trebbiano and Greco grapes.

Torre Saracena (I.)

A red wine from Taranto, in the southwestern Apulia region; made from Malvasia Nera and Negroamaro grapes.

Torrepalino, Cantino Sociale (I.)

A co-op winery in Solicchiata, Sicily; produces red and white Etna wines.

Torres, Viñedos (Sp.)   1870

A large estate in Vilafranca de Penedès, Tarragona district, Catalonia region; produces several red, white and rosé wines made from native and French grapes, some of which are purchased; Coronas (red), Esmeralda (white), Sangre de Toro (red) and Viña Sol (white) are the most well-known; some wines have the word "*Gran*" preceding the name, indicating a superior wine; also owns vineyards and a winery in Chile. 1,000 acres.

Torres de Serrano (Sp.)

Ordinary red and white wines from the Valencia region of east central Spain.

Torrette (I.)

A red wine from west of Aosta, in the Valle d'Aosta region; made from the Petit Rouge grape.

Torricella (I.)

A rare, white wine from the Chianti Classico district, in the Tuscany region; made from the Malvasia grape.

Torrontes (Sp.)

A white grape grown in the Galicia region.

Torrontes Sanjuanino (Arg.)

An important white grape.

Tortochot, Domaine G. (F.)

An estate in Gevrey-Chambertin, Côte de Nuits district, Burgundy. 26 acres, including 1 acre of Chambertin, 1.6 acres of Charmes-Chambertin, 1 acre of Mazis-Chambertin, .7 acre of Clos de Vougeot, .8 acre of Gevrey-Chambertin Lavaux St.-Jacques and 2 acres of Champeaux.

Toscana (I.)

The Italian spelling of Tuscany.

Toso, Pascual (Arg.)

A winery in San José, in the Mendosa region; produces Cabernet Sauvignon, Riesling and sparkling wines.

Totara Vineyards (N.Z.)   1950

A winery in Thames, south of Aukland, North Island; produces Chenin Blanc, Müller-Thurgau, Chasselas, and a Muscat flavored wine called "Fu Gai."

Touche, Château la (F.)

An estate in Vallet, Muscadet de Sèvre-et-Maine district, Loire Valley. 60 acres.

Tour, Domaine de la (F.)

An estate in the Lirac district, southern Rhône region; produces red and rosé wines. 80 acres.

Tour Blanche, Château La (F.)

An estate in Bommes, Sauternes district, Bordeaux; classified in 1855 as a *Premier Cru*; since 1910 it has been run as an agricultural school; since 1954 it has been run by the Ministry of Agriculture. 6,000 cases. 70 acres.

Tour-Blanche, Château La (F.)

An estate in St.-Christoly, Médoc district, Bordeaux; classified in 1978 as a *Cru Bourgeois*. 12,000 cases. 60 acres.

Tour de By, Château La (F.)

An estate in Bédagan, Médoc district, Bordeaux; classified in 1978 as a *Cru Grand Bourgeois*. 30,000 cases. 148 acres.

Tour-Carnet, Château La (F.)

An estate in St.-Laurent, Haut-Médoc district, Bordeaux; classified in 1855 as a *Quatrième Cru*; named after Jean Caranet, or Carnet (d. 1485); known as early as 1354. 15,000 cases. 80 acres.

Tour d'Elyssas, Domaine de la (F.)   1966

An estate in Granges, Coteaux du Tricastin district, southern Rhône region; produces red and rosé wines. 250 acres.

Tour-Figeac, Château La (F.)

An estate in St.-Émilion, Bordeaux; classified in 1955 as a *Grand Cru Classé*; was a part of Château Figeac until 1879. 8,000 cases. 35 acres.

Tour-Haut-Brion, Château La (F.)

An estate in Talence, Graves district, Bordeaux, next to La Mission Haut-Brion, and owned by La Mission; classified in 1959 as a *Cru Classé* for red wine only. 20 acres. 3,000 cases.

Tour Haut-Caussan, Château La (F.)

An estate in Blaignan, Médoc district, Bordeaux; classified in 1978 as a *Cru Bourgeois*. 4,000 cases. 20 acres.

Tour du Haut-Moulin, Château La (F.)

An estate in Cussac, Haut-Médoc district, Bordeaux; classified in 1978 as a *Cru Grand Bourgeois*. 10,000 cases. 65 acres.

Tour-de-Lirac, Domaine de (F.)

An estate in Lirac, southern Rhône region.

Tour-Martillac, Château La (F.)

An estate in Martillac, Graves district, Bordeaux; classified in 1959 as a *Cru Classé* for red and white wine. 50 acres, 5,000 cases of red; 10 acres, 500 cases white.

Tour du Mirail, Château La (F.)

An estate in Cissac, Haut-Médoc district, Bordeaux; classified in 1978 as a *Cru Bourgeois*. 6,000 cases. 25 acres.

Tour-de-Mons, Château La (F.)

An estate in Soussans-Margaux, Haut-Médoc district, Bordeaux; classified in 1932 as a *Cru Bourgeois*. 12,000 cases. 60 acres.

Tour-du-Pin-Figeac, Château La (F.)

An estate in St.-Émilion, Bordeaux; classified in 1955 as a *Grand Cru Classé*; formerly, the two estates were one property, this half owned by M. Giraud. 6,000 cases. 25 acres.

Tour-du-Pin-Figeac, Château La (F.)

An estate in St.-Émilion, Bordeaux; classified in 1955 as a *Grand Cru Classé*; formerly, the two estates were one property, this half owned by A. Moueix. 4,000 cases. 18 acres.

Tour-Saint-Bonnet, Château La (F.)

An estate in St.-Christoly, Médoc district, Bordeaux; classified in 1978 as a *Cru Bourgeois*. 18,000 cases. 100 acres.

Tour Saint-Joseph, Château La (F.)

An estate in Cissac, Haut-Médoc district, Bordeaux; classified in 1978 as a *Cru Bourgeois*. 45 acres. 10,000 cases.

Touraine AOC (F.)

A large region around Tours, east of the Anjou region, in the Loire Valley; the most well-known wines are Vouvray, Montlouis, Bourgueil and Chinon.

The Touraine AOC designation is for red, white and rosé wines; the red and rosé made from the two Cabernets, Cot, Gamay, Pineau d'Aunis, Pinot *Meunier* and other grapes; the white are made from Chenin Blanc, Arbois, Sauvignon and Chardonnay grapes, and can be sweet or dry. In addition, three villages may use the Touraine AOC with the name of the village added: Touraine-Amboise, Touraine-Azay-le-Rideau and Touraine-Mesland.

Tourelles, Château des (F.)

An estate in Blaignan, Médoc district, Bordeaux; classified in 1978 as a *Cru Bourgeois*. 12,000 cases. 45 acres.

Touriga Francesa (P.)

A red grape, one of 16 first quality grapes used to make Port wine; similar to the Cabernet Franc grape.

Touriga Nacional (P.)

A red grape, one of 16 first quality grapes used to make Port wine.

Tourigo (P.)

A red grape grown in the Dão region and in the northeast.

Tourmaline, Domaine de la (F.)

An estate in Saint-Fiacre, Muscadet de Sèvre-et-Maine district, Loire Valley. 75 acres.

tourne (F.)

A malady caused by bacteria attacking tartaric acid, which causes the wine to become gassy, with a bad aroma; similar to acescence.

Tourtouil, Domaine de (F.)

An estate in Tavel, southern Rhône region.

Toussaints, Les (F.)

A *Premier Cru* vineyard in Beaune, Côte de Beaune district, Burgundy. 16 acres.

Toutigeac, Château (F.)

An estate in Turgon, Entre-deux-Mers, Bordeaux; produces red and white wines. 375 acres.

Toyon Winery and Vineyards (U.S.) 1972
winery 1980

A small winery in Healdsburg, Sonoma County, California; produces Cabernet Sauvignon, Zinfandel, Chardonnay and Gewürztraminer wines. 5,000 cases.

trabalhadores (P.)

Barefoot men who trod the grapes in *lagares* before mechanical crushers were adopted; some growers still use the old method.

Traben-Trarbach (G.)

A pair of villages on either side of the Mosel River, in the Mosel-Saar-Ruwer region, Bereich Bernkastel (Mittel-Mosel), Grosslage Schwarzlay. The vineyards are: Burgweg, Gaispfad, Hühnerberg, Königsberg, Kräuterhaus, Kreuzberg, Schlossberg, Taubenhaus, Ungsberg, Würzgarten, Zollturm and Rosengarten (*Ortsteil* Starkenburg). 80 acres. There are five more vineyards in *Ortsteil* Wolf.

Trabense (I.)

A dry, sparkling wine from Travo, in the Colli Piacentini district near Piacenza, in the western Emilia-Romagna region; made from Trebbiano, Ortrugo and Malvasia grapes.

tracteur-enjambeur (F.)

A system of cultivating vines by straddling the rows with horse-drawn, wooden-wheeled cultivators (modern ones are machine-driven); first used in 1863 in Savigny, Burgundy.

Tracy, Château de (F.) 1396

An ancient estate in Pouilly-sur-Loire, Pouilly-Fumé district, Upper Loire region. 48 acres.

Traisen (G.)

A village in the Nahe region, Bereich Schoss Böckelheim, Grosslage Burgweg. The vineyards are Bastei, Kickelskopf, Nonnengarten and Rotenfels.

Trajadura (P.)

A white grape grown in the Vinho Verde region.

Trakia (Bul.)

"Thrace," a brand of red and white wines from southern Bulgaria.

Trakya (T.)

"Thrace," red and white wines from Thrace, in northwestern Turkey.

Trameah (Aus.)

A white wine made near Sidney, in New South Wales; made from the Traminer grape by the Penfolds Winery.

Tramin *also* Termano (I.)

A village north of Trento, in the Trentino-Alto Adige region of northeastern Italy, where the Traminer grape is believed to have originated.

Traminac (Y.)

The Yugoslavian name for the Traminer grape or wine.

Traminer *also* Gewürztraminer

A white grape grown in the Alsace region of France, in Germany, Italy (where it is believed to have originated, around the village of Tramin, or Termeno, north of Trento), California and other regions of the world. It gives small yields, is somewhat late-ripening, although earlier than Riesling, has small berries, and gives wines that are low in acid, high in alcohol; also called Savagnin in the Jura region of France, where it is used to make *Vin Jaune*.

Traminer Aromatico DOC (I.)

1. Another name for the Gewürztraminer grape, which produces:
2. A white wine made in the northern Trentino-Alto Adige region of northeastern Italy.

Transdanubia (H.)

A region in western Hungary; includes the Lake Balaton, Villány, Mecsek, Somló and Mór districts.

transfer method *or* process

A technique of making sparkling wine by transferring the wine from the bottles after the second fermentation into a tank under pressure; the sediment is removed in bulk, by filtering; the clear wine is then transferred back to bottles and corked.

Transylvania (R.)

A large region in northwestern Romania; known for the Tîrnave district, which produces mostly white wines.

Trapet Père et Fils, Domaine Louis (F.)

An estate in Gevrey-Chambertin, Côte de Nuits district, Burgundy. 42 acres, including 10 acres of Chambertin, 2.6 acres of Chapelle-Chambertin, 4 acres of Latricières-Chambertin, 2.5 acres of Gevrey-Chambertin Petite-Chappelle and 2 acres of Clos-Prieur.

Trapet-Lalle (F.)

An estate in Comblanchien, Côte de Nuits district, Burgundy. 22 acres, including 4 acres of Nuits-St.-Georges, 1.2 acres of Aloxe-Corton and 10 acres of Côte de Nuits-Villages.

trasiego (Sp.)

The racking of the wine off the lees.

travaso (I.)

The racking of the wine off the lees.

Travers, Domaine des (F.)

An estate in the commune of Cairanne, in the Côtes du Rhône-Villages district, southern Rhône region.

Traversagna, Tre Torri di (I.)

A vineyard near Gattinara, in the northern Piedmont region, which produces a Spanna wine made by Vallana.

Trebbianino Val Trebbia DOC (I.)

A white wine from the Trebbia River Valley, south of Piacenza, in the northwestern Emilia-Romagna region; it is made dry, sweet or fizzy from Ortrugo, Malvasia, Trebbiano, Moscato and Sauvignon Blanc grapes.

Trebbiano d'Abruzzo DOC (I.) since 1972

A white wine from the Abruzzo region; made from Trebbiano d'Abruzzo, Trebbiano Toscano grapes or both, with Malvasia Toscano, Cococciola and Passerina grapes.

Trebbiano d'Abruzzo, *also* Trebbiano Toscano (I.)

A white grape grown in many regions of Italy; also called Trebbiano Nostrano in some places; also called St.-Émilion and Ugni Blanc in France.

Trebbiano Giallo (I.)

A white grape grown in northern Italy and the Latium region; also called Rossetto and Greco.

Trebbiano Nostrano (I.)

A white grape grown in northern and central Italy; also called Trebbiano d'Abruzzo or Trebbiano Toscano.

Trebbiano di Romagna DOC (I.)

1. A white grape grown in the Emilia-Romagna region, which produces:

2. A white wine from the eastern part of the Emilia-Romagna region.

Trefethen Vineyards (U.S.)   1886, 1968
first wine 1973

A winery north of Napa City, Napa Valley, California; formerly the Eshcol winery; first vintage was the 1973 Chardonnay, then the 1974 Cabernet Sauvignon; also produces Johannisberg Riesling, white Pinot Noir and several blended wines. 40,000 cases. 600 acres.

Treixadura (Sp.)

A white grape grown in the Galicia region; it is the same as the Trajadura of Portugal.

Tremblay, Jacques (F.)

An estate in La-Chapelle-Vaupelteigne, Chablis district, Burgundy. 20 acres, including 5 acres of Fourchaume.

Trenel Fils (F.)

A merchant in Charney-Lès-Mâcons, Beaujolais district, Burgundy; produces several Beaujolais wines.

Trentadue Winery and Vineyard (U.S.)
1969

A winery and vineyard in Geyserville, Alexander Valley, northern Sonoma County, California; produces numerous varietals and sells grapes to other wineries, especially to Ridge Vineyards. 24,000 cases. 200 acres.

Trentino DOC (I.)

A large district covering the southern half of the Trentino-Alto Adige region; produces varietal wines: Cabernet Sauvignon, Lagrein, Marzemino, Merlot, Moscato, Pinot Bianco, Pinot Nero, Riesling, Traminer Aromatico and *Vin Santo*.

Trentino-Alto Adige (I.)

A region in northeastern Italy, divided into two parts: the Trentino, or southern part, surrounds Trento (Trent), and the northern part, which prior to 1919 belonged to Austria as part of the Tyrol, called the Südtirol, or South Tyrol.

Tressot (F.)

A red grape grown in the Auxerrois district, especially in Irancy, west and southwest of Chablis, in Burgundy.

triage (F.)

The sorting of grapes, by hand, to discard under-ripe and over-ripe fruit.

Trier (G.)

An ancient city in the Mosel-Saar-Ruwer region. It lies between the Saar and Ruwer tributaries of the Mosel River; the 28 vineyards are in Bereich Saar-Ruwer, Grosslage Römerlay, and includes the Karthäuserhofberg vineyards and those of Avelsbach.

Trifesti (U.S.S.R.)

A sweet, white wine from Moldavia, S.S.R.; made from the Pinot Gris grape.

Trignon, Château du (F.)   1888

An estate in Gigondas, southern Rhône region; produces Gigondas, Sablet and Rasteau wines. 120 acres.

Trimbach, F.E. (F.)   1626

A merchant in Ribeauvillé, Haut-Rhin district, Alsace region. 30 acres, including the

Osterberg vineyard (Riesling), the Trottacker vineyard in Ribeauvillé (Gewürztraminer), and 3 acres of Clos St.-Hune.

Trimoulet, Château (F.)

An estate in St.-Émilion, Bordeaux; classified in 1955 as a *Grand Cru Classé*. 7,500 cases. 40 acres.

Trincadeira (P.)

A red grape grown in the Alentejo, Algarve, Bairrada and Ribatejo regions, and appears to be the same as, or similar to the Periquita grape.

Trinquevedel, Château de (F.)

An estate in Tavel, southern Rhône region. 60 acres.

tris (F.)

A successive picking of selected, fully-ripened grapes over a period of days or weeks, an expensive process usually done in the Sauternes district, Bordeaux.

Tristo di Montesecco (I.)

A white wine from Montesecco, northwest of Jesi, in the northeastern Marches region; made from Trebbiano Toscano, Riesling Italico, Pinot Grigio and Malvasia di Candia grapes.

Trittenheim (G.)

A village in the Mosel-Saar-Ruwer region, Bereich Bernkastel, Grosslage Michelsberg. The vineyards are: Altärchen, Apotheke, Felsenkopf and Leiterchen. 750 acres.

trocken (G.)

Dry, containing less than 9 grams of sugar per litre; used on labels in Germany since 1976.

Trockenbeerenauslese (G.)

German for "a selection of dried berries," a rare and expensive process used to make an expensive, sweet white wine, usually from only the best grape varieties in a great vintage year.

Troême *also* Troesmes
also **Clos-de-Troême (F.)**

A *Premier Cru* vineyard in Beines, Chablis district, Burgundy; usually included as part of the Beauroy vineyard.

Trois Domaines, Les (Mor.)

An estate in the Guerrouane district, southwest of Meknes; produces red and rosé wines.

Trois-Moulins, Château (F.)

An estate in St.-Émilion, Bordeaux; classified in 1955 as a *Grand Cru Classé*. 2,500 cases. 10 acres.

Troisième Cru (F.)

Third Growth, a designation of red wines from the Haut-Médoc district, in Bordeaux, the third highest category of *châteaux*.

Trollat, Raymond (F.)

An estate in St.-Jean-de-Muzols, St.-Joseph district, northern Rhône region; owns St.-Joseph – 7.5 acres.

Trollinger (G.)

A red grape from the South Tyrol, also grown in the Württemberg region of Germany; big, dark blue grapes, late-ripening, high in acid; also called Gross-Vernatsch, Frankentaler, Meraner Kurtraube and Blauer Malvasier.

Tronquoy-Lalande, Château (F.)

An estate in St.-Estèphe, Haut-Médoc district, Bordeaux; classified in 1978 as a *Cru Grand Bourgeois*. 5,000 cases. 45 acres.

Troplong-Mondot, Château (F.)

An estate in St.-Émilion, Bordeaux; classified in 1955 as a *Grand Cru Classé*. 15,000 cases. 65 acres.

Trotonoy, Château (F.)

An estate in Pomerol, Bordeaux; made mostly from Merlot grapes; makes a wine similar to that of Château Pétrus. 4,000 cases. 25 acres.

Trottevieille, Château (F.)

An estate in St.-Émilion, Bordeaux; classified in 1955 as a *Premier Grand Cru*. 4,500 cases. 20 acres.

Trousseau (F.)

A red grape grown in the Arbois district of the Jura region; it is believed to be the same grape as the Bastardo of Portugal.

Trübstoffe (G.)

The solid particles in new wine which are present before the wine is racked off.

Truluck Vineyards and Winery (U.S.) vines 1971, winery 1976

A winery in Lake City, South Carolina; produces red, white and rosé wines from French hybrid and some *vinifera* grapes. 120 acres.

Tschaggele *also* Tschaggelevernatsch (I.)

A red grape grown around Merano, in the northern Trentino-Alto Adige region; also called Tschaggelevernatsch, in German.

Tsimlyanskoye (U.S.S.R.)

A sweet, red, sparkling wine from Rostov, in southwestern Russia.

Tsinandali (U.S.S.R.)

A white wine grown in Georgia, S.S.R.

Tsingtao (China)

A province in the Shantung peninsula; produces dry red and white wines, high in alcohol.

Tualatin Vineyard (U.S.)   1977

A large vineyard and winery in Forest Grove, Tualatin Valley, northwestern Oregon; produces Pinot Noir, Chardonnay, Gewürztraminer and Johannisberg Riesling wines; originally from purchased grapes. 15,000 cases. 75 acres.

Tudal Winery (U.S.)   1979

A winery in St. Helena, Napa Valley, California; produces Cabernet Sauvignon and Chardonnay wines, some from purchased grapes. 2,000 cases. 10 acres.

Tudernum (I.)

Red and white wines from Todi (Tudernum is Latin for "Todi"), in the northern Umbria region.

Tullbagh WO (S. Af.)

An important town and district north of Capetown and Paarl; produces mostly white wines. It has three well-known estates: Montpellier, Theuniskraal and Twee Jongegezellen.

Tulloch (Aus.)   1893

An old winery in Pokolbin, Lower Hunter Valley, New South Wales; produces Hunter Riesling (made from the Sémillon grape), Chardonnay, Hermitage and Cabernet Sauvignon wines.

Tulocay Winery (U.S.)   1975

A winery in Napa City, Napa Valley, California; produces Cabernet Sauvignon, Pinot Noir, Zinfandel and Chardonnay wines from purchased grapes. 2,000 cases.

tun (E.)

A large cask equal to two pipes, or four hogsheads, or 954 liters (252 gallons).

Tunina (I.)

An unusual white wine from the Collio district of the Friuli-Venezia Giulia region; made from Pinot Bianco, Chardonnay, Sauvignon Blanc and some Picolit grapes.

Tunisia

An independent country in North Africa, owned by France until 1956. Wine controls date from 1942; AOC, VDQS, VS (*Vins Supérieurs*) and VCC designations put into effect in 1957. The most important districts are Côteaux de Carthage, Haut Mornag, Sidi Rais and Muscat Sec de Kelibia. Vines date back to the Roman era; European grapes are mostly grown: Carignan, Alicante-Bouchet, Cinsault, Ugni Blanc, Clairette de Provence, Grenache and the native Beldi. 90,000 acres.

Tuquet, Château Le (F.)

An unclassified estate in Beautiran, Graves district, Bordeaux; produces red and white wines. 15,000 cases. 80 acres.

Turgeon and Lohr Winery (U.S.)   1974

A winery in San José, Santa Clara County, California; produces Chardonnay, Riesling, Fumé Blanc, Chenin Blanc, Cabernet, Gamay, Petite Sirah, Pinot Noir, Zinfandel wines and a sweet Chardonnay. 100,000 cases. 300 acres in Monterey County.

Turkenblut (G.)

"Turk's Blood," a red version of *Kalte Ente* (Cold Duck).

Turkey

A country in southwestern Asia. The wine industry has been growing since 1928, when the Moslem religion ceased to be the state religion; the most important wines are from central and southeastern Anatolia; made mostly from native grapes. 10 million gallons. 750,000 acres.

Turner Winery (U.S.)   1979

A winery in Lodi, San Joaquin Valley, California; produces Cabernet Sauvignon, Zinfandel, Napa Gamay, Gamay Beaujolais, Chardonnay, Johannisberg Riesling, Chenin Blanc, Sauvignon Blanc and generic jug wines. 40,000 cases. 575 acres.

Turruntés (Sp.)

A red grape grown in the Rioja region.

Tursan VDQS (F.)

A designation for red, white and rosé wines from around Geaune, north of Pau, in the Southwest region; the red and rosé wines are made from Tannet, Cabernet Sauvignon, Cabernet Franc and Fer grapes; the white is made from the Baroque grape.

Tuscany (I.)

Toscana, an important region of central Italy; produces the famous red wines of Chianti, Brunello di Montalcino, Vino Nobile di Montepulciano and Carmignano.

Twee Jongegezellen EWO (S. Af.)   1950

Afrikaans for "Two young friends," a famous estate in the Tulbagh district, north of Cape Town and Paarl; produces Riesling, Steen, Sauvignon Blanc and Frontignac wines. 600 acres.

Tyland Vineyards (U.S.)   1979
vineyard 1971

A vineyard and winery in Ukiah, Mendocino County, California; produces Cabernet Sauvignon, Zinfandel, Gamay Beaujolais, Chardonnay, Chenin Blanc, Gewürztraminer and Johannisberg Riesling wines. 250 acres. 7,000 cases.

tyna (Tun.)

An aged red wine.

Tyrell's (Aus.)   1858

An old, experimental winery in Pokolbin, Lower Hunter Valley, New South Wales; produces Chardonnay, Sémillon (Hunter Riesling), Sauvignon Blanc, Pinot Noir, Cabernet Sauvignon, Merlot, Malbec and blended wines; bottled with inventory vat numbers. 100 acres. 50,000 cases.

U

Ughetta (I.)

A red grape grown in the Oltrepò Pavese district, in the Lombardy region.

Ugni Blanc (F.)

A white grape grown in southern France; also called St.-Émilion in Cognac, and Trebbiano in Italy.

Ugni Rosé (F.)

A pink version of the Ugni Blanc grape grown in Palette, in the Provence region.

Uhlheim, Schlosskellerei (A.)

A merchant in Ilz, Steiermark (Styria) region; produces wines from several districts in Austria.

Uiterwyk Estate EWO (S. Af.)   1946

An estate in the Stellenbosch district; produces Cabernet Sauvignon, Pinotage, Cape Riesling and Columbar wines. 300 acres.

Uitkyk Estate EWO (S. Af.)   1973

An estate in the eastern Stellenbosch district; produces a wide range of red and white wines. 400 acres.

Ukraine (U.S.S.R.)

A republic of the U.S.S.R.; produces sweet red and white wines; the best-known districts and wines are Massandra, Chorny Doktor and Ai-Danil.

Ull de Llebre (Sp.)

Another name for the Tempranillo grape; also called Cencibel and Ojo de Liebre.

ullage

The air space in a bottle or cask. If this space is larger than normal it is an indication that air is seeping in and that the wine is evaporating.

Umani Ronchi (I.)

A winery in Osimo Scalo, the Marches region; produces Rosso Cònero, Rosso Piceno, Rosato, Sangiovese, Verdicchio and other wines, made from their own and purchased grapes. 100,000 cases. 250 acres.

Umbria (I.)

A region in central Italy, between Florence and Rome; famous for Orvieto and Torgiano wine.

Umstadt (G.)

A *Bereich*, one of 2 in the Hessische Bergstrasse region.

Undhof, Weingut (A.)   1792

An estate and merchant in Stein, in the Wachau region; produces numerous wines from their own and purchased grapes. 12,000 cases. 40 acres.

Undurraga, Viña (Ch.)   1885

A winery in Santiago, central Chile, the leading winery in Chile; produces red and white wines. 600 acres. 450,000 cases.

Ungstein (G.)

A village in the Rheinpfalz region, Bereich Mittelhaardt-Deutsche Weinstrasse, Grosslagen Kobnert, Honigsäckel and Hochmess. The vineyards are: Michelsberg, in Grosslage Hochmess; Herrenberg, Nussriegel and Weilberg, in Grosslage Honigsäckel; and Bettelhaus and Osterberg, in Grosslage Kobnert.

Union Vinicole pour la Diffusion des Vins d'Alsace (F.)

A group of growers in Alsace who have pooled their resources to produce and market better wines; they control 15% of the market.

United States

The leading wine producing states are California, New York, Ohio, Oregon, Virginia and Washington; the most important is California, with about 500 wineries with 750,000 acres producing 500 million gallons; second is New York, with fewer than 100 wineries with 43,000 acres producing 150 million gallons. 853,000 acres.

Université du Vin (F.)   1978

A professional wine school in Suze-la-Rousse, in the Rhône region.

Unterhaardt (G.)

The former name of the northern section of the Rheinpfalz region; since 1971 it has been joined to the Mittelhaardt district to form Bereich Mittelhaardt/Deutsche Weinstrasse.

Upper Douro also Alto Douro (P.)

The region in northern Portugal, along the Douro River, where Port wine is made.

Upper Loire (F.)

A region in the western Loire Valley consisting of the Ménétou-sur-Loire (Ménétou-Salon), Orléans, Pouilly-Fumé, Quincy, Reuilly and Sancerre districts.

Uruguay

A country in South America; grows European, local and hybrid grapes, including: Harriagne (Tannet), Vidiella, Cabernet Sauvignon, Pinot Noir, Merlot, Sémillon, Sauvignon, Grignolino, Lambrusco, Carinena, Malvasia, Pedro Ximénez and Riesling. 15 million gallons. 50,000 acres.

Ürzig (G.)

A village in the Mosel-Saar-Ruwer region, Bereich Bernkastel, Grosslage Schwarzlay. The vineyards are: Würzgarten and Goldwingert. 165 acres.

Utah (U.S.)

A state in the western United States. Brigham Young had wines made in 1847 for Communion and for sale, but after 1910 wine was no longer made because of church doctrine and economics. There are presently no wineries of any commercial significance.

Utiel-Requeña DO (Sp.)

1. A district comprising the two towns of Utiel and Requeña, west of Valencia, in eastern central Spain, which produces blending wines called *viño de doble pasta* as well as:

2. Red, rosé and white wines, made from Bobal, Cencibel and Garnacho grapes.

uva (I., Sp.)

A grape.

Uva d'Oro (I.)

A red grape grown in the eastern part of the Emilia-Romagna region around Comacchio; also called Fortana.

Uva di Spagna (I.)

In Sardinia, another name for the Carignano or Carignane grape.

Uva di Troia (I.)

A red grape grown in the Apulia region; also called Summarello.

iveira (P.)

A tree vine; a vine trained to climb up the trunk of a suitable tree, an old method of growing vines in the Vinho Verde region.

d'Uza, Clos (F.)

An unclassified estate in St.-Pierre-de-Mons, Graves district, Bordeaux; shares the same property as Château St.-Pierre and Château Queyrats; produces white wine. 7,000 cases. 85 acres.

Uzzano, Castello di (I.)

An estate in Greve, Tuscany region; produces Chianti Classico wines. 40,000 cases. 300 acres.

V

V.C.C. (F.)

The abbreviation for *Vin de Consommation Courante* (Wine for Every Day Consumption), a classification below the VDQS wines, passed in 1955 by the *Institut des Vins de Consommation Courante*, organized in 1953; it replaced the *Vin(s) de Table* classification.

V.D.N. (F.)

The abbreviation for *Vins Doux Naturels* (Natural Sweet Wines), fortified, sweet, red, white and rosé wines from the Rhône, Languedoc and Roussillon regions of southern France; usually made from Muscat grapes. In the Rhône region - Muscat de Beaumes-de-Venise VDN (from Muscat grapes) and Rasteau VDN (red or white, from Grenache grapes); in the Languedoc region - Muscat de Frontignan VDN, Muscat de Lunel VDN, Muscat de Miréval VDN and Muscat de Saint-Jean-de-Minervois VDN (all white, made from the Muscat grape); in the Roussillon region - Banyuls (also with *Grand Cru* or *Rancio* added) VDN (red or white), Côtes d'Agly VDN (red, white and rosé), Grand Roussillon VDN (red, white and rosé), Maury VDN (red), Muscat de Rivesaltes VDN (white), and Rivesaltes VDN (red, white and rosé). Grenache, Malvoisie and Maccabéo grapes can also be used.

V.D.Q.S. (F.)

The abbreviation for *Vins Délimités de Qualité Supérieure* (Delimited Wines of Superior Quality), laws passed in 1949 which designate and control the quality of the secondary wines of France, similar to the AOC laws.

V.I.D.E. (I.)

The abbreviation for *Vini Italiani di Eccellenza* (Italian Wines of Excellence), an association of wine producers in Milan, organized in 1977 to promote and provide a seal of approval for wines of high quality.

Vorm. (G.)

The abbreviation for *Vormund*, a guardian, or trustee.

V.Q.P.R.D. (F.)

The abbreviation for *Vin de Qualité Produit en Regions Déterminées* (Quality Wine Produced in Specific Regions), a European Common Market category which includes DOC and DOCG wines of Italy, AOC, VDN and VDQS wines of France, QbA and QmP wines of Germany and some wines of Luxembourg.

V.S. (Tun.)

Vins Supérieurs, a catagory of superior wines of Tunisia.

Vaccarèse (F.)

A red grape grown in the Rhône region, and one of 13 used to make Châteauneuf-du-Pape wine.

Vacheron, Jean (F.)

An estate in Sancerre, Upper Loire region; produces red and white Sancerre wines. 45 acres.

Vacqueyras AOC (F.)

1. A commune in the Côtes du Rhône-Villages district, southern Rhône region, which produces:

2. Red, white and rosé wines made from the usual grapes of the district.

Vaduz *also* Vaduzer (Liech.)

1. A city (the capitol) and district in Liechtenstein, which produces:

2. A light, red wine made from the Blauburgunder grape.

Vaihingen (G.)

A village in the Württemberg region, Bereich Würtembergisch Unterland, Grosslage Stromberg. The only vineyard in Höllisch Feuer.

Vaillons (F.)

A *Premier Cru* vineyard in Chablis, Chablis district, Burgundy; also includes the Beugnons, Châtains, Les Lys and Séché vineyards.

Val, Clos du *also* Climat du Val (F.)

A *Premier Cru* vineyard (in part) in Auxey-Duresses, Côte de Beaune district, Burgundy. 23 acres.

Val d'Arenc, Domaine du (F.)

An estate in Bandol, in the southern Provence region.

Val Panaro (I.)   1951

A winery in San Cesario sul Panaro, Emilia-Romagna region; produces Lambrusco and Malvasia wines. 200,000 cases.

Val-des-Rois, Domaine du (F.)

An estate in Valréas, in the Côtes du Rhône-Villages district, southern Rhône region; produces wines from Grenache, Syrah, Cinsault and Gamay grapes. 30 acres.

Val di Suga (I.)

An estate in Montalcino, Tuscany region; produces Brunello and Merlot wines. 55 acres.

Val Verde Winery (U.S.)   1919

An old winery near Del Rio, southwestern Texas; produces dry and sweet red and white wines from hybrid grapes. 30 acres.

Val Wine Company, Clos du (U.S.)
1st wine 197

A winery in Yountville, Napa Valley, California; run by Bernard Portet, of France; produces Cabernet Sauvignon, Zinfandel, Merlot and Chardonnay wines; made from purchased grapes until the 1975 Estate Bottled Cabernet Sauvignon. 120 acres plus 170 in the Carneros district. 25,000 cases.

Valais (Sw.)

A canton and region on the Rhône River east of Geneva, in southwestern Switzerland; produces Dôle, Fendant and Ermitage wines. 9,000 acres.

Valbuena (Sp.)

A red wine from the Vega Sicilia estate in north central Spain, aged in oak for 3-5 years instead of 10 years for the better Vega Sicilia wine.

Valcalepio DOC (I.)

1. A district west of Lake Isea, in the central Lombardy region, which produces:

2. Red and white wines; the red wine is made from Merlot, Cabernet Sauvignon and sometimes Marzemino grapes and the white wine is made from Pinot Bianco and Pinot Grigio grapes.

Valcarceia (Sp.)

In the Rioja region, another name for the Monastrel grape.

Valdadige DOC (I.)

1. A long, narrow district along the Adige River, from Merano south to the Veneto region, which produces:

2. Red and white wines, made from any of the grapes grown in the region.

Valdenz (G.)

A village in the Mosel-Saar-Ruwer region, Bereich Bernkastel (Mittel-Mosel), Grosslage Kurfurstlay. The vineyards are: Carlsberg, Elisenberg, Grafschafter Sonnenberg, Kirchberg and Mühlberg. 350 acres.

Valdeorras DO (Sp.)

1. A district around El Barco de Valdeorras, in the southeastern Galicia region, northwestern Spain, which produces:

2. Red and white wines. The red wine is made from Garnacha de Alicante, Mencía, Tempranillo and Gran Nero grapes and the white wine is made from 90% Xerez grapes and some Godello, Treixadura and Valenciana grapes.

Valdepeñas DO (Sp.)

1. Formerly Val de Peñas ("Valley of Stones"), a town and district in the southwestern part of the La Mancha region, in central Spain, which produces:

2. Red and white wines, the best of which are considered to be from the towns of Los Llanos and Las Aberturas. The red wine is made from Cencibel, Monastrel and Tintorera grapes and the white wine is made from Lairén, Palomino, Moscatel and other grapes.

Valdiguié (F.)

A red grape grown in the Languedoc, Provence, Rhône and Savoie regions.

Valea Călugărească (R.)

"Valley of the Monks," a state-run experimental vineyard in the Dealul Mare district, Wallachia region; famous for red wines made from Cabernet Sauvignon, Merlot and Pinot Noir grapes.

Valençay VDQS (F.)

A district southeast of Tours and west of Reuilly, in the Touraine region, Loire Valley; produces red and rosé wines made from Gamay, Cabernet Franc, Cabernet Sauvignon, Cot and Pinot Noir grapes, and white wine from Pineau Menu (Arbois), Chardonnay, Chenin Blanc and Romorantin grapes.

Valencia (Aus.)

One of 3 wineries in Western Australia taken over by Hardy's. Valencia is in the Swan Valley district; produces Malbec Rosé and Verdelho wines.

Valencia DO (Sp.)

A city and district in the Levante region, in east central Spain; produces red and white wines.

Valenciana (Sp.)

A white grape grown in the Galicia region.

Valentini, Edoardo (I.)

An estate in Loreto Aprutino, Abruzzi region; produces Montepulciano and Trebbiano wines. 2,000 cases. 125 acres.

Valette, Éts. (F.)

A merchant in Mâcon, Burgundy region.

Valgella DOC (I.)

A red wine from the Valtellina district, in the northern Lombardy region; made from 95% Nebbiolo grapes.

Vallana & Figlio, Antonio (I.)

An estate in Maggiora, Piedmont region; produces Boca, Barbera, Bonarda and several single-vineyard designated Spanna wines.

Valle d'Aosta (I.)

A region in northwestern Italy, the smallest in the country; produces two DOC wines: Donnaz and Enfer d'Arvier.

Valle Isarco DOC (I.)

1. A valley and district along the Isarco River, northeast of Bolzano, in the Trentino-Alto Adige region, which produces:

2. White varietal wines made from Gewürztraminer, Müller-Thurgau, Pinot Grigio, Sylvaner, and Veltliner grapes as stated on the label.

Vallé de la Marne (F.)

A district along the Marne River, west of Épernay, in the Champagne region; planted mostly with Pinot Noir grapes.

Valle Redondo (Mex.)

A district near Tecate and Tijuana, in the Baja California region near the United States border.

Vallerots, Les (F.)

A *Premier Cru* vineyard (in part) in Nuits-St.-Georges, Côte de Nuits district, Burgundy. 24 acres.

Valley of the Moon (U.S.)   1944

A large winery in Sonoma, Sonoma County, California; produces mostly jug wines and some varietals. 50,000 cases. 200 acres.

Valley View Vineyard (U.S.)   1977

A vineyard in Ruch, near Jacksonville, Rogue River Valley, southwestern Oregon; produces Cabernet Sauvignon and Chardonnay wines. 6,000 cases. 25 acres.

Valley Vineyards (U.S.)   1970

A winery in Morrow, northeast of Cincinnati, Ohio; produces wines from native and hybrid grapes. 40 acres.

Vallunga, Fratelli (I.) 1970

A winery in Marzeno di Brisighella, Emilia-Romagna region; produces Albana, Marègia, Rosso Armentano, San Marten, Sangiovese, Trebbiano and sparkling wines. 85 acres.

Valmur (F.)

A *Grand Cru* vineyard in Chablis, Chablis district, Burgundy.

Valozières, Les (F.)

A *Premier Cru* vineyard in Aloxe-Corton, Côte de Beaune district, Burgundy. 16 acres.

Valpantena (I.)

A red wine from a part of the Valpolicella district, in the Veneto region, similar to Valpolicella.

Valpolicella DOC (I.)

1. A district northwest of Verona, in the Veneto region, which produces:

2. A red wine made from up to 70% Corvina, up to 30% Rondinella and up to 15% Molinara grapes.

Valsangiacomo fu Vittore, Fratelli (Sw.)
1831

An estate and merchant in Chiasso, Ticino region; produces red and rosé wines from their own and purchased grapes. 35 acres.

Valtellina DOC (I.)

1. A district around Sondrio, in the northern Lombardy region, which produces:

2. A red wine made from at least 70% Nebbiolo grapes (called Chiavennasca in this district), and some Pinot Nero, Merlot, Pignola, Rossola and Brugnola grapes. There are four areas entitled to the "*Superiore*" pedigree: Grumello, Inferno, Sassella and Valgella.

Vannières, Château des (F.)

An estate in La Cadière d'Azur, Bandol district, in the Provence region; produces Bandol and Côtes de Provence wines. 130 acres.

varietal wine

A wine made from one grape, or mostly one grape, which shows the typical character and taste of that grape and from which the wine gets its name.

Variety 439 (U.S.)

A red hybrid grape – a cross of Minnesota #78, a cold-resistant wild grape clone, and Seibel 11803; developed in Wisconsin by Elmer Swenson; also called Norvin or Swenson's Red.

Varogne (F.)

A vineyard section of Hermitage, in the northern Rhône region; produces red wines.

Varoilles, Les *or* Clos des *also* Véroilles (F.)

A *Premier Cru* vineyard in Gevrey-Chambertin, Côte de Nuits district, Burgundy. 15 acres.

Varoilles, Domaine des (F.)

An estate in Gevrey-Chambertin, Côte de Nuits district, Burgundy. 25 acres, including Clos des Varoilles Monopole – 15 acres, La Romanée – 2.5 acres, Clos du Meix des Ouches – 2.5 acres, Clos du Couvent – 1.2

acres, Charmes-Chambertin – 1.5 acres, Gevrey-Chambertin Champonnets – 1.5 acres, Bonnes Mares – 1.3 acres and Clos de Vougeot – 3.2 acres.

Varro, Marcus (116-27 B.C.) (Lat.)

An ancient Roman historian and author. He wrote *Rerum Rusticum Libri* (or *De Re Rustica*), in which he describes vines and wines; written during the reign of Caesar and Augustus Caesar.

Vaselli, Conte (I.)

An estate in Castiglione in Teverina, Latium region; produces Orvieto Classico and other wines.

Vassalli Della Gada (Sw.)   1870

An estate in Cupolago, Ticino region; produces Merlot wines. 10 acres.

Vasse Felix (Aus.)   1967, 1st wine 1972

A winery in the Margaret River district, Western Australia; produces Cabernet Sauvignon (blended with Malbec and Shiraz), Rhine Riesling and Gewürztraminer wines. 20 acres.

vat

A large container made of wood, glass, stainless steel or cement, used to ferment and blend wines.

Vatican, La Cuvée du (F.)

An estate in Châteauneuf-du-Pape, southern Rhône region. 40 acres.

Vaucoupin (F.)

A *Premier Cru* vineyard in Chichée, Chablis district, Burgundy. 15 acres.

Vaucrains, Les (F.)

A *Premier Cru* vineyard in Nuits-St.-Georges, Côte de Nuits district, Burgundy. 15 acres.

Vaud (Sw.)

A canton and region around Lake Geneva; produces Dézaley and Aigle wines. 9,000 acres.

Vaudésirs, Les (F.)

A *Grand Cru* vineyard in Chablis, Chablis district, Burgundy.

Vaudevey (F.)   1983

A newly formed *Premier Cru* vineyard in the Chablis district, Burgundy.

Vaudieu, Château de (F.)

An estate in Châteauneuf-du-Pape, southern Rhône region. 73 acres.

Vaugiraut (F.)

A *Premier Cru* vineyard in Chichée, Chablis district, Burgundy; usually considered a part of the Vogros vineyard.

Vaulorent (F.)

A *Premier Cru* vineyard in Poinchy, Chablis district, Burgundy; usually considered a part of the Fourchaume vineyard.

Vaupulent (F.)

A *Premier Cru* vineyard in Fontenay and La Chapelle-Vaupelteigne, Chablis district, Burgundy; usually considered a part of the Fourchaume vineyard.

Vauvry (F.)

A *Premier Cru* vineyard in Rully, Côte Chalonnaise district, Burgundy.

vecchio (I.)

Old, usually meaning aged for 3 years in wood before bottling.

Vecchio Samperi (I.)

A dry, white wine from northwestern Sicily; made from Grillo grapes using the *solera* system; similar to Marsala.

Veeblanc (C.)

A white hybrid grape – a cross of Cascade and Seyve-Villard 14-287; grown in Canada.

Veedercrest Vineyard (U.S.)   1972

A vineyard on Mt. Veeder, northwest of Napa City, Napa County, California, with a winery in Emeryville, north Alameda

County; produces Cabernet Sauvignon, Pinot Noir, Chardonnay, Johannisberg Riesling and Chenin Blanc wines. 300 acres. Closed down in 1983.

Veeport (C.)   **1961**

A red hybrid grape developed by Ollie Bradt in Canada, in 1961.

Vega Sicilia (Sp.)

A red wine from east of Valladolid, on the River Duero, in north central Spain, named after Santa Cecilia, and made since 1864; when aged for 3 to 5 years it is sold as Valbuena, and the Vega Sicilia Unico is aged in wood for 10 years; made from Cabernet Sauvignon, Merlot, Malbec, Tinto Aragonés, Garnacho Tinto grapes and the white Albillo grape.

Vega Sicilia S.A., Bodegas (Sp.)   **1864**

A well-known estate in Valbuena del Duero, Valladolid district, Old Castile region; produces Vega Sicilia and Valbuena red wines made from Spanish grapes: Tinto Aragonés, Garnacha and Albillo, and French grapes: Cabernet Sauvignon, Merlot and Malbec. 2,700 acres.

velho (P.)

Old.

Velletri DOC (I.)

A town southwest of Rome, in the Castelli Romani district, Latium region; produces red wine made from Cesanese, Montepulciano, Sangiovese, Bombino Nero, Merlot and Ciliegiolo grapes and white wines from Malvasia, Trebbiano and other grapes.

Veltliner (A., G.)

The Grüner Veltliner grape, a white grape grown in Austria, Hungary, Czechoslovakia and California.

Venčac-Oplenac (Y.)

A district south of Belgrade, in the northern part of the Republic of Serbia; produces mostly red varietal wines made from Cabernet Sauvignon, Cabernet Franc, Merlot, Gamay, Pinot Noir, Prokupac and Plovdina grapes.

vendage (F.)

The harvest; the vintage year.

vendangeoir (F.)

A press-house, a term used in the Champagne region.

vendemmia (I.)

The vintage, or vintage year.

vendimia (Sp.)

The grape-harvesting, or harvest time; the vintage.

Venegazzù *also* **Venegazzù della Casa (I.)**

Red and white wines from the Venegazzù del Montello estate in Volpago del Montello, northeast of Treviso, in the eastern Veneto region. The red wine is made from Cabernet Sauvignon, Cabernet Franc, Malbec and Merlot grapes and the white wine is made from Pinot Bianco with some Riesling Italico grapes.

Venegazzù del Montello (I.)   **1940**

An estate in Volpago del Montello, northwest of Treviso, in the Montello e Colli Asolani district, eastern Veneto region; produces Prosecco, Pinot Bianco, Pinot Grigio, Venegazzù and sparkling wines. 50,000 cases. 125 acres.

venencia (Sp.)

A small silver cup on a long handle, used in the Sherry region for taking samples from Sherry casks.

Veneri, Ruggero (I.)

An estate in Spello, Umbria region; produces Merlot wine.

Veneto (I.)

A region in northeastern Italy centered around Venice and Verona; produces and exports a large variety of wines; the largest DOC producing region in Italy; famous for

Valpolicella, Bardolino, Amarone and Soave wines. 225 million gallons.

Ventana Vineyard (U.S.)   **vines planted 1973, 1st wine 1978**

A vineyard and winery in Soledad, Monterey County, California; produces many varietal wines, including Chardonnay, Pinot Blanc, Johannisberg Riesling, Chenin Blanc and Sauvignon Blanc; also sells grapes to other wineries. 300 acres.

vente sur souches (F.)

Sold on the vine; i.e., an advance sale of wine before the grapes are harvested.

véraison (F.)

The maturing stage of the grapes, when the color begins to change.

verbessern (G.)

To improve the must with the addition of sugar; to sugar the wine.

Verbesserung (G.)

The improvement of must by the addition of sugar. The same as chaptalization or gallization.

Vercots, Les (F.)

A *Premier Cru* vineyard in Aloxe-Corton, Côte de Beaune district, Burgundy. 10 acres.

Verdea (I.)

A white grape grown east of Pavia, in the Lombardy region.

Verdea (Gr.)

"Green wine" from the Island of Zante (Zakinthos), off the western coast of the Peloponnese region.

Verdeca (I.)

A white grape grown in the Apulia region, and used to made Locorontondo and Martinafranco wines; also grown in the Campania region.

Verdejo (Sp.)

A white grape grown in Peñafiel, in the Old Castile region, in north central Spain.

Verdelet (F.)

A white hybrid grape, Seibel 9110 – a cross of Seibel 5,455 and Seibel 4,938; fruity and spicy.

Verdelho (P.)

1. A white grape used to make white Port and Madeira wine; also called Gouveio.

2. A semi-sweet Madeira wine.

Verdelho Tinto (P.)

A red grape grown in the Vinho Verde region.

Verdello (I.)

A white grape grown in the Marches, Tuscany and Umbria regions; one of several used to make Orvieto and Torgiano wine.

Verdicchio (I.)

1. A white grape grown in the Latium, Marches and Piedmont regions, one of several used to make Orvieto and Verdicchio wines.

2. Any of several districts in the Marches region, in east central Italy: V. dei Castelli di Jesi DOC from Jesi, V. di Matelaca DOC from Matelaca, southwest of Jesi, V. di Montanello from Montanello, southeast of Jesi, V. Pian delle Mura, south of Matelica, near Serrapetrona. Each produces:

3. A white wine, sometimes sparkling as well, made from 80% Verdicchio grapes with some Trebbiano and Malvasia grapes.

Verdignan, Château (F.)

An estate in St. Seurin de Cadourne, Médoc district, Bordeaux; classified in 1978 as a *Cru Grand Bourgeois*. 25,000 cases. 115 acres.

Verdil (Sp.)

A white grape grown in the Alicante district of southeastern Spain.

Verdiso (I.)

A white grape and wine from Conegliano, in the northeastern Veneto region.

verdolino (I.)

A pale green wine.

Verdot (F.)

See **Petit Verdot.**

Verdun Estate EWO (S. Af.)

An estate in the Stellenbosch district; known for Gamay wines.

Verduzzo (I.)

A white grape grown in the Friuli and Veneto regions.

Verduzzo *also* Verduzzo Friulano DOC (I.)

A white wine from the Colli Orientali district, in the Friuli-Venezia Giulia region; made from the local Verduzzo grape.

Vered (Is.)

A rosé wine from the Binyamina district, Samaria; made from the Malbec grape.

Vereinigte Hospitien, Güterverwaltung (G.)

An estate in Trier, Mosel-Saar-Ruwer region; owns vineyards in Serrig and Wiltingen, Trier, Piesport, Bernkastel, Graach and Zeltingen; owns several several *monopoles* as well as part of the Scharzhofberg vineyard. 110 acres.

Vergelesses, Les *or* Aux (F.)

A *Premier Cru* vineyard in Savigny-lès-Beaune, Côte de Beaune district, Burgundy; part of the vineyard is in Pernand-Vergelesses. 42 acres.

Vergelesses Bataillière, Les (F.)

A *Premier Cru* vineyard in Savigny-lès-Beaune, Côte de Beaune, Burgundy. 42.5 acres.

Vergennes *also* Vergeness (U.S.)

An American red hybrid grape grown in Vermont and New York.

Vergennes, Les (F.)

A *Grand Cru* vineyard in Ladoix-Serrigny, Côte de Beaune district, Burgundy; it may use the name of Corton (white) or Corton-Charlemagne. 6 acres.

Vergenoegd Estate EWO (S. Af.)   1969

An estate in the Stellenbosch district; known for Cabernet Sauvignon, Shiraz and Cinsaut wines. 300 acres.

Verger, Clos du (F.)

A *Premier Cru* vineyard in Pommard, Côte de Beaune district, Burgundy. 6 acres.

Vergers, Les (F.)

A *Premier Cru* vineyard in Chassagne-Montrachet, Côte de Beaune district, Burgundy. 23.5 acres.

Vergil (Lat.)

See **Virgil.**

Verín (Sp.)

A village and district in the Galicia region of northwestern Spain; produces red and white wines.

verjus (F.)

1. Grapes from a late or second flowering; they are very acidic, since they don't have time to ripen.

2. Verjuice, the juice of green, or unripe grapes.

Vermentino (I., F.)

1. A white grape grown in the Liguria region, Sardinia and Corsica (French); a strain of the Malvasia grape.

2. A white wine from the Liguria region and Sardinia made from the Vermentino grape.

Vermentino di Alghero (I.)

A dry, white wine from Alghero, in northwestern Sardinia; made from the Vermentino grape.

Vermentino di Gallura DOC (I.)

1. A large district on the Gallura peninsula, in northeastern Sardinia, which produces:

2. A dry, white wine made from 95% Vermentino grapes.

Vermiglio (I.)

An early (13th century) name for red wine from the Florence district, which is now the Chianti district; also called Florence Red.

vermouth

A red, or white, apéritif made from wine, sugar syrup or mistelle, alcohol, herbs and spices. It is mixed, pasteurized, refrigerated, filtered and bottled. The word is derived from the German *Wermuth* (wormwood); first made in 1786 in Turin, by Antonio Carpano.

Vernaccia (I.)

A white grape grown in the Tuscany, Marches and Sardinia regions and elsewhere in Italy.

Vernaccia di Cannara (I.)

A sweet, red wine from Cannara and Bevagna, in the central Umbria region; made from Cometta and Corvetta grapes; usually *frizzante*.

Vernaccia Nera (I.)

A red grape grown in the southern Marches region and in Sardinia.

Vernaccia di Oristano DOC (I.)

1. A local white grape grown around Oristano, Sardinia, unrelated to other grapes called Vernaccia.

2. Dry and sweet white wines from the Tirso River area near Oristano, in west central Sardinia; made from overripe Vernaccia di Oristano grapes; when fortified, the wine is similar to Sherry; the *flor* method of vinification is used but without the *solera* system.

Vernaccia di San Gimignano DOC (I.)

A white wine from San Gimignano, northwest of Siena, in the central Tuscany region; made from the Vernaccia grape; known since 1643.

Vernaccia di Serrapetrona DOC (I.)

A sparkling red wine, dry or sweet, from Serrapetrona, south of Matelica, in the southwest Marches region; made from the Vernaccia di Serrapetrona grape or the Vernaccia Nera and some Sangiovese grapes.

Vernatsch (I.)

The German name for the red Schiava grape in the northern Trentino-Alto Adige region, in northeastern Italy.

Vernay, Georges (F.)

An estate in Condrieu, in the northern Rhône region; owns 15 acres of Condrieu, 4 acres of Côte-Rôtie and some St.-Joseph.

Vernous, Château (F.)

An estate in Lesparre, Médoc district, Bordeaux; classified in 1978 as a *Cru Bourgeois* Being Reconstituted. 6,000 cases. 45 acres.

Véroilles, Les *also* Varoilles (F.)

A *Premier Cru* vineyard in Gevrey-Chambertin, Côte de Nuits district, Burgundy. 15 acres.

Verquière, Domaine de (F.)

An estate in Sablet, in the Côtes du Rhône-Villages district, southern Rhône region. 120 acres, including vineyards in Sablet, Rasteau and Vacqueyras.

Verseuil, En (F.)

A *Premier Cru* vineyard in Volnay, Côte de Beaune district, Burgundy. 2 acres.

Vertzami (Gr.)

A red grape grown on the Island of Levkas, in west central Greece.

Verwaltung (G.)

An administration; a management.

Vespaiolo (I.)

1. A local white grape grown in Breganze, in the central Veneto region; also called Bresparolo.
2. A white wine made from the Vespaiolo grape.

Vesuvio DOC (I.)

Red, white and rosé wines from 12 villages around the southern face of Mount Vesuvio, in the Campania region. The red wine is made from Piedirosso and Olivella grapes (locally called Palombina and Sciascianoso) with some Aglianico grapes and the white wine is made from Coda di Volpe grapes (locally called Caprettona) and some Verdeca, Falanghina and Greco grapes.

Veuve Clicquot-Ponsardin (F.)   1772

A Champagne firm in Reims; produces Brut, Vintage Brut, Rosé and La Grande Dame. 6.5 million bottles. 650 acres.

Vevey Festival (Sw.)

"Fête des Vignerons," in French. A great wine fest held since the 17th century in the commune of Vevey, southeast of Lausanne, on Lake Geneva, in the Vaud region.

Viano Winery, Conrad (U.S.)   vines 1920
                                   winery 1946

A vineyard and winery in Martinez, Contra Costa County, California; produces Cabernet Sauvignon, Zinfandel, Barbera, Gamay, Zinfandel rosé, Grey Riesling, Port and Sherry wines. 60 acres.

Vicchiomaggio, Castello (I.)

An estate in Greve, Tuscany region; produces Chianti Classico and Paleo Bianco wines. 70 acres.

Vichon Winery (U.S.)   1980

A winery in Oakville, Napa Valley, California; produces Chardonnay, Chevrier (since 1983 called Chevrignon), a blend of Sémillon and Sauvignon and Cabernet Sauvignon wines; made from grapes purchased from Napa Valley. 30,000 cases.

Victoria (Aus.)

A province in the southeastern corner of Australia; vines were first planted here in 1838; vineyards are scattered in various districts from east to west; famous for muscat dessert wines and Tokay wine made from the Hárselevü grape.

Victoria Berg, Königin (G.)

An estate in Hochheim, Rheingau region, named after Queen Victoria; owns the *monopole* vineyard Hochheimer Königin Victoria Berg. 12 acres.

Vidal, J. L. (F.)

A French hybridizer, the late director of the Fougerat Station in Bois-Charentes; known for developing the Vidal Blanc hybrid grape.

Vidal Blanc (F.)

A white hybrid grape, Vidal 256 – a cross of Ugni Blanc and Seibel 4986; grown in the eastern and midwestern U.S.

Vidal-Fleury (F.)   1781

An estate and merchant in Ampuis, Côte-Rôtie district, Rhône region; owns 20 acres of Côte-Rôtie.

Vidal Wine Producers (N.Z.)   1905, 1908

A winery in Hastings, Hawkes Bay, North Island, owned by the Villa Maria winery; produces Cabernet Sauvignon, Chardonnay, Gewürztraminer, Te Moana Riesling and sparkling wines.

vidange (F.)

Ullage.

Vides di Guadalupe (Mex.)   1972

A winery northeast of Ensenada, in the Baja California region, owned by Pedro Domecq; produces table wines.

Vidiella (Ur.)

A red grape.

vie (R.)

A vine.

viejo (Sp.) *also* **añejo (Sp.)**

Old.

Vieille Ferme, La (F.)   **1971**

A brand of blended red wine from the Côtes du Ventoux district, southern Rhône region; made from purchased Syrah and other grapes of the Côtes du Ventoux and from purchased wines. Made by J.-P. Perrin.

Vien de Nus (I.)

A local red grape grown in the Valle d'Aosta region.

Viénot, Charles (F.)

An old estate in Prémeaux, Côte de Nuits district, Burgundy; owns parcels of Richebourg – 2.5 acres, Corton – 7.5 acres, Nuits-St.-Georges Clos St.-Marc Monopole – 3.6 acres, Clos des Corvées-Pagets – 4 acres, and acreage in Vosne-Romanée and Aloxe-Corton.

Vierthaler, Manfred (U.S.)   **1976**

A winery in Sumner, Washington; produces Johannisberg Riesling and Müller-Thurgau wines. 6,000 cases. 30 acres.

Vietti (I.)

A winery in Castiglione Falletti, in the southern Piedmont region; produces Arneis, Barbaresco, Barbera, Barolo, Dolcetto, Freisa, Grignolino, Nebbiolo and Moscato wines.

Vieux Château Certan (F.)

An estate in Pomerol, Bordeaux. 7,000 cases. 35 acres.

Vieux Chêne, Domaine du (F.)

An estate in Camaret, Côtes du Rhône district, southern Rhône region; produces red wine made from Grenache, Syrah, Cinsault and Muscardin grapes. 45 acres.

Vieux Clocher, Le (F.)

An estate in Vacqueyras, in the Côtes du Rhône-Villages district, southern Rhône region.

Vieux Moulin de Tavel, Les (F.)

An estate in Tavel, southern Rhône region. 100 acres, 17 acres in Lirac.

Vieux Robin, Château (F.)

An estate in Bégadan, Médoc district, Bordeaux; classified in 1978 as a *Cru Bourgeois*. 6,000 cases. 25 acres.

Vieux Télégraphe (F.)   **1900**

An estate in Châteauneuf-du-Pape, southern Rhône region; produces red wine made from 75% Grenache, 15% Syrah, 5% Cinsault and 5% Mourvèdre grapes. 6,000 cases. 122 acres.

vigna *also* **vigneto (I.)**

A vineyard.

Vigna del Curato (I.)

An estate in Sappanico, the Marches region; produces Moscato, Rosso Piceno and Verdicchio wines.

Vigna Vecchia (I.)

An estate in Radda, Tuscany region; produces Chianti Classico wines. 15,000 cases.

vignaiuolo (I.)

A grower.

Vignamaggio (I.)

An estate in Greve, Tuscany region; produces Chianti Classico wine.

vigne (F.)

1. A vine.

2. A vineyard, or small parcel of vineyard.

Vigne Blanche, La *also* **Clos Blanc de Vougeot (F.)**

A *Premier Cru* vineyard in Vougeot, Côte de Nuits district, Burgundy, the vineyard from which the Clos Blanc de Vougeot white wine is made. 7 acres. A *monopole* of l'Héritier-Guyot.

Vigne de l'Enfant Jésus (F.)

A section of the Grèves vineyard in Beaune, Côte de Beaune district, Burgundy (a *Premier Cru*); a *monopole* of Bouchard Père et Fils. 10 acres.

Vigne-au-Saint, La (F.)

A *Grand Cru* vineyard in Aloxe-Corton, Côte de Beaune district, Burgundy; a *monopole* of Louis Latour. 6 acres.

Vigneau, Château (F.)

A former estate in Bommes, Sauternes district, Bordeaux; in 1855 the name of what is now Château Rayne-Vigneau.

Vignelaure, Château (F.)

An estate in Rians, in the Côteaux-d'Aix-en-Provence district, Provence region. 110 acres.

vigneron (F.)

A wine-maker, grower or vineyard worker.

Vignerondes, Aux *also* Aux Vignes Rondes (F.)

A *Premier Cru* vineyard in Nuits-St.-Georges, Côte de Nuits district, Burgundy. 9 acres.

vigneronnage (F.)

In Beaujolais, a tenant working a vineyard; the practice of renting out a vineyard; also called *métayage*. See also **fermage**.

Vignerons de Chusclan, La Cave des (F.) 1939

A co-op winery in the commune of Chusclan, Côtes du Rhône-Villages district, southern Rhône region; produces red, white and rosé wines. 130 members, 1,500 acres.

Vignerons de Saumur (F.)

A co-op winery in St. Cyr-en-Bourg, Saumur-Champigny district, Anjou region, Loire Valley; produces Saumur Blanc, Saumur Rouge, Saumur-Champigny, Crémant de Loire, Mousseux and other wines. 200,000 cases. 1,800 acres.

Vignes Franches, Les (F.)

A *Premier Cru* vineyard in Beaune, Côte de Beaune district, Burgundy. 25 acres.

Vignes Rondes, Les (F.)

A *Premier Cru* vineyard in Monthélie, Côte Chalonnaise district, Burgundy. 7 acres.

vignoble (F.)

A vineyard, or estate; a wine district or region.

Vignoles (F.)

A white hybrid grape – a cross of Pinot Noir and Seibel 6905; also called Ravat 51.

viile (R.)

A vineyard.

Vila Nova de Gaia (P.)

A village opposite Oporto, on the River Douro, in northern Portugal, where most Port lodges (warehouses) are located.

Vila Real (P.)

A region in Portugal, north of the Douro region; produces red and rosé wines.

villa (I.)

A manor; a wine estate.

Villa Armando (U.S.)   1902, 1962

A winery in Pleasanton, Livermore Valley, Alameda County, California; produces red and white jug wines and some varietal wines. 150,000 cases. 200 acres.

Villa Bianchi (U.S.)   1974

A winery in Fresno, San Joaquin Valley, California; produces jug wines. 160 acres.

Villa Cerna (I.)

An estate in Castellina in Chianti, Tuscany region; produces Chianti Classico wines. 40,000 cases. 150 acres.

Villa di Corte (I.)

A rosé wine from east of Florence, in the Tuscany region; made from the grapes used for Chianti wine.

Villa Dal Ferro (I.)

An estate in San Germano, in the Colli Berici district, Veneto region; produces varietal wines from French and Italian grapes,
labeled with special names. The red wines
are: Le Rive Rosse, made from Cabernet
Sauvignon and Cabernet Franc grapes,
Campo del Lago, from Merlot and Rosso
del Rocolo, from Pinot Nero. The white
wines are: Bianco del Rocolo, made from
the Pinot Bianco grape, Busa Calcara, from
Riesling Renano and Costiera Granda,
from Tocai Friulano.

Villa d'Ingianni (U.S.)   1973

A small winery between Lake Seneca and
Lake Keuka, Finger Lakes region, New
York; produces wines from Johannisberg
Riesling, Delaware, Baco Nero and other
grapes.

Villa Maria Wines (N.Z.)   1961

A winery in Mangere, North Island, with
other properties as well; produces Traminer, Chardonnay, Riesling Sylvaner, Cabernet Sauvignon, Pinotage and
Melesconera wines made mostly from purchased grapes. 20 acres.

Villa Medeo (U.S.)   1974

A winery in Madison, Indiana; produces
wines from hybrid grapes. 11 acres.

Villa Mt. Eden (U.S.)   1881, 1970
                                    1st wine 1975

An old, revived winery in Oakville, Napa
Valley, California; produces Cabernet Sauvignon, Pinot Noir, Napa Gamay, Chardonnay, Chenin Blanc and Gewürztraminer wines; uses some field-crushing. 85
acres.

Villa Sachsen, Weingut (G.)

An estate in Bingen, Rheinhessen region;
owns vineyards in Bingen. 65 acres.

Villa Santelia (I.)

A white wine from the Cirò district, in the
east central Calabria region; made mostly
from Greco grapes.

Villa a Sesta (I.)

An estate in San Gusmè, Tuscany region;
produces Chianti Classico wine. 6,000
cases.

Villadoria, Marchese (I.)

A brand name used by CE.DI.VI., a company in Rivoli, Piedmont region; produces
Dolcetto, Barbera, Grignolino, Barolo and
other wines.

Village-de-Volnay (F.)

A *Premier Cru* vineyard (in part) in Volnay,
Côte de Beaune district, Burgundy. 33
acres.

Villagrande (I.)

An estate in Milo, Sicily; produces Etna
wines. 8,000 cases. 75 acres.

Villaine, A. et P. de (F.)

An estate in Rully, Côte Chalonnaise district, Burgundy; produces Bourgogne
AOC wine. 30 acres.

Villamagna (I.)   17th cent.

An estate in Contrada Montanello, the
Marches region; produces Rosso Piceno,
Verdicchio and other wines. 8,500 cases. 40
acres.

Villamont, Henri de (F.)   1964

An estate and *négociant* in Savigny-lès-
Beaune, Côte de Beaune district, Bur-
gundy. 16 acres, including 1.2 acres of
Grands Échézeaux, 5 acres of Savigny Clos
des Guettes and some Chambolle-
Musigny.

Villány-Siklós (H.)

A district in the southern Transdanubia
district consisting of the towns of Villány
and Siklós, in southwestern Hungary; produces red wine mainly from the Pinot Noir
grape. Officially rated red wine of Excellent Quality. 5,000 acres.

Villard, Pierre (Sw.)   1955

A small estate in Geneva; produces Pinot
Noir, Chardonnay, Chasselas and Gamay
wines. 8 acres.

Villard, Victor (F.)

A French hybridizer whose daughter married Bertille Seyve, Jr.(1895-1959), which accounts for the name Seyve-Villard, used for the hybrid grapes developed by B. Seyve, Jr.

Villard Blanc

A white hybrid grape: Seyve-Villard 12375 – a cross of S. 6,468 and S. 6,905.

Villard Noir

A red hybrid grape: Seyve-Villard 18315 – a cross of S.7,053 and S.6,905.

Villegeorge, Château (F.)

An estate in Avenson, Haut-Médoc district, Bordeaux. Classified in 1932 as a *Cru Bourgeois Exceptionnel* and in 1966 as a *Cru Grand Bourgeois Exceptionnel*, but not classified in 1978. 25 acres. 3,000 cases.

Villemaurine, Château (F.)

An estate in St.-Émilion, Bordeaux; classified in 1955 as a *Grand Cru Classé*. 3,500 cases. 16 acres.

Villeneuve, Château De (F.)

An estate in Souzay-Champigny, Coteaux du Saumur district, Anjou region, Loire Valley; produces red and white wines. 60 acres.

Villeroy, Domaine du Château de (F.)

An estate in the Vins des Sables district, Languedoc region; owned by Domaines Viticoles des Salins du Midi; produces red and white wines.

Villots, Domaine des (F.)   1646

An estate in Verdigny, Sancerre district, Upper Loire region, Loire Valley. 15 acres.

vin (F.)

Wine. *Vin rouge* is red wine, *vin blanc* is white wine, *vin rosé* is pink wine, *vin gris* is a pale rosé, *vin vert* is a wine made from unripe grapes, and *vin jaune* is a special yellow wine, a little like Sherry.

vin alb (R.)

White wine.

vin de l'année (F.)

"Wine of the year," this year's wine; a very young wine, a term usually applied to young Beaujolais when first shipped in the spring after the vintage.

vin d'ardoise (F.)

French for "wine from *ardoise*," in the Anjou region, made from grapes grown in hard schist soil.

Vin Biondo (I.)

A sweet, white, spumante wine from the Montalcino district, in the Tuscany region; made from the Muscadelletto grape.

Vin de Blanquette (F.)

The term for non-sparkling Blanquette de Limoux wine, made from the same grapes.

Vin de Bugey VDQS (F.)

A designation for red, white and rosé wines from several villages around Belley, east of Lyons, just west of the Savoie region. The red and rosé wines are made from Gamay, Mondeuse, Pinot Noir and Poulsard grapes, and the white is made from Altesse, Aligoté, Chardonnay, Jacquère, Mondeuse Blanc and Pinot Gris grapes. Some villages have the right to add the village name.

Vin des Chanoines (I.)

A red wine from Aosta, in the Valle d'Aosta region; made from the Gamay grape.

vin chaud (F.)

Mulled (warmed) wine.

vin de la comète (F.)

A descriptive designation given to a good vintage year if the year includes the appearance of a comet. The most famous one was in 1811.

Vin du Conseil (I.)

A dry, white wine made at the Regional Agricultural School near Aosta, in the Valle d'Aosta region; made from the Petite Arvine grape.

Vin de Consommation Courante or VCC (F.)

"Wine for Daily Consumption," a category of wine that was designated in 1955 for *vin ordinaire*, the lowest category of French wines, formerly known as as *Vin de Table* (table wine).

Vin de Corse AOC (F.)

The general appellation for red, white, rosé and VDN wines from Corsica, with the delimited district name added on the label.

vin cotto (I.)

"Cooked wine," a wine made from must that is cooked until it becomes a sweet syrup, after which fresh must is added, and then the mixture is fermented until 18-20 degrees of alcohol is obtained. The resulting wine can be either dry or sweet.

vin de coupage (F.)

A blending wine, a wine used to correct a deficiency in another wine.

vin de cru (F.)

A wine from one village only, and not blended with wine from other villages, a term used in the Champagne region, usually found in the Côte des Blancs *communes* of Crémant and Avize.

vin cuit (F.)

A boiled-down grape syrup or wine.

vin de cuvée (F.)

The first pressing, or *serre*, in the Champagne region; it gives the best quality wine.

vin diable (F.)

"Devil wine," wine that has undergone a second fermentation in the bottle in the spring and which pops the cork or explodes the bottle; also called *saute bouchon* (cork-popper).

Vin Doux Naturel or VDN (F.)

A fortified, sweet, white, red or rosé wine from the Languedoc, Roussillon and Rhône regions in southern France; made from the Muscat, Grenache and other grapes. In the Rhône region – Muscat de Beaumes-de-Venise VDN (from Muscat grapes) and Rasteau VDN (red or white, from Grenache grapes); in the Languedoc region – Muscat de Frontignan VDN, Muscat de Lunel VDN, Muscat de Miréval VDN and Muscat de Saint-Jean-de-Minervois VDN (all white, made from the Muscat grape); in the Roussillon region – Banyuls VDN, also with *Grand Cru* or *Rancio* added (red or white), Côtes d'Agly VDN (red, white and rosé), Grand Roussillon VDN (red, white and rosé), Maury VDN (red), Muscat de Rivesaltes VDN (white), and Rivesaltes VDN (red, white and rosé). Malvoisie and Maccabéo grapes can also be used.

vin fin (F.)

"Fine wine," wine of high quality.

vin flétri (Sw.)

A sweet wine from the Valais region; made from over-ripe or dried grapes.

Vin Fou (F.)

French for "mad wine," a white, sparkling wine made in Arbois, in the Jura region.

vin de garde (F.)

A wine for laying down, i.e. for aging in the bottle.

Vin du Glacier (Sw.)

A white wine from the Valais region, stored at high altitudes in the Alps.

vin de goutte (F.)

Free-run wine; not pressed.

vin gris (F.)

A pale pink wine, a rosé of a very light color.

vin d'honneur (F.)

"Wine of honor," a wine for special occasions or ceremonies.

vin jaune (F.)

"Yellow wine," a wine from the Jura region of eastern France, made from Savagnin grapes which are harvested late, pressed into wine and sealed into barrels for at least 6 years during which time a film (*flor*, or *fleur*) forms on the surface as in Sherry wine. This film is made up of microorganisms which give a nutty taste and a yellow color to the wine. The wine is very long-lived. Château-Châlon is the most well-known *vin jaune*.

vin de liqueur (F.)

1. A sweet wine, either naturally sweet or fortified with brandy.

2. A sweet wine which has been fortified with brandy and is added to Champagne to bring it up to the desired sweetness; a *liqueur d'expédition*.

vin de Macadam (F.)

An old Parisian term for new, sweet, white wine which is drunk in open air cafés, overlooking Macadam-paved streets and squares; the term is mostly applied to wines from the Bergerac district.

vin de marque (F.)

A trade-mark wine; a commercial blend, usually with no regional identification.

vin de médecine (F.)

A wine used as a booster to strengthen a weaker wine.

vin de messe (F.)

Altar wine; wine used during the Mass.

Vin dei Molini (I.)

A rosé wine from Faedo, north of Trentino, in the Trentino-Alto Adige region; made from a blend of Schiava and Riesling grapes.

vin mousseux (F.)

A sparkling wine.

vin muté (F.)

Partially fermented wine; the fermentation is stopped by the addition of brandy; used in making apéritifs.

Vin Nature de la Champagne (F.)

The name formerly used for a still wine from the Champagne region; the legal name now in use is Coteaux Champenois.

Vin Noble du Minervois VDQS (F.)

A designation for sweet, white wine from the Minervois district, in the Languedoc region; made from late-harvested Muscat, Malvoisie, Maccabéo and Grenache grapes. Minimum alcohol is 13%.

vin nouveau (F.)

"New wine," a very young wine, with a slight effervescence; a term usually applied to Beaujolais wines shipped on or sometime after November 15.

vin ordinaire (F.)

"Ordinary wine," a common, inexpensive wine.

vin de paille (F.)

"Straw wine," a wine made in the Jura region of eastern France for which grapes are dried for at least 2 months on beds of straw before pressing. This results in a rich, long-lived, yellow wine. Soleil de Sierre, from the Valais region in Switzerland, is also a *vin de paille*.

Vin de Pays (F.)   1968
                                revised 1973, 1979

A designation for a local wine of a specific region for local consumption, a classification below VDQS wine; usually light, typical of the region, and low in alcohol, and therefore does not age or travel well.

vin de presse (F.)

"Press wine," the wine made from the juice squeezed in the wine press, as opposed to free-run juice.

vin de primeur (F.)

Very young wine, the first wine of the vintage; the same as vin *nouveau*.

vin de réserve (F.)

In the Champagne region, a wine which has been set aside from a previous vintage in order to be blended with wine from the current vintage, so as to maintain a consistant style from year to year.

vin roşu (R.)

Red wine.

Vin Ruspo (I.)

A special type of rosé wine from the Carmignano district, in the Tuscany region; made from a mixture of red and white grapes.

Vin de Sables VCC (F.)

The red, white and rosé wine from the Sables du Golfe du Lion district, covering a large area of sandy soil south, southeast and southwest of Montpellier, in the Languedoc region; made from a large number of grape varieties common to the region.

Vin Santo (I.)

"Holy wine," a wine primarily from the Tuscany and Umbria regions; made from semi-dried grapes which are aged in sealed barrels for 3 years; mostly white, some red; can be dry, semi-dry or sweet but always 16-17% alcohol content.

Vin de Savoie AOC (F.)   AOC in 1973

One of the AOC designations for red, white and rosé wines from the Savoie region, in southeastern France; the white wine is made from Altesse, Jacquère or Roussette, Chardonnay, Chasselas and Aligoté grapes and the red and rosé made from Mondeuse Noir, Gamay, Pinot Noir and other local grapes. Other designations may include certain *communes* and sparkling wines.

vin de tête (F.)

In the Sauternes district, Bordeaux region, wine made from the first crush, i.e. the best wine; also called *crème de tête*.

vin de tuffeau (F.)

Wine made from grapes grown in *tuffeau* (calcareous) soil in Saumur, Anjou region, Loire Valley.

vin d'une nuit (F.)

"One-night wine," wine that has fermented for only one day and one night by carbonic maceration; made in St.-Saturnin, in the Coteaux du Languedoc district of the Languedoc region, southern France (the Midi); the wine is very light and fruity.

vin uşor (R.)

Light wine.

vin vert (F.)

"Green wine," from the Roussillon region (the Midi), a white wine made from early-harvested Maccabéo grapes.

viña (Sp.)

A vineyard.

Viña, La (U.S.)   1977

A winery in Anthony, Mesilla Valley, southern New Mexico; produces wines from *vinifera* grapes. 50 acres.

Viña Madre (U.S.)   1972, 1978

A winery in Roswell, Pecos Valley, in southern New Mexico; produces wines from many *vinifera* grape varieties, including Cabernet Sauvignon, Zinfandel and Barbera. 40 acres.

Viña Vista (U.S.)   1971

A winery in Cloverdale, Alexander Valley, northern Sonoma County, California; produces Cabernet Sauvignon, Petite Sirah, Zinfandel, Chardonnay, Johannisberg Riesling and Sangiovese wines mostly from purchased grapes. 4,000 cases.

vinage (F.)

The addition of alcohol to wine in order to strengthen the wine.

vinasse (F.)

A cheap, bad wine.

Vincent (C.)

A red hybrid grape developed in Canada by Ollie Bradt; also grown in New York.

vine

1. A woody, climbing plant of the *Ampelidaceae* family; *Vitis* is a *genus* of this family.
2. The grape vine or plant.

viné (F.)

1. Fortified.
2. Wine to which brandy has been added.

Vine Hill Wines (U.S.)   **1977**

A small winery in Santa Cruz City, Santa Cruz County, California; the site of the old Schermerhorn Vineyard, owned by the Smothers Brothers; produces Cabernet Sauvignon, Zinfandel, Johannisberg Riesling, Gewürztraminer and Chardonnay wines; also owns some vines in Sonoma County.

viñedo (Mex.)

A vineyard.

Viñedos Del Rio, Los (U.S.)

A vineyard in Healdsburg, Russian River Valley, Sonoma County, California; produces Chardonnay, Napa Gamay and Merlot wines, owned by the Louis Martini Winery.

vinello (I.)

A little, thin wine; referring to a poor wine or a light, fresh wine.

vinettino *also* **vinetto (I.)**

A little, thin wine; a poor wine.

vineyard

An area of land planted with grape vines.

Vinhão (P.)

A red grape grown in the Vinho Verde region.

vinho (P.)

Wine. *Vinho branco* is white wine, *vinho clarete* is light red wine, *vinho rosado* is rose wine, *vinho tinto* is red wine and *vinho verd* is a specially made, young, red or white wine.

vinho do ano (P.)

Fresh, young wine; not aged.

vinho canteiro (P.)

A Madeira wine made by a natural process of heating in the sun and not by artificia heating (*estufado*).

vinho claro (P.)

New wine.

vinho consumo (P.)

Ordinary, common wine.

vinho espumante (P.)

Sparkling wine.

vinho generoso (P.)

A fortified wine of special quality.

vinho liquoroso (P.)

Fortified wine.

vinho maduro (P.)

Mature wine; aged wine.

vinho de mesa (P.)

Table wine.

Vinho de Ramo (P.)

An unfortified table wine from the Upper Douro region, where Port is made.

vinho surdo (P.)

Sweet must with added alcohol; used to adjust the sweetness of Madeira wines.

vinho trasfugado (P.)

Madeira wine which has been heated and racked off the lees.

Vinho Verde (P.)

1. A region in northwestern Portugal, which produces:

2. "Green wine," i.e. young red (70%) or white wine, slightly fizzy or effervescent, made in a traditional method using malo-lactic fermentation and retaining the semi-sparkle; usually drunk very young. 65,000 acres of vines, grown in granite soil.

vinícola (Mex.)

A winery.

Vinícola de Ensenada (Mex.)

A large winery in Ensenada, Baja California region; produces numerous types of wines.

viniculture

The study and art of wine making.

vinifera

A species of the *genus Vitis*, the European grape used to make most wines.

Vinifera Wine Cellars (U.S.)   1962

A winery in Hammondsport, on Lake Keuka, Finger Lakes region, New York, owned by Konstantin Frank & Sons; produces Riesling, Chardonnay, Pinot Noir and Muscat Ottonel wines. 6,000 cases. 80 acres.

vinification

The process of making wine from grapes.

vinification ferré (F.)

The practice of heating the must in wine-making to give a uniform character to different wines; first attempted in 1927 by Drouhin, in Beaune, Burgundy.

Vinitaly (I.)

An important wine fair, the largest in the country, held in Verona.

vino (I.)

Wine. *Vino bianco* is white wine, *vino rosato* is rosé wine, *vino rosso* is red wine.

vino (Sp.)

Wine. *Vino blanco* is white wine, *vino clarete* is a light, red wine, *vino rosado* is rosé wine, *vino tintillo* is a pale, red wine, *vino tinto* is red wine, and *vino verde* is a red, or white, young wine with a slight sparkle.

vino de aguja (Sp.)

Wine with a slight sparkle; similar to Vinho Verde of Portugal.

vino da arrosto (I.)

A full-bodied red wine to drink with roasted meats.

vino de color (Sp.)

Concentrated grape juice used for coloring and sweetening wines.

vino corriente (Sp.)

Ordinary, common wine; also called *vino comun*.

vino de doble pasta (Sp.)

A wine, usually red, from the Alicante district, in the Levante region, east central Spain; made from the second pressing of grapes (after free run juice, or *vino de lagrima*, is run off) with crushed grapes added. This produces a very thick, dark, high-alcohol wine used for blending.

vino dulce (Sp.)

Very sweet wine used for blending.

vino espumoso (Sp.)

Sparkling wine.

vino generoso (I., Sp.)

Wine that is high in alcohol; Sherry-like wine.

vino de lágrima (Sp.)

Free-run juice; the juice obtained from grapes prior to crushing.

vino de lusso (I.)

Delux wine; expensive or in a luxury class.

vino madre (I.)

New wine which has been boiled down; used to sweeten dessert wines.

vino da meditazione (I.)

"Meditation wine," a term applied to sweet wines of high alcohol content (19% and up); intended to be sipped slowly and pensively; also called *Vin Santo* in the Tuscany and Umbria regions and *Vino Santo* in the Trentino-Alto Adige region.

Vino Nobile di Montepulciano DOCG (I.)

A red wine from Montepulciano, in the southeastern Tuscany region; made from 50-70% Prugnolo, 10-20% Canaiolo Nero, 10-20% Malvasia del Chianti and Trebbiano Toscano and up to 8% Mammolo grapes.

vino novello (I.)

New wine, drunk within 3 months of the harvest, similar in style to Beaujolais *nouveau* wine.

vino da pasto (I.)

Ordinary table wine.

vino de pasto (Sp.)

Ordinary table wine.

vino de prensa (Sp.)

Press wine, i.e. wine that is pressed out of the lees and mixed with the lowest portion of the fermented wine, after the rest of the wine has been drawn off; it is used as a blending wine.

Vino Quinado (Sp.)

Sugared wine with quinine and essence of orange rind added.

vino quotidiano (I.)

Everyday wine; ordinary wine for daily use.

Vino Santo (I.)

A sweet white wine of 14% alcohol from an area around Lake Toblano, west of Trento, in the southern Trentino-Alto Adige region; made from Nosiola and Pinot Bianco grapes, semi-dried and aged in small barrels. See also **Vin Santo.**

vino da taglio (I.)

Unclassified wine used for cutting or blending.

vino tierno (Sp.)

The new, sweet Málaga wine used for blending.

vino de la tierra (Sp.)

Ordinary wine; regional wine.

vino valiente (Sp.)

"Valiant wine," a very strong, full-bodied, coarse wine.

vino de yema (Sp.)

1. "The yolk of the wine," the top section of the wine in the vat after fermentation.

2. Wine made from the first pressing.

3. A superior quality wine.

vinosity

A main characteristic of wine; an assertive, winey taste.

Vinòt (I.)

A red *vino novello* (new wine) from the southern Piedmont region; made from the Nebbiolo grape; to be drunk young, like Beaujolais *nouveau*. Produced by Gaja.

Vinprom (Bul.)

The official Bulgarian state agency responsible for handling and controlling the vineyards and wines.

Vins Délimités de Qualité Supérieure (F.)

"Delimited Wines of Superior Quality," a designation of quality wines ranked below the AOC wines; originated in 1949 and strictly controlled. Abbreviated V.D.Q.S., they are generally found in southern France and in the Loire Valley.

Vins d'Entraygues et du Fel VDQS (F.)

Red, white and rosé wines from Entraygues, north of Rodez, in the Southwest region. The red and rosé wines are made from Cabernet Sauvignon, Cabernet Franc, Fer, Gamay, Merlot, Negrette and other grapes; the white is made from Chenin Blanc and Mauzac grapes.

Vins d'Estaing VDQS (F.)

Red, white and rosé wines from d'Estaing, north of Rodez, in the Southwest region. The grapes used are the same as above.

Vins du Haut Poitou VDQS (F.)

Red, white and rosé wines from Poitiers, southwest of Tours, in the Loire Valley. The red and rosé wines are made from Cabernet Sauvignon, Cabernet Franc, Gamay, Pinot Noir and other grapes; the white is made from Chardonnay, Chenin Blanc, Pinot Blanc and Sauvignon grapes.

Vins de Lavilledieu VDQS (F.)

A designation for red wine from an area northwest of Toulouse, near the Garonne River, in the Southwest region; made from Fer, Mauzac, Négrette and other grapes.

Vins de Marcillac VDQS (F.)

Red and rosé wines from Rodez, in the Aveyron department, the Southwest region; made from Fer grapes, with some Cabernet, Gamay, Merlot and other grapes.

Vins de la Moselle VDQS (F.)

One of 2 officially demarcated wines of the Lorraine region, in northeastern France for red and white wines (the other being Côtes de Toul VDQS), the red made from Gamay, Pinot Noir and Pinot Gris grapes, and the white from Pinot Blanc and Sylvaner grapes.

Vins de l'Orléanais VDQS (F.)

Red, white and rosé wines from Orléans, in the Upper Loire region, Loire Valley. The red and rosé wines are made from Cabernet, Pinot Noir and Pinot Meunier grapes, and the white is made from Chardonnay and Pinot Blanc grapes.

Vins du Thouarsais VDQS (F.)

Red, white and rosé wines from Bressuire and Thours, southeast of Angers, in the Anjou region, Loire Valley. The red and rosé wines are made from Cabernet Sauvignon and Cabernet Franc grapes and the white is made from Chenin Blanc grapes.

Vintage Character Port (P.)

A high-quality Port blended from the best Cima Corga wines from different vintages.

Vintage Port (P.)

A Port wine from a good vintage declared so by any individual Port company, made from the best vineyards, aged in 630-liter oak casks for 2 years, then blended and bottled. It is aged for at least 10 years in the bottle and can be aged for up to 30 years or longer. Since 1975 all Vintage Port has been bottled at the lodges in Portugal. The wine must be decanted for it throws a crust or sediment when aged; it accounts for 2% of the total Port production.

vintage wine

Wine from grapes grown in one season, or vintage year, which are made into wine and bottled the following year; not blended with wine from other vintages.

vinum picatum (Lat.)

Resinated wine, or wine with pitch added, similar to Greek Retsina, produced in the Côte-Rôtie district near Vienne, in the first century A.D. Mentioned in Columella's *De re rustica*, c. A.D. 60, Martial's (40-105 A.D.) *Epigrams*, and in Pliny's (23-79 A.D.) *Natural History*.

Viognier (F.)

A white grape grown in the Rhône region, especially in the Condrieu (including Château-Grillet) and Côte-Rôtie districts.

Violland, Léon (F.)   1844

An estate in Beaune, Côte de Beaune district, Burgundy. 25 acres, including 11 acres of Beaune Montée Rouge, 5 acres of Savigny Les Marconnets, 10 acres of Pommard and some Corton, Corton-Charlemagne and Beaune Clos du Roi.

Viosinho (P.)

A white grape, one of 16 first quality grapes used to make Port wine.

Virely, Cuvée Pierre (F.)

A red wine from the Hospices de Beaune, Côte de Beaune district, Burgundy. Not made separately since 1968, the *cuvée* was composed of the following vineyard in Beaune: Les Cent-Vignes.

Virgil *also* Vergil (70-19 B.C.) (Lat.)

The ancient Roman poet; wrote about the vine in *Georgics II*.

Virgin Hills (Aus.)   1968

A winery in Kyneton, south of Bendigo, central Victoria; produces Cabernet Sauvignon, Shiraz, Malbec, Pinot Noir, Traminer and Rhine Riesling wines. 45 acres.

Virginia (U.S.)

A state in the eastern U.S. It has several new wineries, growing mostly French hybrid grapes and some *vinifera* grapes. 1,000 acres.

Virginia Dare (U.S.)

A famous wine from North Carolina during the first half of the 20th century, produced by Paul Garrett in North Carolina; made from Scuppernong grapes blended with Concord grapes and some California wine; it is now made in Canandaigua, N.Y. by the Richard's Wine Cellar of Virginia, but with less Scuppernong in the blend.

Viria, La (F.)

A vineyard in Côte-Rôtie, Côte Brune section, in the northern Rhône region.

Visconti (I.)   1908

A winery in Desenzano del Garda, Lombardy region; produces Bardolino, Lugano, Merlot, Oltrepò Pavese and other wines.

Vista, Viña (U.S.)   1971

A winery in Cloverdale, Alexander Valley, northern Sonoma County, California; produces Cabernet, Chardonnay, Petite Sirah, Riesling, Sangiovese and Zinfandel wines, mostly from purchased grapes. 4,000 cases.

Vital (P.)

A white grape grown in western Portugal.

vite (I.)

A vine.

Viti (Sw.)

A red wine from the Ticino region, in southeastern Switzerland; made from the Merlot grape.

Viticole des Carmes, Domaine (F.)

An estate in Aloxe-Corton, Côte de Beaune district, Burgundy; run by La Reine Pédauque; owns 45 acres of Mâcon and some Savigny.

viticulteur (F.)

A vine-grower, usually one who owns his own vineyard.

viticulture

The science and art of grape-growing.

vitigno (I.)

A grape variety.

Vitis labrusca

A species of grape vines native to North America, which includes the varieties Catawba, Concord, Fredonia, Isabella and Norton; grown in the eastern U.S.

Vitis riparia

A species of grape vines native to North America, frequently used in the production of hybrids and as a stock on to which *vinifera* vines are grafted.

Vitis rotundifolia

A species of grape vines native to North America, which includes the varieties

Campbell's Early, Carlos, Magnolia, Noble, Scuppernong and Thomas; grown in the southeastern U.S.

Vitis vinifera

The most important species of grape vines used for wine; its origins have been traced to the Middle East. All of the great wines in Europe, Australia, California and elsewhere are made from *vinifera* grapes, which include Cabernet Sauvignon, Pinot Noir, Merlot, Syrah, Gamay, Barbera, Nebbiolo, Sangiovese, Chardonnay, Sauvignon Blanc, Sémillon, Muscat, Palomino, and numerous others.

Viura (Sp.)

A white grape grown in the Rioja region; an approved DO grape; also called Alcañon, Alcañol and in the Catalonia region, Macabeo.

Vlasotinci (Y.)

A town and district in southern Serbia; produces mostly red and rosé wines made from Prokupac and some Plovdina grapes.

Voarick, Émile (F.)

An estate in Mercurey, Côte Chalonnaise district, Burgundy. 125 acres, including 2 acres of Aloxe-Corton Clos des Fiètres, 2.5 acres of Beaune Montée, 2.5 acres of Mercurey Clos-du-Roi Monopole, 7.5 acres of Château Beau and 20 acres of Givry.

Voarick et Fils, Michel (F.)

An estate in Aloxe-Corton, Côte de Beaune district, Burgundy. 35 acres, including 1.2 acres of Corton Renardes, 2.5 acres of Languettes, 1 acre of Clos du Roi, 3.3 acres of Corton-Charlemagne, 8 acres of Pernand-Vergelesses, 10 acres of Aloxe-Corton and manages the vineyards of Hospices de Beaune Corton Cuvée Dr. Peste; also runs the Domaine Henri Poisot.

Vocoret et ses Fils, Domaine Robert (F.)

An estate in Chablis, Chablis district, Burgundy. 30 acres, including 3 acres of Les Clos, 1 acre of Valmur, 7.5 acres of Blanchot

and some Montée de Tonnerre, Beugnon, Forêts, Séchet and Châtain.

Voge, Alain (F.)

An estate in Cornas, northern Rhône region. 12 acres.

Vogüé, Domaine Comte Georges de (F.)

An old estate in Chambolle-Musigny, Côte de Nuits district, Burgundy. 30 acres, including Musigny – 17 acres, Musigny Blanc – 1.2 acres, Bonnes Mares – 7 acres, Chambolle-Musigny Les Amoureuses – 1.2 acres and Chambolle-Musigny – 5 acres.

Voigny, Château (F.)

An unclassified estate in Preignac, Sauternes district, Bordeaux. 1,800 cases. 15 acres.

Voillot, Joseph (F.)

An estate in Volnay, Côte de Beaune district, Burgundy. 25 acres, including Volnay – 10 acres, Pommard Pézerolles – 2.6 acres, Pommard – 5 acres and Meursault *Premier Cru* – 1 acre.

Voiret, Domaine (F.)

An estate in Beaune, Côte de Beaune district, Burgundy. 37 acres, including Beaune Aux Cras – 1.7 acres, Pertuisots – 4 acres, Les Grèves – 1 acre, Les Avaux – 1.2 acres, Les Aigrots – 1 acre, Les Teurons – 1 acre, *Premier Cru* – 7.5 acres and Côte de Beaune Grande Châtelaine – 2.5 acres.

Voirosses (F.)

A *Grand Cru* vineyard (in part) in Aloxe-Corton, Côte de Beaune district, Burgundy.

Vojvodina (Y.)

A province north of the Republic of Serbia. It includes the districts of Fruška Gora, Banat and Subotička Peščara; produces red and white varietal wines.

volatile acidity

Acetic acid, a component of spoiled or partially spoiled wine.

Volkach (G.)

A village in the Franken region, Bereich Maindreieck, Grosslage Kirchberg. The only vineyard is Ratsherr.

Vollrads, Schloss (G.)   1335

A famous estate in Winkel, Bereich Johannisberg, Grosslage Honigberg, Rheingau region; owned by Graf Matuschka-Greiffenclau, qualifies as an *Ortsteil*; also handles the wines of Weingut Fürst Löwenstein estate (40 acres) in Hallgarten. 115 acres.

Volnay AOC (F.)

A commune in the Côte de Beaune district, Burgundy; produces a delicate, perfumed, red wine and some whites which are usually sold as Meursault. It has 14 *Premiers Crus*. 210,000 gallons. 525 acres.

Volpaia, Castello di (I.)

An estate in Radda, Tuscany; produces Chianti Classico, Coltassala and Vin Santo wines. 18,000 cases. 100 acres.

volpino (I.)

Foxy taste, as in American grapes of the *Vitis labrusca* family.

Volxem, Weingut Bernd van (G.)

An estate in Wiltingen, Bereich Saar-Ruwer, Mosel-Saar-Ruwer region. 25 acres, including vineyards in Wiltingen: Scharzhofberg, Gottesfuss, Klosterberg, Braunfels, Schlangengraben and Schlossberg.

vonkelwyn (S. Af.)

Sparkling wine.

Vorlese (G.)

The early harvesting of grapes.

vörös (H.)

Red.

Vose Vineyards (U.S.)   1978

A winery in Napa City, Napa Valley, California; produces Cabernet Sauvignon, Zinfandel, Chardonnay, Sauvignon Blanc and white Zinfandel wines. 5,000 cases. 20 acres.

Vosgros *also* Vogiras (F.)

A *Premier Cru* vineyard in Chichée, Chablis district, Burgundy; usually includes the Vaugiraut vineyard.

Vöslau *also* Bad Vöslau (A.)

A village south of Vienna; produces mostly red wines made from the Blauer Portugieser grape.

Vosne-Romanée AOC (F.)

A famous commune in the Côte de Nuits district, Burgundy; the home of Romanée-Conti, one of the world's most famous red wine. It has 5 *Grands Crus* and 10 *Premiers Crus*. 172,000 gallons. 425 acres.

Vosne-Romanée, Château de (F.)

The name of the estate of Abbé Liger-Belair. 4 acres, including La Romanée Monopole – 2 acres, and Vosne-Romanée les Regnots – 1.7 acres. The wines are now handled by Bouchard Père et Fils (formerly handled by Bichot).

Vougeot AOC (F.)

A commune in the Côte de Nuits district, Burgundy; it gets its name from the River Vouge, a stream which separates it from Chambolle-Musigny; produces mostly red wine and some white. Clos de Vougeot is its one *Grand Cru*. 154 acres, the Clos taking up 125 acres.

Vougeot AOC, Clos de (F.)

A famous *Grand Cru* vineyard of the commune of Vougeot, Côte de Nuits district, Burgundy; started in 1150 by Cistercian Monks. 75 owners, 107 different plots. 125 acres.

Vouvray AOC (F.)

1. A commune and district in the Touraine region of the Loire Valley, which produces:
2. White wines from Vouvray and 8 other nearby communes; made from the Chenin Blanc, or Pineau de la Loire grape; usually made sweet or semi-sweet, seldom dry.

Voyat, Ezio (I.)

An estate in Chambave, Valle d'Aosta region; produces Chambave Rouge and Moscato wines.

Voyen, Clos *also* Les Voyens (F.)

A *Premier Cru* vineyard in Mercurey, Côte Chalonnaise district, Burgundy.

Vranac (Y.)

1. A red grape grown in southern Yugoslavia, which produces:
2. A red wine from the Republics of Montenegro and Macedonia, made from the Vranac grape.

Vraye-Croix-de-Gay, Château (F.)

An estate in Pomerol, Bordeaux. 1,200 cases. 15 acres.

Vugava (Y.)

A white grape grown in the Dalmatia region of the Republic of Croatia.

Vuignier & Fils, Louis (Sw.)   1957

An estate in Grimisuat, Valais region; produces Fendant, Pinot Noir, Humagne, Petite Arvine, Johannisberg, Malvoisie and other wines. 85 acres.

W

W.G.S. (A.)

The abbreviation of *Weingütesiegel* (Quality Wine Seal), a numbered neck label on Austrian wines that are guaranteed to be quality wines; the wines are officially tested and approved.

W.O. (S. Af.)   1973

The abbreviation for *Wyn van Oorsprong* (Wines of Origin), a law and system which guarantees the truthful labeling of all wine in the country, instituted in 1973.

W.O.S. (S. Af.)   1973

The abbreviation for *Wyn van Oorsprong Superior* (Superior Wines of Origin), the designation for superior quality wines in South Africa; the wine must be made from 100% of the grape named on the label.

Wwe. (G.)

The abbreviation for *Witwe* (widow).

Wachau (A.)

An important district in the Lower Austria region, west of Vienna, along the Danube River. The most important villages are Spitz, Weissenkirchen, Dürnstein and Loiben; produces white wine made from the Grüner Veltliner grape.

Wachenheim (G.)

A village in the Rheinpfalz region, Bereich Mittelhaardt/Deutsche Weinstrasse, Grosslagen Mariengarten, Schenkenböhl and Schnepfenflug. The vineyards are: Altenburg, Belz, Böhlig, Gerümpel, Goldbächel and Rechbächel in Grosslage Mariengarten; Fuchsmantel, Königswingert, Mandelgarten, Odinstal and Schlossberg in Grosslage Schenkenböhl; and Bischofs-

garten and Luginsland in Grosslage Schnepfenflug. 1,000 acres.

Wachstum (G.)

A winegrower; also called *Kreszenz*; neither term has been in use since 1971.

Wagner Vineyards (U.S.)   1977

A winery in Lodi, on the eastern shore of Lake Seneca, Finger Lakes region, New York; produces wines from native, French hybrid and some *vinifera* grapes. 125 acres. 40,000 cases.

Waldmeister (G.)

The woodruff plant; the flavor of the leaves is an ingredient in May wine.

Waldulm (G.)

A village in the Baden region, Bereich Ortenau, Grosslage Schloss Rodeck. The vineyards are: Kreuzberg and Pfarrberg.

Walker Wines (U.S.)   1979

A winery in Los Altos Hills, Santa Clara, California; produces Cabernet Sauvignon, Gamay, Barbera, Petite Sirah and Chardonnay wines from purchased grapes. 1,000 cases.

Wallachia (R.)

A large region in southern Romania; includes the districts of Argeş, Drăgăşani, Segarcea, Dealul Mare and Murfatlar.

Walluf (G.)

A village in the Rheingau region, Bereich Johannisberg, Grosslage Steinmächer. The vineyards are: Berg Bildstock, Oberberg and Walkenberg, in Walluf proper (also called Niederwalluf), and Fitusberg and

Langenstück, in Oberwalluf. The wine is mostly sold abroad as Rauenthaler Steinmächer.

Walporzheim (G.)

A village in the Ahr region, Bereich Walporzheim /Ahrtal, Grosslage Klosterberg. The vineyards are Alte Lay, Domlay, Gärkammer, Himmelchen, Kräuterberg and Pfaffenberg. Red wine made from Pinot Noir, Portugieser and other grapes accounts for over half of the production.

Walporzheim/Ahrtal (G.)

A *Bereich*, the only one in the Ahr region, and which has only one *Grosslage*: Klosterberg.

Wälschriesling

See **Welschriesling**.

Wanne *also* Wannen (F.)

A famous *Grand Cru* vineyard in Guebwiller, Haut-Rhin district, Alsace region.

Wantirna Estate (Aus.)   1963

An estate in Wantirna South, Victoria; produces Cabernet Sauvignon, Merlot, Pinot Noir, Chardonnay and Rhine Riesling wines. 2,000 cases. 10 acres.

Wantz, Charles (F.)

A merchant in Barr, Bas-Rhin district, Alsace region; produces wines made from purchased grapes.

Warner Vineyards (U.S.)   1938

A winery in Paw Paw, southeastern Michigan, the largest in the state; produces wines from hybrid grapes: M. Foch, Chelois, De Chaunac, Chancellor, Aurora and Seyval Blanc, from their own and purchased grapes; also sparkling wines. 500 acres.

Warre & Company (P.)   1670

A producer of Port wine in Vila Nova de Gaia, the oldest British Port firm. Owner of Quinta da Cavadinha.

Washington (U.S.)

A state in the northwestern United States, the third in grape production in the country. Vines were planted as early as 1872 but there were no wineries before 1933. New wine laws of 1969 allowed the sale of wine by privately-owned stores. 25,000 acres.

Water Wheel (Aus.)

A winery near Bendigo, Central Victoria; produces Shiraz, Cabernet Sauvignon and Cabernet Franc wines.

Wawern (G.)

A village in the Mosel-Saar-Ruwer region, Bereich Saar-Ruwer, Grosslage Scharzberg. The vineyards are: Goldberg, Herrenberger, Jesuitenberg and Ritterpfad. 100 acres.

Wehlen (G.)

A village in the Mosel-Saar-Ruwer region, Bereich Bernkastel, Grosslage Münzlay. The vineyards are Klosterberg, Nonnenberg and Sonnenuhr. 400 acres.

Wehrheim, Weingut Engen (G.)

An estate in Nierstein, Rheinhessen region; owns vineyards in Nierstein. 25 acres.

Weibel Champagne Vineyards (U.S.) 1939
                                                    1972

A winery west of Ukiah, Mendocino County, California, a part of Weibel, of Warm Springs, Alameda County. Produces a large selection of still and sparkling wines. 650 acres in Mendocino and Sonoma Counties, 1000 acres in Warm Springs.

Weil am Rhein (G.)

A village in the Baden region, Bereich Markgräflerland, Grosslage Vogtei Rötteln. The vineyards are: Schlipf and Stiege.

Weil, Weingut Dr. R. (G.)   1868

An estate in Kiedrich, Rheingau region; owns parts of vineyards in Kiedrich: Sandgrub, Wasseros, Grafenberg and Klosterberg. 45 acres.

Wein (G.)
Wine.

Weinbach, Domaine (F.)   1885
An estate in Kaysersberg, Haut-Rhin district, Alsace region. 60 acres in Kaysersberg and Kientzheim.

Weinbauer (G.)
A wine-grower.

Weinbauorte (G.)
The German word for a wine village; also called *Gemeinde* and *Gemarkung*.

Weinberg (G.)
A vineyard or holding; part of a *Lage* or site; also called *Weingarten* .

Weinbergsrolle (G.)
A Vineyard register; an official list of site names and their location.

Weingarten (G.)
A vineyard or holding; part of a *Lage* or site; also called *Weinberg*.

Weingarten (F.)
A section of the Brand vineyard in Turkheim, Haut-Rhin district, Alsace region.

Weingut *plural:* Weingüter (G.)
A wine estate.

Weingutesiegel (A.)
Quality Wine Seal, a numbered neck label on Austrian wines of quality, which have been officially tested and approved.

Weinheim (G.)
A village in the Baden region, Bereich Badische Bergstrasse/Kraichgau, Grosslage Rittersberg. The vineyards are: Hubberg and Wüstberg.

Weinheim (G.)
A village in the Rheinhessen region, Bereich Wonnegau, Grosslage Sybillenstein. The vineyards are: Heiliger Blutberg, Hölle, Kapellenberg, Kirchenstück and Mandelberg.

Weinmesse (G.)
A wine exchange where wines are sold.

Weinsäure (G.)
Wine acid.

Weinsberg (G.)
A village in the Württemberg region, Bereich Württembergisch Unterland, Grosslage Salzberg. The vineyards are Althälde, Ranzenberg and Schemelsberg.

Weinviertel (A.)
German for "Wine Quarter," a district north of Vienna, in the Lower Austria region. The most important villages are: Eggenburg, Falkenstein, Haugsdorf, Hollabrunn, Mailberg, Matzen, Poysdorf, Pulkau, Ravelsbach, Retz, Wolkersdorf and Zistersdorf.

Weissburgunder (A., G.)
An important grape grown in Styria, southeastern Austria and in Germany; believed to be a mutation of Pinot Gris, which is itself a mutation of the Pinot Noir; yellow-green berries, sweet, low acidity; also called Pinot Blanc and White Burgundy.

Weissherbst (G.)
A full-bodied rosé wine from the Baden region; made from Blauer Spätburgunder grapes, sometimes with Traminer or Riesling added; legally labelled *Rosee* since 1971.

Welschriesling *also* Wälschriesling (A.,Y.)
A white grape grown in Austria and Yugoslavia. It ripens early, moderate yield, large berries; no relation to the Johannisberg Riesling; also called Riesling Italico, or Italian Riesling.

Welder (U.S.)
A white muscadine grape grown in the southeast.

Weltevrede Estate EWO (S. Af.)

An estate in the Robertson district, east of Capetown; produces white wines.

Wendouree Cellars (Aus.)   1895

A winery in the Clare/Watervale district, South Australia; produces long-lived reds and Port wines.

Wente Brothers (U.S.)   1883

An old winery in Livermore, Livermore Valley, Alameda County, California; produces Cabernet Sauvignon, Pinot Noir, Gamay Beaujolais, Petite Sirah, Zinfandel, Chardonnay, Sémillon, Grey Riesling, Sauvignon Blanc, Johannisberg Riesling and Chenin Blanc wines. Over 1 million cases. 900 acres in Livermore, 800 acres in Monterey.

Werner'sches Weingut, Domdechant (G.)   1780

An estate in Hochheim, Rheingau region. 35 acres, including parts of vineyards in Hochheim: Domdechaney, Hofmeister, Hölle, Kirchenstück, Reichestal, Stein, Steilweg and Sommerheil.

West Vineyards, Mark (U.S.)   1972
1st wine 1976

A winery in Forestville, Russian River Valley, Sonoma County, California; produces Pinot Noir, Riesling, Chardonnay and Gewürztraminer wines. 15,000 cases. 60 acres.

Western Australia (Aus.)

A Province of Australia which has vineyard districts in the southwestern corner, around Perth. These districts are: Swan Valley, northeast of Perth, Mount Barker, south of Perth and Margaret River, on the southwestern coast; produces red, white and fortified wines.

Westfield (U.S.)

An American red grape of the *labrusca* family.

Westfield Wines (Aus.)   1922

A small winery in the Swan Valley district, northeast of Perth, in Western Australia; produces Sémillon, Verdelho, Cabernet Sauvignon and Vintage Port wines. 3,000 cases. 5 acres.

Wetshof, De *also* Dewetshof (S. Af.)

An estate in the Robertson district, well-known for producing Riesling wine.

Westhofen (G.)

A village in the Rheinhessen region, Bereich Wonnegau, Grosslage Bergkloster. The vineyards are: Aulerde, Benn, Brunnenhäusen, Kirchspiel, Mornstein, Rotenstein and Steingrube.

Weyher (G.)

A village in the Rheinpfalz region, Bereich Südliche Weinstrasse, Grosslage Ordensgut. The two vineyards are Heide and Michelsberg.

Wheeler Vineyards, William (U.S.)   1981

A winery in Healdsburg, Sonoma County, California; produces Cabernet, Chardonny and Zinfandel wines. 30 acres. 15,000 cases.

White Marsh Cellars (U.S.)   1983

A winery in Hampstead, Maryland; produces Chardonnay, Riesling and Seyval Blanc wines. 18 acres.

White Mountain Vineyards (U.S.)   1965, 1969

A winery in Belmont, New Hampshire; produces Maréchal Foch and blended wines from hybrid grapes. 150 acres.

White Pinot (U.S.)

1. In California, another name for the Chenin Blanc grape.

2. A dry, white wine from California made from the Chenin Blanc grape.

White Port (P.)

Port wine made from red and white grapes or from white grapes alone. The skins are separated from the must soon after fermentation begins so as not to give too much color to the wine; it is made sweet or dry.

White Riesling (U.S.)

Another name for the Johannisberg Riesling grape, or the wine it produces.

white rot

A vine disease characterized by the formation of a fungus on ripening berries, which causes them to split; also called *rot blanc* in French.

White Shiraz (Aus.)

1. Another name for the Trebbiano or Ugni Blanc grape.

2. A white wine made from the White Shiraz grape.

White Zinfandel (U.S.)

A white wine made from the Zinfandel grape; made in California, the wine usually has a faint tinge of pink.

Whitehall Lane Winery (U.S.)   1980

A small winery in St. Helena, Napa County, California; produces Cabernet Sauvignon, Chardonnay and Sauvignon Blanc wines. 25 acres. 6,000 cases.

Wibelsberg (F.)

A *Grand Cru* vineyard in Andlau, Bas-Rhin district, Alsace region. 35 acres.

Wickham Vineyards (U.S.)   1981

A winery in Hector, on Lake Seneca, Finger Lakes region, New York; produces several varietal wines. 175 acres.

Widmer's Wine Cellars (U.S.)   1888

A large winery in Naples, on the southern tip of Lake Canandaigua, New York; produces generic blends and varietals including: Niagara, Isabella and Salem; also owned 500 acres in California from 1970. 235 acres in N.Y.

Wiederkehr Wine Cellars (U.S.)   1880

A winery in Altus, northwestern Arkansas; produces wines from French hybrid grapes, Delaware, Campbell's Early and Cynthiana as well as Cabernet Sauvignon, Johannisberg Riesling, Chardonnay, Gewürztraminer, and sparkling wines. Over 500 acres.

Wiemer Vineyard, Herman J. (U.S.)   1979

A winery in Dundee, on Lake Seneca, Finger Lakes region, New York; produces Pinot Noir, Riesling, Chardonnay and Gewürztraminer wines. 35 acres.

Wien (A.)

The German name for Vienna, the capital of Austria; produces *Heurige* wines. 1,800 acres.

Wienerwald *also* Wienerwald-Steinfeld (A.)

The Vienna Woods, a district south of Vienna, in the Lower Austria region; includes the towns of Baden, Vöslau and Gumpoldskirchen.

Wiesloch (G.)

A village in the Baden region, Bereich Badische Bergstrasse/Kraichgau, Grosslage Mannaberg. The vineyards are: Bergwälde, Hägenich and Spitzenberg.

Wildbacher (I.)

1. A red grape, originally from Austria, grown in the northeastern Veneto region around Conegliano, Italy, which produces:

2. A red wine.

Wildwood Vineyard (U.S.)

A vineyard in Kenwood, in eastern Sonoma County, California; produces grapes for Château St. Jean Chardonnay and Cabernet wine. 300 acres.

Willamette Valley (U.S.)

An important region in northwestern Oregon with a cool climate, especially suitable for growing the Riesling grape.

Willard (U.S.)

An American white grape of the *Vitis rotundifolia* species.

Williams & Humbert Ltd. (Sp.)   1877

A Sherry producer in Jerez de la Frontera; produces several types of Sherry, including "Dry Sack" (*amontillado*), "Canasta Cream" and "Pando" (*fino*).

Willm, A. (F.)

A merchant in Barr, Bas-Rhin district, Alsace region; owns 10 acres of Kirchberg (Riesling) and the Clos Gaensbroennel – 17 acres (Gewürztraminer).

Willow Creek (U.S.)

A vineyard west of Paso Robles, in San Luis Obispo County; produces Zinfandel grapes for the Monterey Peninsula Winery.

Willow Creek Cellars (U.S.)

A brand of varietal and generic wines (Robert Haas Selection) from Souverain Cellars, in Geyserville, northern Sonoma County, California.

Willow Creek Winery (U.S.)   1975

A small winery in McKinleyville, Humboldt County, California; produces Cabernet Sauvignon, Zinfandel, Petite Sirah, Chardonnay, Gewürztraminer and Green Hungarian wines, some from purchased grapes. 3 acres.

Willowside Vineyards (U.S.)   1975

A vineyard and winery in Santa Rosa, Sonoma County, California; produces Zinfandel, Pinot Noir, Chardonnay and Gewürztraminer wines. 3,000 cases. 25 acres.

Willyabrup Vineyard (Aus.)

An estate in the Margaret River district, Western Australia; produces Rhine Riesling and Cabernet Sauvignon wines.

Wilmont Wines (U.S.)   1976

A winery in Schwenksville, Pennsylvania. 5 acres.

Wiltingen (G.)

A village in the Mosel-Saar-Ruwer region, Bereich Saar-Ruwer, Grosslage Scharzberg. The vineyards are: Braune Kupp, Braunfels, Gottesfuss, Hölle, Klosterberg, Kupp, Rosenberg, Sandberg, Schlossberg, Schlangengraben and the Scharzhofberger estate. 800 acres.

Windsor, Château (Is.)

A red wine from Israel made from the Carignan grape; produced by the Carmel Winery.

wine

Fermented grape juice. It contains: water, sugars, alcohols, esters, acids, minerals, nitrogenous substances, acetaldehyde, phenolic substances, color pigments, vitamins and it also produces CO_2 gas which is usually allowed to escape.

Wine and the People (U.S.)   1970

A winery in Berkeley, northern Alameda County, California; produces Cabernet Sauvignon, Pinot Noir and Chardonnay wines from purchased grapes; also a special Chardonnay from Winery Lake Vineyard, Napa Valley; also sold as Berkeley Wine Cellars.

wine fountain

A fountain which uses wine and is set up on special, rare occasions; originating as far back as 1474 in Urach, Germany where it was used at a wedding, it was also known to Egypt, Greece and Rome and is still used today in Europe.

wine society

An organization which promotes wine and conducts meetings and wine festivities; also called *confrérie* in France.

winery

A company or building where wine is made; also, a wine estate.

Winery Lake Vineyard (U.S.)

An old vineyard, replanted in 1961, in the Carneros Creek district, Napa Valley, California; grows Chardonnay, Riesling, Merlot, and Pinot Noir grapes for Acacia, Belvedere, La Crema Viñera, Cuvaison, Martin Ray, Veedercrest and Wine and the People wineries. 225 acres.

Winery Rushing (U.S.)   1977

A winery in Merigold, Mississippi; produces wines from muscadine grapes. 35 acres.

Wines of Origin (S. Af.)   since 1973

English for *Wyn van Oorsprong* (WO), a system of guaranteeing the origin of the wine as stated on the label, similar to the French AOC designation; it includes 14 districts.

Wines of Origin Superior (S.Af.)   1973

An official designation (W.O.S.) for superior quality wines.

Winkel (G.)

A village in the Rheingau region, Bereich Johannisberg, mostly in Grosslage Honigberg. The vineyards are: Bienengarten, Dachsberg (in Grosslage Erntebringer), Gutenberg, Hasensprung, Jesuitengarten, part of Klaus, Schlossberg and the famous estate of Schloss Vollrads, regarded as an *Ortsteil*. 650 acres.

Wintrich (G.)

A village in the Mosel-Saar-Ruwer region, Bereich Bernkastel (Mittel-Mosel), Grosslage Kurfürstlay. The vineyards are: Grosser Herrgott, Ohligsberg, Sonnenseite and Stefanslay. 675 acres.

Winzer (G.)

A wine grower; one who cultivates grapes and makes wine from them.

Winzerverein (G.)

A wine-growers co-operative; also called *Winzergenossenschaft*.

Winzergenossenschaft (G.)

A wine-growers co-operative; also called *Winzerverein*.

Wisconsin (U.S.)

A state in the north central United States; produces very little wine except for cherry wines, etc. There is one 20-acre winery which grows hybrid and *vinifera* grapes.

Witfrans (S.Af.)

The Palomino grape.

Wollersheim Winery (U.S.)   1867, 1973

A winery in Prairie du Sac, near Sauk City, Wisconsin; originally built in 1867, formerly the Haraszthy winery (c. 1840); produces Seyval Blanc, Aurora, M. Foch, Riesling and Chardonnay wines, some from purchased grapes. 20 acres.

Wöllstein (G.)

A village in the Rheinhessen region, Bereich Bingen, in Grosslage Rheingrafenstein. The vineyards are: Äffchen, Haarberg-Katzenteg, Hölle and Ölberg.

Wonnegau (G.)

A *Bereich*, one of 3 in the Rheinhessen region.

wood *also* in wood

Pertaining to a wooden cask or barrel; aged in wood, e.g., a wood Port.

wood Port

Port wine that has been aged in wood casks for at least 2-3 years for Ruby Port and longer for Tawny Port.

Woodbury Estate (Aus.)

A vineyard of Tollana Winery, in Eden Valley, a part of the Barossa Valley district, South Australia.

Woodbury Vineyards (U.S.)   1979

A vineyard and winery in Dunkirk, Chautauqua region, New York; the first *vinifera* planting (1976) in this region; produces Chardonnay, Riesling, Gewürztraminer, Cabernet Sauvignon, Dutchess, Niagara and de Chaunac wines. 45 acres.

Woodbury Winery (U.S.)   1977

A winery in San Rafael, Marin County, California; produces Port wines made from Cabernet Sauvignon, Zinfandel, Pinot Noir and Petite Sirah grapes, grown in Sonoma County. 4,000 cases.

Wooden Valley Winery (U.S.)   1932

A winery in Fairfield, Solano County, California; produces varietal, jug and dessert wines. 50 acres.

Woodley (Aus.)   1856

An historic winery in Glen Osmond, near Adelaide, South Australia; produces Queen Adelaide Claret and Queen Adelaide Riesling wines from purchased grapes.

Woodside Vineyards (U.S.)   1961

A small winery in Woodside, San Mateo County, south of San Francisco, California; produces Cabernet Sauvignon, Pinot Noir and Chardonnay wines; owns 3 acres of the once-famous La Questa Vineyard. 5 acres.

woody

A term used to describe a wine having the smell and/or taste of wood; depending on the wine and the degree of woodiness, this can be a positive or a negative characteristic.

Wooton (E.)   1973

A vineyard in North Wooton, Shepton Mallet, Somerset; produces white wines made from Schönburger, Müller-Thurgau and Seyval Blanc grapes. 6 acres.

Worcester WO (S. Af.)

An important town and district northeast of Capetown and Paarl; there are co-operatives but no estates in this district; produces Cinsaut, Pinotage, Chenin Blanc, Palomino, Sémillon, Muscat d'Alexandre and Colombar wines.

Worden (U.S.)

A red grape of the *labrusca* family; grown in Florida.

Worms (G.)

A city in the Rheinhessen region, Bereich Wonnegau, Grosslage Liebfrauenmorgen. There are 20 vineyards, including the famous Liebfrauenstift-Kirchenstück, from which Liebfraumilch wine originated. Originally 2,400 acres, now only 400 acres.

Wunsch et Mann (F.)

An estate and merchant in Wettolsheim, Haut-Rhin district, Alsace region. 35 acres.

Württemberg (G.)

A region centered around Heilbron, Stuttgart and the Neckar River; the *Bereiche* are: Remstal-Stuttgart, Württembergisch Unterland, Kocher-Jagst-Tauber and Beyerische Bodensee; produces red and white wines. 20,000 acres.

Württembergische Hofkammer Kellerei (G.)

An estate in Stuttgart, in the Württemberg region; owns vineyards in several villages. 60 acres.

Württembergisch Unterland (G.)

A *Bereich*, one of 4 in the Württemberg region.

Würtzburg (G.)

A city in the Franken region, Bereich Maindreieck, and the center of the production of *Steinwien*. The vineyards are: Abtsleite, Innere Leiste, Kirchberg, Pfaffenberg, Schlossberg, Stein and Stein/Harfe. 750 acres.

Würzer (G.)

A white grape – a cross of Gewürztraminer and Müller-Thurgau; developed at the State Research Institute, Alzey, Rheinhessen region in 1932.

wyn (S. Af.)

Wine.

Wynberg (S. Af.)

The first district to produce wine in the Cape province.

Wyndham Estate (Aus.)   1928

A large winery in the Hunter Valley region, New South Wales; produces many varietals, including: Johannisberg Riesling, Chardonnay, Sauvignon Blanc, Gewürztraminer, Cabernet Sauvignon and blended wines. 250,000 cases. 1,000 acres.

Wynn's (Aus.)   1918

A winery in the Coonawarra district, South Australia, formerly the Riddoch Winery; produces Cabernet Sauvignon, Shiraz claret and *méthode Champenoise* sparkling wines. 4,500 acres.

X

Xampán (Sp.)
"Champagne," sparkling wine.

Xarel-lo (Sp.)
A white grape grown in the Catalonia region; used to make sparkling and still wines; also called Pansa Blanca.

Xeito (Sp.)
Red and white wines from the Ribeiro district, Galicia region, northwestern Spain; produced by the Bodega Cooperativa de Ribeiro.

Xenophon (431-355 B.C.) **(Gr.)**
The ancient Greek historian, author of *Anabasis*, in which he wrote about the wines of the Black Sea region.

Xérès (F.)
Sherry.

Xeres (Lat.)
The ancient Roman name for the city of Jerez, Spain.

Xerez (Sp.)
A white grape grown in the Galicia region.

Xiros (Gr.)
Dry.

Xynisteri (Cyp.)
A white grape grown in Cyprus.

Xynomavro (Gr.)
A red grape grown in Macedonia, northern Greece.

Y

"Y" *also* **Ygrec (F.)**

A dry, white wine made by Château d'Yquem, in Sauternes, Bordeaux region; made since 1959. 2,000 cases.

Yakima (U.S.)

A river, city, county and wine region in south central Washington.

Yakima River Winery (U.S.)

A small winery in Prosser, Yakima Valley, Washington; produces Chardonnay and Riesling wines. 25 acres. 4,000 cases.

Yaldara, Château (Aus.)   1947

A winery in the Barossa Valley, north of Adelaide, South Australia; it has replicas of various European wine structures; produces mainly sparkling wines.

Yalumba (Aus.)   1883

A winery of S. Smith & Son in Angaston, Barossa Valley district, South Australia; produces Rhine Riesling, especially from the Pewsey Vale vineyard, Claret, Chardonnay, Traminer and Sherry and Port wines. 1,200 acres.

Yamanashi (J.)

An important district (prefecture) west of Tokyo, central Japan.

Yapincak (T.)

A white grape grown in Turkey.

Yarra Valley (Aus.)

A district in southeastern Victoria, near Melbourne; produces mostly Cabernet Sauvignon wine.

Yarra Yering (Aus.)   1969

A winery in Coldstream, Yarra Valley district, Victoria; produces blended red wines in Bordeaux and Rhône styles. 30 acres.

Yarrinya, Château (Aus.)   1971

A winery in Dickson's Creek, Yarra Valley district, Victoria; produces Cabernet Sauvignon, Shiraz, Pinot Noir, Rhine Riesling and Gewürztraminer wines. 135 acres.

Yayin (Biblical)

Wine.

Yearlstone (E.)

1. A winery in Bickleigh, Devon, England, with 1.5 acres, which produces:

2. A white wine made from Chardonnay, Siegerrebe, Madeleine Angevine and Triomphe d'Alsace grapes.

yeast

A group of microscopic, unicellular fungi which cause fermentation. The *Saccharomyces cereviseae* and *Saccharomyces hayanus* types are useful in wines and the *Saccharomyces acidifaciens* and other types are harmful.

Yecla (Sp.)

A district southwest of Valencia, in southeastern Spain; produces mostly strong red wine made from the Monastrell grape.

Yellow Muscat (H.)

A white grape; also called Sárgamuskotály.

Yellowglen (Aus.)   1971

A winery near Ballarat, Victoria; produces Shiraz, Cabernet Sauvignon and sparkling wines, some from purchased grapes. 100 acres.

Yerassa (Cyp.)

A village south of Mt. Olympus, on the island of Cyprus, one of 3 important villages which produce Mavrodaphne wine.

Yerba Buena (U.S.)   1977

A winery in San Francisco, California; produces a variety of wines from purchased grapes.

yeso (Sp.)

Gypsum, or calcium sulphate, sprinkled on grapes before crushing them, in order to achieve the desired degree of acidity; also called plastering; used in the Sherry region.

Ygrec *also* "Y" (F.)

A dry white wine made by Château d'Yquem, Sauternes, Bordeaux; made since 1959. 2,000 cases.

Yon-Figeac, Château (F.)

An estate in St.-Émilion, Bordeaux; classified in 1955 as a *Grand Cru Classé*. 10,000 cases. 50 acres.

York Creek Vineyard (U.S.)

A well-known vineyard on Spring Mountain, in the hills above St. Helena, Napa Valley, California; was once part of La Perla vineyard; grows Cabernet, Petite Sirah and Zinfandel grapes for Ridge and Freemark Abbey wineries. 100 acres.

York Mountain Winery (U.S.)   1882

A winery in Templeton, San Luis Obispo County, California; produces Cabernet Sauvignon, Zinfandel, Pinot Noir, Chardonnay, Chenin Blanc and Johannisberg Riesling wines.

Young Vineyard, Robert (U.S.)   1963

A vineyard in Alexander Valley, Sonoma County, California; produces Cabernet, Chardonnay, Sauvignon Blanc, Gewürztraminer and Riesling grapes for Château St. Jean, Felton-Empire and Belvedere wineries. 275 acres.

d'Yquem, Chateau (F.)

A famous estate in Sauternes, in the Sauternes district, Bordeaux; classified in 1855 as a *Premier Grand Cru*, the only one so designated, it has been in the same family since 1785; produces a sweet white wine made from 80% Sémillon and 20% Sauvignon botrytized grapes which are picked individually; also makes a dry wine from the same grapes called "Y," or Ygrec. 6,000 cases sweet wine, 2,000 cases dry wine. 250 acres.

Yuga (U.S.)

A red muscadine grape grown in California.

Yugoslavia *also* Jugoslavia

A country in southeastern Europe; the republics of Serbia and Croatia produce 80% of the wine; grows European and many local grapes, the Prokupac is the predominant grape in Serbia. 160 million gallons. 610,000 acres.

Yverdon Vineyards (U.S.)   1970

A winery on Spring Mountain, in St. Helena, Napa Valley, California; produces Cabernet Sauvignon, Napa Gamay, Chenin Blanc and Johannisberg Riesling wines. 5,000 cases. 92 acres.

Yvorne (Sw.)

A village just north of Aigle, in the Chablais district, Vaud region; produces a white wine made from the Chasselas grape.

Z

Z.B.W.(G.)

The abbrebreviation for *Zentralkellerei Badischer Winzergenossenschaften*, a large co-op winery in Breisach, Baden region.

ZD Wines (U.S.)   1969

A winery in Napa City, Napa Valley, California, formerly in Sonoma City; produces Cabernet Sauvignon, Pinot Noir, Merlot, Zinfandel, Chardonnay, Riesling and Gewürztraminer wines mostly from grapes purchased in Carneros Creek. 10,000 cases.

Zaca Mesa Winery (U.S.)   1973

A winery in Los Olivos, Santa Ynez Valley, Santa Barbara County, California; produces Cabernet Sauvignon, Pinot Noir, Syrah, Zinfandel, Chardonnay, Johannisberg Riesling and Sauvignon Blanc wines. 50,000 cases. 250 acres.

Zacatecas (Mex.)

A state in central Mexico, northwest of Mexico City, just south of Parras; it is a new wine district at a very high altitude (7,000 feet). 3,500 acres since 1970.

Začinak (Y.)

A red grape grown in the Republic of Serbia.

Zagarolo DOC (I.)

A town southeast of Rome, near the Castelli Romani district, in the central Latium region; produces white wines from Malvasia, Trebbiano and other grapes.

Zahnacker, Clos du (F.)

A vineyard in Ribeauvillé, Haut-Rhin district, Alsace region, planted since the ninth century, now owned by the village co-op; produces Riesling, Gewürztraminer and Tokay grapes. 3 acres.

Zalema (Sp.)

A white grape grown in the Huelva region of southwestern Spain.

Zamora (Sp.)

A province north of Salamanca; produces Toro and Vega Sicilia wines.

Zandvliet EWO (S. Af.)   1975

An estate in the Robertson district, east of Capetown; produces Shiraz, Cabernet and Pinot Noir wines. 550 acres.

Zante Currant (U.S.)

A red *vinifera* grape grown in California; also called Black Corinth.

Zardetto (I.)   1969

An estate in Conegliano, Veneto region; produces Cartizze, Prosecco and sparkling wines.

Zecca, Conti (I.)

An estate in Leverano, Apulia region; produces Leverano and Donna Marzia Bianco and Rosso wines.

Zéja, Paul (F.)

An estate in Ligré, Chinon district, Touraine region, Loire Valley.

Zelen (Y.)

A white grape grown in the Republic of Slovenia.

Zell/Mosel (G.)

A *Bereich* in the northern part of the Mosel-Saar-Ruwer region, covering about one-third of the region from Coblenz south to Zell; one of 4 in the region.

Zellenberg (F.)

A village north of Colmar, in the Haut-Rhin district, Alsace region.

Zeller Schwarze Katz (G.)

"Black Cat from Zell," a brand-name wine from Zell, in the Mosel-Saar-Ruwer region, Bereich Zell/Mosel, Grosslage Schwarze Katz, which gave its name to the *Grosslage* for the vineyards of Zell and Senheim.

Zellerbach Vineyard, Stephen (U.S.) 1978

A winery in Alexander Valley, northern Sonoma County, California; produces a Cabernet Sauvignon/Merlot blend. 10,000 cases. 70 acres.

Zeltingen-Rachtig (G.)

A village in the Mosel-Saar-Ruwer region, Bereich Bernkastel, Grosslage Münzlay. The vineyards are Deutschherrenberg, Himmelreich, Schlossberg and Sonnenuhr; the wines are sold as Zeltinger followed by the vineyard name. 625 acres.

Zeni (I.)   1882

An estate in Grumo di San Michele all'Adige, Trentino-Alto Adige region; produces Chardonnay, Rosé, Teroldego and Trentino wines. 10 acres.

Zentralkellerei (G.)

A co-operative winery.

Zentralkellerei Badischer Winzergenossenschaften (G.)

A very large co-op winery in Breisach, Baden region, combining 12,000 acres from hundreds of growers, producing several hundred different wines.

Zibibbo (I.)

A white grape grown on the island of Pantelleria, Sicily, off the coast of Tunisia; a large Moscato grape.

Zichron Yacob (Is.)

An important town for wine making, with a large co-op winery, north of Tel Aviv.

Zierfändler (A.)

A local white grape grown in Gumpoldskirchen, south of Vienna; also called Spätrot.

Žilavka (Y.)

A white grape grown in the Republics of Macedonia and Serbia; produces a big, rich, perfumed wine.

Zind-Humbrecht, Domaine (F.)   1959

An estate in Wintzenheim, Haut-Rhin district, Alsace region; owns Herrenweg vineyard (Gewürztraminer), Hengst – 2 acres (Gewürztraminer), Rangen (in Thann) – 10 acres, Clos St. Urban, a total of 65 acres in Turckheim, Gueberschwihr and Thann.

Zinfandel (U.S.)

A red grape grown only in California, although it may be related to the Primitivo grape of the Puglia region, in Italy; produces mostly dry red wine, some sweet red wine and some white wine.

Zinnkoepflé (F.)

A vineyard in Westhalten, Haut-Rhin district, Alsace region; produces Gewürztraminer, Sylvaner and Tokay grapes.

Zisser, Clos (F.)

A vineyard in Barr, Bas-Rhin district, Alsace region; a 12-acre *monopole* of the Klipfel estate.

Zitsa (Gr.)

A white, semi-sparkling wine from Epirus (Ipiros), northwestern Greece; made from the Debina grape.

Zöbing (A.)

A village in the Krems district, in the Lower Austria region.

Zoete Inval Estate, De EWO (S. Af.)

An estate just south of Paarl, in the Paarl district.

Zonin (I.)   1921

An estate in Gambellara, Veneto region; produces Bardolino, Gambellara, Valpolicella and sparkling wines. 4 million cases. 750 acres.

Zonnebloem (S. Af.)

The name for the best quality wines from the Stellenbosch Farmers Winery; produces vintage Cabernet, Pinotage and Riesling wines.

Zoopiyi (Cyp.)

A village south of Mt. Olympus, on the Island of Cyprus, one of 3 important villages which produce Mavrodaphne wine.

Zotzenberg (F.)

A vineyard in Mittelbergheïm, Bas-Rhin district, Alsace region. 175 acres.

Župa (Y.)

A region south of Belgrade, in the Republic of Serbia; produces red and rosé wines made mostly from Prokupac grapes and some Plovdina grapes.

Zweigelt *also* Zweigeltrebe (A.)

An early-ripening, Austrian red grape; also grown in England.

Zwicker (F.)

In the Alsace region, wine that is blended from a mixture of noble and common grapes. An *Edelzwicker* is a blend of only the noble varieties; *Zwicker* is not often made anymore.

Zymotechnology

The study of yeast fermentations.

Zymase

A complex of enzymes found in yeasts which ferments sugar into alcohol and CO_2 gas.

Bibliography

Adams, Leon D.
The Wines of America, third edition. New York: McGraw-Hill, 1984.

Anderson, Burton
Vino. The Wines and Winemakers of Italy. Boston: Little, Brown and Co., 1980.
The Simon and Schuster Pocket Guide to Italian Wines. New York: Simon and Schuster, 1982.

Arlot, John and Christopher Fielden
Burgundy Vines and Wines. London: Davis-Poynter, 1976.

Blumberg, Robert S. and Hurst Hannum
The Fine Wines of California, Third Edition. Garden City, N.Y.: Doubleday, 1984

Broadbent, Michael
The Great Vintage Wine Book. New York: Knopf, 1980.

Chroman, Nathan
The Treasury of American Wines. New York: Rutledge-Crown, 1973.

Churchill, Creighton
A Notebook for the Wines of France. New York: Knopf, 1961.

Debuigne, Gérard
Larousse Dictionary of Wines of the World. New York: Larousse, 1976.

Duijker, Hubrecht
The Great Wines of Burgundy. New York: Crescent, 1983.
The Wines of the Loire, Alsace and Champagne. New York: Crescent, 1983.
The Great Wine Châteaux of Bordeaux. New York: Crescent, 1983.
The Good Wines of Bordeaux. New York: Crescent, 1983.

Fegan, Patrick W.
Vineyards and Wineries of America, a Traveler's Guide. Brattleboro, Vermont: Stephen Greene Press, 1982.

Hallgarten, Fritz
A Guide to the Vineyards, Estates and Wines of Germany. Dallas: Publivin, 1974.

Hanson, Anthony
Burgundy. London: Faber and Faber, 1982.

Jacquelin, Louis and René Poulain
The Wines and Vineyards of France, translated by T.A. Layton. New York, Putnam's Sons, 1962.

Johnson, Frank E.
The Professional Wine Reference, revised edition. New York: Beverage Media and Harper & Row, 1983.

Johnson, Hugh
Pocket Encyclopedia of Wine. New York: Simon and Schuster, 1983.
The World Atlas of Wine. New York: Simon and Schuster, 1978.
Modern Encyclopedia of Wine. New York: Simon and Schuster, 1983.

Lichine, Alexis
Guide to the Wines and Vineyards of France. New York: Knopf, 1979.
New Encyclopedia of Wine and Spirits, third edition. New York: Knopf, 1982.

Masse, William E.
Wines and Spirits. New York: Bramhall House, 1961.

Meinhard, Heinrich
The International Wine and Food Society's Guide to the Wines of Germany. New York: Stein and Day, 1976.

Olken, Charles, Earl Singer and Norman Roby
The Connoiseurs' Handbook of California Wines, third edition. New York: Knopf, 1984.

Penning-Rowsell, Edmund
The International Wine and Food Society's Guide to the Wines of Bordeaux. New York: Stein and Day, 1970.

Peppercorn, David
Bordeaux. London: Faber and Faber, 1982.

Read, Jan
The Wines of Portugal. London: Faber and Faber, 1982.
The Wines of Spain. London: Faber and Faber, 1982.
The Simon and Schuster Pocket Guide to Spanish Wines. New York: Simon and Schuster, 1983.

Robinson, Jancis
The Great Wine Book. New York: William Morrow, 1982.

Roger, J.R.
The Wines of Bordeaux. London: A. Deutsch, 1960.

Roux, Michel Pierre, Pierre Poupon and Pierre Forgeot
A Guide to the Vineyards and Domain(e)s of Burgundy. Dallas: Publivin, 1973.

Roux, Michel Pierre
A Guide to the Vineyards and Châteaux of Bordeaux. Dallas: Publivin, 1972.

Saintsbury, George
Notes on a Cellar-book. New York: Mayflower, 1920.

Schoonmaker, Frank
The Wines of Germany, revised by Peter Sichel. New York: Hastings House, 1980.
Encyclopedia of Wine, revised and expanded by Julius Wile. New York: Hastings House, 1978.

Simon, André
The History of Champagne. London: Octopus Books, 1971.
The Noble Grapes and the Great Wines of France. New York: McGraw-Hill, 1957.
Wines of the World, second edition by Serena Sutcliffe. New York: McGraw-Hill, 1981.

Spurrier, Steven
The Concise Guide to French Country Wines. New York: Putnam, 1983.

Thompson, Bob
The Pocket Encyclopedia of California Wines. New York: Simon and Schuster, 1980.

Wagner, Philip M.
A Wine-Grower's Guide, revised edition. New York: Knopf, 1982.
Grapes into Wine, revised edition. New York: Knopf, 1982.

Younger, William
Gods, Men, and Wine. Cleveland: Wine and Food Society and World Publishing Co., 1966.

Yoxall, H.W.
The International Wine and Food Society's Guide to the Wines of Burgundy, second edition. New York: Stein and Day, 1978